ORIENTAL CERAMIC ART

ORIENTAL CERAMIC ART

ILLUSTRATED BY EXAMPLES FROM THE COLLECTION OF

W. T. WALTERS

*WITH ONE HUNDRED AND SIXTEEN PLATES IN COLORS
AND OVER FOUR HUNDRED REPRODUCTIONS IN BLACK AND WHITE*

TEXT AND NOTES BY

S. W. BUSHELL, M. D.

PHYSICIAN TO H. B. M. LEGATION, PEKING

CROWN PUBLISHERS, INC. : NEW YORK

THE ORIGINAL EDITION OF

THIS WORK WAS PUBLISHED IN TEN VOLUMES

IN 1896 BY D. APPLETON AND COMPANY

————

THIS EDITION IS PUBLISHED

OCTOBER 1980 BY

CROWN PUBLISHERS, INC.

ONE PARK AVENUE

NEW YORK, N.Y. 10016

MANUFACTURED IN THE

UNITED STATES OF AMERICA

ISBN: 0-517-52581X

A GEORGE HORNBY RENAISSANCE EDITION

CONTENTS.

FIG. 1.—Etched Baluster Vase and pair of Hexagonal Bottles, enamelled
with turquoise crackle, artistic French mounting.

THE late William Thompson Walters, of Baltimore, died on November 20, 1894. The work which is here briefly introduced was begun by him nearly fifteen years before. At his death he left it practically completed. It only remained, therefore, for those intrusted with its details to assemble the several parts and discharge the mechanical duties necessary to its publication.

That publication is now entered upon in conformity with his expressed wishes and instructions, and as, had he lived, he would himself have had it. Furthermore, it is done in the belief that it will add one more to the many useful things that were the outcome of his purposeful and well-filled life. Mr. Walters was the first American to create a collection of Oriental ceramics, and in the many years that he devoted to the subject he became more and more impressed with the need there was of some authoritative work respecting it—a work which should treat, with such precision as was possible, of its origin, its history, and its qualities, and take it in at least some slight degree from that vague and indeterminate condition in which all contemporary or recent European writers have left it. Not that the literature of Oriental porcelain is copious in any modern tongue, but that those who have written best about it have had hardly anything to say, while those who have written at any length have been capricious, empirical, and only too misleading. The only way in which this purpose could be effected, if at all, was to seek in China itself whatever historical matter might exist in relation to the one distinguishing art of that country, the art of the potter.

In the introduction, written in 1883, to a very useful and instructive little volume on Oriental art, privately published by Mr. Walters in the ensuing year, he set forth his opinion on this point with a clearness which it is interesting at the present time to recall. " Notwithstanding," wrote Mr. Walters, " the numerous works that have been published on this subject, we have as yet but an imperfect knowledge of the age, history, and meaning of much that appears in collections of Oriental porcelain ; and until some European residing in China, well versed in the subject and well acquainted with the Chinese language, has obtained access to the stores of native collectors, we shall be to a certain extent working in the dark."

The more deeply the subject was looked into the less prospect there seemed to be of a successful issue. The only translation that existed of the writings of a Chinese authority was that made in 1856 by M. Stanislas Julien, of the *Ching-tê-chên T'ao Lu*. This was for years the ultimate reference of students of Chinese ceramics, but, although M. Julien was a great scholar and eminent sinologue, it was of little value and in some essential matters misleading. The difficulty was with the Chinese text. Given a sentence or two in Chinese descriptive of a piece of porcelain, its shape, the quality of its paste, its color, or other of its attributes, and the sinologue who is learned only in the language *per se* may translate it with the profoundest erudition and yet not convey its real meaning ; but if he have before him the actual piece which the Chinese author has been describing, and if he have also a well-founded knowledge of Chinese porcelain, then his translation will be of a very different character and much more instructive. In such matters the Chinese author is perfectly intelligible only when the reader adequately understands the subject. If, for instance, the reader knew that the Chinese writer was discussing celadon, he would not, in translating, read blue for green, although the Chinese word used meant equally blue or green, according to the application made of it. The illustration is a radical one, but it indicates accurately a case in which a very learned sinologue befogged many patient students.

It was while pursuing the matter with the best authorities abroad that Mr. Walters heard indirectly from Prof. A. W. Franks (now Sir Wollaston Franks), of the British Museum, of a translation of a Chinese work called the *T'ao Shuo*, which had been made by Dr. Stephen W. Bushell, of Peking. Dr. Bushell had already become well known as a sinologue, and especially for his unremitting industry in the direction of the ancient literature of porcelain. He had been for many years the medical officer of the British legation at Peking, and had devoted himself to the study of Chinese until he had attained among European scholars the reputation of an authority of the first rank. Prof. Franks was greatly interested in the *T'ao Shuo*, pointed out the importance that it possessed for students of Oriental ceramics, and expressed the hope that it would secure publication. Dr. Bushell's translation of it was accordingly secured for that purpose, and was found to be most instructive and interesting. It was proposed then to publish the translation together with other papers on the subject, including a new version from the Chinese text of the *Ching-tê-chên T'ao Lu*, already done into French by Julien. The whole would have made a considerable and a not unimportant addition to the stock of information relating to Chinese porcelain in the English language. When, however, a year or two later, Dr. Bushell visited the United States and entered upon a discussion of the question with Mr. Walters, it was decided to revise the project and bring out the present work, which contains, so far as all modern knowledge of the subject goes, the best information that Chinese letters convey respecting the origin of porcelain and its history through successive ages.*

Mr. Walters laid the foundation of the present collection nearly forty years ago. As has been said, he was the first in this country to create a collection of Oriental ceramics. The ceramic store of the United States was never great. We have had a modest share of English pottery since our earlier days, but no accumulation of it. Of Oriental porcelain a very little found its way to Colonial families, and only a few traces of it remain. Our first President had a domestic service of Chinese manufacture, and it was very fine in its way; but it belonged strictly to the category of commercial porcelain familiar to the last century as East India china—that is, porcelain made for export from Chinese ports and fashioned for household use or conventional household decoration, and having no relation to the artistic product of the Chinaman's kilns. The remains of this set of china are preserved in the National Museum at Washington. Probably the most artistic of our early acquisitions of Chinese porcelain were the pieces of blue and white that New England ship captains brought back from their voyages to the North Pacific, and of which many interesting examples are still to be found in old New England homes. As far as any broader awakening of taste in the matter of Oriental porcelain is concerned it must be referred to the occasion of the Centennial Exhibition of 1876. Many people had long before acquired an acquaintance with the subject at the great European exhibitions and through the opportunities of foreign travel, but our first popular knowledge of it most undoubtedly dates from our exhibition at Philadelphia. Now there are numbers of collections in the United States, some of them of great extent and value. It can also be confidently said that nowhere else do collectors betray any keener intelligence, or, perhaps, an equal knowledge of the general subject; whereby it has been rightly observed by Chinese and Japanese connoisseurs that if one wants to study fine Oriental porcelain he must come to America.

---

* So far as the Chinese texts relating to processes of manufacture are concerned they are of slight and only incidental interest. They tell about the petuntse and the kaolin, about the composition of glazes and the management of kilns, but no European potter has ever added from them a scintilla to his knowledge. The Chinese potter's formula is not unlike the chemist's analysis of one of Nature's healing waters—it is complete; but in the one case it is indispensable that the application be made by a Chinaman, and in the other that the compounding be done by Nature herself.

The plates in color with which this work is illustrated were made by Louis Prang, of Boston. Several experimental plates were made abroad, and the work of every European house of importance was examined, before Mr. Prang was asked to make lithographs of three pieces of porcelain of different colors. His immediate success determined the question; and when, two years later, some twenty of the plates were shown to French lithographers in Paris, their criticism was that the impressions from the stone had been fortified by color applied with the brush. They could not believe that work of such excellence could be produced by simple lithography. This very satisfactory opinion has been since confirmed by many lithographers, and it is conceded that these plates represent the highest type of work that has been produced in that branch of art. The color of Oriental porcelain is more akin to the color of some brilliant mineral than to the familiar pigments of an artist's palette; and as truth of color was the first requirement, many and serious difficulties had to be overcome. Mr. Prang, however, was equal to the task, and during the years that it was in progress at his house in Roxbury he devoted to it a degree of watchful care and untiring energy that were far from commercial in their inspiration.

WILLIAM M. LAFFAN.

May, 1896.

FIG. 2.—Octagonal Lantern of K'ang-hsi egg-shell
porcelain, decorated in colors. The opposite side
is illustrated in Plate XI.

Editorial Note

The original 1896 edition of this work remains one of the most majestic books ever published in America. One of our problems was to convert its ten volumes of massive 22 x 17 inch size into one volume of manageable proportions. This we have successfully done, yet reduced the text page area by only ten percent. Our great space saving came in the form of margins.

The color illustrations in the original were made by means of lithographic stones, created by Louis Prang, the father of American lithography. The 116 color plates required an average of nineteen stones per subject, with some needing as many as thirty. This could not be done today nor could the rare beauty of these subjects be captured by today's advanced computerized methods of color reproduction alone. Our compromise was to retain as many of the past skills as possible and merge them with some of the present refinements in cameras and film.

Most of the subjects are kept at or near their original reproduction size. Those reduced more were chosen with an eye to their nature and importance. Our sole compromise in this area was to depart occasionally from the numbered sequence. We had to retain the original numeration to conform to the extended notes describing each plate.

ORIENTAL CERAMIC ART

PLATE I

PLATE II

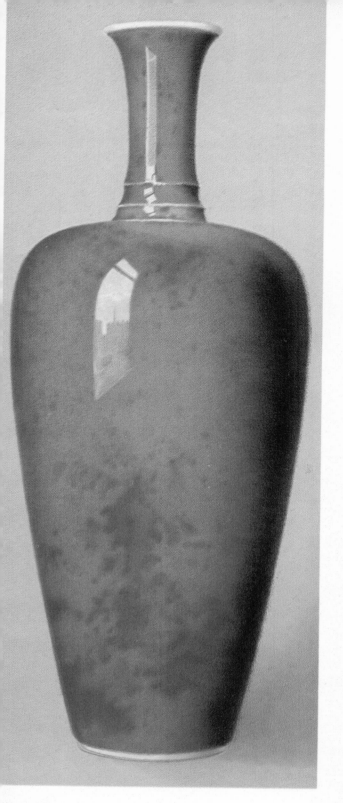

PLATE III

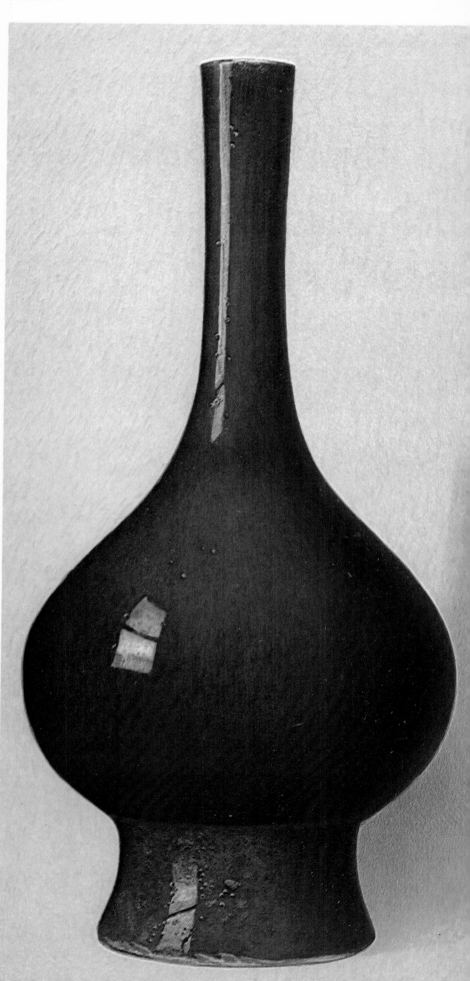

PLATE IV

PLATE V

PLATE VI

PLATE VIII

PLATE IX

PLATE X

PLATE XI

PLATE XII

PLATE XIII

PLATE XIV

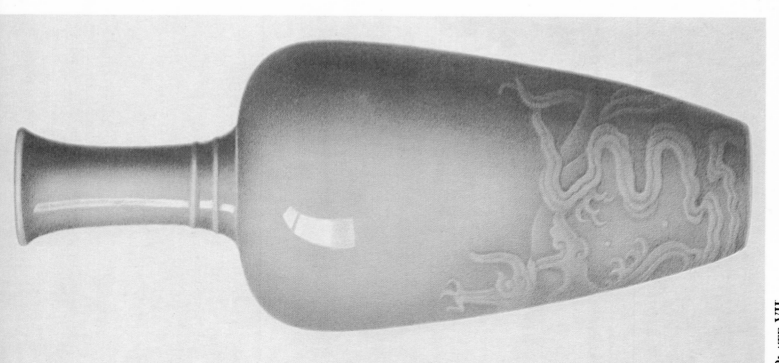

PLATE VII

PLATE XV

PLATE XVI

PLATE XIX

PLATE XX

PLATE XVII

PLATE XXI

PLATE XXV

PLATE XXII

PLATE XXIII

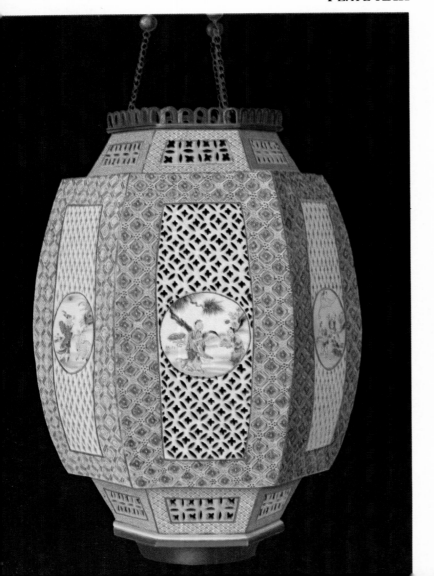

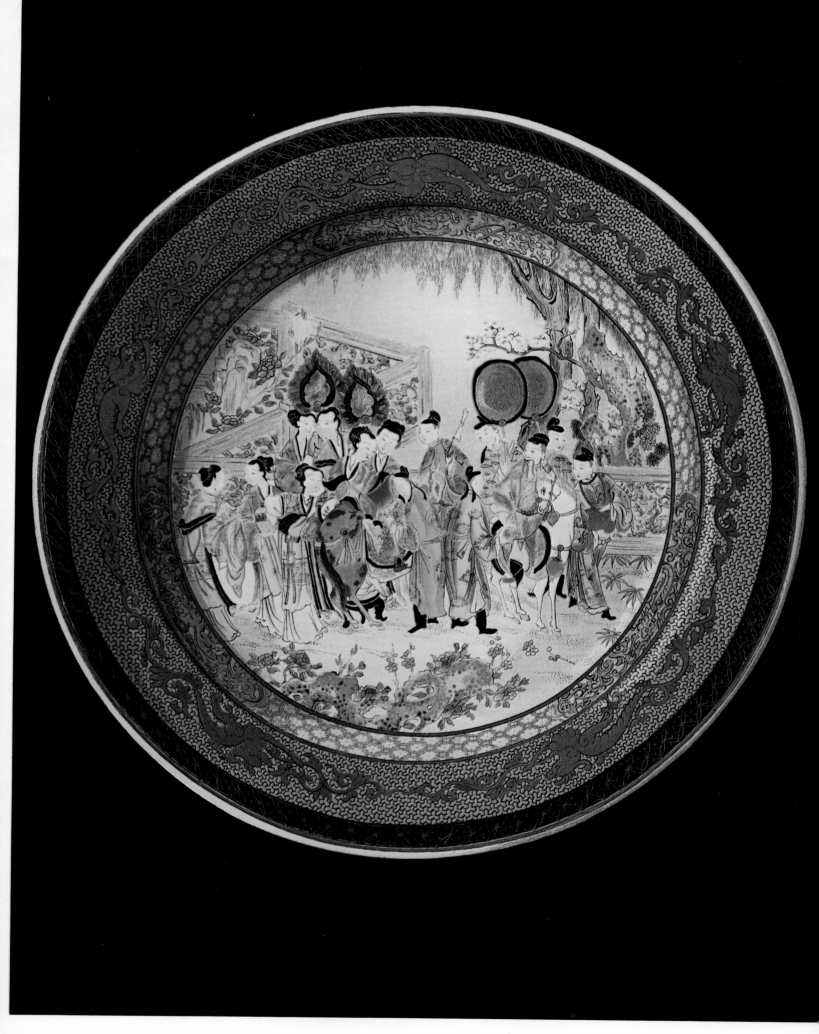

PLATE XXIV

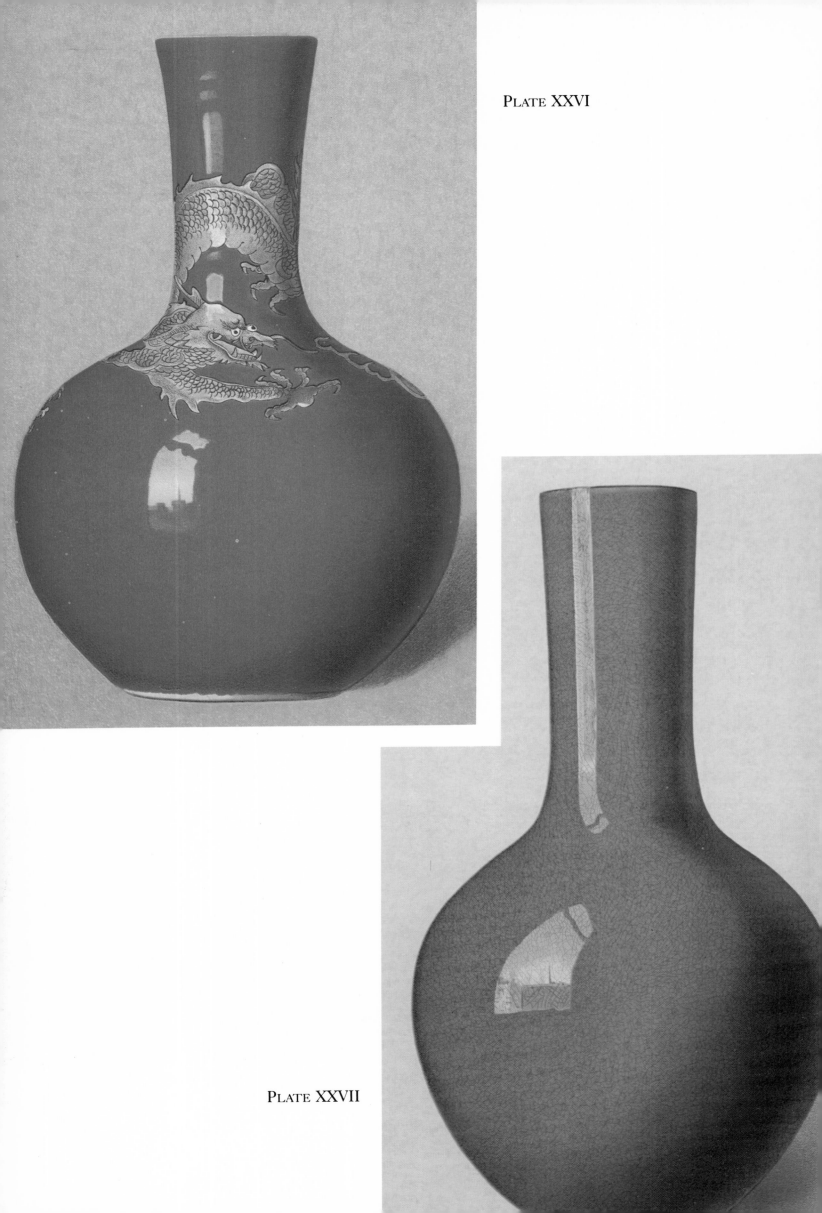

Plate XXVI

Plate XXVII

PLATE XXVIII

PLATE XXX

PLATE XXIX

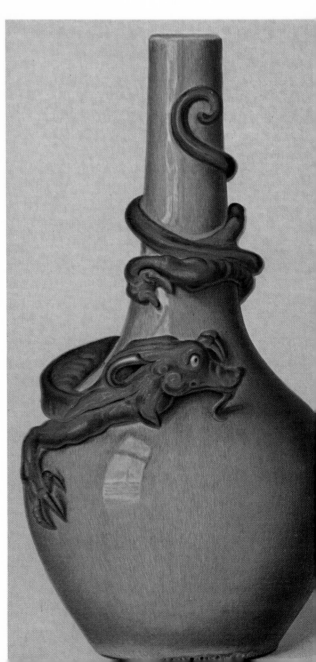

PLATE XXXI

PLATE XXXII

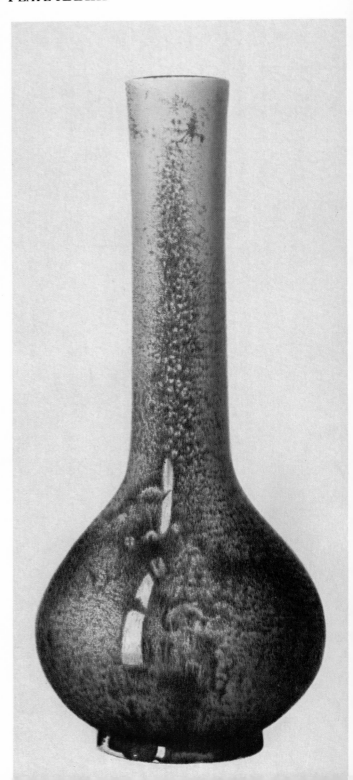

PLATE XXXIII

Plate XXXIV

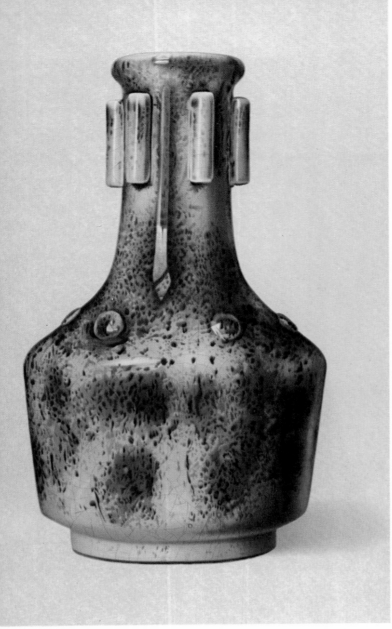

PLATE XXXV

PLATE XXXVI

PLATE XXXVIII

PLATE XXXVII

PLATE XXXIX

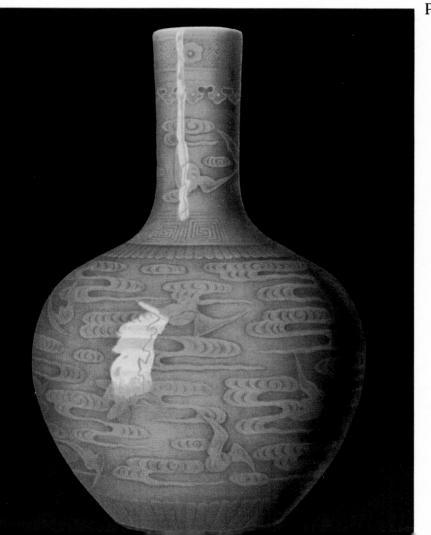

Plate XL

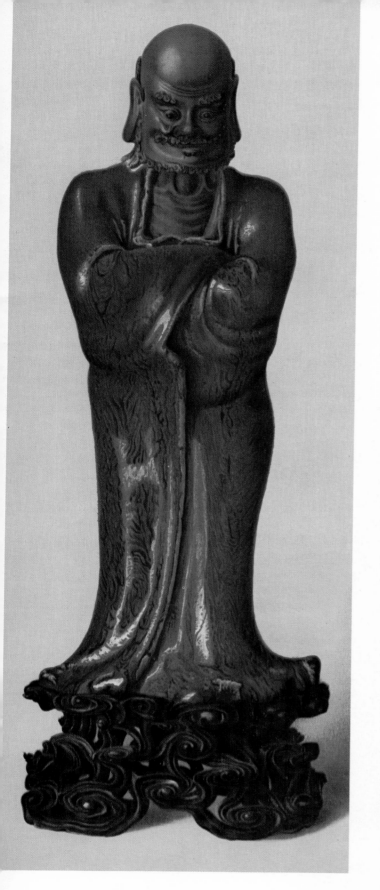

PLATE XLI

PLATE XLII

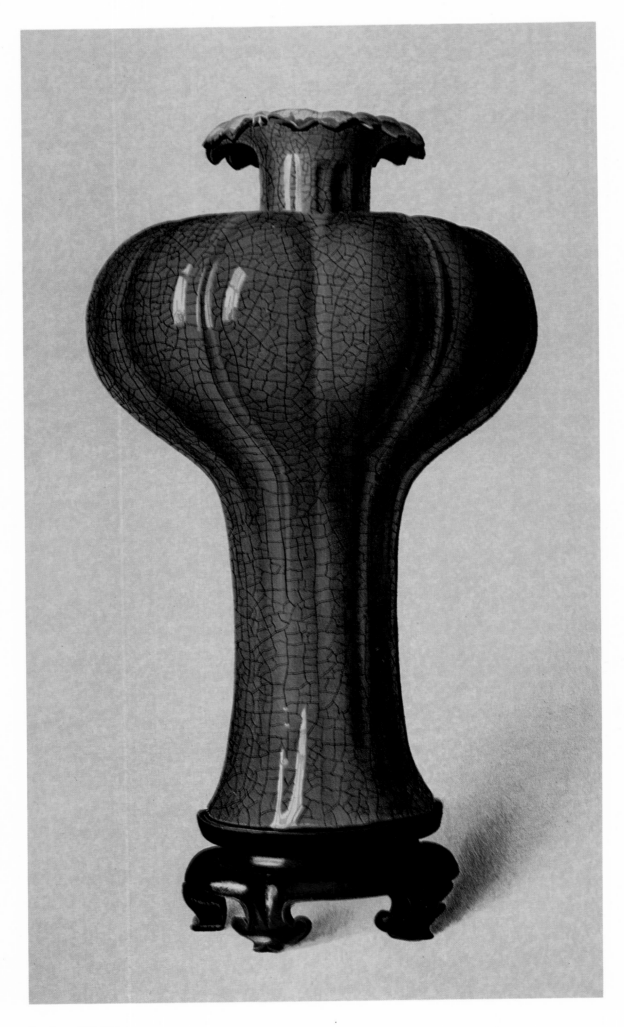

PLATE XLIII

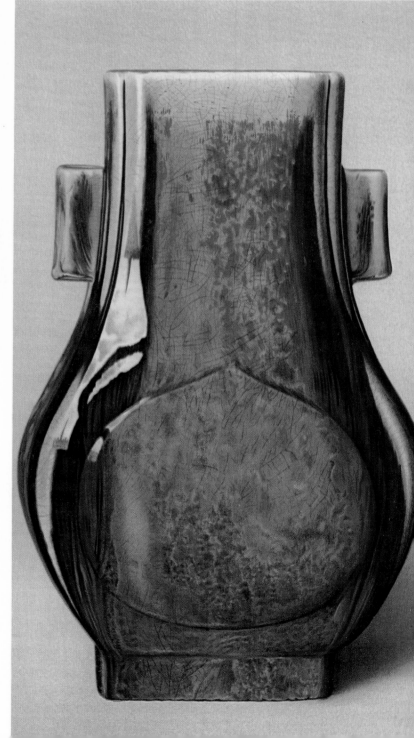

PLATE XLVI .

PLATE XLIV

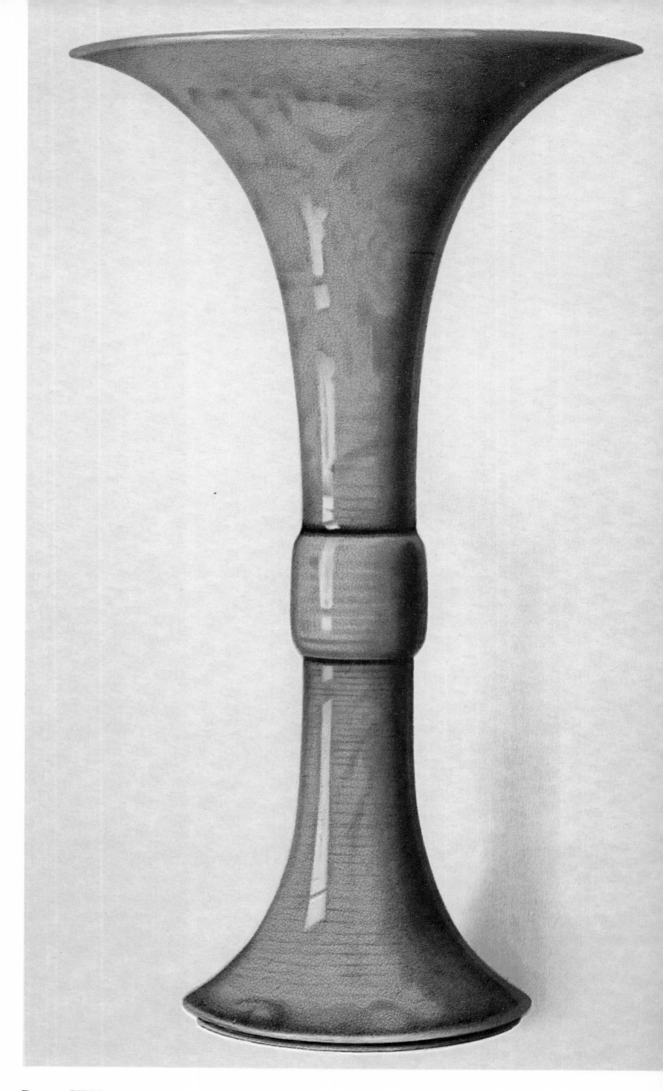

PLATE XLV

PLATE XLVII

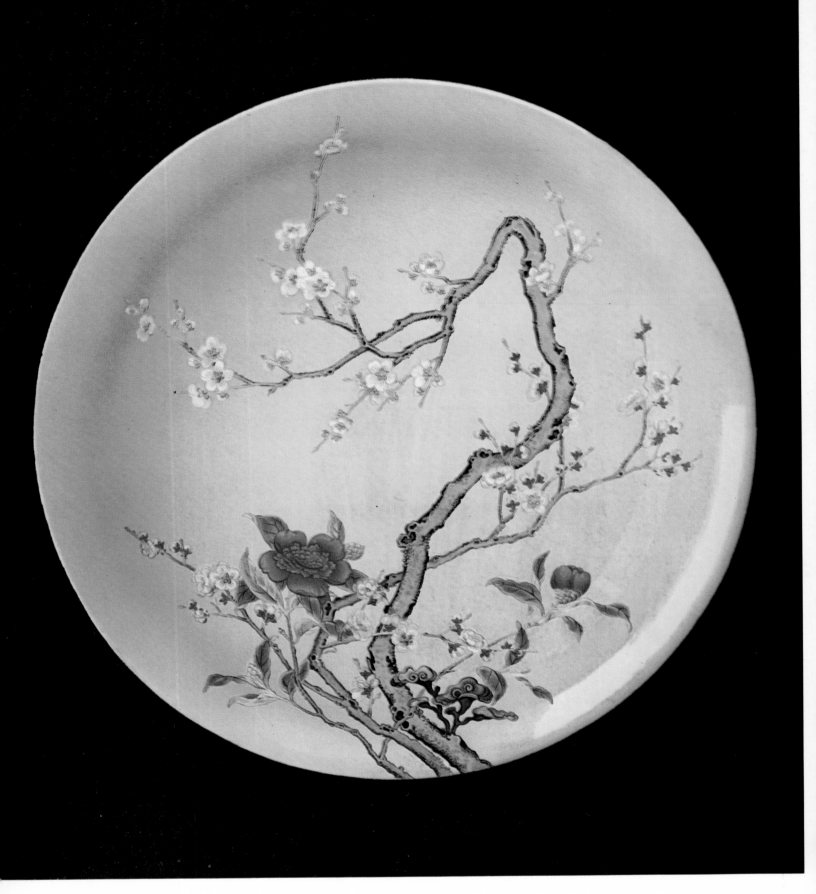

PLATE XLVIII

PLATE XLIX

PLATE LII

PLATE L   PLATE LI

PLATE LIII

PLATE LIV

PLATE LV

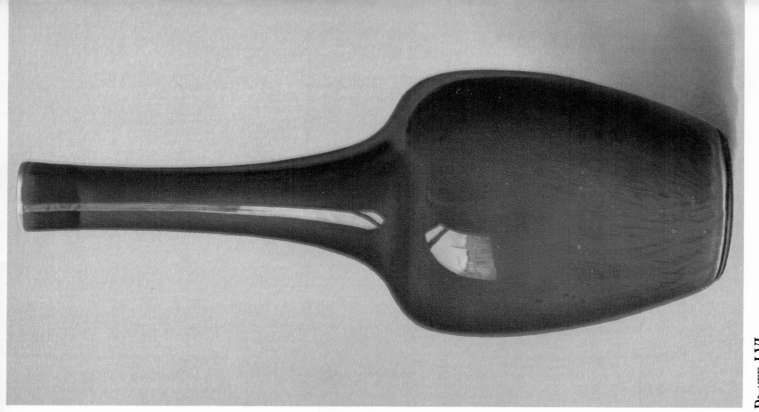

PLATE LVI

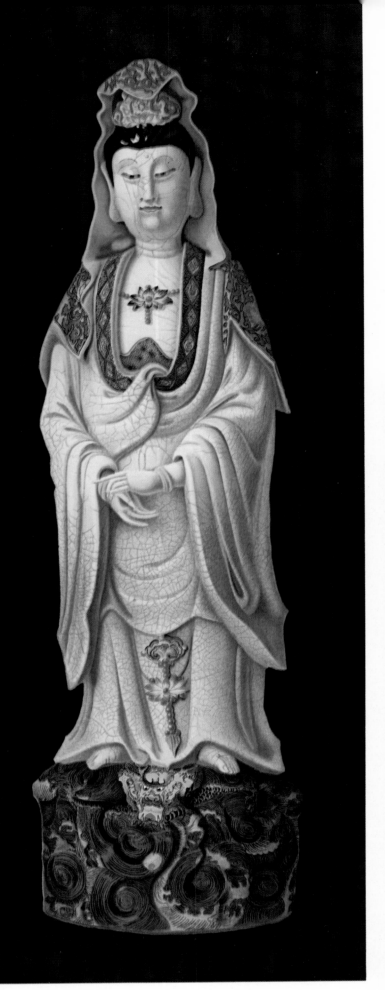

PLATE LXI

PLATE LX

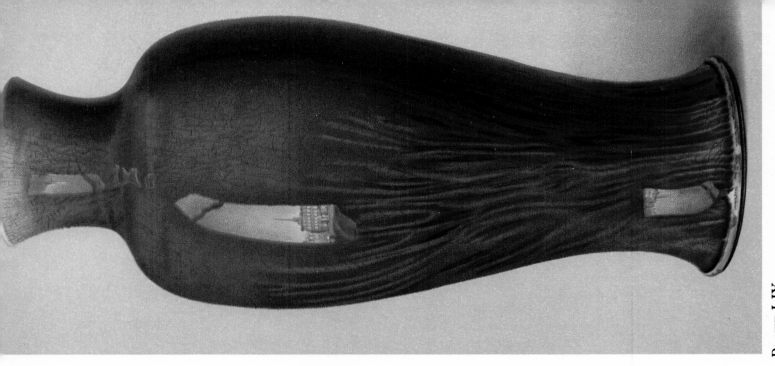

Plate LVII

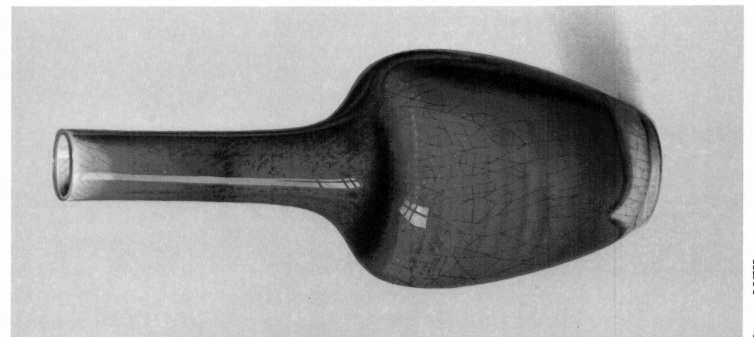

Plate LVIII

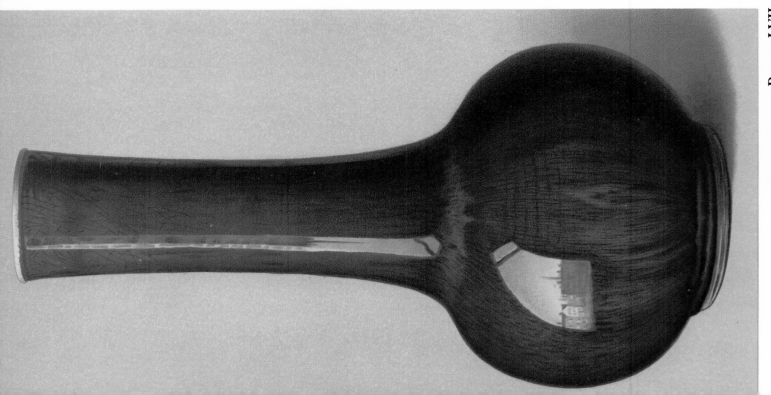

Plate LIX

PLATE LXII

PLATE LXV

PLATE LXVII

PLATE LXIII

PLATE LXIV

PLATE LXVI

PLATE LXVIII

PLATE LXIX

PLATE LXXII

PLATE LXX

PLATE LXXI

PLATE LXXIV

PLATE LXXIII

PLATE LXXV

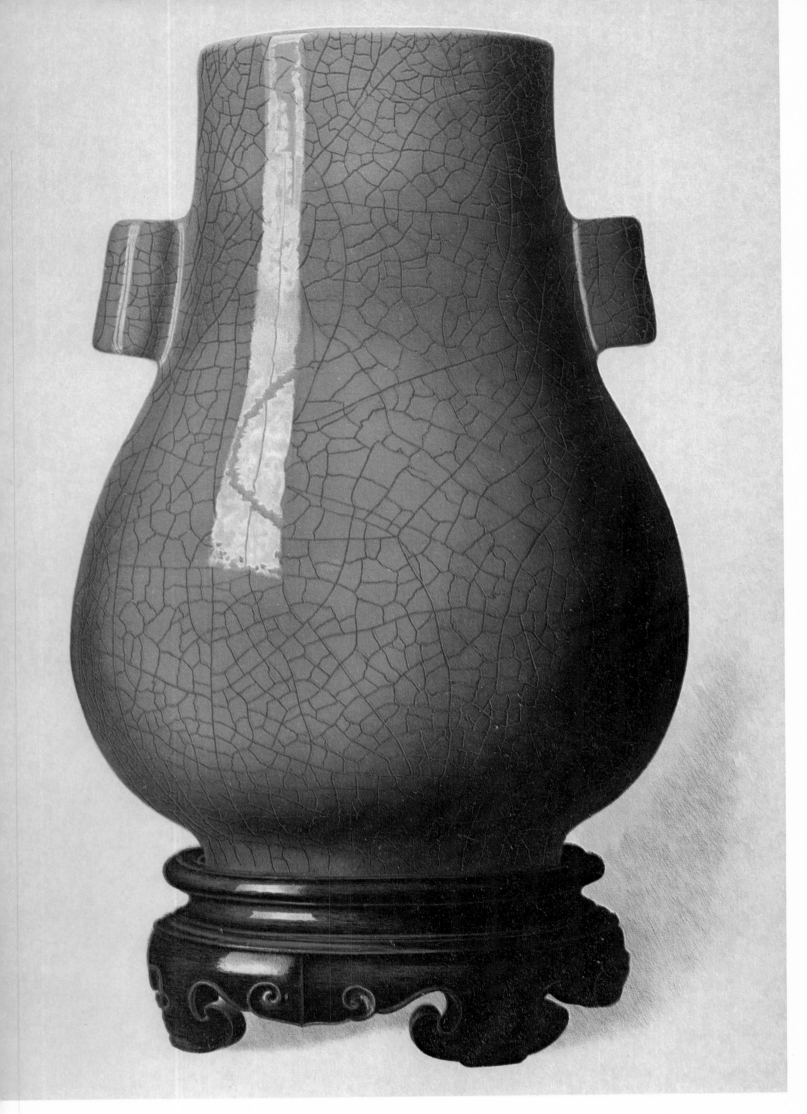

PLATE LXXIX

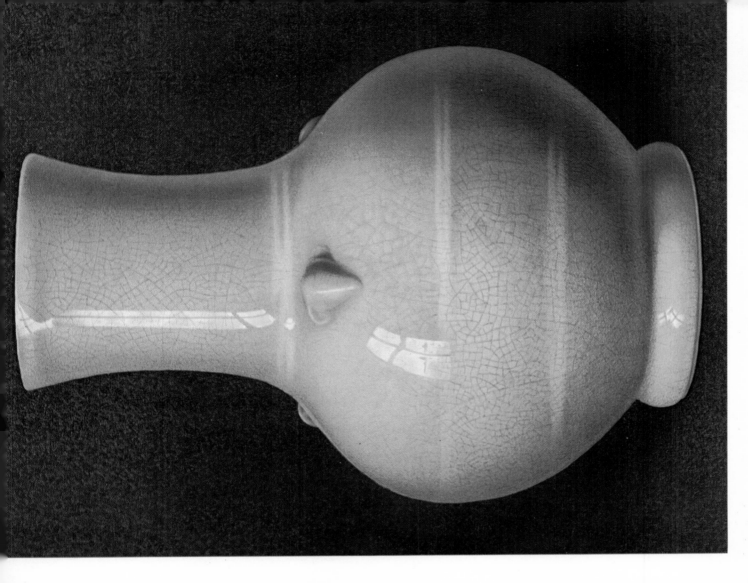

PLATE LXXVII

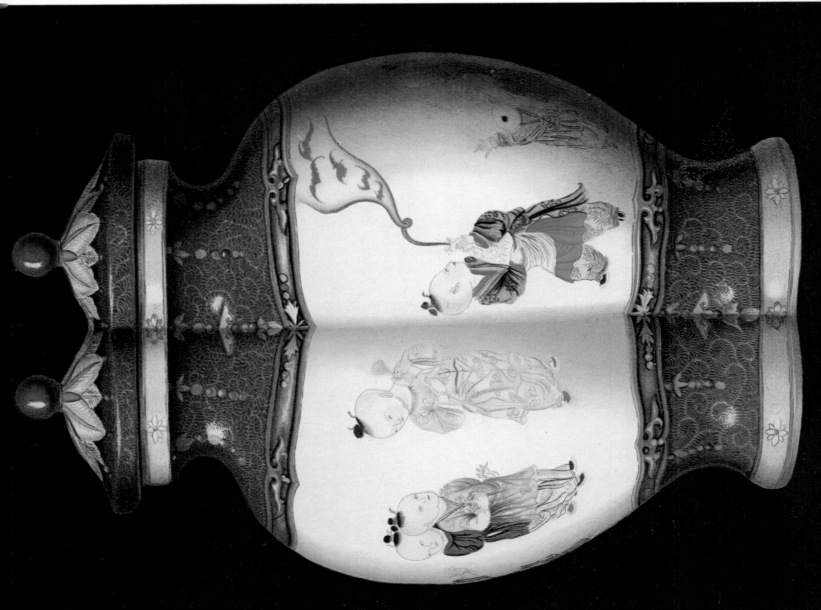

PLATE LXXVI

PLATE LXXVIII

PLATE LXXXII

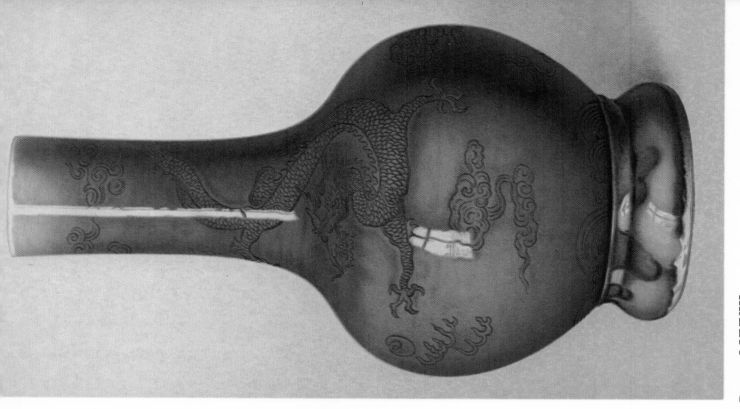

PLATE LXXXIII

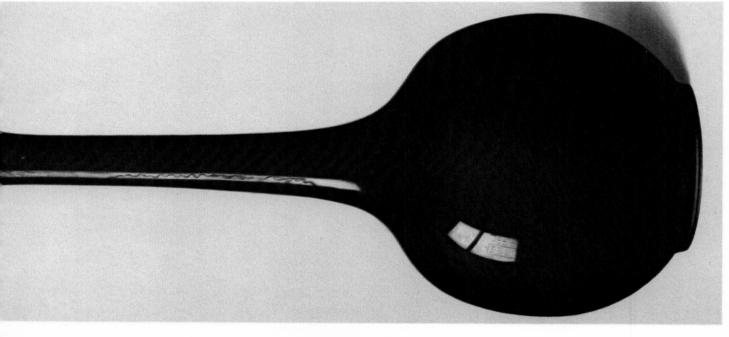

PLATE LXXX

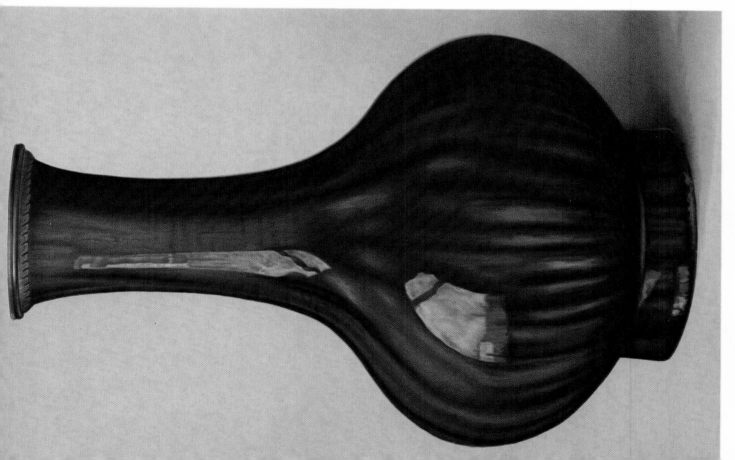

PLATE LXXI

PLATE LXXXIV

PLATE LXXXV

PLATE LXXXVIII   PLATE LXXXVI   PLATE XCVI

PLATE LXXXVII

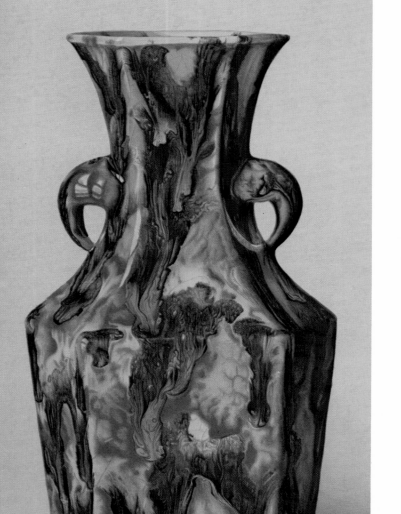

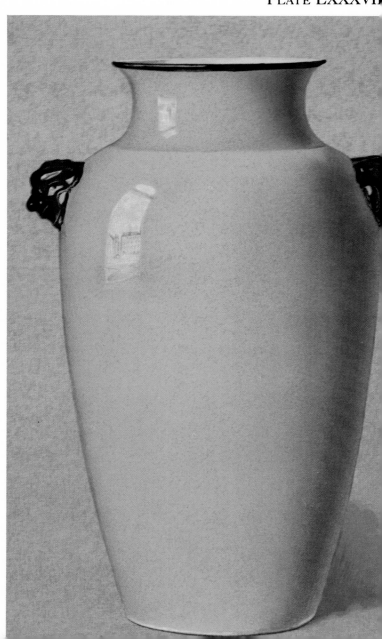

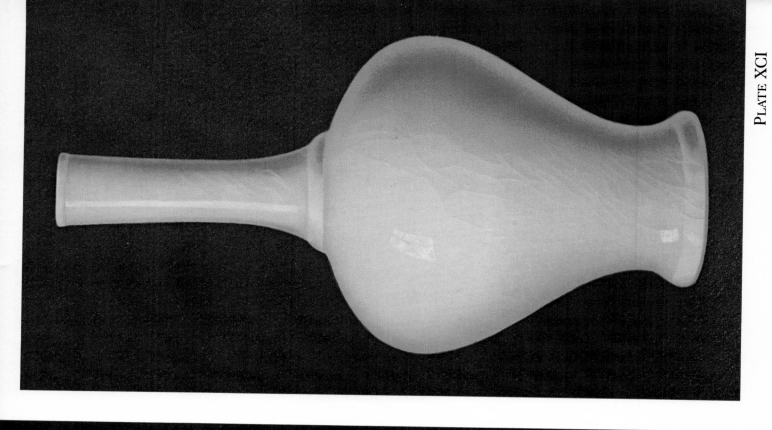

PLATE XCI

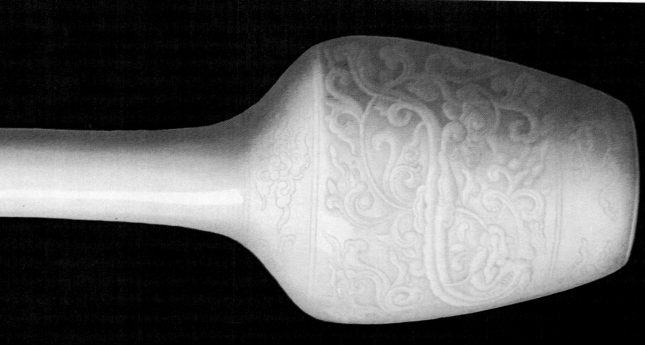

PLATE XC

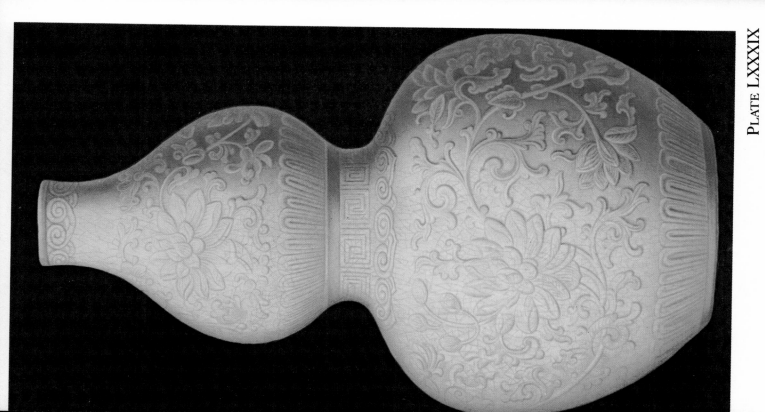

PLATE LXXXIX

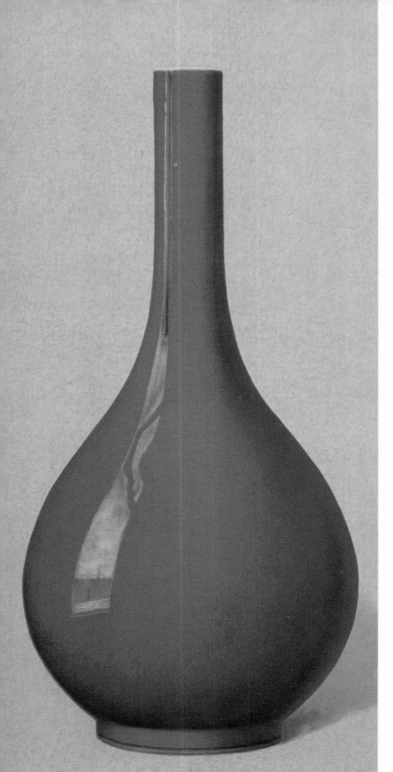

PLATE XCII

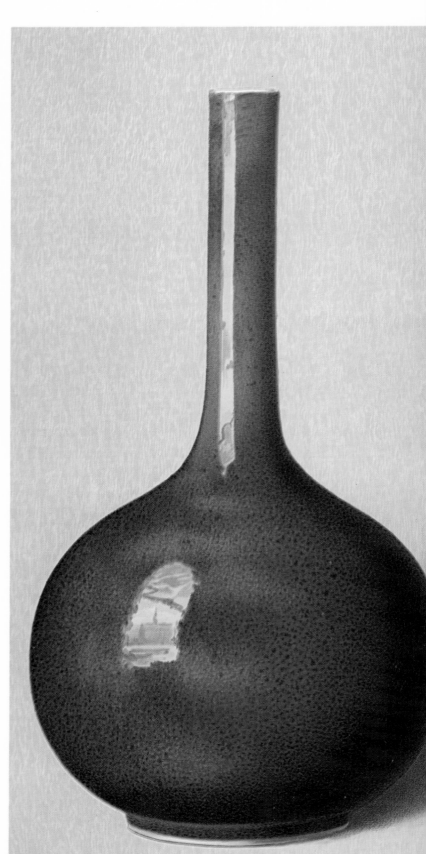

PLATE XCIII

PLATE XCI

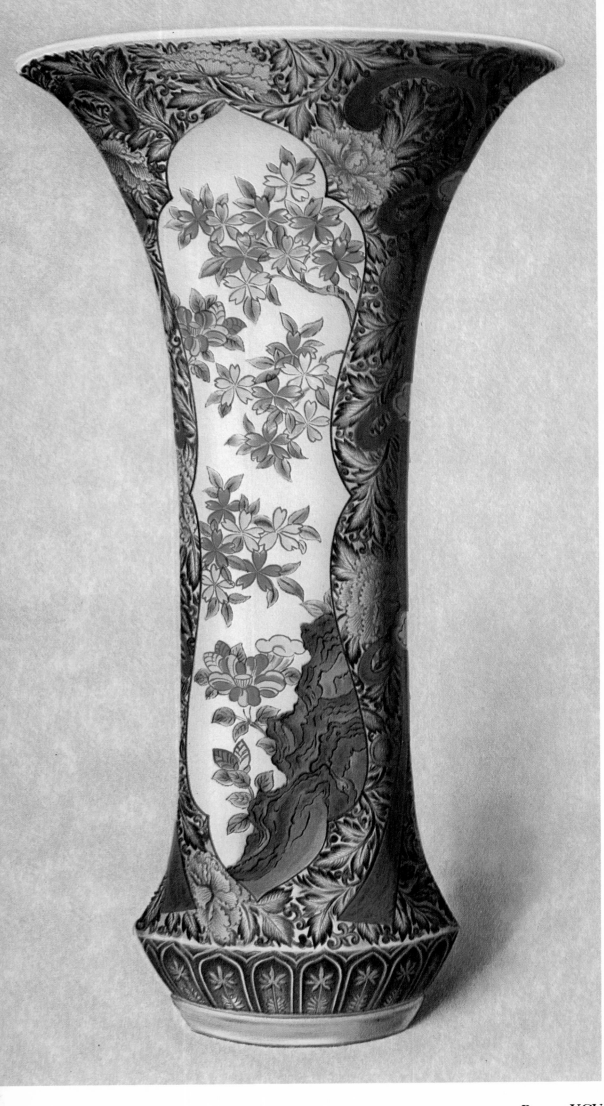

PLATE XCV

Plate XCIX

Plate XCVII

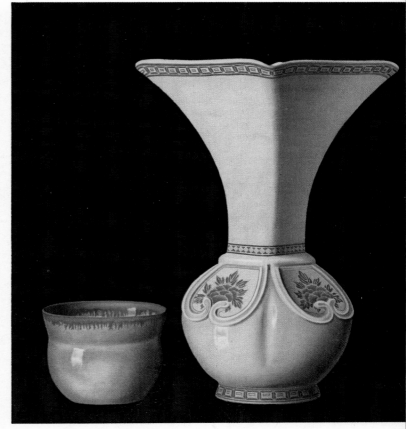

Plate C

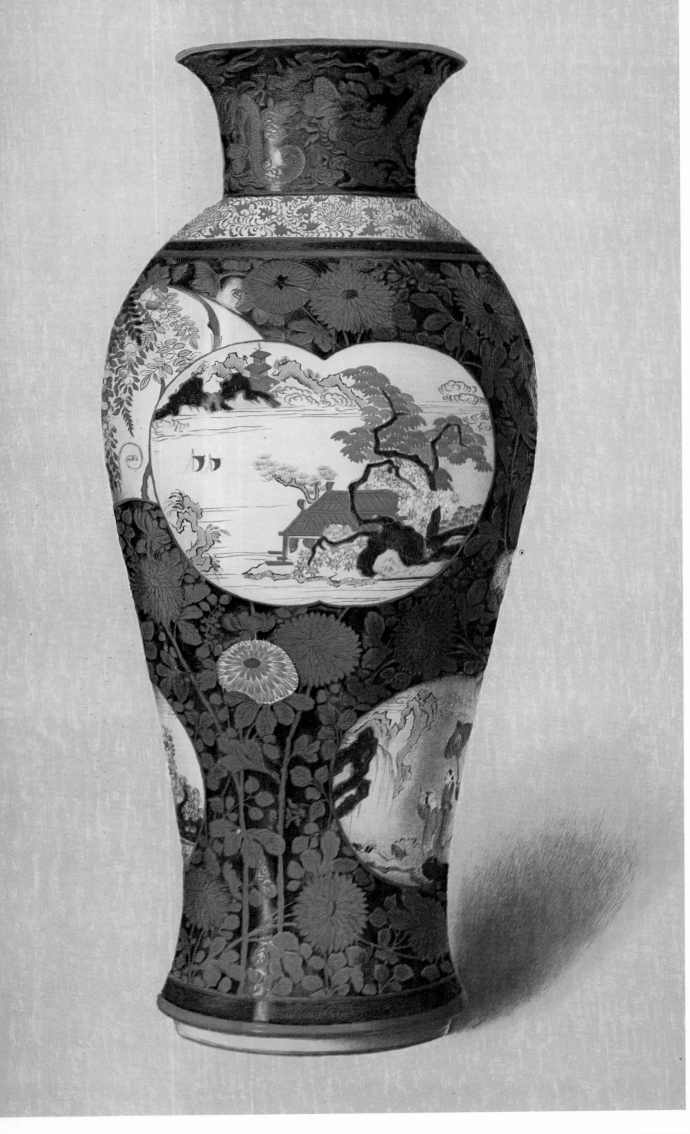

PLATE XCVIII

PLATE CI

PLATE CII

PLATE CIII

PLATE CIV

PLATE CV

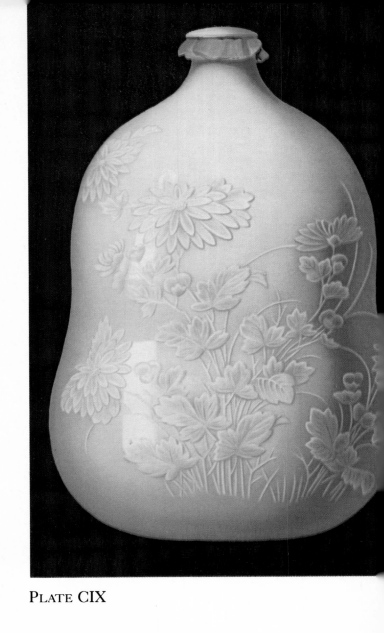

PLATE CVI   PLATE CIX

PLATE CVII

PLATE CVIII

PLATE CX

PLATE CXI

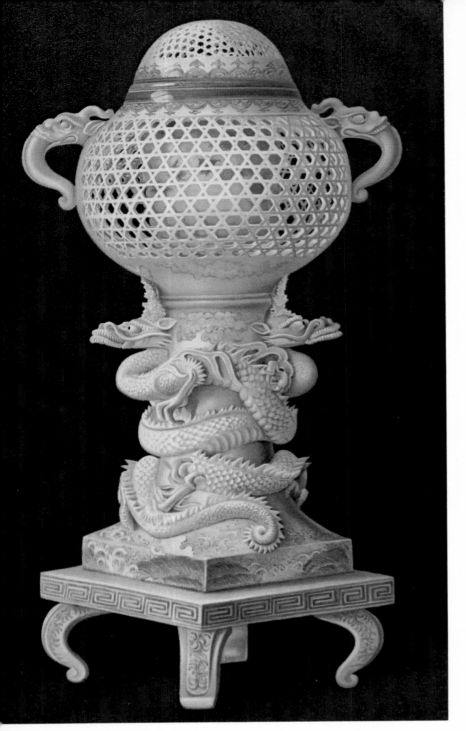

PLATE CXII

PLATE CXIV

PLATE CXIII

PLATE CXV

PLATE CXVI

FIG. 3.—Small Conical Bowl of Yuan dynasty porcelain, with crackled glaze of ivory-white tint; Jar of archaic iron-gray stoneware with a crackled glaze of stone-gray celadon color, specimen of Kuang Yao of Yuan dynasty; Bowl of Yuan dynasty ware (Yuan Tz'ŭ), of reddish-gray body, with crackled purplish glaze, mottled with brown.

ORIENTAL CERAMIC ART.

INTRODUCTION.

DURING a residence of twenty-five years at Peking, as physician to her Britannic Majesty's legation, the study of Chinese ceramics has been my chief distraction. I have obtained access, in the exercise of the duties of my profession, to several palaces and private houses, and have in this way had many opportunities of seeing the treasures of native collectors, which usually are so rigidly closed to foreigners. The Chinese themselves maintain a profound interest in the subject, especially from an antiquarian point of view, and the literature which relates to it is very extensive, ranging as it does over many centuries. The best special work is the *T'ao Shuo*, "A Description of Chinese Pottery," in six books, published in the year 1774, by Chu Yen. The learned author quotes many of the older writers, and describes all the varieties of the potter's skill that became celebrated before the close of the *Ming* dynasty in 1643. I translated this work into English, at the request of the late Mr. W. T. Walters, some years ago, so that I now have it before me for reference. For the older wares there is also the manuscript catalogue, illustrated by eighty-two water-color drawings, of Hsiang Yuan-p'ien, a celebrated collector of the latter half of the sixteenth century, which I brought before the notice of the Peking Oriental Society in 1886,* and which I hope some day to publish in full. The colored illustrations are fairly exact, and are indispensable for the proper comprehension of the text of Chinese writers on this subject, in the absence of actual specimens of the different kinds of porcelain described. The author of the *T'ao Shuo* is not so satisfactory as a guide to the porcelain of the reigning dynasty, of which he gives only a short *résumé* in his first book. For this we must turn to the *Ching-tê-chên T'ao Lu*, the well-known memoirs on the productions of Ching-tê-chên, published in 1815, which were partially translated into French by Stanislas Julien in 1856,† and which have

FIG. 4.—Square Bottle, one of a pair, of the K'ang-hsi Period, with an intense coral-red iridescent ground surrounding reserves painted in colors, Louis XVI mounts.

* *Chinese Porcelain before the Present Dynasty*, by S. W. Bushell, M. D.; extract from the Journal of the Peking Oriental Society, 1886.

† *Histoire et Fabrication de la Porcelaine chinoise*, par M. Stanislas Julien, Paris, 1856.

been the main source of information for all European writers. The translator seems, however, to have had little if any practical acquaintance with Chinese porcelain, and he had, moreover, no native expert at hand to refer to in case of difficulty, so that his rendering of technical points is often erroneous. It is always safer to turn to the original, which is happily no longer rare, as the book has been lately republished in China. Ching-tê-chên, which has been for centuries the seat of the imperial manufactory of porcelain, occupies a place in China like to that which Sèvres does in France or Meissen in Germany. It is, indeed, in the present day the sole source of artistic porcelain in the Chinese Empire. The regulations and detailed accounts of the imperial works are to be found in the different official statistical descriptions of the province of Kiangsi, of the prefecture of Jao-chou-fu, and of the district of Fou-liang, in which the manufactory is situated. But, unfortunately, these books, which at irregular intervals are issued and republished in a revised form by the authorities, are very difficult to procure, even in China. The most complete account is contained in the *Fou-liang Hsien Chih*, the "History of the Walled City of Fou-liang," and I am most grateful to the director of the Bibliothèque Nationale in Paris for his generous loan of this rare work, the eighth book of which includes a long memoir entitled *T'ao Chêng*, or "Porcelain Administration." This edition was published by a commission presided over by Ho Hsi-ling, a member of the Hanlin College and of the National Historiographers' Office, whose preface is dated the third year of *Tao-kuang* (1823), although the

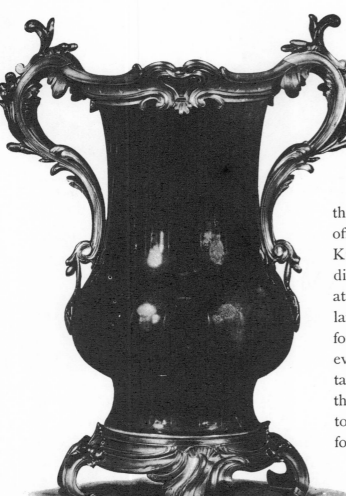

FIG. 5.—Sang-de-Bœuf Vase of the K'ang-hsi period (Lang Yao), with characteristic mottling and streaks of brilliant color; old European mounts.

list of officials in the book is continued up to the twelfth year of the emperor (1832). The first edition, which was published in the period *Hsien-shun* during the *Sung* dynasty, in the year 1270, was burned. The present edition gives twenty-one old prefaces, which are all printed in full, and the first of these is dated 1325. The fifteenth, by T'ang Ying, the most celebrated of the superintendents of the imperial manufactory at Ching-tê-chên, is dated the fifth year of *Ch'ien-lung* (1740). The entire series of these official statistical works, were it possible to obtain it complete, would furnish the most authentic of accounts, in chronological sequence, of the imperial manufacture of porcelain.

Since my return to Peking last year I have succeeded in acquiring a recent edition of the *Chiang-hsi T'ung Chih*, the "General History of the Province of Kiangsi," published in the seventh year of the reigning Emperor *Kuang-hsü*, by an imperial commission presided over by the famous Tsêng-Kuo-fan. It is bound in native fashion in one hundred and twenty volumes, and contains one hundred and eighty books, of which the ninety-third gives the *T'ao-Chêng*, or "Porcelain Administration," of Ching-tê-chên, brought up to date.

FIG. 6.—K'ang-hsi Ovoid Vase of brownish-red monochrome, one of a pair, mounted in silver as bowls with covers.

I am indebted to M. Garnier, the talented director of the museum at Sèvres, for the opportunity to consult a report written by my lamented friend, M. Scherzer, who visited Ching-tê-chên in 1883, at which time he was French consul at the river port of Hankow. It is curious to compare this recent report with the two valuable letters of the old Jesuit missionary Père d'Entrecolles, written from the same place in 1712 and 1722, toward the close of the long reign of the Emperor *K'ang-hsi*, the culminating period of ceramic art in China.* The worthy Father collected his information from his converts among the artists and workmen, and his letters are all the more valuable in that we have so little from native writers during this reign.

From the foregoing some idea may be gained of the material which is available to the student who undertakes to present a general account of Oriental ceramic art. To illustrate such a work there could be no better opportunity than that which is afforded by the W. T. Walters collection. Such is the object which it has been sought here to attain. The illustrations and text have had to be arranged independently, most of the colored plates having been completed beforehand. The text-cuts will be inserted, as far as possible, in appropriate places, and there will be a descriptive list of the figures included later on, which it is hoped will remedy the disjunction which the issue of the book in parts has rendered unavoidable. For text-cuts of the first section a selection has been made from the series of objects of Chinese porcelain mounted in metal, in which the collection is so very rich. The mountings are generally in gilded bronze of French workmanship, dating for the most part from the 18th century. Some of them by the famous Gouthière are of the highest artistic merit, and indicate the vivid appreciation of Chinese colors for the decoration of the luxurious interiors of the time of Louis XV and Louis XVI. It is difficult, indeed, to imagine anything more effective than the

Fig. 7.—Large Celadon Vase of Ming Period, with relief decoration, European metal mounts.

soft changing tints of the turquoise glaze of the vases in Figs. 1 and 20, and of the bowl (Fig. 40), when exhibited in such perfect contrast with the gilded material of their graceful framework. The same may be said of the lovely open-work mounting in gold, fashioned to strengthen the etched turquoise vase of Fig. 8, and of the filigree mounts of the beautifully decorated *K'ang-hsi* vases exhibited in Figs. 11 and 30, lovingly executed and signed by the modern jeweler, Boucheron of Paris. Mountings of Persian and Japanese workmanship will follow in other sections. Some of these mounts are interesting as aids in determining the age of the piece, like the Elizabethan silver-gilt mounting with the hall mark of 1585 of the blue and white Chinese Jug, No. 7,915, in the South Kensington Museum, and the blue and white pieces which are said to have been at Burghley House in the possession of the Cecil family since the days of Queen Elizabeth.

Fig. 8.—Chia-ch'ing Vase with delicately etched designs under a minutely crackled turquoise glaze of soft tone; French mounting in gold.

The Walters collection is remarkable for its single color or monochrome examples, and comprises many choice specimens of brilliant beauty in this attractive branch of art, in which the Oriental potter stands unrivaled. There is room for much difference of opinion on the question of the comparative merits of monochrome glazes and of painted decoration in enamel colors upon porcelain. With the Chinese collector, as with the European or American amateur, it is a matter of taste, and the preference appears to be equally divided.

* *Lettres édifiantes et curieuses,* xviii, pp. 224–296; xix, pp. 173–203, Paris, 1781.

The earliest acquaintance of European collectors with the porcelain of China was confined to monochrome examples, including, of course, blue and white. Of the five-color pieces of the *Ming* period it is difficult to find any trace in the early European collections; and, indeed, it appears that it is only within recent years that such pieces have left China. M. Vogt, the director of the porcelain manufactory at Sèvres, the most recent writer on the subject and a thoroughly competent judge, writes (pages **22, 23**): "The form commands the decoration; the Chinese have wisely preferred simple, absolutely ceramic forms, of which their vase (*potiche*) is the essential type. In this shape, fashioned in one operation, the surface is unbroken from the base to the mouth; it is in reality a cylinder with flowing depressions. For the decoration of Chinese vases, whatever may be the merit resulting from the fantastic art of the composition or from the harmony of the colors, we prefer, for our part, not the decorated vases, but the pieces which have the ground left as they come from the kiln, the beauty of the enamel being the dominant quality

(*la qualité maîtresse*) in ce- the enamel, the more op- no color, no gilding, could absorption of the *flambés ma-fei*, horse's lung—mix- and yellowish-green running over lava, so much chopped-up blood, into enamels; any addition would tea-dust glaze, or the iron-rust of

Mr. Walters wrote, in the in- "Our interest and effort have been characteristic examples of the beau- terial, than of the merely truth, been fully realized; more beautiful, in all these peach-bloom vases, which appreciate, outside China, of form, in perfect finish of play of color, whereby they the warm and varied hues

FIG. 9.—K'ang-hsi Leaf-shaped Fruit Dish, one of a pair, of finely crackled apple-green ground, with sprays of flowers and fruit in open-work relief inside touched with colors, European stands.

ramics. The more beautiful posed it is to decoration; resist the vibrating force of called *lo-kan*, mule's liver; tures of red, blue, violet, the porcelain like a stream of lungs, and liver, as it were, melted spoil the softer colors, such as the the Chinese." *

troduction to his early catalogue, † more in the direction of securing tiful, either in form, color, or ma- curious." This aim has, in for what can be imagined three respects, than the famous he was one of the first to excelling as they do in purity material, and in a diversified have been so aptly likened to of the skin of a peach ‡ ripen-

ing in the sun? They mark the culminating point of Chinese ceramic art. The contemporary vases of similar form of pure white, of the sea-green tint called celadon, or of the pale gray-blue known by the French as *clair de lune*, after its Chinese name of *yueh pai*, are almost as attractive. The crimson and pink monochrome glazes of the succeeding period, derived from gold, are less pure, but have the softness of the muffle stove in which they are developed—a quality which they share with another famous color, the coral red, which is derived from peroxide of iron. The older colors, which attest the pre-eminence of the Chinese potter, include a camellia-leaf green of deepest iridescent sheen, sapphire blue, and powder-blue, apple-green and citron-yellow, a finely crackled turquoise glaze of purest tint, and, last but not least, the celebrated *Lang yao*, or *sang de bœuf*, a broadly crackled glaze imbued with red of marvelous depth, the despair of modern imitators. This is a short list of some of the successes of the Oriental decorator in the line of single colors. Working as he does with impure materials, with the chemical composition of which he is totally unfamiliar, his chief successes are often due

---

* *La Porcelaine*, par Georges Vogt, Directeur des Travaux Techniques de la Manufacture Nationale de Sèvres, Paris, 1894.

† *Oriental Collection of W. T. Walters*, Baltimore, 1884.

‡ "Peach-bloom" is a better name in English for this charming glaze than "peach-blow," because the latter is only applicable to the flower, while the former corresponds to the *peau de pêche*, the term adopted by French ceramists. Neither of the two is Chinese; they generally call it *Chiang-tou Hung*, from its resemblance to the variegated beans of the *Dolichus sinensis* (*Chiang-tou*), which are pink spotted with brown; some call it *P'ing-kuo Hung*, "apple-red." The green mottling which so often accompanies it is termed *P'ing-kuo Ch'ing*, or "apple-green."

to pure hazard. Many other colors will be described later, as well as the decoration of the painted pieces, on which the artist works with the same palette.

According to a Chinese adage, "Knowledge comes from seeing much," and I would like to refer the student to some of the collections available for the study of the subject of Oriental ceramics, and at the same time seize the opportunity of tendering my grateful thanks to the owners of the private collections in the United States which I have had the opportunity of seeing, and from which I have learned not a little. There seems to be a widespread enthusiasm in America for the beauties of Oriental art, and the beautiful objects illustrated in this book have doubtless, by their exhibition in the galleries at Baltimore, helped in no small measure to form a growing taste for the rare and beautiful. There are, so far, no national collections in America, but there are objects of interest in the private collections of Mr. Charles A. Dana, Mr. James A. Garland, and Mr. W. M. Laffan, and in the Avery collection in the Metropolitan Museum at New York, and in the Hippisley collection on loan at the Smithsonian Institution at Washington, of which a catalogue,* rich in Chinese lore, has been published by my friend Mr. Hippisley, who is a sinologue of foremost rank. Among the European collections of most easy access are the Franks collection in the British Museum; the Salting collection, which includes so many

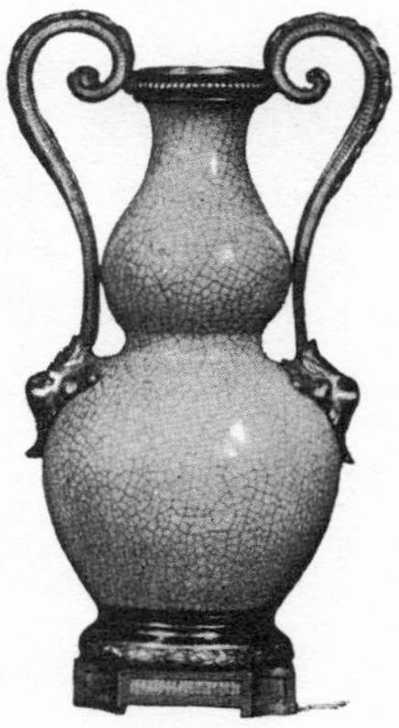

FIG. 10.—Gourd-shaped Vase, one of a pair of gray crackle of the K'ang-hsi Period, with European mounts.

FIG. 11.—Vase of K'ang-hsi Period, decorated in brilliant enamel colors, gilded mounts in Oriental style, signed "Boucheron," Paris.

FIG. 12.—Snuff Bottle with Po-Ku emblems in painted relief on a fret background.

magnificent pieces, in the loan exhibition at the South Kensington Museum; and the Grandidier collection at Paris. Sir Wollaston Franks, who has presented his treasures to the British Museum, is *facile princeps* among European authorities, and the author of a well-known handbook.† M. Grandidier, a critical as well as an enthusiastic admirer of Chinese porcelain, and the compiler of a fine book‡ illustrated by forty-two heliogravures, has recently presented his collection to the republic, and it is already worthily installed in one of the galleries of the Louvre.

The Sèvres Museum contains an Oriental department of considerable value. The museums of Amsterdam and The Hague display a selection of the porcelain brought over in such quantities by the Dutch East India Company in the sixteenth and seventeenth centuries. The Dresden Oriental collection is probably the most ancient in Europe, having been chiefly brought together, according to its former director, Dr. Graesse,△ by Augustus the Strong, King of Poland and Elector of Saxony, between the years 1694–1705. This is the palmy period of the reign of the Chinese Emperor *K'ang-hsi* (1662–1722), to which time most if not all of the more important Chinese pieces in this large collection must be referred. This collection is also remarkable for its series of old Japan jars and beakers decorated with polychrome enamels. It was stored

* *Catalogue of the Hippisley Collection of Chinese Porcelains*, by A. E. Hippisley. Report of National Museum, 1888, Washington, D. C.

† *Catalogue of a Collection of Oriental Porcelain and Pottery*, by A. W. Franks, F. R. S., F. S. A., second edition, London, 1878.

‡ *La Céramique chinoise*, par E. Grandidier, Paris, 1894.

△ *Die K. Porzellan und Gefass-Sammlung zu Dresden*, von Hofrath Dr. J. G. Th. Graesse, Dresden, 1873.

away for many years in the vaults of exhibited in the Johanneum on the

The question of celadon is one problems, and its solution has thrown known, is the name applied to a pecul- which is found distributed through- the eastern and northern coasts of

the Japanese palace, but is now fully opposite side of the river.

of the most interesting of ceramic a flood of light on the intercourse be- tween distant nations in early medi- æval times.* Celadon, as is well iar kind of porcelain of sea-green tint, out southern and western Asia, along

FIG. 13.—Celadon Jar of the Ch'ien-lung Period, with ar- chaic designs worked in slight relief under the glaze, European mounts, parcel gilt and inlaid with enamels.

FIG. 14.—Blue and White Vase, one of a pair, of K'ang-hsi Period, with European mounting.

FIG. 15.—Monochrome Vase, one of a pair, of soufflé cop- per-red (Nien Yao), mounted in metal as ewers.

Africa, and in the adjoining islands, from Ceram and the Key Island on the east to Madagascar and Zanzibar on the west, as well as in Japan and China. A quantity has been dug up in recent times in Cairo, and Persia is a never-failing source of the thick, round dishes with fluted borders, foliated rims, and tooled decoration under the glaze, which Mohammedans value so

FIG. 16.—A Pillow; fine five-colored decoration, with diapered bands. Period of K'ang-hsi.

highly because they are supposed to change color at the contact of poisoned food. The Arabs called them *martabâni*, a name derived from Martabân, one of the states of ancient Siam, the modern Maulmain; and one of their encyclopædists, writing early in the seventeenth century, declared that "the precious magnificent celadon dishes and other vessels seen in his time were

* *Ancient Porcelain : A Study in Chinese Mediæval Industry and Trade*, by F. Hirth, Ph. D., 1880.

manufactured at Martabân." Starting from this, Prof. Karabacek, of Vienna, has lately tried to prove that this old celadon was not Chinese. Others, like Jacquemart, had previously ascribed it to Persia or to Egypt, arguing principally from the difficulty of transporting such large quantities by caravan traffic across Asia. But this difficulty vanishes now that we know from Mohammedan as well as Chinese sources of the long sea voyages undertaken by the Chinese in early times.

Arabian writers speak of fleets of large Chinese junks in the Persian Gulf as early as the ninth century, and their route may be followed in the official annals of the *T'ang* dynasty. Chinese authors of the *Sung* dynasty describe how their ships travelled along the coast of Africa as far south as Zanzibar, which they call Tsang-pa, and copper "cash" of the period have lately been dug up there mixed with fragments of celadon vessels. They carried *ch'ing t'zu*, "green, or celadon, porcelain," and brought back *wu ming yi*, "cobalt mineral." In the next dynasty, when the Mongols ruled Bagdad as well as Peking, the traffic by sea was still more constant. Marco Polo travelled homeward in the suite of a Mongolian princess, and described the route from Zayton to Hormuz; and Ibn Batista, who came to China soon afterward, also alludes to the trade in Chinese porcelain. In the *Ming* dynasty, which succeeded, the ambitious Emperor *Yung-lo* dispatched the fighting eunuch, Admiral Chêng Ho, who carried Chinese arms into Ceylon, and who was again sent on a more peaceful mission by the next emperor, *Hsüan-te*, in the year 1430, to the south coast of Arabia, to the port of Magadoxo in Africa, and to Jiddah, the seaport of Mecca in the Red Sea, to which he carried celadon porcelain, as well as musk, silk, camphor, and copper "cash." This was the time that *Su-ma-li* blue was brought to China. Cobalt had long previously been employed in Persia in the decoration of tiles and other objects of faience. After the appearance of the Portuguese ships in their seas Chinese junks were no more seen, but celadon porcelain was left behind in all the coasts they visited, and there seems little reason to doubt its exclusively Chinese origin.

FIG. 17.—Blue and White Saucer Dish of the K'ang-hsi Period,
decorated with conventional scrolls of lotus design.

FIG. 18.—Eggshell Wine Cup of the K'ang-hsi Period, enameled white, with a delicate scroll in blue round the foot; Eggshell Wine Cup, one of a pair, of the Wan-li Period, with the decoration molded in relief inside under the white glaze.

CHAPTER I.

ORIGIN OF PORCELAIN.

PORCELAIN was invented in China. The exact date of the invention, however, is wrapped in mystery; it is, in fact, hardly likely that it will ever be definitely settled, as it must have been by a gradual progress in the selection of materials, and in the perfection of processes of manufacture, that porcelain was at last evolved from ordinary pottery. For the creation of a scientific classification of ceramic products we are indebted to M. Brongniart,* and it will be well first to define the distinctive characteristics of porcelain. Porcelain ought to have a white, translucent, hard paste, not to be scratched by steel, homogeneous, resonant, completely vitrified, and exhibiting, when broken, a conchoidal fracture of fine grain and brilliant aspect. These qualities, inherent in porcelain, make it impermeable to water, and enable it to resist the action of frost even when uncoated with glaze. These characteristics of the paste, especially the translucence and vitrification, define porcelain very well. If either of these two qualities be wanting, we have before us another kind of pottery; if the paste possess all the other properties, with the exception of translucence, it is a stoneware; if the paste be not vitrified, it belongs to the category of terra cottas or of faience.

FIG. 19.—Large Ewer, for iced syrup, enamelled with a finely crackled purple glaze of aubergine tint, K'ang-hsi Period, Louis XVI mounts.

The Chinese define porcelain, which they call 瓷 (*tz'ŭ*), as a hard, compact, fine-grained pottery 陶 (*t'ao*), and distinguish it by the clear, resonant note which it gives out on percussion, and by the fact that it can not be scratched by a knife. They do not lay so much stress on the whiteness of the paste, nor on its translucency, so that some of the pieces may fail in these two points, when the fabric is coarse; and yet it would be difficult to separate them from the porcelain class. The paste of the ordinary ware, even at Ching-tê-chên, is composed of more heterogeneous materials than that fabricated in European factories, and may even be reduced in some cases to a mere layer of true porcelain earths plastered over a substratum of yellowish gray clay. The Chinese separate, on the other hand, dark-colored stonewares, like the reddish-yellow ware made at Yi-hsing, in the province of Kiangnan, known to us by the Portuguese name of *boccaro*, or the brown stoneware produced at Yang-chiang, in the southern part of

---

* *Traité des Arts Céramiques*, par Alexandre Brongniart, two volumes, 8vo, with Atlas, Paris, 1844.

the province of Kwang-tung, which is coated with colored enamels, and is often put in European collections among the monochrome porcelains.

The Chinese word for pottery in its widest sense is *t'ao*, which includes all ceramic products, from common earthenware to porcelain. Like many of the great nations of antiquity, they claim for themselves the invention of the potter's wheel. M. Brongniart is inclined to admit their claim, and even attempts to trace the route by which it may have reached Egypt, through Scythia and Bactria; but such speculations seem too hazardous. It was certainly known to the Egyptians at a very early period, probably not later than twenty-five hundred years before our era. Scenes depicted at Beni Hassan and at Thebes show us the Egyptian potters at work, and figure the simple wheel, consisting of a flat disk or hexagonal table, placed on a stand, which appears to have been turned with the left hand while the vase was shaped with the right.* The Chinese claims go back to about the same period, as they attribute the invention of the potter's wheel to the director of pottery attached to the court of the fabulous Emperor *Huang Ti*, to whose reign they carry back their cyclical system of chronology, starting from a date corresponding to B. C. 2637. The Emperor *Shun*, whose reign is placed in B. C. 2255–2206, is generally credited with the first improvements in the art of welding clay. Ssŭ-ma Ch'ien, the Herodotus of China, the compiler of the *Shih Chi*, the first of the dynastic histories, says in his biography of *Shun*, that before he came to the throne he made pottery at Ho-pin. This name, by the way, furnishes an explanation for a Japanese seal, figured in the *Franks Catalogue* (Plate XV, Fig. 191), which reads in Chinese *Ho-pin chih liu*, or Offshoot of Ho-pin, a title taken from old Chinese lore to be bestowed on a favorite potter by one of the Japanese feudal princes. Père d'Entrecolles describes the immense value a Chinaman attaches to any pieces of pottery he can attribute to the reigns of *Yao* and *Shun*. Tradition says that *Yao* adored simplicity, and had

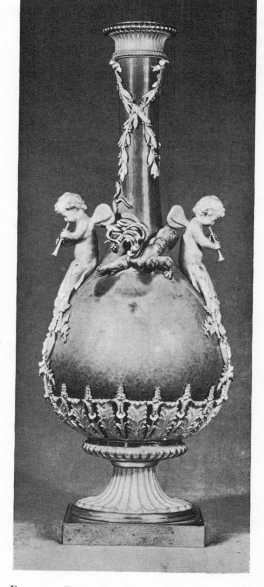

FIG. 20.—Turquoise Vase with dragon in relief, in magnificent bronze mounting of Louis XVI work.

FIG. 21.—Dark "Iron-rust" Glaze flecked with metallic iridescent spots, European mounts.

his sacrificial vessels fashioned of plain yellow earthenware, and that *Shun* was the first to have them glazed, and the credulous collector classifies his prehistoric pieces accordingly.

Coming to more historical times, the period of the *Chou* dynasty (B. C. 1122–249), the third of the Three Ancient Dynasties, its founder, *Wu Wang*, is recorded to have sought out a lineal descendant of the Emperor *Shun*, on account especially of his hereditary skill in the manufacture of pottery, to have given him his eldest daughter in marriage, and to have appointed him feudal ruler of the state of Ch'ên (now Ch'ên-chou Fu, in the province of Honan), to keep up there the ancestral worship of his accomplished ancestor. This noble is supposed to have been the first director of pottery under the new dynasty, an official often alluded to in the *Ceremonial Classic* and in other ancient records of the period.

The *Chou Ritual* has been preserved among the classical books, and consists of an elabo-

* *History of Ancient Pottery*, by S. Birch, London, 1858.

FIG. 22.—K'ang-hsi Vase of pale cobalt blue (T'ien Ch'ing), with Louis XVI mounts.

rate detail of the various officers, with their respective duties. It has been translated into French.* The officers were classed then, as now, under six boards. But when the book was edited in the first century B. C. by Liu Hin, the sixth section, which was that of the Board of Works, was found to be wanting. To supply the deficiency he incorporated the *K'ao kung chi*, an artificer's manual of the same period. This includes a short section on pottery, which gives the names and measurements of several kinds of cooking vessels, sacrificial vases, and dishes, in the fabrication of which the different processes of fashioning upon the wheel and of molding are clearly distinguished. The vessels are described as having been made by two classes of workmen, called respectively *t'ao-jên*, "potters," and *fang-jên*, "molders."

But few specimens of pottery that can be certainly referred to the Three Ancient Dynasties have survived to the present day, although ritual vessels and other antiques of bronze are to be seen in native collections by thousands. These last often have inscriptions upon them, beginning perhaps with the number of the month, the waxing or waning period of the moon, the day of the month and its cyclical number; rarely is the year of the reigning sovereign or feudal suzerain prefixed; never his name, as far as I know. It was during the *Han* dynasty, which reigned from B. C. 202 to A. D. 220, that the system of dividing the reigns into periods of years with honorific titles (*nien hao*) was inaugurated in B. C. 163. This provided for the first time a convenient means of dating vases and other objects.

Bricks and tiles are among the most useful of ceramic products. They may even rank as historical monuments when inscribed. The Chinese antiquary collects them in chronological series to show the changes in the style of the written character, or puts one upon his writing-table for daily use, excavated into the

FIG. 23.—Snuff Bottle of red "boccaro" ware (Yi-hsing), with landscape in white slip painted in colors.

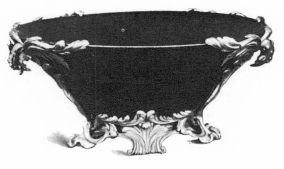

FIG. 24.—Bowl, one of a pair, of the K'ang-hsi Period, enamelled "sur biscuit," with a finely crackled aubergine-purple glaze, European mounts.

FIG. 25.—White Snuff Bottle with a pierced casing carved with nine lions and tasselled balls.

shape of an ink pallet. They were first molded, with the date inscribed on one side, during the *Han* dynasty. Some of the pottery of the period is also inscribed. There is, for instance, a bottle-shaped vase of dark reddish stoneware in the Dana Collection, in New York, molded in the shape of a bronze ritual vessel of the time, enameled with a deep-green iridescent glaze,

* *Le Tcheou, li, ou Rites des Tcheou*, traduit du Chinois par E. Biot, Paris, 1851.

much exfoliated, which is engraved on the surface with a date corresponding to B. C. 133, the second year of the period *Yuan-kuang*. A similar vase in the British Museum, although it has no inscription upon it, evidently dates from about the same time, and specimens of this kind are not uncommon in Chinese collections. The vase illustrated in Fig. 49 is a good example of this class, an ancient stoneware of brownish-red paste, invested with a thin but lustrous glaze of camellia-leaf green, which came from the collection of Chang Yin-huan, formerly Chinese minister at Washington, as a relic of the *Han* dynasty.

There is no word, however, of porcelain so far in Chinese books, and we have to do only with an opaque stoneware, invested with colored glazes. It remained for European writers to ascribe the existence of porcelain to so remote a period, as in the case of the little medicine bottles dug up out of Egyptian tombs that had not, it was supposed, been disturbed before, and which were consequently attributed to the eighteenth century B. C. Their pretensions to such an antiquity have been so abundantly disproved that it is hardly necessary to refer to them here. They must have been fraudulently provided and surreptitiously placed in these tombs by the Arab workmen, who were rewarded whenever any antique was discovered.

Other authorities consider the murrhine vases of the ancients, which were described as " cooked in Parthian fires," and which were so highly valued that the Emperor Nero gave the

FIG. 26.—Crackled Green Celadon Vase of the K'ang-hsi Period, with reserved bands of iron-gray color, elaborate European mounting.

FIG. 27.—Vase of European form mottled with a richly variegated transmutation glaze of the Ch'ien-lung Period, European mounts.

FIG. 28.—Vase of soufflé copper-red of the Yung-chêng Period (Nien Yao), mounted in metal as a small cistern.

equivalent of a quarter of a million dollars for one, to have been made of Chinese porcelain. It is far more probable, as has been suggested by Mr. Nesbitt in his notes on the history of glass-making, that these murrhine vases were made of agates and other hard stones, the colors of which had been modified in the East by heating and staining; and that the false murrhines were glass bowls imitating hard stones, but with various strange tints not to be found in natural stones.

With regard to the origin of porcelain in China, the Chinese themselves confess that previous to the commencement of the *T'ang* dynasty, in A. D. 618, there are no criteria for forming an opinion. The names of some score of different sacrificial vases, drinking vessels, and other objects may be collected from books, but nothing is said about their structure or place of production. It was reserved for a Western scholar to carry back the invention to the *Han* dynasty, and to date it precisely as between B. C. 185 and A. D. 87. These dates, adopted by M. Julien in his preface (*loc. cit.*, p. xx), have been generally followed by writers on the subject, as derived from Chinese records, although based, as we shall show, on fallacious grounds. They are deduced from a short note in the appendix to the memoir on the administration of porcelain in the annals of Fou-liang (*Fou-liang Hsien Chih*, book viii, folio 44), which reads, "The ceramic manufacture of Hsin-p'ing according to local tradition, was founded in the time of the *Han* dynasty, and was probably of strong, heavy, and roughly finished material, moulded and fashioned after methods handed down from ancient times."

Commenting on this passage M. Julien writes: "Sous la première dynastie des *Han*, *Sin-p'ing* était un *hien* [district] qui faisait partie du royaume de *Hoai-yang*, fondé en l'an 185 avant J. C., par l'empereur *Kao-ti* des *Han* occidentaux. Ce royaume fut appelé *Tch'in koue*, dans la deuxième année de la période *Tchang-ho* (l'an 88 après J. C.) du règne des *Han* orientaux. Or, comme la porcelaine parut pour la première fois sous les *Han*, dans le pays de *Sin-p'ing*

FIG. 29.—Square Bottle, one of a pair, of K'ang-hsi Period; powdered blue ground painted in gold with flowers and birds; European mounts.

FIG. 30.—Artistically decorated Vase of the same period and style as Fig. 11, and with similar mounting.

FIG. 31.—Bowl, one of a pair, of Ch'ien-lung turquoise crackle, mounted upon pedestals of German porcelain.

(aujourd'hui *Hoai-ning-hien*, département de *Tch'in-tcheou-fou*, dans le *Honan*), qui a pu appartenir aussi bien au royaume de *Hoai-yang* qu'a celui de *Tch'in*, il s'ensuit qu'on peut en placer l'invention entre les années 185 avant et 87 après, J. C."

The Chinese names of the geographical dictionaries from which these facts are taken are given in footnotes, but all the trouble of reference would have been saved had M. Julien known that Hsin-p'ing was the original name of Fou-liang Hsien. It is recorded in the geographical section of the official annals of the *T'ang* dynasty (*T'ang Shu*, book lx, folio 25) that this walled city was founded under the name of Hsin-p'ing, in the fourth year of the period *Wu-tê* (A. D. 621), with jurisdiction over a tract which formed part of the old district of Po-yang; that it was re-established in the fourth year of *K'ai-yuan* (716), under the new name of Hsin-ch'ang; and that its name was finally changed to Fou-liang (which it has kept to the present day) in the first year of the period *T'ien-pao* (742).

In another part of his book (p. 88), in reference to porcelain made at Hsin-p'ing by Ho Chung-ch'u, in the year 621, for the use of the emperor, Julien strangely identifies this with another Hsin-p'ing, corresponding to the modern Pin-chou, a department in the prefecture of Si-ngan, the capital of the province of Shensi, a city which certainly had this name during the Eastern *Han* dynasty (25–220), but never since, so that this identification involves another anachronism of several centuries. The name signifies "Newly Pacified," and a number of cities seem to have borne it in turn for a brief period.

Hsin-p'ing occurs constantly in different pages of the annals quoted above as the old name of Fou-liang, and it is, besides, referred to more than once in the last three books of the *Ching-tê-chên T'ao Lu*, which are omitted in Julien's translation. An extract, for example, is quoted in book viii, folio 2, from the biography of Chu Sui, styled Yu-hêng, an official under the *T'ang* dynasty, who was superintendent at Hsin-p'ing, when, in the first year of the period *Ching-lung* (A. D. 707), an imperial decree was received by the Governor of Hung-chou, ordering him to supply with all speed a number of sacrificial utensils for the imperial tombs. Chu Sui is described as having pushed on the work so energetically that they were all sent before the end of the year. Hung-chou is the old name of the modern Nan-ch'ang Fu, the chief city of the province of Kiangsi, and Jao-chou, within the bounds of which lies Fou-liang Hsien, is stated in the Annals of the *T'ang* dynasty to have been actually at that time under the jurisdiction of the Governor of Hung-chou.

It seems to me certain that Hsin-p'ing in all these quotations must refer to the same place, which is recorded to have furnished a supply for the imperial court, as early as the seventh century, to be sent to the capital in the northern province of Shensi, and which has been the seat of the imperial potteries since the year 1004, in which Ching-tê-chên was founded, down to the present day. It follows, necessarily, that we must give up the *Han* dynasty as furnishing a certain date for the invention of porcelain. This clears the ground for further research. We know that the word *t'zŭ*, which means porcelain in the present day, first came into use during the *Han* dynasty, and Mr. Hippisley (*loc. cit.*, p. 393) takes this coining of a new word to designate the productions of that age to be a strong argument in favor of the early date. Others, more skeptical, before reaching any decision, ask to be shown actual specimens of translucent body that can be certainly referred to the period.

FIG. 32.—Snuff Bottle molded in basket-work pattern, enamelled turquoise.

In default of such material we will pass on to the *T'ang* dynasty, which ruled over the whole of China for nearly three centuries, during what has been described as a protracted Augustan age, when arts and letters flourished abundantly. During the short-lived *Sui* dynasty (581–617) which immediately preceded the *T'ang* we hear of a kind of green porcelain (*lü tz'ŭ*) invented by a President of the Board of Works named Ho Chou to replace green glass (*liu-li*), the composition of which had been lost. The contemporary annals of the *Sui* dynasty (*Sui Shu*, book lxxxviii, folio 7), which give his biography, say: "Ho Chou had an extensive knowledge of old pictures and a wide acquaintance with objects of antiquity. China had long lost the art of glass-making, and the workmen did not dare to make fresh trials, but he succeeded in making vessels of green porcelain which could not be distinguished from true glass." Considerable progress must have been made about this time in the ceramic manufacture at Fou-liang Hsien, as it is recorded in the geographical account of the district that, in the early years of the reign of the founder of the *T'ang* dynasty, T'ao Yü, a native of the place, conveyed his porcelain to the capital of the empire in the province of Kuan-chung (now Shensi), where his ware, known by the name of "false jade vessels," was all presented to the emperor. The same book records that in the fourth year (A. D. 621) of the same reign an imperial decree was issued ordering the potter Ho Chung-ch'u, referred to above, and other natives of Hsin-p'ing (now Fou-liang), to make a supply of porcelain utensils for the use of the imperial court.

FIG. 33.—Turquoise Crackle Shell, one of a pair, with leaf-shaped covers surmounted by smaller shells, European mounts.

The ceramic ware produced at this time is described to have been of finely levigated paste, thin in body, translucent, and brilliant as white jade. This description seems exaggerated, yet the contemporary name of "imitation jade" is enough, almost, to prove that it must have been really porcelain, taken into consideration with the fact that it was the production of the same district that produces the finest porcelain of the present day. No simile would be more appropriate; for a highly polished bowl of white jade is quite as translucent as the most delicate piece of egg-shell porcelain.

We know that the ceramic art was highly appreciated during the *T'ang* dynasty from the frequent reference to it made in the books of the period. The Buddhist monks had their almsbowls (*po*, Sanskrit *pâtra*) and their ablution vases (*kun-ch'ih-ka*, Sanskrit *kuṇḍika*) made both of porcelain (*t'zǔ*) and of common earthenware (*wa*), preferring the new material on account of its simplicity to the gold, silver, bronze, and precious stones which had been employed previously.

Tea first came into general use as a beverage about this time, and there is a classical treatise on tea, called *Ch'a Ching*, written by Lu Yü in the middle of the eighth century, which is still extant. It contains ten sections, entitled (1) Origin of the Plant; (2) Implements for Gathering; (3) Manufacture of the Leaf; (4) Utensils used in preparing the Infusion; (5) Methods of Boiling; (6) Drinking; (7) Historical Summary; (8) Districts of Production; (9) *Résumé;* and (10) notes on illustrations.

Among the utensils, the bowls (*wan*) used for drinking tea are briefly described, and classified according to the effect of the color of their glaze in enhancing the tint of the infusion, which was made by pouring boiling water upon the powdered tea, the leaves having been previously ground in a mortar. The bowls preferred by the author were those of Yueh-chou, the modern Shao-hsing Fu, in the province of Chehkiang; those of Hsing-chou, now Shun-tê Fu in the province of Chihli, where white porcelain is still produced in the present day, being ranked next. He writes (folio 5): "Yueh-chou bowls are the best. Some persons place Hsing-chou bowls above those of Yueh-chou, but they are,

FIG. 34.—Mug of K'ang-hsi Blue and White, with silver mounting engraved with a crest.

FIG. 35.—K'ang-hsi Vase cut down and mounted as a mug, with a coronet and coat of arms etched upon the cover.

FIG. 36.—White Ch'ien-lung Vase of ancient bronze form, with archaic designs worked in slight relief, impressed seal of the period, European mounts.

in my opinion, mistaken. Hsing-chou porcelain resembles silver, while Yueh-chou porcelain is like jade—the first point in which Hsing is inferior to Yueh; Hsing-chou porcelain resembles snow, Yueh-chou porcelain is like ice—the second point of inferiority; Hsing-chou porcelain being white makes the tea look red, while the Yueh-chou porcelain being green gives a greenish tint to the tea—the third point in which Hsing is inferior to Yueh."

This porcelain, however, was more highly appreciated by others, as one writer of the time observes that "the white teacups of Hsing-chou porcelain, like the brown ink-slabs of Tuan-hsi stone, are prized throughout the empire by high and low alike." Both kinds of porcelain are described as giving out a clear, resonant ring when struck; and a celebrated musician is said, in his biography, to have been in the habit of using ten cups of Yueh-chou or Hsing-chou porcelain to make a musical chime, playing upon them with ebony rods.

The poets of this, the classical age of poetry, make constant reference to porcelain cups in their verses in praise of tea and wine, both favorite subjects for odes. They liken the bowls to curled "disks of thinnest ice," to "tilted lotus leaves floating upon a stream," to "white or green jade." Such similes are applicable only to porcelain. One of the most renowned of these poets, the younger Tu, who lived 803–852, wrote a letter in verse begging for the loan from Wei Ch'u of some white porcelain bowls from the Ta-yi potteries in the province of Ssechuan, which is often quoted: "The porcelain of the Ta-yi kilns is light and yet strong. It rings with a low jade note, and is famed throughout the city. Your Excellency's white bowls surpass hoarfrost and snow. Be gracious to me and send some to my poor mat-shed." The first line praises the quality of the fabric, the second the resonance of the material, the third the color of the glaze.

Arab trade with China was very extensive in the eighth and ninth centuries, when Mohammedan colonies were formed in Canton and other seaport towns. One of the travelers, Soleyman by name, wrote an account of his journey in the middle of the ninth century, which has been translated into French, and he furnishes the first mention of porcelain outside China which may be quoted in confirmation of the Chinese descriptions of the time. He says: "They have in China a very fine clay with which they make vases which are as transparent as glass; water is seen through them. These vases are made of clay."* The Arabs at this time were thoroughly well acquainted with glass, so that this evidence is almost conclusive.

We pass next to the Emperor *Shih Tsung* (954–959) of the Posterior *Chou*, a brief dynasty which reigned just before the *Sung*, who encouraged the manufacture of porcelain at his capital in Honan, now K'ai-fêng Fu. The pieces which were known afterward as *Ch'ai* porcelain, that being the name of the imperial house, were described as being "as blue as the sky, as clear as a mirror, as thin as paper, and as resonant as jade." This eclipsed in its delicacy everything that preceded it. The description refers clearly to an azure-tinted monochrome glaze produced by the use of the native cobaltiferous mineral.

It is probable that no perfect specimens of these delicate wares are still extant, so that we have to be content with only a literary proof of their existence. The Chinese are satisfied with this; they delight in literary research, as much as they dislike digging in the ground, fearing to disturb the rest of the dead. We must be content to wait for future discoveries to satisfy those sceptics who demand tangible evidence of the existence of true porcelain before the *Sung* dynasty. No one, as far as I know, disputes that it existed. But further discussion of this interesting subject must be deferred, meanwhile, to a future chapter.

* *Relation des Voyages faits par les Arabes et les Persans dans l'Inde et à la Chine dans le IXe siècle de l'ère chrétienne*, par M. Reinaud, membre l'Institut, Paris, 1845.

FIG. 37.—Opening Nelumbo in pale green and delicate white porcelain of the period of K'ang-hsi. —Bowl of pale cobalt blue soufflé, mounted with two fish of turquoise crackle.—Delicate blue and white Bowl, with cover surmounted by dog Fu. Decoration of beautifully drawn five-clawed Kilins, with fire emblems. Period of K'ang-hsi.

Fig. 38.—In center, Wine Pot of the Ming Period, turquoise crackle "sur biscuit" splashed with aubergine purple, silver spout and mounts of old work. On left, Yung-chêng Wine Cup, with floral decoration in gold. On right, Tao-kuang Wine Cup, decorated in colors.

CHAPTER II.

RELATIONS OF CHINESE, KOREAN, AND JAPANESE CERAMICS.

THE civilization of China, whether it be indigenous, or derived, as some learned men think, from an Accadian source in western Asia, is certainly much more ancient than that of either Korea or Japan. Those who, like M. Terrien de Lacouperie, would bring it from the Mesopotamian regions, or from the southern shores of the Caspian Sea, place the date of its introduction into China within the third millennium before Christ. The Chinese, who consider, on the other hand, that their culture is entirely of native growth, date it from about the same time, during which the legendary—as distinct from the purely mythical—period of their history begins with Fu-hsi, the reputed founder of the Chinese polity, whose reign is placed by them in B. C. 2852. Their cyclical system of chronology is dated from the reign of *Huang Ti*, the "Yellow Emperor," the first of the periods of sixty years commencing with the year B. C. 2637. He is credited with a full court of officials, who are described as having introduced many of the useful arts, the ceramic art among the rest. The invention of the potter's wheel is generally attributed to his director of pottery. The *Shu King*, or *Book of History*, which has been translated into English by Dr. Legge, and which is one of the most authentic of the ancient classics, begins with the reigns of *Yao* and *Shun*, which immediately precede the "Three Ancient Dynasties" of *Hsia*, *Shang*, and *Chou*, the first that were composed of hereditary lines of sovereigns.

Fig. 39.—K'ang-hsi Blue and White, of brilliant mottled tone, a pair of gourds, with European mounts.

Chou Hsin, the last sovereign of the second ancient dynasty, was an abandoned tyrant, who perished in the flames of the Lu T'ai, or Deer Tower, his luxurious palace of pleasure, in B. C. 1123, the year that he was defeated by Wu Wang, the founder of the *Chou* dynasty. One of the chief feudal nobles of the empire during the reign of the tyrant Chou Hsin was Ki Tzŭ, the Viscount or Chief of Ki. This noble vainly sought to turn the licentious monarch from his evil ways, but was cast into prison, whence he was released by the victorious *Wu Wang* in B. C. 1122. He was offered a high post under the new rule, but declared that he could not recognize the sovereignty of a usurper, and he retired to the country now forming the kingdom of Korea. The peninsula was then inhabited by barbarous tribes, among whom he introduced the first elements of culture, and he was accepted by them as their first ruler, and was so recognized by the new sovereign of China.

Korea is indebted to China for the knowledge of writing, as well as for most of the sciences and useful arts. They use the written characters of China to this day, although they have also an alphabet, derived probably from the Sanskrit, adapted by Buddhist pilgrims from India, who doubtless reached Korea by way of China. There has been frequent intercourse with China throughout historic times. The Chinese invaded the country in force during the *Han* and *T'ang* dynasties, and claim to have reduced it to the condition of a province during the latter *régime*. Most of the Tartar dynasties that have ruled over China, when they emerged from their native wilds on the north of Korea, have first invaded Korea and compelled its submission before overrunning China. The present *Manchu* dynasty is no exception to this general rule. The Koreans, however, were not without some knowledge of pottery in the earliest periods of which we have an account of them from Chinese sources. The Chinese historiographers in the *Han* times mention them as making vessels of unglazed earthenware in archaic forms and designs, similar to those alluded to in the ancient classics of China, and attributed to the ancient emperors *Yao* and *Shun*. Such prehistoric vessels are found everywhere throughout eastern Asia, as well as in North and South America, and are remarkable for the general similarity of their shape and rude ornamentation. This prehistoric pottery has been more thoroughly investigated in Japan, where immense deposits have been discovered in ancient shell mounds at Omori, in the vicinity of Tokio, and elsewhere throughout the country. Several specimens have been figured in special works in Japanese ceramics.* The subject is treated at length by Prof. Morse and Mr. Satow in their papers upon the Shell Mounds of Omori † and Sepulchral Mounds at Kaudzuke.‡

Fig. 40.—Globular Fish Bowl, one of a pair, of turquoise crackle, with tall, elaborate mounts of the period of Louis XVI.

Prof. Morse describes the pottery which he discovered at Omori and other places in Japan as being black, or black with a reddish tinge, or red of various shades, and made of coarse clay. The vessels are in many cases unevenly baked, and with few exceptions they are quite thin; the surfaces are generally smooth; the rims of the vessels, either straight, undulating, or notched, project at intervals into points, or have variously formed knobs. The borders are frequently ribbed within, or marked with one or more parallel lines outside, the lines often inclosing a row of rude dots. The surfaces of the vessels are ornamented with curved lines, bands of oblique lines running in one direction round the vessels, followed by a band of similar lines running in an opposite direction, and sometimes these lines cross each other. The bottoms of some of the pots have matting impressions. These designs have either been roughly incised or, as in the case of the mat marks, impressed, or they are smoothed out of wet clay, or carved in dry clay before baking; and, like all the pottery found in shell mounds throughout the world, these works bear the impression of the cord mark.

In some instances he found that the vessels had been painted with mercury sulphide, but in no example had any attempt been made to paint designs or patterns, except that in some cases the color was applied to interspaces between lines or curves already marked. The objects, discovered mostly in fragments, are grouped as follows: Cooking vessels answering to pots, stewpans, etc.; hand vessels, such as bowls and cups; vessels with constricted necks, possibly used as water bottles; and a few vessels of various forms which may be designated as ornamental jars and bowls. Much difference of opinion exists as to the age of these deposits. None of the fragments shows the least sign of having been thrown or turned; and the supposition therefore is that they were made at a period at least anterior to the use of the potter's wheel in Japan, the invention or introduction of which is referred by the Japanese to the eighth century of our era. Prof. Morse considers them much more ancient, on account of

* See *Japanese Pottery*, by James L. Bowes, Liverpool, 1890.

† Shell Mounds of Omori, by Edward S. Morse, Professor of Zoölogy, University of Tokio, *Memoirs of the Science Department, University of Tokio*, Japan, 1879.

‡ Ancient Sepulchral Mounds in Kaudzuke, by Ernest Satow, *Transactions of the Asiatic Society of Japan*, vol. viii, Yokohama, 1880.

differences in the species of the accompanying fauna as compared with those of the present day; he even thinks that the pottery may have been made by a pre-Aino race.

The most interesting portion of Mr. Satow's report upon the discoveries at Ohoya and Ohomuro is that which refers to the fragments of human figures and of horses, roughly and inartistically molded in soft clay and imperfectly baked, probably by exposure to the sun. Among the traditions of the ceramic industry recorded in old Japanese books is a story relating the making of pottery figures in the third year of the Christian era, to take the place of the persons and animals previously buried around the graves of people of rank, which is probably based upon fact, although it may be untrustworthy as to period. The common version runs as follows: "The Emperor *Suinin* (who is said to have reigned from B. C. 26 to A. D. 70, and to have died at the age of one hundred and forty-one years) signalized his reign by the repeal of a barbarous custom which doomed the imperial retainers, as well as horses and perhaps other animals, on the decease of the sovereign, to be buried alive in holes in the ground around the tomb. In the year 3 A. D. the empress died, and *Suinin*, at the suggestion of his re- | tainer Nomi no Sukuné, called together one hundred of the *hajibé* or potters of | Idzumi province that they might make clay figures of men and horses, to bury | in the place of living victims, as an example for future ages. The workmen | molded the figures under the direction of Nomi no Sukuné and interred them | in a circle around the tomb. The em-

FIG. 41.—Pilgrim Bottle with pierced handles, with flowers in light relief upon a ground of pale cobalt blue, European mounting.

FIG. 42.—K'ang-hsi Blue and White, one of a pair, with European bronze mounting.

FIG. 43.—Five-necked Rosadon of pea-green celadon, with European mounts.

peror rewarded his adviser by conferring upon him and his descendants the office of chief of the potters, with the title of *Hajibé no Tsukasa.*" Mr. Satow, without supporting the correctness of the Japanese dates, adopts the native view that the tumuli explored were really ancient burial places of the imperial family.

The ancient Japanese annals called *Kojiki* state that in the early part of the same reign a Korean prince became naturalized in Japan, and brought with him a noted potter of Shiraki, a principality of Korea, from whom descended the workmen of Kagami no Hazama, in the province of Omi, who for many centuries were reputed for the fabrication of Shiraki ware. This is generally quoted as the first introduction of a foreign element into Japanese ceramic art, although the relics identified with this production are of very primitive construction, scarcely equal to that of the shell heaps, being also handmade, roughly molded, unglazed, and presenting nothing worthy of the name of decoration. The baking was effected in holes dug in the ground. Mr. Ninagawa* says that in the present day the manufacture of handmade pottery in the Shiraki style is carried on at the village of Kimura, in Yamato province, but the workmen now make use of a raised earthen stove.

But the native chronology of these times is very uncertain, and it is not till the fifth cen-

---

* In his work on Japanese pottery entitled *Kwan ko dzu setsu*, published at Tokio, in five parts, with colored illustrations, and a partial translation of the text in French.

tury, when it becomes more accurate, that we can accept Japanese accounts of intercourse with the outside world with any confidence. In the year A. D. 463 the Emperor *Yuriaku* is said to have dispatched an envoy to Korea to engage the services of a skilled potter, which resulted in the advent of a man named Koki, who settled in the province of Kawachi, and there taught the ceramic methods of his people, which gradually spread to other parts of Japan.

The vases figured in Ninagawa's work *Kwan-ko dzu-setsu* as prehistoric are probably more recent than is usually supposed. Many of them contained, when discovered, the curious carved and

FIG. 44.—Large Dish, of Ming celadon of greenish tone, with the decoration etched and tooled in relief in the paste.

polished jade ornaments called, from their shape, *magatama, kudatama,* etc.; and jade, according to Prof. J. Milne, is a stone foreign to Japan, and must have been imported from abroad.

The progress of the art in Japan was confessedly very slow, and aided at every step by Korea or China, although the invention of the potter's wheel is claimed by the Japanese, as well as in quite recent times that of clay seggars. The invention of the wheel is attributed to the Korean Buddhist monk Giδgi, who lived from 670 to 749 A. D. The process of enameling was not adopted till the ninth century, according to Mr. Ninagawa, who states that although glazed ware was known in Japan in the eighth century, the specimens were probably imported, and that glaze was not applied by Japanese potters till the next century. The green glazed tiles used in building the roof of the imperial palace at Uda in 794 are supposed to have been of Chinese manufacture.

Mr. Chamberlain's researches into the ancient writings * have demonstrated that the chronology

* See the introduction to his translation of the *Kojiki*, in the *Transactions of the Asiatic Society of Japan*, 1883.

of the Japanese anterior to the opening of the fifth century of our era is fabricated, and that even the myths and legends, as related in the earliest written documents extant, are so intermingled with imported Chinese elements that much of their suggestiveness is destroyed. He shows the narrow limit of the stock of knowledge possessed by the early Japanese before the commencement of Chinese and Korean intercourse, and that they were certainly not acquainted with a number of the arts and products which figure in true historical periods. "They had no tea, no fans, no porcelain, no lacquer, none of the things, in fact, by which in later times they have been chiefly known. They did not yet use vehicles of any kind. They had no accurate method of computing time; no money; scarcely any knowledge of medicine; neither do we hear anything of the art of drawing, though they possessed some sort of music and poems, a few of which are not without merit. But the most important art of which they were ignorant was that of writing."

The peninsula of Korea, projecting as it does from the northeast of China toward the Japanese islands, has been the route by which the knowledge of many of the arts has traveled to the latter country. Korea, which was anciently divided into three principalities—Kaoli, Petsi, and Sinra— was not united into one kingdom until about the middle of the tenth century, after it had recovered its independence, toward the close of the *T'ang* dynasty in China. In A. D. 463, according to the Japanese report translated by Mr. (now Sir Wollaston) Franks,* some Japanese princes introduced from Petsi a number of colonists, among whom were some potters; but these were stated to have belonged to a Chinese corporation established in Korea. Koreans were also concerned in founding the factory at Karatsu (Hizen) at the end of the seventh century, as well as some other industries, the principal of which was the well-known ware of Satsuma, where the kilns were built on Korean models, and the potters formed a class apart, not being allowed to marry out of their own community. Excepting, however, the Satsuma ware, the Koreans do not appear to have introduced any pottery of remarkable excellence, and we hear nothing of their making porcelain. The real reason why the Japanese attached such a fanciful value to Korean vessels, and why they continued to import Korean potters long after they themselves had made so much progress in the art, was connected with the Tea Ceremonies, a peculiar institution which they adopted from the Chinese, and which has been often described. It is to the Chinese that they are really indebted for their greatest advances; the first good Japanese glazed pottery having been made at Seto, about 1230, by Tôshiro, who had learned the art in China; while the first porcelain made in Japan is attributed to Gorodayu Shonsui, who went to study the manufacture in China, and returned, to settle at Hizen, in the year 1513.

FIG. 45.—Covered Bowl, of pierced work, finely decorated in colors of the best K'ang-hsi Period, European mounting.

The "Father of Pottery," Katô Shirozayémon, more familiarly known as Tôshiro, crossed the sea at the age of twenty, in company with the Buddhist abbot Dôgen, with a view to studying the more advanced processes of the art in China, and returned six years later, in 1229, to carry his experience into practice at the village of Seto, in Owari. He brought back materials with him and made utensils of China clay which are called by tea-drinkers *Kara-mono*, "Chinese ware." The tea jars and tea bowls made from Seto clay by him and his descendants for four generations are known as Ko Seto, "Old Seto." They are fashioned of stoneware, invested with a black, brown, or yellow glaze, and are good in form and color, as well as perfect in technique. Not only have they served as models for Japanese potters down to the present day, but the celebrity of the ware has given the generic name of *Seto-mono*, or "Seto ware," to all subsequent products of the ceramic art.

Gorodayu Shonsui, who brought to Japan the art of porcelain-making, was a native of Isé, and imitated the example set by Tôshiro nearly three hundred years before, by traveling to China to study the technical methods of an art new to his countrymen. He spent several years in Foo-

* *Japanese Pottery*, by A. W. Franks, London, 1880.

chow, during which time he is supposed to have visited Ching-tê-chên, and returned in the eighth year of the Chinese Emperor *Chêng-tê* (A. D. 1513). This reign is celebrated for its blue and white porcelain, decorated in cobalt blue under a white glaze, and we find that this is the kind of decoration that was first produced in Japan. Shonsui took the precaution to import a considerable quantity

Fig. 46.—K'ang-hsi Vase of pure celadon tint, with symbols molded in relief under the glaze, European mounts.

Fig. 47. — Monochrome Coral Red, of perfect tone, enhanced by gilded mounting of artistic European workmanship.

Fig. 48. — Snuff Bottle with Taoist emblems in the pierced outer casing, and two carved panels, displaying the Taoist Fu, Lu, and Shou.

of the *petuntsé, kaolin*, and cobaltiferous manganese used by Chinese potters, and employed them in the making of various small objects, such as bowls, saké bottles, and tea jars, painted in blue under an uncracked glaze. A specimen marked with his name, made by him in China, is preserved at Nara. He settled finally in the province of Hizen, where he built several kilns, and he is regarded not only as the founder of Japanese porcelain, but as the first Japanese ceramist to apply the principles of drawing to the ornamentation of pottery, as the few rude outlines occasionally found upon the older ware scarcely merit the name of painted decoration.

But the materials brought over by Shonsui were soon exhausted, and, in default of native material, he was unable to create a genuine native industry, and his successors could achieve nothing but faïence, although that faïence was no longer plain, but relieved by fairly executed designs under the glaze, copied in part from Chinese models. It was not till the close of the sixteenth century (1599) that a Korean named Risampei, who had been brought over to Hizen after the Korean war by a general of the army under the command of Prince Nabeshima, found the lacking ingredients at Mount Idzumi. He established a new industry in Arita for the production of blue and white ware (*Sométsuké*), and, as the materials were now abundant and cheap, a large quantity of porcelain was turned out. The novelty of the manufacture, as Captain Brinkley observes in his *History of Japanese Keramics*, combined with the popular taste for porcelain already developed by familiarity with the fine specimens China furnished under the *Ming* dynasty, soon made it extremely popular, though he declares that for us it does not possess so much interest, being copied directly from the Chinese blue and white, to which it is considerably inferior in purity and finish.

It is worthy of remark that neither Risampei nor any other among the large number of Korean potters brought over by Taiko's generals could impart to their conquerors a knowledge of decoration in enamels over the glaze. This honor was reserved

Fig. 49.—Ancient Stoneware of the Han dynasty, coated with a dark-green glaze.

for Higashima Tokuzayémon, a potter of Imari, in the same province of Hizen. He is said to have learned from a Chinese visitor to Nagasaki the method of painting with vitrifiable colors upon the glaze, and succeeded, with the assistance of other potters, and after experiments spread over several years, in this new class of decoration. This was about the middle of the seventeenth century. The official Japanese report* says that it was in the second year of *Sho-ho* (A. D. 1645) that the export of pieces ornamented with colored enamels, in gold and silver, etc., was begun, in the first place to a Chinaman named Hachikan, afterward to the Dutch traders. It was made especially for the foreign market, and was distributed by the Dutch, who had a settlement upon the island of Desima, near to Nagasaki, and were allowed exclusive trading privileges, to all parts of Europe, where it afterwards became known as "old Japan." M. Jacquemart † quotes from the Reports of the Dutch East India Company the record that in 1664 eleven ships arrived in Holland with forty-four thousand nine hundred and forty-three pieces of Japanese porcelain. The museum at Dresden is remarkable for a large series of noble jars and vases of the most elaborate form and decoration, which was mainly brought together by Augustus the Strong, King of Poland and Elector of Saxony, between the years 1694–1705.

FIG. 50.—Pilgrim Bottle of the Ch'ien-lung Period, decorated in colors, with Taoist and Buddhist symbols.

The Chinese apply the name of *wu ts'ai*, or "five colors," to this kind of decoration, the Japanese form of which, *go-sai*, is also used in that country, although the name of *nishiki*, or "silken brocade," is much more commonly employed in Japan. The reign of *Wan-li* in China was especially celebrated for its porcelain, decorated in colored enamels, which supplied the first models for the Japanese, even the "mark" being often copied. Ching-tê-chên suffered very much in the wars at the close of the *Ming* dynasty, which was finally overthrown in 1643, and the porcelain industry became almost extinct. Some of the potters perhaps found their way to Nagasaki, conveyed there by the Dutch, who seem to have done much to develop the manufacture in Japan, if indeed they were not the means of introducing it. The old crackled ware of China that has always been so highly appreciated in Japan is imitated there in recent times under the name of *hibi-yaki;* and the sea-green, or celadon, under the name of *seiji-yaki, seiji* being the Japanese form of *ch'ing-tz'ŭ*, or "green porcelain," the ordinary Chinese name of this class.

A recent report ‡ upon Japanese porcelain exhibited at Chicago in 1893, shows how they are still working in the old lines and succeeding in producing marvels of imitative art. The author says that, speaking broadly, there are at present two schools of ceramists in Japan, one of which he calls the Yokohama school, the other the Sinico-Japanese school. The former owes its existence primarily to the demand of foreign exporters and tourist amateurs for brightly ornate and decorative specimens, and produces a mass of objects in the ornamentation of which profusion of color and lavishness of labor are set conspicuously above excellences of technique and chastity

---

* *Le Japon à l'Exposition Universelle de 1878*, publié à Paris sous la direction de la Commission Impériale Japonaise.

† *Histoire de la Porcelaine*, par A. Jacquemart et E. Le Blant, Paris, 1862.

‡ *Artistic Japan at Chicago:* A Description of Japanese Works of Art sent to the World's Fair, by F. Brinkley, Yokohama.

of taste. They figure by hundreds on the shelves of bric-à-brac dealers, decorated with mobs of saints, crowds of warriors, or gardens of flowers painted with microscopic accuracy; but all such were ostracized by the Japanese art critics and ruthlessly excluded from the Fine Arts Section of the Exposition. The latter, the Sinico-Japanese school, has its center at Kioto, and Seifu Yohei figures as its most prominent representative. This potter is placed in the foremost rank for his successes in the celadon, ivory-white, and coral-red glazes. The reproduction of the old Chinese celadon has always been the chief ambition of the Japanese, but no one has ever approached Seifu in this line. Occasional pieces of canary-yellow, turquoise-blue, or aubergine-purple faïence from his kiln are said to have shown the hand of a master of monochromatic glazes, and his canary-yellow glazes with reserved designs in rich blue to have been of K'ang-hsi type. Next to him among the masters of the Sinico-Japanese school is ranked Miyagawa Kozan, of Yokohama, whose essays of the Chinese *yao-pien* or "transmutation" glaze astounded the public, some of his polychrome glazes exhibiting tints of rare beauty, although they never convey the impression of depth and solidity that belongs to the Chinese ware alone. When his first copies of the celebrated *Chiang-tsu-hung* or "peach-bloom" appeared in the market, the astute Chinaman, detecting a golden opportunity, hastened to acquire as many as possible, inclosed them in the traditional silk-lined boxes of his country's collector, and sold them to trustful Occidentals at figures commensurate with the magnitude of the deception. The periodical openings of the kilns at Ota are eagerly watched, and the successful pieces incontinently carried off to New York or Paris by such adroit middle-

Fig. 51.—Large K'ang-hsi Jar, covered with prunus sprays in white reserve on a ground of marbled blue, reticulated with darker lines; mark, a double ring.

men. The third potter of this school is Takemoto Hayata, of Tokio, who excels in the glossy black glaze, sometimes showing tints of raven's-wing green, and hairlike lines of silver or dappling of golden brown, in his reproductions of the old *Chien Yao* of the *Sung* dynasty, which used to turn out the choice cups so highly prized by the *dilettanti* of the Japanese tea clubs.

But these things are not made for the purpose of deception. Like Yeiraku of old, the modern Japanese believes that until a potter can reach the standard of the old masters, he can have no business in attempting to strike out new lines. Who, as Captain Brinkley says, that is familiar with what China achieved prior to the close of the eighteenth century, will deny that the field of reproduction offers ample scope for the genius of any modern expert?

Fig. 52.—Large Plate of the K'ang-hsi Period. Decorated on an order of a Dutch merchant with an armorial design.

CHAPTER III.

INTRODUCTION TO THE CLASSIFICATION OF CHINESE PORCELAIN.—INSCRIPTIONS.—CHRONOLOGY.

THE most satisfactory classification of porcelain would be a chronological one, which should be based upon the actual characteristics of the objects to be classified, with reference to the history of the subject. The classification of Oriental porcelain in European collections has been hitherto mainly empirical. A glance at one of the many works of Albert Jacquemart, so beautifully illustrated by the artistic etchings of Jules Jacquemart, will show how the author confounds Japanese and Chinese specimens, and endows Korea with an elaborately decorated archaic ware of perfect finish which was certainly never produced in that country. In his *History of the Ceramic Art*, for instance, Chapter III,* on Korea, is illustrated by two figures only, and the first of these is a jar (*potiche*) of Chinese blue and white decorated with floral arabesque designs; the second, a Japanese red and gold wine-pot painted with the imperial Kiri-mon, four times repeated; while among the four specimens selected to illustrate Chapter II, on Japan, the second is a Chinese eggshell plate, although only "the vulgar," according to the author, confound such artistically enameled pieces with those of his own Chinese Rose family; the third, a "mandarin jar" with gold filigree ground, is as certainly Chinese; and the fourth, a hexagonal vase "with reticulated open-work panels of vigorous iron-red, framing softly painted medallions," has every appearance of belonging to the same school of art. The Chinese class of *laque burgautée* porcelain again is referred by M. Jacquemart to Japan; and "old Japan" pieces of Imari origin, decorated in colors, are placed by him, on the other hand, among the Chinese ware, because they are often marked underneath with a Chinese *nien hao*, or reign.

It is always unsafe to rely implicitly upon the marks attached to Oriental porcelain. The

* *Histoire de la Céramique*, par A. Jacquemart, Paris, 1873. Translated into English by Mrs. Bury Palliser, *History of the Ceramic Art*, second edition, London, 1877.

Japanese constantly employ Chinese marks, penciled, however, generally in a peculiar style, so as to betray a foreign hand to any one familiar with the native style of writing. The Chinese themselves seldom attach a true mark of date, excepting upon pieces produced at the imperial manufactory. There special writers are retained to pencil the seal, which is outlined in the most approved antique style.

The classification of the modern private fabrics produced at Ching-tê-chên described in the books includes: (1) *Kuan ku ch'i* (官古器), "Imperial ancient ware"; (2) *Shang ku ch'i* (上古器), "Ware of the highest antiquity"; (3) *Chung ku ch'i* (中古器), "Ware of middle antiquity"; (4) *Yu ku ch'i* (泑古器), "Glazed ancient ware"; (5) *Hsiao ku ch'i* (小古器), "Small ancient pieces"; and (6) *Ch'ang ku ch'i* (常古器), "Ordinary ancient ware." It is not pretended that any of these things are really ancient, but the Chinese consumer adores antiquity, and will have nothing called modern; so that we find the commonest of crockery shops or street stalls full of articles of blue and white marked *Hsüan-tê*, and of colored pieces marked *Ch'êng-hua*, that have not the slightest pretension to date from the *Ming* dynasty. The former reign was celebrated for its blue, the latter for its colors, and the ware of to-day must be marked accordingly. It is a mere matter of fashion or custom.

FIG. 53.—Small Jar of the K'ang-hsi Period, with a pale, cobalt-blue ground penciled with floral designs in darker blue; there are two with European mounts, a third with an etched metal cover of Persian work.

The reign of *K'ang-hsi* (1662-1722) is famous both for its dazzling monochrome glazes and for the brilliant enamel colors of its decorated porcelain. The long reign of this emperor forms the culminating period of ceramic art in China; the imperial factory turned out pieces of the finest quality, and the private potteries produced a profusion of ware of every grade, that was circulated throughout the Chinese Empire, and distributed besides

FIG. 54.—Blue and White Garniture of the famed *Lange-Eleizen* pattern. Period of K'ang-hsi. The mark on the foot—Chia-ching nien-chi 1522-1567—is apocryphal, as it invariably is in blue and white examples of this class.

to all parts of the world by the ships of the East India Companies; yet genuine marks of this reign are rare. It is recorded in the annals of Fou-liang that in the sixteenth year of the reign of *K'ang-hsi* (1677), when the imperial factory was rebuilt after the civil wars excited by the rebellion of Wu San-kuei, the governor of the city, Chang Ch'i-chung, issued a proclamation

forbidding the potters of
the name of the reign, or
sacred or classical works,
be broken and the sacred
dust and profaned. The
when he was the official
found with only a double
mark of which it formed
the unofficial ware marked
nature, a spray of flowers,
some propitious symbol, if
the preceding dynasty. I
vases, jars, and beakers,
which occupy a prominent
lections, boldly decorated
perhaps by a ground en-
or yellow, painted either
"biscuit." In spite of the
ground for the common
these large pieces as *Ming*,
fabric, rough execution, and
    A few words on the
China may not be out of
ing to the classification and
porcelain. The Chinese

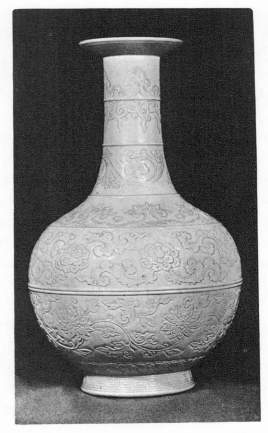

FIG. 55.—Enameled White Vase of the Ch'ien-lung Period, with embossed and etched designs under the glaze.

Ching-tê-chên writing either
texts from any of the
lest the porcelain should
characters trampled in the
imperial pieces of the time
in charge are consequently
ring, a survival of the old
the border, underneath;
with a fanciful artist's sig-
a leaf, a vase, etc., or with
not with a fictitious date of
refer especially to the tall
and the large round dishes,
place in most Oriental col-
in enamel colors, relieved
ameled black, green, buff,
over the white glaze or on
marks, there is slender
practice of classifying any of
even if they be of coarse
so-called archaic aspect.
writing and history of
place here before proceed-
description of marks on
language, I need hardly

say, is monosyllabic, and each word is represented by a separate "character" in the written script. These characters seem to have been originally pictures of natural objects which have been subsequently combined in various ways, as phonetics, and as determinatives or radicals. The radicals in modern use are 214, a number arbitrarily fixed for dictionary purposes, as a means of classifying the 20,000 or more written characters of the language, and of providing a convenient method of coining new combinations. The large majority of the characters in actual use consists of the two parts referred to above—viz., a radical, which gives a clew to the meaning by indicating the particular class of things or ideas to which the combination of which it forms a part belongs, and a phonetic, which conveys some idea of the sound.

    A few words of frequent occurrence in works on ceramics may serve as an illustration, and at the same time afford an opportunity of defining the meanings of the characters. Among the radicals, those referring directly to the subject are the 98th, 瓦, *wa*, a general name for earthenware, which was originally a picture of a round tile; the 108th, 皿, *min*, the ancient form of which resembled a circular dish; while the 121st, 缶, *fou*, applied to ceramic vessels generally, delineated a wine-jar or vase; and the 193d, 鬲, *li*, in its original form showed the mouth, belly, and crooked legs of a three-footed caldron, the upper horizontal line being the cover. In older books these different radicals are often interchanged so that the characters *p'ing*, "vase," and *ying*, "cruse," may be written either with *wa*, "earthenware," or *fou*, "vessel," prefixed to the two phonetics. Some of the characters had originally other radicals, such as *mu*, "wood," *yü*, "jade," *chin*, "metal," or *shih*, "stone," attached to the phonetics, and a study of the ancient forms employed in writing will show the materials of which these utensils were made.

    Wa, 瓦, with the addition of different phonetics, forms 甎, *chuan*, a brick, 甓, *p'i*, applied to fine terra-cotta ware of the period anterior to the Christian era, 瓷, *t'zŭ*, porcelain, and the names of many utensils, such as 罌, *ying*, a cruse, with perforated "ears" for stringing a cord, 甕, *wêng*, a large earthenware jar, etc.

Min, 皿, is the radical of many kinds of vessels of domestic and sacrificial use, such as 盞, *chan*, winecups, 盆, *p'ên*, basins, 杯, *pei*, winecups, 盌, *wan*, bowls, 盂, *yü*, basins, 盒, *ho*, boxes, 盤, *p'an*, dishes, etc.

Fou, 缶, is the radical of a natural group of characters relating to vases, and the like, such as 缸, *kang*, fish-bowl, 窰, *yao*, jar, 缾, *p'ing*, bottle, 罇, *tsun*, sacrificial vase, 罐, *kuan*, covered pot, *t'an*, wine-jar, etc. It forms an integral part of 陶, *t'ao*, a very ancient character, applied to pottery in its widest sense, so as to include all kinds of ware fired in kilns, and of 窰, *yao*, a character of more recent construction, signifying both kiln and, as a secondary meaning, the product of the kiln. Both of these words are used in modern books as synonyms of 瓷, *t'zŭ*, porcelain. The original form of 陶, *t'ao*, was 匋, without the radical 缶, *fou*, place, which was added subsequently, and it is written thus in the ancient dictionary *Shuo Wên*, which defines it as meaning "earthenware," "composed of 缶, *fou*, and 勹, *pao*, the phonetic being omitted." It had two different sounds, *t'ao* and *yao*, both of which are preserved in old names; 陶, *T'ao* (the modern P'ing-yang-fu in Shansi) being the name of one of the principalities of the ancient Emperor *Yao*; *Kao Yao* (皋陶) that of the upright judge of the time of the Emperor *Shun*, the successor of *Yao*. Originally meaning "kiln," *t'ao* is now used to signify "pottery," in its widest sense, including porcelain among the other products of the potter's skill. Unfortunately, the word pottery is often used by us in ordinary parlance to mean faïence and common earthenware, in contradistinction to porcelain, so that the rendering of *t'ao* as "pottery," convenient as it is, may be liable to some misconception. The rendering of *tz'ŭ* as "porcelain" would also be sometimes inappropriate, as the Chinese include in the term any pale stoneware in which the paste has been sufficiently vitrified to produce a clear ring on percussion, although it may be too thick and opaque to transmit light, one of the characteristics on which we rely in our definition of porcelain.

With regard to the transliteration of the Chinese characters into English, the system adopted here is that of Sir Thomas Wade, whose syllabary of the mandarin dialect, explained in his Chinese Course, the *Tzŭ Erh Chi*, is almost universally followed in China, and forms the basis of the two most recent dictionaries of the Chinese language, the large work of Mr. Herbert Giles, and the

Fig. 56.—Brush Pot (Pi T'ung), with the decoration partly in relief, painted in enamel colors and underglaze blue.

small, inexpensive *Pocket Dictionary* of the Rev. Chauncey Goodrich, Peking, 1891, which every one who is interested in the subject ought to possess. The 20,000 characters of the written script are comprised in a syllabary of some 500 sounds. In speaking, these are differentiated into four "tones," which, however, may be disregarded in writing. The vowels and diphthongs must be generally pronounced as in Italian, the consonants as in English. Some consonants at the beginning of words may be aspirated; such as *ch*, *k*, *p*, and *t*, when they have an apostrophe affixed, are written *ch'*, *k'*, *p'*, *t'*, and pronounced accordingly, *t'a*, for example, being read like "hit hard" with the first two and last two letters omitted. The initial *hs* is one of the peculiarities of the Peking

mandarin dialect; *hsing* is pronounced somewhat like "hissing" without the first *i*; another peculiarity is the softening of the initials *k* and *ts* before certain vowels, by which the name of the famous emperor of the last century has become *Ch'ien-lung*, instead of *K'ien-lung*, that of the *Ming* emperor who reigned 1522–1566, *Chia-ching*, in place of *Kia-tsing*. This results from the same philological law which causes similar changes of Latin words in the Italian and French of modern days.

The written script of the Chinese has also become gradually changed in course of time. Its most archaic form is seen in the inscriptions upon ancient bronze vessels dating from the three earliest dynasties, which have been discovered at various times buried in the ground, and illustrated in voluminous works by native antiquarians, such as the *Po ku t'ou*, which was published in thirty books in the reign of *Hsüan-*

FIG. 57.—Libation Cup of "Chien Tz'ŭ," fashioned in the form of a knot of wood with blossoming twigs; on one side a flying stork, on the other a fish and a dragon, a deer, and other archaic designs, in salient relief.

ho (1119–1125), and the *Hsi-Ch'ing ku chien*, the well-known large folio catalogue of the extensive collection of the Emperor *Ch'ien-lung* (1736–1795). Among the most ancient inscribed monuments are the ten stone drums of the eighth century before Christ, preserved in the gateway of the Confucian Temple at Peking, which are engraved with odes in praise of hunting and fishing, written in the antique script which was invented by Chou, the grand historiographer of *Hsüan-Wang* (B. C. 827–780), to replace the archaic ideographic characters.* These are the 篆字, *Chuan tz'u*, the characters in which the ancient annals were written upon tablets of bamboo before the invention of paper. In foreign books they are commonly known as "seal characters," because modern seals are usually engraved in this style. The seals and other marks on porcelain are often penciled in this antique script, so as to require the use of the *Shuo Wên*, an ancient dictionary of A. D. 121, for their decipherment. These characters, called 大篆,

FIG. 58.—Seal, one of a pair, with lions as handles, decorated in enamel colors of the K'ang-hsi Period.

FIG. 59 (bis).—Inscriptions on the two seals: 1. (on left) engraved; the characters come out in white reserve. 2. Carved in relief.

ta chuan, or "greater chuan," were succeeded by the "lesser chuan," *hsiao chuan*, 小篆, which were invented by Li Ssŭ, the notorious minister of *Ch'in Shih Huang*, the emperor of the third century B. C., who burned the old books and built the Great Wall of China.

A pair of porcelain seals in the collection, with lion handles richly decorated in colors, of

* *The Stone Drums of the Chou Dynasty*, by S. W. Bushell, M. D. Transactions of the North China Branch of the Royal Asiatic Society, vol. viii, 1873.

which one is shown in Fig. 58, are inscribed with *chuan t'zŭ*. The inscriptions are seen in Fig. 59. The first, on the left, has three characters in the most archaic script, *Hsiang Shan Shih*—i. e., "native of Hsiang Shan"; the second is inscribed with four characters, *P'ei Shuai-tu Yin*, "seal of P'ei Shuai-tu," the personal name of the individual for whom the seal was made. These were followed almost immediately by the square characters called 隸, *li*, "official," that were first used in writing documents in the official Boards, and were afterward gradually transformed into the regular characters called 楷書, *k'iai shu*, which, first fashioned under the Chin dynasty (265–419), have survived with little modification to the present day, and are employed in printed books as well as in formal written manuscripts. Two different cursive scripts have survived at the same time: the 草書, *ts'ao shu*, or "grass hand," in which the characters are contracted and abbreviated for the quick writer, which was invented by a eunuch of the palace in the first century B. C.; and the 行書, *hsing shu*, or "running hand," in which the characters are rapidly

FIG. 60.—Fuchien Porcelain (Chien Tz'ŭ), one of a pair of ivory white wine cups, with stanzas of verse etched on the sides.

written without raising the pencil, but unabbreviated, which was started by Liu Tê-shêng in the reign of the Emperor *Huan Ti* (147–167).

FIG. 61.—Vase of Ch'ien-lung Porcelain, richly decorated in enamel color, with gilding.

Any of these styles of writing may be found upon porcelain. The "grass hand" is the most difficult for the uninitiated, because the characters are contracted according to the fancy of each individual scribe. The stanzas of poetry which are quoted as labels for pictures are often written in this style; it is found also on the little porcelain bottles which have drifted in such numbers from Egypt into our museums, and which were supposed once to be of fabulous antiquity, until the lines scribbled upon them—"The flowers open, and lo! another year," "Only upon this solitary hill"—opposite rudely outlined flowers, had been traced to poets of the T'ang dynasty.

Such scraps of verses are often written on small pieces, and form, perhaps, the sole decoration, as in the case of a little pair of *blanc-de-chine* winecups from the province of Fuchien, of which Fig. 60 is one. The stanza carved in the paste under the velvety glaze of creamy tone reads:

> "Drunken with wine, I leave in you, sir,
> A libation for the bright moon."

There is always presumed to be in China an intimate connection between the art of poesy and Bacchus, and Luna.

The verses inscribed on vases are usually connected with the subject of the decoration, which is perhaps chosen to illustrate the verse. The vase, for example, in Fig. 61 is decorated in the lower panel with a picture of a hunting scene, to illustrate an ode of the Emperor Ch'ien-lung's composition, which is written in the upper panel and signed with the imperial autograph:*

> "Clouds overspread the vaulted sky, the air at dawn is chill;
> The ring is spread for the hunt, when the sun is but three poles high.
> Clad in warm cloak of sable fur, it seems to me like spring:
> How different for you all round, in your single, unlined coats!"

---

* The name of the emperor is framed in coral-red, the special color of the imperial "vermilion pencil." The character *Ch'ien* is here written in antique script; in other similar inscriptions, as in Fig. 65, below, it is replaced in the first small circular panel by three parallel unbroken horizontal strokes, the first of the eight "trigrams" of divination, which, like *Ch'ien*, conveys the meaning of "heaven."

Another beautiful vase of the same period (Fig. 62), decorated on one side with a view of a picturesque landscape with temples on a wooded hill, representing the island of Yen Yü Shan, "The Hill of Mist and Rain," in the lake at the city of Hangchou, has four stanzas of rhyming verse penciled in black on the reverse side (*b*), perfectly written, and signed in antique style with the seal *Yun Ku,* "Valley of the Clouds." They may be rendered:

FIG. 62.—Ch'ien-lung Vase, finely decorated in delicate enamel colors (*a*); Inscription in black on the reverse side (*b*).

" For miles round, orioles warble at dawn in
the rose-tinted trees;
Both shore hamlets and hill forts show the
wine-flags waving in the breeze.
Here in the Southern Dynasties stood four
hundred and eighty fanes,
And as many wood-circled spires, all half
hidden by mists and rains."

The coral-red bowl of the *Tao-Kuang* Period (Fig. 63) has an inscription reserved in white on the bright-red ground, which also refers to the subject of the decoration, reserved on the other side of the bowl, consisting of sprays of white plum blossoms delicately tinted with soft green and red. The verse, with a fanciful heading inscribed in a leaf-panel "Moon Cut," is signed *Ya Wan,* "Literary Toy," which occurs also as a "mark," as we shall see later. It may be translated:

" The trees, enveloped in clouds of melting, dawn-red tint,
Show leaves of deepest green and flowers of jadelike white;
The buds, like precious pearls, spread out early in the springtime;
The powder-pot of palace beauty sprinkled into snowy flowers."

We will give one more inscription, in verse, from the pen of the Emperor Ch'ien-lung, in Fig. 65, which is a slightly magnified representation of the beautiful little snuff-bottle shown in

FIG. 63.—Inscription upon a Tao-kuang Bowl, decorated with prunus flowers in enamel colors, relieved by a coral-red ground.

FIG. 64.—Snuff-Bottle, decorated in colors.

Fig. 64. It is interesting as devoted especially to the ceramic question, and as giving the views of an illustrious connoisseur, whose poetic effusions, I may mention, are printed and fill some tens of volumes.* The other side of the snuff-bottle (Fig. 64) is decorated in enamel colors with a miniature garden scene containing a rockery and mountain peonies, and a boy carrying a basket from which he is feeding a hen and chickens. The inscription is penciled in black and authenticated by the imperial seal in red affixed below in two small labels. There is also

---

* Wylie, in his *Notes on Chinese Literature* (London and Shanghai, 1867), says that, besides several extensive collections of essays and discourses, this monarch left to posterity a quadruple collection of poems. The first, in forty-eight books, contains 4,150 pieces, composed during the first twelve years of his reign; the second. in one hundred books, contains upward of 8,470 pieces, composed between 1748 and 1759; the third, in one hundred and twelve books, contains 11,620 pieces, written during the next twelve years; and the fourth, also in one hundred and twelve books, includes 9,700 pieces, written between the years 1772 and 1789, the whole work comprising about 33,950 poetical compositions.—*Editor's Note.*

a mark underneath, written in one line of seal characters, *Ch'ien-lung nien chih*, "Made in the reign of *Ch'ien-lung*" (1736–1795). The ode runs:

"Yueh-chou porcelain of the Li dynasty of T'ang is no longer extant: *
The imperial ware of the Chao house of Sung is rare as stars at dawn.
Yet the ancient ritual vessels of Yin and Chou abound in the present day:
Their material, bronze, is stronger; vessels of clay are more fragile.
But though strong and rude they last, the weak and polished perish:
So honest worth wears well in daily life, and should be ever prized.
The Chu dynasty of Ming, going back from to-day, is not so far remote:
And the artistic gems of Hsüan and Ch'êng may be seen occasionally.
Their brilliant polish and their perfect coloring are universally lauded;
And among them the 'Chicken Winecups' are the very crown of all.
The Mutan peonies under a bright sun opening in the balmy spring;
The hen and chicken close together, and the cock in all his glory,
With golden tail and iron spurs, his head held straight erect,
In angry poise ready for combat, as if he heard the call of Chia Ch'ang.
The clever artist has rendered all the naturalistic details
In a style handed down from old time, varying in each period:
But I will think only in my own mind of the ancient Odes of Ch'i,
And not dare to cherish my own ease when it is time to rise early.
    "Composed by the Emperor Ch'ien-lung in the cyclical year *ping-shên*, and sealed by him."

A pamphlet was published early in the nineteenth century with a translation of this inscription and an illustration of the winecup from which it was taken, which is decorated with a picture similar to that described above. It is entitled *Ly-T'ang*, An Imperial Poem in Chinese, by

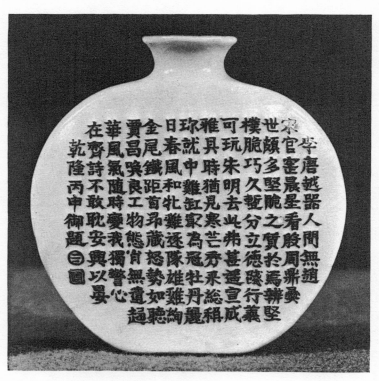

FIG. 65.—Poem by the Emperor Ch'ien-lung in praise of the Ceramic
Art, inscribed upon a snuff bottle, decorated in colors.

Kien-Lung, with a Translation and Notes by Stephen Weston, F. R. S., F. S. A., London, 1809. Dedicated to Sir George Staunton, Bart. It is quoted in *Marks and Monograms on Pottery and*

* The Yueh porcelain of the *T'ang* (618–906) and the "Imperial Ware" (*Kuan Yao*) of the *Sung* dynasty (960–1279) will be described presently. The *Yin* and *Chou* were the last two of the three ancient dynasties B. C. The reigns of the *Ming* dynasty alluded to are those of *Hsüan-tê* (1426–1435) and *Ch'êng-hua* (1465–1487), both famous for their porcelain. Chia-Ch'ang lived in the reign of *Ming Tsung* (926–933), of the After *T'ang*, and was employed by the emperor on account of his skill with fighting-cocks. The Ode of Ch'i, referred to in the last stanza, enjoins the sovereign not to lie in bed after cock-crow. The year *ping-shên* of the cycle corresponds to A. D. 1776.

Porcelain, by W. Chaffers, 1891, seventh edition, pp. 310, 312, "to show the difficulty of translating Chinese." The translation certainly differs from mine. It begins:

"Ly-T'ang, idle and unemployed, in a vacant and joyless hour spake thus: 'Behold the
sun, star of the morning, rise on my furnace and illumine my hall under an imperial dynasty.'
Great is the beauty and high the antiquity of sacred vases," etc.; but I will refer the curious to
the Catalogue of the British Museum, a whole page of which is filled with the titles of the works of
Mr. Weston, who seems to have been a leading light of the Society of Antiquaries of the time.

The marks on Chinese porcelain are written on different parts of the piece. In the more
ancient specimens they occur generally on some part of the surface, written in a vertical or
horizontal panel which forms part of the decoration, because the base is so often left unglazed.
Under the reigning dynasty, on the contrary, the mark is usually either penciled or impressed
underneath the vase or bowl. The inscription generally marks the date according to the native
systems of chronology, of which there are two: first, the cycle of sixty years; second, the *nien-
hao*, or title of the reign of the emperor.

The cycle of sixty is indicated by a combination of the "Ten Stems" with the "Twelve
Branches."

The "Ten Stems" which compose the Denary Cycle are:

1. 甲,	Chia	} Corresponding to the element 木 *Mu*, Wood.	
2. 乙,	Yi		
3. 丙,	Ping	" " " 火 *Huo*, Fire.	
4. 丁,	Ting		
5. 戊,	Wu	" " " 土 *T'u*, Earth.	
6. 己,	Chi		
7. 庚,	Kêng	" " " 金 *Chin*, Metal.	
8. 辛,	Hsin		
9. 壬,	Jên	" " " 水 *Shui*, Water.	
10. 癸,	Kuei		

The "Twelve Branches" which compose the Duodenary Cycle mark the divisions of the
Chinese zodiac, the horary periods of the day, and are equivalent to the animal cycle adopted
from the Tartars. They are:

1.	子,	Tzŭ	鼠,	*Shu*, the Rat.
2.	丑,	Ch'ou	牛,	*Niu*, the Ox.
3.	寅,	Yin	虎,	*Hu*, the Tiger.
4.	卯,	Mao	兔,	*T'u*, the Hare.
5.	辰,	Ch'ên	龍,	*Lung*, the Dragon.
6.	巳,	Ssŭ	蛇,	*Shê*, the Serpent.
7.	午,	Wu	馬,	*Ma*, the Horse.
8.	未,	Wei	羊,	*Yang*, the Goat.
9.	申,	Shên	猴,	*Hou*, the Monkey.
10.	酉,	Yu	雞,	*Chi*, the Cock.
11.	戌,	Hsü	犬,	*Ch'üan*, the Dog.
12.	亥,	Hai	猪,	*Chu*, the Pig.

By joining the first of the twelve to the first of the ten signs the combination 甲 子, *chia-tzŭ*,
is formed, and so on in succession until the tenth sign is reached, when a fresh commencement
is made, the eleventh of the series of twelve "branches" being next appended to the sign 甲,
chia. The sixty combinations thus formed are called the *Chia tzŭ* series, commonly known as
the cycle of sixty. This has been employed from a period of remote antiquity for the purpose
of designating successive days. It was not till the *Han* dynasty, in the century preceding the
Christian era, that it was applied to the numbering of years. The official chronology starts with
the year B. C. 2637, so that the beginning of our era corresponds with the fifty-eighth year of

the forty-fourth cycle. The following table shows the cycles posterior to the Christian era, and will be found useful for the calculation of any given cyclical date:

TABLE I.

CHINESE CYCLES 45 TO 76, OR A. D. 4 TO 1923.

CYCLICAL SIGNS		A.D. 4 / 304 / 604 / 904 / 1204 / 1504 / 1804	A.D. 64 / 364 / 664 / 964 / 1264 / 1564 / 1864	A.D. 124 / 424 / 724 / 1024 / 1324 / 1624	A.D. 184 / 484 / 784 / 1084 / 1384 / 1684	A.D. 244 / 544 / 844 / 1144 / 1444 / 1744
甲	子	04	64	24	84	44
乙	丑	05	65	25	85	45
丙	寅	06	66	26	86	46
丁	卯	07	67	27	87	47
戊	辰	08	68	28	88	48
己	巳	09	69	29	89	49
庚	午	10	70	30	90	50
辛	未	11	71	31	91	51
壬	申	12	72	32	92	52
癸	酉	13	73	33	93	53
甲	戌	14	74	34	94	54
乙	亥	15	75	35	95	55
丙	子	16	76	36	96	56
丁	丑	17	77	37	97	57
戊	寅	18	78	38	98	58
己	卯	19	79	39	99	59
庚	辰	20	80	40	00	60
辛	巳	21	81	41	01	61
壬	午	22	82	42	02	62
癸	未	23	83	43	03	63
甲	申	24	84	44	04	64
乙	酉	25	85	45	05	65
丙	戌	26	86	46	06	66
丁	亥	27	87	47	07	67
戊	子	28	88	48	08	68
己	丑	29	89	49	09	69
庚	寅	30	90	50	10	70
辛	卯	31	91	51	11	71
壬	辰	32	92	52	12	72
癸	巳	33	93	53	13	73
甲	午	34	94	54	14	74
乙	未	35	95	55	15	75
丙	申	36	96	56	16	76
丁	酉	37	97	57	17	77
戊	戌	38	98	58	18	78
己	亥	39	99	59	19	79
庚	子	40	00	60	20	80
辛	丑	41	01	61	21	81
壬	寅	42	02	62	22	82
癸	卯	43	03	63	23	83
甲	辰	44	04	64	24	84
乙	巳	45	05	65	25	85
丙	午	46	06	66	26	86
丁	未	47	07	67	27	87
戊	申	48	08	68	28	88
己	酉	49	09	69	29	89
庚	戌	50	10	70	30	90
辛	亥	51	11	71	31	91
壬	子	52	12	72	32	92
癸	丑	53	13	73	33	93
甲	寅	54	14	74	34	94
乙	卯	55	15	75	35	95
丙	辰	56	16	76	36	96
丁	巳	57	17	77	37	97
戊	午	58	18	78	38	98
己	未	59	19	79	39	99
庚	申	60	20	80	40	00
辛	酉	61	21	81	41	01
壬	戌	62	22	82	42	02
癸	亥	63	23	83	43	03

It will be observed that this table has been cut in two, and the parts placed side by side in order to bring it within the limits of the page. The second column of Chinese characters is but a continuation of the first column of Chinese characters, and each column of figures in the second part of the table is but a continuation of the corresponding column in the first part. The short columns at the top show the date of the beginning of each cycle in regular order, A. D. 4, 64, 124, 184, 244, 304, etc., followed by the years corresponding to the successive years of the cycle. For example, 甲 子, *Chia Tzŭ*, is the cyclical sign of each of the years mentioned above, while 乙 丑, *Yi Ch'ou*, the second cyclical sign, corresponds to the years 5, 65, 125, 185, 245, 305, 365, etc. 甲 午, *Chia Wu*, the thirty-first sign, corresponds to the years 34, 94, 154, 214, etc. Now, if it be wished to ascertain the cyclical year 庚 戌, *Kêng Hsü*, of the period *Tao-kuang* of the *Ch'ing* dynasty, an inspection of Table III shows that the first year of *Tao-kuang* was 1821, and that the period closed with 1850. Turning to Table I, it will be found that a cyclical period began with 1804, and as it would end with 1863, the period *Tao-kuang* naturally falls within that cycle. Fixing 辛 巳, *Hsin Ssŭ*, as the first year of *Tao-kuang's* reign, and going down the column, we reach the sign 庚 戌 we are in search of, and identify it as the year 1850, the last of the reign.

The legendary period of Chinese history (as distinct from the purely mythical ages which preceded, and which, according to the more extravagant chronologers of the country, reach back some two or three millions of years to the creation of the world) begins with *Fu-hi*, the reputed founder of the monarchy, the first year of whose reign is placed in B. C. 2852. He is the first of the *Wu Ti*, or Five Rulers, who are succeeded by the Emperors *Yao* (B. C. 2356) and *Shun* (B. C. 2255), with whose reigns the *Shu Ching*, or "Historical Classic," opens. *Fuh-hi's* immediate successors were *Shên-nung*, the Divine Husbandman (B. C. 2737); *Huang-ti*, the Yellow Emperor (B. C. 2697); *Shao-hao* (B. C. 2597); and *Chuan Hsü* (B. C. 2513). The Emperor *Shun* was succeeded by the Great *Yü* (B. C. 2205), the founder of the first of the twenty-four dynasties which have ruled the empire in succession down to the advent of the reigning Manchu dynasty in A. D. 1644.

TABLE II.

SUCCESSION OF THE CHINESE DYNASTIES.

BEGAN

1. Hsia	夏	B. C. 2205		The Three Ancient Dynasties.
2. Shang *	商	1766		
3. Chou	周	1122		
4. Ch'in	秦	255		
5. Han	漢	206		The usurper *Wang Mang* occupied the throne A. D. 9–23.
6. Eastern Han	東漢	A. D. 25		
7. After Han	後漢	221		Three Kingdoms, 三 國, divided China, the 漢 Han, 魏 Wei, and 吳 Wu.
8. Chin	晋	265		
9. Eastern Chin	東晋	317		
10. Sung	宋	420		This period is known by the collective name of *Nan Pei Ch'ao*, Northern and Southern Dynasties, as the 魏 Wei ruled the north from 420 to 550.
11. Ch'i	齊	479		
12. Liang	梁	502		
13. Ch'ên	陳	557		
14. Sui	隋	589		
15. T'ang	唐	618		
16. After Liang	後梁	907		These short-lived dynasties are known collectively as the 五 代 *Wu Tai*, Five Dynasties.
17. After T'ang	後唐	923		
18. After Chin	後晋	936		
19. After Han	後漢	947		
20. After Chou	後周	951		
21. Sung	宋	960		The Niu-chih Tartars occupied North China (1115–1234) as the *Chin* dynasty 金 朝.
22. Southern Sung	南宋	1127		
23. Yuan	元	1280		Mongolian dynasty founded by *Kublai Khan*.
24. Ming	明	1368		
25. Ch'ing	清	1644		The reigning *Manchu* dynasty.

* In B. C. 1401 the title of this dynasty was changed from *Shang* to *Yin*.

TABLE III.

REIGNS OF THE LAST TWO DYNASTIES.

EMPERORS OF THE 明 MING DYNASTY.

DYNASTIC TITLE, OR MIAO HAO.		TITLE OF REIGN, OR NIEN HAO.		DATE OF ACCESSION.
太祖	T'ai Tsu	洪武	Hung-wu	1368
惠帝	Hui Ti	建文	Chien-wên	1399
成祖	Ch'êng Tsu	永樂	Yung-lo	1403
仁宗	Jên Tsung	洪熙	Hung-hsi	1425
宣宗	Hsüan Tsung	宣德	Hsüan-tê	1426
英宗	Ying Tsung	正統	Chêng-t'ung	1436
景帝	Ching Ti	景泰	Ching-t'ai	1450
英宗	Ying Tsung (resumed government)	天順	T'ien-shun	1457
憲宗	Hsien Tsung	成化	Ch'êng-hua	1465
孝宗	Hsiao Tsung	宏治	Hung-chih	1488
武宗	Wu Tsung	正德	Chêng-tê	1506
世宗	Shih Tsung	嘉靖	Chia-ching	1522
穆宗	Mu Tsung	隆慶	Lung-ch'ing	1567
神宗	Shên Tsung	萬歷	Wan-li	1573
光宗	Kuang Tsung	泰昌	T'ai-ch'ang	1620
熹宗	Hsi Tsung	天啓	T'ien-ch'i	1621
莊烈帝	Chuang Lieh Ti	崇禎	Ch'ung-chên	1628

EMPERORS OF THE 大清, THE GREAT CH'ING DYNASTY.

世祖	Shih Tsu	順治	Shun-chih	1644
聖祖	Shêng Tsu	康熙	K'ang-hsi	1662
世宗	Shih Tsung	雍正	Yung-chêng	1723
高宗	Kao Tsung	乾隆	Ch'ien-lung	1736
仁宗	Jên Tsung	嘉慶	Chia-ch'ing	1796
宣宗	Hsüan Tsung	道光	Tao-kuang	1821
文宗	Wên Tsung	咸豐	Hsien-fêng	1851
穆宗	Mu Tsung	同治	T'ung-chih	1862
The reigning sovereign		光緒	Kuang-hsü	1875

Fig. 66.—Tripod Censer, of archaic aspect, painted with dragons in blue,
under a coarsely crackled glaze.

FIG. 67.—Bowl, decorated in enamel colors, with
imperial dragons upon a coral-red ground.

CHAPTER IV.

MARKS ON CHINESE PORCELAIN.—MARKS OF DATE.—HALL MARKS.—MARKS OF DEDICATION AND
FELICITATION.—MARKS OF COMMENDATION.—MARKS IN THE FORM OF DEVICES.

T
HE "mark" on porcelain is generally understood to be any inscription or device
indicating the time at which the specimen was made, or the make, or the workman, and which forms no part of the decoration. The Chinese word for "mark"
is 欵 *k'uan*, which is usually translated "seal," although the term includes written
inscriptions of the kind indicated above as well as impressed marks. The mark
is generally penciled by a special writer employed for the purpose on the bottom of the piece
before it is fired. The foot, which has been left a solid mass for convenience of handling
during the different operations of the potter, is at last shaved off and polished, and the writer
attaches the seal upon the surface of the unbaked white clay. The glaze is afterward applied,
either by immersion, or by sprinkling, and the piece is ready for
the furnace. The mark is usually written in cobalt blue
under the glaze. This is the case not only in pieces painted
in blue, and in those in which underglaze blue forms part
of the decoration in colors, but also, often, in those enameled
with single colors, and, occasionally, in decorated ware which
has no blue in its painted designs. In other pieces, decorated
in enamel colors, the mark is outlined in one of the colors of
the muffle-stove from the palette of the decorator, such as black
or overglaze blue; while those painted simply in coral red or
gold have seals written underneath over the glaze in the same
color as that employed in the decoration.

FIG. 68.—Yung-chêng Teapot of
Ku Yueh Hsüan type, decorated
with landscapes painted in soft
enamel colors.

This description applies especially to the porcelain produced at the imperial manufactory
at Ching-tê-chên. In the private manufactories a special writer is not employed, the mark being
attached by the artist who paints the decoration. He pencils his signature, a motto, or some
painted device, or perhaps a label descriptive of the picture he has painted, on some part of the
piece. This is not always inscribed underneath the foot, so that we may find the artist's monogram in some cases underneath the piece, in others attached as a signature to the picture, or
following the verses which accompany it. In this same way a descriptive label like "The
mountains are high, the rivers long" (*Shan kao shui ch'ang*) may be written either at the head
of the landscape or under the foot of the vase. In the latter case it often occurs,
written in the seal character, as an ordinary mark of pieces decorated with landscape
paintings. The former case is exemplified by the beautiful little teapot illustrated in
Fig. 68, one of the most perfect specimens of the Ku Yueh Hsüan style in the
collection, which is marked in bright blue enamel underneath *Yung chêng nien chih*, "Made in
the reign of *Yung-chêng*" (1723–35). It is decorated in two broad panels, framed in delicately

tinted floral scrolls, filled with landscapes, penciled in overglaze blue, which are headed by half stanzas of verse, written in black, with two carmine seals attached. On the reverse side is a mountain view with the superscription "The echo-resounding Southern Mountains," sealed *Shan kao,* "The hills are high." In front there is a river scene labeled "A cottage smoking far off on the Northern Islet," and sealed *Shui ch'ang,* "The rivers are long." The definition of a "mark," quoted above from the Franks *Catalogue of Oriental Porcelain,* seems therefore to require some qualification for China, where the mark certainly sometimes forms part of the decoration.

Chinese marks are written either in the antique script known as *chuan,* or seal character, of which there are several varieties, which is so called because it is now principally employed on seals; or in the ordinary modern script, called *k'ai-shu,* used in printed books and formal manuscripts. The running-hand script called *hsing-shu* is rarely employed for marks, although it is often seen in the verses written to accompany the decoration of vases. Chinese writing, it is hardly necessary to say, is read from above downward and from right to left; each character represents a word to a Chinaman, a Korean, or a Japanese, although pronounced differently according to the locality, just as Arabic numerals are pronounced differently in European countries.

These marks may be classified as:
1. Marks of Date.
2. Hall Marks.
3. Marks of Dedication and Felicitation.
4. Marks of Commendation.
5. Marks in the Form of Devices.

I. MARKS OF DATE.

These are of two kinds, the first indicating the number of the year in the cycle of sixty, the second the year of the reigning emperor. The two methods of dating may be combined in the same mark, as in that given in Hooper and Phillips's *Manual of Marks* (p. 190), which reads, *T'ung chih shih êrh nien kuei yu,* or "The twelfth year (*kuei yu*) of *T'ung-chih.*" The eighth emperor of the present *Ch'ing* dynasty, who was canonized as *Mu Tsung,* reigned during the period 1862–74 under the title (*nien hao*) of *T'ung-chih,* and the twelfth year of his reign, A. D. 1873, will be found on the Cyclical Table given above (Table I) to correspond to *kuei yu,* the tenth year of the seventy-fifth cycle. In the *Manual* it is erroneously given as 1874. There is one small point to be noted in Chinese chronology, an ignorance of which has constantly led to miscalculation of dates in foreign books: the whole of the year in which an emperor dies is always reckoned as belonging to his reign, and the reign of his successor does not begin officially until the first day of the first month of the next year, when a new *nien hao* is inaugurated.

Another compound "mark" of this kind is seen in Fig. 38, at the bottom of the little bowl-shaped winecups decorated with the eight Buddhist emblems, displayed in pairs bound with waving fillets, of which the wheel of the law and the conch-shell of victory are in the foreground. The mark, penciled underneath in red, is *Tao kuang kêng hsü nien chih,* "Made in the (cyclical) year *kêng-hsü* of the reign of *Tao-kuang,*" indicating, as may be seen by reference to the Tables, the date of A. D. 1850.

Most of the cyclical dates, however, are given without the reign, which involves an uncertainty as to which of the cycles is intended. Many of these would belong to the reign of *K'ang-hsi,* in the sixteenth year of which (1677) the official in charge of the potteries issued a proclamation forbidding the inscription upon pottery of the sovereign's name, or of any sacred text. To this period is certainly to be referred the cyclical mark, *Yu hsin ch'ou nien chih,* which has excited an interesting discussion. It was first published by Jacquemart and Le Blant (*loc. cit.,* p. 161), taken from a bowl in the Musée Céramique at Sèvres, made of white Chinese porcelain, subsequently decorated with flowers and European figures in Germany during the first half of the eighteenth century, and it was attributed to the right year (1721) from the style of decoration, although the mark was not correctly understood. It was first explained by Sir A. W. Franks (*loc. cit.*, page 208) as meaning "Made in the *hsin-ch'ou* year again [recurring]." The Emperor *K'ang-hsi* came to the throne in the thirty-eighth year of the seventy-second cycle, A. D. 1661, and died December 20, 1722, so that he had reigned for a whole cycle on the recurrence in 1721 of the thirty-eighth year of the cycle, an event unexampled in Chinese history, which has thus happened to be recorded upon porcelain. The bowl in the Franks Collection on which it occurs is described as being of "Chinese egg-shell porcelain, painted inside with a group of flowers and fruit in enamel colors, the outside coated with a delicate rose color." I have seen in a Chinese collection at Peking a "rose-backed" saucer dish with an exactly similar decoration, inscribed underneath with the same mark. These specimens are of interest to us from another point of view, as a proof of the employment of the delicate enamels of the *famille rose* class at this early date.

Another cyclical date, which reads, *Ping-hsü nien chih*, "Made in the year *ping-hsü*," is given by Du Sartel* (p. 95), taken from an octagonal brushpot, painted in blue and white with landscapes and verses. He attributes it to the same reign of *K'ang-hsi*, so that it would indicate the twenty-third year of the seventy-third cycle, which corresponds to A. D. 1706.

Marks of date of the second kind, referring to the reign, give only the *nien hao*, or title of the emperor. A Chinese emperor on his accession loses his personal name, and selects an honorific title instead, by which he continues to be known during his reign, unless he chooses to change it. The new title is not adopted, however, as explained already, till the new year succeeding the death of his predecessor. After his death he is canonized under another new title, the temple name, or *miao hao*, under which he is worshiped in the ancestral temple and referred to in all formal documents of subsequent dates. In former times the *nien hao* was frequently changed during the reign to mark the occurrence of any important event, or for some superstitious reason; but since the accession of the *Ming* dynasty in 1368, the only instance of such a change is that of the emperor canonized as *Ying Tsung*, who adopted on his accession in 1436 the title of *Chêng-t'ung*. He was taken prisoner by the Mongols and dethroned in 1449, and adopted the new title of *T'ien-shun* in 1457, when he recovered the throne on his return to his own country, after a captivity of eight years in Tartary. During the interregnum his brother carried on the government under the title of *Ching-t'ai*, a *nien hao* signalized by the introduction into the palace workshops of the Byzantine process of cloisonné enameling upon metal, which, consequently, is known to this day as "*Ching-t'ai Lan.*"

The reign mark consists usually of six characters, written in two columns of three words, or in three columns of two words, occasionally in one line, either vertically or horizontally. The first character is *Ta*, "great," followed by the name of the dynasty; the next two characters give the *nien hao*; the last two are *nien*, "year" or "period," and *chih*, "made." The first two characters, indicating the dynasty, are often omitted and then the mark consists of only four characters. The dates on the older specimens are generally written in the plain character; those of the present dynasty are often in antique script, inclosed within a square border in the form of a seal, which may be either penciled with a brush or impressed in the paste with a stamp.

Sung and Yuan Dynasties.—It is recorded in the annals of Fou-liang-hsien that during the *Sung* dynasty the Emperor *Chên Tsung*, who founded the imperial manufactory of Ching-tê-chên in the period *Ching-tê* (1004–1007), from which it derived its name, ordered that the four characters *Ching tê nien chih*, "Made in the period *Ching-tê*," should be inscribed on the ware made for the palace. The Franks Collection contains a vase enameled olive-green and touched with gold to imitate patinated bronze, in the ornate style of the reign of *Ch'ien-lung* with a seal of this period penciled in gold; and also a bowl painted in blue, with a *nien hao* of a later

---

* La Porcelaine de Chine. Par O. du Sartel, Paris, 1881.

reign underneath, being marked (see No. 1) *Ta Sung Yuan fêng nien chih*—i. e., "Made in the period *Yuan-fêng* (1078–1085) of the great *Sung*"; but doubts are suggested as to the authenticity of either of these two pieces, which doubts I would venture to emphasize.

豐 大
年 宋
製 元

No. 1.

The period of *Hsüan-ho* (1119–1125) of the reign of *Hui Tsung*, the eighth emperor of the *Sung* dynasty, is represented, so far as its *nien hao* is concerned, by two pieces in the Walters Collection. The first, a pure white vase of fine shape and perfect technique, illustrated in Plate XC, with the decoration worked in relief and etched, consisting of a broad band of fungus scrolls, traversed by a pair of horned lizardlike dragons, extending round the middle, and of symbols encircled by fillets above and below, is marked in underglaze blue (see No. 2), *Hsüan ho nien chih*, "Made in the period *Hsüan-ho.*" The second (Fig. 69) is a small quadrangular vase with swelling body and receding neck, composed of a very fine, dark-brown paste, invested with a purplish mottled gray glaze, overlaid with a whitish gray overglaze, which runs down in a rich unctuous mass not reaching to the base of the vase. It has the mark, in two characters only, of *Hsüan-ho*, the same *nien hao*, which is carved in the center underneath, and filled in with grayish-white enamel. This comes from the Brinkley Collection. It is of perfect technique and finish

年 宣
製 和

No. 2.

FIG. 69.—Vase, of dark-colored paste, invested with two coats of glaze in the style of the Sung dynasty, and marked "Hsüan-ho."

—too much so, indeed, to belong really to such an early date— and it seems to be a reproduction of the Kuan Yao, the "imperial ware" of the *Sung* dynasty which was made at the capital K'ai-fêng-fu; and the first piece appears to me to be a clever reproduction of the porcelain made at Ching-tê-chên at the same time, which was described to resemble the purest white jade. I would refer both pieces to the reign of *K'ang-hsi* (1662–1722), with all deference to my learned friend Captain Brinkley, in whose catalogue* his piece is attributed to the reign of *Chia-ching* of the *Ming* dynasty. I may just mention here that the Japanese have recently gained no small reputation in Peking for their expert reproductions of ancient *Sung* porcelain. Their marvelous skill in olden days in the decoration of pottery with mingled glazes of brilliant tints was no doubt likewise of Chinese origin and inspiration.

The emperors of the *Yuan* dynasty (1280–1367) gave no special patronage to the porcelain manufacture, and no *nien hao* of this period is found among marks on porcelain, although the mark of *Chih-chêng*, the last reign of this dynasty, is occasionally found on the foot of cloisonné enamels on copper, and the titles of some of the other reigns on ritual utensils of bronze.

Ming Dynasty.—In the *Ming* dynasty, which succeeded the *Yuan*, the imperial factory was rebuilt at Ching-tê-chên by *Hung-wu*, the founder of the new line, whose reign is represented in collections by a few pieces, of somewhat doubtful authenticity, inscribed (see No. 3) *Ta Ming Hung wu nien chih*, or simply *Hung wu nien chih*, with the name of the dynasty omitted.

Those marked with the *nien hao* of his son, *Ying-lo* (1403–1424), the third of the line, include more veritable specimens, with marks both in the plain character (see No. 4) and in an antique seal script (see No. 5). The latter is found especially on the white eggshell bowls characteristic of this period, with decoration worked in relief or etched in the paste, of which Fig. 70 is an illustration of a remarkable example, which has the mark *Yung lo nien chih* faintly engraved at the bottom underneath the glaze. Some other bowls of this date are described in Chinese books as molded in the same form as the one just mentioned, with the figures of two lions, lightly impressed under the white glaze in the interior, playing with a brocaded ball, and having inside the ball the same seal faintly etched in the paste in four tiny characters,

武 大
年 明
製 洪

No. 3.

年 永
製 樂

No. 4.

No. 5.

* *Rare Chinese Porcelains*, New York, 1893, p. 13.

not nearly so large as grains of rice, the exterior of these bowls being decorated in blue and white.

The reign of *Hsüan-tê* (1426–35) is celebrated for the excellence of its blue and white as well as for its blue and red monochromes, and it shares with that of *Ch'êng-hua* (1465–87), which

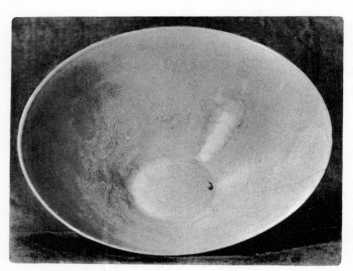

is famed especially for its colored decoration, the distinction of being the *Ming* mark most frequently found on porcelain. The two intervening reigns were occupied by battles with the Mongols, and their titles are not recorded among marks. The two *nien hao* of *Hung-hsi* (1425) and *T'ai-ch'ang* (1620) are also conspicuous for their absence, due probably to the fact that each lasted less than a year. All the other *nien hao* of the *Ming* dynasty are represented.

FIG. 70.—White Eggshell shallow Bowl, with the mark of Yung-lo in antique seal script, engraved in the paste (No. 5, p. 39).

The usual form of the mark of *Hsüan-tê* (1426–35) is (No. 1) *Ta Ming Hsüan tê nien chih,* "Made in the period *Hsüan-tê* of the great *Ming* [dynasty]." This is sometimes etched in the paste; occasionally the last four characters are impressed with a square seal so as to appear in relief. The seal form (No. 2), which has been copied from the Franks *Catalogue,* Plate III, Fig. 24, is described there by the author as taken from a specimen which is "probably modern." It is the form so frequently found on the incense pots of bronze, for the manufacture of which this reign was specially celebrated.

The mark of *Ch'êng-hua* (1465–87) is very common. It has been more frequently forged than any other, and only a very small proportion of the pieces so marked can be genuine. The usual form is (No. 3) *Ta Ming Ch'êng hua nien chih,* "Made in the period *Ch'êng-hua* of the great *Ming* [dynasty]." The inscription of (No. 4) *Ta Ming Ch'êng-hua yuan nien yi yu,* "The first year of *Ch'êng-hua* of the great *Ming* [dynasty] *yi yu* (of the cycle)" occurs on a square vase decorated in enamel colors in the Salting Collection, which fixes the date most precisely, in twofold fashion, as A. D. 1465; the style and coloring of the decoration, however, belong to the reign of *K'ang-hsi* (1662–1722) of the Manchu dynasty. The four-character mark (No. 5) *Ch'êng hua nien chih* also occurs, either penciled or impressed, in the plain character as well as in the antique script shown in No. 6. Most of the so-called old crackle of archaic type, with mask handles and encircling bands of iron-gray paste in the midst of the stone-colored ground of the clumsy vase, is stamped underneath with this last form of the mark, which, in these cases, is evidently fictitious.

The mark (see No. 7) *Ta Ming Hung chih nien chih,* "Made in the period *Hung-chih* (1488–1505) of the great *Ming* [dynasty]," is found on bowls and dishes enameled yellow, and on a few rare pieces of porcelain of peculiarly heavy solid material decorated in colors of a very archaic type.

The mark (see No. 8) *Ta Ming Chêng tê nien chih,* "Made in the period *Chêng-tê* (1506–1521) of the great *Ming* [dynasty]," is comparatively rare. It occurs, however, on bowls decorated with green dragons as well as on pieces of blue and white porcelain. It was in this reign, we are told, that a new supply of Mohammedan blue (*Hui ch'ing*) was obtained from the west, and there is an interesting collection of porcelain of the period with Arabic inscriptions in the British Museum. It is exhibited in a glass case together with several sacrificial vessels of bronze, which are marked with the same *nien hao*, and decorated with medallions of Arabic scrolls—another proof of the prevalence of the Mohammedan religion in China at this time.

The mark (see No. 1.) *Ta Ming Chia ching nien chih*, "Made in the period *Chia-ching* of the great *Ming* [dynasty]," represents the next reign (1522–1566), which is characterized by the deep blue of its painted decoration on porcelain. The mark often occurs in a vertical or horizontal line written in a panel in the midst of the decoration. In the large round dish, three feet across, which will be described presently, there is a horizontal panel outside, near the rim, with the exceptional inscription, *Ta Ming Chia ching liu nien chih*, "Made in the sixth year of *Chia-ching*" (1527). The big globular vase illustrated in Plate XLIX has the ordinary form of the mark boldly written underneath in the same deep, strong blue with which the jar is decorated.

The two marks (see No. 2) *Ta Ming Lung ch'ing nien chih*, "Made in the period *Lung-ch'ing* (1567–1572) of the great *Ming* [dynasty]" and (No. 3) *Ta Ming Wan li nien chih*, "Made in the period *Wan-li* (1573–1619) of the great *Ming* [dynasty]," are always coupled together by the Chinese with regard to their porcelain, which is very similar in type. The reign of *Wan-li*, being much longer than that of his predecessor, is more frequently found. The Japanese are fond of counterfeiting Chinese marks, especially those of *Wan-li* and *Chia-ching*, and these very often occur on Imari pieces which have no pretensions to be contemporary, and which at once betray their alien origin by the peculiar style in which the mark is written.

The marks (see No. 4) *Ta Ming T'ien ch'i nien chih*, "Made in the period *T'ien-ch'i* (1621–1627), of the great *Ming* [dynasty]" and (No. 5) Ta Ming *Ch'ung chên nien chih*, "Made in the period *Ch'ung-chên*" (1628–1643) of the great Ming dynasty, are very rare, and occur generally on inferior pieces. The only exception that I am aware of is in the case of a series of little globular vases marked underneath with the single character *T'ien*, "Heaven," said to be a contraction of the *nien hao* T'ien-ch'i. I have seen them decorated in color, as well as painted in blue, and in both cases resembling good specimens of the preceding reign of *Wan-li*. There is one described in the *Catalogue of Blue and White Oriental Porcelain exhibited by the Burlington Fine Arts Club in London in 1895*, although the mark which is figured in Plate III, Fig. 22, of the *Catalogue*, is erroneously deciphered there as *Tai*, "Great." A mark of dedication on a temple sacrificial vase, dated the ninth year of *Ch'ung-chên* (1636), will be noticed later. The Chinese were too busily occupied during the last two reigns of the *Ming* dynasty in disputing the advance of the rising Manchu power to pay much attention to the porcelain manufacture, and the records are absolutely silent on the subject.

Ch'ing Dynasty.—Date marks of the reigning dynasty are found, like those of the *Ming*, consisting either of six characters, or of four only, with the first two, the name of the dynasty, omitted. A new fashion of writing the characters in antique script, in the form of an oblong or square seal, came into vogue in the reign of *K'ang-hsi*, and in the nineteenth century the majority of the pieces made in the imperial factories at Ching-tê-chên are dated in that way. The mark of the first reign, *Shun-chih* (1644–1661), is very rare, and it is doubtful whether there is a genuine instance of a seal mark, although one is figured here for the sake of completeness. The seal mark of *K'ang-hsi*, even, is not common, although I have seen it on authentic pieces. It was not till the reign of *Ch'ien-lung* that the date came to be more often inscribed in the seal character than in the ordinary plain script.

The first emperor of the new Manchu dynasty reigned eighteen years under the title of *Shun-chih* (1644–1661). There is a record of large fish-bowls and veranda plaques having been ordered by him from Ching-tê-chên for the decoration of the palace at Peking, such as had been supplied in the reign of *Wan-li* of the *Ming* dynasty, but the mandarins in charge were obliged to reply that it was impossible to produce them. The mark occurs in the plain

大明嘉靖年製
No. 1.

大明隆慶年製
No. 2.

大明萬曆年製
No. 3.

大明天啟年製
No. 4.

大明崇禎年製
No. 5.

character (see No. 1), *Ta Ch'ing Shun chih nien chih*, "Made in the reign of *Shun-chih* of the great *Ch'ing* [dynasty]," on small pieces both of enameled and of blue and white porcelain, decorated in the style of the later emperors of the *Ming*. It is almost as rare, however, as the marks of the last two reigns of the former dynasty, and without the mark the few specimens that I have seen could hardly have been distinguished from *Wan-li* productions. With regard to the seal mark (see No. 2), it is probably always fictitious.

The next reign, that of *K'ang-hsi* (see No. 3), lasted for the long period of sixty-one years (1662–1722). The early part of his reign was occupied in consolidating the Manchu rule in the south of China, and in fighting with the viceroy Wu San-kuei, who had declared himself independent. The potteries suffered much in this rebellion, and the imperial factories were burned to the ground during the troubles which lasted from the twelfth to the sixteenth year. They were rebuilt in this last year (1677), and a new era in the history of the ceramic art was inaugurated. Earlier in the reign the manufactory had been under the direction of the governors of the province, among whom Lang T'ing-tso was the most celebrated, as the inventor of the brilliant *sang-de-bœuf* glaze, which is called after him, *Lang Yao*. In the year 1677 the official in charge issued a proclamation forbidding the inscription of the imperial *nien hao*, or of any sacred text, upon porcelain, which, in consequence, had to be marked with the hall-mark of the manufacturer, with the signature of the artist decorator, or with some pictorial or fanciful device. Many of the finest pieces of this time were not marked at all, although a double ring in blue is often found underneath, surviving as an empty relic of the old mark. We are not told when the decree was rescinded. The first imperial commission for the porcelain works was appointed at Peking in 1680, and arrived in Ching-tê-chên in the following year. One of its most important members was Ts'ang Ying-hsüan, who became subsequently famous for his monochrome glazes, shades of "eel-skin yellow," varying from brownish old-gold tints to olive, and "snake-skin green," with its brilliant iridescent sheen, and who is generally credited with the invention of the mottled "peach-bloom," and the pure pale-blue *clair de lune*, the finest pieces of which have underneath, the six-character mark of the *K'ang-hsi* (see No. 3) period, delicately penciled in underglaze cobalt blue. The little eggshell winecup (Fig. 18) shows the ordinary method of inscription of the mark at this time, encircled with a doubled ring. The characters are so minute as almost to require a lens for their decipherment.

The seal mark also read (see No. 4), *Ta Ch'ing K'ang-hsi nien chih*, "Made in the reign of *K'ang-hsi* of the great *Ch'ing* [dynasty]," has been often counterfeited, but, as I have already observed, I have seen it on undoubtedly genuine pieces.

The title of this reign means "Peace and Joy," and a quaint mark penciled in blue under another eggshell winecup, Fig. 71 which is decorated with a picture of lotus plants and water-birds, painted in blue and filled in with the pure red and the deep brilliant greens of the early *K'ang-hsi* period, must be referred to it. The mark reads, *Hsi ch'ao chi wan chih chên*, "A gem among rare trinkets of the reign of joy," and was no doubt written in this peculiar way to avoid the inscription of the full *nien hao*, forbidden by statute at the time, lest it should be profaned on the dust heap.

FIG. 71.—Eggshell Winecup of the K'ang-hsi period, decorated in brilliant enamel colors.

The pair of mandarin ducks swimming in the water and the kingfisher flying above are perfect in their miniature painting. The verse, penciled in blue—

"The root is jade buried in the mud:
In the bosom lurk pearls of liquid dew"—

is sealed with the character *Shang*, "A Gift," inclosed in a small panel. The verse refers to the jadelike whiteness of the lotus root, which makes a favorite sweetmeat, and to the pearly drops of water which collect upon the leaves, and are taken by the Buddhists as types of the sacred "jewel of the law."

The succeeding emperor, *Yung-chêng*, reigned from 1723–1735. The porcelain of the time is characterized by its finished technique as well as by its crisp decoration and delicate col-

No. 1.

No. 2.

No. 3.

No. 4.

No. 5.

No. 6.

oring. The superintendents of the imperial factory were Nien Hsi-yao, distinguished for the purity of his monochrome glazes, and T'ang Ying, the most famous of all, a fertile inventor and wonderful reproducer of ancient colors, whose name we shall meet very often in subsequent pages. The private kilns of the time also turned out a quantity of fine work, in emulation of the imperial manufactory, as shown by the eggshell tea services and the beautiful ruby-backed plates, which were made principally for export to Europe. The Walters Collection is rich in these, and it contains some of the largest imperial pieces as well, like the magnificent round dishes, one of which

FIG. 72.—Yung-chêng Bowl, richly decorated with the enamel colors of the *famille rose.*

is illustrated in Plate XLVIII, and the pilgrim bottle shown in Plate XLVII. Both of these are marked in the ordinary script (see No. 1), *Ta Ch'ing Yung-chêng nien chih*, "Made in the reign of *Yung-chêng* of the great *Ch'ing* [dynasty]." A rare eggshell bowl from one of the private kilns, very richly decorated, in enamel colors of the *famille rose* and gilding, with a scene of family life, surrounded by diapered grounds and floral brocades, is seen in Fig. 72. It is marked in underglaze cobalt blue with the six-character inscription written in stiff archaic style inside a double ring. The seal form of the same mark (shown in No. 2), occurs more rarely.

The reign of the next emperor, *Ch'ien-lung*, was nearly as long as that of his grandfather *K'ang-hsi*, and he terminated it by abdicating after the completion of a full cycle of sixty years (1736–1795). The porcelain is generally good and very plentiful, and is so similar to the productions of *Yung-chêng* that the two reigns are often classed together under the same heading. The mark of *Ta Ch'ing Ch'ien-lung nien chih*, "Made in the reign of *Ch'ien-lung* of the great *Ch'ing* [dynasty]," occurs in both the common (see No. 3) and seal characters, though more generally in the latter (see No. 4), one of the forms of which in four characters, with the name of the dynasty omitted, is seen in No. 5.

No. 7.

No. 8.

No. 9.

No. 10.

The Emperor *Chia-ch'ing*, the son of *Yung-chêng*, reigned 1796–1820. The best porcelain of the earlier period is equal to that of the preceding reign, but toward the end it indicates a gradual process of degeneration. The mark, which occurs less frequently in the ordinary script (see No. 6), is *Ta Ch'ing Chia-ch'ing nien chih*, "Made in the reign of *Chia-ch'ing* of the great *Ch'ing* [dynasty]," which is shown in No. 7.

Tao-kuang succeeded his father in 1821, and reigned till 1850. Some of the finest work of this time was lavished upon ordinary table services, and rice bowls with this mark are eagerly sought by collectors, like the medallion bowl with an etched spiral ground of crimson *rouge d'or*, brocaded with flowers of Fig. 73, which has underneath it a square seal penciled in blue (see No. 9), *Ta Ch'ing Tao-kuang nien chih*, "Made in the reign of *Tao-kuang* of the great *Ch'ing* [dynasty]." Specimens of the mark in the ordinary script (see No. 8) are less commonly met with. The son of *Tao-kuang*, who succeeded his father, reigned under the title of *Hsien-fêng*, A. D. 1851–1861. During the early part of his reign some fine work was produced at the imperial factory, which is usually found marked in full (see No. 10), *Ta Ch'ing Hsien-fêng nien chih*, "Made in the reign of *Hsien-fêng* of the great *Ch'ing* [dynasty]," penciled in red in the common script. The mark from this time onward seems, for

the most part, to have been relegated to the private potters, and is usually indifferently penciled (see No. 1). In the sixth year of this reign the province of Kiangsi was devastated by
the Taiping rebels, and Ching-tê-chên especially was almost depopulated, and the porcelain
industry has never since recovered.

No. 1.

The next emperor who ascended the throne
adopted the title of *T'ung-chih*, and reigned
1862–1874. The porcelain is marked (see Nos.
2 and 3) *Ta Ch'ing T'ung chih nien
chih*, "Made in the reign of *T'ung-chih*
of the great *Ch'ing* [dynasty]." A good
idea of the productions of the imperial factory is gained from an official list of the
palace indents of the year 1864, which we
will extract presently from the provincial statistics of the time.

No. 2.

No. 3.

No. 4.

FIG. 73.—Tao-kuang Medallion Bowl, richly decorated in colors, with flowers displayed upon an
etched *rouge-d'or* ground of crimson tint.

This last emperor was succeeded by his
cousin, who was enthroned under the title of *Kuang-hsü* in 1875, and is still reigning. The imperial ware (*kuan yao*) of the present day is usually marked in ordinary
characters (see No. 4) *Ta Ch'ing Kuang-hsü nien chih*, "Made in the reign of
Kuang-hsü of the great *Ch'ing* [dynasty]." But the ceramic art is in these days at
its lowest ebb in China, and its productions may be dismissed in the native phrase
as "not worth collecting." Still less worthy of consideration is the porcelain of the
private kilns (*ssŭ yao*), which is sometimes marked with a rudely outlined seal (see
No. 5), usually, however, inscribed with a mark of one of the older reigns of the
most transparently fictitious character.

There is another form of this date mark to be noticed, in which the character
yü, "imperial," is substituted for *nien*, "year." This form, which means that the
piece bearing it was made by special order of the emperor, occurs also on specimens of carved jade and of *cloisonné* enamels on copper produced in the imperial works of the
period indicated. I have seen the following four instances on porcelain, of which the second,
figured in Hooper's *Manual* (*loc. cit.*), is given here as an example of the series.
These are :

1. *K'ang-hsi yü chih* (1662–1722).
2. *Yung-chêng yü chih* (1723–1735).
3. *Ch'ien-lung yü chih* (1736–1795).
4. *Chia-ch'ing yü chih* (1796–1820).

The accompanying mark, penciled in red, is found underneath the "chicken-
cups" (*chi kang*) made by order of the Emperor *Ch'ien-lung*, and inscribed with
the poem of his own composition, which I translated in the last chapter. One
of them is illustrated in the pamphlet which is quoted there, and the illustration
is better than Mr. Weston's grotesque translation of the inscription. These are
the most prized of teacups among Chinese virtuosos of the present day, and the
curio dealers of Peking ask a hundred taels for a perfect pair—the same price
that used to be asked by the dealers of the last dynasty for their prototypes, the
tiny eggshell *chi kang* winecups of the famous reign of *Ch'êng-hua*. The seal
(see No. 7), is to be read *Ta Ch'ing Ch'ien-lung fang ku*—i. e., "Copy of antique
of *Ch'ien-lung* (1736–1795) of the great *Ch'ing* [dynasty]." The cups are decorated in colors, like the little snuff-bottle with the same inscription in the Walters
Collection, with a picture of a rockery with peonies growing upon it, and a boy
feeding a hen and chickens from a basket. See Fig. 64.

This seems to be the place for a seal mark of one character of not infrequent occurrence
in collections, which has not been hitherto deciphered (see No. 8). It is said to signify *Chih*,

"By Imperial Order," and is found on *K'ang-hsi* porcelain of the most artistic decoration, the mark varying considerably, however, in the shape and arrangement of the strokes in different cases. The first form is taken from a magnificent round dish, twenty-eight inches in diameter, decorated in brilliant enamel colors of the *K'ang-hsi* period, with a party of ladies in boats, gathering lotus flowers in a lake, while other gayly dressed damsels are looking on from a pavilion, the borders of the dish being filled with richly brocaded diapers interrupted by medallions of flowers. The

No. 1.

No. 2.

second form (see No. 1), which is apparently a variation of the same mark, is taken from a square beaker of the same period, decorated on the four sides with flowers relieved by a black ground in the style of Plate IX, and is a rare instance of an inscription in this peculiar class of decoration, which is almost always unmarked.* The third form (see No. 2) is taken from a large blue and white dish belonging also to the *K'ang-hsi* period. This appears to me to be intended for another character called *chih*, a synonym of *chih*, "to make," which, however, also means "by order." They are examples of a large and varied category of marks introduced at a time when the use of the proper *nien hao* was forbidden by the authorities.

2. HALL—MARKS.

The term "hall" is used here in its most comprehensive sense, reaching from the palace or pavilion of the emperor down to the shed of the potter, so as to include the reception hall of a noble, the library of a scholar, the studio of an artist, and the shop of a dealer. The Emperor of China stamps his ode with the seal of the pavilion in which he has just composed it, the official in charge of the imperial manufactory attaches his hall mark to the porcelain produced there, the artist or writer uses the name of his studio as a *nom de plume*, the dealer has his trading hall-mark inscribed on the porcelain made for sale at his shop, and the potter occasionally authenticates his productions with his own mark. The hall-mark on porcelain may belong to any one of these different classes, and it may mean made *for* the particular hall, as well as *at* the hall, the name of which is inscribed on the piece, the clew being sometimes suggested by the meaning of the name. For example, of two new hall-marks supplied by this collection, the one *Yi yü t'ang chih* must be "Made *at* the Ductile Jade Hall," while the other, in which the name *Ssŭ kan ts'ao t'ang* is taken from a line in one of the *Ancient Odes* of Chinese classical times, would in all probability be "[Made *for*] the Straw [i. e., thatched] Pavilion on the River Bank."

The usual word employed for "hall" is 堂, *t'ang*, but we find also other terms of similar meaning used occasionally in its stead in inscriptions on porcelain, such as 閣, *ko*, a "palace pavilion," 亭, *t'ing*, a "summer-house," 齋, *chai*, a "studio," 軒, *hsüan*, a "balcony or railed terrace," or a porch projecting beyond the eaves, 山房, *shan-fang*, a "mountain retreat," and other synonyms.

The mark (see No. 3) *Jên ho kuan*, "Hotel of Benevolence and Harmony," is often cited as the earliest instance on record of a hall-mark, and it would appear to denote the establishment for which the vase was made. It is quoted from the *Ni ku lu*, a little book on antiquarian subjects, published early in the sixteenth century, in which the author describes a bottle-shaped vase of white Tingchou porcelain of the *Sung* dynasty in his own collection, as "having upon it this inscription, fired in the glaze, in the handwriting apparently of one of the Ni family, father or son," referring to two famous calligraphists of the eleventh century.

仁
和
館

No. 3.

The fashion of inscribing upon porcelain made for the imperial palace the name of the particular pavilion for which it was intended seems to have begun in the reign of *Yung-chêng*.

* Another form of this mark, in which the first part of the character is more correctly penciled, is given in the Franks *Catalogue*, Plate XIII, Fig. 130. It is deciphered there as "*Fan*, the maker's name," but the Chinese experts that I have consulted refuse to pass this reading.

Of the two examples which I give, the first (see No. 1), *Lang yin ko*, "Pavilion for Moonlight Recitation," occurs on a flower-pot decorated in colors of the reign of *Yung-chêng* (1723–1735), the second (see No. 2), *Tz'ŭ shu ko*, "Pavilion for Presentation of Books," is inscribed upon the covers of a pair of circular boxes of the kind used for holding incense or chips of fragrant wood. They are eight inches in diameter, and are painted in red and blue with bats flying among clouds, and marked on the foot with the ordinary seal of the *Chia-ch'ing* period (1796–1820).

No. 1.

FIG. 74.—Rice Bowl of the Tao-kuang period, painted in enamel colors. Mark, *Shên-tê-t'ang*.

There are two other hall-marks which are generally referred by Chinese authorities to the palace, viz. (see No. 3), *Ching wei t'ang chih*, "Made at the Hall of Reverent Awe," which is attributed to the *Ch'ien-lung* period (1736–1795), and (see No. 4) *Shên tê t'ang chih*, "Made at the Hall for the Cultivation of Virtue," which is said to have been the name of a pavilion founded by the Emperor *Tao-kuang* (1821–1850), and by him given a name chosen from the classics (*The Great Learning*, chap. x, p. 6).

No. 2.

No. 3.

"Hence the sovereign will first take pains about his own virtue." This mark is much sought after by Chinese collectors. There is an example of it here in the bowl (Fig. 74), which is decorated in delicate enamel colors with butterflies relieved by a monochrome ground of soft coral-red tint. It has been conjectured that it might be the hall name of the official in charge of the imperial factory, but this could hardly be, as in China it would be contrary to etiquette for a subject to select one from such a text. There is a saucer dish in the Franks Collection (No. 387 in the catalogue) marked (see No. 5) *Shên tê t'ang po ku chih*, "Antique (*po ku*) made for the Shên tê Pavilion," and the learned author thinks that "from peculiarities of make it is probable that this dish is of the early part of the reign of *Kang-he*," so that the "antique" must be well executed if our account of the origin of this mark be correct. The form of the ordinary seal of the reign with *po ku* is common enough on jade carvings from the imperial workshops, which are usually fashioned after ancient models, and are marked in this way to indicate the fact.

No. 4.

No. 5.

A hall-mark quoted in Hooper's *Manual* (*loc. cit.*, p. 205) as taken from a bowl, one of a pair, the other being marked as above, is (see No. 6) *Chan ching chai chih*, "Made for the Retreat of Quiet Stillness," so that this mark would probably belong to the same period as that of Shên tê t'ang.

No. 6.

The last palace marks which we will give here are taken from a pair of beautiful bowls, examples of the finest work of the present day; inferior, however, it must be confessed, both in technical details and in tone of coloring, to the porcelain of the reign of *Ch'ien-lung*, which is said to have furnished the models. These bowls are in the possession of Sir Nicholas O'Conor, K. C. B., her Britannic Majesty's late envoy plenipotentiary at Peking, who has kindly permitted me to copy the marks. They are decorated in enamel colors inside and out, with floral sprays of roses and wistaria, the stems of the latter winding over the rim, so as to cover the interior of the bowl with gracefully trailing blossoms; a single magpie is perched on one of the branches; and the whole is relieved by a monochrome ground of soft gray-green tint. On the outer surface near the rim is the hall-mark (see No. 7) *Ta Ya Chai*, "Abode of Grand Culture," and near it, in a small oval panel framed by dragons, the motto (see No. 8) *T'ien ti yi chia ch'un*, "Spring throughout heaven and earth as one family!" Underneath there is another mark penciled in red (see No. 9), *Yung ch'ing ch'ang ch'un*, "Eternal Prosperity and Enduring Spring!" These bowls are interesting from

No. 7.

No. 8.

No. 9.

the fact that they are part of a dinner service made specially at the imperial factory at Ching-tê-chên for the empress dowager, who has ruled China for so many years, and who is noted as being herself a clever artist and calligraphist. She is said to have sent down some bowls and saucer dishes of the *Ch'ien-lung* period from the palace at Peking as patterns to be copied at Ching-tê-chên. *Ta ya Chai* is the name of one of the new pavilions in *Ch'ang Ch'un Kung*, "The Palace of Enduring Spring," on the western side of the "Prohibited City," at Peking, where this empress, the "Western Buddha," as she is colloquially called by the Pekingese, resided until she removed to the new palace which was prepared for her at the termination of the emperor's long minority. The propitious mark underneath the world-embracing motto in the dragon label, and the decoration, all point to spring, of which season the *Wistaria Sinensis* is one of the floral emblems.

FIG. 75.—Teapot of early K'ang-hsi period, painted in blue with touches of "Nankin yellow" and black.

堂 怡
製 玉

No. 1.

草 斯
堂 干

No. 2.

綠
漪
堂

No. 3.

奉
先
堂

No. 4.

The ordinary hall-marks are so numerous that it would be quite useless to attempt to give a complete list. They are found on porcelain of the present dynasty from the reign of *K'ang-hsi* downward. It would be useful to arrange them in chronological sequence had we sufficient material at our command. At present it is only possible to make a short selection for illustration here, beginning with the two unedited marks in the Walters Collection, that have been already quoted.

The first, one of the earliest of the class that we have met with, is inscribed on the bottom of the square teapot (Fig. 75), which is decorated with dramatic and domestic scenes in blue and white of the *K'ang-hsi* period, and has rims and borders of canary or "Nankin yellow." The upright rim is surrounded by small panels of floral sprays of the four seasons; the knob of the cover is carved in open work, with the character *lu* ("rank") encircled by a four-clawed dragon penciled in blue; and the handle is tinted black on a pale-yellow ground to imitate basket work. The mark is (see No. 1) *Yi yü t'ang chih*, "Made at the Ductile Jade Hall," and is such as would be likely to be chosen by a potter, using white jade as a well-worn simile for fine porcelain.

The other is a *Ch'ien-lung* vase with the rim and foot incased in metal mounts (Fig. 76), which is enameled with a minutely crackled turquoise glaze of soft, charming tone. The decoration, delicately etched in the paste under the glaze, consists of a pair of five-clawed dragons pursuing the effulgent disk of omnipotence in the midst of cloud scrolls and lightning flames.

FIG. 76.—Ch'ien-lung Turquoise Vase, with imperial dragons engraved under the finely crackled glaze. European mounts.

The foot, colored brown underneath, has the mark engraved in the paste (see No. 2), *Ssŭ kan ts'ao t'ang*, "The Straw (i. e., thatched) Pavilion on the River Bank." The name is taken from a text in the ancient *Minor Odes of the Kingdom*, Book xiv, Ode 5, the first line of which is, "By these banks (*Ssŭ kan*) has the palace risen."

The above mark is curious for the omission of the word *chih*, "made," in which it agrees with the two hall-marks that follow (see No. 3): *Lu yi t'ang*, "The Pavilion with the Waving Bamboos," and (see No. 4) *Fêng hsien t'ang*, "The Hall for the Worship of Ancestors." The former occurs on *K'ang-hsi* pieces decorated in colors, with either a white or a mazarine blue ground; the latter on more modern porcelain, is that which is usually inscribed on ritual vessels, perhaps as an indication of their being intended for use in the ancestral temple.

Another unpublished mark occurs more than once in the Walters Collection, which must be included in this class, although the word "hall" happens to be omitted in its composition. The first piece (Fig. 67) is a rice-bowl of lotus-flower design, with an eightfold foliated wavy rim, and eight petals molded in relief round the foot, decorated with dragons and tiny sprays of flowers relieved by a coral-red ground. The second, illustrated in Fig. 77, is one of a pair of four-lobed winecups, with indented rims, painted in delicate enamel colors, with the eight Taoist

FIG. 77.—Winecup, one of a pair, with processions of Taoist immortals painted in delicate enamel colors.

genii crossing the sea. Chung-li Ch'üan and Lü Tung-pin are seen on the left of the picture mounted upon a dragon, which is guided by a damsel swimming in front, holding up a flaming jewel. Lan Ts'ai-ho and Ho Hsien-ku are still upon the shore; the former is scattering flowers from his basket, as if to propitiate the waves; the latter, the virgin member of the sacred group, carries a lotus cup upon a stick and a small branch of twin peaches upon her shoulder. A few white jasmine flowers and buds, painted in soft tints, are sprinkled over the interior of the cup, as if to imbue its contents with their fragrance. The mark in all three cases is in the seal character, penciled in red (see No. 1), *Hsieh chu tsao,* "Made for [or at] the Hsieh Bamboo [Hall]." Compare the mark figured in the Franks *Catalogue* (Plate VI, Fig. 72), which is read (see No. 2), *Hsieh chu chu jên tsao,* "Made for [or by] the lord [Chu jên] of the Hsieh Bamboos." Hsieh is the name of the valley in the Kun-lun Mountains where Ling Lun, minister of the fabulous Emperor *Huang Ti,* is said to have cut bamboo tubes of different lengths when he is supposed to have invented the musical scale and fashioned the first musical instruments. The style and coloring of these bowls indicate the reign of *Tao-kuang* (1821–50), or perhaps *Chia-ch'ing* (1796–1820).

No. 1.

No. 2.

The next mark, which is taken from a brush cylinder (pi t'ung), carved in open work to simulate a clump of bamboos growing from rocks, and tinted in delicate

FIG. 78.—Eggshell Winecup of K'ang-hsi period, decorated in brilliant colors.

enamel colors of the *Ch'ien-lung* period, is to be read (see No. 3) *Lü chu shan fang chên ts'ang,* "Precious Treasure of the Green Bamboo Mountain Lodge."

Another six-character hall-mark of the same time is (see No. 4) *Ching lien t'ang fang ku chih,* "Made as a copy of an antique at the Ching-lien Hall." This would be the mark of an official or scholar posing as an admirer of Sung Ching-lien, a supporter of the founder of the *Ming* dynasty in the fourteenth century, and a distinguished commentator on the classics.

A hall-mark indicative of a lover of flowers, which was first published by Jacquemart and Le Blant (*loc. cit.,* p. 188), is *Tzŭ tz'ŭ t'ang chih,* "Made at the Hall of Purple Thorn" (see No. 5), taken by them from a charming vase, decorated with figure subjects, in the possession of M. Holtrop, librarian to the King of Holland. There is another hall-mark (see No. 6) published on the following page of the same book, taken from a bowl enameled green outside, yellow inside, with fish and water plants, with the reading, *T'ien mao t'ang chih,* "*Fabriqué dans la salle du ciel voilé.*" The second character, however, is *ch'ang* ("prosperity"), not *mao,* which has an extra horizontal stroke at the bottom, so that we must read instead, "Hall of Heaven-sent Prosperity," which is a common trading-hall name in China.

No. 3.

No. 4.

No. 5.

No. 6.

I have been permitted to select four winecups from my own collection to illustrate the subject of hall-marks. Fig. 78 is a cup of the thinnest eggshell texture and most translucent glaze, decorated in colors, with pale-green bamboo and red dianthus flowers; a bat, emblem of happiness, is flying across with *chi ch'ing,* the jade symbol of good fortune, in his mouth; there is a short inscription penciled in black behind, "A propitious prayer for a thousandfold harvest"; and a couple of fragrant jasmine blossoms are painted inside. The mark penciled in red on the bottom of the cup is *Chih hsiu ts'ao t'ang*, "The Straw (i. e., thatched) Pavilion adorned with Variegated Fungus." It is a specimen of the reign of *K'ang-hsi* (1662–1722). The next, Fig. 38 (*a*), delicately painted in gold with sprays of chrysanthemum flowers, is attributed to the reign of *Yung-chêng* (1723–35); it is marked underneath in red, *Ching ssǔ t'ang chih*, "Made for the Pavilion of Classical Bookcases."* The third is a tiny cup, Fig. 79, of the reign of *Ch'ien-lung* (1736–95), decorated in delicate enamel colors with a combination of the three propitious plants, symbols of longevity—the fir, bamboo, and blossoming prunus (*Sung, chu, mei*). The mark penciled underneath in red is *Pao shen chai chih*, "Made for the Retreat where Virtue is Precious." The fourth, Fig. 80, one of a pair of winecups referred to the reign of *Chia-ch'ing* (1796–1820), which are covered inside and out with flying bats painted in red, fifty on each cup, and have the circular form of the character *shou* ("longevity") emblazoned on the bottom of each in red and gold. The decoration conveys the felicitous phrase, *Shuang shou po fu*, "Twofold longevity and the hundred happinesses." The mark penciled underneath in red is *Fu ch'ing t'ang chih*, "Made at the Hall of Happiness and Good Fortune."

FIG. 79.—Ch'ien-lung Winecup, decorated in delicate enamel colors.

The Chinese potter lavishes some of his choicest work on the decoration of these little winecups, and many more might be selected with other marks, but space is limited, and these few must suffice for the present.

Toward the end of the reign of *K'ang-hsi*, glass works were founded at Peking under the direct patronage of the emperor, with the assistance of the Roman Catholic missionaries. The production was known as *Kuan liao*, or "imperial glass"; it included pieces colored in mass, pieces made of layers of different color superimposed and subsequently carved, and pieces either of clear or of opaque white material, painted with translucent enamels of different colors. These last are commonly known in the present day as *Ku Yueh Hsüan*, because the hall-mark, *Ku Yueh Hsüan chih*, "Made at the Ancient Moon Terrace," is often inscribed underneath. Tradition says that one of the directors of the factory named *Ku*, whose patronymic was a character composed of *Ku*, "ancient," and *yueh*, "moon," broke it up into its two component parts to form his studio name. The accompanying mark is engraved underneath a bowl of this kind, which is fabricated of white glass and is colored brown, the outside of the bowl being etched with a landscape of hill scenery touched with the same brown enamel. The Emperor *Yung-chêng* is said to have been enamored of the new art and to have sent down to Ching-tê-chên some of the finest specimens, to be reproduced in porcelain under the auspices of the celebrated T'ang Ying. The objects which were produced in this and the succeeding reign of *Ch'ien-lung* are among the most precious of treasures; they have a paste of peculiarly vitreous aspect, white, and fine-grained, and are decorated in translucent enamels, often with European subjects. The variety is known as *Fang Ku Yueh Hsüan*, "Imitations of the Ancient Moon Terrace [Work]." The teapot figured in the last chapter is a notable example of this beautiful style of decoration. The Chinese exquisite will pay in the

FIG. 80.—Chia-ch'ing Winecup, painted in red with touches of gold.

---

* There is a pair of teacups with this mark in the Hippisley Collection (*Catalogue*, Nos. 120 and 121), "*Teacups* (a pair) with covers, of thin white Yung Chêng porcelain, decorated with two imperial five-clawed dragons pursuing sun amid clouds, all in deep red, the clouds, the dragons, and the scales of the latter being outlined in bright gold; covers bear similar decoration. Mark, *Ching ssǔ t'ang*, an imperial or princely hall-mark as yet unidentified."

present day over a hundred taels for a little *Ch'ien lung* snuff-bottle of clear glass, lightly touched with a design in colors, authenticated by this mark; and much more for a small porcelain vase of the variety, decorated with a pastoral scene of European style in enamels of the *famille rose*.

塵定
軒製
No. 1.

Another unedited hall-mark with the word *hsüan*, found on decorated porcelain of the *Ch'ien-lung* period, is (see No. 1) *Chên ting hsüan chih*, literally, "Made in [or for] the Dust-fixed Terrace." "Dust" (*ch'ên*) is the "world" in Buddhist metaphor, and *ting* ("immovable") is the word used by Buddhists to convey the idea of mental abstraction, so that we should render this hall-name, "Terrace of Abstraction from Mundane Affairs."

碧雲
堂製
No. 2.

Some of the earliest hall-marks have names referring to the quality of the porcelain, distinguishing either the fineness of the paste or the brilliancy of the coloring. One of those already given, "Hall of Ductile Jade," refers to the fine fabric, while the accompanying mark (see No. 2) of the same early period, which is penciled in blue under a small vase with celadon-glazed body, with a ring of chocolate-brown tint round the shoulder, and having the neck decorated with peaches in underglaze blue touched with peach-color, refers to the coloring, being *Pi yün t'ang chih*, "Made at the Hall of Moss-Green-Jade Clouds."

奇玉
堂製
No. 3.

林玉
堂製
No. 4.

To the former class, also, belong the following marks: (see No. 3) *Chi yü t'ang chih*, "Made at the Hall of Rare Jade"; (No. 4) *Lin yü t'ang chih*, "Made at the Hall of Forest Jade"; and (No. 5) *Yü t'ang chia ch'i*, "Beautiful Vessel of the Hall of Jade," which occurs both in the ordinary script and in "seals" of varied style, of which one with the third character imperfect is given here in No. 6.

玉堂
佳器
No. 5.

堂製
益右
No. 8.

Of the latter class, No. 7, which reads, *Ts'ai jun t'ang chih*, "Made at the Hall of Brilliant Colors," a frequent mark on porcelain decorated in enamel colors, is another example.

No. 6.

堂製
養和
No. 9.

Among other marks of commercial character, which may be either those of potters or of dealers in the ware, are: (No. 8) *Yi yü t'ang chih*, "Made at the Hall of Profit and Advance"; (No. 9) *Yang ho t'ang chih*, "Made at the Hall for the Cultivation of Harmony"; (No. 10) *Ta shu t'ang chih*, "Made at the Great Tree Hall"; and (No. 11) *Ch'ü shun Mei yü t'ang chih*, "Made at the Beautiful Jade Hall of Riches and Success." The last of these is a compound name, of which the first part, *Ch'ü shun*, must be that of the shop or trading firm,

堂製
彩潤
No. 7.

堂製
大樹
No. 10.

玉堂製
聚順美
No. 11.

who eulogize their ware under the title of beautiful jade, a comparison often met with.

The above hall-names represent generally the marks of the factory. The individual name of the potter is rarely found attached to his work in China, which differs in this respect from Japan. In the ivory-white porcelain of the province of Fuchien it is sometimes found, etched in the paste under the glaze. In the colored stoneware of the province of Kuang-tung the name of the potter occurs more frequently, being stamped in the paste under the foot of the piece, so that the inscription appears either in intaglio or in relief. The mark (No. 12) *Ko Ming hsiang chih*, "Made by Ko Ming-hsiang," for instance, is not uncommon on vases of reddish paste from these potteries, of such archaic aspect that they have been mistaken for ancient specimens of the *Sung* dynasty.

No. 12.

One curious seal, shown in No. 13, taken from an antique crackle vase of porcelain of gray tone, decorated with propitious inscriptions worked in reserve and filled in with colored glazes of the *Ming* period, gives the name of an individual potter. Read in inverse fashion, from left to right, it is *Wu Chên hsien yao*—i. e., "Pottery [from the Kiln] of Wu Chên-hsien."

No. 13.

Another mark which must not be omitted from the list is that of Hao Shih-chiu, the celebrated and scholarly potter who flourished at Ching-tê-chên in the reign of *Wan-li* (1573–1619)—a poet, too, whose merits were often sung in contemporary verse. He chose as

No. 1.

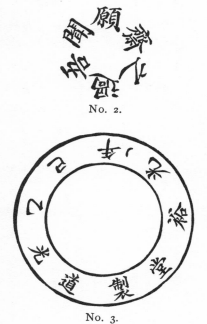

No. 2.

his sobriquet *Hu yin Tao jên*, "The Taoist hidden in a pot" (No. 1), a sympathetic device for a ceramic artist, which was adopted from an old legend of a Taoist recluse who, according to an ancient book on the Taoist Immortals, possessed the magic faculty of concealing himself within the pilgrim's gourd which he carried on his girdle. This mark was inscribed by him underneath his delicate eggshell winecups of pure white and dawn-red tints, each of which was said to have weighed less than the forty-eighth part of a Chinese ounce. A verse may be quoted here which a fellow-poet wrote to him:

"In your search after the philosopher's stone, you strive in the market place.
Far from the rustling furs and changing clouds, your heaven is a teapot.
I know you, sir, only as the maker of those dawn-red winecups,
Fit to be launched from the orchid arbor to float down the nine-bend river."

No. 3.

The last stanza refers to the *Lan T'ing* or "Orchid Pavilion," where, in the fourth century of our era, a party of celebrated scholars used to meet to drink wine and compose verses. The scene with the cups floating down the river has been a favorite subject for Chinese pictorial art ever since.

This section may be closed by two unusually elaborate hall-marks, both of which happen to be written in circular form. The first (see No. 2) comes from the foot of a large rice-bowl, decorated with flowers, fruit, and birds, in enamel colors of the *Ch'ien-lung* period. Our Chinese wood engraver, who was instructed to mark the top of each block for the benefit of the printer, was nonplussed by this one, and when asked why he had omitted the usual mark, he exclaimed, "How could I tell where to begin to read?" To obviate this difficulty, we have put it with the first character at the top, and, proceeding in the ordinary way to the left, we find the quaint inscription, *Yuan wên wu kuo chih chai*, "The Retreat [*chai*] where I wish to hear of my transgressions."

The second (see No. 3), which is penciled in red round the circumference of the hollow foot of a tazza-shaped bowl, exhibits, in combination, the *nien hao*, the cyclical date, and the hall-mark of the maker. It is read, *Tao kuang yi ssŭ nien Kuang yü t'ang chih*—i. e., "Made at the Hall of Brilliance and Riches, in the cyclical year *yi-ssŭ* of the reign of *Tao-kuang*." This year will be found, on referring to the Tables in the last chapter, to correspond to A. D. 1845. The bowl, which is mounted upon a tall, hollow stem, spreading at the foot, is decorated in blue, with the eight Taoist genii crossing the sea,

FIG. 81.—Tall Ewer, painted in blue, with phœnixes and storks flying in clouds in the characteristic style of the Ming dynasty, mounted in metal and studded with turquoises and garnets.

the intervals being occupied by waving fillets, and the stem covered with sea-waves; the interior of the bowl is painted with a large circular *shou* ("longevity") symbol, encircled by a ring of five bats, emblems of the *wu fu*, or five happinesses or blessings, namely, longevity, riches, peacefulness and serenity, the love of virtue, and an end crowning the life.*

* See Mayer's *Chinese Reader's Manual*, p. 312.

3. Marks of Dedication and Felicitation.

This heading is selected to comprise all the marks, not included in the last class of " Hall-Marks," that imply dedication to some particular institution, individual, or purpose, as well as those expressive of wishes of happy augury for the future possessor of the piece. The next heading, " Marks of Commendation," will take the remainder of the written marks—viz., those eulogizing the material or referring to the decoration of the porcelain. Some of the hall-marks might have come under these headings, as the official in charge of the imperial manu-factory will sometimes have a set of sacrificial vases, or a dinner service, inscribed with the hall-mark of the friend or patron for presentation to whom it was specially made; or the potter, as we have seen, will choose a hall name descriptive of the jadelike texture of his porcelain or the brilliancy of its color. It was more convenient, however, to treat the hall-marks separately.

樞
府

No. 1.

One of the earliest marks of dedication is that of (No. 1) *Shu fu*, " Imperial palace," which was inscribed on some of the porcelain made for the use of the emperor during the *Yuan* or Mongol dynasty (1280–1367). We shall find a specimen described in our manu-script album of the sixteenth century, in which this mark is incised on the foot of a little vase underneath the ivory-white glaze. The decoration of this vase consists of dragons and cloud-scrolls lightly etched in the paste; and the author, in his description of the piece, gives us the interesting information that the porcelain of this period was fashioned on the lines of that of the Ting-chou manufacture of the early *Sung* dynasty, and that it in turn supplied models for the pure white porcelain which distinguished the reigns of *Yung-lo* and *Hsüan-tê* of his own (*Ming*) dynasty, which was also ornamented with designs incised at the point underneath the glaze.

The sacrificial vessels intended for use in religious worship often used to have the object for which they were designed marked upon them, like the white altar cups of the reign of *Hsüan-tê* (1426–35), which were inscribed 壇, *t'an*, " altar," according to the author of the *Po wu yao lan*. The same book describes sets of white altar cups made at the imperial factory in the reign of *Chia-ching* (1522–66), which were marked inside with the characters 茶, *ch'a*, " tea "; 酒, *chiu*, " wine "; 棗湯, *tsao t'ang*, " decoction of jujubes "; and 薑湯, *chiang t'ang*, " decoction of ginger "; in-dicating the different offer-ings presented in the cups when the emperor officiated at the Taoist altar.

Inscriptions of dedica-tion to particular temples are not uncommon, and are often lengthy. Jacquemart quotes one (*loc. cit.*, page 166) inscribed on a trum-pet-shaped vase, which is composed of twelve charac-

No. 2.

ters, indicating that it was a ritual vase " made for the temple of Fou lou tsiang in [1636] the ninth year of *Ts'ung-chêng*, in summer, on a propitious day." Marks of this reign, the last of the *Ming* dynasty, are very rare, and there is no little reason for regarding them as, for the most part, apocryphal.

The longest I have met with is that reproduced above in No. 2. It is inscribed on the base of a pricket candlestick of elaborate design, painted in blue with conventional scrolls and formal foliations, one of a pair twenty-eight inches high, now in my own possession. They were made in the year 1741 (the sixth of *Ch'ien-lung*), by T'ang Ying, the famous director of the imperial porcelain manufactory, the successor of the still more illustrious scholars and artists Lang and

Nien, and dedicated by him to a Taoist temple at Tungpa, a town situated on the northern bank of the canal which connects T'ungchou with Peking.*

"Reverently made by T'ang Ying of Shên-yang, a Junior Secretary of the Imperial Household, and Captain of the Banner, promoted five honorary grades, Chief Superintendent of Works in the palace Yang-hsin Tien, Imperial Commissioner in Charge of the three Customs Stations of Huai, Su, and Hai, in the province of Kiangnan, also Director of the Porcelain Manufactory, and Commissioner of Customs at Kiukiang, in the province of Kiangsi; and presented by him to the Temple of the Holy Mother of the God of Heaven at Tungpa, to remain there through time everlasting for offering sacrifices before the altar; on a fortunate day in the spring of the sixth year of the Emperor *Ch'ien-lung.*"

FIG. 82.—Wine-Pot, molded in the form of the character *fu*, "happiness," decorated in soft-toned colors of early K'ang-hsi date.

Among marks of dedication to institutions I will quote two. One is a seal mark shown in No. 1 (*Burlington Fine Arts Club Catalogue of Blue and White, loc. cit.*, Plate II, Fig. 17), from a plate with flanged brim decorated with eight horses reserved in white on a delicate blue ground, which is to be read *Shu-ch'ang*, indicating that it was made for the Shu-ch'ang Kuan, a college of the Hanlin Yuan, the national university at Peking.† The other (see No. 2) is a mark in the plain character (Franks' *Catalogue, loc. cit.*, Plate XII, Fig. 150), *Shuai fu kung yung*, "For the public use of the general's hall," from an old bowl painted in blue, with four-clawed dragons emerging from the sea and pursuing jewels in the clouds.

No. 1.

公 師
用 府

No. 2.

雅 聖
集 友

No. 3.

友
來

No. 4.

Two marks of more private character are (No. 3) *Shêng yu ya chi*, "For the Elegant Circle of Revered Friends," and (No. 4) *Yu lai*, "For Coming Friends"; both of which occur on porcelain painted in blue, of no great artistic value.

Porcelain utensils are sometimes ordered from Ching-tê-chên by shops in different parts of China to be inscribed with the hall-name of their firm and an advertisement of the wares sold there, and we will give one specimen here as an example. It is a little circular gallipot of fine porcelain, decorated in blue on

FIG. 83.—Blue and White Bottle of the K'ang-hsi period, with floral emblems and felicitous symbols.

the cover, with a son offering a present to his aged parents, and on the sides with a landscape, which has underneath an inscription written in underglaze blue in five columns, to

---

* This temple, like so many of those in the vicinity of Peking, is now in ruins. The candlesticks formed part of the sacrificial set of five vessels (*Wu kung*) made for the principal altar of the temple. I saw the two flower vases with trumpet-shaped mouths belonging to the set, but their inscriptions had been purposely erased. The tripod incense burner which once figured as the centerpiece of the altar set had long before been broken and lost.

† See Mayer's *Chinese Government*, p. 25.

indicate the particular shop for which it was made. This reads, *Ching tu Chêng yang mên wai Ta shan lan hsi t'ou lu pei Yun hsiang ko hsiang huo shou yao p'u* (see No. 1); which may be translated, "Yun Hsiang Ko, or 'Cloudy Fragrance Hall,' a shop for scented wares and pre-pared drugs, at the west end of the Ta-shan-lan, on the north side of the street, outside the Great South Gate of the Capital [Peking]."

No. 1.

The only Mongol mark that I have ever seen inscribed on porcelain may be classed as a mark of dedication. It occurs pen-ciled in surface red on the bottom of bowls and saucer-shaped dishes of three different sizes, forming a dinner service, decorated with bright enamel colors and gold in the style of the imperial ware of the *Tao-kuang* period. The interior contains Buddhist symbols of happy augury alternating with longevity characters; the exterior is occupied by the seven precious emblems of a *chakra-vartin*, or universal sovereign, posed upon lotus thalami on a floor of sea waves, and delineated in the traditional manner of the Lama sect. The inscription written within a panel (see No. 2) is *Bara-gon Tumed*, in Mongolian script. This is the name of the Right or Western Wing of the Tumed Banners, a principality of south-ern Mongolia. A daughter of the Emperor *Tao-kuang* was given in marriage to the hereditary prince of these Mongols, who was granted a palace in Peking, and the service with this mark was no doubt made at the imperial manufactory at the time as part of the wedding outfit.

No. 2.   No. 3.

Marks of felicitation are very common, and occur on porcelain of all periods, more especially on articles intended for presents. One of the most common is the *Shuang hsi*, or "twofold joy" symbol (No. 3), the special emblem of wedded bliss, a combina-tion of two *hsi* ("joy") characters placed side by side. This sym-bol is pasted on the lintels of the door on the happy occasion, and is also inscribed on porcelain articles intended for wedding pres-ents either as a mark or as part of the decoration. Two forms of it are published in Hooper's *Manual* (*loc. cit.*, page 198), but wrongly deciphered, "(?) *Ke*, a vessel, vase, ability, capacity."

No. 4.

No. 5.

A curious combination of a date-mark with a felicitous formula (see No. 4) has been taken from the bottom of a set of saucer-shaped dishes, decorated in blue and white of the *Ming* period, where it was found penciled in blue in antique script. The square panel in the middle inclosing the motto *Tê hua ch'ang ch'un*, "Virtue, Culture, and Enduring Spring," is sur-rounded by a circle inclosing the inscription *Wan li nien tsao*, "Made in the reign of *Wan-li*" (1573–1619).

A mark of the same period occurs in the Franks Collection (*Catalogue, loc. cit.*, Plate VI, Fig. 74) with the inscription, written as a legend of a medal pierced with a square hole, in the form of an ordinary Chinese "cash" (see No. 5), which reads, *Ch'ang ming fu kuei*, "Long Life, Riches, and Honor." It is taken from a shallow bowl, five and a quarter inches in diameter, which is described in the following words: "In the inside is a circular medallion with a stork amid clouds, painted in a dark blue; round this a broad band of pale green, over which is a running pattern in gold consisting of flowers and scrolls; outside, two branches of flowers with a bird on each, painted in dark blue. The same mark occurs on a bowl of similar decoration in a German mounting of silver gilt of the sixteenth century." We find the mark in the Walters Collection upon the tall ewer of graceful form (Fig. 81) decorated in the style and coloring of the *Wan-li* period, with blue phœnixes and storks flying among clouds. It is studded all over with uncut turquoises and garnets arranged alternately, mounted in gilded settings of Persian or Indian workmanship, shows traces of gilded rings, and is fitted at the upper and lower rims and at the end of the spout with engraved metal mounts. The mark is written underneath in underglaze blue encircled by a double ring. Among other marks of similar meaning are (No. 1), *Fu kuei ch'ang ch'un*, "Riches, Honor, and Enduring Spring"; and (No. 2) *Fu kuei chia ch'i*, "A Perfect Vessel of Wealth and Honor," which is found on old specimens of blue and white, inscribed both in the ordinary character and in the seal script.

The most frequent vows of the Chinese are offered for the threefold blessings of happiness, rank, and longevity, and the deities who confer these gifts are the most ardently worshiped of any. We shall find the three gods constantly represented upon porcelain, with their respective characters, perhaps, in the background. See, for example, the vase illustrated in Plate XVIII, which is blazoned with the two large characters, *Fu*, "Happiness," and *Shou*, "Lon-

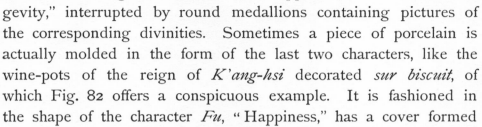

No. 1.

No. 2.

No. 3.

No. 4.

No. 5.

gevity," interrupted by round medallions containing pictures of the corresponding divinities. Sometimes a piece of porcelain is actually molded in the form of the last two characters, like the wine-pots of the reign of *K'ang-hsi* decorated *sur biscuit*, of which Fig. 82 offers a conspicuous example. It is fashioned in the shape of the character *Fu*, "Happiness," has a cover formed of the first "dot" of the hieroglyph, and is inscribed on the handle and spout with archaic forms of the *shou* ("longevity") character. These forms are almost infinite, and a not uncommon decoration of a pair of vases or bowls consists of a hundred different forms of the character *fu* balanced by a hundred of the *shou* hieroglyphs. A favorite decoration of blue and white in the *Ming* dynasty consisted of a pair of dragons holding up in their claws *shou* characters instead of the traditional jewels.

The three characters, *fu, lu, shou*, occur constantly also as marks, either conjointly or singly. The compound marks in one of the seal forms (see No. 3), and in the ordinary script (see No. 4), are appended. The single-character marks are found on porcelain of all ages. The little ivory-white plate of ancient *blanc de Chine*, which is inlaid with Oriental gold work set with uncut rubies and emeralds, and which figures as the oldest piece in the Dresden Museum, having been originally brought to Europe by a crusader from Palestine, we are told by the late curator, Dr. Graesse, is inscribed underneath with the character *fu*. One of the forms of the mark *lu*, "rank," is shown here (see No. 5), taken from a saucer-dish of brilliant blue and white attributed to the *K'ang-hsi* epoch. But of them all, the character *shou* ("longevity") is the most frequent and variable, and it is found in an endless variety of shapes, in circular, oval, and diamond-shaped medallions, in addition to the ordinary oblong forms. One of the oblong forms is inscribed on the snuff-bottle shown in Fig. 102. An oval form is seen in the right-hand panel upon the blue and white vase (Fig. 83), the other panel in front displaying the seal character *ch'ien*, "heaven." Three of the circular medallions are displayed upon each of the two basket-work bands encircling the crackled vase (Fig. 84). One of the oblong forms of the character *shou*,

often found on good blue and white porcelain of the kind that used to be highly appreciated in Holland, is commonly known there as the "spider mark" (see No. 1).

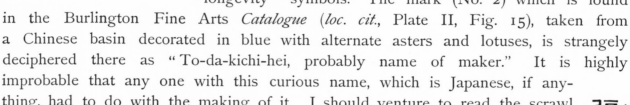

The *fylfot* or *svastika* symbol, the peculiar variety of the cross with the four arms bent at right angles in the same direction, which dates from prehistoric times and is found in all parts of the world,* occurs in China as a mark on porcelain, either plain or inclosed in a lozenge with looped angles, or enveloped in a waving fillet. This symbol is clearly shown in Plate LXII, in a small panel upon the swelling neck of the vase, where it alternates with the "jewel" symbols. It is a synonym of *Wan*, "10,000," in Chinese, and two or four of these symbols are often interwoven symmetrically with the circular form of the *shou* character so as to form an ornamental monogram, to be read *Wan shou*, "For myriads of ages." This is the special birthday vow of his subjects for the Emperor of China, and it corresponds to the Persian "O King, live forever!" The monogram with two *svastika* symbols, one on either side, is displayed prominently in the center of the pilgrim bottle illustrated in Fig. 50, developed, as it were, in the bosom of a sacred lotus blossom. Fig. 85, the gourd-shaped vase enameled in *K'ang-hsi* colors with rich designs of floral brocade pattern, also exhibits on the neck a combination of red *svastika* and yellow *shou* symbols.

FIG. 86.—Statuette of K'uei Hsing, the star-god of literature, posed upon a fish-dragon, painted in enamel colors.

Many of the marks which are passed by as undecipherable are curious forms of these "happiness" and "longevity" symbols. The mark (No. 2) which is found in the Burlington Fine Arts *Catalogue* (*loc. cit.*, Plate II, Fig. 15), taken from a Chinese basin decorated in blue with alternate asters and lotuses, is strangely deciphered there as "To-da-kichi-hei, probably name of maker." It is highly improbable that any one with this curious name, which is Japanese, if anything, had to do with the making of it. I should venture to read the scrawl as simply a variation of *Fu shou*, "Happiness and Longevity."

No. 1.

No. 2.

No. 3.

Another vow of similar meaning is often found inscribed in large antique characters upon bowls as part of their external decoration, or put underneath as a mark, written either in the seal character or in common script. It is read (see No. 3), *Wan shou wu chiang*, ["May you live for] myriads of ages, never ending!" A second mark of this kind is *Fu shou shuang ch'üan*, "Happiness and long life both complete." A longer mark (No. 4) is the oft-repeated formula, *Shou pi nan shan, Fu ju tung hai*, "The longevity of the southern hills, the happiness of the eastern seas." We shall find a still more extended version of this propitious formula directed to be penciled upon blue and white bowls in the imperial factory during the *Ming* dynasty in the reign of *Chia-ching* (1522–66), viz., *Shou pi nan shan chiu, Fu ju tung hai shên*—i. e., "May your life be longer than that of the southern hills, your happiness as deep as the eastern seas!" The "isles of the blessed" are placed by the Taoist legend-mongers somewhere in the Eastern seas, and their "star of longevity shines down from the southern heavens upon immemorial hills." The last felicitous mark of this kind that we will give is (No. 5), *T'ien kuan tz'ŭ fu*, "May the rulers of heaven confer happiness!"

The single propitious characters, 吉, *chi*, "good fortune," 發, *fa*, "prosperity," and 慶, *ch'ing*, "congratulations," occur as marks; also the propitious combinations (No. 6), *Ta chi*, "Great good fortune," and (No. 7) *Chi hsiang ju i*, "Good fortunes and wishes fulfilled," the last mark being written usually in the seal character, as in that given here.

No. 4.

No. 5.

No. 6.

No. 7.

* *La Migration des Symboles*, par le Comte Goblet d'Alviella, Paris, 1891, v, chap. ii, De la Croix Gammée.

A mark often found on the cylindrical vessels, which are used by the Chinese writer or artist as brushpots (*pi-t'ung*), is *Wên chang shan tou*, "Scholarship equal to the Hills and the Great Bear" (see No. 1), implying the wish that the happy possessor, when he wields his brush-pencil, may attain the exalted heights of the Tai Shan, the ancestral mount of China, and of the *pei tou*, the polar constellation, the celestial abode of his special deity, the god of literature, whose image appears in Fig. 86. The mark of (No. 2) *Chuang yuan chi ti*, "May you obtain the degree of chuang-yuan!" occurs also on cylinder vases of this kind. This degree is the highest attainable in the state examinations, and the chief object of ambition for every candidate as a first step upon the ladder leading to high official rank.

山文
斗章

No. 1.

及狀
第元

No. 2.

鼎奇
之石
珍寶

No. 3.

鼎奇
之玉
珍宝

No. 4.

如奇
玉珍

No. 5.

如奇
玉玩

No. 6.

珍博
玩古

No. 7.

寶文
鼎玉

No. 8.

錦南
玉川

No. 9.

珍艸
蕭𤧜

No. 10.

4. MARKS OF COMMENDATION.

This heading is intended to comprise the rest of the written marks on porcelain, those that refer to the quality of the material, comparing it to fine jade and other rare stones and jewels, or to the character of the decoration with which the piece is painted. They go back as far as the *Ming* dynasty, and are frequently found penciled in seal characters, as well as in common script, on specimens dating from the *Wan-li* period (1573–1619).

A few of these eulogistic marks selected from the many are: (No. 3) *Chi shih pao ting chih chên*, "A gem among precious vessels of rare stone"; (No. 4) *Chi yü pao ting chih chên*, "A gem among precious vessels of rare jade," in which the character *pao*, "precious," is written in a contracted form; (No. 5) *Chi chên ju yü*, "A gem rare as jade"; (No. 6) *Chi wan ju yü*, "A trinket rare as jade"; (No. 7) *Po ku chên wan*, "A jeweled trinket of antique art"; (No. 8) *Wên yü pao ting*, "A precious vessel of worked jade"; (No. 9) *Nan ch'uan ch'in yü*, "Brocaded jade of Nan-ch'uan," an ancient name of Ching-tê-chên, which it derived from its situation on the "southern" bank of the Chang "river." A mark of commendation in the seal script, which is found upon blue and white pieces, is (No. 10) *Jo shên chên ts'ang*, "To be treasured like a gem from the deep"; it occurs also in the common character.

Among two-character marks of similar signification are: (No. 11) *Hsi yü*, "Western jade"; (No. 12) *Chên yü*, "Precious jade"; (No. 13) *Wan yü*, "Trinket jade"; (No. 14) *Chên yü*, "Genuine jade"; (No. 15) *Yü chên*, "Jade jewel"; (No. 16) *Chên wan*, "Precious trinket"; (No. 17) *Ya wan*, "Artistic trinket"; (No. 18) *Pao shêng*, "Of unique value"; and (No. 19) *Ku chên*, "Antique gem." A quaint mark, found underneath a blue and white cup, is (No. 20) *Yung shêng*, which means "Ever full," if it refer to the cup, "Ever prosperous," if it be the hall-name of the potter.

Any of the above characters may occur singly as marks, and we very often find *Yü*, "jade," *Chên*, "gem," *Pao*, "precious," etc. The mark *Ch'üan*, shown in No. 21, signifies "perfect," and is one of the most frequent. Some services of porcelain are inscribed underneath with different single characters, which are intended to be read consecutively to form sentences when the plates or dishes are arranged in proper order. The copper "cash" of the first half of the seventeenth century were also cast with single characters on the reverse, which could be read consecutively when a series of the coins happened to be available, so that this curious practice is not peculiar to porcelain.

西
玉

No. 11.

珍
玉

No. 12.

玩
玉

No. 13.

真
玉

No. 14.

玉
珍

No. 15.

珍
玩

No. 16.

雅
玩

No. 17.

宝
勝

No. 18.

古
珍

No. 19.

永
盛

No. 20.

全

No. 21.

Marks referring to the decoration are not so common as those praising the make. Two have already been given, *Shan kao shui ch'ang*, "The hills are lofty, the rivers long," found on pieces painted with landscapes, and the mark *Yung ch'ing ch'ang ch'un*, "Ever-flourishing,

enduring spring," which applies to the floral decoration of the bowl as well as to the name of the palace of the empress dowager for which the dinner service on which it occurs was made.

A mark (see No. 1), *Tsai ch'uan chih lo*, "[I] know that they rejoice in the water," found upon porcelain decorated with fishes and water-plants, and evidently referring to the subject, requires a word of explanation. It is taken from the works of Chuang Tzŭ, the celebrated philosopher of the fourth century B. C., who is related to have had the following discussion with Hui Tzŭ, a rival philosopher:

No. 1.

Chuang Tzŭ.—How the fish are enjoying themselves in the water!

Hui Tzŭ.—You are not a fish. How can you know?

Chuang Tzŭ.—You are not I. How can you know that I do not know that the fish are rejoicing?

No. 2.

Another mark referring to the subject of decoration occurs upon saucer-shaped dishes painted in colors with lotus flowers and reeds (see No. 2), *Ai lien chên shang*, "Precious gift for the lover of the lotus." The mark (No. 3) *Tan kuei*,

No. 3.

"Red olea fragrans," a floral metaphor for literary honors in China, is found inscribed underneath bowls decorated inside with a scholar holding a branch of this symbolical flower.

The private seal of the artist-decorator, which is usually attached to the painting or appended to the scraps of verse which accompany the picture, like the seal on the beautiful *K'ang-hsi* vase illustrated in Plate VI, which is the studio name or *nom de plume* of the artist, (see No. 4) *Wan shih chü*, "The Myriad Rock's Retreat," or the seal on the little winecup in Fig. 71, which is simply *Shang*, "A

No. 4.

No. 5.

gift," is not infrequently found underneath the foot of the piece as a mark. Such marks are found on porcelain of all qualities, and some of the finest pieces of the *K'ang-hsi* period are inscribed with them, especially in the class decorated in enamel colors. The next mark of the same kind (No. 5), inscribed *Chu shih chü*, "The Red Rock Retreat," is taken from a set of *K'ang-hsi* bowls decorated with agricultural scenes, with poems attached, celebrating the successive steps in the cultivation of rice.

Such marks are called by Chinese connoisseurs *chia k'uan*, or "private marks," and are even by them passed by generally as illegible, and as hardly worth the trouble of deciphering.

No. 6.

They form the majority of those marks found in every collection of Chinese porcelain which have to be labeled "undeciphered," although a collection of such artists' monograms would not be without interest if arranged in proper chronological order. They are rarely found before the present dynasty, but M. du Sartel (*loc. cit.*, page 105) figures a typical example, "Taken from a vase similar to others marked with the period *Lung-ch'ing*" (1567–1572)

The mark numbered 6 is attached to a stanza of verse written on the back of the charming eggshell vase with undulatory glaze decorated in sepia with a spray of chrysanthemum and a single head of spiked millet, as shown in Fig. 87. The seal, outlined in vermilion, the only touch of bright color, is "Ta," the artist's name, the two characters above it being *Chin ku*, "The Golden Valley," his place of abode. The verse—

A spray plucked from the garden of Tung-li:
A precious flower rescued from the frosty blast of winter—

is a quotation from the Buddhist monk Wu-k'o, who refers in it to the Tung-li garden of T'ao Yuan-ming, the "lover of the chrysanthemum." A pair of vases of the *K'ang-hsi* period, formerly in the Marquis Collection at Paris, like the one in European mounting illustrated in Fig. 88, which have a pale cobalt-blue monochrome body, a ring of dark brown round the shoulder, and a dragon encircling the neck painted in blue and dark brown or maroon, are marked underneath with a typical private mark, a seal (see No. 1) containing two characters, which look like a corruption of *fu shou*, "Happiness and longevity."

It may be useful to give here a table of the Chinese numerals, in their ordinary and more complex forms, as an assistance in deciphering dates. They occur alone, among the earliest marks, engraved underneath flowerpots, saucers, and other specimens of the Chün-chou porcelain of the *Sung* dynasty, which is distinguished for the brilliant colors of its *flambé* glazes.

Yi - - -	一	壹	1
Erh - -	二	貳	2
San - - -	三	參	3
Ssŭ - - -	四	肆	4
Wu - -	五	伍	5
Liu - -	六	陸	6
Ch'i - -	七	柒	7
Pa - - -	八	捌	8
Chiu - -	九	玖	9
Shih - -	十	拾	10
Pai - - -	百		100
Ch'ien - -	千		1,000
Wan - -		萬	10,000

5. Marks in the Form of Devices.

This heading is intended to comprise all marks of pictorial character, whether merely ornamental, or symbolical in their signification. As examples of purely ornamental marks, two may be selected for illustration. The first (see No. 2) is taken from a small *K'ang-hsi* plate of the finest quality, painted in blue with four-clawed dragons. The second (see No. 3) occurs on blue and white, painted for the European market, decorated with foreign designs, and accompanied by inscriptions in foreign letters, often incorrectly written. A tall covered cup and saucer with this mark is illustrated by Jacquemart and Le Blant (Plate XVI, Fig. 1), painted with a medallion containing a European king and queen seated, and with kneeling figures in panels, which has inscribed round the edge, "L'Empire de la vertu est etabli jus q'au bout de l'uners [Univers]." Another cup of Oriental porcelain painted in blue, with the same mark, is described in the Franks Catalogue (No. 583) as having a copy of a European picture of the sea, with a siren rising from the waves, and a label inscribed "Gardes-vous de la syrene!"

No. 1.

No. 2.

No. 3.

The symbolical devices are very numerous, and of such varied origin that it will be necessary to consider them in some detail. The Chinese are very fond of the philosophy of numbers, and of arranging all kinds of objects in sets or "numerical categories," and the symbols of divination and of Confucianism, Taoism, and Buddhism are all grouped in this way, usually in sets of eight, the number of the *pa kua*, the eight ancient trigrams. The individual members of the different sets may not all occur as marks, but the groups are so constantly used in the decoration of porcelain, either alone or in combination with other designs, that it will save repetition to dispose of them here once for all. It will be convenient to arrange the devices under the following five subdivisions:

1. *Symbols of Ancient Chinese Lore.*—*Pa kua* and *Yin yang. Pa Yin*, "Eight Musical Instruments." *Shih-êrh Chang*, "Twelve Ornaments embroidered upon ancient sacrificial robes."

2. *Buddhist Symbols.*—*Pa Chi-hsiang*, "Eight Emblems of Happy Augury." *Ch'i Pao*, "Seven Paraphernalia of a *chakravartin*, or universal sovereign."

3. *Taoist Symbols.*—*Pa An Hsien*, "Attributes of the Eight Immortals, Emblems of Longevity."

4. *The Hundred Antiques (Po Ku).*—*Ch'in, Ch'i, Shu, Hua*, " The Four Elegant Accomplishments." *Pa Pao*, "The Eight Precious Objects," etc.

5. *Devices intended to be read in "Rebus" fashion.*

1. *Symbols of Ancient Chinese Lore.*

The most ancient of these are the *Yin-yang* symbol of dualism, which represents the creative monad or ultimate principle, divided into its two elements of darkness (*yin*) and light (*yang*), and the *Pa kua*, the eight trigrams formed by different combinations of broken and unbroken lines, also representing respectively the same two dualistic elements. They are seen modeled upon the four sides of the *flambé* vase illustrated in Plate XXIII, each of the sides of which displays two of the trigrams, separated by the *yin-yang* symbol. This last is represented by the circle in the middle, which is divided by a spiral line into its two essential elements, the negative *yin* and the positive *yang*; the former, the darker half, corresponding to darkness, earth, femininity, etc., the other half corresponding to light, heaven, masculinity, and the like. The trigrams begin with three unbroken lines representing "heaven," and end with three broken lines representing "earth," the intermediate diagrams being different combinations of these two lines, representing vapor, fire, thunder, wind, water, and mountains. A ceaseless process of revolution is held to be at work in Nature, during which the various elements of properties indicated by the diagrams mutually extinguish and give birth to one another, and thus produce the phenomena of existence. The development of the *Pa kua* is attributed to *Fu-hi*, the legendary founder of the Chinese polity, who is believed to have lived early in the third millennium B.C.; a dragon-horse appeared out of the water of the Yellow River and revealed the first plan to him. *Wên Wang*, the virtual founder of the *Chou*, the third of the Three Ancient Dynasties, during his imprisonment at the hands of the tyrant *Shou*, in the twelfth century B.C., devoted himself to the study of the diagrams, and appended to each a short explanatory text. These explanations, with certain amplifications by his son, the famous *Chou Kung*, "Ducal Prince of Chou," constitute the ancient work known as the *Book of Changes*, of the *Chou* dynasty, which, with the commentary added by Confucius, forms the *Yi Ching*, or *Canon of Changes*, the most venerated of the Chinese classics. The entire system of this work, which serves as a basis for the philosophy of divination and geomancy, and is largely appealed to as containing not only the elements of all metaphysical knowledge, but also a clew to the secrets of Nature and of being, reposes upon the eight trigrams.*

FIG. 89.—K'ang-hsi Vase, with relief modeling, filled in and decorated with enamel colors, without underglaze blue or gold.

The Eight Musical Instruments, *Pa Yin*, of ancient times, which were made of as many different materials, are found in the decoration of porcelain as a complete set, as well as sometimes, though rarely, separately, as marks. They are:

1. *Ch'ing*, "Sounding Stone," which is suspended upon a frame and struck with a wooden

---

* See Mayer's *Chinese Reader's Manual*, p. 333; and Legge's *Yi King*, in *Sacred Books of the East*, vol. xvi (Oxford, 1882).

hammer. It is usually made of jade carved in the form of a mason's square, with a hole pierced near the angle for suspension. Being a homonym of *Ch'ing*, "Good Fortune," it often figures with that meaning on the rafters of houses, etc.

2. *Chung*, "Bell," made of metal, clapperless, and suspended, to be struck by a mallet. Bells as well as sounding stones are hung in sets upon frames to produce musical chimes.

3. *Ch'in*, "Lute," with strings of silk. This often occurs as a mark, usually wrapped in its brocaded case.

4. *Ti*, "Flute," made of bamboo.

5. *Chu*, "Box," made of ordinary wood, with a metal hammer inside.

6. *Ku*, "Drum," covered with skin.

7. *Shêng*, "Reed Organ," a mouth instrument dating from very early times, in which the body or wind-chest

No. 1.

is made of gourd, with seventeen reed pipes of different lengths inserted at the top.

8. *Hsüan*, "Icarina," made of baked clay, in the shape of a cone pierced with six holes.

Several of these musical instruments are seen inclosed in small medallions in the decoration of the vase shown in Fig. 89. They may all be found figured in a learned paper on *Chinese Music*, by Mr. J. A. Van Aalst,* who is himself a cultivated musician.

The next series of symbols derived from ancient Chinese lore are the Twelve *Chang*, or "Ornaments," with which the sacrificial robes used to be embroidered. They are referred to in the earliest of the Chinese classics, where the Emperor *Shun* desires at this remote period "to see these emblematic figures of the ancients."† The robes

FIG. 90.—Ch'ien-lung Ritual Wine Vessel, painted in blue with Buddhist emblems.

of the emperor had all the twelve figures painted or embroidered upon them; the hereditary nobles of the first rank are said to have been restricted from the use of the sun, moon, and stars; those of the next two degrees were further restricted from mountains and dragons; and by a continually decreasing restriction five sets of official robes were made indicating the rank of the wearers. The figures are taken from an official edition of the *Shu Ching*, or *Historical Classic*, referred to below, the illustrations of which date from the *Sung* dynasty. The series comprises:

1. *Jih*, the "Sun" (No. 1), a disk supported upon a bank of clouds, with the three-legged solar bird inside. In the works of Hwai Nan Tzǔ, who lived in the second century B. C., this fabulous bird is alluded to as inhabiting the sun. The sun in Chinese dualism is the concrete essence of the masculine principle in Nature, the source of brightness and energy.

No. 2.

2. *Yueh*, the "Moon" (No. 2), a disk supported upon the clouds, containing a hare, under the shade of a cassia tree, occupied with pestle and mortar, pounding the drugs of immortality. The moon is the concrete essence of the feminine principle in Nature; it is inhabited by the hare and the three-legged toad, and there grows the tree (the cassia) which confers immortality on those who eat its leaves. The Chinese "old man of the moon" (Yueh

* *China. Imperial Maritime Customs. Chinese Music.* By J. A. Van Aalst. Published by order of the Inspector General of Customs, Shanghai, 1884.

† *The Chinese Classics.* Translated by Dr. Legge, v. iii. *The Shoo King*, p. 80.

Lao) is popularly said to tie together with an invisible cord the feet of those who are predestined to a betrothal.

3. *Hsing Chên*, the "Stars," represented by a stellar constellation of three stars connected in Chinese fashion by straight lines (No. 1).

4. *Shan*, "Mountains," which have been worshiped in eastern Asia from prehistoric times (No. 2).

5. *Lung*, "Dragons," a pair of the fabulous five-clawed scaly monsters (No. 3), resembling somewhat in shape the huge saurians which paleontologists have brought to light in recent years.

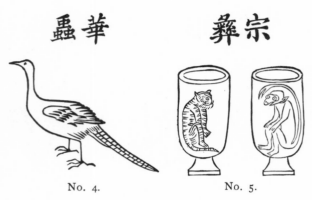

No. 1.   No. 2.   No. 3.

6. *Hua Chung*, the "Variegated Animal" (No. 4)—i. e., the pheasant, or "flowery fowl" of the Chinese.

7. *Tsung Yi*, the "Temple Vessels" (No. 5), used in the services of the ancestral temple, of which one was said to have had the figure of a tiger upon it, another that of a kind of monkey—animals distinguished for their filial piety, according to the commentators on the classics.

8. *Ts'ao*, "Aquatic Grass" (No. 6).

9. *Huo*, "Fire" (No. 7).

10. *Fên Mi*, "Grains of Rice" (No. 8). These are also often represented on the pierced medallions of ancient jade, the earliest tokens of value in China.

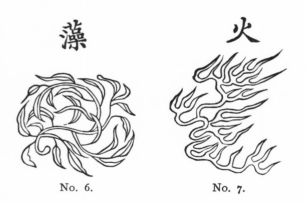

No. 4.   No. 5.

11. *Fu*, an "Axe" (No. 9).

12. *Fu* (No. 10), a "Symbol" of distinction, to which no special signification is attached, and which seems to have been of purely ornamental origin. It is used in the sense of "embroidered," in modern phraseology, and often occurs as a mark on porcelain of decorative character.

No. 6.   No. 7.

2. *Buddhist Symbols.*

Buddhism was first heard of in China some two centuries before Christ, and Buddhist priests came from India as early as the first century of the Christian era, bringing with them images, pictures, and books, and a knowledge of the elaborate symbolism of the new religion, much of which had been borrowed from pre-existing Indian sources. Lamaism, the Tibetan form of Buddhism, was introduced much later, under the influence of the Mongol dynasty which ruled China in the thirteenth century, and this is the cult which is chiefly affected by the Manchu Tartars who now occupy the throne at Peking.

Of the Buddhist symbols found upon porcelain the most frequent are the eight symbols of good fortune, known by the name of *Pa Chi-hsiang, pa* meaning "eight," *chi-hsiang*, "happy omens." They were among the auspicious signs figured on the sole of the foot of Buddha; they are constantly used in the architectural decoration of temples, and are displayed in porcelain, stone, or gilded wood

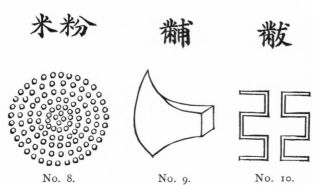

No. 8.   No. 9.   No. 10.

upon the altar of every Buddhist shrine. They are usually drawn round with fillets, and are:

1. The "Wheel" (Chinese *Lun*, Sanskrit *Chakra*), the sacred wheel of the law, which appears whirling in the air enveloped in flames, as the sign of the advent of a *Chakravartti Rajâ*, a "Wheel King," or universal monarch (No. 1). This is sometimes replaced by the large hanging Bell (Chinese *Chung*, Sanskrit *Ghanta*), which is struck with a mallet on its outer rim during Buddhist worship.

2. The "Shell" (Chinese *Lo*, Sanskrit *Sankha*), the conch-shell trumpet of victory, which is also blown during certain religious ceremonies (No. 2).

3. The "Umbrella" (Chinese *San*, Sanskrit *Chattra*), the state umbrella (No. 3) held over the head of personages of rank throughout the East, a well-known symbol of sovereignty (" Lord of the White Umbrella ").

FIG. 91.—Snuff-Bottle, with Buddhist symbols molded in relief.

No. 1.

No. 2.

No. 3.

No. 4.

4. The "Canopy" (Chinese *Kai*, Sanskrit *Dhvaja*), hung with streamers and jeweled tassels (No. 4).

5. The "Flower" (Chinese *Hua*, Sanskrit *Padma*), properly the sacred lotus, a rose-colored variety of the *Nelumbium speciosum*, but often represented in China by a peony or some other flower (No. 5).

6. The "Vase" (Chinese *P'ing*, Sanskrit *Kalasa*), which may have a flower and miniature *ju-i* scepter placed inside, or perhaps a trio of peacock's feathers (No. 6).

7. The " Fish " (Chinese *Yü*, Sanskrit *Matsya*), the golden fish, represented in pairs (No. 7), an emblem of fertility.

8. The "Entrails" (Chinese *Chang*, Sanskrit *Srîvatsa*). The " lucky diagram," an angular knot (No. 8) formed of a line without beginning or end, an emblem of longevity. It was customary in ancient times to cut open the abdomen of the sacrificial victim and to augur from the position of its entrails.

No. 5.

No. 6.

No. 7.

No. 8.

These *Pa Chi-hsiang* form the principal motive of decoration of the blue and white ritual wine-pot in Fig. 90, the swelling body of which is decorated with the set of eight, encircled by waving fillets, and supported by conventional flowers of Indian lotus. The conch-shell, umbrella, and canopy are seen in the picture. The same symbols are molded in relief so as to project upon the scrolled background of the accompanying snuff-bottle (Fig. 91), and one can distinguish on the side illustrated the umbrella and the flame-encircled wheel, flanked by the flower upon the right and the vase on the left. The large pilgrim bottle shown in Fig. 50 has its circumference filled with the same Buddhist emblems of good fortune, while the large round medallions display at the front and back of the vase the eight attributes of the Taoist genii, with other symbols of longevity and happiness. This vase forms altogether a perfect mine of religious symbolism, with the emblems of different religions reposing upon it side by side, in a way that does not strike a Chinese mind as unnatural or inconsistent.

The "Seven Gems" (in Chinese *Ch'i Pao*, in Sanskrit *Sapta Ratna*) are taken from the porcelain service which was made for the daughter of the Emperor *Tao-kuang*, who was given in marriage to the Tumed Prince, and which has been already described in the illustration of its Mongol mark of *Baragon Tumed*. They are the attributes of the universal monarch, such as Prince Siddhârta would have been had he not become a Buddha, and they are often figured in Buddhist temples upon the base of his throne. They comprise:

No. 1.

1. The "Golden Wheel" (No. 1), *Chin Lun*, the victorious jeweled wheel of a thousand spokes which heralds the advent of a *Chakravartî Râja*, or "Wheel King."

2. The "Jadelike Girl" (No. 2), *Yü Nü*, the beauteous consort, who fans her lord to sleep, and attends him with the constancy of a slave.

No. 2.

3. The "Horse" (No. 3), *Ma*, which appears to symbolize the horse-chariot of the sun, implying a realm where the sun never sets, as well as the celestial steed which springs Pegasus-like from the clouds to deliver the sovereign from any danger. It carries on its back the sacred alms-bowl.

4. The "Elephant" (No. 4), *Hsiang*, the white elephant which was borrowed from Indian Buddhism by the Buddhist kings of Burmah and Siam, and which seems to be Indra's elephant Airâvata. He carries the sacred jewel of the law.

No. 3.

5. "Divine Guardian of the Treasury" (No. 5), *Chu Ts'ang Shên*, the minister who regulates the affairs of the empire.

6. "General in Command of the Army" (No. 6), *Chu Ping Ch'ên*, with drawn sword and tiger shield, who conquers all enemies.

No. 4.

7. "Wonder-working Jewels" (No. 7), *Ju I Chu*, in Sanskrit *Chintā-mani*, fulfilling every wish. They are figured here as a bundle of jeweled wands bound round with a cord.

No. 6.

The Buddhist symbols which occur most frequently as "marks," either in simple outline or bound with fillets, or inclosed in panels of different form, are the lotus flower (No. 8), which is usually accompanied by a few waving reeds, the palm leaf (No. 9), on which the scriptures were written in ancient times, the pair of fish, the *srivatsa*, or endless knot, and the *svastika* symbol. This last, which has been already referred to, is a mystic diagram of great antiquity and wide distribution, mentioned in the Râmâyana and found in the rock temples of India, among all the Buddhistic people of Asia, and even as the emblem of Thor among Teutonic nations.

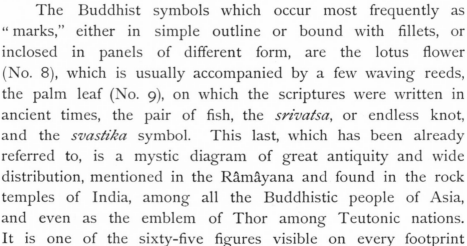

No. 5.

No. 7.

It is one of the sixty-five figures visible on every footprint (*Sripâda*) of Buddha. In China it is the symbol of Buddha's heart—i. e., of the esoteric doctrines of Buddhism—and is the special mark of all deities worshiped by the Lotus School. The images of Kuan Yin, the god (or goddess) of mercy, have sometimes a lotus flower, sometimes a *svastika*, figured on the breast.

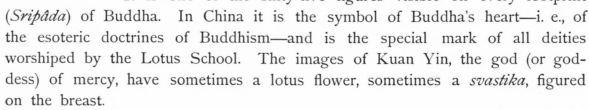

No. 8.

3. *Taoist Symbols.*

The Taoist set of eight symbols are comprised in the *Pa An Hsien*, the attributes of the eight Taoist genii or immortals. They are:

No. 9.

1. The "Fan" (*Shan*) carried by Chung-li Ch'üan, with which he is said to revive the souls of the dead.

2. The "Sword" (*Chien*) of supernatural power, wielded by Lü Tung-pin.

3. The "Pilgrim's Gourd" (*Hu-lu*) of Li T'ieh-kuai, the source of so many magical appearances.

4. The "Castanets" (*Pan*) of Ts'ao Kuo-ch'iu, who always has a pair in his hand.

5. The "Basket of Flowers" (*Hua Lan*), borne by Lan Ts'ai-ho.

6. The "Bamboo Tube and Rods" (*Yu Ku*), a kind of miniature drum carried by Chang Kuo.

7. The "Flute" (*Ti*), upon which Han Hsiang Tzŭ plays.

8. The "Lotus Flower" (*Lien Hua*) of the virgin damsel Ho Hsien Ku.

The fan is sometimes replaced by the fly-whisk (*ying shua*), the pilgrim's gourd is nearly always accompanied by the crooked iron staff (*kun*) of the lame beggar, and the flower basket

FIG. 92.—The mark shown on the foot of the tall vase in Fig. 93; the sacred *ling-chih* fungus enveloped in tufts of grass.

by the spade (*chan*) of the florist. These Taoist symbols are constantly met with in Chinese art as architectural designs, patterns of wall paper and domestic furniture, etc., as well as in the decoration of jade, bronze, and porcelain. They occupy the large central medallion on the two sides of the *Ch'ien-lung* pilgrim bottle decorated in colors, shown in Fig. 50, being represented there as bound together in pairs with waving fillets, displayed upon a ground filled with cloud scrolls and sprays of conventional flowers. The palm-leaf fan and the sword are seen tied together, the castanets and the drum with its two rods inside, the gourd, crooked staff, and flute, the basket of flowers and the lotus.

The emblems of longevity which so frequently occur as marks are mostly of Taoist origin, or connected with Taoist mythological legends, and they may consequently be referred to here. The greatest desire of a Chinaman is for long life, which is reckoned as the first and chief of the five happinesses, and the Taoist hermits, like the mediæval alchemists, spend their time in the search after the elixir of immortality.

The most prominent position in the mystical fancies of the Taoists is given to the peach. The most ancient superstitions of the Chinese attributed magic virtues to the twigs of the peach, and the fabulists of the *Han* dynasty added many extravagant details to the legends already existing. The divine peach-tree which grew near the palace of the goddess *Hsi Wang Mu*, whose fruit ripened but once in three thousand years, was celebrated by them as conferring the gift of immortality. The peach as an emblem of longevity is found as a mark (No. 1) in combination with a bat, the homonym of *fu*, "happiness."

A still more common emblem of longevity is the sacred fungus (*ling-chih*), the *Polyporus lucidus* of botanists, distinguished by the brightly variegated colors which it develops in the ordinary course of its growth. When dried it is very durable, and it is placed upon the altar of Taoist temples and often represented in the hands of their deities. It is occasionally seen held in the mouth of a deer, and one of these animals always accompanies *Shou Lao*, the longevity god. The fungus is specially valued when a tuft of grass has grown through its substance, and this is carefully preserved with the dried specimen. The tuft of grass is generally found, too, in the mark, and has been a puzzle to collectors, who have often described the peculiar combination as a cockscomb or some other flower, under the idea that a fungus could not have leaves. In the mark photographed in Fig. 92, from the foot of one of a pair of blue and white gourd-

No. 1.

FIG. 93.—Tall Vase, one of a pair, richly decorated in pure cobalt blue with medallions of diverse form in the midst of floral scrolls.

shaped vases of the *K'ang-hsi* period, Fig. 93, the fungus is represented in the middle of five such tufts of grass. In the other mark (No. 1), a more frequent form, it is accompanied by a few blades only.

No. 1.

Three other plants which figure as emblems of longevity are the *Sung, Chu, Mei*, the Pine, Bamboo, and the Prunus, the first two because they are evergreen and flourish throughout the winter, the prunus because it throws out flowering twigs from its leafless stalks up to an extreme old age. The accompanying mark (No. 2), reproduced in facsimile from a large bowl with flaring mouth, decorated inside and out with dramatic scenes in the most brilliant blue, of the *K'ang-hsi* period, is composed of two tiny twigs of prunus blossom encircled by the usual double ring.

FIG. 94.—Large Flat Dish of the K'ang-hsi period, decorated in colors, including red, yellow, black, overglaze cobalt blue, pale purple, light green, coffee-brown, and touches of gold.

Among the animal emblems of longevity are the deer, the tortoise, and the stork, all of which occur occasionally as marks. The hare (No. 3) is found more frequently than any as a mark. It is the animal sacred to the moon, where the Taoists believe it to live, pounding with pestle and mortar the drugs that form the *elixir vitæ*. It is said to live a thousand years, and to become white when it has reached half its long span of life. The stork, in the form that is usually figured as a mark, is seen inclosed in a small circular medallion in the decoration of the gourd-shaped vase in Fig. 85; it is the patriarch of the feathered tribe, attaining a fabulous age, and is the aërial courser of the Taoist divinities, often represented

No. 3.

No. 2.

bringing from a paradise in the clouds the tablets of human fate which it carries in its beak. The tortoise is also sometimes seen accompanying the longevity god, and the common felicitous phrase

Kuei ho ch'i shou means, "May your longevity equal that of the tortoise [*kuei*] and stork [*ho*]!" As a mark, however, it is rare in China, although more commonly used in Japan in the form of a tortoise with a hairy tail composed of strings of confervoid growth.

4. *The Hundred Antiques (Po Ku).*

The expression *Po Ku*, which is constantly used in the description of Chinese art, refers to the almost infinite variety of ancient symbols and emblems, derived from all kinds of sources, sacred and profane, which form a common motive in the decoration of porcelain and other art objects. Although the word "hundred" is used vaguely as a noun of multitude, it is not a mere figure of speech, as it would not be a difficult matter to enumerate more than that number of antique symbols appertaining to this category. These antiques sometimes form the sole decoration of vases; sometimes they are grouped in panels of diverse form, as in the blue and white "hawthorn" jars in which the floral ground is interrupted by medallions; in other cases they are arranged singly within the bands of floral brocade or diaper which encircle the borders of a round dish or other piece.

The tall two-handled blue and white cup illustrated in Plate XIV is decorated, for instance, with groups of these symbols, the intervals of the conventional borders of foliated design being filled with paraphernalia of the scholar and artist—books on tables, brushes in vases, water receptacles, and scroll pictures, enveloped with waving fillets and mixed with tasseled wands and double diamonds, symbols of literary success.

The large and beautiful plate (Fig. 94) painted in brilliant enamel colors of the *K'ang-hsi* period, with a broad band of peony scrolls penetrated by archaic dragons around the rim, succeeded by narrower rings of fret, displays in the interior a typical example of the *Po Ku* style of decoration, artistically carried out. The center piece is a tall, graceful vase with rings hanging upon open scrolled handles, decorated with sprays of lotus, standing upon a tripod pedestal, filled with a bouquet of peonies, floral emblems of literary success leading to wealth and honor. A low vase with wide, bulging body, decorated with dragons at the side, holds peacocks' feathers, emblems of high rank. On the other side, a lion-shaped censer upon a four-legged stand is emitting a cloud of incense shaping above into the forms of a pair of storks, symbols of long life and of conjugal felicity. A second set of incense-burning apparatus, a bundle of scroll pictures tied up in a brocaded wrapper, a *ju-i* ("wish-fulfilling") scepter or wand, a musical stone, and other felicitous symbols, and a sword with a paper-weight in the foreground, fill in the picture. The background is a scroll picture partially unrolled to show a pine-clad mountain with pavilions and temples, a representation of the Taoist paradise, the immemorial hills (*Shou Shan*) where their immortal hermits are wont to wander.

The *Po Ku* symbols, like those of the Buddhist and Taoist cults, are also often arranged in numerical categories. The sets most frequently met with are the *Pa Pao* or "Eight Precious Things," and the "Four Accomplishments of the Scholar." These occasionally occur in the ornamental borders of plates and vases, generally bound with fillets, and they are also found singly as marks. The usual set of the *Pa Pao* comprises:

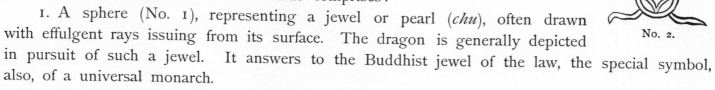

No. 1.

No. 2.

1. A sphere (No. 1), representing a jewel or pearl (*chu*), often drawn with effulgent rays issuing from its surface. The dragon is generally depicted in pursuit of such a jewel. It answers to the Buddhist jewel of the law, the special symbol, also, of a universal monarch.

2. A circle inclosing a square (No. 2). This represents a "cash" (*ch'ien*), the ordinary money of the Chinese, which is a round copper coin pierced with a square hole in the center for convenience of stringing. A couple of them may be united by a fillet, or a long line form an ornamental border to a plate. Sometimes the god of riches will be seen emerging from the clouds at night, with a string of such "cash" whirling round his shoulders, in the act of filling a treasure chest, while the guards are sleeping beside it.

3. An open lozenge (*fang-shêng*) with ribbons entwined round it (No. 1). This is a symbol of victory or success. A pair of such objects interlaced make a common symbol, a pattern for jewelry, or worn in the front of the caps of boys, conveying the idea *T'ung hsin fang shêng*, or "Union gives success."

No. 1.

4. A solid lozenge (No. 2), another form of the same symbol (*fang shêng*). A musical stone of jade or a plaque of bronze may be fashioned in this shape.

No. 2.

5. A *ch'ing*, or musical stone of jade (No. 3). Also cast in sonorous metal. Struck with a hammer, it is a very ancient musical instrument, and minute directions for its manufacture are found in old books. A set of sixteen, of different size and thickness, form the *pien ch'ing*, or "stone chime." It is also a Buddhist musical instrument. On account of the similarity of the sound of its name with that of the word *ch'ing*, which means "happiness" and "good luck," it is often seen in symbolical decorations on the rafters of a house, the side of a winecup, etc.

No. 3.

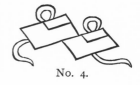

No. 4.

6. A pair of books (*shu*) strung together by a ribbon (No. 4). This symbol is generally found as one of the four which represent the elegant accomplishments of the Chinese scholar, the other three being *ch'in*, *ch'i*, and *hua*, the lyre, the chess-board, and scroll paintings.

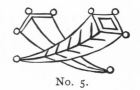

No. 5.

7. *Chüeh*, a pair of horns (No. 5). The rhinoceros horn used to be considered an object of great value in China, and was elaborately carved into winecups, girdle clasps, and many other things. A horn brimming with good things is emblematic of plenty, like the cornucopia of our own classical times.

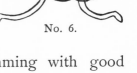

No. 6.

8. An artemisia leaf (the *ai yeh*, shown in No. 6). A fragrant plant of good omen, used from ancient times for the "moxa." The Buddhist priest at his ordination places small balls of the dried leaves upon his head and ignites them to burn a number of spots into the skin. At the festival of new moon in the fifth month every householder nails to the posts and windows of his house some leaves of the artemisia and sweet flag, tied together in bundles, to dispel noxious influences.

These objects are sometimes seen borne by a procession of fantastic figures representing tribute bearers from abroad. The set is variable, and any one of the members may be replaced by a branch of coral, a silver ingot, a brush and cake of ink, etc., or by a *svastika* symbol, or by one of the Buddhist emblems of good fortune, such as a lotus flower, conch shell, or pair of fishes. These symbols, as the eight aquatic jewels (*Shui pa pao*), represent the treasures of the sea, and are pictured in combination with winged sea-horses and other monsters floating upon the waves of the sea—a common decoration of the interior of bowls and dishes.

FIG. 95.—Decorated in brilliant enamel colors of the K'ang-hsi period, with medallions displayed upon a scrolled ground of coral-red.

FIG. 96.—Vase of the K'ang-hsi period, painted in coral-red, pale green, and gold.

The "Four Accomplishments" of the Chinese scholar—music, chess, calligraphy, and painting—are known by the collective title of *Ch'in Ch'i Shu Hua*, and are represented by the articles named in the title, viz.: (1) a lyre wrapped in its embroidered case; (2) a chess- or rather *gô*-board, with round boxes for the white and black "men"; (3) a pair of books placed side by side or tied together with a fillet; and (4) a couple of scroll pictures. They are inclosed in panels within a diapered band encircling the shoulder of the vase illustrated in Fig. 95, and each one of the four occupies a prominent position in the successive panels of the vase shown in Fig. 96, so that it is unnecessary to illustrate them separately. They all occur, besides, as marks. The exercise of the four accomplishments is a common motive of decoration for figure subjects, and some of the finest vases of the *K'ang-hsi* period, both blue and white and brilliantly enameled in colors, exhibit bevies of busy damsels or parties of *literati* gathered in four groups, which are depicted either on the same vase, or on a pair of bowls of the same set, two of the groups being displayed in the latter case on the sides of each of the bowls.

The vase just alluded to (Fig. 96), which is referred to the *K'ang-hsi* period, is decorated in coral red and pale green with touches of gold, with floral brocades and diapered bands of varied pattern, surrounding four large panels with indented corners which are filled with selections of these *Po Ku* designs. The four sides have been separately photographed, to give an idea of the variety of the devices.

FIG. 97.—One of the panels of the vase shown in Fig. 96, exhibiting the *Po Ku* style of decoration.

The first picture (Fig. 96) shows the outline and decoration of the vase; the other three give the successive panels, starting from the first and proceeding round the vase from left to right. The first panel has in the center a three-legged censer of complex form with dentated ribs, and a cover surmounted by a one-horned grotesque lion; the corners are occupied by a folding chess-board, with two boxes for the "men," a pair of horn cups bound with fillets, an open book, and a magic wand (*ju-i*) with its fungus-shaped jeweled head, a cylindrical pot (*pi-t'ung*) with a picture scroll, a feather whisk, and two brushes inside, and a water receptacle with tiny ladle near at hand; two cups and a fluted incense box with palm-leaf cover fill in the intervals.

The second panel (Fig. 97) contains a vase of "hawthorn" pattern interrupted by bands of triangular fret, mounted upon a stand, with an emblematic spray of blossoming prunus inside; in the corners a lyre in its brocaded case tied with ribbons, the staff and fan of the mendicant friar, a jar of wine (*chiu tsun*) with a ladle inside and a winecup near at hand, a censer decorated with trigrams, and a covered incense box beside it: in the intervals are a waterpot (*shui-ch'êng*), a libation cup, the round "cash" symbol, a lozenge displaying a *svastika* symbol,

FIG. 98.—Another panel of the vase shown in Fig. 96.

FIG. 99.—The fourth panel of the vase shown in Fig. 96.

and two interlacing rings, an archaic form of money and of the earliest hieroglyph representing it.

The third panel (Fig. 98) has as its center-piece a tripod censer with dentated ribs and upright loop handles; two books, having their volumes inclosed in the usual cloth cases, and a *Ju-i* wand tied with a fillet, *below*, a sacred alms-bowl, the holy grail of Buddhism, reposing on a bed of *Ficus religiosa* leaves, and a pair of casta-nets, *above*; a palette and pair of brushes, the "cash" symbol, a palm leaf, and the interlacing lozenge-symbol (*fang-shêng*) filling in the intervals.

The fourth panel (Fig. 99) exhibits a tall vase of graceful form, decorated with an archaic dragon, containing a branch of coral and two peacock's feathers, emblems of high rank, with a couple of scroll pictures tied together with a cord half hid-den by the vase, a bundle of rolls of silk and a flute, a palm-leaf fan and Buddhist rosary on either side of its neck; a low table with four divisions filled apparently with nuts, having two tea-cups in their saucers beside it, a waterpot and a foot rule, a third small cup, and the inter-lacing ring-symbol, complete the emblematic decoration.

This is enough to show the great variety of the *Po Ku* symbols. Two of them, which often occur separately as marks, are the *pao ting* (No. 1), or precious censer, a bronze antique with either three or four legs, which is often roughly shaped, so that it was mistaken by Jacquemart for a model-ing table; and *fu*, the ornamental symbol (No. 2) which formed one of the designs embroidered in olden times upon sacrificial robes.

5. *Devices intended to be read in "Rebus" fashion.*

The Chinese language being monosyllabic, and hav-ing comparatively few vocables to express the myriads of written characters, lends itself readily to puns, and a subclass is necessary for devices of this kind. The idea of *Ling Hsien Chu Shou*— i. e., "The Sacred Genii worshiping the Lon-gevity God"—is involved, for instance, in a floral device consisting of interlacing sprays of polyporus fungus, narcissus flowers, bamboo twigs, and peach fruit;* the fungus is called *ling-chih*, the narcissus, *shui hsien hua*, or "the water fairy," *chu*, "bamboo," is used as a "re-bus" for "worship," which has the same sound, and the peach suggests the deity of longevity, whose special attribute it is. Again, a device which often occurs as a mark on porcelain is composed of a bat,

No. 1.

No. 2.

FIG. 100.—Artistically decorated Vase of the Ch'ien-lung period, enameled with a celadon glaze of typical shade.

* This floral device is carved in the bottom of a magnificent dish of white jade, the "brush-washer" (*pi-hsi*) of a Chinese writer or artist, now in the Walters Collection.

a peach, and a couple of "cash" united by a fillet, and is read *Fu Shou Shuang Ch'üan*—i. e., "Happiness and Longevity both complete"; the bat (*fu*) is a homonym of (*fu*) "happiness"; the peach is the sacred fruit of longevity (*shou*), and *ch'üan*, the ancient term for "cash," means also "perfect." We have had this last character already as a single mark. Dozens of such curious conceits might be cited.

The richly decorated vase of the *Ch'ien-lung* period enameled in colors with gilding, illustrated in Fig. 100, which has flowers of the four seasons in its four large panels—the magnolia

FIG. 101.—Yung-chêng Dish, decorated in brilliant enamel colors, with sprays of magnolia, pyrus, and tree-peony. (Companion in Plate XLVIII.)

yulan and peonia of *spring*, the hydrangea, pinks (dianthus) and flags (iris) of *summer*, the oak with acorns and russet leaves and the chrysanthemums of *autumn*, the blossoming plum and early roses of *winter*—has the two oblong panels on the neck occupied by an emblematical device

FIG. 102.—Snuff-bottle, inscribed with the character *shou*, "longevity."

of this kind, which is composed of a chain of symbols hung with knotted ribbons and jeweled beads. It suggests the felicitous motto, *Chi ch'ing yu yü*—i. e, "Good Fortune and Abundance of Riches"; the hanging musical plaque of jade of triangular form (*chi-ch'ing*) suggests the homophone "good fortune"; and the pair of fishes (*yü*) involves the idea of prosperity and abundance (*yü*), which is read with the same vocable, although written with a different character.

The accompanying mark (No. 1) has already been published in the Franks *Catalogue*, so often referred to (Plate VII, 88), taken from a pair of circular trays, which are decorated, in colors with gilding, with ladies engaged in two out of the "four accomplishments," viz., painting and chess. The first exhibits "two ladies, one seated at a table with a brush in her hand, the other (her attendant) standing with a hand-screen behind the former, a stand with vases, etc."; the second has "three ladies seated on a carpet and playing at a game somewhat like chess, in the background a stand

No. 1.

with vases, stool with tea things, etc." The mark, which is composed of a pencil-brush (*pi*), a cake of ink (*ting*), and a magic wand (*ju-i*) symbolizes the phrase *Pi ting ju-i*—i. e., "May [things] be fixed as you wish!" The same mark occurs also on blue and white porcelain of good style.

The decoration of the pair of eggshell winecups, of which one is shown in Fig. 78, includes another "rebus" in the shape of two flying bats (*fu*), with triangular plaques of jade (*chi-ch'ing*) in their mouths, suggesting the felicitous phrase *Shuang fu chi ch'ing*—i. e., "Twofold Happiness and Good Fortune."

The magnificent *Yung-Chêng* dish, illustrated in Fig. 101, would also be suggestive to a Chinese mind, and it would imply, from its floral decoration, the felicitous sentence, *Yü t'ang fu kuei*, or "Jade Halls for the Rich and Noble," the three flowers displayed in the interior of the dish being the magnolia (*yü-lan*), the double pyrus (*hai-t'ang*), and the tree-peony, which is often called the *fu-kuei* flower, as the special floral emblem of riches and high rank. Many of the titles of Chinese art designs are of this alliterative character, and suggest at once the conventional details which make up the composition.

FIG. 103.—An Eggshell Plate, of very fine, white, translucent paste; the decoration, in gold and sepia, composed of an inscription in Arabic. The central design embodies the familiar Mohammedan Confession of Faith: "*La Ilâh illa-l lâh wa Muhammad rasûl-a-llâh,*" or, "There is no deity but God, and Muhammad is his messenger." The border embodies the opening lines of the Qurân, as commonly recited in prayer: "*Bismi-l-lâhi-rrahmâni-rrahîm. Al hamdu lillâhi rabbi-l alamîn arrahmâni rrahîm mâliki yaumi-ddin. Iyyâka n'abudu wa iyyâka nasta'in. Thdîna-ssirâṭa-l-Mustagîm Siraṭa-llazîna an'amta 'alayhem. Gayri-l-magḍubi 'alayhem wala-ḍḍallîn.*" Which, being translated, reads: "In the Name of God the Compassionate, the Merciful! Praise be to God, the Lord of the Universe, the Compassionate, the Merciful, the Ruler of the Day of Judgment! Thee do we worship, and Thee do we ask for assistance. Lead us in the right path, the path of those upon whom Thou art gracious, and not of those upon whom Thou art angry, nor those who go astray!"

FIG. 104.—Tz'ŭ-chou whiteware: (a) Wine Flask, decorated in shades of brown; (b) Double Gourd, painted in brown; (c) The Twin Genii of Taoist Fable, mounted with a tube for incense, painted in brown.

CHAPTER V.

CLASSIFICATION OF CHINESE PORCELAIN.—PRIMITIVE PERIOD.—SUNG DYNASTY.—JU YAO.—KUAN YAO.—TING YAO.—LUNG-CH'ÜAN YAO.—KO YAO.—TUNG-CH'ING YAO.—CHÜN YAO.—THREE FACTORIES AT CHI-CHOU, CHIEN-CHOU, AND TZ'Ŭ-CHOU.—UTENSILS OF SUNG PORCELAIN.

IT has already been shown in Chapter I, from the evidence of contemporary writers, that porcelain must have been known in China at least as early as the *T'ang* dynasty. But the jadelike resonant white ware of Hsin-p'ing, the modern Ching-tê-chên, in the province of Kiangsi, and the cups of Ta-yi, in the Ssŭchuan province, so often celebrated by the poets of the period, together with the enameled bowls of Yueh-chou and the other colored fabrics described in the early books on tea, have long since disappeared. Even the famous porcelain of the After *Chou* dynasty, which reigned A. D. 951–960, known at the time as imperial ware, subsequently as Ch'ai Yao, after the name of the reigning emperor, who decreed that it should be produced " blue as the sky, clear as a mirror, thin as paper, resonant as jade," is described by modern collectors as almost a phantom, and as being so rare that in the present day fragments are set in gold like jewels, to be worn in the front of the cap.* The author of the *Ch'ing pi ts'ang*, a little book on art published in 1595, writes: " I have seen a broken piece of Ch'ai Yao made into a ring and worn on the girdle, the sky-blue color and brilliant polish of which corresponded to the description as given above, but it differed in being thick." It seems hardly necessary, therefore, to include these different wares in our classification, or to occupy our space with any of the other less important productions which are described in the older books, but are not seen in collections of the present day.

It is different when we come to the *Sung* dynasty, which began in 960 and lasted till 1280, when it was overthrown by Kublai Khan, the grandson of the famous Genghis Khan and the founder of the *Yuan* dynasty, which ruled China till it was in its turn succeeded by the native *Ming* dynasty in the year 1368. We have actual specimens of the porcelain of these times in our possession and can compare them with the descriptions of the writers on ceramic subjects. They agree in having a certain primitive aspect, being invested generally with glazes of single colors of uniform or mottled tint, with plain or crackled surface, so that the two dynasties are justly classed together by M. Grandidier,† whose classification of Chinese porcelain I propose to follow here, arranged as it is in chronological order after a Chinese model:

* This practice of cutting fragments of broken porcelain into oval plaques for mounting into buckles for girdles, or buttons for the tobacco pouch, is useful for the study of the rarer glazes, and for comparison with any unbroken specimens which we have before us for classification. They show the thickness of the glaze as well as the texture of the paste, both of which are important criteria for determining the age of a piece.

† *La Céramique chinoise*, avec 42 héliogravures par Dujardin, par Ernest Grandidier, Paris, 1894.

1. Primitive period, including the *Sung* dynasty (960–1279) and the *Yuan* dynasty (1280–1367).

2. *Ming* period, comprising the whole of the *Ming* dynasty (1368–1643).

3. *K'ang-hsi* period, extending from the fall of the *Ming* dynasty to the close of the reign of *K'ang-hsi* (1662–1722).

4. *Yung-chêng* and *Ch'ien-lung* period (1723–1795).

5. Modern period, from the beginning of the reign of *Chia-ch'ing* in 1796 to the present day.

This classification gives five fairly well marked ceramic classes, and as a rule it will not be found difficult to decide from the style, from the method of decoration, or from the colors employed, to which of these classes a particular piece should belong.

FIG. 105.—K'ang-hsi Bowl, with a broad band of svastika fret in white relief, interrupted by medallions; mark, a lotus flower.

The first, or Primitive period, is named from the comparatively simple character of its ceramic productions. This must be stated with some qualification, however, as many of the different processes of decoration were introduced, and it will be seen that there were considerable advances in the ceramic productions, before the end of the period, when they are compared with the really primitive porcelain of the *T'ang* dynasty. At first the pieces were either plainly fashioned on the wheel, or molded, and invested with glazes of different color, the brilliance of which constituted the chief charm. Afterward more work was lavished on the paste, which was worked in relief, engraved, or carved in open-work designs. The delicacy of some of the molded decoration of this period in the interior of the white bowls and platters of the Ting-chou kilns, with phœnixes flying through floral scrolls, and other elaborate designs, has, indeed, hardly been surpassed since.

Among the monochrome glazes are found whites of various tones, grays of bluish and purplish tints, greens from pale sea-green celadon to deep olive, browns from light chamois to dark tints approaching black, bright red, and dark purple. Especially notable are the pale purple, often speckled with red spots; the brilliant grass-greens of the Lung-ch'üan porcelain, called *ts'ung-lü*, or "onion-green," by the Chinese; the yueh-pai, or *clair de lune*, a pale gray blue, and the *aubergine*, or deep purple (*ch'ieh tzŭ*), of the Chün-chou ware; these last kilns were also remarkable for the brilliance of their *yao-pien*, or "transmutation" mottled tints, due to the varied degrees of oxidation of copper silicates.

Painted decoration was more sparingly employed, although in the province of Chihli both the Ting-chou and Tz'ŭ-chou porcelains were painted with brown flowers, as we learn from the *Ko ku yao lun*, a work published in the fourteenth century. The same book describes the vases produced at Yung-ho-chên, in the department of Lu-ling-hsien, in the province of Kiangsi, as ornamented with painted designs. The potteries here were closed during the wars at the end of the *Sung* dynasty, and the majority of the potters fled to Ching-tê-chên, and seem to have initiated the potters there in new methods of decoration.

FIG. 106.—Small Water Vessel of Wan-li porcelain, in the form of one of the large fish-bowls of the time, decorated in under-glaze blue and enamel colors; mark of the period in blue underneath, within a double ring; carved wood stand; silver cover of Japanese work.

As early as the tenth century cobalt blue, as we learn from the official annals of the *Sung* dynasty (*Sung Shih*, book 490, f. 12), was brought to China by the Arabs, under the name of *wu-ming-yi*. It had long been used in western Asia in the decoration of tiles and other articles of faïence. It was first employed in China, probably, in the preparation of colored glazes, as we know nothing of painting in blue before the *Yuan* dynasty.

The decoration of porcelain *sur biscuit* with glazes of different colors, which prevailed in the early part of the *Ming* dynasty, must also have begun in the *Sung*, if we are to accept the statement quoted in the *T'ao Shuo*, that the celebrated image of Kuan-yin * enshrined in the Buddhist temple Pao-kuo-ssŭ at Peking dates from that dynasty. The bonzes of the temple confidently assert it, claiming also that it is a miraculous likeness, in that the goddess herself descended into the furnace while it was being fired and fashioned the ductile clay in her own image; and they point triumphantly to the laudatory verses composed by the Emperor *Ch'ien-lung*, which are engraved upon the carved blackwood pedestal of the shrine, which supports and screens the sacred image, made by imperial order in the palace workshop of the *Nei-wu-fu*, as sufficient evidence. It is a finely molded figure about a foot high, seated upon a lotus pedestal of the same material, colored crimson, with the chin supported by the right hand, the long taper fingers drooping gracefully, and the elbow resting upon the knee. The face, the right arm, the breast, and the left foot, which is extended in an awkward pose to exhibit the sole, are bare, covered with an opaque white enamel.

From the necklet, which is yellow, hangs a square network of yellow beads attached to the inner garment girdling the waist, which is colored red-brown of charming mottled hue. The figure is loosely wrapped in flowing drapery of purest and bluest turquoise tint, with the wide sleeves of the robe bordered with black and turned back in front to show the yellow lining; the upper part of the cloak is extended up behind over the head in the form of a plaited hood, which is also lined with canary yellow. The brow is encircled by a tiara of gold and crimson, with a tiny image inlaid in the front, and flower designs in relief on either side. The right hand holds a circular mirror, with Sanskrit characters carved in open work, enameled, of dark-brown color, surrounded by a halo of golden flames. †

Fig. 107.—Bowl, with the lower fluted part a pale green celadon monochrome, the upper part encircled by a band of clouds in white relief, inclosing dragons in peach-bloom tints.

The ordinary decoration of painting in enamel colors upon porcelain previously fired, and subsequently fired again in the muffle stove to fix the colors, was certainly unknown at this period. We read occasionally, it is true, of butterflies, birds, fish, or fabulous beasts, outlined by some magic transformation on the surface of celadon vases, but these appear to be merely accidental resemblances of the colored patches so often produced during the firing of these glazes. Such reddish or purple stains occurring on ancient pieces, from partial oxidation of the coloring material, are specially prized by collectors as marks of authenticity, and an artificial patch is usually daubed on in modern imitations to deceive the unwary.

A general idea of the form and coloring of the porcelain may be gathered from the water-

---

* The Goddess of Mercy.

† I have had the privilege of paying several visits to the shrine of this goddess, who has, somehow, an irresistible fascination. The prior of the monastery assures me that his records show that the image has been there since the foundation of the temple in the thirteenth century, and I see no reason to doubt his assertion. The colors are of the same type as those of the finest flower-pots and saucers of the Chün-chou porcelain of the *Sung* dynasty. A Chinese author of the *Ming* period writes that there must have been porcelain decorated in colors during the *Sung* dynasty, basing his statement on this very image of Kuan-yin. Most people have been led astray by its traditional name of Yao-p'ien—i. e., "Furnace Transmutation"—and imagined, like Dr. Hirth, that it was invested with an ordinary *flambé* glaze. The colors, the turquoise-blue, canary-yellow, brown of "old gold" and "dead leaf" tones, crimson and red-striped purple, are laid on in perfect contrast, and make one almost understand the rhapsodies of some of the older ceramic writers about the brilliancy of the colors produced at the Chün-chou kilns. The image is considered too sacred to be photographed or even portrayed in colors by a profane artist.

color illustrations of the album of the sixteenth century to which I have already briefly referred. It was described in a paper read by me before the Peking Oriental Society in 1886, and published there in the journal of the Society, which is, however, difficult to procure, so that I may perhaps be forgiven for repeating part of the description. The album, bound in four volumes, between boards of sandalwood, came from the library of the palace of the hereditary princes of Yi. It is entitled *Li tai ming tz'ŭ t'ou p'u*, 歷代名瓷圖譜, *Illustrated Description of the Celebrated Porcelain of Different Dynasties.* The writer, 項元汴, Hsiang Yuan-p'ien, who himself drew and colored by hand the eighty-two illustrations copied from pieces in his own collection and in the collections of his friends, was a native of Chia-hsing-fu, in the province

FIG. 108.—Ch'ien-lung Vase, with soufflé body flecked with *rouge-d'or*, and bands of floral scrolls in rich colors of the *famille rose*.

of Chekiang, a celebrated con-
teenth century. The author
referred to, includes his name
by him in book ii, f. 3, and
is relied upon by connoisseurs
the authenticity of a picture to
   The first leaf contains an
ace, which runs : " In ancient
living in the midst of the
and made pottery as a
that even before the
ties the art of molding
existence. But very
elapsed, and his gen-
that no examples of
vived. Passing on to
and *Chin* dynasties, we
mention of potters, in
cups of Chi Shu-yeh and
Ching - shan. Successors
daily work produced an
the reign of the house of *Ch'ai*,
celebrated for its ceramic ware,
search for mere fragments of
able to find any, and declare it
   " Next to the Ch'ai pot-
Ju, Kuan, Ko, and Ting fol-
we come to our own dynasty,
the reigns of *Yung-lo*, *Hsüan-*

noisseur who lived in the six-
of the *Ch'ing pi ts'ang*, already
in the list of collectors given
the seal of Hsiang Yuan-p'ien
to this day as a guarantee of
which it is attached.
introduction by way of pref-
times, while *Shun* was still
fields, he tilled the ground
means of livelihood ; so
Three Ancient Dynas-
clay was already in
many years have
eration is so remote
his work can have sur-
the *Ch'in, Han, Wei,*
come to the earliest
the case of the wine-
the wine-vessels of Hsü
of these two men in their
abundant quantity, down to
which was the first to become
so that in the present day men
this porcelain without being
to be but a phantom.
tery, we have the porcelains of
lowing for inspection, till finally
and have before us porcelain of
tê, Ch'êng-hua, and *Hung-chih,*

to compare with the specimens of the *Sung*, which it even surpasses, excelling both in texture and form as well as in brilliancy of coloring.

   " I have acquired a morbid taste for refuse (literally ' scabs '), and delight in buying choice specimens of the *Sung, Yuan,* and *Ming,* and in exhibiting them in equal rank with the bells, urns, and sacrificial wine-vessels of bronze, of the Three Ancient Dynasties, the *Ch'in,* and the *Han.*

   "With the aid of two or three intimate friends, who meet constantly both day and night for discussion and research, I have selected a series of pieces out of those that I have seen and that I possess myself and compiled this book. I have painted the specimens in colors and given the source of each one, so that I may preserve them from being lost and forgotten, and be able to show them to my friends. Say not that my hair is scant and sparse and yet I make what is only fit for a child's toy ! "

   "Written by Hsiang Yuan-p'ien, styled Tzŭ-ching, native of Chia-ho."

   The signature is accompanied by two seals in antique script, impressed in vermilion, " The

Seal of Hsiang Yuan-p'ien," and *Mo lin Shan jên*, "A dweller in the hills at Mo-lin." The author is described, in the voluminous *Imperial Cyclopædia of Celebrated Writers and Artists*, "as a clever calligraphist as well as a skillful painter and collector of objects of art"; and it also alludes to him as signing his writings with the literary title of *Mo-lin chü shih*, "Retired scholar of Mo-lin."

There are eighty-three illustrations in the album, arranged in order according to the purpose for which the objects figured are intended to be used. They comprise:

Censers for burning incense.

Ink Pallets, Pen Rests, and Water Pots for the library table.

Vases of varied forms for holding flowers.

Jars and Libation Cups for sacrificial wine.

Wine Ewers and little Cups, Teapots and Teacups, Rice Bowls and Dishes for ordinary use.

Rouge Pots and Perfume Boxes for the toilet.

Pagoda enshrining a jade image of Buddha, and a jade jar containing sacred relics from India, presented by the empress to the Porcelain Tower Temple at Nanking.

Oil Lamps and Pricket Candlesticks of elaborate design.

The pieces figured appear to be choice examples of the different kinds of porcelain appreciated by collectors at the time and to have been selected from the best available sources. The forms and ornamental decoration of most of the objects have been modeled after the ancient bronze vessels, which are dug up in such abundance in China and have been figured in illustrated catalogues by many collectors. A detailed description of each piece is written on the opposite page, giving the size and color, the source of the design, the name of the owner, and often the price he had paid. The pictures are usually of the natural size, one on each leaf; sometimes, when small, two on the page. The rarity of the specimens is indicated by the high prices recorded to have been paid—a hundred ounces of silver, for instance, for a pair of tiny eggshell winecups, a price confirmed, as we shall see, by printed books of the time.

FIG. 109.—Vase, fashioned in the form of a sacred fungus, with smaller ones sprouting from its surface, coated with a crackled glaze, overlaid with variegated splashes. Underneath the heavy glaze a decoration in blue is faintly discernible.

Of the 83 objects figured, 42 are attributed to the *Sung* dynasty, A. D. 960–1279, only 1 to the *Yuan* (1280–1367), the remaining 40 to the *Ming* dynasty, of which five reigns are represented: *Yung-lo* (1403–1424) by 1 piece; *Hsüan-tê* (1426–1435) by 20 pieces; *Ch'êng-hua* (1465–1487) by 11 pieces; *Hung-chih* (1488–1505) by 4 pieces; and *Chêng-te* (1506–1521) by 4 pieces. Two of the pieces of the last reign are teapots of red "boccaro" stoneware from the potteries which were founded then by Kung Ch'un at Yi-hsing, in the province of Kiang-nan; all the rest of the *Ming* pieces come from the imperial manufactory at Ching-tê-chên, in Kiangsi province. The *Yuan* dynasty piece marked *Shu fu*, "imperial palace," comes from the same place. The 42 *Sung* specimens are selected from several fabrics famous at the time, and comprise: 3 pieces of *Ju Yao*, "Juchou porcelain"; 10 pieces of *Kuan Yao*, "Imperial porcelain"; 12 pieces of *Ting Yao*, "Tingchou porcelain," the white, purple-brown, and black glazes being all represented; 1 of *Ko Yao*, and 11 of *Lung-ch'üan Yao* from Lung-ch'üan-hsien; 1 of *Tung-ch'ing Yao*, and 4 of *Chün Yao*, "Chün-chou porcelain."

I have arranged the objects described according to their source, and have added a brief description of each of the different kinds of porcelain. The description of each specimen is a literal translation of the author's words.

汝窯, Ju Yao.

The *Ju Yao* was the porcelain made during the *Sung* dynasty at Ju-chou, in the province of Honan, the modern Ju-chou-fu. We are told that the porcelain hitherto sent to the capital from Tung-chou was found to be too fragile, and that a supply was therefore ordered for the use of the court from Ju-chou. The new porcelain resembled the celebrated *Ch'ai* ware of the

preceding dynasty, which was made in the same province, and which the emperor ordered should be of the color of the clear sky in the intervals between the clouds after rain. The glaze is described as being so thick as to run down like melted lard, and as often ending in an irregularly curved line before reaching the bottom of the piece.

The surface was either crackled or plain, and the latter was preferred if the color was perfectly pure and uniform. The color is described by the artist as that of the pale azure-tinted blossoms of the *Vitex incisa*, the "sky-blue flower" of the Chinese, a flowering shrub which is common upon the hillsides in summer throughout central and northern China; it is the *yueh pai*, literally "moon white," of the modern Chinese silk dyer, which we know in ceramic parlance as *clair de lune*, and this is the name given also to the tint of the *Ju Yu*, or "Ju Glaze," of the modern reproductions of the ancient color. This is well shown in Plate LI, 2, an illustration of a *clair de lune* vase of the *K'ang-hsi* period. The tint of the ancient Ju Yao nearly approached

FIG. 110.—Finely crackled Turquoise Gourd of early K'ang-hsi or late Ming date, with archaic designs worked in the paste; old-bronze stand and cover.

that of the *Sung* cup illustrated in Plate XII, 1, only it was of brighter hue and of purer blue.

Three pieces of Ju Yao of the *Sung* dynasty are illustrated in our ancient album, and described by the artist:

"*Vase (Ku)*, of slender, upright, hornlike form, with wide, trumpet-shaped mouth, modeled after an ancient bronze design, with four prominent vertical dentated ridges. It is ornamented with grotesque dragons' heads on a rectangular scroll ground upon the body, and with conventional palm leaves filled in with scrolls round the neck. Specimens of Ju-chou porcelain are extremely rare, and when found are usually plates and bowls, so that a perfect unbroken vase like this is almost unique, and it makes, like other sacrificial wine-vessels of the time, a charming receptacle for flowers. Moreover, it excels in material, form, and color both *Kuan* and *Ko* porcelain, and is far more valuable than either. I saw it at the capital, in the possession of Huang, General of the Guards, who told me that he had given 150,000 'cash' for it."* H. 6½ in.

"*Vase (Ku)*, of solid, rounded, beaker-shaped outline, copied from an ancient sacrificial vessel of bronze, with a band of ogre (*t'ao-t'ieh*) faces on the body, invested, like the last, with a plain uncrackled glaze of pure "vitex-blue" color. A choice specimen of this rare fabric, it makes also a perfect receptacle for flowers." H. 4½ in.

"*Wine Jar (Fu Tsun)*, fashioned in the shape of a duck, after an ancient bronze design, the body being hollow to contain the wine, and the beak forming the spout. From the back springs a vaselike neck, with a movable cover, and a loop handle

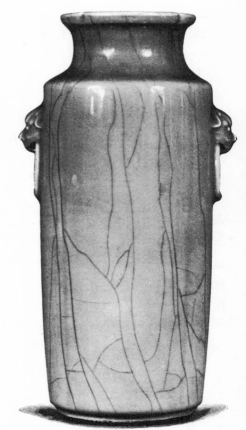

FIG. 111.—Vase of gray-blue color sparsely crackled with red lines, foot rim simulating the ancient Ju Yao of the Sung dynasty.

* The copper "cash" of China has varied in value at different times, but the normal rate of exchange is 1,000 for a tael, or Chinese ounce of silver, which is worth intrinsically about one Mexican dollar and one third.

supported upon grotesque figures. Ornamented with encircling bands of spiral pattern worked in the paste under the 'starch-blue' (*fên ch'ing*) glaze, which is coarsely crackled. The perfect finish of the fabric and the antique character of the coloring and crackled pattern make this a rare specimen of ancient wine-vessels. The duck floats gracefully upon the waves, and men of old made wine-jars in its form, as a symbol that one ought to swim lightly on the surface, and not be drowned in the wine like the drunkard." H. 5½ in., L. 5 in.

官窰, KUAN YAO.

The *Kuan Yao* is the "imperial porcelain" of the *Sung* dynasty, *kuan* meaning "government" or "imperial." The manufactory was founded in the capital Pien-chou, the modern K'ai-fêng-fu, in the beginning of the twelfth century. A few years later the dynasty was driven southward by the advancing Tartars, and a manufactory was founded in the new capital, the modern Hang-chou-fu, to supply the palace with porcelain of the same kind, and the productions of the new kilns founded in the city near the Temple of Heaven was also called Kuan Yao. The same name is used, in fact, for porcelain made in the imperial manufactory at Ching-tê-chên to-day.

The porcelain produced at the old capital seems to have resembled the celebrated Ch'ai ware, which was fabricated probably at the same place, as it was the capital of the After *Chou* dynasty at that time. The glaze of the Kuan Yao was generally crackled, of various tints, of which yueh pai (*clair de lune*) was the most highly esteemed of all, followed by *fen ch'ing*, "pale blue," *ta lü*, "emerald-green" (literally *gros vert*), and lastly *hui sê*, "gray." The Hang-chou ware was made of a reddish paste covered with the same glazes, and we read of iron-colored feet and brown mouths, the upper rim being more lightly covered with glaze and showing the color of the paste underneath.

There is a typical example of this class in the little crackled teacup in this collection figured in Plate XII, 1, and the illustration exhibits very well the tone of color of the crackled glaze and the characteristic brown rim round the edge.

FIG. 112.—Blue and White Bottle, of the Ch'ien-lung period, painted in shades of blue.

The album contains ten illustrations of the imperial porcelain of the *Sung* dynasty, of which the pallet figured as No. 8 indicates clearly the red color of the fabric, exposed in the parts which are left unglazed.

"*Tripod Censer* (*Ting*), fashioned after an old bronze design, with a rounded, three-lobed body composed of three monstrous ogre-like faces with frightful features and protruding eyes projecting from a finely etched scroll ground, three cylindrical feet, and two upright looped ears. The glaze of light bluish tint, as clear and lustrous as a precious emerald, is covered throughout with a network of icelike crackle, so that it is a most choice example of the grand imperial porcelain of the time. This piece likewise came from the palace at Peking. I saw it at Nanking, at the palace of the Governor Chu Hung, Grand Tutor of the Emperor." H. 4 in., D. 4 in.

"*Censer* (*Lu*), of depressed globular form, with two curved loop handles and three mammillated feet, a shape adapted from the bronze work of the *T'ien-pao* period of the *T'ang* dynasty, and often reproduced in the celebrated bronze urns of the reign of *Hsüan-te* of our own dynasty. It is covered with an antique glaze of brilliant depth, pale blue in color, fissured with a reticulation of icelike cracks throughout. From the collection of Chang Chui-chang of Su-chou." H. 1½ in., D. 5 in.

"*Ink Pallet* (*Yen*), copied from a pallet used by the emperor in the Hsüan-ho Palace. The outline is like that of a vase, with loop handles at the sides for passing a string through for hanging the pallet upon the wall. A large oval patch is left unglazed in the middle for rubbing the cake of ink upon, leaving the red paste exposed. The under surface (which is also illustrated) has the figure of an elephant etched upon it, surmounted by a hexagram, which, taken with the vase shape, make the 'rebus' *T'ai p'ing yu hsiang*, 'An augury of great peace.' Like the upper surface, it is invested with a pale bluish glaze crackled throughout, encircled by a red-brown ring left unglazed." L. 5½ in., Br. 4 in.

"*Water Pot (Shui Ch'êng)* of ovoid form, with a slightly flaring mouth, and two small loop handles from which movable rings hang suspended. A band of cicada pattern is engraved round the body, a ring of palmations encircles the foot, and a chain of rectangular scroll, between two lines of dots, surrounds the neck. The glaze of pale bluish tint is uniformly crackled." H. 3 in.

"*Pencil Rest (Yen Shan)*, modeled in the form of a miniature range of hills with a high peak in the middle, covered with a glaze of bluish tint as bright as the vitex-tinted azure sky, crackled throughout with icelike lines. The antique color and the luster of the glaze far excel those of the *Ko Yao* pencil rest figured beside it. It cost me twenty taels of silver at Peking." H. 3 in., L. 4½ in.

"*Vase (Fang Hu)*, of flattened quadrangular section, with a bulging body and a cover surmounted by four spiral projections. Two handles of grotesque heads supporting rings are worked in relief on the front and back of the vase. The glaze of bright greenish-blue is covered with icelike crackle. This vase was in the collection of K'uo Ch'ing-lo, who bought it for fifty taels without the cover. The owner, happening to be fishing one day, found in the boat a cover which had been drawn up in the net, and purchased it for ten strings of cash. It proved to be the original cover, and he wrote some verses in commemoration. Since Ch'ing-lo's death I know not what has become of the vase." H. 8 in., D. 4½ in.

"*Teacup (Ch'a Pei)*, of upright form, with wavy outline and vertically ribbed sides, molded in the shape of a Buddha's-hand citron. Invested outside with a pale blue glaze, white inside, both surfaces traversed with a coarse network of lines like crackled ice." H. 3 in.

FIG. 113.—Vase, bestrid by a dragon in full relief, coated with a grayish glaze, with mottled clouds of olive brown.

"*Libation Cup (Chüeh)*, of ancient bronze design, with three feet and a wide channeled lip. A double band of rectangular scroll ornament encircles the body, which has a loop handle on one side springing from a dragon's head. The glaze is pale blue with icelike crackle throughout." H. 6 in.

"*Libation Cup (Chüeh)*, of design somewhat similar to the last, but more elaborately ornamented with projecting dentated ridges and geometrical scroll patterns. The glaze of sky-blue color without a single line of crackle, and the delicate and complicated ornamentation, executed without a blur, make it a remarkable specimen of this imperial fabric." H. 4½ in.

"*Saucer (Tieh T'o)*, of complex form, modeled after a red lacquer carved saucer of the period, with an engraved decoration executed in the formal scroll patterns characteristic of lacquer work. The glaze is of the light bluish tint of an egg, and is marked with no crackled lines." D. 4½ in.

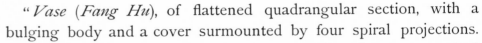

定窰, TING YAO.

Ting Yao is the name applied to the porcelain fabricated in the *Sung* dynasty at Ting-chou, in the province of Chihli. This is well described in the *Ko ku yao lun*, published in 1387, one of the principal works on antiquarian subjects of the *Ming* dynasty:

"Specimens of ancient Ting-chou porcelain in which the paste is finely levigated and the color white and of rich luster are valuable; those of coarser fabric and yellowish color are inferior. Those with tear-drops outside are genuine. Some of the engraved designs are very beautiful. The plain pieces are also good, but those ornamented with painted decoration are less highly esteemed. The best belong to the periods *Hsüan-ho* (1119–25) and *Chêng-ho* (1111–17), but it is difficult to find perfect specimens of these reigns. There is a purple Ting-chou porcelain, the color of which is purple, and a black Ting-chou porcelain colored black like lacquer."

The white variety is known as *Pai Ting* or *Fên Ting, pai* being "white," and *fên*, "flour," to distinguish it from the coarser yellow ware alluded to above, which is called *T'u Ting*, from *t'u*, "earth." The red variety is often referred to by the older poets, and is compared to carved red jade or carnelian. The black kind is extremely rare. Our artist observes: "I have seen over a hundred specimens of the white, and some tens of the purple-brown; but the black is so rare that in my whole life I have met with only one piece, which I figure here."

Pieces of Ting-chou porcelain are probably more common in modern collections than those of any of the other *Sung* dynasty factories. The bowls and dishes are often impressed inside with intricate and elaborate designs, composed principally of the modern peony, lily flowers, and flying phœnixes. The material was very fragile, on which account it used to be the fashion to bind the rims of the pieces made for the use of the palace with copper collars to preserve them from injury. The bowls and dishes seem to have been often placed in the kiln bottom upward, so as to rest upon the rims, which were in such cases left unglazed. The glaze of the best pieces of this ware is of a dull white, when compared with the soft, velvety gloss of the white porcelain of the province of Fuchien. It is less translucent, and of soft "ivory-white" tone.

Northern Ting-chou porcelain has been more imitated, perhaps, than any other. First comes the *Nan Ting*, or "Southern Ting," fabricated after the *Sung* emperors had been driven south by the Mongols in 1127; then the *Hsin Ting*, or "New Ting," a name given to the vases of elegant shape with contracted waist made in the *Yuan* dynasty (1280–1367) by P'êng Chün-pao, a worker in gold. Next, the false *Wên Wang* censers of Chou Tan-ch'uan, the clever potter of the reign of *Wan-li* (1573–1619), who imposed upon the connoisseurs of his time by his reproductions of the incense burner which forms the first illustration in our album, and of others of the same kind.* He worked at Ching-tê-chên, and reproductions of the old Ting Yao are still made there.

Twelve examples of the *Sung* dynasty have been selected for illustration, including six of the white variety, five of the purple, and one black.

"*Censer* (*Ting*), of quadrangular form and oblong section, with two upright loop handles, resting on four legs curving upward below. The body, with eight vertical dentated ridges, is covered with antique designs carved in relief. Copied from a sacrificial vessel dedicated to the ancient sovereign *Wên Wang* figured in the *Po ku t'ou*, an illustrated collection of old bronzes, this censer was made at the imperial factory, and it is perfectly finished with delicate carving fine as bullock's hair or floss silk. It stands square and upright, without leaning a hair's breadth, and is exactly proportioned in every part. The glaze, uniformly lustrous and translucent, is like mutton fat or fine white

* His story is well told by Julien (*loc. cit.*) in pp. xxxiii and xxxiv of his *Preface du Traducteur*.

jade. It is a choice specimen of the fabric of Ting-chou in Chên-ting-fu, worthy to be placed at the head of the incense burners of different factories, and its equal is rarely, alas! to be seen in the present day. It was shown to me in the palace of the Prince of Chin, standing upon a stand of fragrant lign-aloes, with a cover carved out of the same wood crowned by a lizard dragon of moss-green jade." H. 4½ in., Br. 3½ in.

"*Censer* (*Yi*), in the form of a shaped bowl of depressed globular form, rounding in at the neck and slightly expanding at the mouth, resting upon a low circular foot. The neck is encircled by a band of rectangular scroll pattern, interrupted by two handles fashioned as lions' heads in slight relief. The glaze of pure white without stain resembles mutton fat or fine jade, and it forms a beautiful ornament for a scholar's library. It is an old piece which has been preserved for generations in our family cabinet, and I now draw it for my friends." H. 2 in., D. 4½ in.

"*Miniature Vase* (*Hsiao P'ing*), of nearly cylindrical form, slightly bulging in the middle, with two pointed open handles projecting upward from the shoulder. Decorated with two scroll bands, above and below, engraved under a pure white glaze resembling congealed fat." H. 3 in.

FIG. 116.—Tall Yung-chêng Vase, of archaic form, with ribbed embossed body and flowing dragon-handles, a crackled glaze of *clair-de-lune* tint deepening into azure blue when thick, foot rim buff; seal of the period in blue underneath.

"*Sacrificial Jar* (*Hsiang Tsun*), modeled in the form of an elephant, after an ancient bronze vessel made for the ancestral temple. The body is hollowed into a jar for wine, of which the uplifted trunk of the elephant forms the spout and a narrow canopy arching over the saddle makes the handle, which has attached to it a round cover ornamented with geometrical and spiral scroll borders and surmounted by a knob. The rope girths and ornamental details are engraved under the white glaze. It holds about a pint of wine." H. 4½ in., L. 5 in.

"*Willow-basket Cup* (*Liu-tou Pei*), molded in the form of a basket of rounded shape bulging below, with the osier twigs bound with ropes all worked in the paste under the white glaze. This is a novel and curious design for a wine-cup." H. 2½ in.

"*Phœnix Candlestick* (*Fêng Têng*), of elegant form and design, a branched pricket candlestick for three candles. A slender pillar, springing from a square, solid, polished stand, curves at the top to end in a crested phœnix head, from the beak of which hangs a ring chain with a lotus suspended upon it. The stem of the lotus branches below into three flowers to hold the candles, which are shaded by a large overhanging leaf. The natural details are etched in the paste under the white glaze. It is a rare specimen of Ting-chou porcelain, which I use to light my own library." H. 21 in.

"*Tripod Censer* (*Ting*), with plain loop handles and feet springing from grotesque heads. Modeled after an ancient bronze with ogre (*t'ao t'ieh*) faces carved upon the body on the upper part, a band of foliated outline below. The artistic character of the design is executed in the spirit of the Three Ancient Dynasties; the color of the glaze is a warm purple of translucid depth, of the same tint as that of ripe grapes. Ting-chou porcelain is usually white, the purple (*tzŭ*) and black (*mo*) glazes being much more rare, and such a choice example as this of the purple variety is rare indeed. I bought it for ten taels of silver at Peking from the stall of a curio dealer at the Buddhist temple Pao-kuo-ssŭ." H. 3½ in., D. 4 in.

"*Water Pot* (*Shui Ch'êng*), modeled after a tazza-shaped bronze cup of the *Han* dynasty, of oval form, with foliated rim; it has a fluted body, with a scroll-like border composed of coiled silkworms, and a ringed hollow foot. The glaze is purple, of the color of the fruit of the aubergine plant. It is mounted on a carved rosewood stand, with a coral spoon inside, for use on the writing table." H. 2 in.

"*Jar* (*Hu*), modeled after an ancient sacrificial wine-vessel of bronze, of ovoid form and quadrangular section, with a lobed body decorated with a band of scrolled dragons round the shoulder, a chain of interrupted fret encircling the foot. Two loop handles terminating in horned heads project from the neck with rings suspended upon them. The glaze is deepest amethyst, of the color of very ripe grapes, and beautifully lustrous. I saw it in the palace of the Prince of Chiang-yu, where I painted the picture for my friends." H. 6 in.

FIG. 117.—Duck-headed Vase of the K'ang-hsi period, enameled with a celadon glaze of typical shade.

"*Small Vase* (*Hsiao P'ing*), of the kind once used for divining stalks, adapted for flowers upon the writing table. The body, of square section slightly expanding upward, is carved in a formal, zigzag pattern; it has a round mouth and a low, circular foot. The glaze is purple, of deepest tone and beautiful color." H. 4 in.

"*Wine Vessel* (*Chia*), of a characteristic bronze form, with three pointed feet, a plain loop handle and two studs on the upper rim. It is decorated with bands of grotesque dragons' heads carved in relief. The color of the glaze is purple, like the aubergine fruit, and the decoration is very finely carved. I got it from a fellow-citizen in exchange for a winecup of jade." H. 4 in.

"*Duck-headed Vase* (*Fu Tsun*), of black Ting-chou porcelain. A bottle-shaped vase with swelling body and ringed neck, which curves over to end in a duck's head, the orifice of the vase, defined by a lip, being in the convexity of the curved neck. The black color painted upon the head and neck gradually fades away below into the body of the vase, which is enameled white. The black glaze is of the greatest rarity in Ting-chou porcelain. In my whole life I have seen over a hundred specimens of the white, some tens of purple, but only this one of black." H. 6 in.

龍 泉 窯, LUNG-CH'ÜAN YAO.

The *Lung-ch'üan Yao* is the porcelain that used to be made at Lung-ch'üan-hsien, in the prefecture Ch'u-chou-fu, in the southern part of the province of Chekiang. During the early part of the *Sung* dynasty the factory was at Liu-t'ien, some twenty miles distant from the walled city of Lung-ch'üan, and under its jurisdiction. Two brothers named Chang, who are said to have lived here in the twelfth century of our era, are celebrated for their productions. The elder, called for that reason Chang Shêng yi, introduced a new glaze, distinguished by its crackled texture, which became known as *Ko Yao*, or the "Elder Brother's Porcelain." "Chang Secundus," Chang Shêng êrh, fabricated his ware on the old lines, only improving the luster and color of the green glaze, so that his productions continued to be called by the old name of Lung-ch'üan Yao.

These potteries furnished the main source of the famous old celadon and crackled porcelains, which were exported at this time from China to all parts of Asia, as well as to the eastern and northern coasts of Africa. They constitute the *Ch'ing Tzŭ*, 青 瓷, the "green porcelain," *par excellence* of the Chinese, and are well known to the Japanese, who esteem them very highly by the same name, which they pronounce *Seiji*. During the *Sung* dynasty there was considerable commercial intercourse by sea between China and the Mohammedan countries, and we read in both Arabian and Chinese books of the time of "green porcelain" as one of the articles of trade. The Chinese describe it as carried as far as Zanzibar, which they call

---

* This curious form is still in use in China, as shown in Fig. 117, which is a celadon piece in the collection referred to the *K'ang-hsi* period.

Tsangpa, and are curiously confirmed by the discovery there in some old ruins, during Sir John Kirk's residence as H. B. M. consul-general, of a quantity of celadon vessels, principally in fragments, mixed with Chinese coins of the *Sung* dynasty.

The Arabs and Persians call this peculiar porcelain *martabâni*, and value it very highly from its fancied property of detecting poisoned food by changing color. The name comes from Martabân, one of the states of ancient Siam; and Prof. Karabacek, of Vienna, has lately tried to prove that it is not Chinese, basing his theory mainly upon a passage quoted from the encyclopedist Hâdji Khalifa, who died in 1658, that "the precious magnificent celadon dishes and other vessels seen in his time were manufactured and exported at Martabân, in Pegu." But there is no evidence that porcelain was ever made at Maulmain (Martabân), Rangoon, or elsewhere in Burma. Others have attributed it, with as little success, either to Persia or to Egypt, because so much has been discovered there, but neither of these countries produced true porcelain, although they excelled in the decoration of faïence. An Arab manuscript in the Bibliothèque Nationale at Paris, treating of the life and exploits of Saladin, mentions that this emir presented in the year 1171 forty pieces of this kind of Chinese porcelain to Nur-ed-din.

Marco Polo, after his travels in China in the thirteenth century, seems to have been the first in Europe to use the name of "porcelaine" to describe this product of the far East. It had probably been applied previously only to shells, and Marco Polo applied the same term to the cowries which he found used as money in Eastern countries. The crusades were apparently the earliest means of introduction of specimens of this ware to the West. Dr. Graesse relates that the most ancient piece in the Dresden Museum was brought by a crusader from Palestine. Perhaps it came through Egypt. A present of porcelain vases was sent in 1487 by the Sultan of Egypt to Lorenzo de' Medici, and it is mentioned about the same time in the maritime laws of Barcelona as one of the articles imported into Spain from Egypt.

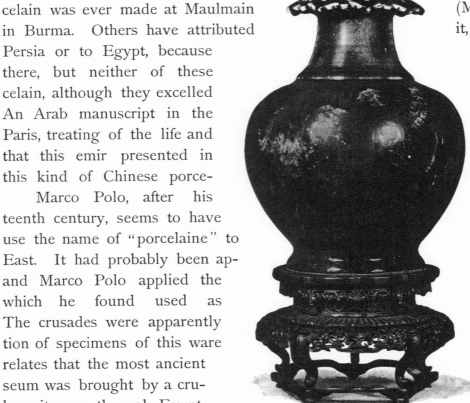

FIG. 118.—Ch'ien-lung Vase, of transmutation (Yao-pien) glaze, exhibiting the characteristic splashes of purple, and deep crimson flecked with pale blue.

It is curious that the earliest specimen of porcelain that can be now referred to as brought to England before the Reformation, viz., the cup of Archbishop Warham, at New College, Oxford, is of the sea-green or celadon kind.

The glaze of the Lung-ch'üan porcelain is of a monochrome green color, varying from bright grass-green, the tint of the Chinese olive, a species of canarium, through lighter intermediate shades to palest sea-green. The term celadon is well known to collectors as applied to these different shades of color. Céladon was the name of the hero of the popular novel *L'Astrée*, written by Honoré d'Urfé in the seventeenth century, who used to appear on the stage dressed in clothes of a kind of sea-green hue of a gray or bluish tint. This shade became fashionable, and the name was borrowed to describe a similar shade in the color of Chinese porcelain. This peculiar shade, however, is specially characteristic of the Lung-ch'üan porcelain of the *Ming* period, made in the city of Ch'u-chou-fu, to which place the manufactory was removed early in the *Ming* dynasty. It was here that the characteristic large dishes were made marked underneath with a ferruginous ring, showing the portion of the paste left unglazed, so as not to adhere to the support in the kiln. The older pieces attributed to the *Sung* dynasty are completely covered with glaze under the foot, and are generally of a more decided grass-green color, approaching the emerald-green tint of jadeite, which seems to have been the effect especially aimed at. The decoration was either worked in relief or engraved in the paste, and its effect was enhanced by the different shades of color produced by the varying depth of the glaze. The vessels are often fluted or ribbed, and with wavy or foliated rims; some have a peony or a lotus blossom, fish or dragons, sprays of flowers or geometrical patterns etched in the paste. Others have a pair of fishes worked in relief in the bottom, or a pair of rings attached outside to handles.

The accompanying illustration (Fig. 119) is taken from a little dish of typical *Sung* celadon in the Walters Collection. The glaze is crackled, of a greenish-brown tone approaching that of the olive, shot and flecked with bright grass-green, the tint of onion sprouts. A pair of fish are worked in bold relief in the paste underneath the glaze as if swimming round inside the dish. The rim of the foot, unglazed, shows a reddish buff paste. There is no "ring" underneath.

FIG. 119.—Small Dish of ancient Sung dynasty celadon, with two fish modeled in relief; a crackled glaze of brownish tone shot with grass-green.

The other cut (Fig. 120) represents a celadon dish etched inside with a spray of peony, which is attributed to the *Ming* dynasty. The sides are fluted in the interior and correspondingly ribbed underneath. The glaze is of sea-green shade, varying in tone according to its depth. The under surface of the dish, which is about a foot in diameter, has been photographed, to show the pe-culiar ferruginous ring with its ragged edges, where the paste, left bare, is fired of a reddish buff color.

Our album contains eleven specimens of Lung-ch'üan porcelain attributed to the *Sung* dynasty.

"*Water Pot (Shui Ch'êng)* for the writing table, in the shape of a globular tazza-like bowl, with a cylindrical foot slightly spreading at the base, and a round cover with a knob on the top. The cover is etched with a radiating geometrical pattern, the bowl decorated with sprays of chrysanthemum flowers alternating with *Polyporus* fungus heads mingled with grass. The flowers stand out in strong relief as if painted in a picture. The glaze is bright green, of the color of fresh moss or of willow twigs as they hang down in early springtime." H. 4 in.

"*Water Pot (Shui Ch'êng)*, modeled after a bronze casting of the *T'ang* dynasty, of glob-ular form, with a slightly flaring mouth and three small mammillated feet. The shoulder has two handles worked in relief as lions' heads with curling mane holding rings; above and below them the body is circled with interrupted chains of rectangular and spiral fret, etched under the glaze, which is translucent and lustrous, of the color of moss-green jade or nephrite." H. 2½ in.

"*Vase (Hu)*, bottle-shaped, with a bulging body, contracting to a slender neck, which swells again to a bulbous enlargement to end in a small orifice defined by a light lip. The nar-rowest part of the neck is marked by a prominent ring. Vases of this form, copied from an old bronze figured in the *Po ku t'ou*, are esteemed for holding peonies and orchids of different kinds, because the small mouth prevents the water giving out a bad odor. The glaze is bright green, of the color of young onion sprouts, so that the color is as beautiful as the form is distinguished. It always stands on the dining-table in my own house." H. 6 in.

"*Flower Vase (Hua Nang)*, with several mouths, of crackled Lung-ch'üan porcelain, of a depressed ovoid form bulging below, it contracts above to an oval mouth which is surrounded by four other smaller tubular mouths springing from the shoulder of the vase. The color of the glaze is as green as parrots' feathers and crackled like broken ice, a rare variety of this ware, adapted for displaying the colors and mingling the fragrance of different kinds of roses on a small table. It is enshrined in the Chi-hsiang-an Temple of my native city." H. 3 in., Br. 4½ in.

"*Small Vase (Hsiao P'ing)*, of hexagonal form, with a low circular foot, and a lip sharply drawn into a round mouth, covered with a brilliant glaze of the color of a fresh green cucum-ber." H. 3½ in.

"*Miniature Vase* (*Hsiao P'ing*), for a single flower, of semiglobular form, flattened below, with a tubular neck, having two loop handles at the sides strung with slender movable rings. Invested with a bright monochrome coat of green, it makes a charming receptacle for a small flower like a dwarf orchid, a balsam, or a sprig of jasmine." H. 2 in.

"*Palm-Leaf Vase* (*Chiao Yeh P'ing*), fashioned in the form of a whorl of palm leaves surrounding a hollow stem adapted to hold water for flowers. The veining of the leaves is engraved in the paste, and the surfaces are colored green, light or dark, according to their natural shades, showing that the ancient workmen spared no pains in the fabrication even of a little work of art like this." H. 6 in.

"*Rhinoceros Jar* (*So Tsun*), a sacrificial wine-jar for the ancestral temple, modeled after an ancient bronze vessel figured in the *Po ku t'ou*. It is molded in the form of a hornless rhinoceros, with the body hollowed out to hold wine, the peaked saddle on its back being hinged in front to make the cover of the jar. The convoluted folds of the skin and the other natural details are worked in the paste so as to be picked out in darker shades in the bright green glaze of the color of young onion sprouts. In the present day porcelain is much used for sacrificial vessels in place of gold and copper. The altars are not so luxuriously furnished, but the resources of the people are not infringed upon, so that it should not be lightly esteemed. I saw this jar at Nanking, in the hall of a Taoist temple for the worship of Heaven." H. 4½ in., L. 4½ in.

FIG. 120.—The bottom of a Fluted Celadon Dish of Lung-ch'üan Yao of the Ming dynasty, showing the typical "ferruginous ring."

"*Gourd-shaped Jar* (*P'ao Tsun*), molded as a wine-vessel, in the form of a recumbent gourd of elongated oval shape, curving up at the neck to a round orifice, which is fitted with a ringed cover. A long, curved handle, with a dragon's head at each end, is attached to the gourd by ring chains. The cover and shoulder of the jar are decorated with plain and foliated bands picked out under the glaze, which is of the usual green color." L. 6 in.

"*Wine-Vessel* (*Yu*) of the form of an ancient bronze sacrificial vessel of that name, with the finest details of the metal work carefully finished to a hair's breadth. The body, of flat quadrangular section, is contracted above to an oval orifice which is fitted with a rounded cover. To the two loop handles on the shoulder of the vase are attached ring chains hanging down from the ends of a curved rod by which the jar can be suspended. The sides are decorated with foliated panels, the rims with brocaded bands and formal borders, and the outlines of deer and dragons of antique design fill in the intervals. The glaze is a bright grass-green." H. 4 in.

"*Oil Lamp* (*Yu Têng*), copied from a bronze design. The lipped saucerlike receptacle is poised on the tip of a leafy branch which springs from a foliated pedestal, while from underneath the branch a second support curves down, to end below in chicken's claws. The glaze is of the color of green onion sprouts, the form of antique elegance." H. 4 in.

哥 窰, KO YAO.

Ko Yao, which means "Elder Brother's Ware," was the name referred to already as having been given to the ceramic production of Chang the elder, who was a potter of Liu-t'ien, in

Lung-ch'üan-hsien, in the twelfth century of our era. The porcelain which he made was distinguished especially for its crackled glaze, which was described as having the appearance of being "broken into a hundred pieces," or as looking "like the roe of a fish." It had also the iron-gray foot and the red mouth which characterized some of the older fabrics of the *Sung* dynasty, and is said to have almost rivaled the *Kuan Yao*, "the imperial porcelain of the period." The color of the glaze varied from bluish gray or celadon to rice color or stone gray.

This was the original Ko Yao; the name has since been extended to include almost all kinds of porcelain covered with crackled monochrome glazes, of the different shades of celadon, gray, and white. So we have Ko Yao of the *Yuan* dynasty, which was fabricated in large quantities at the same pottery, but was far inferior to the old porcelain both in grain and in color. Specimens of this are brought to our museums in modern times from Borneo and other islands of the Eastern Archipelago as far east as Ceram, among other old relics of Chinese porcelain which the natives prize so highly. Mr. Carl Bock, in his *Head-Hunters of Borneo*, alludes to these: "Among his [the Dyak's] greatest treasures are a series of *gudgi blanga*, a sort of glazed jar imported from China, in green, blue, or brown, ornamented

FIG. 121.—Crackled Archaic-looking Cup, a folded lotus leaf with a crouching dragon as a handle; Ko Yao, so called, of the present dynasty.

with figures of lizards and serpents in relief. These pots are valued at from one hundred to as much as three thousand florins (£8 to £240) each, according to size, pattern, and, above all, old age, combined with good condition. According to the native legend, these precious vases are made of the remnants of the same clay from which Mahatara (the Almighty) made first the sun and then the moon. Medicinal virtues are attributed to these wares, and they are

FIG. 122.—Small Censer of ancient crackle (Ko Yao of the Sung dynasty), Carved Rosewood Stand, and Cover with a ling-chih knob of carved white jade.

regarded as affording complete protection from evil spirits to the house in which they are stored."

There is also a modern Ko Yao made at Ching-tê-chên up to the present day in the pattern of the old ware.

There is only one piece of Ko Yao of the *Sung* dynasty illustrated in the album, a small pencil-rest covered with a crackled glaze of purplish celadon which can hardly be distinguished from that of the *Kuan Yao*, viz.:

"*Brush Rest (Yen Shan)*, made after a bronze model of the *Han* dynasty, as a miniature range of hills with four peaks of irregular height, and covered with a glaze of pale bluish celadon crackled like broken ice. Of antique form and lustrous color, it forms an artistic rest for the skilled pen of the writer." H. 1 in., L. 4 in.

We can add three pieces from the Walters Collection which are referred to the *Sung* dynasty: (1) A miniature censer (*Hsiang Lu*), shown in Fig. 122, covered with a thick grayish speckled glaze, traversed by a crackled network of brown lines, with three feet of dark iron-gray color surrounded at their base with brown lines of stain. (2) A small water pot (*Shui Ch'êng*), shown in Fig. 123, invested inside and out, as well as under the foot, with a thick, unctuous translucent glaze of dark brownish-gray tone crackled throughout; the mouth tinged copper-red, the foot-rim dark iron-gray. (3) A little vase, with mask-handles in relief (Fig. 124) of light gray crackle, covered with a deep rich glaze fissured with a network of dark lines connected by a few more superficial lines, and with the same glaze under the foot; the foot-rim shows a pale iron-gray paste.

東 青 窰, Tung-Ch'ing Yao.

Tung-ch'ing Yao, which means "Eastern celadon porcelain," is the name of the porcelain which was fabricated at private factories in the vicinity of K'ai-fêng-fu, the Eastern capital, during the Northern *Sung* dynasty (A. D. 960–1126). It resembled the imperial porcelain of the time, but was of coarser make and paler color, and it was never crackled.

The name of *Tung-ch'ing* has survived to the present day as that of the typical celadon glaze, so well illustrated in Plates VII and XXXVIII. The first syllable of the name is, however, generally written with another character of the same sound meaning "winter," changing the expression to "winter green" or "ever-green," and this is the form used in the imperial lists of to-day.

FIG. 123.—Water Receptacle of ancient gray-brown crackle upon a carved wood stand.

The one piece of the *Sung* dynasty figured here is described as follows:

"*Water Bowl* (*Hsi*), resembling in shape an octagonal flower-pot, with an eight-lobed body resting on a circular foot, and a foliated rim round the top. It is decorated outside in panels with formal sprays of flowers, including the plum blossom, polyporus fungus and grass, peony and bamboo, etched in the paste under the glaze, which is of the color of plumes of kingfisher feathers painted on in several layers, with its surface raised in faint millet-like tubercles. Made for washing the brushes of an artist, it is well adapted for the decoration of a dinner table with an open-work rockery, or for growing flowering bulbs of narcissus." H. 5 in.

鈞 窰, Chün Yao.

Chün Yao is the name given to the porcelain fabricated at Chün-chou from the early part of the *Sung* dynasty, which began in the year A. D. 960. This corresponds to the modern district of Yü-chou, in the province of Honan. It was not ranked high among the potteries of the period, because the material was not so finely levigated, and because the forms were generally original, instead of being copied from classical designs. The glazes were, however, remarkable for their brilliancy and for their varieties of color, including as they did the *flambé* or transmutation glazes, composed of flashing reds, passing through every intermediate shade of purple to pale blue. This was not much appreciated at the time, being described as a failure in the firing of one of the pure monochromes, but its reproduction in the hands of more recent potters is universally regarded as one of the chief triumphs of Chinese ceramic art.

The author of the *Po wu yao lan,* one of the best of the antiquarian works published near the end of the *Ming* dynasty, written by Ku T'ai, in sixteen books, and printed in the reign of *T'ien-ch'i* (1621–27), says in the fifth book, which is the one devoted to ceramics: "Chün-chou porcelain includes pieces of vermilion red, of bright onion-green, vulgarly called parrot-green, and of *aubergine* purple. When these three colors, the first red as mineral rouge, the second green as onion sprouts or kingfisher feathers, and the third purple dark as ink-black, are pure and without the least change of color,

FIG. 124.—Small solid Vase with mask handles of gray crackle of the Sung dynasty.

they comprise the highest class. Underneath the piece one or two numerals are often inscribed as marks. The colors of pig's liver, of flaming red, and of blues and greens mingled in blotches like a child's tear-stained face, are due only to insufficient firing of the above three colors; they are not distinct varieties of glaze. Such vulgar names as 'nasal mucus' and 'pig's liver' only provoke ridicule. The flowerpots and saucers of this porcelain are of great beauty, but the other things, like the barrel-shaped seats, the censers and round pots for incense, the square vases and jars with covers, all these have the paste composed of yellow sand, so that they are of coarser fabric. The new pieces made in the present day are all fabricated out of Yi-hsing clay, so that, although the glaze is somewhat similar to the old, and the work as well finished, they will not resist wear and tear."

The image of the Buddhist divinity Kuan Yin in the Pao Kuo Ssŭ at Peking, described already, exhibits a rare and brilliant combination of these different colors in the glazes with which it is invested. The flowerpots and saucers referred to by the author quoted above are the specimens seen in modern Chinese collections that are valued at such very high prices in their own country that few genuine examples are exported. There are two remarkable examples, however, in the Walters Collection which seem from their mountings to have come out of one of the imperial collections at Peking—a pair of bowl-shaped flowerpots. One of them is illustrated in Plate XCIV, showing the stippled gray-blue glaze spotted with darker tints. The companion flowerpot is enameled with a ground color of darker tone and more thickly flecked with crimson passing into purple. Their preservation is due to the thickness and solidity of the material, and they figure in the cultured interior of a Chinese house to display the flowering bulbs of the narcissus or the dwarf shrubs of the blossoming plum, which flower at the new year, the one great national holiday. The marks are the numerals 1 to 9 deeply engraved underneath in the paste, either singly or repeated; in the last case, for example, the number is carved inside one of the feet, as well as on the base of the flowerpot or saucer.

FIG. 125.—Water-pot of Sung dynasty, Chün Yao, with dragon molded in relief, invested with a thick unctuous glaze of *clair-de-lune* color, showing a patch of *aubergine* with shaded border.

Fig. 125 is a picture of a little water-pot, *shui-ch'êng*, of the ancient Chün Yao of the *Sung* dynasty, such as a Chinese writer loves to put on his table, and it is marked underneath with the character *san*, "3," carved in the paste. An archaic dragon is modeled on one side in bold relief so as to lift up its head above the rim. It is covered with a rich, deep, finely crackled glaze, of *yueh-pai* or *clair-de-lune* color, with a patch of deep *aubergine* tint shaded with lighter purple round the edge. It shows in miniature two of the characteristic colors of the time. It had been shattered into fragments, and when first seen was coated with lac dating from the *Ming* dynasty, which has since been scraped off.

These things were reproduced with some success by T'ang Ying in the reign of *Yung-chêng*, 1723–35. His productions may be distinguished by their perfect execution and finish, the texture being finer and the paste whiter than in the originals. A beautiful example of his work is seen in Fig. 126, showing a shallow bowl mounted upon three foliated feet, modeled in the shape of one of the bowls of Chün Yao made in the *Sung* dynasty for the cultivation of narcissus bulbs, and enameled with a copper-red glaze of mottled tint exhibiting a pink ground flecked with darker red spots. The bottom, coated with a grayish glaze, is engraved with the character *san*, "3." The seal of the period *Yung-chêng* is impressed in the paste in the middle underneath. This seal had been filled in with cement, plastered over and artificially tinted, showing that the bowl had been intended to figure as a relic of the *Sung*; and it is really such a perfect reproduction as to be liable to deceive the very elect, had it not been marked with the reign in which T'ang Ying flourished, as well as with the numerical mark of the older *régime*.

Our artist figures four specimens of Chün-chou porcelain of the *Sung* dynasty in the manuscript album, all of darkest purple-brown, or *aubergine* color.

"*Jar* (*Tsun*), of ovoid form, slightly expanding above the short neck to a circularly rimmed mouth. The two handles which project from the neck are fashioned in open-work relief as phœnixes, with crested heads and bodies terminating below in spiral curves. The numeral *wu*, '5,' is inscribed under the base as a mark. The glaze is dark purple-brown. The source of the design can not be traced, although the elegance of the form and the artistic finish of the work are such as no common potter could have executed. Chün-chou used at the time to be ranked at the bottom of the potteries of the *Sung* dynasty, yet this jar in its perfect form and beautiful color makes a receptacle for flowers equal to any one either of *Ju, Kuan, Ko,* or *Ting* porcelain. Its "mark" is an additional proof that it is really a Chün piece. I am now the fortunate possessor." H. 3½ in.

"*Miniature Vase (Hsiao P'ing)*, of oval form, with a bulbous neck shaped like a 'head' of garlic. It is enameled with a glaze of mottled blue and purple (*ch'ing tzŭ*), and is of the colors vulgarly known as 'ass's liver and horse's lung.' It is in my own collection, and is one of the tiniest of vases, little more than an inch high, fit to hold a single pearl orchid or a jasmine flower."

"*Wine-Pot (Hu)*, of depressed oval form, with a short neck ending above in a circular mouth, a tiny spout at one end, and a minute solid triangular handle at the other. It must originally have had a small round cover, which is now lost. The surface is covered with formal floral sprays and spiral scrolls worked in relief under the glaze, which is of *aubergine* purple color. Specimens of Chün-chou porcelain are often, like this piece, of novel original design, as the potters did not usually copy the antique. Of the colors used in its decoration none excelled the vermilion red (*chu hung*) and the *aubergine* purple (*ch'ieh tzŭ*), of which this is a fine example; the moonlight white (*yueh hsia pai*), or *clair de lune*, and the pale green (*yu ch'ing*) being both inferior glazes, when compared with the others. It holds about a pint of wine." H. 3 in., D. 5 in.

FIG. 126.—Shaped Dish with three scrolled feet of the Yung-chêng period, modeled after the style of the ancient Chün Yao of the Sung dynasty; mounted upon two stands of carved wood.

"*Dragon Lamp* (*Chiao Têng*), molded in the form of a grotesque hornless dragon, with its coiled scaly body hollowed into a receptacle for the oil, its serpentlike head elevated with protruding tongue and open mouth to receive the wick. The glaze is bluish purple of the color of ripe grapes. It is a lamp of rare design, lifelike and awe-inspiring, and illuminates the whole room when lighted." H. 16 in.

Magnificent pieces of this Chün-chou fabric are to be seen in Chinese collections, remarkable for the brilliant and variegated coloring of the rich, unctuous, liquescent glaze, which exhibits all the transmutation tints of the copper silicates in their pristine perfection. The material is generally, however, a reddish stoneware rather than porcelain. I have just seen a large tripod censer with rounded bowl and receding neck thickly imbued with a mottled opalescent glaze of *clair-de-lune* type, contrasting with the red color of a pair of archaic dragons worked in bold relief round the hollow of the neck, and partially reserved between two irregularly undulating lines of glaze. The dragons form a frieze, half hidden, as it were, in azure-tinted clouds.

THREE OTHER MANUFACTORIES.

There were several other manufactories in different parts of China during the *Sung* dynasty, of which three must not be omitted, although their productions are not illustrated in our album. These are (1) Chi-chou, in the province of Kiangsi, celebrated for its crackled porcelain; (2) Chien-chou, in the province of Fuchien, famous for its black teacups, of priceless value for the tea ceremonial of the time; and (3) Tz'ŭ-chou, in the province of Chihli, where a peculiar kind of stoneware, enameled white and painted in brown, is fabricated down to the present day.

(1) The *Chi-chou Yao,* 吉 州 窰, was made at Yung-ho-chên, in Chi-chou, which corre-

sponds to the modern Lu-ling-hsien in the prefecture Chi-an-fu, in the province of Kiangsi.* The *Ko ku yao lun* says that the colors of the porcelain were white and purple-brown, like that of Ting-chou, but that it was thick and comparatively coarse in fabric, and not worth so much money; and that in the *Sung* dynasty there were five manufactories, of which that of the Shu family was the most celebrated. Some of the smaller pieces were decorated with painting, and one of the daughters of the family, called Shu Chiao, or "The Fair Shu," was a skillful artist. The *Sui Ch'i,* 碎噐, or crackled vases, were, however, the most famous productions of this factory, and rivaled the similar vases of Ko Yao, which they resembled in color and in being reticulated with lines like fissured ice. Tradition says that during the troubles at the close of the *Sung* dynasty, when the famous minister Wên T'ien-hsiang (1236–82) came to this place, the porcelain was transformed in the kilns to jade, and that the potters fled in boats down the river to Ching-tê-chên, where they settled, and continued for generations to make this crackled ware.

(2) The *Chien Yao,* 建窰, was the original porcelain produced at the ancient Chien-chou, in the province of Fuchien. This corresponds to the modern prefecture Chien-ning-fu. The manufactory, which was established at Chien-an at the beginning of the *Sung* dynasty, was moved afterward to Chien-yang. In the *Yuan* dynasty, which succeeded the *Sung,* this last place became still more famous for its ceramic production. During the *Sung* the shallow bowls and cups with everted rims, enameled with a black glaze speckled with white, which sometimes ran down in brown drops, were appreciated above all others at the tea ceremonies. They were called "hare's fur cups" or "partridge cups," from their resemblance in color to the skin of the common hare and to the plumage of the *Perdrix cinerea.* They were thick and heavy and kept hot a long time — another quality for which they were highly prized by the old "tea-tasters."

FIG. 127. — Tall Vase, one of a pair, of early K'ang-hsi period, with molded and etched decoration under a crackled turquoise glaze of pure bluish tint; European mounts.

The practice of the competitors at these tea parties was to grind the tea leaves to fine dust and put a little of the powder into each of the cups, to fill the cup with boiling water, and stir up the mixture with a bamboo whisk. After the powder had subsided the tea was drunk, and the cup was again filled with water, the process being repeated as long as any trace of tea-dust remained visible at the bottom of the cup. The more "waters" the tea would bear the better it was considered; and the dark-colored cups of Chien-an were valued, for one reason, because they showed the slightest trace of pale yellow dust as long as any of the tea lasted.

The Chinese ceremonial was afterward adopted in Japan at their tea clubs, which have been so often described. The Japanese also showed an immense appreciation for the "hare-skin" glaze of the teacups of Chien-an, which they imported for their own use and valued at such fabulous prices. Three cups with silver rims, attributed to the twelfth century A. D., from the collection of the Japanese archæologist, Ninagawa Noritane, are described in one of Captain F. Brinkley's catalogues † as being about five inches in diameter and two and a half inches deep, and as having a lustrous black glaze covered with yellowish metallic-looking lines.

These potteries have long been extinct. The porcelain fabricated in the province of Fuchien

---

* Julien, in the preface of his work (*loc. cit.*), places this factory correctly in Kiangsi province, but refers it on page 16 of the text to Kuangsi, in the southeast of China, and on page 76 to Shensi, in the far northwest.

† *Collection of Japanese, Chinese, and Korean Porcelain, Pottery, and Faïence,* p. 96.

in the present day, and still known as *Chien Yao*, or *Chien Tz'ŭ*, is the well-known *blanc-de-Chine* variety, with a soft-looking, velvety glaze, which comes from Tê-hua, of which the libation-cup shown in Fig. 57 is a typical specimen.

(3) The *Tz'ŭ Yao*, 磁窑, was the ware produced at Tz'ŭ-chou, which was formerly under the jurisdiction of the prefecture Chang-tê-fu, of Honan province, but is now under Kuang-p'ing-fu, in the province of Chihli. The ceramic ware is made out of a peculiar kind of white clay found here, and is really an opaque white stoneware rather than porcelain, covered with a dull, white glaze, and decorated with floral and other designs painted in dark brown or dull

blue. The forms of the pieces and the style of decoration in the present day are of archaic character, and are often wrongly classed as Korean. They include figures of deities, of Taoist and Buddhist saints, as well as vases and jars, and all kinds of common utensils. At the present day these potteries supply the coarser articles used by the common people of Peking and throughout northern China. There is a general resemblance in the ware to the old Ting Yao, which was made in the vicinity, Ting-chou being within the bounds of the same prefecture of Kuang-p'ing-fu.

The *Ko ku yao lun*, referring to the production of the *Sung* dynasty, says that good specimens of Tz'ŭ-chou ware resembled the products of Ting-chou, only their glazes exhibited no traces of tears. They comprised both engraved and painted decorations, and the plain pieces fetched as high prices as those of Ting-chou. He adds, however, that the production of his own times (fourteenth century) was not worthy of description.

FIG. 128.—Ewer of early K'ang-hsi blue and white, painted with panels of cross-hatched design ; Persian metal mounts.

Three modern pieces of this ware are reproduced in Fig. 104 to show its archaic character and peculiar style of decoration : (*a*) A Wine Flask, *Chiu P'ing*, painted in two shades of brown, with a floral spray. (*b*) A gourd-shaped vase, *Hu-lu P'ing*, painted in dark brown, with the character *fu* (" happiness ") above and a spray of flowers below. (*c*) Twin Figures of Two Merry Genii, *Ho Ho Erh Hsiang*, with a tube, intended to hold a stick of incense when placed upon a Taoist altar, projecting from the shoulder of one of the figures ; the details of the costume being picked out in lighter and darker brown.

Some Utensils of Sung Porcelain.

The short account of porcelain of the *Sung* dynasty given above may be supplemented by a list, condensed from the fifth book of the *T'ao Shuo*, of some of the other articles fabricated at the time that have not been already alluded to. The books from which the author usually quotes are those describing the artistic furniture and paraphernalia of the scholar's library, so that utensils for the use and ornament of the writing-table occur on every page of his book, in the same way as such things fill the greater part of our manuscript album.

"A *Vase* (*P'ing*), of white Ting-chou porcelain, which the author of the *Ni ku lu* bought at Hsiu-chou, with four handles, fired with the inscription *Jên ho kuan*, ' Hotel of Benevolence and Harmony,' written obliquely across, in the handwriting apparently of one of the Mi family, father or son." The author refers here, no doubt, to Mi Fei, a famous calligraphist of the eleventh century A. D.

"*Vases* (*P'ing*), of Kuan, Ko, and Ting porcelain, the finest of which are the slender beakers with trumpet-shaped mouths, with a brilliant blue glaze sinking into the ' bone,' speckled with vermilion spots rising in relief ; the others, to be chosen for the scholar's library, should be the low and graceful vases shaped like paper beaters, those with goose necks, like aubergine fruit, like flower jars or flower bags, the receptacles for divining stalks, or the bulrush-shaped vases. Vases called *p'ing* were used in ancient times both for drawing water and for holding wine; the Buddhist used them for ceremonial cleansing; it was not till the *Sung* dynasty that they were used for flowers. Flower vases of bronze, which are not liable to breakage by frost, should be used in the winter and spring, of porcelain in the summer and autumn. Large vases are preferred for the hall and reception room, small ones for the library. Copper and porcelain are esteemed above gold and silver, to cultivate simplicity; rings and pairs should be avoided, and rarity be the quality specially aimed at. The mouth should be small, the foot thick, so that the vase may stand firmly and not emit vapor. If the mouth be large, a tube of tin should be fitted inside, to hold the flowers upright."

"*Ink Pallet* (*Yen*), of Ko Yao, belonging to Ku Lin, engraved with a rhyming verse of four lines: 'Neither the fine clay pallets of the Ts'ung Tower nor the ancient tiles of the Palace of Yeh, Are equal to those of Ko porcelain in its antique elegance. These are green as the waves of spring, and hold water most perfectly: So that even pallets of the finest stone must be ranked below them.'"

"A *Pencil Rest* (*Pi Ko*), of white Ting-chou porcelain, molded in the form of a boy lying upon a flower."

"*Waterpots* (*Shui Ch'êng*) for the writing-table from any of the different potteries, shaped like a fish-bowl, like a Buddhist *patra* or alms-bowl, with ribbed sides, in the form of a chrysanthemum flower with hollow center," etc.

"*Water Pourers* (*Shui Chu*), little vessels with spouts, in the form of an upright or recumbent gourd, of a pair of peaches, of two lotus capsules, a herd-boy lying upon a cow, or a toad."

"*Larger Waterpots* (*Hu*), with handle and spout, fashioned like a gourd with the leafy stem trailing round, like an aubergine plant with the stem and leaves attached to the fruit, like a camel, this last adapted to serve also as a pencil rest," etc.

"*Dishes for washing Brushes* (*Pi Hsi*), of imperial (*Kuan*) and Ko porcelain, are of many kinds, being round and saucer-shaped, of the form of an althæa flower, with a rim of the foliated outline of a Buddhist stone gong, a lotus leaf with tilted margin, a joint of sugar-cane with everted mouth," etc.

"Those of Lung-ch'üan celadon porcelain comprise round dishes with a pair of fishes inside molded in relief under the glaze, chrysanthemum flowers, Buddhist alms-bowls, plaited and fluted platters."

"Among Ting-chou white pieces are barrels bound round with three hoops, vessels molded in the shape of a plum-blossom, a girdle ring, or a woven basket of osier; others have a cup in the middle to dip the brush in, encircled by a saucerlike rim to rub it on; and any one of the numerous small round dishes of this ware may be selected for use as a pencil washer."

FIG. 129.—Sacrificial Vase, of archaic form, with two handles in the shape of alligator-like dragons; the crackled glaze of mottled purple and green resembles that of the flambé vase in Plate XXIII.

"*Paper Weights* (*Chên Chih*), molded in the form of coiled dragons, of lions and drums, of playing boys and grotesque monsters."

"*Seals* (*Yin*), with handles of varied design, copied from ancient seals of jade, gold, and copper."

"*Seal-Color Boxes* (*Yin-Sê Ch'ih*), for holding vermilion, include square, octagonal, and plaited boxes of Kuan and Ko porcelain, and the beautiful square caskets of Ting-chou fabrication with floral designs molded over the exterior."

"*Censers* (*Lu*), of varied form and design, are generally modeled after ancient sacrificial vessels of bronze. Incense was introduced into China by the Buddhists, who used the censers of elaborate design called *Po-shan Lu*. The Chinese, however, used these outside the temple, but made their censers for private use after indigenous designs of bronze. The porcelain censers of the *Sung* dynasty in turn furnished models for the bronze censers of the reign of *Hsüan-tê* (1426–35), which are well known in collections. The incense-burning apparatus in ordinary use consists of three pieces, comprising a box with cover to hold the incense, and a vase to hold the miniature poker, tongs, and shovel, which are made of metal, in addition to the censer. The *Vases* (*Chu P'ing*) selected for this purpose must be low and solid, so as to stand firmly without being overbalanced. The *Incense Boxes* (*Hsiang Ho*) of white Ting-chou porcelain and the productions of Ching-tê-chên are preferred, those from Chün-chou being usually of comparatively coarser fabric. Sometimes they are nested, the outer box inclosing one or more smaller ones."

FIG. 130.—Vase of graceful form, artistically painted in delicate colors of the Yung-chêng period.

"*Paste Pots* (*Hu Tou*) include tall jars of Chien-chou porcelain, black outside, white within; jars of Ting-chou porcelain of oval form, fashioned in the shape of a bulb of garlic or of a bulrush head; and square vessels of Ko Yao, like a corn measure, with a horizontal bar stretched across the top as a handle."

"Of *Reading Lamps* (*Shu Têng*) the best are the oil lamps with three nozzles of white Ting-chou porcelain."

Porcelain Pillows (*Tz'ŭ Chên*) were much used in summer during the *Sung* dynasty, being supposed to be good for preserving the eyesight. The palace of the Emperor *Ning Tsung* (1195–1224) is described as having been full of them. Pillows of smaller size were made for supporting the head of the dead body in the coffin, and these are often discovered in old tombs. For this reason the author of the *K'ao p'an yü shih* prescribes that only those pillows of ancient porcelain that are two and a half feet long and over six inches broad should be used, and he insists firmly on the injunction that the "corpse pillows," which were generally only one foot in length, even if made of the finest Ting-chou ware, and most elaborately decorated with molded designs, must be ruthlessly discarded. One of these pillows, dug up from an ancient tomb, is described as having had the well-known verse of the poet Tu inscribed upon it in four stanzas, beginning "Wearing a girdle studded with a hundred jewels."

"*Watering Pot* (*Hua Chiao*), of imperial porcelain (*Kuan Yao*), with the inscription upon it: 'Red oh! as dawn-hued drops scattered by fishes' tails: Rich oh! as early rain sprinkling the pear blossoms.' These similes might refer either to the fabric, of rich red paste, or to the glaze, the most highly appreciated tone of which was a pale purple flecked with red spots."

Mottled Hare-Fur Teacups (*T'u-mao-hua Ch'a-ou*), of Ting-chou porcelain, are often referred to in books on tea of the *Sung* dynasty as specially suitable for use at the competitive tea-tasting parties; they were covered with an iron-gray glaze. In an oft-quoted line in his ode on boiling tea in the examination-hall, the poet Su Tung-p'o, who wrote in the eleventh century, alludes to teacups from the same factory enameled red: "In flowered porcelain of Ting-chou, like carved red jade."

The *Hare-Fur Cups* (*T'u-mao Chan*), of Chien-an, in Fuchien province, were first described by Ts'ai Hsiang, a native of that province, in his account of the tea-plant, entitled *Ch'a Lu*, which was written in the eleventh century. He says: "Tea being of a pale whitish tint, black is the most suitable color for cups. Those made at Chien-an are of a soft black color, spotted like the fur of a hare. These cups are rather thick and retain the heat, so that they cool very slowly when once warmed. For these reasons they are highly prized, and there is nothing produced at any of the other potteries to rival them."

"A *Face Cup** (*Jên-mien Pei*), a wine-cup molded in the form of a man's face, of imperial porcelain of the *Sung* dynasty, is alluded to by the author of the *Ni ku lu* as being in the collection of Hsiang Yuan-tu." This collector seems to have been the brother of Hsiang Yuan-p'ien, the author of our manuscript Album. The *Ni ku lu*, a book on objects of art, was written by Ch'ên Chi-ju in the sixteenth century, so that the author and our artist must have been contemporaries.

"A *Double Wedding Cup* (*Ho-Ch'êng Pei*) of Ko Yao" is also described in the work just quoted, as molded in the form of twin peaches, standing in a saucer of the same material hollowed out in the center for their reception. The peaches were detached for use as wine-cups. At the marriage ceremony in China the bride and bridegroom must each drink in succession three cups of wine. The vessels are mentioned in the ancient ritual books, which prescribe that a wine-jar (*tsun*) filled with wine should be placed upon the altar on the east side of the door, with a basket tray upon its south holding four single cups (*chüo*) of the shape of the old libation cups, and one double cup (*ho-ch'êng*) which was a split gourd. In ancient times these cups were carved out of shell, as well as split from gourds; in modern times they are made of porcelain, gold, silver, and copper, or of hard stone. Some of the jade cups are beautifully carved and ornamented outside with appropriate symbols in open-work relief; a composite cup, for example, fashioned in the form of two interlacing lozenges, or a pair of linked hollow rings, emblems of union and success, overlaid with peaches and bats, symbols of longevity and happiness, and with the *shuang hsi*, or "double joy" hieroglyphs, special attributes of wedded bliss, displayed upon their surface.

"A *Stem Cup* (*Pa Pei*), of octagonal shape, of Ko Yao, in the collection of Hsiang Yuan-tu." The name of *pa pei* (literally "handled cup") is applied in China to the tazza-shaped cups used for tea or wine, just as the *pa wan* are the tazza-shaped rice-bowls, with high cylindrical stems. Cups with handles at the sides like our tea-cups are rarely seen in China even now; they were quite unknown in early times.

"*Bowls decorated in Blue* (*Hua Ch'ing Wan*), of Jao-chou porcelain." The *Ko ku yao lun* describes these bowls produced in the imperial potteries of Jao-chou in the *Sung* dynasty as being of thin texture and translucent material, painted in blue on a white ground, and as but slightly inferior to the Ting-chou porcelain of the period. This refers to the earliest porcelain of Jao-chou, which became so famous in after times.

Wên Chên-hêng, the author of the *Ch'ang wu chih* quoted in the *Ching-tê-chên T'ao-lu*, book ix, gives the following short account of *Sung* porcelain: "The Ch'ai

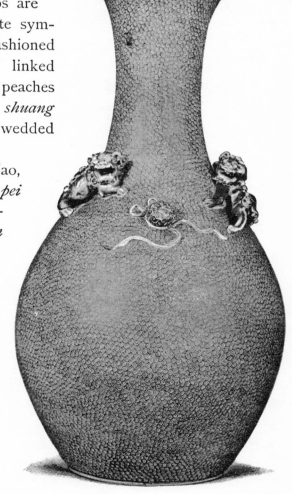

FIG. 131.—Vase, with three lions in full relief upon the shoulder pursuing brocaded balls, roughly decorated in enamel colors, with gilding.

porcelain (of the preceding dynasty) is the most valuable of all, but not a single piece remains; it is said to have been blue as the sky, clear as a mirror, thin as paper, ringing like a musical stone. Of the porcelains called Kuan, Ko, and Ju, the best is of pale blue (or green) color,

---

* A cup of this peculiar form, of pale blue, uncrackled Ju-chou porcelain of the *Sung* dynasty, is mentioned among the things sent from the palace at Peking by the Emperor *Yung-chêng* as a model for T'ang Ying to reproduce at Ching-tê-chên.

the whitish glaze comes next, the ash-gray last; that crackled with lines like fissured ice of the color of eel's blood is ranked highest, a black reticulation in the pattern of the petals of plum-blossom next, minute broken lines lowest. In Chün-chou porcelain rouge-red color is the best; the green, like fresh onion sprouts or emerald jade, and the inky purple, come next; the mixed colors are not so much appreciated." Again, the "Kuan Yao has the glaze crackled like claws of crabs, the Ko Yao like roe of fish. The Lung-ch'üan porcelain is very thick and of comparatively coarse workmanship."

"For Flower Vases good specimens of Kuan, Ko, and Ting porcelain should be selected; an ancient vase of gall-bladder shape, or one molded like a branch of a tree, a small divining-

FIG. 132.—A grayish-white crackle with reddish spots, interrupted by encircling bands and ring handles of iron-gray biscuit.

rod receptacle, or a paper-beater vase; as to the others, like those with decoration engraved under the glaze, the painted blue and white, the aubergine and gourd-shaped vases, the medicine jars with small mouths, flattened bodies, and contracted feet, and the new Chien-chou vases, none of these are so suitable for the study of a simple scholar; the goose-neck bottles and the hanging wall-vases also are not all of good style."

"Among flower-vases of Lung-ch'üan and Chün-chou porcelain there are some very large ones, measuring two or three feet in height, which are well adapted to display old branches of the blossoming plum at New-Year's time."

"In white Ting-chou ware we have Pencil Rests (*Pi Ko*) of three hills, of five hills, and of children reclining on flowers; among the Brush Pots (*Pi T'ung*) of ancient manufacture, a joint of bamboo is the most valued form, but it is difficult to find one large enough. Those of old celadon, with fine decoration worked under the glaze, may also be chosen. More elaborate forms, like that of a drum pierced at the top with holes for the brushes and the cake of ink, although ancient, are in bad style. Brush Washers (*Pi Hsi*) of Kuan and Ko porcelain include althæa-blossom dishes, dishes with rims foliated like the outline of a hanging gong, lotus-leaves with the margin tilted up all round, and sugar-canes with expanded mouth; those of Ting-chou comprise three-hooped tubs, plum-blossoms, and square saucer-shaped receptacles. Brush Washers of Lung-ch'üan porcelain include round dishes with a pair of fish, chrysanthemum flowers, and vessels with hundred-fluted sides. Among Water Droppers (*Shui Chu*), for the pallet, of the Kuan, Ko, and Ting-chou wares, there are square and round upright gourds, recumbent gourds, twin peaches, lotus capsules, and aubergine pots with leaves trailing round. For Seal-color Boxes (*Yin Ch'ih*), the square-shaped, of Kuan and Ko fabrication, are the best; those of Ting-chou, the octagonal and many-lobed shapes, come next; those painted in blue on a white ground, and the oval boxes with covers, are not so much valued."

"*Waterpots* (*Shui Chung-Ch'êng*), for the writing-table, are often made of copper, but copper becomes corroded and infects the water, so that it injures the brush, for which reason porcelain is considered to be a preferable material. Among such receptacles of Kuan and Ko fabrics there are miniature fish-bowls, Buddhist alms-bowls, and round cups drawn in at the mouth. For Ink Pallets (*Pi Yen*), the small, round, shallow dishes, either of Ting-chou or of Lung-ch'üan ware, serve excellently. There are Paste-Pots (*Hu-Tou*), of Ting-chou fabrication, of the shape of garlic bulbs, and oval jars with covers; and of Ko ware in the form of a square corn-measure with a rodlike handle across the mouth."

This account shows how much porcelain was coming into general use before the close of the *Sung* dynasty. One of the principal causes was the growing scarcity of copper and consequent monetary difficulties, which provoked the passage of sumptuary laws, making the possession of bronze articles a penal offense, after every available object had been collected for the mint and melted down into "cash." Most of the objects of art had previously been modeled in copper or other metals, and the corresponding things when first made of porcelain were generally fashioned, as we have seen, after the older bronze designs. An early vase of Ting-chou porcelain, for example, will be found to be molded in the same shape, with grotesque mask-handles in relief, and chiseled with rings and borders of similar ornamental frets as were employed previously in the decoration of bronze work.

Some of the larger pieces produced at these last kilns are remarkably fine examples of the potter's art, excelling in the graceful curves of their classical outline and in the perfect finish of the ornamental details, which are worked in flowing relief or graved with the point

FIG. 133.—Large, heavy Vase of the Sung dynasty. Exceedingly dense body
and deep indented glaze of livid red, purple, and gray.

under the soft-looking glaze of ivory-white tint. This glaze has usually a finely crackled surface, and being of a soft, absorbent nature it is often mottled and stained with age. The reproduction of these *Fên-Ting* vases at Ching-tě-chên taxed all the energies of the celebrated T'ang Ying in the first half of the eighteenth century, and his handiwork is valued at its weight in gold by collectors of the present day, more highly even than the original models, which are not so often seen out of China. The Koreans worked in the same lines, and the earliest Satsuma ware produced under their influence in Japan, with its finely crackled ivory-white texture, offers a surprising resemblance to the old Chinese *Fên-Ting* porcelain.

The specimens of *Sung* porcelain were generally sent down from the collections in the palace at Peking as models of monochrome coloring, and it would be very interesting to have a complete catalogue of the ancient relics preserved there. There are manuscript lists in existence compiled by the Chamberlain's department, of which I have seen two or three, detailing the articles of furniture and art objects contained in the halls of the several palaces. I have had the opportunity of consulting one of these in the library of Mr. H. R. Bishop, of New York. It is the official list of the contents of the Shu Ch'ing Yuan, one of the palaces in the Western Park at Peking, dated the thirteenth year of *Chia-ch'ing* (1808). The objects of art catalogued are of bronze, *cloisonné* enamel, carved red lac, jade, and porcelain, and offer, no doubt, a fair representation of the collections in the other parts of the palace.

There are eighty-four pieces of porcelain on exhibition, of which seventeen are attributed to the *Sung* dynasty, being referred to six of the different potteries referred to above, and confirming in their character the accounts quoted from the books.

1. *Ju Yao.*

Pencil Rest (*Pi Shan*), in the form of a miniature range of hills.
Brush Washer (*Pi Hsi*), a fluted dish modeled in the shape of a rose-mallow flower.

2. *Kuan Yao.*

Fluted Dish (*P'an*), of rose-mallow design.
Vase (*P'ing*), with a girdle in open-work carving.

3. *Ting Yao.*

Dish for holding quinces (*Mu-kua P'an*), mounted with a copper rim.
Beaker-shaped Vase (*Hua Ku*), of *Fên-Ting*, with a piece broken out, and cracked.
Shallow Bowl (*Hsi*), of *Fên-Ting*, with copper-mounted rim, upon two rosewood stands.
Olive-shaped Vase (*So-lan P'ing*), with a copper band round the rim.
Jar, with Cover (*Kai Wan*).
Round Dish (*P'an*), with a copper rim.

4. *Lung-ch'üan Yao.*

Jar, with Cover (*Kai Kuan*).

5. *Ko Yao.*

Two round, fluted *Dishes* (*P'an*), of rose-mallow design.
Shallow Bowl (*Hsi*) for washing brushes.
Round, fluted *Dish* (*P'an*), of chrysanthemum design.
Waterpot (*Shui Ch'êng*), with a coral spoon inside.

6. *Chün Yao.*

Double Gourd Vase (*Hu-lu P'ing*).

FIG. 134.—Small Vase of archaic character. A coarse, black, crackled ground, with a bold design in dark violet-blue.

FIG. 135.—Snuff-bottles: (1) Blue and white; (2) White paste, modeled in high relief, and surmounted by the dog Foo; (3) Perforated and reticulated design in Fên-ting white paste.

CHAPTER VI.

YUAN DYNASTY.

IN the thirteenth century A. D. China was overrun by the Mongols and was gradually conquered by them, the *Sung* dynasty being driven into the sea. A new dynasty with the title of *Yuan* was founded in 1280 by Kublai Khan, the grandson of the famous Mongol Genghis. In 1368 the *Yuan* dynasty was overthrown, the Mongols expelled to the north of the Great Wall, and a native dynasty once more ruled, under the title of *Ming*. The Mongols consequently reigned with their capital at Khanbalik, or Cambalu, "City of the Khan," the modern Peking, for less than a century altogether.

After the Mongol conquest the principal provincial posts were given to Tartars, who seem to have cared only for the money they could wring out of such native industries as remained after the war, without caring to support them in any way. Many of the old potteries disappeared about this time, and Ching-tê-chên began to occupy the prominent position in the ceramic field which it has held ever since. In 1296, the second year of the reign of the second emperor, *ping shên* of the sexagenary cycle, Fou-liang-hsien was promoted to the rank of a chou city, a Mongol being appointed governor (*darugha*) of Fou-liang-chou, as it was now called. Ching-tê-chên was made a customs station, and the superintendent of the potteries was appointed commissioner, with the title of *t'i-ling*. In the period *Tai-ting* (1324–27) the governor of the province of Kiang-si was appointed superintendent of the potteries (Chien t'ao), and ordered to go there whenever an imperial requisition was issued, and to close the imperial manufactory after the work was finished, pending the issue of a new decree.

The first edition of the *Annals of Fou-liang-hsien* had been issued during the *Sung* dynasty in the cyclical year *kêng wu* (1270), of the *Hsien-shun* period. Before this its events had been recorded in the *Annals of Po-yang*, which were published in the year 1215. In the *Yuan* dynasty a new edition of the *Annals of Fou-liang* was compiled by the native scholar Ts'ang T'ing-fêng and published officially in the period *Chih-chih*, the cyclical year *jên-hsü* (1322). This edition included a special memoir on the porcelain manufacture, *T'ao chi lüo*, by Chiang Ch'i, which is found reprinted in every subsequent edition of the *Annals*, as well as in the *Statistical Descriptions* of the prefecture of Jao-chou-ju, and of the province of Kiang-si. This is the earliest account in any detail of the ceramic industry which we have, and I will translate it here, omitting only some of the less interesting passages, such as the author's diatribes upon the excessive taxation levied upon the industry in his time:

"The potteries at Ching-tê-chên contained formerly more than three hundred manufactories. The porcelain produced in its workshops was of pure white color and without stain, so that the merchants who carried it for sale to all parts used to call their ware 'Jao-chou Jade.' It was compared with the red porcelain of Chên-ting-fu, and with the emerald-green ware of Lung-ch'üan-hsien, and found to surpass them both in beauty.*

"The furnaces are carefully measured by the officials, and their length in feet and the number of workmen employed in each one are recorded upon the registers, to fix the proportion of tax to be levied; neither the size of the fire, nor the number of channels, chimneys, and vent-holes being reckoned or put on the register.

"The potters are given land to cultivate for their living, and not paid regular wages; they are settled round the masters of the factories, and called together by their orders when necessary, which is called 'opening the works.' When they have cased the ware in the seggars (*hsia*), these are placed carefully in different parts of the furnace so that the contents may be properly fired, which is called 'firing the kilns.' At the time of lighting the fire the amount of silver fixed on the register, including the tax for the workmen passing in and out, according to the kiln table, must be paid; this is called 'reporting the fire.' After the fire has been kept up one day and two nights it is stopped, and when the furnace is opened the merchants throng to buy and select the best pieces; this is called 'choosing the porcelain.' For settling the accounts of the sale an accountant is employed in each factory, and dealers are licensed by the officials, who examine the accounts; this is called the 'shop license.' For carrying the porcelain to the river licensed porters are employed, who are provided with papers to enter the quantity carried and the number of journeys for which the merchants have to pay; these are called 'porterage tickets.' Such are the general regulations of the manufactories.

FIG. 136.—Gourd overspread with a network of the gourd-vine, with five bats in the meshes; pale blue monochrome glaze, touched in parts with copper-red.

"Throughout the province of Chê (Chekiang), both east and west, they prefer the yellowish-black or brown ware, which is produced in the potteries of Hu-t'ien; in the provinces of Chiang (Kiangnan), Hu (Hukuang), Ch'uan (Ssŭch'uan), and Kuang (Kuangtung), the greenish-white or celadon ware which comes from the kilns of Ching-tê-Chên proper.

"The bowls (*wan*) engraved with fish and waves and those of tazza shape with high feet, and the dishes (*tieh*) with the glaze shaded in different tones and those ornamented with 'sea eyes' and 'snow-white flowers,' are the kinds which sell profitably in Ch'uan (Ssŭ-ch'uan), Kuang (Kuangtung), Ching and Hsiang (Hunan and Hupei). The large dishes (*p'an*) of horse-shoe shape and of 'betel-nut' glaze, the large bowls (*yü*) of lotus-blossom design, and the square forms with indented corners, the rice-bowls (*wan*) and the platters (*tieh*), with painted decoration, with silvery designs, with fluted sides, and with encircling strings, these are sold readily in Kiangnan, Chekiang, and Fuchien provinces. The different kinds have all to be selected to please the fancy of the consumer of each district.

"There are many different forms of censers (*lu*) made for burning incense, in the form of fabulous lions (*ni*), of the ancient bronze sacrificial vessels *ting* (three-footed and four-footed)

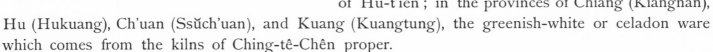

* The red porcelain of Ting-chou, in the prefecture of Chên-ting-fu, used to be compared to carved carnelian by the poets of the *T'ang* dynasty. The other ware alluded to is the old celadon porcelain of Lung-ch'üan, which was often of bright grass-green tint during the *Sung* dynasty.

and *yi* (bowl-shaped), of the ancient caldrons with three hollow legs called *li*, of the ritual form used for the worship of heaven (*chao-t'ien*), with elephants as feet (*hsiang t'ui*), like square scent-caskets (*hsiang lien*), or round tubs (*t'ung-tzŭ*). The various kinds of vases (*p'ing*), for flowers and ornament, include trumpet-mouthed beakers (*ku*), bladder-shaped vases (*tan*), bottle-shaped vases with handles and spouts (*hu*), vessels of Buddhistic form for ceremonial ablution (*ching*), vases shaped like gardenia flowers (*chih tzŭ*) or like lotus leaves (*ho yeh*), double gourds (*hu lu*), musical pipes (*lü kuan*), vases with animal mask-handles (*shou huan*) and glass forms (*liu-li*); and there are many other empty names and fine distinctions difficult to define, which are really of value to nobody but the dealer.

"Speaking generally, the porcelain consumed in the two Huai provinces (Kiangsu and Anhui) consists of the inferior pieces rejected by the provinces of Kiang (Kiangsi and Kiangnan), Kuang (Kuangtung), Min (Fuchien), and Chê (Chekiang); the native dealers sell such to them under the name of *huang tiao*, or 'yellow stuff,' because the color of the glaze is inferior, and the ware is only fit to be thrown away. The above is a short *résumé* of the kinds of porcelain articles made.

"In winter the paste freezes, and porcelain can not be fired. When the pieces are newly shaped they are very soft, and must be carried with care into the fire-chamber. As to the firing the proper time can not be exactly fixed, so that it is necessary to look through the aperture of the kiln to see whether the porcelain is properly baked, judging by the white heat of the fire.

"The porcelain earth prepared from Chin-k'êng stone is used in the fabrication of the finest porcelain, the rocks produced at Hu-k'êng, Ling-pei, and Chieh-t'ien being of the second class. The different earths brought from Jên-k'êng, Kao-shan, Ma-an-shan, and Tz'ŭ-shih-t'ang are red in color and are used only in the fabrication of the seggars and molds. If these be mixed with the other kinds in the preparation of the paste, it is of inferior quality, and the porcelain is not worth buying. It is in the hills of Yu-shan that the mountain brushwood is collected to make the ashes used in the preparation of the glaze. The method followed is to pile the lime burned from the stone in alternate layers with this brushwood mixed with persimmon (*Diospyros*) wood, and to burn the two together to ashes. These ashes must be combined with the 'glaze earth' brought from Ling-pei before they can be used. The pieces after they have been glazed are fired either upright or bottom upward. There are several distinct branches of work divided between the potters, the seggar-makers, and the preparers of the earth; the pieces before they are fired are fashioned by the different processes of throwing the paste on the wheel, finishing it with the knife on the polishing wheel, and finally by glazing it; the decoration is executed by molding, by

Fig. 137.—Yao-pien Vase, in the form of three coalescent gourds tied with a ribbon, exhibiting a play of mottled crimson and purplish tints.

painting, or by carving the ornamental designs. The different steps in the ceramic manufacture are kept distinct, and all provided with technical names.

"The kilns are inscribed on the register according to their measurement, and heavy fines are inflicted if they are lighted without authority. The glaze must be stamped in three grades of color according to its quality, and severe punishment follows the use of the wrong grade. The official inspectors must be bribed at every step, and if the slightest rule be infringed even the shop-dealers and the porters are made jointly responsible and punished. The penal regulations are both numerous and minute; yet, where formerly the revenue was most rich and abundant, there is now nothing but complaint of its insufficiency. Still the total amount of taxes has been increased by a large percentage. There are contributions levied for the governor of the province, who is superintendent, and for his deputies, for the monthly expenses of the officials of Jao-chou, and for the police of Ching-tê-chên, besides an allowance for the widows and orphans of the potters, the total mounting up to a monthly sum of over 3,000 strings of 'cash.' Then there are levies in spring and autumn for the soldiers, taxes for sacred holidays and the worship of heaven and earth, presents and money for the periodical repair of the examination halls, making one hundred and fifty strings more, all exacted by the officials on pain of instant punishment. I can give personal testimony, as I have seen for several tens of years past how the successive superintendents of this place have constantly, when transferred to other posts, left in debt to citizens of the chou.

FIG. 138.—Small Cup of white porcelain, with pierced sides, inclosing Taoist divinities in salient relief, touched with colors.

" Inquiring for the cause of this failure of revenue, there are five reasons: 1. The opening of the factories for work depends upon the abundance or scantiness of the harvest. 2. The porcelain manufactures in Lin-ch'uan, Chien-yang, and Nan-fêng have diverted much of the profit. 3. If the payment of the taxes be delayed a day, the police runners come knocking at the gate and devour everything like caterpillars. 4. The prisons are without jailers, and the proper officials have deserted their posts, so that dishonest men have nothing to fear. 5. The permanent local officials are banded together, and if an honest official should by chance be sent, he is immediately accused by them and the place made too hot for him. The times are bad, and it is useless to look for the honest officers of olden days," etc.

The potteries of Hu-t'ien referred to in this memoir were at Fou-liang-hsien, in the vicinity of Ching-tê-chên, from which they were separated by a small river. They were closed during the *Ming* dynasty, and are now represented only by ruins in a small hamlet with a pagoda on the southern bank of the river.

The other three potteries alluded to in the last paragraph of the memoir were situated at different stages on the overland route from Ching-tê-chên to Ch'üan-chou, the chief city of the province of Fuchien at that time, and the principal port for foreign trade, as we are told by Marco Polo and by Arab writers of the time.

Lin-ch'üan-hsien was in the prefecture of Fu-chou-fu, Nan-fêng-hsien in the prefecture of Chien-chang-fu, both in the province of Kiangsi. The porcelain of the former place is described as having been of finely levigated clay, thin, and generally of white color with a tinge of yellow, and to have been sometimes decorated with rough painting. That of Nan-fêng, made of similar material, was slightly thicker; the pieces were often decorated with painting in blue, while others are said to have resembled the coarser yellowish variety of Ting-chou ware. Chien-yang-hsien was in the province of Fuchien, nearer to Ch'üan-chou; it was already in existence in the *Sung* dynasty, and we have seen above that it was celebrated then

FIG. 139.—Small Teapot, one of a pair, of turquoise crackle, artistically fashioned in the form of a lotus flower, the cover a lotus leaf, the handle a dragon, and the spout an alligator with gaping mouth.

for the production of the black tea-bowls which were so highly appreciated at the competitive tea clubs of the time under the name of "hare-fur cups."

Chien-yang must surely have been the factory referred to by Marco Polo as situated in the province of Fuchien, and as being the seat of the production of the porcelain exported to all parts of the world from Ch'üan-chou, which was known to him by its Persian name of Zayton. The name of the factory given by him may be a local rendering of Chien-chou, the old name of the department. The only other factory that we know of in the province was that of Tê-hua, which was not founded till later, in the *Ming* dynasty.

He says (Yule's *Marco Polo*, Book II, chap. lxxxii): "Let me tell you also that in this province there is a town called Tyunju, where they make vessels of porcelain of all sizes, the finest that can be imagined. . . . Here it is abundant and very cheap, insomuch that for a Venice groat you can buy three dishes so fine that you could not imagine better."

Soon after Marco Polo, Ibn Batuta, an Arab, came to this port, of which he writes (*Voyages d'Ibn Batoutah*, traduits par Défrémery et Sanguinetti, t. iv, p. 256): "On ne fabrique pas en Chine la porcelaine, si ce n'est dans les villes de Zeïtoun (Ch'üan-chou) et Sincalan (Canton). Elle est faite au moyen d'une terre tirée des montagnes qui se trouvent dans ces districts; laquelle terre prend feu comme du charbon. . . . Les potiers y ajoutent une certaine pierre qui se trouve dans le pays; ils la font brûler pendant trois jours, puis versent l'eau par-dessus, et le tout devient une poussière, ou une terre qu'ils font fermenter. Celle dont la fermentation a duré un mois entier, mais non plus, donne la meilleure porcelaine; celle qui n'a fermenté que pendant dix jours, en donne une de qualité inférieure à la précédente. La porcelaine en Chine vaut le même prix que la poterie chez nous, ou encore moins. On l'exporte dans l'Inde et dans les autres contrées, jusqu'à ce qu'elle arrive dans la nôtre, le Maghreb (Morocco). C'est l'espèce la plus belle de toutes les poteries."

FIG. 140.—Three-lobed Vase, with lions in relief, coated with a variegated transmutation glaze, splashed with olive-brown and crimson patches of mottled tint.

Another manufactory which acquired some renown under the *Yuan* dynasty was that of Ho-chou, in the province of Kiangnan, where a goldsmith named P'êng Chün-pao produced imitations of the white porcelain of Ting-chou, of good color but very fragile, which were called at the time "New Ting-chou Porcelain," and the best of which, it was said, could hardly be distinguished from the genuine old ware.

The porcelain produced at the imperial manufactory at Ching-tê-chên is briefly described in the *Ko ku yao lun*, which says, under the heading of "Ancient Jao-chou Porcelain": "The porcelain made at the imperial factory was thin, translucent in texture, and very fine. It included plain bowls drawn in at the waist, and bowls with unglazed rims, which, although thick, were of pure white color and perfectly translucent. These were as good as the Ting-chou bowls, although not so high in price. The white bowls made in the *Yuan* dynasty, with small feet and molded decoration, which have inscribed inside the mouth, *Shu fu*, or 'imperial palace,' are also very fine. There was, besides, green porcelain and decoration in many colors, but these are considered to be more common. Another variety of porcelain was of greenish-black color, penciled with designs in gold; this consisted chiefly of wine-pots (*chiu hu*) and wine-cups (*chiu chan*), which are extremely beautiful." The author, speaking of these wine-pots adds: "Such things were unknown in China before the *Yuan* dynasty, when so many novel forms were introduced. In former times the wide shallow bowls called *p'ieh* were preferred for drinking tea because they were so easily dried and did not retain the dregs. Vases were used for the hot water; ewers and pots with spouts were new things for tea and wine; so were the tall upright teacups (*ch'a chung*) with saucers, and the stem wine-cups (*pa pei*) with tray. Neither these nor the bowls (*yü*) with lips were known in the wares of the *Sung* dynasty, either in imperial or in Ting-chou porcelain."

There is one specimen of this dynasty in our illustrated album which is described as follows:

"*Small Vase (Hsiao P'ing)* of imperial porcelain (*Shu fu Yao*) of the *Yuan* dynasty, bottle-shaped, with a globular body receding to a slender neck, which ends in a bulging garlic-shaped enlargement surrounding the circularly rimmed mouth. It is decorated with dragons with two-horned bearded heads and serpentine bodies with three-clawed legs, coiling through spiral scrolls of clouds, all etched in the paste under the white glaze. The pure white porcelain of our own dynasty of the reigns of *Yung-lo* and *Hsüan-tê*, with the decoration faintly engraved under the glaze, was all made after the style of this imperial porcelain. The *Shu fu* porcelain itself was modeled after the fabrication of Ting-chou under the northern *Sung* dynasty, and this vase has its form and glaze, as well as its style of decoration, all designed like a Ting-chou piece. The vase has underneath the mark *Shu fu*, 'imperial palace,' engraved in the paste under the glaze. Its form and size adapt it for ornamenting the middle of a small dinner-table, with a

FIG. 141.—Bowl of Yuan dynasty ware (Yuan Tz'ŭ), of reddish-gray body, with crackled purplish glaze, mottled with brown.

spray of narcissus, begonia, golden lily, or dwarf chrysanthemum put inside. It is now in my own library." H. 4 in.

We have but few authenticated pieces of the *Yuan* dynasty in modern collections, so that this specimen is of special interest, as belonging to a transition period, and connecting the molded and etched dishes of the *Sung* dynasty, which are often seen with rims bound round with copper collars, with the eggshell cups and bowls of the reign of *Yung-lo* at the beginning of the fifteenth century. The other kinds of porcelain, such as the celadons and the crackled wares, show similar transition characters; and the massive stoneware cups and bowls, known commonly as *Yuan* porcelain (*Yuan Tz'ŭ*), found throughout northern China, can hardly be distinguished from ceramic productions of the *Sung*. They are characterized by a thick glaze of unctuous aspect, finely crackled throughout, usually of pale lavender tint speckled with red, which often only partially covers the surface, so as to leave the lower part of the bowl bare. Another glaze is of a light sky-blue color, sparsely crackled or uncrackled, which often exhibits a ferruginous crimson stain at some point, of accidental origin, but much appreciated by Chinese collectors of the present day. The vase illustrated in Plate XII, 2, is a typical example of the period, with its finely crackled *clair-de-lune* glaze stained with a red ferruginous blotch.

One of the massive bowls (H. 3 in., D. 6½ in.) of the *Yuan* dynasty is shown in Fig. 141. It is composed of a reddish-gray ware of intense hardness, invested with a crackled glaze of pale purple tint, mottled with darker spots, and becoming brown at the edges, which runs down in a thick mass underneath, covering only two thirds of the surface, and ending in an irregularly undulating line. The smaller bowl (H. 1½ in., D. 4¼ in.), exhibited in Fig. 3 (*a*), is an example of the crackled ware of the period of hard, gray, dense texture, covered with a thick, lustrous glaze of ivory-white tone, minutely crackled with a reticulation of dark lines; the lower third and the foot underneath are left unglazed.

The Mongols conquered nearly the whole of Asia and a large part of eastern Europe; they sent fleets for the conquest of Japan as well as to Java; and Chinese junks sailed every year from the port of Ch'üan-chou to the Persian Gulf, carrying among other cargo, we are told, greenish-white or celadon porcelain. Many of the crackled vessels treasured by the natives of Borneo and other islands of the Pacific are to be referred, doubtless, to this time.

Some of these last-mentioned relics seem, however, to have come from the potteries of the province of Kuangtung, being made of a dark-brown stoneware covered with mottled glazes, often brilliantly colored. This is the Kuang Yao, which is still made and

FIG. 142.—Jar of archaic iron-gray stoneware, with crackled glaze of gray celadon; specimen of Kuang-Yao of the Yuan dynasty.

exported from Canton at the present day. Some of this ware was crackled, like the vase shown in Fig. 142, which is a specimen of Kuang Yao attributed to the *Yuan* dynasty.

FIG. 143.—Miniature Censer (two inches in height),
with a grayish-white crackled Ko Yao glaze.

CHAPTER VII.

MING DYNASTY.—REIGNS OF HUNG-WU, YUNG-LO, HSÜAN-TÊ, CH'ÊNG-HUA, HUNG-CHIH, CHÊNG-TÊ, CHIA-CHING, LUNG-CH'ING, WAN-LI, T'IEN-CH'I, CH'UNG-CHÊN.

THE *Ming* dynasty reigned in China from 1368 to 1643, when it was overthrown by the Manchus, who still occupy the throne at Peking. The emperors of the *Ming* dynasty patronized the ceramic art, and the manufacture of porcelain made considerable advances down to the reign of *Wan-li*, during which such large sums were lavished that the censors vigorously protested against the expenditure of so much money on mere articles of luxury. The manufacture became gradually concentrated at Ching-tê-chên, where the potters collected from all parts and established themselves round the imperial manufactory. From this time forward artistic work in porcelain became a monopoly of this place, and the productions of other potteries are noticed only by way of parenthesis, as they generally confined themselves to the fabrication of coarser ware for everyday consumption, while Ching-tê-chên produced the more decorative kinds, which were distributed from its kilns throughout China and sent from the most accessible seaports to all parts of the world.

The mass of native ceramic literature is now so great as to be rather embarrassing, and we will depend chiefly on the official annals of Fou-liang-hsien and on the *T'ao Shuo*, the author of which devotes his third book to a general account of the porcelain of the *Ming* dynasty, and his sixth book to a description of particular specimens of the ceramic art, arranged chronologically under the reigns to which they belong.

洪武, HUNG-WU (1368–98).

The founder of the dynasty established his capital at Nanking, and, according to the official records, in the second year of his reign (1369) the imperial manufactory was built at Ching-tê-chên, on the south side of the Jewel Hill, which was inclosed within the wall surrounding the manufactory, and formed its "protecting hill," according to Chinese geomantic science. Offices were also built on the eastern side for the Tao-t'ai of Chiu-chiang (Kiukiang), who was stationed here to superintend the fabrication of porcelain for the use of the palace, and to forward it annually to the capital.

永樂, YUNG-LO (1403–24).

Hung-wu was succeeded by his grandson, who was soon, however, deposed by his uncle, the powerful viceroy of the northern provinces, who declared himself emperor in 1403, under the title of *Yung-lo*, and made Peking, the famous Cambalu, or city of the Mongol khans, once more the capital of the Chinese Empire, as it remains to the present day. The *Yü Ch'i Ch'ang*, or "Imperial Porcelain Manufactory," at Ching-tê-chên, continued, as before, to furnish imperial ware for the use of the court, which was sent all the way to Peking by water, the boats traveling from the potteries down the Chang River to Jao-chou-fu, across the Poyang Lake, down the great river

Yangtsŭ to Chinkiang, and thence by the Grand Canal to Tientsin, and by the river Paiho to their final destination.

The imperial porcelain of this reign was distinguished for its white enamel, which is described as having been often pitted on the surface, or perforated by "palm-eye" spots. It was engraved with ornamental designs etched in the paste underneath, or decorated both in cobalt blue and in colors. It is generally ranked by native connoisseurs below that of the reigns of *Hsüan-tê* and *Ch'êng-hua*, but above that of *Chia-ching* and later reigns.

FIG. 144.—Superficially crackled copper-red glaze of varied tones of mottled hue, passing into pale green above, deepening below where superfluous drops have been removed by the wheel.

The blue and white variety is described in the *Po wu yao lan*, which says: "The cups (*pei*) of form adapted to be grasped by the hand, with an upright rim, a waist drawn in, and a glazed foot encircled by an unglazed ring, which were ornamented in the interior with a pair of lions playing with brocaded balls, and had inscribed inside, at the bottom, the seal mark, either in six characters, *Ta Ming Yung lo nien chih*, 'Made in the reign of *Yung-lo* of the great *Ming* dynasty,' or in four characters (the name of the dynasty being omitted) no larger than so many grains of rice. These were of the first class. The cups decorated with mandarin ducks in the interior were ranked next. Those with flowers in the interior came after the last. The cups were painted outside in blue of a deep brilliant color, in designs of artistic beauty. They have been handed down from distant times and their value is correspondingly high. The imitations of modern times are not worth looking at."

The white porcelain of this period, alluded to above, is still better known. It is often of eggshell thinness, and has supplied models for some of the most perfect productions of T'ang Ying in the eighteenth century. There is a fine large bowl in the Walters Collection (Fig. 70), the fellow of one thus described in the Franks *Catalogue* (*loc. cit.*, page 2): "BOWL. One of a pair. Thin ivory-white Chinese porcelain. Very small base and wide rim, in which are six indentations. Inside are two five-clawed dragons, very faintly engraved in the paste and glazed over. In the center an inscription, also engraved under the glaze, in an ancient seal character, being the mark of the period Yung-lo, 1404–1424. H. 2¾ in., D. 8½ in."

A small white cup of different form, with low upright sides springing from a circular rimmed foot, is illustrated in our album, and described as follows:

"*Cup* (*Pei*) of *Yung-lo* eggshell porcelain (*to-t'ai tz'ŭ*), with dragons and phœnixes engraved under the glaze. The form and design of these cups are very beautiful, and they can be used either for tea or for wine; they are very thin, not thicker than paper, and are for this reason called *to t'ai*, or 'bodiless.' This is a most delicate specimen of the kind, and it has dragons and phœnixes upon a scrolled ground very finely etched upon its surface. It is marked underneath with the six characters *Ta Ming Yung lo nien chih*, 'Made in the reign of *Yung-lo* of the great *Ming* dynasty,' cleverly engraved under the glaze. There are several of these cups preserved, although they are rare even in choice collections. I have figured this one in order to give a general idea of their character, so that collectors of taste may be able to recognize a genuine specimen and not grudge a liberal sum to acquire it. For my successors who may not be so fortunate as to find one even, the picture may be of some value. I copied it in Peking from a cup in the possession of a prince of the imperial blood." H. 1½ in., D. 3 in.

宣德, HSÜAN-TÊ (1426–35).

The reign of *Hsüan-tê* is celebrated for its ceramic productions as well as for its artistic work in bronze, and it is generally considered by Chinese authorities as sharing with that of

Ch'êng-hua a pre-eminent position among the reigns of the *Ming* dynasty; *Hsüan-tê* being un-rivaled in the brilliance of its painting in blue and in the purity of its red decoration; *Ch'êng-hua* in the artistic treatment of its combinations of different colors. The "five colors" in the decorated pieces of the *Hsüan-tê* period were laid on too thickly, so as to stand out in prominent relief when the piece had been fired, while those of *Ch'êng-hua* were applied with less lavish profusion, so that the result resembled a good painting in water-colors. The colored decoration in both reigns seems to have been effected by the use of glazes of different colors, laid upon a white unglazed or "biscuit" ground. The process of decoration of porcelain previously glazed and fired with enamel colors, which were afterward fixed in the muffle stove, was not discovered or introduced till much later in the *Ming* dynasty. This is specially known by the distinctive name of *Wan-li Wu ts'ai*, literally "five-colored [porcelain] of the *Wan-li* period."

The brilliancy of the blue which distinguished this reign is said to have been due to the importation from the West of a foreign product known as blue of *Su-ni-p'o*. In other books of the period it is called *Su-ma-li* or *Su-ma-ni* blue, which are evidently variations of the same name,

FIG. 145.—Altar Vase, modeled in the form of a Buddhist dâgaba, decorated with mythological subjects in early K'ang-hsi style; greens predominate among the enamel colors; no blue or gold.

but whether this be the name of the came, still remains to be proved. The the reign of *Ch'êng-hua*, which de-ores. Hsiang Yuan-p'ien, in his de-*Hui-hui Ch'ing*, "Mohammedan blue," thors of the time more especially to the of *Chia-ching* by the eunuch viceroy of

The yet more famous red glaze of It was applied in several ways—either porcelain, sometimes left plain, some-or in combination with the white glaze; a similar way to the cobalt blue, and glaze. The red designs are de-glaze so as to dazzle the eyes. it was prepared by powdering and amethystine quartz seems into the glaze to give it greater not, however, have been due amethysts would become col-the furnace; its application it must have been a copper

The white porcelain re-*Yung-lo*, which it even ex-The white "altar cups" of this *wu yao lan* as finely made, form, with the character *t'an*, inside; and the white "tea-ferior to the "altar cups," convexity in the middle under-like rim, brilliant and translu-inside with dragons and phœ-

color, or of the country from which it supply is reported to have failed before pended solely on native cobaltiferous scriptions, generally uses the term of which is applied by other ceramic au-cobalt blue imported in the later reign the province of Yunnan.

the period was derived from copper. as a monochrome glaze upon "biscuit" times chiseled with ornamental designs; or painted on in decorative designs, in subsequently covered with the white scribed as shining through the

Some Chinese writers assert that rubies obtained from the West, really to have been introduced transparency; the color could to this, because rubies and orless in the intense heat of under the glaze shows that silicate.

sembled that of the reign of celled in texture and finish. reign are described in the *Po* richly glazed, and of perfect "altar," inscribed in the bottom cups," *ch'a chan*, as hardly in-being of rounded form with a neath encircled by a thread-cent as fine jade, decorated nixes delicately chiseled, and

with the mark *Ta Ming Hsüan tê nien chih*, "Made in the reign of *Hsüan-tê* of the Great *Ming*," also etched under the white glaze, which exhibited a faintly tuberculated surface like the peel of an orange.

The same book describes stem cups decorated with red fish, and others painted in blue with dragonlike pines and flowering plum-trees, stemmed wine-cups painted in blue with historical scenes and sea monsters, bowls on high bamboo jointed feet, and teacups painted with illustrations of classical poetry. The large rice-bowls of monochrome vermilion are characterized as being red as the sun, with rims of white color—like the *sang-de-bœuf* bowls of more recent times. Flower vases (*hua tsun*) of low, beaker-shaped form with trumpet mouths; barrel-shaped garden seats (*tso tun*) of deep green ground, some with brocaded designs carved in openwork filled in with colors, others of solid form, overlaid with many-colored designs; barrel seats of dark blue overlaid with colored decoration like carved *lapis lazuli,* as it were, inlaid with flowers, others painted with blue flowers in a white ground, and others crackled like fissured ice—all those are comprised in this book and described as novelties unknown in former times. Flat jars (*pien kuan*) and cylindrical jars (*t'ung kuan*) for honey preserves, oil-lamps of varied forms, receptacles for birds' food (*chiao shih p'ing*) to hold seed and water, and bowls for fighting crickets (*hsi hsuai p'ên*) occur in the same list. The bowls of pure white "biscuit" ornamented with designs in worked gold are alluded to in the poetry of the time as of exceeding beauty. There were two families named Lu and Tsou, at Su-chou-fu, famed for their cricket bowls, which were elaborately finished with delicately chiseled and embossed work, and the names of Ta Hsiu and Hsiao Hsiu, elder and younger daughters of the craftsman Tsou, have been handed down as having executed the finest work of all. The game of fighting crickets was then a favorite pastime; thousands were staked on the event, and no expense was spared on the decoration of the materials.

FIG. 146.—Beaker-shaped Vase, imperial yellow monochrome of the Ch'ien-lung period.

These barrel-shaped seats are still to be seen occasionally in Chinese gardens side by side with seats of similar form from the earlier Chün-chou potteries of the *Sung* dynasty. Such large pieces are usually of stoneware rather than porcelain, the technique resembling that of the image of Kuan-yin, enshrined in the Buddhist Temple Pao-kuo-ssŭ at Peking, which has already been described. I have seen other Buddhist figures of antique design with the details filled in with colored glaze of the early *Ming* period, notably in the Dana collection at New York, together with some of the large, wide, solid jars of the time, with Taoist figures inclosed in the carved openwork casing, picked out in turquoise, purple, green, and yellow. The colors differ from the ordinary colored enamels of later times in being composed of a lead flux.

To M. du Sartel is due the credit of first calling attention to these jars and of referring them correctly to early *Ming* times. He figures three in Plate II of his work *La Porcelaine de Chine,* already cited, with the following description (page 155):

"No. 2. Jarre à mettre le vin, en porcelaine grise et épaisse. Le décor, de style archaïque, coloré en émaux de demi-grand feu sur biscuit, se compose de bordures à faux godrons, celle du haut soutenant des lambrequins ornés de fleurs et reliés entre eux par des cordons de perles avec pendeloques. Le corps du vase est occupé par un paysage courant, présentant sur deux faces opposées un personnage symbolique. Ce décor, dessiné par des filets en relief, est en partie resté en biscuit avec quelques teintes jaunâtres et en partie bleu turquoise, sur fond bleu foncé. Hauteur 0ᵐ 42. Coll. O du Sartel.

"No. 3. Potiche analogue au vase précédent, décorée de nélumbos en fleur. Hauteur 0ᵐ 35. Coll. Léon Fould, à Paris.

"No. 4. Autre potiche de même espèce, mais dont le décor, sur fond bleu turquoise, présente quelques parties émaillées violet clair. La panse est occupée par un paysage courant, avec sujet hiératique montrant Chéou Lao entouré des emblêmes de la longévité, et recevant la visite mystérieuse des saints personnages, ses disciples, les Pa-Chen. Hauteur 0ᵐ 35. Coll. O. du S."

Our album is rich in specimens of this reign, and a description of these will give a better idea of the ceramic art of the time than any number of quotations from Chinese books which might be extended indefinitely. There are no less than twenty illustrations given, including seven of blue and white pieces, and thirteen decorated in colored glazes, among which the red predominates, two of these being wholly invested with red as a monochrome glaze.

"*Antique Censer* (*Yi Lu*), with fish handles, decorated with deep red, in the guise of ruddy dawn clouds disappearing in bright sunshine. The form of this censer is modeled after an ancient bronze sacrificial vessel figured in a collection published in the period *Shao-hsing*, 1131–62. The upper two-thirds of the surface is enameled with a deep red glaze of the warmest tint of ruddy dawn clouds; the lower part is white, pure as driven snow, and the red and white melt into each other in wavy lines, dazzling the eyes. It stands pre-eminent among the celebrated' porcelains of different dynasties; the whole surface is strewn with faint, milletlike tubercles, and it is truly a precious jewel of rare value. I saw it at Nanking, in the collection of Chu Hsi-hsiao, the governor of the city, who told me that it originally came from the imperial palace, given to one of the princes as part of his monthly allowance, and that he purchased it afterward from the prince for three hundred taels of silver. Even for a thousand taels it could not be bought now." H. 3 in., D. 3½ in.

"*Water-Dropper* (*Shui Chu*), for the ink pallet, decorated with colored glazes. Taken from an old bronze design, the vessel is molded in the form of twin persimmons (*Disospyros shitze* fruit) hanging upon a leafy branch, the stem of which is hollowed to make the spout. The color of the fruit is as red as fresh blood, with slightly raised millet marks; the leaves are green; the sepals and stalk are brown; exactly like a picture from Nature, by the artist Hsü Tsung-ssǔ. It is a rare jewel for the ornament of a scholar's library, which I bought, with two ink pallets of porcelain, also figured, from Hsü, a high official of Wu-mên." H. 2½ in., D. 3½ in.

"*Wine-Pot* (*Chiu Hu*), with an open scrolled handle and a spout molded in the shape of a phœnix head, covered with a monochrome glaze of deep red color. It was copied from a carved jade wine-pot used by the emperor. The body, of slender, vaselike form, swelling above and curving gracefully inward toward the foot, is chiseled with cloud scrolls and ornamental bands of geometrical and spiral pattern; it is surmounted by a conical cover encircled by rings of foliated design. The spout is the feathered neck of a phœnix, projecting as it were from the cloudy background, and terminating in a crested head with open beak. Among the different kinds of porcelain of the reign of *Hsüan-tê* the deep red was the most highly valued of all. In the preparation of the glaze, red precious stones from the West were pulverized, and after it had been fired, flashes of ruby-red color shone out from the depths of the rich glaze so as to dazzle the eyes. There is no other porcelain to rival this. The piece figured is in the collection of Huang, General of the Guards at Peking, who told me that he bought it for two hundred ingots of silver in paper notes [nominally about six hundred pounds sterling, although the Government paper currency was then at a considerable discount], from one of the chief eunuchs of the palace." H. 6½ in.

FIG. 147.—Yung-chêng White Vase, with a dragon upon it in undercut relief, painted in soft cobalt blue of mottled tint.

"*Rouge-Pot* (*Lu Hu*) molded in the shape and size of a persimmon fruit (*Diospyros shitze*) and decorated with colored glazes. The lobed fruit, of deep red color, has a short, wide spout of the same tint projecting at one end, a branch joining the handle at the other, colored brown, with a green twig winding round in openwork relief so as to display the green leaves worked upon the red skin of the fruit. The cover is the calyx of four segments, with the stalk curving upward to form its handle. The red is of rich color, like fresh blood; the brown and green are true to life. It came out of the palace, where it had been used by one of the imperial princesses to hold vermilion for painting her lips and face. It was priced very high, over one hundred taels, by a curio seller at the temple Pao-kuo-ssŭ,* at whose stall I saw it when at the capital." H. 2½ in., D. 3¼ in.

"*Tazza-shaped Cup* (*Pa Pei*), decorated with three red fishes on a white ground. The form is taken from wine-cups of jade of the *Han* dynasty. The glaze, of the aspect of congealed fat, is white as driven snow, and the three fishes of deep red color, vigorously outlined, are crimson as fresh blood with flashes of ruby tint of dazzling brilliance. It is truly a rare gem of this highly prized class. At the foot of the cylindrical stem, which expands toward the base, there is faintly engraved under the paste the six-character mark *Ta Ming Hsüan tê nien chih*, 'Made in the reign of *Hsüan-tê* of the Great *Ming*.' I bought this cup for twenty-four taels from a collector at Shao-hsing-fu." H. 3 in., D. 3 in.

FIG. 148.—Wine Pot of rustic form enameled *sur biscuit*, with crackled glaze of turquoise and aubergine tints combined with touches of apple-green; cover immovable, the wine being poured in through a hole in the bottom.

"*Tazza-shaped Cup* (*Pa Pei*), of the same shape and size as the above, decorated with three pairs of red peaches on a white ground. The shaded red, of the tint of red cherries or of precious garnets, flames out from the depth of the glaze, very different from the modern imitations of these wine-cups, which are made by painting the red color over the glaze, and which remind one only of dull, ferruginous clay.† These cups are very rare, only three or four being known to exist within the four seas."

"*Conical Wine-Cup* (*Tou Li Pei*), with a handle boldly fashioned in openwork relief in the form of an archaic dragon (*ch'ih-lung*), decorated in colors. The ground inside and out is engraved with cloud scrolls under the white glaze; the band of scrolled ornament which encircles the rim is picked out in blue, while the dragon, which is coiled half round the cup, with its teeth and fore-claws fixed in the rim and its bifid tail opposite, is glazed deep red. The dragon stands out conspicuously in blood-red relief from the mutton-fat tinted ground; only one or two of these beautiful little cups are known, and a hundred taels is not considered too much to pay for a specimen. I figure this one from the collection of the Lieutenant-Governor of Nanking." H. 2 in., D. 3 in.

"*Small Wine-Cup* (*Hsiao Chan*), of rounded shallow form with circularly rimmed foot, decorated outside with three fishes of deep red color on a snow-white ground. The fish are no bigger than flies, yet the several scales and spines are chiseled under the *sang-de-bœuf* glaze. It holds one *hu*—i. e., less than two ounces." H. ¾ in., D. 3 in.

FIG. 149.—Globular Bowl of lavender crackle, with European mounts.

"*Palace Rice-Bowl* (*Kung Wan*), of gracefully modelled shape, springing from a small circularly rimmed foot, decorated outside with three fishes of *sang-de-bœuf* color upon a snow-white ground, rising in milletlike granules. It is figured from the collection of Liang, one of the chief eunuchs at Peking, who obtained it himself from the palace of the emperor." H. 2½ in., D. 7 in.

"*Dish* (*Hsi*), for washing brushes in, of circular form with a flat bottom and upright sides, decorated with red fishes swimming in undulating waves, penciled in deep red on a snow-white ground. One pair of fishes, instinct with life and movement, is painted on the bottom of the dish inside, and three smaller fishes are swimming round outside." H. 1 in., D. 5. in.

"*Palace Dish* (*Kung Tieh*), saucer-shaped, springing from a circular foot, covered outside

---

* This is the Buddhist temple already alluded to as containing the ancient porcelain image of Kwan Yin. It is situated in the southern or Chinese city of Peking, and is one of those thrown open at stated days every month for a kind of fair, when its courts are thronged with peddlers and curio dealers, who spread their stalls on both sides of the way to attract visitors.

† We know from other sources that the art of painting porcelain in the red prepared from copper silicate failed toward the end of the *Ming* dynasty, so that in the reign of *Chia-ching* (1522–66) even the imperial potters petitioned to be allowed to decorate it instead with the iron-red produced by the incineration of iron sulphate.

with a monochrome glaze of deep red color, over five-clawed dragons, and clouds delicately chiseled in the paste. Marked underneath with the six-character seal *Ta Ming Hsüan tê nien chih*, 'Made in the reign of *Hsüan-tê* of the Great *Ming*,' engraved under the glaze." D. 7 in.

"*Perforated Box (Ch'uan Hsin Ho)*, painted in deep red on a white ground. A small round box, with a lid of the same shape, fashioned in the likeness of a 'cash' of the period, having a square hole passing through the middle for tying it on the corner of a handkerchief, when used as a casket for scent. It is decorated outside with encircling bands of spiral fret, and has the inscription on the cover, written also in red, *Hsüan tê t'ung pao*, 'Current money of *Hsüan-tê*,' a reproduction of the ordinary legend of the coins of this reign." H. ½ in., D. 1 in.

"*Relic Pagoda (Shê-li T'a)*, of white "biscuit" porcelain decorated in colors (*wu ts'ai*). This is a relic shrine in the form of a pagoda, one foot and a half high, of seven stories. Each story is six-sided, surrounded by a carved open-work railing, and hollow inside. In the first story there is an altar with a little vase of white jade standing upon it containing three grains of sacred relics (*shê-li* = Sanskrit *śarîra*) of Buddha. The seven stories are all hung around the eaves with tiny gold bells only half an inch long. Within the chamber of the fifth story there is a little sacred image of Buddha, of jade, about eight-tenths of an inch high, with fine features and venerable figure, seated upon a lotus throne, exactly like the large Buddha enthroned for worship in ordinary religious temples. This image of Buddha, the temple bonze assures me, was brought as tribute to China from a foreign country. The body of the pagoda shows the intrinsic color of the porcelain, and the different colors are cleverly painted on in turns, the tiles emerald-green, the railings red, the walls white, and the windows yellow. The relics emit every day at noon and midnight a radiance of colored light. I myself saw the rays emitted on both occasions, and was convinced thereby of the deep mysteries of the doctrine of Buddha. The stand is inscribed with the mark written in blue in a horizontal line, *Ta Ming Hsüan tê nien chih*, 'Made in the reign of *Hsüan-tê* of the Great *Ming*.' I saw this shrine at Nanking at Pao-ên-ssŭ (the famous Porcelain Pagoda Temple destroyed by the Taiping rebels) in the house of the prior of the monastery, who told me that it had been sent from the palace at Peking in the reign of the Emperor *Lung-ch'ing*, by special order of the empress-dowager, who bestowed it upon the temple, to be preserved and reverently worshiped there."

Fig. 150.—Vase, decorated in coral-red, with green and gold of the K'ang-hsi period.

The remaining seven pieces of this reign illustrated in the album are painted in blue on a white ground. The decoration is minutely finished, with borders of fret and encircling bands of rectangular and spiral chains, executed with fine strokes of the brush, so as to remind one of the delicate finish of the chiseled bronze and carved cinnabar-lac work of the period.

Fig. 151.—A Water Receptacle for the writing-table, of white porcelain touched with colors and gilding.

"*Ink Pallet (Yen)*, of oval form, with dragons and clouds etched round the sides, painted in blue, with a band of triangular fret round the upper border, and a double oval ring underneath. The form, an oval slab, with a crescentic depression at one end, is copied from a jade pallet used by one of the emperors of the *Sung* dynasty. The color of the glaze is white as driven snow, rising into faint milletlike elevations; the blue, penciled in finest strokes, is brilliant and deep as congealed ink, so that it is really a beautiful specimen. There are two five-clawed imperial dragons delicately chiseled in the paste under the glaze, surrounded by cloud scrolls into which they are plunging their heads. The mark written underneath in blue, in a vertical line, in the middle of the oval ring, is *Ta Ming Hsüan tê nien chih*, 'Made in the reign of *Hsüan-tê* of the Great *Ming*.'" L. 3½ in.

"*Small Vase* (*Hsiao P'ing*), in the shape of a three-jointed cylinder of bamboo, with the joints and margins picked out in blue, and the extremities ornamented with lines of little rings painted in blue. The blue is the 'Mohammedan *gros bleu*,' the *Hui-hui ta ch'ing* of the period, brilliant and dazzling to the eyes. The upper ring of circles is interrupted by a line of six characters, not much larger than mosquito claws, but perfectly clear, written in blue, *Ta Ming Hsüan tê nien chih*, the mark of the reign. I have had this piece in my possession since I was a boy; it has been in my cabinet over fifty years, and is growing old with me." H. 2½ in.

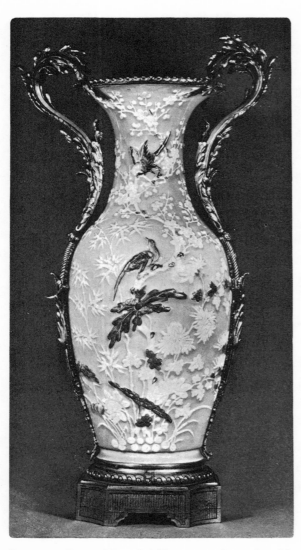

FIG. 152.—Large K'ang-hsi Vase, one of a pair, with relief decoration in white slip or touched with blue, upon a celadon background; European mounts.

"*Jar* (*Hu*), modeled in the form of a goose, and painted in blue. The goose is always referred to in the classics as a domestic bird of watchful nature, a terror to robbers, and the form was originally chosen for a wine-vessel as a warning against nightly intoxication. The feathers and other natural details are outlined in blue of brilliant color; the glaze is sprinkled with milletlike elevations, and it is altogether a fine specimen of the reign of *Hsüan-tê*. It holds about one pint of wine." L. 6 in.

"*Elephant Jar* (*Hsiang Tsun*), painted in blue, of rounded ovoid form with bulging body, springing from a low foot, with a receding shoulder and a slightly flaring mouth, surmounted by a round cover. The cover has standing upon it the figure of an elephant, molded in full open-work relief, of plain white. The two ring handles upon the shoulder of the jar hanging from grotesque heads are outlined in blue, and the jar, as well as the cover, is surrounded by several plain bands of blue. It is of ancient bronze design, and holds nearly two pints." H. 6½ in.

"*Teacup* (*Ch'a Pei*), decorated in blue with a dragon pine. Of upright form, rounded below, and slightly hollowed at the sides, it is modeled, probably, in the form of a jade wine-cup of the *Han* dynasty. The glaze is as translucently white as mutton fat or fine jade, rising in millet tubercles, and the blue is deep and clear, painted in the Mohammedan *gros bleu* of the time. The fir-tree is designed with a gnarled trunk like a huge coiled dragon, and lifelike orchids and fungus spring naturally from the ground beneath, evidently drawn by the pencil of a celebrated landscape-painter. I bought a set of four of these tea-cups from a high official at Wu-hsing." Diam. 2½ in.

"*Sacrificial Vessel* (*Yi*), painted in blue on a white ground, of ancient bronze design, with an oval body, having a broad lip at one end, supported upon four straight cylindrical feet, and a prominent cover with a horned dragon's head molded in relief projecting over the lip. The ground is whiter than snow, the blue of deep tint is painted in the first-class Mohammedan color, and both blue and white are marked alike with milletlike elevations. Decorated with blue bands of rectangular and spiral fret round the neck of the vessel, and with blue lines outlining the rim and relief details of the cover. An important specimen of the reign of *Hsüan-tê*, which I got from a collector of Wu-mên, in exchange for two manuscript volumes of verse written by a calligraphist of the *Yuan* dynasty." H. 5 in.

"*Four-burner Lamp* (*Ssŭ T'ai Têng*), with blue decoration on a white ground. A lamp of complex form, with an oval receptacle, which has four curved spouts projecting from it, one on each side, to hold the wicks, springing from a rimmed foot, and surmounted by a conical cover of four-lobed outline. A flat dish with an upright rim stands underneath. The shoulder is looped for chains to suspend the lamp to a horizontal bar, which is also looped in the middle to support the cover, and perforated for a cord to hang the whole apparatus from the ceiling. It is painted in brilliant blue with encircling bands and chains of spiral fret, and with medallions and foliations of formal pattern. On the foot is inscribed in blue, in a horizontal line, the mark *Ta Ming Hsüan tê nien chih*, 'Made in the reign of *Hsüan-tê* of the Great *Ming.*'" H. 5 in., D. 4½ in.

There are thirteen specimens of this reign in the Shu Ch'ing Yuan palace at Peking, according to the official list quoted above, of which seven are painted in blue on a white ground, viz.:

1. Receptacle for Flowers, *Hua Nang*, in the form of a square corn-measure with a bar-handle stretching across the top.

2. Ink-Jar, *Mo Kuan*.

3. Double Cylinder Vase, *Shuang Kuan P'ing*.

4. Vase with swelling shoulder and small neck, used for a spray of plum-blossom, and hence called *Mei P'ing*.

5. Pair of upright Teacups, *Ch'a Chung*.

6. Water-Pot, *Shui Ch'êng*, for the writing-table.

7. Rice-Bowl, *Wan*. The next is a large round Dish, *P'an*, of monochrome, copper-red, *Chi hung*, followed by a Plum-blossom Vase, *Mei P'ing*, with painted decoration in red on a white ground, the remaining four being round fluted Dishes, *P'an*, of rose-mallow design, enameled celadon (*tung-ch'ing*).

成化, CH'ÊNG-HUA (1465–87).

There is an interval of thirty years between the close of the last reign and the beginning of that styled *Ch'êng-hua*. The emperor who reigned under the title of *Hsüan-tê* was succeeded by his son, who reigned under the title of *Chêng-t'ung* from 1436 to 1449, when he was captured by the Mongols and kept prisoner in Mongolia for seven years, during which his brother ruled with the title of *Ching-t'ai* from 1450 to 1456. The emperor returned then to the throne and reigned till his death, under the new title of *T'ien-shun*, the only instance of a change of *nien-hao* during the *Ming* dynasty; his reign lasted till 1464, when he died, and was succeeded by his son, who reigned as *Ch'êng-hua*, from 1465 to 1487. In the reign of *Hsüan-tê* the imperial porcelain manufactory at Ching-tê-chên had been placed under the charge of a director specially appointed by the emperor to superintend the work. In the first year of *Chêng-t'ung* this appointment was abolished, as we learn from the official annals, which state that so many of the people were enlisted for military service that the imperial works had to be closed. In the fifth year of *Ching-t'ai* (1454) it is recorded in the *Yü-chang Ta shih chi*, another descriptive work on the province of Kiangsi, of which Yü-chang is an ancient name, that the annual amount of porcelain requisitioned from Jao-chou-fu was reduced to one third,

FIG. 153.—Jar, painted in dark blue of brilliant tone, with the "Eight Taoist Immortals" crossing the sea; mark of the Wan-li period underneath.

so that, in addition to the abolition of the office of director, the supply since drawn from private sources was also diminished. In the following twenty years there is no official mention of porcelain, excepting the fact that in the year *ting-ch'ou* of the cycle (1457) when the emperor recovered the throne, a eunuch was again sent from the palace to Ching-tê-chên as director, and the imperial manufactory was re-established as before, although we know nothing whatever of the ceramic production of this reign.

The porcelain of *Ch'êng-hua*, on the contrary, is constantly referred to, and it disputes with that of *Hsüan-tê* the supremacy of the *Ming* period, according to the opinion of different connoisseurs. The general verdict upon their relative merit is that *Hsüan-tê* stands first in the brilliancy of its red derived from copper, and in the purity and depth of its blue imported from abroad, while it is excelled by *Ch'êng-hua* in artistic decoration in colors. The exotic supply of blue had failed before this reign, and only native ores of cobalt were available.

FIG. 154.—Vase, painted in enamel colors relieved by a black ground, with a mouth-piece proceeding from the shoulder, mounted with metal as part of a *narghili*.

The author of the *Po wu yao lan* says: "In the highest class porcelain of the reign of *Ch'êng-hua* there is nothing to excel the stemmed wine-cups with shallow bowls and swelling rims decorated in five colors with grapes; these are more beautiful even than any of the cups of *Hsüan-tê*. Next to these come the wedding-cups decorated in colors with flowers and insects, or with a hen and chicken, the wine-cups of the shape of a lotus-nut painted with figure scenes, the shallow cups decorated with the five sacrificial utensils, the tiny cups with flowering plants and butterflies, and the blue and white wine-cups that are as thin as paper. There are also small saucer-shaped plates for chopsticks painted in colors, round boxes for incense, and little jars of varied shapes fitted with covers, all of artistic beauty and worthy of admiration." *

With reference to the celebrated "Chicken Cups" *Chi Kang*, there is an ode composed upon them in the works of Kao T'an-jên, a writer of the seventeenth century, also known as Kao of Chiang-ts'un, with the following note attached †: "The wine-cups of *Ch'êng-hua* porcelain are of many different kinds, all artistically designed and perfectly finished, with the colors laid on in dark and light shades, the fabric strong and of translucent texture. The 'chicken cups' are decorated with Moutan peonies and with a hen and chicken under the flowers, instinct with life and movement." ‡ Among other decorative subjects painted upon these wine-cups given by the same writer is a beautiful damsel holding up a candle to look at *hai-t'ang* (cydonia) flowers, called "Rosy beauty lit up by a flaring silver flame". Then there are "Brocaded Cups," with medallions of flower sprays and fruit painted on the four sides; "Swing Cups," with a party of young girls swinging; the "Dragon-Boat Cups," with boats racing in the great dragon festival; "Famous-Scholar Cups," which have Chou Mao-shou on one side admiring his beloved lotus, and T'ao Yuan-ming on the other with his favorite chrysanthemum flowers beside him; "Wa-wa Cups," with five little boys playing together; and "Grape-Trellis Cups," with a grapevine growing

FIG. 155.—Celadon Vase, molded in relief with the outlines of two fishes; European mounts.

upon a frame. Others are decorated with fragrant flowers, with fish and water-weeds, with gourds and aubergine fruit, with the eight Buddhist emblems of good fortune, with the flowers of the utpala, a dark variety of lotus, and with conventional sprays of the sacred lotus of

---

* The official list of the art objects in the Shu Ch'ing Yuan palace at Peking, referred to above, includes four little saucer-shaped plates, *hsiao tieh*, of this reign, decorated in colors, inclosed in a rosewood box, and a perfume sprinkler, *chiao*, also painted in "five colors."

† M. Julien, in his preface (*loc. cit.*, p. xxx), translates this note from the *T'ao Shuo*, but strangely misconceives the heading, as he translates Ch'êng, the contracted form of *Ch'êng-hua*, into "fabriquait," and transforms ko-chu, "ode-note," into a proper name. Thus he provides two names for this reign in his list of celebrated potters. Here is what he says: "Dans la periode *Tch'ing-hoa*, figure avec honneur, un artiste que le Traité sur la porcelaine [*T'ao-choue*] appele Kao-than-jin. Il fabriquait des jarres ornées de poules. Un autre ouvrier, nommé Ko-tchou, faisait de jolies tasses pour le vin." Many of the "marks" in Julien's work are of a like fictitious origin, so that the book, useful as it is, must be used with caution.

‡ We have seen in the chapter on Marks how these "chicken cups" were copied in the reign of *Ch'ien-lung*, who sent one of the originals from the palace as a model, together with a poem of his own composition, to be inscribed on the reverse side of the cup. These copies are now valued by the Chinese connoisseurs at many times their weight in gold.

India, etc. All of these cups are described as artistically painted, translucent in color, and of strong texture.

The price of these little cups was already very high even before the end of the *Ming* dynasty. The Emperor *Wan-li* is said to have always had a pair of them placed on his dinner-table which were valued at 100,000 cash, equivalent to 100 taels of silver. The *P'u shu t'ing chi*, "Memoirs of the Book-Sunning Pavilion," written by Chu Yi-tsun in the beginning of the present dynasty, relates how the author "on the days of new moon and full moon often went, while staying at Peking, to the fair at the Buddhist temple Tz'ŭ-ên-ssŭ, where rich men thronged to look at the old porcelain bowls exhibited on the stalls there. Plain white cups of *Wan-li* porcelain were several taels of silver each, those with the mark of *Hsüan-tê* or of *Ch'êng-hua* ranged from twice as much and more, up to the chicken cups, which could not be bought for less than five twenty-tael ingots of pure silver, yet those who had the money did not grudge it, estimating the pottery of this period as more valuable than the finest jade."

The eleven specimens figured in our album to illustrate the porcelain of this reign are all decorated in colors, neither the blue and white nor the monochrome "copper red" of the period being represented.

FIG. 156.—Tall Vase, elaborately decorated in the *famille verte* style of the K'ang-hsi period.

"*Melon-shaped Wine-Pot* (*T'ien-Kua Hu*), decorated in colors. The body, of oval form and indented outline, molded in the natural form of the lobed fruit, is colored yellow, and passes above into a rounded cover, the handle of which, colored brown and green, is designed as the stalk of the fruit. The spout and handle of the wine-pot are formed of convoluted branches, with the chiseled details colored brown, round which tendrils wind in open-work relief, and from which spread leafy twigs, to decorate the surface of the wine-pot with leaves, tendrils, and miniature gourds, contrasting in their tones of shaded green with the surrounding bright yellow ground. In the porcelain of the reign of *Ch'êng-hua*, that painted in different colors is the most highly valued, because at this time the designs were executed in the palace by the most celebrated artists, and the colors were laid on in their different shades with finished skill. This wine-pot, of the natural size of a melon, with the skin and branchlets of the color of the original, and the two surfaces of the leaves appropriately shaded, is a conspicuous example. It holds nearly 1½ pints of wine." H. 5 in., D. 3 in.

"*Wine-Cup* (*Chiu Pei*), fashioned in the form of a purple *yulan* flower (*Magnolia conspicua*). The bowl, with indented rim, is formed of the petals of a bursting blossom, enameled in bright colors, white inside, purple outside, springing from the green calyx; the foot, carved in open-work relief, is a branching twig, enameled brown, ending in small leaves of shaded green." H. 2 in., D. 2½ in.

"*Tazza-shaped Wine-Cup* (*Pa Pei*), decorated in colors with grapes. Of delicate form and fabric, with a round shallow bowl slightly everted at the lip, mounted upon a high cylindrical stem spreading at the base. The bowl is encircled outside with a festoon of grapes with trailing tendrils, painted in colors upon a white ground of slightly grayish tone. The leaves are bright emerald-green; the grapes hang down like bunches of purple amethysts, drawn with the utmost delicacy. The glaze rises into faint milletlike elevations, and the decoration is in perfect taste and antique coloring, making this a choice specimen of the rare productions of a famous reign, and it is of correspondingly high value. It is figured from the collection of Wang Sun-chi of Chin-sha, who says that he purchased it for sixty taels from the sub-prefect of Hsüan-ch'êng.

It is marked underneath in blue with the inscription, written in a horizontal line, *Ta Ming Ch'êng hua nien chih*, 'Made in the reign of *Ch'êng-hua* of the great *Ming*.'" H. 2½ in., D. 2½ in.

"*Two Small Wine-Cups* (*Hsiao Pei*), decorated in colors with flowers and insects. Of rounded form, with slightly swelling lips, and low, circular feet, they are so thin and delicate that each cup weighs less than one-third of an ounce. They are decorated outside with miniature garden scenes, with the cockscomb, narcissus, aster, and grass sprouting from the green, dotted ground, the flowers, minute as flies' heads or mosquitoes' claws, filled in with crimson, green, and yellow, and with flying dragon-flies and crawling mantis insects as minutely finished after life. The amount of work lavished upon each little cup is surprising, and they are choice specimens of the art work of this celebrated reign, which are well worth one hundred taels a pair. Now, indeed, it is far easier to get the money than to find such cups. I saw them at Peking at the house of Huang, General of the Imperial Guards." H. 1½ in., D. 2 in.

FIG. 157.—Vase, of dark brown (tzŭ-chin) monochrome ground, with reserve medallions painted in blue; mark, a palm-leaf; bronze cover of Persian work.

"*Two Wine-Cups* (*Kang Pei*), decorated in colors, one with a pair of geese swimming, the other with fighting-cocks in a garden. The cups, which are extremely thin and delicate, with flat bottoms and slightly swelling sides, are modeled in the shape of the large porcelain bowls used for goldfish, from which they take their name of *kang*. The ground is a pure white, on a material as translucent as the diaphanous wing of a cicada, and they are most minutely painted in colors after Nature. The geese are playing in the waves with wings erect, and water-plants occupy the intervals. The cocks are standing on each side of a tall crimson cockscomb sprouting from a brown, grassy rockery, and small, yellow butterflies are flying in the air above. These two little cups, which are very rare and precious, have been in our family for many years." H. 1½ in., D. 2 in.

"*Miniature Cup* (*Hsiao Pei*), molded in the form of a chrysanthemum-flower, painted in colors. The bowl, white inside, has two concentric rings of petals outside, colored yellow, which make the rim dentated; the handle is the projecting brown stalk of the flower, carved in open-work with a green leaf attached, and another shaded green leaf in the opposite side of the cup makes its lip." D. 1½ in.

"*Miniature Cup* (*Hsiao Pei*), fashioned in the shape of a knotted tree-stump, painted in colors. The surface of irregularly knotted outline, terminating above in a convoluted rim, is colored brown, the interior being white; a loop projects at one end, strung with a ring, which forms the handle of the cup. This cup, like the chrysanthemum cup described above, holds only a single sip of wine; both are in the possession of my respected friend, Chang Yuan-lung." H. 1 in., D. 2 in.

FIG. 158.—Triple Gourd Vase, one of a pair, of turquoise crackle of deep tone, becoming almost black in the depths of the grooves; European mounts.

"*Rouge-Box* (*Yen-chih Ho*), painted in colors. A small circular box, with a cover of the same form, decorated with spiral scrolls in green, contrasting charmingly with the bright yellow ground. It came out of the imperial palace, where it had been used by one of the ladies of the court to hold cosmetics for the lips and cheeks. The decoration is artistic and clearly defined, and it might be used as a casket for incense, for ground tea, for betel-nuts, or for prepared perfumes. It has been for a long time past in my own cabinet." H. ¾ in., D. 1 in.

"*Lotus-Flower Lamp* (*Lien-Hua Têng*), of elaborate form, decorated in colors. The design is that of a lotus plant, the green, cup-shaped center of the flower forming the receptacle for the oil, being mounted upon its stalk in the midst of the peltate leaves. Another broad folded leaf with a convoluted margin is spread out as a support at the base, and from the top of this spring two other leaves, the larger one, elevated upon a long curved stem to overhang the lamp, being balanced by a small leaf on the other side of the floral receptacle. The leaves are shaded in green tints with the veining indicated on the two surfaces; the petals of the lotus are painted pale pink, darkening at the tips. This lamp, of an antique style far excelling the rough work of the present day, is in the possession of Chu Tz'ŭ-pu, a physician living at Wu-sung." H. 7 in.

宏治, HUNG–CHIH (1488–1505).

The emperor *Ch'êng-hua* was succeeded by his son, who reigned for eighteen years under the title of *Hung-chih.*

This reign is distinguished especially for its monochrome glaze of yellow color, which is of two shades, the one compared by the Chinese with the tint of a boiled chestnut, the other with the soft yellow of a freshly opened hibiscus-flower. Bowls and saucer-shaped dishes of this pale yellow color, with the mark of *Hung-chih* underneath, are not uncommon. There is a bowl of thin fabric, 7¼ inches in diameter, covered inside and out with a pale yellow glaze, with a mark of this period, No. 39 of the Franks *Collection*, and the only specimen of this *nien-hao* in Jacquemart's List is a "soucoupe émaillée jaune jonquille" (*loc. cit.*, p. 174).

Three pieces of monochrome yellow are figured in our album, together with one other specimen of the reign, a wine-pot decorated in green and brown on a similar yellow ground, a rare example, which, as the artist suggests, could hardly be distinguished from a production of the preceding reign of the *Ch'êng-hua* period.

"*Small Incense-Burner (Hsiao Ting)*, modeled in the shape of one of the sacrificial vessels used in ancient times for offering corn on the altar, made of ancient bronze. The body of oblong form, with rounded corners, is horizontally ribbed, and decorated with a band of interrupted fret engraved round the rim; it is molded on four legs swelling at the top, and has two upright loop handles. The cover, of vaulted form, with triangular projections upon the four corners, is chiseled with a border of similar fret. It is enameled with a yellow glaze of the color of a boiled chestnut. The form, known by the name of 'oak basket,' is of antique artistic beauty, and specially suitable for burning incense upon the altar. I obtained it at Wu-mên from the cell of the bonze Hu-ch'iu." H. 2 in., D. 3 in.

"*Gourd-shaped Wine-Pot (Hu-lu Hu)*, of pale yellow ground, decorated in colors. The porcelain of the reign of *Hung-chih* is celebrated for its pale yellow, but it also included some pieces decorated in colors, fit to be compared with those of the *Ch'êng-hua* period, like

FIG. 159.—Large Celadon Vase of the Ming period, with fluted base and bands of floral decoration, worked in relief under the glaze.

this beautiful wine-pot. It is modeled in the shape of a slender gourd with a contracted waist, the brown stalk of the gourd curving upward as the handle of the small round cover; a branch winds downward to form an open convoluted handle for the wine-pot, round which wind tendrils in open-work relief, and from which spring branchlets and tendrils to ornament the surface with smaller gourds, green leaves, and tendrils, all worked in relief and shaded in green to contrast with the yellow ground; a small hollow gourd of the same form and yellow tint projects upward as the spout of the ewer. It holds over a pint of wine. I acquired it from my fellow-citizen, Chu, a doctor of literature." H. 5 in.

"*Teacup* (*Ch'a Pei*), one of a pair, molded in the shape of a hibiscus-blossom. The bowl of graceful floral form, with flaring indented rim and vertically ribbed sides, springing from a circular foot; it is white inside, and enameled outside with a glaze of a delicate yellow tint resembling that of the petals of the bursting hibiscus flower. I have seen many specimens of *Hung-chih* porcelain, but nothing to surpass these two little cups in beauty of form and color. I got them from a friend in exchange for a copy of the *Thousand Character Classic*, written in running hand by Wên Wei-chung." H. 2¾ in.

FIG. 160.—Tripod Censer of Lang Yao crackle, with mottled streaks of *sang de bœuf*, passing occasionally into pale apple-green; wood stand, and cover with carved steatite knob.

"*Dragon Wine-Vessel* (*Pan Ch'iu Yu*), modeled in the form of an ancient sacrificial vessel of bronze. The body of rounded form is enveloped, as it were, in the wings of two dragons, worked upon it in relief; the two heads of the monsters are worked in salient relief upon the cover, and four dragons' legs form the feet of the vessel. The whole is covered with a bright monochrome glaze of a pale yellow tint, like that of the petals of the hibiscus flower, without spot or flaw, making it a choice example of the period. I saw it in the collection of the historiographer Chou, of the province of Shansi." H. 4 in.

正 德, CHÊNG–TÊ (1506–21).

The mark of this emperor, son of the preceding, who reigned under the title of *Chêng-tê*, is not so very rare in collections, although the porcelain of the period is hardly distinguished for any special excellence in either material or decoration. In the beginning of the reign one of the eunuchs of the palace was dispatched to Ching-tê-chên to superintend the fabrication of porcelain for the court, and he is recorded to have rebuilt the imperial manufactory called Yü-ch'i-ch'ang, which has continued to furnish the annual supplies, with occasional brief intermissions, ever since. The work remained in the hands of the eunuchs during the whole of this reign, in spite of constant complaints of their cupidity and oppression both from the officials and from the potters, and it was not till the first year of the next reign that this *régime* was abolished.

The supply of cobalt-blue from western Asia had failed since the reign of *Hsüan-tê*, when it had been brought by Chinese ships which went as far west as the coast of Africa; in the reign of *Chêng-tê*, as we learn from the *Shih wu kan chu*, it came again by a new route, under the name of *Hui ch'ing*, or "Mohammedan blue," which "a high eunuch, while acting as governor of the province of Yunnan, obtained from foreign countries; it was melted with stone to make imitation sapphires, which were valued at twice their weight in gold; and when it was found that it could be fired, it was used in the decoration of porcelain, the color

FIG. 161.—Wide-mouthed Bottle, one of a pair of coral-red monochrome penciled with floral arabesques in gold; mounting and covers of Persian metal work etched with hunting scenes, etc.

of which surpassed the old." Such intercourse is confirmed by an interesting case in the Oriental department of the British Museum, filled with Chinese bronzes with Arabic scrolls collected by the learned curator, most of them inscribed with marks of this reign, mixed with several specimens of blue and white porcelain with similar Arabic inscriptions, which must have been painted in China at the same time. I will quote the description of one of these pieces, which is numbered No. 147a in the Franks *Catalogue*:

"*Ink Apparatus.* Chinese porcelain, painted in blue. It consists of an oblong slab for rubbing Indian ink, with a hole at one end for water; over this fits a loose cover, the top of which is decorated with one square and two circular compartments, containing Arabic inscriptions to the following purport: 'Strive for excellence in penmanship, for it is one of the keys of livelihood,' and the Persian word 'Writing-case.' The spaces are filled with formal scrolls. Mark of the period, Ching-tih, 1506–1522. L. 9¾ in., W. 5½ in. It was recently obtained in Peking, and was therefore probably originally made for a Chinese Mohammedan, not for exportation."

In addition to blue and white, we have monochrome pieces of this reign enameled yellow, and others decorated in colors, applied sometimes over the white glaze, but usually *sur biscuit.* When over the glaze, they may be used in combination with cobalt-blue and copper-red applied previously under the glaze. A favorite decoration of the time is that of the five-clawed imperial dragon, with the details engraved in the paste and filled in with green, in the midst of scrolled clouds or imbricated waves. The green dragons are sometimes relieved by a yellow ground, as in the vase marked *Chêng tê nien chih,* "Made in the reign of *Chêng-tê,*" described by Jacquemart (*loc. cit.,* p. 175) in these words:

"Vase de forme basse à fond jaune sur biscuit, avec le dragon impérial gravé et réchampi en vert. Coll. de Mme. Malinet."

The Vase shown in Fig. 162 is decorated in this style, and marked also with the seal-mark *Chêng tê nien chih,* incised underneath in archaic characters under the glaze, but it appears to be a production of the beginning of the eighteenth century. It is decorated on the front and back with flowers and butterflies engraved in the paste, and inlaid with green and white enamels, relieved by a purplish-brown ground with brilliant iridescent tints.

FIG. 162.—Vase, with incised decoration, inlaid with enamel colors in the style of the Ming dynasty; mark of the reign of Chêng-tê.

This is the most recent reign represented in our Chinese manuscript album, and it is illustrated by two pieces, both of them invested with a monochrome yellow glaze of orange tint.

"*Libation Cup (Chüeh),* modeled in the form of an ancient sacrificial wine-cup of bronze, with a plain rounded bowl, encircled by a band of three rings in slight relief passing round within the loop of the strap handle, mounted upon three pointed feet, and with two knobs projecting upward at the base of the wide lip. It is enameled with a rich yellow glaze of the tint of a boiled chestnut, rising in faint elevations like the skin of a plucked fowl. It is a choice example of the porcelain of *Chêng-tê* on account of the antique beauty of its form and the artistic simplicity of its coloring." H. 5½ in.

"*Phœnix and Tortoise-supported Lamp (Fêng Kuei Têng),* modeled after an ancient bronze design. The receptacle for the oil, a round pan with fluted sides and a projecting handle, is poised upon a ball supported on the crested head of a phœnix, which stands upright, with wings outspread, on the back of a tortoise. The ornamental details are engraved in the paste, and covered with a monochrome glaze of the rich yellow tint of a boiled chestnut."

The other pieces attributed to this reign are two teapots of colored stoneware, or terra cotta, from the potteries of Yi-hsing-hsien, in the prefecture of Chang-chou, in the province of Kiangsu. These are situated not far from Shanghai, a few miles up the river, near the western shores of the T'ai-wu Lake, and are well known in the present day for their production of the red "boccaro" ware, which is preferred to porcelain by the Chinese for the infusion of tea. The teapots figured in the album are both unglazed, of the natural color of the fired paste, one being fawn-colored, the other brick-red, and both of them are endowed with the curious property of changing to green when they have tea inside.

They are included here as instances of *yao-pien,* or "furnace transmutation." The Chinese have a taste for the marvelous, and describe several kinds of *yao-pien,* produced by the creative power of the fire. One of the old poets relates how music once proceeded spontaneously from a pair of vases during a banquet; a modern collector boasts that a bowl of *Sung* porcelain of his would keep meat or water fresh for an indefinite time. An official, again, gravely reports to the emperor how a whole firing of porcelain slabs for which he was responsible had been transformed in the kiln into beds and boats with all the furniture complete, and how the potters in their fright had destroyed them. Sometimes a vase would appear with a stain on its surface of different color from that of the ground, and this would take the outline of a dragon, a bird, or a butterfly. The above transmutations are all ascribed to miraculous agency. The last kind of "furnace transmutation" ascribed, on the other hand, to human ingenuity, is where the materials of the glaze have been purposely combined to produce the wonderful play of brilliant colors peculiar to the well-known *flambé* glaze, with its flashing streaks of crimson and blue, mingling into every intermediate shade of purple. Here is the description of the artist:

Fig. 163.—Ch'ien-lung Vase, with an imperial dragon worked in relief in the paste, coated with a finely crackled turquoise glaze, transmuted to crimson round the foot where the glaze has "run."

"*Teapot* (*Ch'a Hu*), of *Ming* dynasty, Yi-hsing *yao-pien* or 'furnace-transmutation' ware, made by Kung Ch'un. The potteries of Yi-hsing date from our own sacred dynasty in the reign of *Chêng-tê*, when a celebrated potter lived there named Kung Ch'un, a native of Yi-hsing, who made utensils of earthenware for drinking tea, which were often fortuitously transmuted in the kiln like this teapot. Its original color, a grayish brown like that of felt, changes to a bright green when tea is put in, and gradually returns to its proper color, line by line, as the tea is poured out. This is only a curious accidental peculiarity, and yet modern virtuosos prize it most highly. Both this and the following brick-red teapot were made by Kung. I saw them both in the capital, in the palace of one of the princes, who had bought them from Chang, a high official of Nanking, for 500 taels. This one is a plain teapot of hexagonal section, with an angular spout and a broad, overarching handle, about 4½ inches high."

"*Teapot* (*Ch'a Hu*), of *Ming* dynasty, Yi-hsing *yao-pien* ware, made by Kung Ch'un. Of slender oval form, with a foliated handle and a curved spout. The color of the paste, a vermilion red, changes to bright green like the preceding, so as to show the height of the tea inside. This is a wonderful example of the miraculous power of heaven and earth, a *lusus naturæ* that I could not have credited had I not seen it with my own eyes." H. 5 in.

嘉靖, CHIA–CHING (1522–66).

The last emperor was succeeded by his cousin, another grandson of the Emperor *Chêng-hua*, and his reign is almost as celebrated for its porcelain as that of his grandfather. He reigned for forty-five years under the title of *Chia-ching*. In the beginning of his reign the appointment of eunuchs as superintendents was abolished, and the assistant prefects of the circuit were ordered to officiate in annual rotation as directors of the imperial manufactory, and to provide the funds for the work. This last was no mean task, as it is recorded that in the twenty-fifth year (1546) 120,000 taels of silver were levied from the province as a yearly subsidy, in addition to the provisions for the workmen; and that in 1554 this sum was increased by 20,000 taels, in addition to which the private potters were required to undertake the supply of the largest fish-bowls, and were heavily taxed besides. In 1565 one of the subprefects of Jao-chou-fu was ordered to reside permanently at Ching-tê-chên as director; but this change did not succeed, and early in the next reign the old plan of annual rotation was reverted to.

The supply of Mohammedan blue which was imported by the Yunnan route in the preceding reign continued to arrive, and this reign is especially celebrated for the brilliance of its blue decoration; it was preferred to be very dark in color, in which it differs from the porcelain of *Hsüan-tê*, the other reign famous for its blue and white, the blue of which is usually pale in tone. The best blue of the period was prepared by mixing one part of calcined *shih-tzŭ ch'ing*, or "stone blue," the native cobaltiferous ore of manganese, with ten parts of imported blue, as the latter had a tendency to "run" if used alone. A mixture in the same proportions was also employed, suspended in water, to produce the beautiful mottled blue ground for which this reign is also remarkable; the thin *purée* of blue, *hun-shui ch'ing*, as it was called, being spread with a brush on the paste, so as to fill in the interstices of the penciled decoration, which was either reserved in white, or subsequently filled in with canary yellow or coral red. Sometimes the decoration was penciled over the mottled blue ground with strokes of stronger blue.

Decoration in other colors also occurs, but not to the same extent as in the subsequent reign of *Wan-li*. The colored glazes in the reign of *Chia-ching* were used either as monochromes, including a turquoise-blue derived from copper, in addition to the dark and sky-blue grounds derived from cobalt, the yellow, the brown, and the red; or to form colored grounds to relieve the blue decoration. The monochromes are either plain, or spread over designs previously incised in the paste. The blue paintings are relieved either by red, brown, or yellow; occasionally ornamental designs reserved in the blue mottled ground were colored red or yellow, forming an attractive variety. The art of decoration in copper-red seems to have altogether declined, owing to the substitution of a coral-red glaze derived from iron, prepared by the roasting of crystals of iron sulphate, which was much less expensive and more easily fired. The officials memorialized the emperor to be allowed to use this even for the sacrificial vessels required for the altar of the Temple of Heaven.

The white "altar cups" made for the emperor to use on Taoist altars, and inscribed with the name of the offerings they were filled with, were called by the same name, *t'an chan*, as the exquisite "altar cups" of the older reign of *Hsüan-tê*, but they were slightly yellowish in tinge and less delicate in finish, because the supply of the best porcelain earth from the Ma-ts'ang Hills was already beginning to fail. These white cups are described in the *Po wu yao lan* as resembling jade in appearance, and as having the characters *ch'a*, "tea," *chiu*, "wine," *ts'ao t'ang*, "jujube decoction," and *chiang t'ang*, "ginger decoction," etched inside under the glaze. The same book refers to the decoration of all kinds of porcelain objects in blue and in colors of this reign, and selects as gems the shallow wine-cups with foliated rims, loaf-shaped bottoms, and circularly rimmed feet decorated outside in colors with three fishes, and the tiny round rouge-boxes no larger than "cash" delicately painted in blue.

FIG. 164.—Ming Vase, decorated in green, vermilion, and amber enamel colors penciled with black.

Some of the pieces of porcelain produced in this reign are remarkable for their large size. A vender of sweetmeats has for years plied his trade in the eastern gateway of the imperial palace at Peking with his honey preserves piled up in two immense round dishes over three feet in diameter. They are decorated with five-clawed imperial dragons disporting in clouds, boldly painted in dark underglaze blue, displayed upon an enameled ground of mottled canary yellow, and are "marked" near the upper rim, *Ta Ming Chia ching liu nien chih*, "Made in the sixth year (1527) of the reign of *Chia-ching* of the great *Ming*." He regards them as an heirloom on which his luck depends, and has refused the most tempting offers, declaring that nothing shall induce him to part with them.

The designs used in the decoration of the imperial porcelain are found in a long list in the *Fou-liang-hsien Chih*, which gives all the annual indents from the eighth year, the previous records having, according to these official annals, been burned. The list is interesting, but too long for insertion here, and we will only extract the indents of the two years referred to above, which correspond to 1546 and 1554 A. D.

1. For the Twenty–fifth Year of Chia–ching (a. d. 1546).

Large Fish-Bowls (Kang), 300, decorated with a pair of dragons enveloped in clouds, painted in blue on a white ground, or reserved in white upon blue.

Jars fitted with Covers (Kuan yu Kai), 1,000, of blue ground with sprays of conventional paradise flowers (*pao hsiang hua*) and arabesque designs (*hui-hui hua*).

Bowls (Wan), 22,000, blue inside and out, decorated with dragons coiling through flowers.

Banquet Bowls (Shan Wan), 11,500, of larger size, of blue ground, decorated inside with scepter-framed medallions inclosing phœnixes in pairs; outside, with phœnixes flying through flowers.

Round Dishes (P'an), 31,000, painted inside in blue on a white ground, with sea-waves and dragons in the midst of clouds, and outside with nine dragons.

Saucer Plates (Tieh), 16,000, painted inside and outside in blue on a white ground, with a pair of dragons in the midst of clouds.

Teacups (Ch'a Chung), 3,000, painted in blue and white, decorated outside with dragon medallions and water caltrops (*Trapa bicornis*); inside with dragons and clouds reserved on a blue ground.

Wine-Cups (Chiu Chan), 18,400, painted in blue and white, decorated outside with a pair of dragons in clouds; inside, with dragons and clouds reserved on a blue ground.

2. For the Thirty–third Year of Chia–ching (a. d. 1554).

Bowls (Wan), 26,350, with a blue ground, decorated with a pair of dragons in clouds.

Plates (Tieh), 30,500, of the same design.

Wine-Cups (Chan), 6,900, white inside, blue outside, with the typical flowers of the four seasons.

Large Fish-Bowls (Yü Kang), 680, decorated with blue flowers on a white ground.

Teacups (Ou), 9,000, with foliated rims, of greenish white (*ch'ing pai*) or celadon porcelain.

Bowls (Wan), 10,200, decorated outside with lotus flowers, fish, and water plants, painted in blue on a white ground; inside, upon a blue ground, with dragons and phœnixes passing through flowers, and with a band of dragons and flowers round the rim.

Teacups (Ou), 19,800, of the same pattern.

Libation Cups (Chüeh), 600, with hill-shaped saucers (*shan-p'an*) to support the three feet, of blue color, decorated with sea-waves and a pair of dragons in clouds.

Wine-Pots or Ewers (Hu), 6,000, of white porcelain.

The list of *Chi Ch'i* or "sacrificial vessels" enumerated in the same book on one of the other occasions comprises ten *Mao Hsüeh P'an*, "Dishes for the hair and blood" of sacrificial victims; forty *Tieh*, "Platters"; four *T'ai Kêng Wan*, "Bowls for plain broth"; ten *Ho Kêng Wan*, "Bowls for savory broth"; one hundred *Chiu Chung*, "Wine-cups"; twenty-three *Chüeh*, "Libation cups of tripod form"; eighty *Pien Tou P'an*, "Tazza-shaped Bowls and Dishes" for offerings of bread, fruit, etc.; six *T'ai Tsun*, "Large Wine-Jars" with swelling body and two mask handles of monsters' heads; six *Hsi Tsun*, "Rhinoceros Jars," modeled in the form of a rhinoceros carrying on its back a vase with cover; two *Chu Tsun*, like tall cylindrical cups; and four *Shan Lei*, "Hill and Thunder" cups, so called from the scrolled designs engraved upon them. These ritual forms, which are still in use at the present day, are all figured in book xxv of the *Illustrations of the Institutes of the Reigning Dynasty (Ta Ch'ing Hui Tien T'ou)*. They are enameled of different colors, according to the temple for which they are made: *Blue* for the Altar of Heaven and for the Temple of the Land and Grain; *yellow* for the Altar of Earth, for the worship of the god of agriculture and of the goddess of silk; *red* for the Altar of the Sun; and *white* for the Altar of Jupiter, the "year star" of the Chinese.

In the year 1544 we find the enormous order of 1,340 sets of table services, *cho ch'i*, each consisting of twenty-seven pieces, comprising five *kuo tieh*, "fruit dishes," five *ts'ai tieh*, "food dishes," five *wan*, "bowls," five *yun tieh*, "vegetable dishes," three *ch'a chung*, "tea-cups," one *chiu chan,* "wine-cup," one *chiu tieh,* "wine-saucer," one *cha tou,* "slop receptacle," and one *ts'u chui,* "vinegar cruse or ewer." Of these services, 380 sets were painted in blue, with a pair of dragons surrounded by clouds; 160 were enameled white, with dragons engraved in the paste underneath; 160 were of monochrome brown of the *fond-laque* or "dead-leaf" tint (*tzŭ chin*); 160 of monochrome turquoise-blue (*ts'ui ch'ing sê*); 160 of coral or iron-red (*fan hung*), "instead of bright copper-red (*hsien hung*)"; and 160 were enameled brilliant green (*ts'ui lü*).

The designs of the decorated porcelain of this time are said to have been principally derived from ancient embroidery and brocaded silks. They are conveniently described in the *Ta'o Shuo,* in a list which we extract, under the following six headings:

1. Painted in Blue on a White Ground.
2. Blue Porcelain.
3. White Inside, Blue Outside.
4. White Porcelain.
5. Brown Porcelain.
6. Mixed Colors.

1. Painted in Blue on a White Ground.

Bowls (Wan), decorated with dragons pursuing jewels, and outside with weighing-scales and playing children.

Bowls with the ground, inside and out, filled with graceful beauties.*

Bowls with medallions framed by bamboo leaves and the sacred fungus, containing dragons in clouds and dragons and phœnixes passing through flowers.

Bowls decorated outside with dragons emerging from sea-waves, holding up the eight mystical trigrams; inside, with the three alchemists (i. e., Confucius, Lao-Tzŭ, and Buddha) compounding the *elixir vitæ.*

Bowls decorated outside with dragons and with phœnixes and other birds; inside with dragons in the midst of clouds.

Bowls decorated outside with four fish—the mackerel, carp, marbled perch, and another; inside, with birds flying in the midst of clouds.

Wine-Cups (Chan), decorated outside with celestial flowers supporting the characters *Shou shan fu hai,* "Old as the hills, rich as the sea!" inside, with two Taoist genii.

Wine-Cups (Chiu Chan), with a pair of dragons among clouds outside, and dragons and clouds upon a blue ground inside.

Wine-Cups with dragons among clouds outside, and soaring dragons inside.

Wine-Cups with dragons of archaic design outside, and storks flying through clouds inside.

Wine-Cups with a pair of dragons painted outside, a pair of phœnixes inside.

Teacups (Ou), decorated outside with playing boys and the typical flowers of the four seasons;† inside, with dragons emerging from water into the clouds, and with flowering plants.

Teacups (Ou), decorated outside with dragons emerging from water; inside, with lions.

Teacups (Ou), with emblems of the six cardinal points of the universe outside; soaring dragons inside.

Cups (Chung), decorated with flowers and with the inscription *Fu shou k'ang ning,* "Happiness, long life, health, and peace!"

Teacups (Ch'a Chung), decorated inside and out with the myriad-flowering wistaria; and outside also with dragons grasping jewels in their claws.

Cups (Chung), with playing boys outside; dragons among clouds inside.

Teacups (Ch'a Chung), decorated outside with dragon medallions and water caltrops; inside, with dragons and clouds reserved on a blue ground.

---

* Referring, perhaps, to the slender, graceful figures of Chinese damsels called *Lange Lysen* by the old Dutch collectors, corrupted to "Long Elizas" in the auction catalogues of to-day.

† The tree peony of spring, the lotus of summer, the chrysanthemum of autumn, and the plum of winter.

Cups (Chung), with clouds and dragons outside, floral medallions inside.

Wine Vases (Chiu Tsun), beaker-shaped, decorated with the fir, bamboo, and plum.

Saucer-shaped Dishes (Tieh), filled inside and out with bevies of graceful beauties.

Dishes (Tieh), with cranes, inside and out, flying through clouds.

Dishes (Tieh), decorated outside with dragons enveloped in Indian lotus flowers; inside, with phœnixes flying through flowers.

Dishes (Tieh), decorated outside with fruit-bearing lotus plants; inside, with medallions of flowers.

Dishes (Tieh), with the same decoration outside; dragons and phœnixes inside.

Dishes (Tieh), with phœnixes flying through flowers outside; sporting dragons, both ascending and descending inside.

Jars (Kuan), with covers, decorated with a set of eight precious symbols supported upon branching scrolls of the sacred fungus.

Jars (Kuan), with the eight Taoist immortals crossing the sea.

Jars (Kuan), decorated with Pao-lao Revels—Processions of children in masquerade costume at the new year.

Jars (Kuan), decorated with peacocks and moutan peonies.

Jars (Kuan), decorated with lions sporting with embroidered balls.

Jars (Kuan), with a set of eight precious symbols supported upon interlacing sprays of conventional flowers of paradise.

Jars (Kuan), decorated with graceful beauties, and with different kinds of fish feeding upon water-weeds.

Jars (Kuan), decorated with the eight famous horses—the chariot team of the ancient sovereign *Mu-Wang* of the *Chou* dynasty.

Jars (Kuan), decorated with mountain landscapes of the province of Ssŭ-ch'uan, with waterfalls and flying lions.

Jars (Kuan), with the eight mystic trigrams supported by waves and flames of fire.

Octagonal Jars (Pa-pien Kuan), with a picture of the sea and flying dragons on each of the eight sides.

Vases (P'ing), bottle-shaped, decorated with hoary lions and dragons.

Vases (P'ing), decorated with scrolls of the sacred fungus and the floral emblems of the four seasons.

Large Round Dishes (P'an), decorated outside with the floral emblems of the four seasons; inside, with a landscape containing three rams (*San yang k'ai tai*), types of the revivifying power of spring.

Dishes (P'an), decorated outside with nine dragons and flowers; inside, with dragons mounting from the sea into the clouds.

Dishes (P'an), decorated with ocean views containing flying lions and with dragons upholding the two characters *fu shou*, "happiness and long life."

Dishes (P'an), decorated outside with four Taoist divinities; inside, with cranes flying through clouds.

Dishes (P'an), painted outside with clouds and dragons; inside, with the band of eight Taoist immortals worshiping *Shou Lao*, the god of longevity.

Fruit Boxes (Kuo Ho), of circular form with rounded covers, decorated with dragons and cranes in the midst of clouds.

Boxes decorated with hoary lions and dragons on a blue ground.

Boxes (Ho), painted with dragons and phœnixes and a group of Taoist immortals displaying longevity characters.

Large Bowls (Kang), for keeping goldfish, decorated with a pair of dragons enveloped in clouds.

Fish-Bowls (Kang), painted inside with dragons and clouds.

Tall Jars (T'an) for wine, of ovoid form, with a slender base swelling upward to a rounded shoulder, and a rim cover fitting over the small mouth, decorated with the eight precious symbols (*pa pao*) and the eight Buddhist emblems of good augury (*pa chi-hsiang*), supported by interlacing sprays of lotus, with a pair of scales and playing children.

Tall Wine-Jars (*T'an*), decorated with the hundred different forms of the character *shou*, "longevity," supported by interlacing sprays of lotus.

Double Gourds (*Hu lu*), painted with different designs. Ten thousand vases of this characteristic shape, with contracted waist, are recorded to have been decorated in the year 1547.

Ritual Bricks (*Pai Chuan*). These were inlaid in the floor of the audience hall or of a temple, to mark the proper place for the worshiper to prostrate himself.

Wine Seas (*Chiu Hai*),* decorated with different designs.

2. BLUE PORCELAIN.

Bowls (*Wan*), enameled dark blue. Bowls of sky-blue color and Bowls of turquoise blue.

Dinner Bowls (*Shan Wan*), decorated outside with a pair of phœnixes flying through flowers; inside, upon a blue ground, with scepter-framed medallions inclosing phœnixes in pairs.

Wine-Cups (*Chiu Chan*), enameled dark blue.

Tazza Cups (*Pa Chung*), enameled dark blue.

Teacups (*Ou*), decorated outside with lotus flowers, fishes, and water-weeds; inside, upon a blue ground, with dragons and phœnixes enveloped in flowers, and with a floral band interrupted by dragons round the rim.

Teacups (*Ch'a Chung*), enameled dark blue.

Saucer Plates (*Tieh*), enameled dark blue. Plates of sky-blue and Plates of turquoise blue.

Plates (*Tieh*), with phœnixes and cranes engraved in the paste under the blue glaze.

Jars (*Kuan*), decorated with interlacing sprays of flowers of paradise (*pao-hsiang hua*) and with arabesques (*Hui-hui hua*).

Jars (*Kuan*), with dragons engraved in the paste under the blue glaze.

Large Dishes (*P'an*), blue inside and out, with the interior decorated with sea-waves and dragons, the exterior with a ground of cloud scrolls, displaying either three gilded lions or three gilded dragons. One hundred of these were painted in the year 1552, together with one hundred and eighty of the tripod libation-cups (*chüeh*), with saucers, all decorated in the same ornate style.

Fish-Bowls (*Kang*), with a blue ground decorated with a pair of dragons, and clouds.

Fish-Bowls decorated outside with a pair of dragons in clouds and scrolls of fairy flowers upon a blue ground.

Fish-Bowls of plain dark-blue monochrome glaze prepared from first-class cobalt.

Tall Jars (*T'an*), of ovoid form, for wine, decorated with a pair of dragons in the midst of clouds, enveloped in flowers.

Bricks (*Chuan*), of dark-blue porcelain.

3. WHITE INSIDE, BLUE OUTSIDE.

Bowls (*Wan*), decorated outside with a pair of dragons in the midst of clouds.

Wine-Cups (*Chan*), with a pair of dragons in clouds and with birds flying.

Wine-Cups (*Chan*), decorated with the floral emblems of the four seasons.

4. WHITE PORCELAIN.

Bowls (*Wan*), with crested sea-waves engraved under the white glaze.

Wine-Cups (*Chiu Chan*) and *Libation-Cups* (*Chüeh Chan*), with phœnixes and cranes engraved under the glaze.

Teacups (*Ch'a Ou*), with oval foliated rims.

Teacups (*Ch'a Chung*), with dragons engraved under the white glaze.

---

* The form of these is unknown; perhaps they were like our punch-bowls.

Wine-Cups (Chiu Chung), enameled pure white (*t'ien pai*).

Wine-Ewers (Chiu Hu), *Vases (P'ing)*, *Jars (Kuan)*, and *Dishes (P'an)* of pure white.

Tall Ovoid Jars (T'an), with crested sea-waves incised under the white glaze.

5. BROWN PORCELAIN.

Bowls (Wan), enameled of "brown gold" (*tzŭ chin*) color, with dragons engraved in the paste.

Bowls (Wan), enameled of golden yellow (*chin huang*) color, with dragons engraved in the paste.

Saucer-shaped Plates (Tieh), of "brown gold" color, with incised dragons under the glaze.

Plates (Tieh), of golden yellow color, with dragons incised under the glaze.

6. MIXED COLORS.

Bowls (Wan) and *Plates (Tieh)*, enameled coral red with iron oxide (*fan hung*); substituted for the bright red (*hsien hung*) derived from copper.

Bowls (Wan) and *Plates (Tieh)*, enameled of emerald-green color (*ts'ui lü sê*).

Bowls (Wan), decorated in yellow with phœnixes flying through fairy flowers displayed upon a blue ground.

Teacups (Ou), painted in blue with dragons and clouds, inclosed in a yellow ground.

Wine-Cups (Chan) and *Libation-Cups (Chüeh)*, decorated in yellow with phœnixes flying through fairy flowers, displayed upon a blue ground.

Boxes (Ho), enameled yellow with dragons and phœnixes engraved under the glaze.

Large Dishes (P'an) and *Saucer-shaped Plates (Tieh)*, painted in yellow with a pair of dragons and clouds reserved in a ground enameled of "brown gold" color (*tzŭ-chin*).

Jars (Kuan) of crackled ware (*sui ch'i*), of which there is only one entry, in 1542, when three hundred were made.

Teacups (Ou), with foliated rims of greenish-white or celadon porcelain (*ch'ing pai tz'ŭ*), of which nine thousand were provided in the year 1554.

Large Fish-Bowls (Yü Kang), enameled pea-green (*tou ch'ing*).

Globular Bowls (Po) of the shape of the Buddhist *patra*, or alms-bowl, with embossed designs under the plain glaze.

隆慶, LUNG-CH'ING, 1567–72.

The son of the last emperor, who succeeded him, reigned under the title of *Lung-ch'ing*, and died after a short reign of six years. The porcelain made at Ching-tê-chên during this period is usually described, together with that of the next reign of *Wan-li*, under the combined heading of "Porcelain of *Lung* and *Wan*." It resembled, on the other hand, the ceramic productions of *Chia-ching*, especially in the dark color of its cobalt-blue decoration. The emperor was devoted to the pleasures of the seraglio, and his libertine temperament is reflected in the decoration of the porcelain, which is notorious for its erotic character, while the government of the country gradually fell into the hands of the eunuchs of the palace.

FIG. 165.—Figure of a Cat, with crackled transmutation enamel of mottled tints imitating tortoise-shell.

In the fifth year of this reign (1571) Hsü Shih, the President of the Censorate, presented a memorial to the emperor, remonstrating with him upon the enormous amount required by the eunuch in charge of the imperial household, who had stated that the supply of the different kinds of porcelain had run short, and required no less than 105,770 table services, pairs, and single pieces, to be furnished within eight months, including bowls, wine-cups, and teacups enameled inside and out of brilliant copper-red, as well as a quantity of the largest fish-bowls and square boxes. The memorialist stated that the art of firing the expensive copper-red had been lost; that large fish-bowls, with such broad bottoms and bulging sides as were drawn in the patterns, could hardly be fired unbroken; that the designs of those to be decorated in the "five colors" were too elaborate to be successfully produced; and that the square boxes in three tiers were a novelty of most difficult fabrication. He prayed, therefore, that *fan hung* or "iron red" might be used instead of the *hsien hung* or "copper red," and that the rest of the things referred to might be reduced to one or two tenths of the amount required by the eunuchs. Moreover, that because of the devastation of the potteries by flood and fire, and the flight of hundreds of the workmen, he recommended that instead of such a large total installment of fifteen thousand pieces being required at monthly intervals, the word "monthly" should be altered to "yearly," or even that the quantity should be required at intervals of two years.

FIG. 166.—Wine Pot, fashioned in the form of a lotus pod, and painted *sur biscuit* with green and yellow enamels.

The lists of the things supplied in this reign, according to the official statistics in the annals of the city of Fou-liang-hsien (*Fou-liang-hsien Chih*), include:

Table Services (*Cho Ch'i*), decorated in blue on a white ground with a pair of dragons among clouds, with phœnixes flying through vermilion flowers, with a joyous meeting (symbolized by magpies), with pheasants of different kinds, with sprays of chrysanthemum blossoms, with interlacing scrolls of paradise flowers, with the sacred fungus, and with grapes.

Bowls (*Wan*), painted outside in blue, with dragons and phœnixes upon a floral ground; in the "five colors," with a bevy of beauties and with sprays of cut flowers; inside in blue, with medallions of dragons and phœnixes, with the pine, bamboo, and plum, with iris flowers or flags.

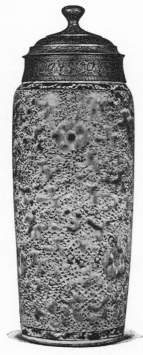

FIG. 167.—Ming Vase, with arabesque decoration in underglaze blue filled in with red and green enamels; copper mounts of Persian work.

Round Dishes (*P'an*), decorated in blue and white outside, with pairs of dragons and phœnixes surrounded by clouds, with nine dragons and sea-waves, with interlacing scrolls of paradise flowers; inside with dramatic scenes, with groups of the sacred fungus, with the emblematic flowers of the four seasons.

Saucer-shaped Plates (*Tieh*), decorated in blue and white outside, with pairs of dragons and phœnixes in clouds, with bamboo shrubs and the sacred fungus, with dragons and clouds amid sprays of flowers, with the pine, bamboo, and plum; inside with medallions inclosing dragons, and with the emblematic flowers of the four seasons.

Wine-Cups (*Chung*), decorated in blue and white outside, with a pair of dragons in clouds, with fu-jung (*Hibiscus mutabilis*) flowers, with magpies typical of a joyous meeting, with interlacing bands of exotic pomegranates and arabesques; inside with pheasants flying through flowers, with blue pied ducks and lotus flowers, with dramatic scenes, with lions, with historical subjects, with a pair of weighing scales; and others enameled monochrome yellow, with dragons etched in the paste under the glaze.

Teacups (*Ou*), decorated in blue and white; outside, with dragons and phœnixes surrounded by flowers, with the eight Buddhist emblems of happy augury, with five dragons and lightly penciled sea-waves, with the typical flowers of the four seasons emblazoned with the four characters *Ch'ien k'un ch'ing t'ai* —i. e. "May heaven and earth be fair and fruitful!"—with the eight Taoist immortals worshiping the god of longevity, with the sacred lotus of India; inside, with flying fishes, with nine dragons, painted red, in the midst of blue sea-waves and fishes, with the pine, bamboo, and plum, with dragons and phœnixes in the midst of a floral ground.

Jars with Covers (*Kuan*), decorated in blue and white, with a pair of dragons coiling through clouds, with phœnixes flying through flowers, with lions sporting with embroidered balls, with interlacing scrolls of moutan peonies; decorated, on a blue ground, with flowers and fruit and with birds of various kinds reserved in white; painted in "five colors" with dragons in the midst of clouds, with fairy flowers of paradise, with flowering plants and butterflies or other insects.

Vases (*P'ing*), decorated in blue and white, with dragons and phœnixes enveloped in flowers, with playing boys carrying branches of flowers in their hands,* with jasmine flowers, with arabesques and fairy flowers of paradise.

Wine-Cups (*Chan*), decorated outside in blue and white, with soaring dragons and with the sacred fungus, in "five colors," with curved waves and plum flowers; inside, with dragons in the midst of clouds, with althæa flowers, with the pine, bamboo, and plum; and others enameled white, with dragons and clouds etched in the paste under the glaze.

Basins (*P'ên*), decorated outside in blue and white, with dragons and clouds, in "five colors," with bevies of beauties, with familiar or with dramatic scenes, with historical subjects, with lotus flowers and dragons; inside with dragons and clouds, with scrolled waves and plum blossoms.

Censers (*Hsiang Lu*), for burning incense, decorated, in blue and white, with a pair of dragons in clouds, with arabesques of flowers and fruit, with birds of various kinds, with nine dragons and lightly penciled sea-waves, with lotus flowers; decorated in red and white, with a pair of dragons and clouds, with interlacing sprays of fairy flowers of paradise.

Incense Boxes (*Hsiang Ho*), decorated, in blue and white, with a pair of dragons soaring into the clouds, with the pine, bamboo, and plum, with separate sprays of chrysanthemum flowers.

Slop Receptacles (*Cha Tou*), of square form, decorated, in blue and white, with a pair of dragons in clouds, with phœnixes and flowers, with sea-waves and sea monsters, with lions sporting with embroidered balls, with joyous magpies on a floral ground, with pheasants.

Vinegar Ewers (*Ts'u T'i*), decorated, in blue and white, with pairs of dragons and phœnixes in the midst of clouds, with flowering plants and quadrupeds, with pheasants flying through flowers, with lions playing with embroidered balls, with single sprays of the typical flowers of the four seasons.

FIG. 168.—Ewer for iced sirup, of the Ch'ien-lung period, decorated in enamel colors, with gilding, dragon handle, and unicorn-surmounted cover.

Tall Wine-Jars (*T'an*), of ovoid form, decorated, in blue and white, with pairs of dragons and phœnixes in the midst of clouds, with outdoor scenes containing wild animals, with flying fishes, with the typical flowers of the four seasons, with the eight Buddhist emblems of happy augury; *Jars* with gilded decorations of peacocks and tree-peonies. All these have covers with the figure of a lion molded upon them.

萬 歷, WAN-LI (1573–1619).

The emperor who reigned for forty-seven years under the title of *Wan-li* was the son of the last. The manufacture of porcelain increased to a remarkable extent during his long reign,

---

* This is the decoration penciled in blue upon the melon-shaped body of the wine-pot with the Elizabethan silver mounting bearing the hall-mark of 1585, which was referred to in my introductory chapter as being in the South Kensington Museum. Four pieces of Chinese blue and white porcelain in silver-gilt mounts are described in the *Catalogue of the Burlington Fine Arts Club*, referred to above, from the Burghley House Collection, said to have been in the possession of the Cecil family since the days of Queen Elizabeth.

and the Chinese declare that there was nothing that could not be made of it. It was stimulated by the large orders for export to foreign countries, which came from Europe as well as from western Asia. The Emperor *Wan-li* is said to have sent a present of large blue and white vases to *Jehangir*, the Mogul Emperor of India, which were kept in the palace at Agra until it was sacked by the Mahrattas in 1771. Blue and white porcelain of this reign has been discovered recently in large quantities in Ceylon, as well as in Persia, and a collection

of the famous "dragon vases," of Poland and Elector of Saxony, the Great of Prussia, in exchange may be seen in the Johanneum

In the preceding reigns the white, with the addition occasion-blue designs, or to make, on the in a single color displayed mottled blue. The rare pieces as it were, with the same col-of *Wan-li* that we find a new amel colors introduced, the vitreous blue combined with a metallic oxides, of the same in enameling upon copper. painted upon porcelain which and fired, and fixed by a sec-This forms the typical *Wan-li* tion in colors." The enamel combination with underglaze lines and part of the decora-the first firing. The applica-color was not employed ap-*K'ang-hsi*, as described by valuable letters, and this distinguishing the produc-may be inferred confidently blue has been fired as a sil-colors, so that it stands out of the white glaze, is subse-

Fig. 169.—Club-shaped Vase, of powder blue ground of the K'ang-hsi period, with white reserved medallions painted in blue.

which Augustus the Strong, King obtained, it is said, from Frederick for a regiment of tall grenadiers, at Dresden.

decoration was mainly in blue and ally of colored glazes to relieve the other hand, a decoration penciled upon a surrounding ground of decorated in colors were inlaid, ored glazes. It is in the reign process of decoration in en-colors being composed of a small proportion of different composition as those employed These enamel colors were had been previously glazed ond firing in the muffle stove. *wu ts'ai* or "*Wan-li* decora-colors were often used in cobalt-blue in which the out-tion had been penciled before tion of cobalt as an overglaze parently till the reign of Père d'Entrecolles in his point supplies a means of tions of the two reigns. It that any piece in which the icate like the other enamel in relief above the surface quent to the *Wan-li* period.

The principal objection to this mode of applying the cobalt-blue is that the color has a tendency to scale off, and this is the reason that the old method of painting it on under the glaze, even when combined with enamel colors, remains in vogue to the present day.

The wholesale production of the reign of *Wan-li* is shown by the abundance of porcelain of this time in the present day at Peking, where a garden of any pretension must have a large bowl or cistern for goldfish, and street hawkers may be seen with sweetmeats piled up on dishes a yard in diameter, or ladling sirup out of large bowls; and there is hardly a butcher's shop without a cracked *Wan-li* jar standing on the counter to hold scraps of meat. This is the *Ming Tz'ŭ*, the porcelain of the *Ming* dynasty, *par excellence*, of the Chinese, with its perfectly vitrified glaze and brilliant style of coloring, characteristic of the period, but of coarse paste and often clumsy in form, the bottom of the vase generally unglazed, and the mark inscribed outside near the rim. It is very different from the porcelain which so frequently figures as *Ming* in European collections, and which is usually to be referred to the reign of *K'ang-hsi*, although often bearing a fictitious mark of the *Ming* dynasty.

We find Wang Ching-min, one of the Supervising Censors, remonstrating, in the year 1583, with the emperor upon the extravagance of the orders for the palace. He protests against the expense of the pricket candlesticks (*chu t'ai*), the large slabs for screens (*p'ing fêng*), and the brush-handles (*pi kuan*). There must of course, he says, be a sufficient provision of bowls, plates, and cups of different form for the table service of the sovereign, and no deficiency should be permitted in the vases and dishes required for sacrificial worship; but with regard to the other things, the apparatus for chess, with boards and jars for holding the black and white pieces, this is a mere pastime; and even the screens and brush-handles, the ornamental vases and jars, the boxes for incense and the censers, are not of such urgent necessity. The numbers are, he declares, much too large—20,000 boxes (*ho*) of different pattern, 4,000 vases (*p'ing*), and 5,000 jars (*kuan*) with covers, of diverse shape and decoration, mounting up with the bowls and other things to a total of over 96,000. He, moreover, prays that the dragons, phœnixes, and other decorative designs should be all painted in plain blue, without the addition of other colors, because enameling in colors (*wu tsa'i*) and openwork carving (*ling-lung*) were both of difficult execution and too meretricious in style. He quotes in his memorial the ancient Emperor *Shun*, whose vessels are said to have been unvarnished, and the great *Yü*, who refused to have his sacrificial bowls of wood chiseled, as models to be imitated. The result of this appeal was the lessening by one half of the number of pricket candlesticks, *gô*-boards, screens, and brush-handles.

The following list, taken from the same official source as that of the last reign, will give some idea of the decorative designs used in the imperial potteries.

I. Painted in Blue on a White Ground.

Bowls (*Wan*), decorated outside with pairs of dragons and phœnixes in the midst of clouds and lotus flowers, with interlacing sprays of Indian lotus, with fairy flowers of paradise; inside, with a medallion of dragons in clouds and a border of dragons interrupted by the eight Buddhist emblems of happy augury, with crested sea-waves, and a border of propitious clouds, with fragrant plants, and with scrolled waves and plum-blossoms.

FIG. 170.—Ch'ien-lung Vase of archaic bronze form, with embossed and etched designs enhanced by the varied tones of the finely crackled turquoise glaze.

Bowls (*Wan*), decorated outside with dragons in the midst of clouds, with fishes and lotus flowers, with playing boys, with the seal characters *Fu shou k'ang ning*—i. e., "Happiness, longevity, wealth, and peace!"—with arabesques of flowers, with sea monsters, with lions sporting with embroidered balls; inside, with storks flying in the clouds, with a bunch of lotus fruit, with lilies, with propitious scrolls of clouds; and with the inscribed mark *Ta Ming Wan li nien chih*, "Made in the reign of *Wan-li* of the great *Ming* [dynasty]."

Bowls (*Wan*), decorated outside with medallions of dragons in clouds, with a pair of phœnixes, with brocaded designs and sea-waves, with *Fu*, *Lu*, and *Shou*, the gods of happiness, rank, and longevity, with branches of sacred fungus; inside, with a pair of dragons holding longevity characters in their claws, with jasmine flowers, and painted in enamel colors inside, with phœnixes flying through the typical flowers of the four seasons.

Bowls (*Wan*), decorated outside with longevity subjects, with harvest fruits, with emblems of the midsummer holiday—sprigs of acorns and artemisia, hung up in China on the fifth day of the fifth moon—with lotus flowers, and fishes feeding upon waterweeds; inside, with a full-faced dragon coiled in clouds upon a blue ground at the bottom, and the pine, bamboo, and plum round the rim.

Bowls (*Wan*), decorated outside with a pair of dragons in the midst of clouds, with the eight Taoist immortals crossing the ocean, with boxes of the typical flowers of the four seasons; inside, with a full-faced dragon with archaic longevity characters, with *ju-i* scepters, with hibiscus flowers, and with bamboo sprays and branches of fungus round the rim.

Dishes (P'an), decorated outside with dragons in clouds and phœnixes, in pairs, enveloped in flowers, with interlacing sprays of fairy flowers, with the pine, bamboo, and plum; inside, with branches of the typical flowers of the four seasons, with arabesque scrolls of fruit, with *ju-i* scepters, with the pine, bamboo, and plum, and with bamboo sprays and branching fungus round the rim.

Dishes (P'an), decorated outside with dragons and lotus flowers, with dragons and phœnixes enveloped in flowers, with the pine, bamboo, and plum, with illustrations of poetry, with familiar scenes, with historical subjects, with playing boys; inside, with scrolls of clouds, with sprays of fragrant bamboo and sacred fungus round the rim, and with dragons, clouds, and conventional flowers incised under the glaze.

Dishes (P'an), decorated outside with medallions of archaic lizard-like dragons, with branches of sacred fungus, with *ju-i* scepters and fairy flowers, with exotic pomegranates and fragrant flowers; inside, with a dragon in the center holding the four characters *Yung pao wan shou*—i. e., "Ever protecting for myriads of ages!"; round the border, with phœnixes and fairy flowers, the inscription *Yung pao hung fu ch'i t'ien*—i. e., "Ever insuring abundant happiness reaching to the heavens!"—and with playing boys.

FIG. 171.—K'ang-hsi Vase of the finest class, richly decorated in colors, exhibiting the supernatural Ch'i-lin (ki- or ky-lin) in its traditional form, and the grotesque Chinese lion; European mounts.

Dishes (P'an), decorated outside with interlacing sprays of lotus, with dragons and phœnixes supporting a set of eight precious symbols, with flowers and fruit, with the pine, bamboo, and plum, with Sanskrit *dharani* or invocations, with branches of the typical flowers of the four seasons; inside, with a dragon surrounded by flowers, in the middle, and round the borders with scattered branches of the flowers of the four seasons, with familiar scenes, with historical subjects, with bamboo sprays and the sacred fungus, with longevity pictures, and with moutan peonies.

Plates (Tieh), decorated outside with phœnixes flying through flowers, with flowers, fruit, and birds, with floral emblems of long life, with a bevy of beauties, with wild animals among trees, with dragons and lotus leaves; inside, with a set of eight precious symbols and antique dragons, with Sanskrit invocations supported upon fairy-flower scrolls, with dragons and phœnixes, with familiar scenes, and with historical subjects.

Plates (Tieh), decorated outside with interlacing branches of the tree-peony supporting eight precious symbols, with crested sea-waves, with the Indian lotus in enameled colors, with fabulous monsters, and with a group of beauties; inside, with a pair of dragons among clouds, with dragons and phœnixes worked in the paste under the glaze, with flowers of paradise, with lions sporting with embroidered balls, with the eight Buddhist emblems of happy augury, with propitiously scrolled clouds and branches of sacred fungus, with flowers and fruit.

Plates (Tieh), decorated outside with the jasmine and interlacing sprays of fairy flowers, with archaic lizardlike dragons bringing branches of sacred fungus; inside, with dragons and phœnixes painted in enamel colors, encircled round the rim with the inscription *Fu ju tung hai*—i. e., "Rich as the eastern ocean!"—with the eight Buddhist emblems upon a brocaded ground, encircled round the border with a set of eight precious symbols borne upon scrolls of fairy flowers.

Plates (Tieh), decorated outside with chains of bamboo sprays and sacred fungus, with flowers and fruit, with a set of eight precious symbols, with pairs of dragons in clouds and phœnixes; inside, with dragons in the midst of the typical flowers of the four seasons, with longevity scenes enameled in colors, with pictures of family life, with sacred peach trees; round the rim, with grapes.

Wine-Cups (Chung), decorated outside with a pair of dragons among clouds, with interlacing bands of exotic pomegranates, with lions sporting with embroidered balls; inside, with dragons among clouds surrounded by flowers, with propitious scrolls of clouds and a border of fragrant plants, with nine dragons painted in red in the midst of blue sea-waves, with water birds and lotus flowers enameled in colors, and with Buddhist invocations in Sanskrit round the sides.

Wine-Cups (Chung), decorated outside with wreaths of peaches having archaic longevity characters inscribed upon the fruit, with interlacing sprays of the flowers of the four seasons, with Sanskrit Buddhist invocations; inside, with storks flying in clouds, with jewels emitting effulgent rays, pursued by a pair of dragons among clouds worked in the paste under the glaze, with lotus flowers and fishes, with sea-waves penciled upon a blue ground.

Teacups (Ou), decorated outside with dragons and phœnixes in the midst of flowers, with the eight Taoist immortals worshiping the god of longevity, with arabesque scrolls of conventional fairy flowers; inside, with dragons and clouds in a medallion, with fishes and lotus flowers, with a river scene and reeds, with Sanskrit invocations supported by flowers.

Teacups (Ou), decorated outside with medallions of dragons and scrolled clouds, with bamboo sprays and sacred fungus, with fishes and water-weeds painted in enamel colors; inside, with longevity characters in seal script, with *ju-i* scepters, with moutan peony flowers, and with *ju-i* wands enameled in colors.

FIG. 172.—Typical " K'ai-pien " Vase, with a decoration penciled in soft blue under the crackled glaze of ivory-white tone and delicate texture.

Wine-Cups (Chan), decorated outside with dragons among clouds, with jasmine flowers, with birds, with graceful ladies, with playing boys, with the eight Buddhist emblems of happy augury supported upon scrolls of sacred fungus; inside, with grapes, with sprays of the flowers of the four seasons, with Buddhist *dharani* in Sanskrit script, with garlands of the floral emblems of longevity.

Wine-Cups (Chan), decorated outside with a pair of dragons among clouds in the midst of flowers, with familiar scenes, with historical subjects, with nine monsters in blue surrounded by red sea-waves; inside, with *ju-i* wands and fragrant flowers, with plum flowers upon scrolled waves, with pheasants flying through flowers, with red sea-waves rising into white crests.

Wine-Cups (Chan), decorated outside with pairs of dragons and phœnixes surrounded by clouds; inside, with yellow hibiscus flowers, with twining scrolls of sacred fungus, with chrysanthemum flowers enameled in colors.

Boxes (Ho), decorated with dragons in propitious scrolls of clouds, with dragons and phœnixes in the midst of flowers, with the inscription *Fêng t'iao yü shun, T'ien hsia t'ai p'ing*—i. e., "With favorable winds and seasonable rains, may peace prevail throughout the world!" with a symbolical head having the hair dressed in four puffs bearing the characters *Yung pao ch'ang ch'un*—i. e., "Ever preserving lasting spring!"— with the eight mystic trigrams and the monad *yin-yang* symbol, with Taoist divinities holding the characters *Ch'ien k'un ch'ing tai*—i. e., "May heaven and earth be fair and fruitful!"

Boxes (Ho), decorated with fabulous monsters paying court to the celestial dragon, with brocades of scroll pattern, with a group of beautiful forms, with diapered grounds, with hibiscus flowers, with interlacing lozenges (*fang-shêng*), with flowers, fruit, and birds, with flowering plants and insects.

Boxes (Ho), inscribed *Wan ku ch'ang ch'un, Ssŭ hai lai ch'ao*—i. e., "Through myriads of ages everlasting spring, and tribute coming from the four seas"—decorated on the covers with dragons, with the typical flowers of the four seasons, with familiar scenes, and with historical subjects.

Boxes (Ho), inscribed *T'ien hsia t'ai p'ing, Ssŭ fang hsiang ts'ao*—i. e., "Peace prevailing throughout the world, and aromatic plants from the four quarters"—decorated with *ju-i* scepters, and on the covers with arabesques, with figure scenes, and with lozenge symbols enameled in colors.

Boxes (Ho), decorated with familiar scenes and with historical subjects; and on the covers with dragons and clouds, with playing boys, with the typical flowers of the four seasons; and enameled in colors with dragons and clouds, with flowers, fruit, and birds, with longevity seal characters supported upon scrolls of sacred fungus.

Cups (*Pei*), decorated outside with winged lions flying over sea-waves, with interlacing sprays of the typical flowers of the four seasons, with antique dragons carrying jasmine flowers, with branches of sacred fungus, with pomegranates; inside, with hibiscus flowers, with tree peonies, with scrolled sea-waves, with fairy flowers.

Cups (*Pei*) and *Saucers* (*P'an*), decorated outside with moutan peonies; in gold, with chrysanthemums, with hibiscus flowers, with the typical flowers of the four seasons; in enamel colors, with a set of eight precious symbols, with grapes, with bees hovering round a blossoming plum; inside, with hibiscus flowers, with moutan peonies, with seal longevity characters; in enamel colors, with lotus flowers, with figures of ancient coins.

Chopstick Saucers (*Chu P'an*), decorated outside with dragons in the clouds and sea-waves; inside, with the center worked in relief, encircled by clouds and dragons.

Wine Seas (*Chiu Hai*), decorated with scrolls of gilded lotus flowers supporting longevity characters in antique seal script.

Censers (*Hsiang Lu*), decorated with the eight mystical trigrams and the monad *yin-yang* symbol, with branches of sacred fungus, with landscapes, with dragons and clouds.

Censers (*Hsiang Lu*), decorated outside with lotus flowers, with fragrant plants and *ju-i* wands, with dragons and clouds worked in relief, with arabesques and fragrant flowers, with dragons surrounded by clouds, with branches of sacred fungus, with conventional fairy flowers, with branches of sacred fungus carved in openwork, with figures of ancient "cash."

FIG. 173.—Unicorn Monster of Ming period, coated with a gray crackled glaze, touched with blue and dark green.

Vases (*P'ing*), decorated with dragons and phœnixes enveloped in flowers, with pictures of animal life, with the ginseng plant and sacred fungus, with argus pheasants and tree-peonies, with storks flying through clouds, with the eight trigram symbols, with the hemp-leaved lotus of India.

Beaker-shaped Vases (*Hu P'ing*), decorated with medallions of dragons surrounded by the typical flowers of the four seasons, with religious inscriptions in Sanskrit script supported upon scrolls of Indian lotus, with phœnixes flying through flowers of the four seasons, with grapes and slices of watermelon, with dragons holding up the characters *shêng shou*—i. e., "Wisdom and long life"—with leafy sprays of apricot, with gilded fishes swimming among water-weeds enameled in colors.

Flower Vases (*Hua P'ing*), modeled in the shape of one of the halves of a double gourd (*hu-lu*), split longitudinally, so as to hang against the wall, decorated with dragons among clouds, with wild geese in reeds, with the pine, bamboo, and plum.

Flower Vases (*Hua P'ing*), decorated with flowers and fruit, with pictures of birds, with flowering plants and butterflies, with familiar scenes, with historical subjects.

Flower Vases (*Hua P'ing*), decorated with phœnixes flying through the typical flowers of the four seasons, with groups of beautiful figures; and, in enamel colors, with dragons enveloped by the flowers of the four seasons, with a set of eight precious symbols supported upon scrolls of sacred fungus, with strings of jewels and fragrant plants.

Jars (*Kuan*), decorated with landscapes, with flying lions, with dragons and clouds, with peacocks and moutan peonies, with the eight Taoist immortals crossing the ocean, with the four "lights" worshiping the star of longevity, and six cranes symbolizing the cardinal points of the universe; and *Jars* enameled in colors with familiar scenes and historical subjects.

Slop Receptacles (*Ch'a Tou*), decorated with a pair of dragons in the midst of clouds, and with a string of magpies flying through flowers.

Slop Receptacles (Ch'a Tou), decorated with dragons and clouds, with arabesques of fragrant plants, with familiar scenes, with historical subjects, with flowers and fruit, with branches of sacred fungus.

Vinegar Ewers (Ts'u Ti), decorated with a pair of dragons among clouds, with interlacing scrolls of fairy flowers.

Chess-Board (Ch'i P'an), decorated with dragons surrounded by clouds.

Hanging Oil-Lamps (Ching T'ai), decorated with dragons mounting from sea-waves into clouds, with the typical flowers of the four seasons, with gilded chrysanthemums and hibiscus flowers.

Pricket Candlesticks (Chu T'ai), decorated with six storks flying to the six cardinal points of the universe, with the sacred fungus supporting a set of eight precious symbols and fairy flowers, with *ju-i* scepters and dragons in clouds.

Pricket Candlesticks (Chu T'ai), decorated with jewel mountains in the midst of the sea and with dragons in clouds, with medallions containing boys seated, with twigs of *Olea fragrans* in their hands, with water-plants, lotus-leaf borders, and flowers.

Jars for Candle-Snuff (Chien Chu Kuan), decorated with dragons and phœnixes among clouds enveloped in typical flowers of the four seasons.

Screens (P'ing), decorated round the border with brocaded bands inclosing flowers, fruit, and birds, in the center with a pair of dragons grasping jewels in their claws.

Pencil-Brush Handles (Pi Kuan), decorated with brocaded designs, with conventional fairy flowers and sacred fungus surrounded by clouds, with the river pictures and writings discovered in ancient times.

Brush-Pots (Pi Ch'ung), of cylindrical form, decorated with dragon medallions and a set of eight precious symbols.

Perfume-Boxes (Hsiang Lien), decorated with kilin (*ch'i-lin*) and ornamental medallions, with winding scrolls of conventional fairy flowers, with spiral bands inclosing flowers and fruit, with the eight Buddhist emblems of happy augury, with branches of the sacred fungus, with plum blossoms and sea-waves.

Fan Cases (Shan Hsia), decorated with dragons in clouds and borders of spiral fret.

Pencil Rests (Pi Chia), decorated with borders of sea-waves surrounding three dragons in the midst worked in high relief with openwork carving, and with landscape pictures.

Pallet Water-Pots (Yen Shui Ti), decorated with couchant dragons, with elephants carrying vases of jewels, with familiar scenes.

Betel-nut Boxes (Pin-lang Lu), decorated with familiar scenes, with historical subjects, with fragrant plants and lotus petals.

Hat Boxes (Kuan Lu), decorated with brocaded grounds interrupted by round medallions, and with dragons coiling through branches of the typical flowers of the four seasons.

FIG. 174.—Fluted Vase, encircled by a dragon in salient open-work relief, invested with a finely crackled turquoise glaze of mottled tone.

Handkerchief Boxes (Chin Lu), decorated outside with round medallions upon a brocaded ground, with a pair of dragons grasping the eight characters, *Yung pao ch'ang shou, ssŭ hai lai ch'ao,* meaning "Ever preserving long life, Homage coming from the four seas!" with familiar scenes, with historical subjects, with the typical flowers of the four seasons; inside, with branches of the sacred fungus, with the pine, bamboo, and plum, with blossoming orchids.

Garden Seats (Liang Tun), barrel-shaped, carved in pierced openwork with designs of a pair of dragons grasping jewels in their claws, with flying dragons, with lions, with sea-horses.

Wine-Jars (T'an), of tall ovoid form, decorated with propitious scrolls of clouds, with a hundred dragons, with a hundred storks; others enameled in colors with a hundred deer and inscribed *Yung pao ch'ien k'un*—i. e., "Ever protecting heaven and earth!"

Garden Bowls (*Kang*), for fish or flowers, decorated with fishes and water-weeds, with a set of eight precious symbols and fragrant plants, with lotus flowers, with groups of graceful forms, with sea-waves and plum-blossoms.

There are two typical examples in the collection of the blue and white porcelain of this period which have been illustrated to show the general style of decoration. The first, Fig. 153, is a jar with a procession of the eight Taoist genii crossing the sea holding up their several emblems, *Pa Hsien kuo hai*, which is inscribed underneath with the "six-character mark" of the reign inclosed within a double ring. The second, Fig. 81, is a tall ewer with long spout and flowing handle, decorated with phœnixes and storks flying among scrolled clouds, subsequently mounted with metal of Oriental workmanship and studded all over with precious stones.

2. PAINTED IN ENAMEL COLORS.

Chess Boards (*Ch'i P'an*), decorated with dragons among clouds.

Brush Handles (*Pi Kuan*), decorated with sea-waves and clouds and ascending and descending dragons.

Brush Cylinders (*Pi Ch'ung*), decorated with dragons and sea-waves, and with the typical flowers of the four seasons in circular medallions.

Flower Vases (*Hua Tsun*), with trumpet-shaped mouths, decorated with waving fillets and *ju-i* wands, with landscape pictures, with groups of sacred fungus.

Pricket Candlesticks (*Chu T'ai*), decorated with jewel mountains in the midst of the sea, with dragons and clouds, with familiar scenes, with historical subjects, with sprays of fragrant plants and rings of lotus petals.

Candle-Snuff Jars (*Chien Chu Kuan*), decorated with dragons enveloped in clouds, and with phœnixes flying through the typical flowers of the four seasons.

Fish-Bowls (*Kang*), decorated with flowers interrupted by medallions containing landscapes, with dragons ascending and descending through blue clouds, with phœnixes in couples.

Perfume-Boxes (*Hsiang Lien*), decorated with fragrant plants, with fir-leaf pattern brocades pierced in open-work, with the typical flowers of the four seasons.

Jars (*Kuan*), decorated with circular medallions on a brocaded ground, with the typical flowers of the four seasons, with fruit and birds, with the eight precious symbols.

Fan Cases (*Shan Hsia*), decorated with dragons and clouds and borders of spiral fret.

FIG. 175.—Crackled Celadon Vase of early Ming or Yuan period, lightly etched under a thick unctuous glaze of green tone.

Pencil Rests (*Pi Chia*), decorated with mountain landscapes and carved in pierced open-work.

Handkerchief Boxes (*Chin Lu*), decorated with the typical flowers of the four seasons.

Slop Receptacles (*Ch'a Tou*), decorated with dragons in clouds and arabesque scrolls, with the typical flowers of the four seasons.

Fish-Bowls (*Kang*), decorated with dragons ascending and descending through clouds, with arabesques and sprays of fragrant flowers.

3. PAINTED IN MIXED COLORS.

Teacups (*Ou*), plain white inside, decorated outside with waving fillets and exotic pomegranates, penciled in reserve upon a blue ground.

Fish-Bowls (*Kang*), white inside, and with a blue ground outside, decorated with pairs of dragons in the midst of clouds, with lions playing with embroidered balls, with interlacing scrolls of gilded lotus flowers, with conventional fairy flowers.

Brush Cylinders (Pi Ch'ung), decorated with white flowers reserved upon a blue ground, and with white dragons enveloped in the typical flowers of the four seasons in the same style of decoration.

Wine-Jars (T'an), of tall ovoid form, with a blue ground, decorated with a pair of dragons in clouds grasping antique *shou* ("longevity") characters, with winged threadlike dragons flying through a field of sacred fungus, with woods and wild animals, with familiar scenes, with historical subjects, and with the picture of the hundred boys.

Barrel-Seats (Liang Tun), decorated in enamel colors with lotus flowers and dragons encircled by clouds; and others enameled with a monochrome yellow ground, inclosing lotus flowers penciled in brown.

Teacups (Ch'a Chung), enameled yellow inside and out, with dragons in the midst of clouds and conventional flowers engraved in the paste under the glaze.

Censers (Hsiang Lu), enameled white inside, and decorated outside with designs painted in enamel colors surrounded by a yellow ground, with archaic lizardlike dragons carrying branches of sacred fungus, with the typical flowers of the four seasons, with fragrant plants and arabesque scrolls.

Vases (P'ing), of plain white porcelain, with phœnixes in couples and conventional fairy flowers engraved in the paste under the glaze.

Banquet Dishes (Shan P'an), enameled white inside, decorated outside with dragons in the midst of clouds, penciled in red, green, yellow, or brown.

It is a long list, but useful in supplying authentic materials as an aid to the proper classification of porcelain. It has been compiled from the series of lists of porcelain sent to Ching-tê-chên from the palace, so that each heading of bowls, for example, may comprise 10,000 or more, of different size and style of dec-

FIG. 176.—Pilgrim Bottle, decorated with imperial dragons in two underglaze colors, copper-red and cobalt-blue; mark, Ch'ien-lung.

oration. It is useful, too, in a negative tant decoration or peculiar color not quent invention.

way, as we may infer that any impor- included in the list was of subse-

The decorative designs were patterns of ancient brocades and is so rich. The author of the third century A. D. official emperor of robes of bro- designs of intertwining ground; and he quotes peror *Jên Tsung* of the in the period *Ching-yu* his " ceremonial hat blue gauze worked with and kilins, having the with dragons and scrolled compares these designs with the decoration of porcelains. names of ancient brocade " Phœnixes in Clouds," Ducks," " The Myriad Gems," nixes in Couples," " Pea- " The Fungus Plant," " Large

for the most part taken from the embroidered silks in which China *T'ao Shuo* traces back to the notices of presents from the caded silks, woven with dragons on a crimson a decree of the Em- *Sung* dynasty, issued (1034–37), ordering that should be made of dark medallions of dragons interspaces filled in clouds in gold," and he those used subsequently in He cites as well-known patterns: "Coiling Dragons," " Kilin," " Lions," " Mandarin " Dragon Medallions," " Phœ- cocks," " Sacred Storks," Lions in their Lair," " Wild

Geese nesting in the Clouds," "Phœnixes enveloped in Cloud Scrolls," "The Lily as an Emblem of Fertility," "The Hundred Flowers," "Phœnixes hidden in Flowers," "Group of Eight Taoist Immortals," "Dragons pursuing Jewels," "Lions sporting with Embroidered Balls," "Fish swimming among Water-Weeds"; and all of these were reproduced by the artists on imperial porcelain. The addition of colored monochrome grounds was also suggested, he thinks, by brocades, accounting thus for the mottled blue, the plain yellow, and the brown or "burnished gold" grounds given in the list. He estimates that about two-thirds of the designs in the *Ming* dynasty were imitated from brocades, the remaining third being either taken from Nature or copied from antiques; while of modern Chinese porcelain forty per cent are enameled in foreign style, in thirty per cent the designs are taken from Nature, twenty per cent have antique designs, and only ten per cent brocade patterns.

The decoration of Chinese porcelain during the *Ming* dynasty was, however, certainly not free from foreign influence. The brilliance of the blue which distinguishes the reign of *Chia-ching* was confessedly due to the cobalt ore called *Hui-hui ch'ing*, or "Mohammedan blue," which was imported from abroad, to be used in the imperial manufactory, and we occasionally meet in the descriptions of the designs with the expression *Hui-hui Wên*, or "Mohammedan scrolls," which I have translated "arabesques." There was frequent intercourse with Persia after the conquest of that country by the Mongols, at which time Hulugu (1253–64), the grandson of Genghis Khan, brought over a thousand Chinese artificers to his new country; and, later, Shah Abbas (1585–1627) is said to have settled a colony of Chinese potters at Ispahan. Previously to this, as we have seen before, in the account of the production of the reign of *Chêng-tê*, porcelain had been painted in blue, with Arabic inscriptions, at Ching-tê-chên, after designs probably sent for the purpose from Persia.

Among the vases in the collection attributed to the reign of *Wan-li* is Fig. 167, decorated with floral arabesques in underglaze blue, and in emerald-green and vermilion-red enamels, with metal mounts of Persian work; and Fig. 164, a vase of the same cylindrical form, with birds, fruit, and flowers on a diapered ground, penciled in black filled in with brilliant enamels.

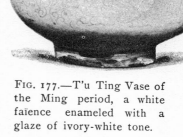

FIG. 177.—T'u Ting Vase of the Ming period, a white faïence enameled with a glaze of ivory-white tone.

Fig. 173 shows a unicorn monster in blue and dark green over a crackled ground; Fig. 174 a vase of turquoise crackle in bold openwork relief; and Fig. 38 (*b*) a little wine-pot enameled in turquoise blue and aubergine purple.

The three pieces of Lung-ch'üan celadon now to be mentioned date from an earlier time in the *Ming*: Fig. 159 shows a large solid vase, decorated in relief with bands of peony and chrysanthemum scrolls; Fig. 44 a large fluted dish, with foliated rim nearly two feet across, engraved under the glaze with fruit and flowers; and Fig. 175 a beaker-shaped vase of crackled celadon, with foliated rim and ribbed body, and an etched decoration under the green lustrous glaze.

The last specimen of the dynasty illustrated here is a *T'u Ting* vase of the yellowish-gray ware peculiar to the Ting-chou potteries in the province of Chihli, Fig. 177, with a molded and carved decoration under the soft-looking glaze of ivory-white tone. It is of archaic aspect and design, with a dragon coiled around the neck pursuing the jewel of omnipotence among the clouds, and swells at the rim in the form of a bulb of garlic.

天啓, T'IEN-CH'I (1621–27) AND 崇禎, CH'UNG-CHÊN (1628–43).

The last two emperors of the *Ming* dynasty reigned under the titles of *T'ien-ch'i* and *Ch'ung-chên*, but they were too busily engaged in repelling the invasion of the Manchu Tartars in the north to pay much attention to the patronage of the ceramic art. It is consequently remarkable only for its gradual decline, which is shown by the few dated pieces of these two periods that exist in collections, and which differ from other porcelain of the dynasty only in their imperfect finish and comparatively coarse decoration.

The only exception that I know of is in the case of certain small water-jars of globular shape marked underneath with a single character *T'ien*, "heaven," which the Chinese call *T'ien Tzŭ Kuan*, or "Heaven-Character Jars." They say that the inscription is only a contraction of the *nien-hao*, T'ien-ch'i; and the style of coloring, resembling that of the preceding reign of *Wan-li*, confirms this supposition. I have seen specimens painted in blue and white as well as brilliantly decorated in vivid enamel colors.

To sum up in a few words the decorated porcelain in the *Ming* dynasty:

1. The favorite color was blue, which was painted on the piece before it was glazed or fired. Usually this formed the sole "blue and white" decoration; occasionally it was relieved by a monochrome ground, or, on the other hand, it formed a mottled cobalt ground surrounding designs penciled in some other single color.

2. The earliest decoration in different colors was in colored glazes, combined with either a feldspathic or a lead flux, which were applied *sur biscuit* and fired in the ordinary furnace.

3. The art of decorating porcelain in vitreous colors, such as had been used previously in painted and *cloisonné* enameling upon metal, and which were painted on over the ordinary white glaze and subsequently fired a second time in the muffle stove, was of later introduction, and flourished especially in the *Wan-li* period.

4. The blue that was generally used in combination with the enamel colors was always laid on under the glaze. It was not till the seventeenth century, in the reign of *K'ang-hsi*, that a cobalt blue of vitreous character was invented, to be applied over the glaze like the other colors, and fired like them in the muffle stove.

FIG. 178.—K'ang-hsi Blue and White Jar, one of a pair, similar in style to that shown in Fig. 114, and mounted like it to form a garniture; mark, a lozenge tied with a fillet, in a double ring.

FIG. 179.—A Group of Snuff-bottles of the reigns of Yung-chêng and Ch'ien-lung.

CHAPTER VIII.

TECHNIQUE DURING THE MING PERIOD.—COLORS.—EMBOSSING.—CHISELING.—OPENWORK
CARVING.—GILDED DECORATION.—DECORATIONS IN ENAMELS.—FIRING.

THERE is an abundance of material in the official records of the *Ming* period for an account of the technique of the manufacture of porcelain, but here we have space for only a short abstract.

The best porcelain-earth (*t'ao t'u*), also called *kuan t'u*, or "government earth," was obtained from the Ma-ts'ang Mountains, near Hsin-chêng-tu, within the limits of the district of Fou-liang-hsien, where it was mined in four different places, the names of which are given. This earth is described as of rich plastic structure, with sparkling silvery spots of crystalline mica disseminated throughout, which indicates its kaolinic character derived from the decomposition of granite. It was brought down the river, the Chang Ho, to Ching-tê-chên in boats, four days being spent on the journey in winter and autumn, when the river was low; less than two days in the time of spring floods. The price paid for this earth at the imperial manufactory was seven tael-cents of silver for each picul of one hundred cat-ties.* In the eleventh year of the reign of *Wan-li* (1583) Chang Hua-mei, director of the manufactory, reported in a memorial to the emperor that the hillsides had been mined and countermined in every direction, and that so much extra labor was required to extract the earth that it was necessary to increase the price to ten tael-cents a picul. In spite of this, the supply of kaolin from these hills soon became exhausted, and it had to be brought from Wu-mên-t'o, where a new source of a similar earth had been discov-  ered; this place was twice as far away, although within the bounds of the district of Fou-liang-hsien, and as no more money was paid, it was diffi-cult to get it in sufficient quantity. Several other kinds of porcelain-earth were brought to Ching-tê-chên from Po-yang-hsien and other neighboring districts, but these were not considered good enough for the imperial manufactory.

FIG. 180.—Small Vase of white "Fên Ting" porce-lain, with lightly etched decoration under the pit-ted undulatory ("orange-peel") glaze of ivory-white tone.

The supply of petuntse, the feldspathic mineral employed in com-bination with the above "porcelain-earth" in the preparation of the paste, was obtained from Yü-kan-hsien, in the south, and from Wu-yuan-hsien, in the east. The petuntse obtained from Yü-kan was valued at twenty tael-cents for eighty catties, that from Wu-yuan at eighty tael-cents for ninety catties, which were reduced to seventy-two catties after a second washing and levigation. The feldspathic rock was pounded on the hillside where it was found, in mills worked by the mountain torrents, and after it had been washed and purified by levigation it was cut into briquettes or little cubes, hence the name of *pai-tun-tzŭ*, or "white briquettes."

* The tael, or Chinese ounce of silver, is equivalent to about $1.40 (Mexican); the catty to 1⅓ pounds, so that a picul would weigh 133⅓ pounds.

The several kinds of rocks which were ground to form the material for the different glazes are also described in order, and the places of production given. The best were covered with "arbor-vitæ-leaf" marks, the Chinese term for the dendrites which were due to manganese oxide. This was combined with the *lien hui*, 鍊灰, or "purified ashes" made by burning alternate layers of lime and ferns on the mountains called Chang-shan, and washing the residue.

All these different materials were worked and brought to the potteries by private enterprise, tunnels being excavated for miles at vast expense and with a loss of many lives, although each man's load produced only a few cents. Yet, in the thirty-second year of *Wan-li*, the governor of the city, Chou Ch'i-yuan, attempted to make the working of kaolin a government monopoly, till the people rebelled and forced him to withdraw his proclamations. It appears that the potters were always ready to resist oppression, as in the twenty-fifth year of the same reign they had burned the gate-house of the imperial manufactory during a riot, in consequence of which the officials responsible for the affair were recalled to Peking and thrown into prison, where they died.

<h2 style="text-align:center">COLORS.</h2>

Blue occupies a paramount position among the colors of the *Ming* dynasty. We have referred to the blue material brought from abroad by sea during the reign of *Hsüan-tê*, and to the "Mohammedan blue," to which the blue and white of *Chia-ching* owes its brilliant tint.

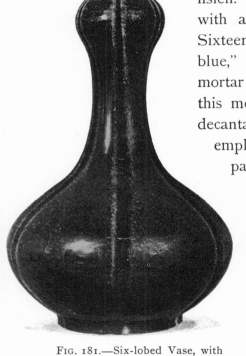

FIG. 181.—Six-lobed Vase, with a copper-red glaze of mottled crimson tint simulating the *sang-de-bœuf* of the Lang-Yao.

There is a long account of this last *hui ch'ing* in the records of Fou-liang-hsien. The best was described as exhibiting vermilion spots when crushed with a hammer, while the ordinary kind was sprinkled with silvery stars. Sixteen ounces of the imported material yielded three ounces of "true blue," otherwise called "crushed blue." The residue was pounded in a mortar with water, filtered through a stratum of broken porcelain, and by this means an additional quantity of about half an ounce was obtained after decantation. This was mixed with native blue in different proportions to be employed for the underglaze decoration of porcelain, a combination of ten parts to one forming the "first-class color," while the "ordinary blue" was composed of six parts of the Mussulman blue mixed with four parts of indigenous ore.

The native material, called 青花料, *Ch'ing hua liao*, or "blue decoration color," is the well-known cobaltiferous ore of manganese, found in many different parts of China, which has been analyzed by M. Ebelmen,* from a specimen obtained from the province of Yunnan. During the *Ming* dynasty the supply for the imperial works was first obtained from Po-t'ang, in the district of Lo-p'ing-hsien, near Jao-chou-fu, in the province of Kiangsi, where it occurred in irregular concretionary masses of peculiar shape. This produced a very dark color, and it is sometimes called by the name of "Buddha's-head Blue," or *Fo-t'ou ch'ing*, the traditional tint of the hair of Sakyamuni being that of lapis lazuli. This source was exhausted in the reign of *Chia-ching*, when the mines were closed in consequence of disturbances, and a new supply was afterward brought from several places in the prefecture of Jui-chou-fu, in the same province, under the name of *Shih tzŭ ch'ing*—i. e., "stone or mineral blue."

After describing the different kinds of blue, the official records give a list of the materials

* The Scientific Works of J. J. Ebelmen, who was Superintendent of the Imperial Porcelain Manufactory at Sèvres for many years, and who died in 1852, have been published in three volumes under the title *Recueil des travaux scientifique de M. Ebelmen, revu et corrigé par M. Salvétat*, Paris, 1861. They include three memoirs of original research on the composition of the materials employed in China in the fabrication and for the decoration of porcelain, prepared in association with M. Salvétat (tome i, pp. 347–455). The materials were sent from Ching-tê-chên by Père J. Ly, "prêtre Chinois de la congrégation de Saint-Lazare," and by M. Itier from Canton, who obtained the colors himself from the palette of a Chinese artist actually engaged in the decoration of porcelain. These memoirs, read before the Academy, are indispensable for the student of modern Chinese ceramic art.

used in the composition of the colored glazes used in the *Ming* dynasty from the reign of *Chia-ching* onward. This is most important and interesting, and the mineral components can be generally identified, as most of them are still in use under the same names.

They include 鉛粉, *ch'ien fên*, "lead carbonate," priced at four tael-cents the catty; 熠硝, *yen-hsiao*, "niter crystals," priced at two tael-cents the catty; 青礬, *ch'ing fan*, "iron sulphate," priced at three "cash" the catty; 黛赭石, *tai chê shih*, "antimony ore," the price of which is not recorded; 黑鉛, *hei ch'ien*, "lead," priced at two tael-cents and eight "cash" the catty; 松香, *sung hsiang*, "turpentine," priced at five "cash" the catty; 白炭, *pai t'an*, "white charcoal," priced at five tael-cents the catty; 金箔, *chin po*, "gold leaf," priced at twenty-five tael-cents the hundred sheets; copper," priced at six tael-

The list of materials prescriptions for the prep-glazes, ten in number al-

1. *Celadon Glaze*, 豆青油, 水, *yu shui*, 鍊灰, *lien hui*, gether. The first two materials silex ground with water, and with ferns, the ingredients of the *t'u*, literally "yellow earth," is a grayish-green tint known to us as of brown if the iron be in excess, time *tou-ch'ing*, or "pea-green"; dents that large fish-bowls were color in the reign of *Chia-ching*. be due to the silicates of lime shade under the influence of a nace, maintaining the iron at a

2. *Brown Glaze*, 紫金油, pared lime ground with water, ized quartz suspended in water. ceramists, passing from the to "dead leaf" and "old proportion of the *tzŭ-chin* iron. The Chinese name which is an appropriate clearer shades. The com- given in full detail by second letter, although he new invention of his time. unburned ware.

FIG. 182.—Beaker-shaped Vase, decorated in brilliant K'ang-hsi colors, greens, brownish-yellow, vermilion, and shaded purples, relieved by a black enameled ground.

and 古銅, *ku t'ung*, "old cents the catty. is followed by a series of aration of the colored together.

Tou-ch'ing Yu, composed of 油 and 黃土, *huang t'u*, mixed to- are feldspathic mineral, or petro- ashes prepared by burning lime ordinary white glaze, and *huang* ferruginous clay. The peculiar "celadon," passing into shades was called by the Chinese at this we have seen in the official in- ordered to be furnished of this The peculiar tint is supposed to and iron developing a greenish reducing atmosphere in the fur- minimum of oxidation.

Tzŭ-chin Yu, composed of pre- mixed with *tzŭ-chin* and pulver- This is the *fond laque* of French darkest bronze or coffee-color gold" according to the mineral, which is rich in means "burnished gold," rendering of some of the position of this glaze is Père d'Entrecolles in his gives it wrongly as a

It is mixed with the ordinary white glaze and applied upon the unburned ware.

3. *Turquoise Glaze*, 翠色油, *Ts'ui sê Yu*, composed of a mixture of *lien ch'êng ku t'ung shui*, a pulverized preparation of copper suspended in water, niter (*hsiao*), and quartz (*shih*). It is uncertain whether laminæ of metallic copper, or an oxide like verdigris, was employed in this mixture. Whichever it was, the result would be a silicate of copper, producing the beautiful finely crackled glaze of turquoise tint known to the Chinese as *ts'ui*, from its resemblance to the color of the plumes of the kingfisher, which they use in jewelry. Bowls and saucer-shaped plates enameled with this monochrome glaze, with the mark of the reign of *Chia-ching* underneath, are not rare.

4. *Bright Yellow Glaze*, 金黃油, *Chin huang Yu*, composed by mixing sixteen ounces of pulverized lead (*hei ch'ien mo*) with one and one-fifth ounces of antimony ore (*chê shih*), and grinding them together in a mortar. *Hei chê shih*, also called *Tai chê shih*, *hei* and *tai* both

meaning "black," is a mineral containing iron and antimony. It was analyzed by Brongniart under the name of *fer oligistique terreux.* The antimony is the source of the yellow, which becomes more or less orange on account of the presence of iron in the ore. It is the "imperial yellow" of collectors, and often occurs as a monochrome glaze, with the marks of all the reigns of this dynasty from *Hung-chih* downward, either plain or enameled over five-clawed dragons and other designs incised in the paste.

5. *Bright Green Glaze,* 金綠油, *Chin lü Yu,* composed by mixing together sixteen ounces of pulverized lead, one and two-fifths ounces of pulverized copper (*ku t'ung mo*), and six ounces of pounded quartz (*shih mo*). The copper is the source of the green, forming a silicate, which is dissolved in the vitrified glaze charged with oxide of lead. The last three glazes in this list—viz., the turquoise, yellow, and green—are often classed, by French writers, with the purple glaze which follows afterward under No. 8, as *couleurs de demi-grand feu.* They differ from the rest in having either a lead or an alkaline flux.

6. *Bright Blue Glaze,* 金青油, *Chin ch'ing Yu,* composed by mixing sixteen ounces of 翠, *ts'ui,* finely powdered, with one ounce of 石子青, *shih tzŭ ch'ing.* The dark blue glaze used by enamelers on metal, colored with silicate of cobalt, is called *ts'ui,* and the *shih tzŭ ch'ing* is the native cobaltiferous ore of manganese found, as we saw above, at Ju-chou-fu, in Kiang-si province. The combination would produce the brilliant sapphire-blue of purplish tint, like the *bleu du roi* of Sèvres, which is occasionally seen in a collection of *Chia-ching* cups. It is distinguished from the ordinary purple glaze of the period by being a *couleur du grand feu.*

7. *Coral-Red,* or *Iron-Red,* 攀紅, *Fan Hung,* composed of one ounce of calcined sulphate of iron (*ch'ing fan*) and five ounces of carbonate of lead (*ch'ien fên*) mixed together with Canton ox-glue (*Kuang chiao*). This is the well-known "coral red" of the muffle stove, which came into vogue in the reign of *Chia-ching,* and seems, from its cheapness and facility of firing, to have completely supplanted the more brilliant copper-red *du grand feu,* which

FIG. 183.—Celadon Vase of the Ch'ien-lung period, with dragons rising from the sea into the clouds, worked in relief under the glaze, which becomes paler over the prominent parts of the design.

made the reign of *Hsüan-tê* so illustrious, and which reappears in the reign of *K'ang-hsi* in the *sang-de-bœuf* glaze of the Lang Yao. With the exception of gold it is the only muffle color in the list, and it is a curious fact that even in the present day the workshops of the decorators in enamel colors at Ching-tê-chên are called *hung tien,* or "red shops," another independent evidence of the early appearance of this glaze.

8. *Purple Glaze,* 紫色油, *Tzŭ sê Yu,* composed of sixteen ounces of pulverized lead (*hei ch'ien mo*), one ounce of cobaltiferous ore of manganese (*shih tzŭ ch'ing*), and six ounces of pounded quartz (*shih mo*). This is the manganese purple formed by the solution of a slightly cobaltiferous oxide of manganese in a lead flux, which is so often found in association with the turquoise glaze, and, like this last, is generally minutely crackled throughout.

9. *Pale Blue Glaze,* 澆青油, *Chiao ch'ing Yu,* composed of *yu shui* and *lien hui,* the in-

gredients of the ordinary white glaze, combined with *shih tzŭ ch'ing*, the indigenous ore of cobalt. *Chiao ch'ing* means literally "watered blue." This is the ordinary blue of the *grand feu*, as M. Salvétat remarks, proved by the presence of lime and petrosilex. The intensity of the blue would depend on the amount of cobalt in the crude material, but it would always have a grayish hue when compared with the bright blue glaze of No. 6.

10. *Pure White Glaze*, 純白油, *Ch'un pai Yu*, composed of pounded feldspathic mineral or petrosilex ground with water (*yu shui*) and incinerated lime (*lien hui*). This is the ordinary white glaze of Chinese porcelain, which was often called at the time *T'ien pai*, *t'ien* meaning also " pure."

Among the other decorative processes described in the records of the imperial manufactory during the reign of *Wan-li* are :

1. Embossing.
2. Chiseling.
3. Openwork Carving.
4. Gilded Decoration.
5. Decoration in Enamel Colors.

1. *Embossed Pieces*, 堆器, *Tui Ch'i*, were made by applying to the surface, before firing, cuttings of the same paste of which they were formed, and working these with a moist brush into the shape of dragons, phœnixes. flowers, or other ornamental designs. The porcelain thus decorated in relief was afterward invested with glaze and finally fired in the kiln.

2. *Engraved Pieces*, 錐器, *Chui Ch'i*, were incised in the paste, as soon as it had been sufficiently dried, with dragons and other designs, chiseled with an iron style, and were subsequently glazed and fired. The work was sometimes so delicately executed that the pattern could be seen only by holding the porcelain up to the light, like the water-mark in paper, and the mark was penciled under the glaze in a similar fashion, which had the special name of 暗花, *an hua*—i. e., "hidden or veiled decoration." These processes were not invented at this time, however, as we often find specimens of Ting-chou porcelain of the *Sung* dynasty with embossed and chiseled ornament.

3. *Openwork Carving*, 玲瓏, *Ling-lung*, of porcelains with ornamental designs in pierced work, is described as having been executed by the potters at this period, although protested against by the censors as too elaborate and costly even for the emperor's palace.

I will pause here a while to describe an openwork vase of the time decorated in colors which is in my collection at Peking. It is bottle-shaped, eighteen inches high, with an ovoid body, gradually tapering into a broad, cylindrical neck, which swells again toward the mouth. The mouth is surrounded by a broad upright lip, which is carved with an open band of ornamental scrolls, and the body is perforated throughout in the interstices of the design, so as

FIG. 184.—Blue and White Jar of the K'ang-hsi period ; mark, palm leaf encircled by a double ring.

to allow an inner solid casing to be visible through an irregular open network, which is carved to represent two pairs of phœnixes displayed flying through clouds. The entire surface of the vase is richly brocaded in colors. The broad outlines of the decoration having been first limned in cobalt-blue of pale shade and penciled with lines of darker blue, the remaining parts are painted in enamel colors, including a rich vermilion red, a green of camellia-leaf tint, and a yellow of palish tone. The yellow parts are outlined in red, the other colors penciled with darker lines of red and green respectively, the last becoming almost black. The two rings of palmations which spread upward and downward to decorate the upper part of the neck exhibit all the four colors, the leaves being painted in regular series—blue, red, green, and yellow. The lower half of the neck is covered with a broad band of peony scrolls, interrupted by two projecting mask-handles, carved in openwork relief, perforated for rings, and enameled to represent lions' heads. The shoulder of the vase is encircled by a floral diaper of lozenge pattern, penciled in red, displaying a ring of the eight Buddhist emblems with waving fillets painted in

underglaze cobalt-blue, and a lightly tions surrounds the base, which is per- large holes, through which straps could sketched border of conventional folia- forated at regular intervals with four be passed.

The vase is a specimen of the "old Japan" Imari pieces, which *chrysanthemo-péonienne*, although crude work. It is interesting, on perfectly finished technique of Fig. 185 exhibits a most excel- gourd is fitted with a revolv- painted with bats flying among the ornamental trellis bands cate profusion of ornamen- in the picture; it is exe- ors, with touches of gilding. trast to the bold execution old *Ming* vase, which is

class which furnished models for the Jacquemart comprised in his *famille* the Japanese copies are of rough the other hand, to compare the the *Ch'ien-lung* period, of which lent example. The waist of the ing belt, and the inner vase is clouds, seen through the rifts of of the outer casing. The deli- tal design is well indicated cuted in fine enamel col- It offers a complete con- and strong coloring of the still not without its charm.

4. *Decoration in Gold,* plied to porcelain that had gold leaf, combined with a bonate of lead, was mixed with brush, and the porcelain was was employed to fire the coral- times applied afterward, and the muffle stove. It was used as well as in combination with mentioned give instances of the with blue and white, directing low hibiscus blossoms to be

描金, *Miao Chin*, was ap- been previously fired. The tenth part by weight of car- gum and spread on with the fired again in the stove that red. A second coat was some- the piece was again fired in solely as a gilded monochrome, other colors. The lists already use of gilding in combination chrysanthemum flowers and yel- penciled in gold.

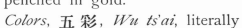

FIG. 185.—Vase, one of a pair, with pierced outer casing and movable belt, decorated in enamel colors, with gilding of the Ch'ien-lung period.

5. *Decoration in Enamel*

Colors, 五彩, *Wu ts'ai*, literally

"in five colors," was only occasionally employed in the imperial manufactory, although it was much used in the private potteries at Ching-tê-chên in the reign of *Wan-li*, when the art of painting in blue declined, from the want of proper materials. The colors employed were vitreous fluxes, containing only a small percentage of metallic oxides, the same that had previously been employed in enameling upon metal. They were painted upon white porcelain that had been fired in the furnace, and then baked a second time in a muffle stove to fix the colors. Some parts of the decoration had often been previously penciled in underglaze cobalt-blue, and the outlines of the designs were usually sketched in the same color.

FIRING.

Several kinds of furnaces are mentioned in the records. The imperial manufactory in the beginning of the reign of *Chia-ching* contained fifty-two furnaces, of which thirty-two were *kang yao*, in which the large fish-bowls were fired, the remainder being either *ch'ing yao*, for baking the ordinary blue and white, or *sê yao*, for firing the colored ware. Later in the reign, when more blue and white was required, it is related that sixteen of the *kang yao* were converted into *ch'ing yao*. Besides these there were the *hsia yao* kilns for baking the clay cases or seggars, in which the porcelain was placed inside the furnace to shield it from the blast of the fire.

The *kang yao* are described as measuring six feet broad in front, six and a half feet broad at the back, and six feet in depth, with rounded top. Only one fish-bowl of the largest size or of the second size could be fired at a time, or two of the third size, placed one above the other. A gentle fire was kept up for seven days and nights, so as gradually to dry the materials, then a fierce fire was raised and maintained for two days, till the seggars were seen to be red all over and emitting rays of white heat. The fire was then stopped, all the orifices sealed up, and the contents were left undisturbed for ten days more before the kiln was opened. The fuel was pine billets, of which one hundred and twenty loads, of one hundred catties, each valued at four tael-cents of silver, were consumed for each firing, ten more being allowed in rainy weather. The largest bowls were valued at fifty-eight taels each, those of the second size at fifty taels, although only twenty and eighteen, afterward raised to twenty-three and twenty taels, used to be paid by the officials for those fabricated at private kilns. The official "squeeze" was tight in China, even four centuries ago.

The *ch'ing yao*, or "blue kilns," were of similar shape to the above, but of smaller size, the corresponding dimensions in Chinese feet being five, five and a half, and four and a half. The charge consisted of about two hundred of the ordinary round dishes and saucer plates; or of one hundred and fifty to one hundred and sixty of those of larger diameter. It would hold twenty-four of the largest bowls, or thirty bowls one foot in diameter, only sixteen or seventeen of the ovoid jars with bulging shoulder called *t'an*, but five hundred to six hundred little wine-cups. The gentle fire lasted two days, the fierce fire twenty-four hours, the period being judged by the state of the seggars as before, after which the furnace was sealed up. From first to last the firing of the blue kilns took five days, and about sixty loads of fuel were consumed, ten more if the charge consisted of large bowls, tall jars, or temple bricks, or if the weather were wet.

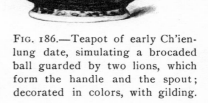

FIG. 186.—Teapot of early Ch'ien-lung date, simulating a brocaded ball guarded by two lions, which form the handle and the spout; decorated in colors, with gilding.

The private kilns for firing blue and white were of larger size and held several times the quantity, the charge consisting of over one thousand of the smaller pieces, yet they are said to have used only about the same amount of fuel. The seggars were piled in tiers and ranged in seven rows; the first two rows next the entrance were filled with coarse pieces, the third row contained a few good pieces, the middle three rows all the best porcelain, and the last three rows next the chimney coarser ware again. In the imperial furnace, where all the porcelain was of the highest class, empty cases stood at the front and back, to screen those in the middle from the blast.

There is no particular account in the official records of the *sê yao*, or furnaces for the colored ware, but in the *T'ien kung k'ai wu*, a small manual of the industrial arts published toward the end of the *Ming* dynasty, there is an illustration showing the form of the open and closed stoves used at the time to fire the porcelain decorated with enamel colors. This picture is reproduced among the woodcuts illustrating the article "Porcelain" in the large Chinese encyclopædia, *T'ou shu chi ch'êng*, in 10,000 books, a copy of which is in the British Museum.

Some of the private potters acquired renown for their ceramic productions in the reign of *Wan-li*, and at this time we begin to hear of copies of antiques, a branch of art so much developed afterward. In the province of Kiang-nan at the "boccaro" potteries of Yi-hsing-hsien, to which reference has already been made, a man named Ou became celebrated for his productions, which were called after him *Ou Yao*. He succeeded in reproducing the crackled glaze of the ancient Ko Yao, and the different colors of the imperial ware and Chun-chou porcelain of the *Sung* dynasty, upon the characteristic brown stoneware of the place. Two of his glazes were afterward copied in turn by T'ang Ying, as we shall see presently.

The imitations of Ting-chou white porcelain made at Ching-tê-chên were still more successful. The *Po wu yao lan* says of these: "The new censers modeled in the form of the four-legged sacrificial *ting* of the ancient sovereign *Wên Wang*, and of the bronzed bowl-shaped *yi* with mask-handles of monsters' heads and halberd-shaped 'ears,' are in no way inferior to the original productions of the Ting-chou potters, and they may even be mistaken for genuine old specimens, if the gloss of the furnace has been removed by friction. The best are those made by Chou Tan-ch'uan." Many stories are told of the marvelous ingenuity of this artist,

FIG. 187.—Blue and White Vase of the K'ang-hsi period; mark, a flower sprig.

who seems to have been on friendly terms with some of the foremost scholars of the time, of which I may quote one: "One day, as Chou Tan-ch'uan was traveling along the river in a merchant boat to the province of Kiang-nan, he landed at Pi-ling to visit his friend T'ang, President of the Imperial Sacrificial Court, and asked to be allowed to look at an ancient Ting-chou censer, the dimensions of which he measured with his fingers, while he took impressions of the chiseled decoration upon paper, which he put in his sleeve, and carried with him back to Ching-tê-chên. Six months later he returned, and when he saw T'ang again he drew from his sleeve a censer, exclaiming: 'Your Excellency has a white Ting-chou censer; I have got its fellow!' T'ang was greatly surprised. He compared it with the ancient censer in his own collection, and there was not a hair's-breadth difference. He tried the cover and the stand of his own, and they fitted exactly. He asked him where he had got it. Chou replied: 'I made it as a copy. I will not deceive you.' The president, delighted, purchased it for forty taels of silver, and put it in his cabinet, beside the original censer, as if they were a pair. Some years later, at the end of the reign of *Wan-li*, Tu Chiu-ju, of Huai-an, after he had seen in a dream a vision of T'ang's ancient censer, succeeded in obtaining from Chun-yü, a grandson of the president, the imitation made by Chou for one thousand taels."

A still more famous potter was the famous Hao Shih-chiu, who adopted the sobriquet of "Hermit hidden in the teapot," and lived in a hut with a broken potsherd for a window, where he capped the verses of his literary friends, and fabricated the delicate wine-cups which people thronged from all parts of the empire to buy. The most beautiful of these tiny cups were the 流霞盞, *liu hsia chan*, or "cups of liquid dawn," invested with undulations of brightest vermilion tint, and the 卵幕盃, *luan mu pei*, or "eggshell cups," of pure translucent white, so thin that they were said to float upon water, and so light that they weighed only half a *chu*— that is, less than a gramme each. He also excelled in the manufacture of teapots, some of which were of pale celadon color, like the old ware of the *Sung* dynasty, but uncrackled; others enameled in reddish shades of brown (*tzŭ chin*) or "dead leaf," made after the "boccaro" teapots of that color fabricated at Yi-hsing-hsien by the Ch'ên family of potters, all of which he inscribed underneath with his own "hermit mark."

An eggshell wine-cup of this reign is shown in Fig. 18, one of a pair fit to be compared with the translucent cups of the hermit Hao Shih-chiu, which have the mark of the reign of *Wan-li* inscribed underneath. Pressed upon a mold before glazing, the decoration appears inside in gentle relief, becoming more visible when the delicate cup is held up to the light filled with yellow Shao-hsing wine. The lineaments of one of the dragons are but dimly visible in the picture.

FIG. 188.—Water Receptacle, with three medallions of archaic dragon scrolls etched under the peach-bloom glaze ; mark, K'ang-hsi.

CHAPTER IX.

CHING-TÊ-CHÊN.—THE IMPERIAL PORCELAIN MANUFACTORY.

BEFORE proceeding to the consideration of the ceramic productions of the present dynasty it is necessary to give a short description of Ching-tê-chên, which, as we have already shown, has long been the chief seat of the porcelain industry in China, where it occupies a more prominent position than does Sèvres, in France, or Meissen, in Germany. It has, indeed, become the exclusive source of artistic porcelain, and supplies the demands of the whole empire, not only for *objets de luxe,* but also for the better class of household porcelain ware, such as dinner services, teapots, and the like. The factories in the other provinces, established where there happened to be available deposits of white plastic clay, furnish only coarse ware for local consumption. The exception is that of Tê-hua, in the province of Fuchien (Fukien), where a kind of white porcelain is produced covered with a soft, velvety glaze of creamy tint, comprising ornamental vases, wine-ewers and wine-cups, teapots, horn-shaped cups of archaic design, etc., and which is especially celebrated for its statuettes of divinities and fantastic figures. This will be referred to more fully in Chapter XXII.

The manufacture of porcelain at Ching-tê-chên, according to local tradition, as it is stated in the official description of the province, dates from the *Han* dynasty (B. C. 206—A. D. 220), but the annalist adds that nothing is known with certainty about the productions of these remote times.

The earliest record of the place in the general annals of the empire is in A. D. 583, the first year of the reign of the last sovereign of the short-lived *Ch'ên* dynasty, who ordered a supply of porcelain plinths (*t'ao ch'u*) to be made there, to serve as pedestals for the support of the wooden pillars of the large palaces which he was building at his capital, Chien-k'ang (the modern Nanking). They were sent, elaborately molded in ornamental designs, in the style of the ordinary plinths carved out of solid stone, but were rejected as not sufficiently solid. A second supply was furnished in due course, but still they were not strong enough for the purpose required, and the imperial decree had to be withdrawn. The plinths of the immense columns which support the roofs of such large buildings are usually made of carved marble or of some other hard stone, and molded white porcelain seems to be the most unsuitable of materials. It is, however, employed with success in Chinese architecture where less strain is required, as in the famous porcelain tower of Nanking, which was rebuilt in the reign of the Emperor *Yung-lo* (1404–24), and formed one

FIG. 189.—Ch'ien-lung Vase, of turquoise crackle, with the ornamental details worked in relief under the glaze.

of the chief ornaments of the ancient capital till the pagoda was destroyed by the Taiping rebels during their occupancy of the city (March 19, 1853, to July 19, 1864). Most museums possess a specimen of the white L-shaped bricks of which it was built, coated with a lustrous white glaze, which were made at Ching-tê-chên. The porcelain of the sixth and seventh centuries must have been of much the same character as these bricks, being always compared by writers of the time to pure white jade.

It was under the name of imitation jade (*chia yü*) that the potters of Hsin-p'ing (the modern Fou-liang) presented their ceramic ware to the founder of the celebrated *T'ang* dynasty in the year 621, when they carried it to the distant capital of Ch'ang-an, in the province of Shensi, and it is said to have rivaled this stone, so precious to the Chinese, in its whiteness, translucency, and musical ring. The new porcelain soon became more widely known, and we find in the official biography of Chu Sui a notice of an imperial decree received by him, when he was Governor of Hsin-p'ing, in the year 707, ordering the production of a set of sacrificial vases for the funeral temple of the Emperor *Chung-Tsung*, the fourth of the *T'ang* dynasty, who had just died. The manufacture seems to have degenerated afterward, and the pale blue ware of other potteries came into wider vogue, the new color being preferred from its enhancing the tints of wine and tea, so that the comparatively coarse fabric of the cups made at these places was overlooked.

It was not until the *Sung* dynasty that regular officials were appointed to superintend the manufacture of porcelain and to send supplies to the capital for the use of the imperial court. The name of Ching-tê-chên dates from this time, and it is derived from that of the period *Ching-tê* (1004–1007), in the first year of which a decree was issued ordering the official in charge of the manufactory to inscribe underneath the pieces the mark *Ching tê nien chih*, " Made in the period *Ching-tê*." The place had been previously known as Ch'ang-nan-chên, from its position on the southern bank of the Ch'ang River, the term *chên*, which may be translated " mart," being applied in China to a few populous centers of trade which are not fortified with regular walls.

Ching-tê-chên is in the province of Kiangsi, on the south of the great Yangtze River, in latitude 29° 16′ north, and longitude 0° 48′ west of the meridian of Peking, according to the

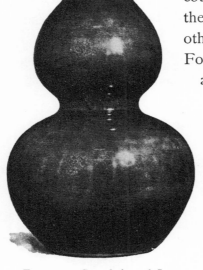

observations of the French missionaries of the eighteenth century. The river Ch'ang, which rises in the mountains which separate the provinces of Kiangsi and Anhui, after a course of about one hundred miles in a southwest direction runs into the Poyang Lake. On its northern bank, about the middle of its course, is the small district town of Fou-liang-hsien, and near its mouth the prefectural city of Jao-chou-fu, which has jurisdiction over this and six other walled towns. Ching-tê-chên is situated about four miles below Fou-liang, on the opposite side of the river, and is under its jurisdiction, although the mandarin in immediate charge is appointed from Jao-chou, with the rank of *T'ung-chih*, or sub-prefect. There is another official in charge of the imperial manufactory, who is usually deputed from the imperial household (Nei Wu Fu) at Peking, and who is at the same time commissioner of the important customs station at Kiukiang, established near the point where the Poyang Lake communicates with the Yangtze. The funds for the porcelain works are directed to be taken from the customs-chest. The commissioner forwards the porcelain by boats to Peking, which go down the Yangtze River to Chinkiang, and thence up the Grand Canal to Tien-tsin. At the junction of the Grand Canal with the Yellow River there is another large customs barrier, with an imperial commissioner, stationed at Huai-an-fu, who used formerly to be *ex-officio* superintendent of the porcelain

FIG. 190.—Gourd-shaped Lang Yao Vase of palish liver-red tint flecked with light spots.

works and privileged to find the funds. T'ang Ying succeeded Nien-si-yao as commissioner of customs at Huai-an-fu in 1736, with the control of the customs of the three provinces of Kiangsi, Kiangsu, and Anhui, and he held the post till he was transferred to Kiukiang, where he remained till 1749, when his successor, Ch'in Yung-chün, was appointed. The annual sum allowed from the Huai-an transit dues had been eight thousand taels. Tang Ying says in his preface to the *Fou-liang-hsien-chih*, dated 1740: " In the sixth year of the reign of *Yung-chêng* (1728) I was appointed to take charge of the imperial potteries. In the first year of *Ch'ien-lung* (1736) I was appointed commissioner of customs at Huai-an, remaining also in superintendence of the potteries, but during my time there, on account of the great distance, I was only once able to visit Ching-tê-chên, when I found everything going on satisfactorily. Last year (1739)* I was transferred to Kiukiang. During my *régime* over ten thousand taels have been devoted yearly to the work, and several hundreds of thousands of articles of porcelain have been provided for the use of the emperor."

To the south of the Poyang Lake, twenty miles distant by river, is the large city of Nan-ch'ang-fu, the capital of the province of Kiangsi, which is full of porcelain shops, its principal staple being the porcelain of Ching-tê-chên, which it distributes to all parts of the south of China. The trade route to Canton passes this city, and large quantities are conveyed thither, consisting partly of finished pieces, partly of plain white porcelain, which has to be decorated in enamel colors by the Cantonese artist before it is finally exported. The journey is made by water with the exception of a day's portage across the Mei-ling pass. This is shown in a series of water-color pictures from Canton, intended to illustrate the porcelain manufacture of China, which hang framed in the British Museum, and which conclude with pictures of the land journey to Canton and of the final packing of the things in boxes for shipment to Western countries.

Fou-liang is situated in a hilly country surrounded by mountains of graphitic granite, from the gradual decomposition of which the kaolinic deposits have been formed. The natives, as the annalist quaintly remarks, partake of the rude and rugged nature of their surroundings. The river runs down a rocky gorge till it reaches Ching-tê-chên, where there is a tract of open country about two miles in length and breadth, bounded on the north and west by the river, which makes a wide curve, on the south by a smaller stream flowing from the west to join the river, and on the east by the Ma-an Shan or "Saddle-back Mountains." These hills supply the red clay for the

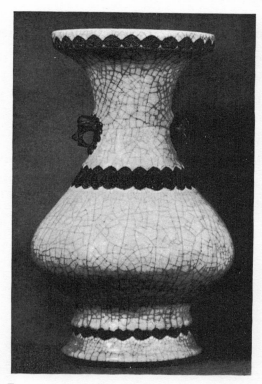

FIG. 191.—Gray Crackled Vase of the Ch'ien-lung period, reserving encircling biscuit bands of fret, and lion's-head handles of iron-gray perforated for rings.

seggars and for the reproduction of antiques with colored bodies. Across the south river is the hamlet of Hu-t'ien-shih, with a pagoda and the ruins of ancient potteries of the *Sung* dynasty. A quantity of potsherds of ancient porcelain were collected from these ruins in the eighteenth century and used as models for monochrome glazes, as will presently be seen. The river strand at Ching-tê-chên is thirteen *li* long, reckoning from the temple of the goddess of Mercy, where it emerges from the hills, to the southwest, where it enters the hills again, re-enforced by the southern stream, and it derives from this its common name of "The Thirteen Li Mart." Within the angle of junction of the two rivers there is an open space of waste ground known as Hsi-kua Chou, or "Watermelon Island," which forms a market-place where the porcelain peddlers display their stalls. The rest of the space is densely packed with streets of shops, temples, and guild-houses, the intervals being filled with the kilns and workshops.

There is a good general map of the place given in the *Ching-tê-chên T'ao lu*, as well as a bird's-eye view of the Yü ch'i ch'ang, the imperial manufactory. I have seen it also penciled in blue upon one of the porcelain slabs of a large screen, with the imperial porcelain manufactory

---

* It was in this year, according to the history of the province of Kiangsi, that the chief commissionership of customs was transferred to Kiukiang, T'ang Ying remaining in charge and retaining also the directorship of the potteries. This city is much nearer to Ching-tê-chên, and the director resided there part of every year to superintend the work in person. Directors were appointed from the imperial household in rotation up to the forty-third year of *Ch'ien-lung* (1778), after which the control was left to the provincial authorities. In the present day the Tao-t'ai of Kiukiang, who is the native commissioner of customs, is also *ex-officio* superintendent of the imperial potteries at Ching-tê-chên.

in the middle, encircled by a number of scattered kilns vomiting flames and smoke from their wide chimneys.

Père d'Entrecolles writes in his first letter,* dated Jao-chou, September 1, 1712: "The sojourn that I make from time to time at King-te-tching, for the spiritual needs of my converts, has afforded me an opportunity of learning the way they make there that beautiful porcelain which is so highly esteemed, and which is exported to all parts of the world. Besides what I have myself seen, I have gathered many particulars from the Christians, among whom there are several who work in porcelain, and from others engaged in its commerce on a large scale. I have assured myself of the truth of their replies by a constant reference to Chinese books treating upon the subject, more especially the annals of *Feou-leam*, the fourth volume of which contains an article on porcelain.

"King-te-tching, which is a dependency of Feou-leam, is hardly more than a good league distant from it, and this last city is under the jurisdiction of Jao-tcheou. The annals do not tell us who was the inventor of porcelain, nor refer to what experiments or to what happy chance the invention is due. They only say that in ancient times the porcelain was exquisitely white and free from any fault, and that the articles that were made of it and transported to other kingdoms were called 'precious jewels of Jao-tcheou.' Lower down they add: 'The beautiful porcelain of sky-blue is all produced at King-te-tching; that made in other places differs widely both in color and quality.'

"In fact, without speaking of the works of pottery which are made everywhere throughout China, and which are never called porcelain, there are some provinces like Fou-kien and Canton where they work in porcelain, but strangers can not be deceived with these products; that of Fou-kien is of a snow white which has no brilliancy, and which is not decorated with other colors. Workmen from King-te-tching carried there formerly all their materials, in the hope that they would reap a rich harvest from the Europeans who drive a large trade with Emouy (Amoy), but it was all in vain; they never succeeded there. The reigning emperor (*K'ang-hsi*), who will ignore nothing, also brought workmen in porcelain to Peking, with everything employed by them in the work; they neglected nothing, in order to succeed under his supervision, yet all their labor was wasted. It is possible that interested motives may have contributed to their want of success; however that may be, it is King-te-tching alone which has the honor of furnishing porcelain for all parts of the world. Even Japan comes to buy it in China.

"King-te-tching only needs to be surrounded by walls to be called a city, and even to be compared with the largest and most populous cities of China. The places called *tching* (*chên*), which are few in number, but distinguished by a large traffic and trade, are not usually walled—perhaps in order that they may grow without hindrance, perhaps to facilitate embarking and disembarking merchandise. King-te-tching is estimated to contain eighteen thousand households, but some of the large merchants have premises of vast extent, lodging a prodigious multitude of workmen, so that the population is said to number over a million souls, who consume daily over ten thousand loads of rice and more than a thousand hogs. It extends for more than a league along the bank of a fine river. It is not, as you might imagine, an indiscriminate mass of houses; the streets are straight as a line and cross at regular intervals; every inch of ground is occupied, so that the houses are too crowded and the streets far too narrow; when passing along you seem to be

FIG. 192.—Bottle of the Ch'ien-lung period, with an embossed and chiseled decoration, painted in green and purple with touches of white, relieved by a monochrome ground of finely crackled yellow of clouded tone.

* *Lettres édifiantes et curieuses*, xviii, p. 224.

in the midst of a fair, and hear nothing but the cries of the street porters trying to force their way through.

"Living is much more expensive at King-te-tching than at Jao-tcheou, because everything consumed there has to be brought from elsewhere, even the wood burned in the furnaces. Nevertheless, it is an asylum for numberless poor families, who can not subsist in the neighboring towns, and employment is found there for the young as well as for the less robust; even the blind and maimed can make a living by grinding colors. In ancient times, according to the history of Feou-leam, there were only three hundred porcelain furnaces at King-te-tching —now there are at least three thousand. Fires are of frequent occurrence, and the god of fire has many temples, one of which has been recently dedicated by the present mandarin. Not long ago eight hundred houses were burned, but the large profits their owners drew from their rental caused their speedy reconstruction.

"The town is situated in a plain surrounded by high mountains. The hill to the east forms a kind of semicircle in the background, while from the mountains at the sides issue two rivers, which unite afterward: one is but small; the other is very large, and forms a splendid strand more than a league long, spreading into a wide basin and losing much of its velocity. This wide space may be seen sometimes filled with two or three long lines of boats, moored close together. The sight with which one is greeted on entering through one of the gorges consists of volumes of smoke and flame rising in different places, so as to define all the outlines of the town; approaching at nightfall, the scene reminds one of a burning city in flames, or of a huge furnace with many vent-holes.

"It is surprising that such a populous place, full of such riches, and with an infinite number of boats coming and going every day, and which has no walls that can be closed at night, should, nevertheless, be governed by a single mandarin, without the least disorder. It must be allowed that the policing is admirable; each street has one or more chiefs, according to its length, and each chief has ten subordinates, every one of whom is responsible for ten houses. They must keep order, under pain of the bastinado, which is here administered liberally. The streets have barricades, which are closed at night, and opened by the watchman only to those who have the password. The mandarin of the place makes frequent rounds, and he is accompanied occasionally by mandarins from Feou-leam. Strangers are hardly permitted to sleep there; they must either spend the night in their boats or lodge with acquaintances, who become responsible for their conduct.

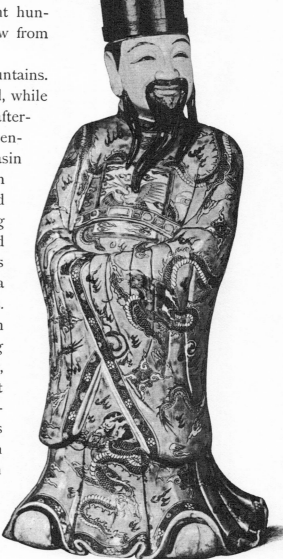

FIG. 193.—Statuette of a Mandarin, in the costume of the highest rank, decorated in brilliant K'ang-hsi colors, with a pale purple ground.

"They tell me that a piece of porcelain, when it comes out from the kiln, has passed through the hands of seventy workmen, and I can well believe it, from what I myself have seen, as their huge workshops have often been for me a kind of Areopagus, when I have proclaimed Him who created the first man out of clay, and from whose hands we proceed to become vessels, either of glory or of shame.

"The boats come constantly down the river, laden with *petuntse* and *kaolin* which have to be purified by decantation, leaving an abundant residuum, which gradually accumulates into large heaps. The clay seggars in the three thousand furnaces last only twice or three times, and very often the whole baking is lost. Some of this *débris* is utilized to fill in the walls which surround all the houses, or is carried to the swampy ground adjoining the river, to make it fit for a market-place, and ultimately for building, for which new ground is always wanted.

Besides, in the flood time, the river carries down much broken porcelain, so that its bed is, so to speak, entirely packed with it, making a refreshing sight for the eyes.

"The mountains all around are covered with tombs; at the foot of one of these is a very large pit encircled by high walls, in which they throw the bodies of the poor who have no money to buy coffins, which is considered the greatest of misfortunes; this place is called *ouan min kem*—that is, 'Pit for the Myriad People'; in the times of plague, which ravages almost every year, the huge pit ingulfs heaps of corpses, which are covered with quicklime to con-

FIG. 194.—Delicate and graceful Vase of the best period of K'ang-hsi. *Pâte sur pâte* modeling of kilin amid surges in fine white beneath a beautiful translucent glaze set off with kilin in strong peach-bloom tint.

sume the flesh. The bonzes, at the end of the year, come to carry away the bones to make room for more, and burn them with a kind of funeral service which they celebrate for the unhappy dead."

The worthy father mentions the Roman Catholic Church, established by the liberality of the Marquis de Broissia, but he does not allude to the imperial porcelain manufactory, which occupies such a prominent place in all the native descriptions and maps. Perhaps it was not in active operation at the time; it was not till four years after the date of his second letter (January 25, 1722) that a new imperial commissioner, Nien Hsi-yao, was appointed superintendent, after a long interval, during which the work was intrusted to the local officials.

The level of the little plain is broken at one point toward the south by a small hill, where, as tradition relates, a general of Ch'in Shih-huang the builder of the Great Wall of China, once tethered his horses, and it derived its original name from this; it was afterward called Tu Shan, "The Solitary Hill," and Chu Shan, "Jewel Hill," the jewel being guarded, according to geomantic notions, by the dragons of the encircling mountain belt. The Yü Yao Ch'ang, "Imperial Porcelain Manufactory," also called Yü Ch'i Ch'ang, was founded on the south side of this hillock in the reign of *Hung-wu* (1368–98), the celebrated founder of the *Ming* dynasty. The annals say: "Tuan T'ing-kuei, style Pao-ch'i, a native of Ch'ing-ch'üan, who was sent by the Emperor *Hung-wu*, with the rank of Secretary of the Board of Works, to superintend the porcelain manufacture, built the *yamên* on the south of Jewel Hill, in spite of the vigorous protests of the natives of

Ching-tê-chên, who objected to being called upon to do any work outside of their own industry." It was afterward burned down, and it was rebuilt in the reign of *Chêng-tê* (1506–21) on its present lines. In the beginning of the reign of *Wan-li* (1573–1619) it was purposely fired by the potters as a protest against the exactions of the palace eunuchs, who, however, were afterward recalled, and eunuchs have never since been put in charge. During the reigning dynasty it has been twice completely razed to the ground: in the fourteenth year of *K'ang-hsi* (1675), in connection with the revolt of Wu San-kuei; and in the year 1855, when Ching-tê-chên was taken by the Taiping rebels and almost depopulated. Their disastrous rule lasted till the third year of *T'ung-chih* (1864), and in 1866 the imperial manufactory was rebuilt by the new superintendent, Ts'ai Chin-ch'ing, with its seventy-two buildings, all raised upon the old foundations.

The outer wall, three *li* (about an English mile) in circuit, incloses the imperial manufactory as well as the Jewel Hill, which forms the "Guardian Hill" of the place on the north. The hill is planted with trees and covered with pavilions, of which the Yü Shih T'ing, "Imperial Verse Pavilion," and the Huan Ts'ui T'ing, "Green Encircled Arbor," stand conspicuously on the crest of the hill. Volumes of odes have been indited in these summer-houses, inspired by the ring of furnace fires outside, the dark background of hill and water, and the calm sky overhead, as the versifiers have sat there sipping their wine or tea. There are three temples inside the inclosure: the Yu T'ao Ling Ssŭ, "Sacred Temple of the Protector of the Potteries," containing the shrine of the Fêng Huo Hsien, the "Genius of the Fire-Blast," a deified potter, the story of whose vicarious sacrifice will be related presently; the Kuan-Ti Miao, "Temple of the (National) God of War"; and the T'u Ti Ssŭ, "Temple of the Gods of the Land." The residence of the superintendent and his *chancellerie* are also inside; that of the sub-prefect of Jao-chou, who is the governor of the place, is built just outside on the right of the main entrance; and the Kung Kuan, the "Public Offices," are also outside on the opposite side of the gate. Inside this great southern gateway stand the drum-tower and gong-tower, one on either side of the avenue leading to the Ta T'ang, the "Principal Hall," which has wings at the sides. Beyond the great hall one comes to a square courtyard with rows of buildings on the right and left for the secretaries, accountants, and attendants, and there is another large hall at the back, behind which are the pleasure-grounds and the Jewel Hill already referred to.

The workshops and stores are on the east and west, outside the courtyard; and the modern arrangement, since the place was rebuilt in 1866, is the following: On the eastern side are two large buildings, each containing six workshops for the making of the *yuan ch'i*, the ordinary "round ware" thrown upon the wheel, including dishes, plates, bowls, cups, and such things; and beyond these, farther east, seven workshops for decorating the pieces in blue and white (*ch'ing hua*). On the western side of the courtyard are three workshops for the artists who decorate in colors (*ts'ai hua*), and another one attached for the carvers of jade and bamboo; the imperial porcelain store (*tz'ŭ ku*), with two separate rooms for the selection of the pieces (*hsüan tz'ŭ*) when they are brought from the kilns; three workshops for the making of vases (*cho ch'i*) fashioned on the wheel, including sacrificial vessels, jars, and ornamental pieces of all kinds; and five workshops for the various operations of molding, carving, and polishing required in the preparation of the square and polygonal vases, and all the complex forms that can not be worked upon the ordinary wheel. Beyond these, farther west, are six workshops for the decoration of the vases and molded pieces in blue and white—three for the application of the glaze, one for grinding the colors used for the *Chün yu*, the reproduction of the old Chün-chou porcelain with a *soufflé*

FIG. 195.—K'ang-hsi Vase artistically decorated in fine colors relieved by an enameled black ground; the mask handles, looped for rings, are left in white biscuit.

glaze, which is commonly known outside China as "robin's egg." Next come three laboratories with muffle-kilns (*lu*) for the second firing of the pieces decorated in enamel colors, which have two kitchens attached for the preparation of the workmen's food; and, finally, seven workshops for the porcelain decorated over the white glaze in foreign style with enamel colors (*yang ts'ai*), for the *soufflé* red (*ch'ui hung*), the monochrome glaze of the *grand feu* derived from copper, and for the monochrome yellow (*Chiao huang*) glaze usually known as "imperial yellow." A list of the objects made in these workshops for the imperial palace in the reign of *T'ung-chih* will be given in a later chapter, and will give a better idea of the work than any mere description.

There is no mention of furnaces in the official account, with the exception of muffle stoves for the second firing of the enameled pieces. In the *Ming* dynasty, as we have seen, the imperial factory contained furnaces for the clay seggars, and separate furnaces for blue and white porcelain, for colored porcelain, and for the large fish-bowls. The last of the fish-bowl kilns (*kang yao*), we are told by T'ang Ying, fell down in the reign of *Ch'ien-lung* and was not rebuilt. In the present day everything is carried outside to be baked in private furnaces, and all the imperial ware is taken to the establishments called *pao ch'ing*, because they guarantee the color of each firing, and are mulcted accordingly for any loss or imperfection.

The furnaces employed for firing porcelain vary widely both in size and shape. They may be grouped generally, according to M. Vogt (*La Porcelaine*, page 178), under the three following types:

1. The cylindrical furnace, with direct flame and vertical axis.
2. The cylindrical furnace, with reversed flame and vertical axis.
3. The semi-cylindrical furnace, with direct flame and horizontal axis.

The first type is that of the furnaces of the *Ming* dynasty in China. They were sometimes built upon a rising slope in a row of five or six communicating cylinders, and this is still the ordinary form in Japan. The second type is a recent European invention for the purpose of economizing fuel and producing a greater regularity in its combustion. The third type is that of the Chinese furnace of the present day; it was formerly also employed in Europe for porcelain, but is now scarcely used there, except for stoneware. Its irregularity fits it all the more for the purpose required. Perfect regularity is essential, according to M. Vogt, for the manufacture of ordinary white porcelain, but not suitable for the production of colors which require different kinds of flame to bring out the different degrees of oxidation or deoxidation required. The colors that resist the heat of the blast-furnace are divided scientifically by French ceramic writers into *couleurs du grand feu* and *couleurs du demi-grand feu*; but in China both of these two classes are fired together in the same charge, the latter being placed near the back of the furnace under the large vent-hole that communicates with the chimney, where the heat is less intense than it is in the middle of the furnace. (*loc. cit.*, page 188), "whose "So the Chinese" porcelain is so diversified, employ a methodically irregular furnace which allows them to execute, in the same firing, all the fantasies inspired by their special genius as accomplished *porcelainiers*. They are able, in fact, in one operation, thanks to the irregularity of their furnace, to fire successfully the crackles, which are of difficult fusibility, the *flambé* reds and the celadons, which require reducing flames, the blue under the glaze, the blacks which fuse so readily, as well as the series of turquoise, green, yellow, and violet enamels; while in

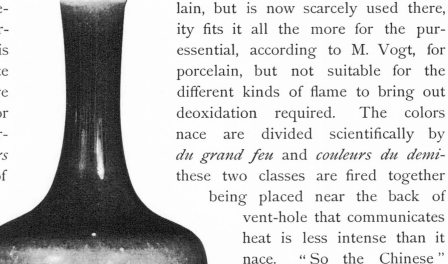

FIG. 196.—Lang Yao Vase of *sang-de-bœuf* tints, with streaked body, whitish rim, and crackled base of mottled apple-green.

Europe, with our furnaces of regular type, three or four different firings would be required to obtain the same results."

We are indebted for a sketch of one of the large modern furnaces to M. F. Scherzer, who, when he was French consul at Hankow, spent three weeks at Ching-tê-chên in 1883 studying the porcelain manufacture. It must have been no easy task, as he wrote to me at the time that he could hardly venture to look out of his close sedan-chair without being pelted with potsherds by the unruly potters. His plans, with vertical and horizontal sections, are copied in the book just quoted (page 189), and accompanied by a full description. The Chinese furnace contains the three essential parts of such structures—viz., the fire, the laboratory, and the chimney. The fire, however, is not outside the furnace, as is usually the case; it is actually inside the laboratory, in such a way that combustion is effected in the midst of the objects that are being fired, without any loss of heat. The laboratory, which is rectangular in shape, passes above into a vaulted roof of cylindrical outline. The rectangular portion below is incased in a massive thickness of earth; the vaulted cylindrical roof is free. Outside the furnace there are staircases on both sides, by which the firemen go up to the top of the massive earth casing to watch the effect of the fire, looking through apertures in the roof intended for the purpose which are covered at other times with movable tiles. The dimensions, according to M. Scherzer, are larger now than they were in the time of Père d'Entrecolles, the height being as much as five metres, the length twice as much, or ten metres, and the breadth three and a half metres. In 1722 the height was three and a half metres, the length double the height, and the breadth equal to the height. Pine-wood in billets is the ordinary fuel used in China. The large trunks of the trees are floated down the river as rafts, the smaller branches being brought down in boats. The bundles, or "loads," so often referred to in Chinese descriptions, are made to weigh one hundred catties, or one hundred and thirty-three pounds, and about two hundred of these "loads" are stated to be required for each firing.

FIG. 197.—Vase decorated with brilliant enamel colors of the K'ang-hsi period.

FIG. 198.—Box for Seal Vermilion, with glaze of typical
peach-bloom tints; mark, K'ang-hsi.

CHAPTER X.

THE K'ANG-HSI PERIOD.

A NEW dynasty of Tartar origin began to rule China under the title of *Ch'ing*, or "Pure," in the year 1644, after the last emperor of the *Ming* or "Illustrious" dynasty had hanged himself upon a tree on Prospect Hill, in the grounds of the palace at Peking. The young emperor, still a minor, was enthroned with the title of *Shun-chih*, and his rule was gradually extended over the south of China; the Chinese general, Wu San-kuei, who had first invited the Manchus into the country to assist in putting down a native rebellion, being made viceroy of the provinces of Yunnan and Kueichou in the far southwest.

The new officials of the province of Kiangsi were all at their posts in the second year, and, according to the annals of the province, the director of the imperial porcelain factory at Ching-tê-chên and the other officers there were appointed with the same duties and titles as in the *Ming* dynasty, and continued to carry on the work in similar lines. The mark of the first reign of the new dynasty is very rare, and the porcelain that bears it is hardly to be distinguished from that of the later reigns of the *Ming* dynasty. Doubtless, supplies were forwarded to Peking for the use of the palace, but the only notices of the appointment of commissioners are in connection with requisitions which they fail to execute.

FIG. 199.—A Group of Snuff-bottles of the period of K'ang-hsi.

The first record is that of an imperial decree in the eleventh year of the reign of *Shun-chih* (1654), ordering the fabrication of a number of "dragon bowls" (*lung kang*) for the palace gardens, which were to be two and a half feet high, three and a half feet in diameter at the mouth, with sides of the thickness of three inches, and bottoms of the thickness of five inches. For four years they worked diligently under the orders of four *tao-t'ai*, who were specially appointed in yearly succession from Jao-chou, and under the personal supervision of the governors of the province Lang T'ing-tso and Chang Chao-lin, but their efforts were in vain, and the last named, who was governor from 1656 to 1664, had finally to present a memorial begging for the withdrawal of the decree.

The dragon bowls required were the large fish-bowls which are usually placed upon stands in the courtyards of Chinese houses, and which are used for the cultivation of the lotus and other water-plants, as well as for goldfish. They were called *lung kang,* or "dragon bowls," because they were usually decorated with dragons, although other decorations also occur. The author of the *Ching-tê-chên T'ao lu* gives among the designs the following:

"Bowls painted in blue with a pair of dragons in clouds, surrounded by conventional paradise flowers; bowls painted in blue with a pair of dragons enveloped in clouds; some painted in blue with dragons in clouds and with bands of lotus petals; others painted in blue with four dragons in a ring sporting above a floor of sea-waves; also bowls of pea-green celadon color."

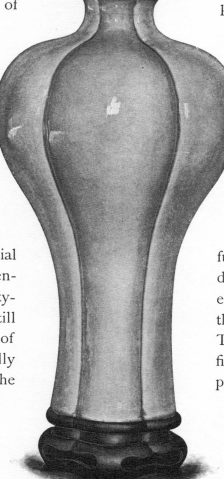

FIG. 200.—Imperial-Yellow Vase of the K'ang-hsi period.

The two which stand in my own garden, in the British legation at Peking, and which are both marked *Ta Ming Wan li nien chih* in underglaze blue, are decorated one, which is twenty-seven inches in diameter at the rim, has four five-clawed dragons, enveloped in clouds, painted round the sides, a band of waves beating upon rocks at the base, and scroll borders above and below; the other, of the same diameter, but only one foot high, is decorated with mandarin ducks swimming in a lake, with lotus flowers growing in the water. The largest dragon bowls were fired in special furnaces, as described in Chapter VIII, one at a time, with an expenditure of over seven tons' weight of fuel, and cost at the time forty-eight taels of silver each.

It was not, by the way, till the early part of the reign of *Ch'ien-lung,* under the direction of T'ang Ying, that such large porcelain fish-bowls were successfully produced by him, according to the provincial statistics, with mouths ranging in diameter from three and a half to four feet, and sides from one and three-fourths to two feet in height, and invested with colored glazes of three kinds: (1) Eel's-skin yellow (*shan-yü huang*), (2) cucumber-green (*kua-p'i lü*), (3) spotted yellow and green (*huang lü tien*). The fish-bowls (*yü kang*) of the K'ang-hsi period, though smaller, are occasionally very richly decorated in colors; they are generally catalogued in Europe as "cisterns."

In the sixteenth year of *Shun-chih* (1659) another imperial decree was issued, ordering from Ching-tê-chên the supply of a quantity of oblong plaques of porcelain for inlaying on the partition walls of open verandas, which were to be three feet high, two and a half feet broad, and three inches thick. A commission was sent down from the Board of Works, with a high Manchu official named Ka-pa as president, and Wang Jih-tsao as secretary, who were associated with the provincial *tao-t'ai* Chang Ssŭ-ming, and proceeded to Ching-tê-chên to superintend the work, but they also failed, and in the following year the Governor of Kiangsi, Chang Chao-lin memorialized the emperor to stop the work.

The task must really have been more difficult than that of the large fish-bowls, of which Père d'Entrecolles asserts that over two hundred were fired without a single success, for he says later in the same letter (*loc. cit.,* page 282): "European merchants demand sometimes from the Chinese workmen plaques of porcelain, of which one piece shall make the top of a table or of a stove, as well as frames for pictures: these things are impossible; the largest and longest plaques made measure only about a foot, and if an attempt is made to pass that, whatever thickness may be given, they become warped. Thickness, in fact, does not facilitate the execution of these works, and this is why, instead of making the plaques thick, they are made with two faces united inside by cross-pieces so as to leave the interspaces hollow. Two openings are left in the sides so that they may be mounted in woodwork or inlaid in the backs of chairs, where they show very prettily." The plaques referred to here are, indeed, sometimes very effective, being decorated in the brilliant enamels of the period and enhanced by gilding. They are either rectagonal or circular in outline, and are usually decorated with figure-scenes of dramatic or historic interest on one side, and with birds and flowers on the other. Perfect examples, however, are rare, because the Chinese so often saw them in two with the jade-cutter's

Fig. 201.—Pilgrim Bottle of the K'ang-hsi period, with dragons in relief covered with a copper-red glaze of peach-bloom type.

wheel, and frame the two sides as companion pictures, adapted either for hanging on the wall or for standing on the table, mounted upon coral pedestals in the usual fashion.

The reign of *Shun-chih* may, in fact, be entirely neglected from a ceramic point of view, and we may pass on at once to that of his successor, *K'ang-hsi* (1662–1722), which is unquestionably the most brilliant epoch in the ceramic art of China, and is distinguished by the purity and brilliancy of its single colors, as well as for the splendid coloring and perfect technical finish of its painted decoration. The special triumphs of the ceramic art which have excited the enthusiastic admiration of ardent collectors in the West, as well as in China, are nearly all the productions of this one period. It is sufficient to mention the magnificent *sang-de-bœuf* red of the Lang Yao vases, the charming play of colors and perfect technique of the "peach-bloom class," and the soft purity of the *clair-de-lune* and celadon glazes—all of which are well represented in the colored illustrations. The decorative effect of cobalt-blue is brought out of the depths of the translucent white glaze of the time in a way that has not been rivaled before or since. The coloring material was blown upon the raw body of the vase, and either left as its sole ornament, as in Plate XCIII, or penciled over the surface with designs of gold, or combined with enamel colors, as in Plate XXVI, or it was mixed with the glaze, as in the sky-blue bottle illustrated in Plate LXXIV; it was painted on with a brush in the large class of "blue and white," which also has its enthusiastic admirers, appearing as blue upon a white ground, as in the graceful vase shown in Plate LXXIII, or as a blue ground with the decoration in white reserve, as in the fascinating "hawthorne" ginger-jars, of which a choice example is reproduced in Plate II. The wonderful variety of the decoration in colors is just as remarkable; the five colors of the Chinese—blue, green, yellow, red, and black—appearing on the same piece in brilliant contrast, some-

Fig. 202.—Peach-bloom Vase, with gadroon border, exhibiting the characteristic mottled play of color; mark, K'ang-hsi.

times relieved by black, yellow, purple, or green grounds, sometimes enhanced by touches of gold. Green in shaded tones occupies a conspicuous place among the characteristic colors of this period, and the term of *famille verte*, introduced by Jacquemart, had its origin therein.

It was in the reign of *K'ang-hsi* that Chinese porcelain was first imported on a large scale into Europe. Previous importations had been confined mainly to celadon and blue and white. The Dutch were the chief importers through their East India Company, and we read of cargoes containing many thousands of pieces. These must have been mainly, if not entirely, composed of porcelain made at the time; the merchants of Canton, Amoy, and Foochow being in constant communication with Ching-tê-chên, as we know from Chinese accounts. So we find most of the early European collections, like that of the museum at Dresden, consisting almost exclusively of productions of this time. The great majority of the objects in more recent collections also date from the reign of *K'ang-hsi*, partly because they were recruited from Holland and Germany, but principally because of the pre-eminent artistic value of the ceramic work of the time, which causes it still to be sought out from all parts of China.

The "marks" of this period, as was explained in Chapter IV, are rarely genuine. It may be held generally, as Sir Wollaston Franks observes, that little reliance can be placed upon Chinese marks; the specimens, as he remarks, are at any rate not older than the dates on them, but may be much more modern. A visit to the commonest crockery shop in China will confirm this; the blue and white pieces will generally be found marked *Hsüan-tê*, and those enameled in colors *Ch'êng-hua*, because these two reigns of the *Ming* dynasty had a great reputation for these two branches of decorations; the larger vases and jars provided for wedding-presents will probably have seals of the reigns of *K'ang-hsi* or *Ch'ien-lung* inscribed underneath; as the shops are not kept by curio dealers, nobody is taken in; it is simply a custom of the trade. So it was with the *K'ang-hsi* potters, who were wont to inscribe a *Ming* mark like that of *Chia-ching* on the blue and white vase shown in Plate LXXIII, or of *Ch'êng-hua*, as on the white vase, with etched dragon of Plate XXXIX; or to fly at higher game still and suggest the reign of *Hsüan-ho* of the *Sung* dynasty, although the charming effect of their chiseled work under a translucent glaze, as indicated in Plate XC,

FIG. 203.—Double Fish Vase, decorated in enamel colors with gilding of the K'ang-hsi period.

approached probably that of carved white jade more nearly than any production of the more remote period they inscribed underneath.

Early writers on ceramic subjects in Europe were inclined to accept such marks of date as genuine; later authorities, with greater plausibility, regard them as indicating copies or reproductions of porcelain actually made at the particular period inscribed. I am not prepared to go even so far as that. M. Grandidier, for example, writes (*loc. cit.*, page 154): "The epoch Tching-hoa has bequeathed to us a series of grand vases which will always find frantic admirers, and which are worthy of their great reputation on account of the boldness of the decoration and the intensity of the colors. Those of the shape called 'lancella' are composed of a jar surmounted by a trumpet-mouthed beaker; others are quadrangular or ovoid; some have the form of a straight beaker, of a square baluster or of a rounded baluster; the group includes besides some

FIG. 204.—K'ang-hsi Vase with a grayish crackled glaze of celadon type mottled with red, becoming more intense in the grooved parts.

statuettes of divinities. The grounds display three principal shades—yellow, dark green approaching black, and clear, limpid green. The decorations comprise rocks in different tones of green, trunks of trees and branches in manganese-violet, plants, flowers, or animals in white, blue, yellow, green, or violet. Figures are more rare at this epoch, and occupy a subordinate place in the composition. This fabrication did not cease with the fall of the Ming, and many of the pieces attributed to the Ming period came out of the Chinese workshops of the first years of Khang-hi. The Salting collection in London contains such vases, seventy centimetres high, with a ground of blackish green, yellow, or green, which are ornamented with green rocks, with branches of peach-tree laden with white flowers, with flowering sprays of peonies, magnolias, water-lilies, snowy hydrangeas, etc., which are marked Tching-hoa. Of the similar pieces in my own collection, . . . although some were fabricated under Tching-hoa,

the majority are only superb reproductions executed during the first years of Khang-hi. Their marks, apocryphal as they are, are yet a precious means of instruction, in that they give us the date of the primitive type." Again (page 166): "The early Khang-hi period is a transition epoch; the traditions of the old Chinese dynasty are still honored. The ancient principles and the old methods, preserved with great pains during forty years of civil war, are perpetuated in the ceramic field, and flower for the last time during the first ten or fifteen years of Khang-hi. So the specimens have not yet quitted the livery of the Ming, the brilliant livery of that brilliant dynasty, and proclaim proudly, by their beauty, the progress achieved under the earlier reign; they bear the Ming decorations, whether they be simple copies, or whether they be veritable originals, inspired by more ancient works."

For examples of the type referred to in the above quotations turn to Plate LV for an illustration of a wine-pot decorated in colors on a white ground, and to Plate IX for that of a quadrangular vase painted in enamel colors relieved by an enameled black ground. There are few collectors, I believe, outside of China, who do not cherish these things as relics of the *Ming* dynasty; there is no Chinese connoisseur, on the other hand, who would not attribute them all to the reign of *K'ang-hsi.* The end of the *Ming* dynasty was an age of criticism, and we have a host of writers on ceramic subjects, but not one of them refers to such large vases as existing in the reign of *Ch'êng-hua;* had they existed at such an early date they could hardly have been overlooked. Nor are there any figured in the illustrated album of the sixteenth century which has been described in Chapter V, although it gives a wine-pot and several wine-cups of the period decorated in colors. The expert confesses the difficulty of distinguishing between an original *Ch'êng-hua* piece and a *K'ang-hsi* copy, and I would, with all deference, propose that they shall all be classed as *K'ang-hsi* productions until proofs of antiquity any better than those of archaic style and ancient mark be brought forward.

Fig. 205.—Lang Yao Vase with the lower part of richly mottled *sang-de-bœuf* tints, the upper half a gray-green celadon tinged with pink.

In the beginning of the reign of *K'ang-hsi*, Lang T'ing-tso was still viceroy. In the preceding reign we found him mentioned as personally supervising the work of the imperial potters at Ching-tê-chên. He was appointed governor (*hsün-fu*) of the province of Kiangsi in 1654, and was promoted to be viceroy (*tsung-tu*) of Kiangsi and Kiangnan in 1656. In the last year of the reign of *Shun-chih* the viceroyalty was divided: Lang T'ing-tso remained the *tsung-tu* of Kiangnan, and Chang Chao-lin was promoted to be *tsung-tu* of Kiangsi. The provinces were reunited in the fourth year of *K'ang-hsi* (1665), with Lang T'ing-tso as viceroy, and he retained the post till 1668, when he was succeeded by Ma-lo-chi, a Manchu of the Yellow Banner. I have given these particulars of the career of the celebrated viceroy, who was a Chinese native of the northern border and an early adherent of the invading Manchus, because the name Lang Yao,* applied to the remarkable ceramic productions of this time, is generally supposed by the most competent Chinese authorities to have been derived from him. *Yao* in its widest sense means "pottery" as well as "potteries," "porcelain" as well as "kiln," and the ceramic production of this time has retained the name of the viceroy, in the same way as the names of Ts'ang Ying-hsüan, Nien Hsi-yao, and T'ang Ying, who were in turn superin-

* This name has been derived by some Chinese of less weight from that of Lang Shih-ning, an artist *protégé* of the Jesuits, who also lived in the reign of *K'ang-hsi,* and whose pictures are still highly appreciated. A note following the description of a bottle in the Franks Collection (*loc. cit.,* page 8), "covered with a deep but brilliant red glaze," says: "This specimen is from Mr. A. B. Mitford's collection, and is thus described in the catalogue: 'A bottle: *Lang yao-tzé,* porcelain from the Lang furnace. The Lang family were a family of famous potters who possessed the secret of this peculiar glaze and paste. They became extinct about the year 1610; and their pottery is highly esteemed and fetches great prices at Peking.'" The family is apocryphal and the porcelain antedated, but the story is generally accepted by later writers, like M. Grandidier, who gives it (page 160) under the reign of *Wan-li,* without, however, acknowledging the source of his information.

tendents of the imperial potteries, were afterward given to the *Ts'ang Yao, Nien Yao,* and *T'ang Yao,* names which the respective productions of their times retain to this day.

The Lang Yao *par excellence* is characterized by a rich, deep glaze of crackled texture imbued with the crimson mottled clouds of blood-red tone, which have earned for it the name of *sang-de-bœuf,* by which it is generally known. The color is not uniform, but flashes in streaks of varied shade produced by the action of the furnace flames on the copper silicate to which the color is due. It is more homogeneous, however, than the *flambé* reds of later times which, in common parlance, share with it the name of *sang-de-bœuf.* Sometimes a quite modern piece of *chi hung,* or "sacrificial red," so-called because, like the Lang Yao itself, it was made after the color of the ancient sacrificial cups of the reign of *Hsüan-tê,* will appear accidentally, as it were, clothed in a rich garb rivaling in intensity that of the finest Lang Yao vase. An intentional imitation, although it may approach in brilliancy of tone the rich coloring of the original, always fails in some point of technical detail. The color requires perfect fluidity of the enamel to bring it out in perfection—a condition which the modern potter can not attain without the glaze "running," so that it becomes very thin on the upper rim, which often appears nearly white, and runs down to collect in thick drops round the foot, which has to be subsequently ground down on the wheel. All attempts to reproduce this beautiful color in the West have also failed, principally, it is said, because it is so difficult to seize the exact moment, a few seconds more or less in the duration of the firing being sufficient to ruin the beauty of the fugitive tint.

FIG. 206.—Vase of powder blue ground, with a floral decoration in gold.

The principal means of distinguishing the veritable Lang Yao consists in the perfect potting of the piece, evidenced by the mathematical regularity of the white line of enamel which often defines the rim and the condition of the foot, as well as in the tone of coloring in the crackled glaze. The condition of the foot is always a special criterion to the Chinese connoisseur, who looks especially at the paste when it is left unglazed round the circular rim, to distinguish the productions of different periods. The bottoms of these vases are described as exhibiting glazes of three kinds, having *ping-kuo ti,* "bases of apple-green (crackle)," *mi-sê ti,* "bases of rice-colored (crackle)," or *pai-tz'ŭ ti,* "bases of plain white porcelain."

If the piece be entirely green, it is a specimen of *Lü Lang Yao,* or "Green Lang Yao." This is always crackled; it is of a uniform apple-green (*p'ing-kuo ch'ing*) shade, paler than that of the brilliant green monochromes which distinguish the later part of the reign; the rims are defined by a line of translucent white enamel, and the technique is that of the ordinary Lang Yao; the rare pieces that I have seen are small in size. The color has been called a copper celadon, but it is better, I think, to restrict the term celadon to the sea-green tint produced by a protoxide of iron.

In addition to the magnificent vases and censers of *sang-de-bœuf,* we have a variety of miscellaneous articles, intended for domestic use, such as saucer-shaped dishes, basins, bowls, tazza-shaped cups, and the like, and occasionally we even find a round box of the type adapted to hold seal-vermilion, or a small snuff-bottle, representing the class. The glaze, always crackled, varies from an intense blood-red, through intermediate shades of paler hue, till it becomes sometimes almost pink; in other cases it darkens into a dull maroon, or a liver-colored tint. The bowls are of solid make, heavy-footed, expanding at the mouth to a thin, spreading rim, which is defined by a white line. There is a series of bowls of the same shape as the red bowls, which are decorated generally with birds and flowers, painted in the brilliant enamel colors of the early *K'ang-hsi* period, which are considered by the Chinese to be productions of the same kilns, and which are also classified by them under the heading of Lang Yao. These bowls are characterized by a deeply crackled glaze of pale greenish tone which is traversed by red lines, and on the surface of this crackle the enamel decoration, boldly designed, is laid on with a free brush, so that the colors, especially the cobalt-blue, stand out in prominent relief. These bowls would be classed under the heading of "Green Lang Yao," decorated with enamels.

To return to the annals of the province. In the tenth year of *K'ang-hsi* (1671) the governor was ordered to supply the ritual sets of sacrificial vessels required by the emperor in the worship of the different temples at Peking. He dispatched officials from Jao-chou and Fou-liang to Ching-tê-chên to superintend the work and see that it was executed in accordance with the imperial decree. The sacrificial vessels required were all fabricated and successfully fired, the necessary funds being provided on a liberal scale, so that neither money nor materials were levied from the people, and the things were sent on in successive batches to the capital, as soon as they were finished, as required by the decree.

But troubles supervened in connection with the rebellion of Wu San-kuei, the viceroy of Yunnan, who threw off his allegiance to the Manchu emperor in 1674, and headed the last expiring efforts of the native Chinese against the rule of the Tartars. The imperial factory at Ching-tê-chên was burned to the ground in the following year. The death of Wu San-kuei, which occurred in 1678, was followed in a few months by a final triumph of the imperial forces, and the province of Kiangsi was soon afterward pacified. In the ninth month of the nineteenth year (1680) an imperial decree was issued ordering the production of a quantity of imperial porcelain for the use of the palace, and at the same time a board of commissioners was selected from the officials of the Nei Wu Fu, or "Imperial Household," and directed to proceed to Ching-tê-chên to superintend the work. The first commission was composed of Hsü T'ing-pi, secretary (*Lang-chung*) of the Treasury of the Privy Purse, and Li Yen-li, an assistant secretary. The second commission, appointed two years later, was headed by Ts'ang Ying-hsüan, secretary of the Imperial Parks Department of the Board of Works, who is stated to have arrived at Ching-tê-chên in the second month of the twenty-second year (1683), and who at once took over the superintendence of the imperial manufactory. We are not told how long he remained in charge. After his time the work was carried on by the provincial officials, as there seems to have been no appointment of another imperial commission till the next reign.

FIG. 207.—Vase with molded floral decoration painted in blue and maroon relieved by a crackled *sang-de-bœuf* ground of brilliant tone.

To Ts'ang Ying-hsüan is due the brilliant renaissance of the ceramic art in China which distinguishes the reign of *K'ang-hsi*. T'ang Ying, who ultimately succeeded to the office, in his *Life of the God of the Furnace Blast*, bears testimony to his genius when he writes: "When Ts'ang was director of the porcelain works the finger of the god was often seen in the midst of the furnace fire, either painting the designs or shielding them from harm, so that the porcelain came out perfect and beautiful." The writer of the *Ching-tê-chên T'ao-lu* says, in his description of the Ts'ang Yao, that the porcelain made by him was of fine rich material and thin translucent texture, that all the different colors were produced, and that among them the four most beautiful colors were the snake-skin green with iridescent hues, the eel-skin yellow of brownish shade, the turquoise-blue, and the variegated yellow, although the monochrome yellow, the monochrome purple, and the monochrome green glazes, as well as the *soufflé* red and the *soufflé* blue, were all remarkably fine. He adds that all these different glazes were copied afterward by T'ang Ying. We may add that the peculiar brilliancy of these well-known *K'ang-hsi* colors is inimitable.

The porcelain was still called by the old name of *Kuan Yao*, or "imperial ware," to distinguish it from the productions of the private potters. Among the things sent to the palace, according to the official list, were fish-bowls (*kang*), flower-pots (*p'ên*), basins (*yü*), round dishes (*p'an*), beaker-shaped vases (*tsun*), censers (*lu*), vases (*p'ing*), jars with covers (*kuan*), saucer-plates (*tieh*), bowls (*wan*), teacups and wine-cups (*chung, chan*). The decorative designs used included fabulous dragons enveloped in clouds, birds, and four-footed beasts, fishes swimming in water green with moss, and flowering plants of all kinds. The porcelain was either painted in colors, or chiseled in relief, or faintly engraved under the glaze, or carved in open-work: all these different processes are declared to have been cleverly executed in the imperial workshops at this period.

Another famous glaze appeared in this reign which challenges the supreme position generally accorded by lovers of the ceramic art to the Lang Yao *sang-de-bœuf.* I refer, of course, to the "peach-bloom" (*peau-de-pêche*), also called sometimes "crushed strawberry" (*fraise écrasée*), which is another example of the decorative power of the same protean color, being due to a fortuitous mingling of the silicates of copper. Although not so intense and brilliant as the *sang-de-bœuf*, it has a special charm of its own in its soft, velvety tones, which remind one of the coloring of the rind of a peach ripening in the sun. The prevailing shade is a pale red, becoming pink in some parts, in others mottled with russet spots, displayed upon a background of light-green celadon tint. The last color occasionally comes out more prominently and deepens into clouds of bright apple-green tint. The varied shades of color are well represented in the illustrations, as will be appreciated by reference to Plates III, LI (a), LII, and L. The vases illustrated here are all marked in full, underneath, with the "six-character mark" of the reign, beautifully written in a minute script, which is penciled under the glaze in cobalt-blue.

FIG. 208.—K'ang-hsi Vase, decorated in enamel colors interrupted by powder blue medallions penciled in gold.

The Chinese prize the subdued beauty of this glaze above all others for the decoration of their writing-tables, and most of the objects originally adapted for this purpose are of comparatively small size. They call it by the special name of *p'ing-kuo hung*, or "apple-red," and they distinguish also the accessory *p'ing-kuo ch'ing*, or "apple-green" clouds, and the *mei-kuei tzŭ*, or "rose-crimson" mottled spots. This comparison with the mingled red and green shades of a rosy-cheeked apple is apt enough, especially as the same idea is often brought out in the form of the object; two favorite designs, for example, of the little water-bottles intended to be used with the writer's pallet are the *p'ing-kuo tsun*, or "apple-jar," which is molded as an exact facsimile in size and shape of the fruit, and its fellow, the *shih-liu tsun*, or "pomegranate-jar"; I have seen these two shapes only in China. Another native name for this "peach-bloom" glaze, which is the one that is commonly used by the Chinese dealer, is *chiang-tou hung.* This might be rendered "haricot-red," the *chiang-tou* being a small kidney-shaped bean of variegated pink color with brown spots, largely cultivated at Peking and other parts of China, the *Dolichos sinensis* of botanists.

Among the other specimens of the peach-bloom class in the collection are (Fig. 188) a small water receptacle for the writing-table modeled in the traditional form of the wine-jar of Li T'ai-po, the famous poet of the eighth century, from which it derives its name of *T'ai-po tsun*; and Fig. 198, a circular box for the vermilion used for impressing seals, another indispensable adjunct of the writing-table of the Chinese scholar. Fig. 202 shows a vase similar in form to the one illustrated in Plate LII, which has been mounted in Japan. Fig. 201 is a pilgrim bottle with a copper-red glaze of "peach-bloom" type, which differs from the rest in being unmarked.

There is one class of these vases in which the base of the neck is encircled by the form of an archaic dragon, modeled in full under-cut relief, which is enameled with a bright apple-green glaze of uniform tint, contrasting vividly, as a complementary color, with the red shades of the vase. Fig. 209 exhibits one of these dragon-encircled bottles which has the usual mark inscribed on the foot underneath.

The last piece to be noticed here is a little bowl-shaped wine-cup of egg-shell texture invested, inside and out, with a "peach-bloom" glaze displaying all the typical tints (Fig. 210). The mark underneath is that of the reign of *Hsüan-tê* of the *Ming* dynasty, but the perfection of the technique and the character of the glaze indicate the *K'ang-hsi* period, and the mark would perhaps be intended to show that the aim of the potter was the reproduction of one of the celebrated "sacrificial red wine-cups" of the older reign, which, we know, were tinted with the same coloring material.

FIG. 209.—Peach-bloom Vase, with a dragon molded in salient relief on the shoulder, enameled bright apple-green; mark, K'ang-hsi.

The first "peach-bloom" vases that reached the United States seem to have come from Peking, out of the famous collection of the hereditary Princes of Yi,* the source also, by the way, of the sixteenth century album that has been so often referred to. The founder of this line of princes was the thirteenth son of the Emperor *K'ang-hsi*. T'ang Ying refers to him (*Chiang hsi t'ung chih*, book xciii, folio 10) as having, in the eighth month of the year 1723, personally announced to him by command of his brother, the Emperor *Yung-chêng*, his own (T'ang Ying's) appointment to be director of the imperial potteries, and we may gather from this that the prince was interested in the development of the ceramic art. After his death the hereditary rank of imperial prince (Ch'in Wang) was conferred upon his descendants, a unique honor, as it is the rule in China for each generation to descend one step in the scale of nobility till they become commoners.

His descendant in the fifth generation was the notorious Yi Ch'in Wang, to whom the empress-regent sent a silken cord in 1861, so that he might expiate by his suicide his mismanagement of the Anglo-French war. A young scion of his house was chosen at the same time to succeed him, instead of one of his own sons, as an additional punishment, and it is he who is currently reported since he grew up to have taken to dissipated ways, and to have wasted the valuable collections of his ancestral palace. It may be of some interest to see traced back, in this way, to a son of the Emperor *K'ang-hsi*, a collection that was no doubt formed in his reign, the gems of which excited such interest in ceramic circles on their first appearance, and which will always rank as triumphs of decorative art.

FIG. 210.—Wine Cup of eggshell texture, covered inside and out with mottled peach-bloom glaze of typical coloring; mark, Hsüan-tê.

The vases, though small in size, are generally of fine technique and graceful form. They share these characteristics with some others of similar make and shape enameled with different glazes, which are often marked in the same style, and evidently belong to the same period. Perhaps the most beautiful of the monochrome glazes of this class is the *yueh pai*, or *clair-de-lune*, of uniformly pale sky-blue tint, which is illustrated in Plate LI (b), but the soft, celadon shades displayed in the illustration (Plate VII), which is modeled in the graceful lines of one of the finest of the "peach-bloom" vases, are almost as charming. Two other vases are given in Plate L, under the heading of Peach-Bloom Transmutations, one of which is a pearl gray of pinkish hue, with traces of mottled red lurking inside the neck, while the other is marbled with variegated splashes of green, passing from emerald to

* In the *Catalogue of the Art Collection formed by the late Mrs. Mary J. Morgan, New York, 1886*, it is noted that several of the "peach-blow or crushed-strawberry vases" came "from the private collection of I Wang-ye, a Mandarin prince," which must be the one I refer to. *Wang Yeh* is "Prince" in colloquial Pekingese, and *Yi* is sometimes written *I*.

intense olive tones, a striking instance of the kiln transmuted green (*yu lü*), which we shall meet with presently in Chapter XVIII.

These two glazes, the *sang-de-bœuf* and the *peau-de-pêche*, were not employed exclusively as single colors; they were used also in combination with other forms of decoration, and some of the most brilliant blue pieces of the period are occasionally seen with the painted designs relieved by one of these colors in place of the ordinary white ground. A remarkable example is seen in the vase illustrated in Fig. 207, the ground of which is a typical "Lang Yao" crackled glaze, exhibiting all the different *sang-de-bœuf* tones, passing from paler shades into deepest crimson. The neck and shoulder of the vase are ribbed, and the decoration is modeled in relief in the paste, and filled in with underglaze cobalt-blue, with touches of copper-red. It consists of a flowering lotus springing from a groundwork of crested waves, and a pair of swallows, one of them perched on a lotus stalk, the other flying. The large, naturally folded lotus leaves, lifted upon rough tuberculated stems, and the birds, are painted in blue; the flowers and buds are shaded in addition, in wavy lines of maroon tint within the blue outlines. The foot, which is enameled white with a tinge of green, has no mark inscribed.

FIG. 211.—Crackled Baluster Vase, with lightly incised decoration invested with a brilliantly mottled glaze of peach-bloom type.

The rare baluster-shaped vase in Fig. 211, which is engraved in the paste with a lightly etched design of a pair of dragons mounting into the clouds from a line of scrolled sea-waves, and is enameled with a brilliant crackled glaze of bright green passing into olive at the edges, is invested with a thick over-glaze of "peach-bloom" type, collecting in mottled clouds of "crushed-strawberry" tint, laid on so thickly that the forms of the dragons are scarcely visible in the interstices of the clouds. The foot, encircled by a broad, unglazed rim, has concentric lines of grayish-white crackle in the middle, with no mark attached.

The "iron-red," prepared by the incineration of green vitriol (iron sulphate), called also "coral-red" from the tone of color, which is quite distinct from that of the "copper-reds" which we have been considering, is found among the single colors of this time, although much less frequently than in succeeding reigns. In the reign of *K'ang-hsi* this color was employed more largely in painted decoration: either alone, as in the egg-shell bowl in Plate LXVII; or in combination with gold, as in the club-shaped vase in Plate XXVIII; or as one of the different colors comprised in the ordinary polychrome decoration of the muffle oven.

The brilliant blues derived from cobalt were brought out with vivid intensity in this reign, which is unrivaled for its monochrome blues, as well as for the beauty of its blue and white decorated porcelain. The calcined cobaltiferous ore of manganese was either mixed with the white glaze to produce the gray-blue illustrated in Plate LXXIV, or it was blown through gauze upon the raw white body of the piece and subsequently glazed over to produce the magnificent effect of powder blue, so well represented by the artist in Plate XCIII. This "powder-blue," also called "Mazarin-blue," or sometimes *bleu fouetté*, from its whipped aspect, may be either left as the sole decoration of the vase, or it may be painted over with ornamental designs in gold, fixed by a second firing in the muffle stove. The vase in Fig. 206, which is decorated in gold with sprays of chrysanthemum and bamboo, is an example of the last style of decoration. In other cases, again, the powder-blue ground is interrupted by medallions of varied form, which are filled with designs, either executed at the same time in blue, or painted after the first firing in enamel colors; an example of a decorated powder-blue vase is illustrated in Plate XVIII. A decorated vase, on the other hand, may have powder-blue panels interrupting the main decoration, as in the interesting vase in Fig. 208, which deserves a word of description. It is painted in brilliant enamel colors with gilding, the body with chrysanthemum scrolls traversed by lizard-like dragons, the neck with butterflies and flowers on a pale-green background dotted with black, with flying storks, and phœnix medallions; the shoulder has a band of floral brocade with pictures in foliated panels, and the upright rim of the mouth is encircled by a green border with a black fret; the twelve panels, fan-shaped, quatrefoil, oblong, or in the form of a leaf or pomegranate, which interrupt the painted decoration, are filled in with a powder-blue *soufflé* ground, outlined in gold, and painted over in gold with landscapes, Taoist temples, flying geese, fighting cocks, sprays of flowers, etc.

Another monochrome glaze invented at this period was the brilliant black called *wu chin*, or "metallic black," by the Chinese, which is sometimes called "mirror black," after Père d'Entrecolles, who compared it to the color of our burning mirrors. It differs from the black of the painted vases, which is of duller aspect, and often of greenish tone, and gives more the impression of being a lacquered surface. It is prepared by mixing some of the calcined cobaltiferous manganese ore with the ordinary white glaze and adding a certain proportion of the ferruginous

FIG. 212.—Tall Triple Gourd of the K'ang-hsi period, with a white center, decorated in colors between mirror-black segments with underglaze reliefs. Companion in Plate LXI.

clay, which produces the *tzŭ-chin*, the which will be referred to presently. overlaid with a gilded decoration, alliterated in course of time, as in the in the pair of large, triple, gourd- and Fig. 212. The charming little its the brilliant intense black with guishes some of the finest dec-

The brown glaze just referred the French potteries as *fond laque*, from a dark bronze hue to the color authors by many names, such as *lait*," etc.; the Chinese name of gold," is as characteristic as any, prefixing *hung*, "red," or *huang*, dominance of either of these two was rarely used alone; it was or other ornamental designs, face enamel colors, as in the two beaker-shaped vases illus- combination is the most com- in huge quantities in Dutch to old inventories which have Jacquemart and others, and old trade name of "Bata- of this class, with the bulg- brown, and the neck decorated pinks, bands of fret, and floral neath with a double ring, a *hsi* period. Fig. 215 presents the "brown-gold" ground that body is succeeded by an en- the shoulder, as well as the

fond laque, or coffee-colored glaze, The mirror-black glaze is usually though this often becomes almost ob- tall vase shown in Plate LXXX, and shaped vases illustrated in Plate LXI vase illustrated in Plate LXII exhib- iridescent surface, which distin- orated pieces of the time. to, which is known technically in may be noticed next. It ranges of old gold, and is known to ceramic "chocolate," "dead leaf," "*café au tzŭ-chin*, which means "burnished and they distinguish the shade by "yellow," according to the pre- colors in the brown. This glaze usually interrupted by medallions which were decorated in sur- garniture of three jars and trated in Fig. 213. The last mon of all; it was imported ships of the time, according been recently published by the decoration still retains its vian." Fig. 214 shows a vase ing body enameled yellowish in blue, with formal sprays of diaper, which is marked under- favorite mark of the *K'ang*- a vase of similar style, in which invests the lower half of the circling band of crackle, and beaker-shaped neck, is painted

in blue with flowers and butterflies; it has no mark underneath, but evidently belongs to the same period as the last. Another mode of decoration was effected by overlaying the brown glaze with designs in white slip; a bottle-shaped vase of this kind is seen in Fig. 216, displaying in its somewhat crude decoration two vases of flowers and a conventional beaded border executed in slip; it is an example of a class of vases decorated by the Chinese in Persian style for export to that country; a similar one, indeed, is erroneously figured by Jacquemart under the heading of Persian porcelain. Père d'Entrecolles tells us that designs were also painted at this time in metallic silver on the surface of this brown glaze, and that the combination was pretty and effective. I have never seen a specimen, perhaps on account of the fugitive nature of the silver decoration, which is easily tarnished and rubbed off by wear.

The "turquoise-blue" and "aubergine-purple" are two colors, dating from previous times, which may be bracketed together, as they offer several analogies, and are, moreover, often used in combination in the decoration of the same piece. The glazes are applied *sur biscuit,* and have a finely crackled or *truité* texture. The turquoise glaze called *Kung-chüo lü,* or "peacock-green," by the modern Chinese, although it is also known in books as *fei-ts'ui,* from its resemblance to the blue plumes of the kingfisher, which are used in jewelry, is prepared by combining copper with a nitre flux. The *ch'ieh p'i tzŭ,* or "aubergine-purple," is derived from the common ore of manganese and cobalt, calcined and mixed like the last with nitre and pulverized quartz. The Walters Collection is very rich in turquoise crackle of different periods, including,

FIG. 213.—Garniture of Three Jars and Two Beakers, with reserve panels, decorated in colors, relieved by a coffee-brown ground.

as it does, considerably over a hundred pieces, some magnificent specimens of which, with bronze mounts by Gouthière, and which are attributed to the reign of *K'ang-hsi,* have already been figured. It is frequently seen on Buddhist images, lions, and other monsters, *magots,* and grotesques of all kinds, such as those which were so eagerly sought after by collectors of the eighteenth century. Aubergine-purple, as a single color, occurs principally on small vases. The two glazes used together make a very effective combination, as in the large lions mounted upon square pedestals, which rank among the chief ornaments of the Dresden Museum. The colors in these pieces are boldly laid on with a free brush and with no attempt at symmetry; in some cases the purple is flecked with a brush in a rain of drops upon the turquoise ground; in others the paste is worked in relief for the reception of the colors which enhance the outlines previously tooled in the paste. The wine-pot shown in Fig. 217 is an illustration of this last method, which dates from very ancient times; it is composed of grayish paste molded in the shape of a peach, with a hole in the bottom for the introduction of a liquid, and has the spout and handle fashioned in the form of twigs from which leaves proceed to decorate the surface of the pot, upon which they are worked in relief and filled in with turquoise, contrasting brightly with the surrounding purple enamel. These colors are said to develop better when there is a mixture of common clay with the ordinary hard kaolinic ingredients of the plate, which is seen to be the case in this small wine-pot.

The same manganese mineral was used in the preparation of the purplish brown, which was one of the three single colors used for enameling the bowls, cups, and saucer-dishes of the imperial dinner services, on which it takes a brownish claret tint, due to an excess of lead in the

flux and a minimum of alkali. The other two colors were a bright green of camellia-leaf tint, and deep yellow, the special imperial color, and the services were either plain or etched with dragons under the glaze. The services of similar style, enameled in pure white (*t'ien pai*) over five-clawed dragons engraved in the paste, were used only when the court was in mourning.

The imperial yellow color is exhibited in Plate V upon a jar with a "six-character mark" of this reign. The "eel-skin yellow," or *shan yü huang*, which is of brownish tint, is seen in Plate LXXXIII upon a vase etched underneath the glaze with dragons; and again in Plate XXV upon a tripod censer, a still more typical example, where it is of less translucent aspect, and mottled in character. The variegated yellow glaze (*huang tien pan*), which has been alluded to as another of the inventions of Ts'ang Ying-hsüan, seems to refer to the peculiar spotted glaze of piebald aspect dabbed all over with spots of yellow, green, purple, and white, which is anything but attractive to an ordinary eye; the Chinese call it by the appropriate name of "tiger-skin" (*hu-p'i*).

The green glazes, which are specially characteristic of the reign, are displayed in all their variety in the colored illustrations, ranging from the *ta lü* or *gros vert* of Plate IV to the pale gray-green celadon tint of Plate XV. Green is almost as prominent among the single colors as it is in the painted decorations in enamel. The same enamels were, of course, used in both the monochrome and the polychrome styles, and comparison often

affords a most useful aid to the determination of the age of a doubtful piece. The crackled green glaze called *kua-p'i lü*, or "cucumber-green," is more characteristic of the *Ch'ien-lung* epoch, although the striking vase shown in Plate LXXXI, with its "cucumber-green" glaze streaked with mottled tints of deepest olive, may well be a *K'ang-hsi* piece, judging from its exceptional brilliancy. The remarkable vase which is so carefully reproduced in Plate LXXIX, with the iridescent bar reflected in a play of rainbow colors from its crackled emerald-green surface, is also generally attributed to this period. One of the green glazes was known in the imperial factory by the name of *shê-p'i lü*, because it resembled in its deep luster the beautiful iridescent hue of the skin of a serpent, like the monochrome glaze in Plate LXXXII, which is spread over the surface of a decorated vase, so as nearly to conceal the original decoration in its intense metallic luster. The same green was occasionally used to enhance the effect of a blue and white piece, touches of green or encircling bands being added to the original design, in the same way that bands of "dead leaf" or "old gold" were some-times attached at this period; an example of which may be seen by referring to the chapter on Marks.

The white glaze of the Ching-tê-chên porcelain of this period is very pure in tint and perfectly translucent in texture, as is well exhibited in the imperial dinner services, etched with dragons, that have just been alluded to, and is fairly represented in the beautiful white vase illustrated in Plate XC, which is attributed to the *K'ang-hsi* reign, in spite of its *Sung* dynasty mark. It is even surpassed in purity and lustrous depth of glaze by the charming little vase shown in Fig. 218, which is molded in the form of a magnolia blossom, with the details etched under the glaze, the graceful flower being mounted upon a twig worked in open-work relief at the foot, and which bears also a couple of buds, that serve as additional support to the delicate vase. This white is distinct from that of the porcelain of the province of Fuchien, which is either of ivory-white or of creamy tint; the objects, moreover, of the Fuchien ware are composed of a paste of characteristic quality, and should have a separate corner reserved for them in every collection.

FIG. 217.—Wine-pot of gray biscuit, worked in relief, filled in with glazes of turquoise blue and aubergine purple.

There is another class of plain white porcelain, modeled on the lines of the ancient Ting-chou ware, which is remarkable for its soft-looking, fragile aspect, in which it reproduces the quality of its prototype, a white *faïence* of fine texture, that can be scratched by a point of sharp steel. The reproductions have only the aspect of soft porcelain, however, although it is the fashion to describe them as such in catalogues; there is nothing produced at Ching-tê-chên that is not composed of hard kaolinic paste. The class I am alluding to is called by the name of

FIG. 218.—White Flower-Vase, of charming design and perfect technique, simulating a magnolia blossom, with two buds rising from the same stalk.

Fên-Ting, after that of the finest ware of the *Sung* dynasty; the glaze is generally crackled, although plain pieces occur, like the delicate little water receptacle in Fig. 219, which is fashioned after an old Ting-chou design with two looped handles, in the shape of a pair of archaic dragons, mounted upon the rim. Of the reproductions of the crackled Ting-chou porcelain, there are two varieties generally attributed to the reign of *K'ang-hsi*. The first is represented by a series of small, solid, compact vases of graceful outline, of which two specimens are illustrated in Figs. 220 and 221; the soft-looking glaze, with which these are invested, is traversed by a very close reticulation of fine, brown lines, and mottled with clouds of light buff tint; the rims of both vases are defined by lines of plain white, and the technique generally is that of the early *K'ang-hsi* period. The second variety, of later development, is characterized by a more delicate fabric, often becoming of egg-shell thinness, and by a whiter glaze, approaching an ivory-white tone. Two notable examples are shown in the colored illustrations: the first, in the sparsely crackled vase of Plate XCI; the second, in the typical *Fên-Ting* gourd, of perfect beauty and finish, which is so well reproduced in Plate LXXXIX. This last, ornamented with floral sprays and bands of fret and conventional scroll, worked in slight relief in the paste, underneath the minutely crackled glaze, which is of characteristic ivory-white tint. Fig. 222 displays another graceful egg-shell vase, with a molded decoration of a four-clawed dragon pursuing an effulgent jewel, executed under a widely crackled ivory-white glaze, with undulatory surface. Fig. 223 is that of a small, minutely crackled square vase, with ribbed corners and four central bosses, carved in open-work, with branches of peach fruit, which is modeled in the ritual form of one of the receptacles for "divining straws," used in Taoist temples.

FIG. 219. — White uncrackled Fên-Ting Waterpot of egg-shell texture, with dragon handles.

The fabrication of this peculiar *Fên-Ting* porcelain was continued at Ching-tê-chên in the succeeding reigns of *Yung-chêng* and *Ch'ien-lung*, and it is not always easy to refer a particular piece positively to one of the three reigns. The same paste and glaze were used contemporaneously in the preparation of the class of blue and white crackled porcelain, which is called by the same name of *Fên-Ting* by the Chinese, and which forms the so-called "soft paste" blue and white of American collectors.

The "soft paste" blue and white porcelain is called by the Chinese by the names of *sha-t'ai,* "sand-bodied," or *chiang-t'ai,* "paste-bodied," and when the glaze is crackled it is distinguished by the addition of the term *k'ai p'ien,* or "crackled." Its composition will be given from Père d'Entrecolles' Letters in the next chapter. The paste has a

FIG. 220.—Bottle with crackled glaze shot with mottled clouds of buff color.

soft, porous aspect, but it is really of intense hardness, so that it can not be scratched by steel. The glaze is generally crackled; even when it is not so as it comes from the kiln, it becomes crackled in course of time. The surface of the glaze is undulatory and often pitted, the characteristics of the *chü-p'i,* or "orange-peel" glaze of Chinese ceramic authors. It is consequently more porous and absorbent than the ordinary glaze, and often becomes discolored by age. It has been suggested that "soft glaze" would be a better name than "soft paste" for this class, but the latter term is sanctioned by usage and may be employed with the proviso that it has nothing in common with the "soft porcelain" of Chelsea, or the *porcelaine tendre* of early Sèvres. One of the chief

FIG. 221. — Finely Crackled Vase of clouded buff tint, with reticulation of brown lines.

characteristics of these pieces is their lightness when handled, which is really surprising, as the fabric is not specially thin. The blue is usually of a grayish tone, and the strokes of the brush are very neatly and clearly defined, so that the picture looks, as Père d'Entrecolles remarks, as if it were painted upon vellum instead of on ordinary paper. The pieces are rarely marked; if there be a date inscribed, it will be of *Hsüan-tê* (1426–1435) of the *Ming* is described to have been pale, of of the blue in modern Japanese

There is a small specimen of trated in Plate LXVIII, a minia- well the peculiar ivory-white color "jade"—not an infrequent mark typical example of the uncrackled exhibited in Fig. 224, which pre- thirteen inches high, of very light soft-toned blue, under the pitted with three formal upright sprays folded peltate leaf, a blossom, stems. Chains of rectangular fret complete the simple decoration, toned blue of pure tint. There is

Fig. 172 shows a choice speci- glaze, with a minutely reticulated tint, over emblematic designs deli- decoration consists of nine lions, neck, disporting with brocaded ported on banks of scrolled clouds conveys the felicitous wish, "Chiu

FIG. 222. — Ivory-white Fên-Ting Vase, of very delicate texture, with dragon molded in relief. The glaze, with undulatory surface, is sparsely crackled.

found to be probably that of the reign dynasty; the blue of this latter period much the same tint, in fact, as that Hirado porcelain.

this crackled blue and white illustrature teapot, which displays very of the glaze; it is marked *yü,* during the *K'ang-hsi* period. A "soft paste" blue and white is sents a baluster vase (*mei p'ing*), material, which is decorated in undulatory "orange-peel" glaze, of lotus, each composed of a and a bud, rising on separate encircling the base and shoulder which is neatly etched in a soft- no mark underneath.

men of the crackled *Fên-Ting* undulating surface of ivory-white cately sketched in soft blue. The five on the body, four on the balls tied with waving fillets, sup- and enveloped in flames. This *shih t'ung chü*"—i. e., "A family

of nine (sons) living together," a pun on the word *shih,* which means "family" as well as "lion." In the same way the five bats in the cloud scroll encircling the receding shoulder of the vase suggest the "five happinesses" (*wu fu*), and the band of prunus blossom round the foot a flourishing longevity. The foot has the same crackled glaze spread underneath, with no mark attached.

The beautiful little cup in Fig. 37 is a *K'ang-hsi* production of the same class. It is modeled in the form and style of the *Hsüan-tê* period, and is decorated in a similar underglaze blue with a pair of five-clawed dragons pursuing jewels among clouds and flames, on the sides, and with a second pair of dragons upon the rounded cover, which is surmounted by a mythological animal; there is no mark underneath.

Passing on to the ordinary blue and white (*ch'ing hua pai ti*— i. e., "painted in blue on a white ground"), the reign of *K'ang-hsi* is unquestionably the finest period, when the cobalt comes out in its full inimitable brilliancy from the depths of a rich translucent glaze. The white ground has often a slight bluish tint, but it is not so blue as it was in the *Ming* dynasty; in the succeeding reigns it becomes creamy, or is even almost opaque, so as to be chalky in aspect. The blue is not generally so full and strong as in the reign of *Chia-ching* of the *Ming* dynasty, but it is graded, so as to produce a charming modulation, and a palpitating quality of color, which we rarely find in earlier work, hardly ever in more recent times; it is never flat or dead. As Mr. Cosmo Monkhouse says in his recent introduction to the *Burlington Fine Arts Club Catalogue*, which has been already cited: "It would take a long time to exhaust the number of changes which the Chinese ring upon the many tints of blue and white—white sometimes white as curds, sometimes grayish, sometimes tinged with the faintest blue, like the film inside a bird's egg. But if the white is varied, what of the blue? Sometimes brilliant and opaque as lapis lazuli, sometimes pure and trembling as a sapphire, now almost black, now wholly

FIG. 224.—Baluster Vase, of light porous material, painted in soft-toned blue under the undulatory "orange-peel" glaze, which is not crackled.

gray, sometimes warm as purple, sometimes cold as a wintry sky. Whatever quality is taken is of course used throughout, but even this allows for great variation in shade; a dark and light blue are nearly always employed, and three, if not more, distinct tones are often seen on the same piece."

Blue and white has always seemed to fascinate the artist, and Mr. Whistler has cleverly illustrated the style of the porcelain of this period,* and not without catching some of the spirit of the Chinese decorator. It is interesting to compare his work with that of our artist; the slender-necked, globular bottle illustrated in Plate XLII happens to have been drawn by him in Plate XXIV, No. 255, in the work just quoted.

FIG. 223.—Crackled Fên-Ting Vase, of the conventional form used for divining rods, with bosses on the four sides carved in openwork as branches of peach fruit.

Blue and white may be divided into two classes: blue upon white, and white upon blue, the latter comprising those examples in which the blue predominates to the extent of furnishing the ground upon which the untouched portions of the white porcelain beneath form the design of the decorations.

This is seen in the vase just referred to. Of the sixteen pieces of blue and white selected here for illustration, no less than thirteen are attributed to the reign of *K'ang-hsi*, although the marks of *Hsüan-tê*, *Ch'êng-hua*, and *Chia-ching* are inscribed on three of the objects. The reign always occupies this preponderating position in good collections. Plate II displays a magnificent example of the white upon blue class, the sprays of prunus shining in white reserve on the jar, which is covered all over, in the intervals of the floral decoration, with a reticulated ground of pulsating blue.

Before proceeding further with the description of the decorated porcelain, it seems advisable

---

* *A Catalogue of Blue and White Nankin Porcelain*, forming the collection of Sir Henry Thompson. Illustrated by the autotype process from drawings by James McN. Whistler, Esq., and Sir Henry Thompson: London, 1878.

to submit a scheme of classification under which its many varieties may be conveniently arranged. In its main lines I propose to follow Brongniart, who was the first, in his *Traité des Arts Céramiques*, which is still the classic of the art, to divide the colors used in the decoration of porcelain into three classes:

A. Couleurs de grand feu.
B. Couleurs de demi-grand feu.
C. Couleurs de petit feu ou de moufle.

The colors employed in China which resist the most intense heat of the furnace are the cobalt-blue, the copper-red, and the sea-green celadon and deep-brown glazes, which are both derived from iron. The first two are painted with a brush on the raw white body of the piece (*sur le cru*), and subsequently covered with glaze, so that they are both underglaze colors, and the porcelain requires but one firing. The other two are applied as glazes previously prepared, in which the coloring material is mixed with a feldspathic flux combined with lime.

The second class of colors (*de demi-grand feu*) are fired in the same furnace as those of the first class (*de grand feu*), but the pieces are placed in the more temperate parts of the furnace, near the chimney at the back, and below the level of its lower orifice, where they escape the direct blast of the fire. The colors are three in number—turquoise-blue derived from copper, manganese-purple, and yellow prepared from an iron ore containing antimony. The glazes, together with the white glaze which accompanies them, are combined with a nitre or lead flux, and applied *sur biscuit*, the piece having been previously fired, unglazed, in the large furnace. This class comprises the typical *San ts'ai*, or "Three-color" decoration of the period.

FIG. 226.—Vase, with decoration worked in relief, painted in colors of the *grand feu* blue, maroon, and celadon; mark, K'ang-hsi.

The third class includes the enamel colors of the muffle stove, which are the same as those used in painted and *cloisonné* enameling upon copper. They are previously combined with a flux composed of powdered quartz, oxide of lead, and alkalies, into a kind of glass, which retains in solution a small percentage of the metallic oxide dissolved in the vitreous mass in the form of silicate. The coloring matters used in China are comparatively few, being oxide of copper for the greens, gold for crimson and pink, oxide of cobalt for the blues, oxide of antimony for the yellows, arsenious acid for the white and for moderating the tint of the other colors. Oxide of iron gives coral-red, and impure oxide of manganese black; these two colors are generally applied directly, mixed with white-lead and glue, as they will not combine with silica. The enamel colors are painted upon white porcelain that has been already glazed and fired, and which has to be baked a second time in the gentle heat of the muffle stove to fix the colors. This is the typical *Wu ts'ai*, the "Five-colored" or Polychrome Decoration of the Chinese. The enamel painting may be executed, also *sur biscuit* or upon a crackled ground, or upon one partially or wholly invested with one of the highly fired, single colors, such as celadon, for example, or in combination with portions of decoration previously painted in one or more of the

FIG. 225.—Vase, decorated in underglaze copper-red of maroon tint, with a pair of five-clawed dragons; mark, K'ang-hsi.

underglaze colors. The changes that may be rung by the different combinations are almost infinite ; some have been already described, others will follow later. Meanwhile the decorated porcelain of this reign will be grouped according to the scheme :

TABLE OF DECORATED PORCELAIN.

A. Colors of the grand feu.
 1. Decorated in underglaze cobalt-blue.
 2. Decorated in underglaze copper-red.
 3. Decorated in mixed colors.

B. Colors of the demi-grand feu.
 4. Decorated in glazes of several colors.

C. Colors of the Muffle Stove.
 5. Decorated in overglaze iron-red.
 6. Decorated in sepia.
 7. Decorated in gold and silver.
 8. Decorated in mixed enamel colors.

 1. *Decorated in Underglaze Cobalt-Blue.*—This class has been briefly noticed already. The blue and white, which is its normal decoration, is sometimes relieved by one of the monochrome grounds, such as " Nankin " yellow or coral-red, as it used to be in the preceding dynasty, or it may still continue to be combined with touches of enamel colors, as it was in the *Wan-li Wu-ts'ai*, the typical polychrome decoration of the reign of *Wan-li*. In the beautiful little vase illustrated in Plate LXII, which is decorated in brilliant mottled blue of this period, the intervals between the panels are filled in with sprays of prunus, painted in delicate enamels, relieved by an iridescent black enameled ground.

 2. *Decorated in Underglaze Copper-Red.*—The coloring material is painted with a brush in the same way as the blue upon the raw, white body of the porcelain ; the glaze is blown on as soon as the piece is sufficiently dry, and it is afterward fired in the large furnace. The color comes out generally of a dull maroon tint, occasionally it is a bright ruby-red, or it may develop " peach-bloom " tints. The snuff-bottle illustrated in Plate XXXVII (2), which is painted with landscapes in maroon-red, is an example of this decoration. A fine specimen of the *K'ang-hsi* period is presented in Fig. 225. Another follows in Fig. 229.

 3. *Decorated in Mixed Colors of the grand feu.*—This class is illustrated in Fig. 226 by a vase which may be thus described : A tall, ovoid vase, seventeen and a quarter inches high, with the decoration of a four-clawed, two-horned dragon rising from the waves of the sea on either side, executed in relief, and painted in three colors—underglaze blue, maroon, and celadon. The bodies of the dragons are brown, the manes are penciled in blue, the effulgent jewels which they are pursuing are of shaded brown. The crested waves at the base, which are painted in blue, have rocks rising out of them, on both sides, of sea-green celadon tint.

FIG. 227.—K'ang-hsi Vase, with relief decoration painted in underglaze cobalt-blue, maroon, copper-red, and celadon.

The mark, written underneath in blue within a double ring, is *Ta Ch'ing K'ang hsi nien chih*—i. e., " Made in the reign of *K'ang-hsi* of the great *Ch'ing* [dynasty]." A vase of the same type is shown in Fig. 227, with raised outlines decorated in the same three colors—blue, maroon and celadon—displaying the combat between the tiger, king of land animals, and the dragon, prince of the powers of the air.

4. *Decorated in Glazes of the demi-grand feu.*—This may be characterized as the typical decoration in three colors (*San ts'ai*). It must be distinguished from the *San ts'ai* decoration of the muffle stove, where the turquoise-blue is replaced by a green of camellia-leaf tint, which is sometimes penciled with black, while the other two colors remain the same. The latter has a plain surface, the former is *truitée*—i. e., crackled all over with a minute reticulation of fine superficial lines. A combination of two of the colors—turquoise and purple—is found in the little peach-shaped wine-pot shown in Fig. 217.

FIG. 228.—Vase of the K'ang-hsi period, richly decorated in brilliant enamel colors.

5. *Decorated in Iron-Red.*—This color, which is prepared from peroxide of iron, produced by the incineration of iron sulphate, being the same as that used for the coral-red monochromes, is penciled upon the surface of the white glaze, and fixed by being fired in the muffle stove. This decoration is the *Ts'ai Hung*, or "Painting in Red," of the Chinese. No more beautiful illustration of it could be imagined than that of the egg-shell bowl of this period, decorated with dragons, which is presented in Plate LXVII. This decoration in coral-red is often combined with gold, as in the club-shaped vase of the reign of *K'ang-hsi*, displayed in Plate XXVIII, in which the effect of the soft red, penciled in two shades, is enhanced by touches of gilding, with the addition of a spot or two of black to define the eyes of the dragons.

6. *Decorated in Sepia.*—This decoration, although described as making its appearance late in the reign of *K'ang-hsi*, is more characteristic of the succeeding reigns, especially of that of *Ch'ien-lung*. It is the *Ts'ai Shui Mo*, or "Painting in Ink," of the Chinese, and, like the last, it is often thrown out effectively by touches of gold. A striking example of painting in sepia is illustrated in Fig. 230, a ruby-backed plate with a picture of a "dragon barge" towed in procession, which is probably the work of a *Ch'ien-lung* artist.

7. *Decorated in Gold and Silver.*—The metals, finely pulverized, were combined with oxide of lead by means of a little gum penciled upon the glaze and fixed in the muffle stove. Painting in gold (*Ts'ai Chin*) on a white ground was not so common in this reign, so we must refer to a wine-cup of the next reign, illustrated in Fig. 38 (*a*). In the reign of *K'ang-hsi* gold was lavished in the richest decoration of large vases enameled with the mazarin-blue and mirror-black grounds. Silver was chiefly employed in the ornamentation of the coffee-brown or dead-leaf ground. Both colors, especially the silver, resist wear and tear badly, so that only indistinct traces of the original designs may perhaps be detected in pieces that have survived to the present day.

8. *Decorated in Mixed Enamel Colors.*—This class includes the great majority of the decorated pieces of the time. Some of the varieties have been referred to already, and it has been explained how a brilliant green of shaded tones, usually laid on in thick patches, predominates among the colors, so that pieces of the old *famille verte*, even if they bear earlier marks of date, are generally to be attributed to this reign. The cobalt-blue, which during the *Ming* dynasty had been applied under the glaze, is now generally overlaid in the same way as the other enamel colors and fixed at the same firing. The other colors are red, yellow, and black, completing the "five colors" of the enameler. When blue and red are absent, we have the three-colored (*san ts'ai*) decoration of the muffle stove. The coloring of this inimitable period has an unmistakable *cachet* to an accustomed eye, which enables it to be distinguished at a glance from any repro-

duction, whether native or European. The two club-shaped vases illustrated in Plates VI and XVII are picked specimens of the richest ornamentation in enamel colors; the egg-shell lantern in Plate XI and the statuette of the goddess Avalôkita in Plate LX are both fine examples of the *famille verte.* It will be sufficient to add a cursory description of two more pieces as typical examples of the *Wu ts'ai* and *San ts'ai* enamel decoration.

The first, Fig. 228, is a richly and artistically decorated vase of the *Wu ts'ai* class, painted in the most brilliant enamel colors of the *K'ang-hsi* period, with a few touches of gold. It is covered with panel pictures of varied form, displayed upon floral and diapered grounds, and separated by a band of floral diaper encircling the shoulder, interrupted by medallions containing butterflies. There are eight panels on the body arranged in two rows, of which the lower panels, representing lotus-leaves and other foliated designs, contain a grotesque lionlike monster standing upon a rocky shore; a pair of peacocks on a rockery with peonies; a pair of phœnixes by a spreading dryandra-tree; a warbler perched upon a prunus-tree with roses underneath. Of the panels in the upper row, two are filled with vases containing symbols of rank and honor, the incense-burning apparatus, and books, scroll pictures, lyres, and chess, the emblems of the "four liberal arts." The other two contain a pair of storks on a pine, with a peach floating in

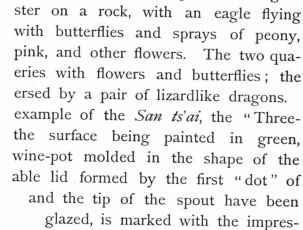

the waves below, and a grotesque mon-overhead. The interspaces are filled chrysanthemum, lotus, begonia, aster, trefoil panels on the neck contain rock-ground between is a spiral diaper trav-

The second (Fig. 82) is a choice colored" decoration of the muffle stove, purple, and yellow enamels. It is a character *fu*, "happiness," with a mov-the written hieroglyph. The handle replaced in metal. The base, un-sion of the stuff in which the and borders are enameled pale ("longevity") characters of dif-and green, upon a pale yel-which is precisely similar on of scrolled bands of lotus de-white and purple blossoms, in-outlined with purple. In the framed in green relief, con-emblems of longevity: on the rock with the sacred fungus

ster on a rock, with an eagle flying with butterflies and sprays of peony, pink, and other flowers. The two qua-eries with flowers and butterflies; the ersed by a pair of lizardlike dragons. example of the *San ts'ai*, the "Three-the surface being painted in green, wine-pot molded in the shape of the able lid formed by the first "dot" of and the tip of the spout have been glazed, is marked with the impres-paste was pressed. The rims green. The spout has *shou* ferent style, alternately purple low ground. The decoration, front and back, is composed sign with green foliations and closed in a pale yellow ground middle are two foliated panels taining pictures of various front a pine overspreading a growing upon it, an axis deer,

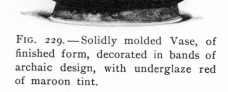

FIG. 229.—Solidly molded Vase, of finished form, decorated in bands of archaic design, with underglaze red of maroon tint.

and a sacred stork; on the back, a peach-tree with a clump of bamboos, a tiger, and a pair of birds flying, all painted in the same soft colors.

There is a class of porcelain decorated *sur biscuit*, with colored glazes, comprising two or three of the above tints, which is not, properly speaking, painted. The designs, generally of floral character, having been previously worked in the paste and engraved with the point, the piece is fired; the details are afterward filled in with glazes of different colors, and the piece is fired again in the muffle stove. There are bowls, for example, with the *K'ang-hsi* mark under-neath, engraved outside with branches of flowers growing from rocks—colored maroon, green, and white—relieved by a ground of imperial yellow, enameled plain yellow inside. The saucer-dishes etched in the paste inside with a pair of dragons surrounded by scrolled waves, with one of the dragons colored green, the other purple, and the surrounding ground yellow, come under the same class. The Chinese distinguish them by the appropriate name of *Huang Lü Huan*— i. e., "Yellow and Green in Panels."

FIG. 230.—Rose-backed Eggshell Plate, painted in sepia, with a
picture of the "Dragon Procession."

CHAPTER XI.

LETTERS OF PÈRE D'ENTRECOLLES.

THESE letters, which have been already referred to more than once, were originally published in the *Lettres édifiantes et curieuses*, and they brought the first detailed account of the manufacture of Chinese porcelain to Europe. The two letters embody the results of the personal observations and researches of the Jesuit missionary, and of the information gathered from such of his Chinese converts as were engaged in the industry. They are dated Jao-chou, September 1, 1712, and King-tê-chên, January 25, 1722. When the second letter was written the long and brilliant reign of the Emperor *K'ang-hsi* was fast drawing to its close. Two years later—that is to say, in the second year of his successor, *Yung-chêng*—the Roman Catholic religion was rigorously proscribed, the foreign missionaries were exiled to Macao, and their churches throughout the different provinces were either converted into secular schools or destroyed, so that we get no more letters on the subject. These two were written at a most interesting time—at a time too in respect to which there is a complete dearth of Chinese information, so that no apology is needed for giving here a *précis*, in the form of an abridged translation, as literal as possible, of the writer's own words. The second letter, which is mainly supplementary and explanatory, has been interwoven with the first to save space, and at the same time to maintain the continuity of the subject. I have slightly modified the orthography of the Chinese words for the sake of uniformity, with the exception of that of the first two words that occur. These have since become classical in Europe, and are to be found in the dictionary of the Académie Française:

"The material of porcelain is composed of two kinds of earth, one called *pe-tun-tse*, the other named *kao-lin*. The latter is disseminated with corpuscles which are somewhat glittering,*

* Crystals of mica. (The notes are added by the translator.)

176

the former is simply white and very fine to the touch. At the same time that a great number of large boats come up the river from Jao-chou to King-tê-chên to be loaded with porcelain, almost as many small ones descend from Ki-mên, laden with *pe-tun-tse* and *kao-lin* made into the form of bricks, for King-tê-chên itself produces none of the materials. *Pe-tun-tse*, of which the grain is so fine, is nothing but pulverized pieces of rock extracted from quarries, to which this form is given. It is not every stone that is suitable; if so, it would be useless to go for it into the next province.* The good stone, the Chinese say, ought to have a slight tinge of green. The rocks are first broken into pieces with iron hammers, and the fragments are finely pulverized in mortars by means of levers which have stone heads mounted with iron. These levers are worked incessantly, either by men or by water-power, in the same way as the tilt-hammers in paper-mills. The powder is thrown into a large jar full of water, and stirred strongly with an iron shovel. When it has been left a few moments to settle, a kind of cream forms at the top four or five fingers thick; this is taken off and poured into another vessel full of water. The operation is repeated several times until only the coarse residuum which sinks to the bottom is left; this is taken back to be crushed again in the mortar.

"With regard to the second jar, into which has been thrown all that was collected from the first, after waiting until a kind of paste has formed at the bottom, and the supernatant water is perfectly clear, the water is de- | canted without disturbing the sedi-
ment. The paste is emptied into | a large kind of wooden case, the
bottom of which is filled with a bed | of bricks, over which is stretched a
cloth of the size of the interior of | the case; this cloth is filled with
the paste, it is covered with an- | other cloth, and then with a flat
layer of bricks, which press out | the water. Before it has become
quite dry and hard, the paste is | divided into little squares, which

Fig. 231.—Covered Bowl of the K'ang-hsi period, with Taoist figures in relief, enameled *sur biscuit* in yellow, green, manganese purple, and white.

Fig. 232.—K'ang-hsi Jar, blue and white decoration, with alternating grounds of white and mottled blue.

Fig. 233.—Censer of the K'ang-hsi period, with buff-tinted finely crackled glaze; stand and cover of carved wood.

are sold by the hundred. The name of *pe-tun-tse* is derived from the white color and the shape of these *briquettes*. There would be nothing to add to this work if the Chinese were not in the habit of adulterating their merchandise; but people who roll little grains of paste in pepper-dust to mix with genuine pepper-corns would hardly care to sell *pe-tun-tse* without mixing it with coarser matters, so that it has to be again purified at King-tê-chên before it is fit for use.

"*Kao-lin* requires a little less labor than *pe-tun-tse;* Nature has done the greater part. It is found in mines in the bosom of certain mountains, which are covered outside with a reddish earth. These mines are fairly deep; it is found there in masses, and is also made into square *briquettes* by the same method that I have described above. It is to *kao-lin* that fine porcelain owes its strength, and it is only a combination with the soft earth that fortifies the *pe-tun-tse*, which is derived from the hardest of rocks. A rich merchant told me that some years ago the

* Ki-men-hsien is in the prefecture of Hui-chou-fu, in the province of An-hui, near the source of the Chang River, which flows by Ching-tê-chên.

English or Dutch had had purchased for them some *pe-tun-tse*, that they took to their country to make porcelain with, but that, having taken no *kao-lin*, their enterprise failed, as they confessed afterward.   The Chinese merchant said to me, laughing, 'They wanted to have a body with no bones to sustain the flesh.'

"Besides the boats laden with *pe-tun-tse* and *kao-lin*, with which the river bank at King-tê-chên is lined, others are found filled with a whitish and liquid substance.   I have long known that this substance was the oil (or glaze) that gives porcelain its whiteness and its luster, but I did not know its composition, which I have at last learned.   This oil is derived from the hardest stone.   The same kind of rock which is used in the preparation of the *pe-tun-tse* can also be employed for the extraction of the glaze, but the whitest pieces are picked out from the heap, and those which have the greenest spots.   The history of Fou-liang says that the best stone is that which has spots upon it like the leaves of the arbor vitæ,* or reddish marks like sesamum seeds.   The rock must first be well washed, and then prepared in the same way as the *pe-tun-tse*.   When there has been collected in the second jar the purest part of the matter that has been levigated in the first jar with all the usual precautions, to every hundred pounds or so of the cream one pound is added of a stone or mineral like alum, named *shih-kao;*† it must have been first roasted in the fire, and then pounded; it acts like rennet in giving a certain consistence, although the matter is always carefully kept in a liquid state.

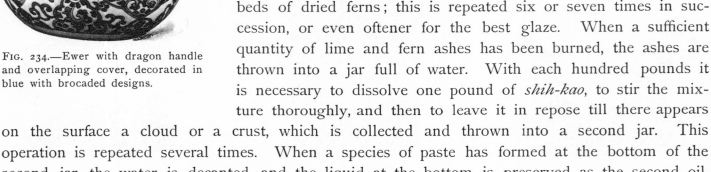

Fig. 234.—Ewer with dragon handle and overlapping cover, decorated in blue with brocaded designs.

"This stone glaze is never used alone; it is mixed with another material which forms its essence.   This is its composition: Large pieces of quicklime are reduced to powder by sprinkling water upon them, and covered with a bed of dried ferns, upon which is spread another layer of quenched lime, and so on in succession, one layer upon the other; then the ferns are set on fire.   After everything is burned, the ashes are spread upon new beds of dried ferns; this is repeated six or seven times in succession, or even oftener for the best glaze.   When a sufficient quantity of lime and fern ashes has been burned, the ashes are thrown into a jar full of water.   With each hundred pounds it is necessary to dissolve one pound of *shih-kao*, to stir the mixture thoroughly, and then to leave it in repose till there appears on the surface a cloud or a crust, which is collected and thrown into a second jar.   This operation is repeated several times.   When a species of paste has formed at the bottom of the second jar, the water is decanted, and the liquid at the bottom is preserved as the second oil, to be mixed with the preceding.

"For a proper mixture, the two *purées* must be of the same thickness, which is tested by dipping in squares of *pe-tun-tse*.   With regard to the quantity of the ingredients, the best glaze that can be made is a combination of ten measures of the first *purée* of stone with one measure of that made of the lime and fern ashes; the most sparing never put less than three measures to one.   The merchants that sell the liquid sometimes dilute it with water, and conceal the fraud by adding a proportionate quantity of *shih-kao* to thicken it.

"Before explaining the method of applying the glaze it is necessary to describe the fabrication of the porcelain.   In the less frequented parts of King-tê-chên are vast sheds, surrounded by walls, in which one sees ranged, story above story, a great quantity of jars of earth.   Inside these walls live and work an infinite number of workmen, each of whom has his allotted task. A piece of porcelain, before it leaves them to be carried to the furnace, passes through the hands of more than twenty persons.

* Dendrites of manganese oxide.

† Gypsum, or sulphate of lime.   The action of this is supposed to be purely mechanical, quickening precipitation.

"The first work consists in purifying anew, by the same process of levigation and decantation, both the *pe-tun-tse* and the *kao-lin*. After having been purified, the two materials are combined in certain proportions: the finest porcelain is made of equal parts; for an inferior kind they use four parts of *kao-lin* to six parts of *pe-tun-tse*; the least that can be put is one part of *kao-lin* to three of *pe-tun-tse*.

"When mixed, the material is thrown into a large hollow or pit, well paved and cemented throughout, where it is trodden and kneaded to weld it to a proper consistence; this is very hard work, and it goes on incessantly, so that the Christians employed can not even come to church without providing substitutes.

"From the mass thus prepared, lumps are taken and put upon large slates, where they are kneaded, beaten, and rolled in every sense, taking the greatest care that there shall be no hollows left, and no admixture of foreign bodies. A hair, a grain of sand, would ruin all the work. From such elements are produced so many beautiful works of porcelain, some fashioned upon the wheel, others made simply by molds, and finished afterward with the polishing-knife.

"The plain, round pieces are all made in the first fashion. A cup, when it comes off the wheel, is very imperfectly shaped, like the top of a hat before it has been put on the shaping mold. The foot is only a piece of clay of the diameter that it is intended to have ultimately, and it is not excavated with the knife until all the other operations are finished. The cup, as it comes from the wheel, is first handed to a second workman, who is seated beneath. It is passed by him to a third, who presses it on a mold, and gives it its shape; this mold is fixed upon a kind of wheel. A fourth workman polishes the cup with

FIG. 235. — Eggshell Plate of pale-green celadon tint, overlaid with a decoration in white, and with over-glaze blue round the borders.

a knife, especially round the rims, and makes it thin enough to be transparent; each time he scrapes it, it must be moistened carefully, or it will break. It is surprising to see the rapidity with which the vases pass through so many different hands, and I am told that a vase that has been fired has gone through the hands of seventy workmen.

"Large objects of porcelain are made in two pieces: one half is lifted upon the wheel by three or four men, who support it on each side while it is being shaped; the other half is fitted upon the first when it is sufficiently dried, and is cemented to it with porcelain earth, mixed with water (i. e., slip), which serves as mortar or glue. When quite dry, the place of junction is pared with a knife, inside and outside, so that, after glazing, there remains no inequality of surface. Handles, ears, and similar adjuncts are attached by means of slip in the same way. This refers principally to the porcelain which is made in molds, or by handwork, such as fluted pieces, or those of bizarre shape, such as animals, grotesques, idols, the busts ordered by Europeans, and such like. These objects, when molded, are made in three or four pieces, which are fitted together, and finished afterward

FIG. 236.—Hexagonal Tripod Censer with overlapping cover pierced in openwork; of Ko Yao crackle, attributed to the K'ang-hsi period.

with instruments adapted for excavating, polishing, and working the various details that have escaped the mold. As for flowers and other ornaments, which are not in relief, but, as it were, *in intaglio*, these are impressed on the porcelain with seals and molds; reliefs, ready prepared, are also put on, in the same way almost as gold lace is attached to a coat.

"I have lately investigated the subject of these molds. When the model of the piece of porcelain to be made is in hand, and it is such as can not be shaped upon the wheel by the potter, they press upon the model some yellow clay, specially prepared for molding; the clay is impressed in this way, the mold being composed of several pieces of pretty large size, which are left to harden when they have been properly impressed. When they are used, they are put near the fire for some time, and then filled with porcelain earth to the thickness the piece is to have, and this is pressed into every part with the hands. The mold is held to the fire for a moment, to detach the "squeeze" from the mold. The different pieces which have been separately molded in this way are joined together afterward with a slip (Fig. 231). I have seen animals of massive proportions fabricated by these means; after the mass has been left to harden, it is worked into the desired form, and finished with the chisel; and, finally, each of the parts worked separately is adjusted. When the object has been finished off with great care, the glaze is put on, and it is then fired; it is painted afterward, if desired, in different colors, and the gold is applied, and then it is fired a second time.

"When the time has come to ennoble the porcelain by painting, it is intrusted to the hands of the *Hua-p'i,** or porcelain painters, who are almost as poor as the other workmen; not so

FIG. 237.—Set of K'ang-hsi Vases, artistically decorated with diapered borders in underglaze blue, inclosing panels painted in colors; European mounts.

astonishing a fact, however, as with a few exceptions they would pass in Europe only as apprentices of some months' standing. All the science of these painters, and indeed of Chinese painters generally, is not based on any principles; it consists only in a certain routine, helped by a vein of imagination limited enough. They are ignorant of every beautiful rule of the art. Still, it must be confessed that they paint flowers, animals, and landscapes, which are much admired upon porcelain as well as on fans and on lanterns of the finest gauze. The work of painting is distributed in the same workshop among a great number of workmen. One has the sole task of outlining the colored rings that are seen on porcelain near the rims of the pieces, another sketches the flowers, which a third paints; this one is for landscapes, that one for birds and for other animals.

"With regard to the colors of porcelain they are of all sorts. In Europe hardly anything is seen excepting a bright blue upon a white ground, but I believe that our merchants have also imported other kinds.† There are some pieces with a ground resembling that of our burning-glasses; others are wholly red, and among these some have the red in the glaze (*yu-li-hung*); others have a *soufflé* red (*ch'ui-hung*), and are strewn with little points somewhat like our miniatures. When these last two kinds come out in perfect success—a work of some difficulty —they are infinitely esteemed and extremely dear.

"Lastly, there are porcelain vases with pictures of landscape scenes painted in nearly all the different colors, enhanced by the luster of gilding. These are very beautiful if no expense is spared; otherwise the ordinary porcelain of this kind is not to be compared with that painted

* Hua-p'i means literally "painter on the raw body" (*sur le cru*), and, like so many terms of the Chinese *atelier*, indicates the greater antiquity of decorating in cobalt-blue than that of painting in enamel colors.

† The two illustrations (Figs. 232 and 234) are specimens of blue and white designs painted for Europe about this time. The cylindrical vase is decorated in alternate bands of blue upon white, and blue with white reserves; and similar vases are often found painted in enamel colors of the period. The other is painted in blue with rich panels of floral brocade.

in azure blue alone. The annals say that in ancient times the people used only white porcelain, probably because the ordinary blue had not yet been discovered.

"The azure blue is prepared in this way: It.is buried in the gravel, which is half a foot thick in the floor of the furnace, and roasted there for twenty-four hours; then it is ground to an impalpable powder, in the same way as the other colors—not on marble, but in a great porcelain mortar, the bottom of which is unglazed, as is also the head of the pestle with which the colors are pounded.

"The red that is made from green vitriol (*tsao-fan*) is prepared by placing about a pound of the iron crystals in a crucible, which is well luted to a second crucible, having in the top a small aperture, covered, however, in such a way that it can be easily uncovered if needful. The whole is surrounded by a large charcoal fire in a reverberating brick furnace. As long as the smoke which rises is all black, the material is not yet fit; but it is as soon as a kind of thin, fine cloud appears. Then they take a little of the material, mix it with water, and try the effect on a piece of pine wood. If it comes out a good red, they take out the brazier in which it is inclosed and partially cover the crucible. When quite cold, a little cake of this red is found at the bottom of the lower crucible, while the finest red lines the upper crucible. One pound of iron sulphate furnishes four ounces of the red used in painting porcelain. This red is combined with five times its weight of white lead, the two powders are passed through a sieve, and mixed together dry. The mixture is incorporated with water thickened with a little ox-glue when it is painted on, so that it may not run down the side of the vase.

FIG. 238.—Finely cracled Turquoise Bottle of the K'ang-hsi period, one of a pair; with European mounts.

"Although porcelain is naturally white, and the glaze serves, moreover, to augment its whiteness, yet there are certain figures in the production of which a peculiar white is painted upon porcelain decorated in different colors. This is prepared by pulverizing a transparent rock,* which is calcined by inclosing it in a porcelain crucible, and by burying the crucible in the gravel floor of the furnace, in the same way as the azure-blue. It is mixed with water, without glue, with twice its weight of white lead, and painted on with a brush. The same white is used for combining with other colors to modify their tints. Added to the ordinary green, for example, in the proportion of two parts of white to one part of green, it makes the pale, clear green, which is often associated with the darker shade.

"With regard to the other colors which are painted on the porcelain for the second firing, the dark green is prepared by combining an ounce of white lead, with a third of an ounce of powdered quartz, and a tenth to a twelfth of an ounce of *t'ung hua p'ien*, which is nothing else than the scum of copper which rises to the surface when the metal is melted. It is necessary to separate carefully the granules of metallic copper which are found mixed with it, as these are bad for the green.

"The yellow color is prepared by combining an ounce of white lead, with a third of an ounce of pulverized quartz, and one fifty-fifth of an ounce of primitive red.† A second workman tells me one fortieth of an ounce of the last ingredient.

"The deep blue with a shade of violet is prepared by mixing one ounce of white lead, with one third of an ounce of pulverized quartz, and one five-hundredth of an ounce of azure-blue. Another workman says four five-hundredths of the blue.

"The black is prepared by mixing the azure-blue mineral with water thickened with ox-glue and a little lime. When this is painted on over the glaze, the black parts of the design are covered with white glaze, which incorporates with the black during the second firing, in the

---

* The *caillou transparent* here spoken of is no doubt arsenious acid, the native arsenical ore, which occurs in large translucid masses. The effect of the decoration in white upon a pale-green celadon ground is seen in Fig. 235.

† The mineral referred to here has been analyzed by Brongniart, and found to be a magnetic iron ore (*fer oligistique terreux*) containing antimony.

same way as the blue is incorporated in the ordinary glaze, when blue and white porcelain is baked in the furnace.

"There is another color called *tsiu*,* from which the deep violet is made. It is found in Canton, and it comes also from Peking, the last being much the best. It sells for about two dollars the pound. This material melts, and when it is melted, or softened, jewelers apply it in the form of enamel to silver objects, such as rings or hairpins. Like the other colors just described, this is used only on the porcelain which is re-fired. It is not roasted like the ordinary azure-blue, but pounded and reduced to the finest powder, which is thrown into a vessel full of water and shaken a little; the water removes some impurities, and the crystal powder, which remains at the bottom, is kept for use. It loses its fine color and appears grayish, but recovers its violet tint as soon as it is fired. It can be painted on, mixed with pure water or with a little glue added.

"To gild or to silver porcelain, a tenth part by weight of white lead is mixed with the gold or silver leaf, which has been previously dissolved by the use of gum. The gold after it has been ground is usually spread with water over the bottom of a porcelain saucer till it forms a little 'gold sky' under the water. This is dried, and, when used, a sufficient quantity is dissolved off by weak glue, mixed with the white lead, and applied in the same way as the enamel colors. Silver comes out with great luster upon the coffee-brown or 'dead-leaf' (*tzŭ-chin*) glaze. If some pieces are painted in gold and others in silver, the silvered porcelain must not be left so long in the little furnace as the gilded; otherwise the silver will disappear before the gold has attained the degree of heat required to give it its proper luster.

"Sometimes porcelain is fired a second time only to conceal some defect, which is painted over with colors. The enameled porcelain, which is very richly colored, is not without attraction for many. When dry it is put into the stove and arranged in tiers and piles, the small pieces within the large, only taking care that the painted parts do not touch. The furnaces may be of iron,† if only small ones are required, but ordinarily they are made of clay. One which I saw was of the height of a man, and almost as broad as one of our largest wine-casks; it was made of several pieces of the same material as the clay segars in which the porcelain is fired, being built of large, rounded pieces, a finger's breadth thick, a foot high, and a foot and a half broad, well cemented together. The bottom of the furnace was elevated about half a foot from the ground, and supported by two or three rows of bricks; the furnace was encircled by a well-built wall of bricks, with three or four air-holes at the bottom. There is a space about half a foot broad between this wall and the furnace, which is left empty for the charcoal fire, except where it is traversed by supporting spurs of masonry. When the charge has been introduced, the top of the furnace is closed with pieces of pottery, similar to those of the sides of the

Fig. 239.—Tall Beaker of K'ang-hsi porcelain, decorated in the characteristic enamels of the period, showing a Court interior, with a dancing-girl, accompanied by an orchestra, performing before the Imperial circle. Height, 30 inches.

* This must be a misprint for *ts'ui*, which is the name of the cobalt-blue glaze used in China by enamelers on copper and silver. It is of somewhat similar composition to the "deep blue with a shade of violet" described just before, and is a characteristic color of the period.

† The furnace used by the *cloisonné* enamelers at Peking is a small iron cylinder with a movable cover. This is imbedded in charcoal, held by a larger outside cylindrical case of iron netting. It is fired in the open courtyard, and the fire is kept up by men standing round wielding large fans.

furnace, which fit inside each other, and are cemented together by mortar or moistened clay. An aperture is left in the middle, to observe when the porcelain is properly baked. A quantity of charcoal is burned at the bottom of the furnace, and also at the same time upon the cover, from which pieces of lighted charcoal are thrown into the space between the brick wall and the furnace. The potsherd which has been put upon the hole in the cover is removed for inspection from time to time, until it appears that all the enamels are thoroughly fired.

"There is a kind of colored porcelain here which is sold at a cheaper rate than that which is painted with the colors of which I have just spoken. To make work of this kind it is not necessary that the materials used should be so fine; cups are taken which have already been baked in the large furnace, without having been glazed, and which are consequently quite white and without luster; they are colored by immersing them in a jar filled with the prepared color, when they are required to be of single color; if they are wished to be of different colors, such as the pieces called *huang lü huan*, which are divided into a variety of panels, one green, another yellow, etc., then the colors are applied with a large brush. This is all the decoration given to this porcelain, excepting that, after it has been fired, a little vermilion is sometimes put upon certain parts, as, for example, upon the beaks of birds; but this last color is not baked, because it would disappear in the furnace, so it lasts but a very short time. After the colors have been applied, the porcelain is re-fired in the large furnace at the same time as other pieces that have not been baked before; care must be taken to place it at the back of the furnace and below the vent, where the fire is not so active, because an intense heat would destroy the colors. The colors adapted for this kind of porcelain are prepared in this way: The green* is made of *t'ung hua*

FIG. 240.—Tall Ovoid Jar with rounded cover, painted in brilliant enamel colors of the best K'ang-hsi period; mark, a double ring.

p'ien (oxide of copper), saltpeter, and powdered quartz reduced separately to an impalpable powder, and mixed together with water. The commonest azure-blue material mixed with saltpeter and pulverized quartz forms the violet. The yellow is made by combining three-tenths of an ounce of iron-red with three ounces of powdered quartz, and three ounces of white lead. The white is made by the addition of four-tenths of an ounce of pulverized quartz to an ounce of white lead. All these ingredients are mixed together with water. This is all that I have been able to gather about the colors of this sort of porcelain, not having any of the workmen among my converts.

"To return to the single colors. The glaze red called *yu-li-hung* is made from granulated

---

* The copper oxide combined in this way with a flux of nitre and silica produces the color we call "turquoise-blue," but which the Chinese call "peacock-green" (*kung-chuo lü*). The decoration *sur biscuit*, described above, fired in the large furnace, is known technically as that of the colors of the *demi-grand feu*.

red copper, and the powder of a certain stone which has a shade of red,* ground together in a mortar with a boy's urine, and mixed afterward with some of the white glaze material. I have not been able to discover the quantities of these ingredients; those who have the secret are very careful not to divulge it. The mixture is applied to porcelain that has not been baked before, and it is not given any other glaze; only special care must be taken that during the

FIG. 241.—Fluted
Vase and Stand
of the K'ang-hsi
period, painted in
soft colors of the
famille verte.

firing the red color does not run down to the bottom of the vase. If the red comes out pure and brilliant and without any stain, it is one of the most perfect achievements of the ceramic art. The porcelain does not ring when struck. I have been assured that when this red is about to be applied, the porcelain is not made of *pe-tun-tse*, but that yellow clay is used in its place to mix with the *kao-lin*, prepared before it and in the same way with the *pe-tun-tse*. The granules of copper which give the red are obtained during the purification of silver ingots, of which there are so many of base alloy in circulation. The refiners, while the melted copper is hardening and congealing, dip a small broom into water, and sprinkle some of it over the liquid copper; the film which then forms on the surface is lifted off with little iron tongs and thrown into cold water, where it forms into granules.

"The *soufflé* red (*ch'ui-hung*) is made in this way: Having prepared the red, a bamboo tube is used which has one of its ends covered with a very close gauze; this is dipped gently into the color so as to cover the gauze, and then, by blowing through the tube, the color is projected upon the porcelain, which will be found strewn all over with little red points. This kind of porcelain is even rarer and dearer than the preceding, because the execution is still more difficult.

"There is also a *soufflé* blue (*ch'ui-ch'ing*) which is much easier to apply successfully. The finest azure-blue, prepared by roasting the cobaltiferous mineral, is mixed with water to a proper consistence, and blown in the same way upon the surface of the unbaked vase; it is allowed to dry, and is then covered with the ordinary white glaze, either alone or mixed with the 'crackle glaze' (*sui yu*), if the porcelain is to be veined. It is finally fired in the large furnace. The cobalt-blue monochrome glaze, whether it be *soufflé* or applied by immersion, may have a decoration traced upon it by artist workmen with the point of a long needle; the needle removes as many little points of the dry azure color as may be necessary to represent the outline of the design, after which the piece is glazed. After the porcelain has been fired, the figures appear as if painted in miniature.

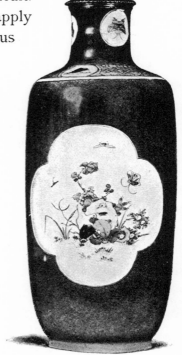

FIG. 242.—Tall club-shaped Vase
covered with a *soufflé* coral-red
ground, with large reserves of
varied form, filled with floral
decorations in K'ang-hsi colors.

"The black porcelain called *wu chin* has also its price and its beauty; it is a brilliant black, somewhat like that of our burning-glasses, which is very effective in combination with the gold decoration with which it is usually associated. The unbaked porcelain is immersed in a fluid mixture composed of prepared azure blue; † it is not necessary to use the finest azure, but it must be rather thick, and mixed with some of the brown mineral (*tzŭ-chin*) and the materials of the ordinary white glaze. For example, to ten ounces of azure pounded in the mortar are added one cup of *tzŭ-chin*, seven cups of *pai yu* (prepared from feldspar), and two cups of the lime and fern-ash mixture. No other glaze is necessary; when the porcelain is fired, it must be placed in the middle of the furnace, and not near the roof, where the heat would be too intense. The gold designs are penciled on afterward, and the piece is fired anew in a particular furnace.

---

* Probably amethystine quartz.

† It should be rather "a *purée* made of calcined cobaltiferous oxide of manganese," the ore which the Chinese used to produce blue, and which, if not covered with glaze, comes out black.

"The glaze referred to just now, called *tzŭ-chin*—i. e., 'burnished gold' (*or bruni*)—I should name rather 'bronze-colored,' 'coffee-colored,' or 'dead-leaf' (*couleur de feuille morte*). It is a recent invention;* for its composition, common yellow clay is taken, levigated in the same way as the *pe-tun-tse*, and mixed with water to the same consistence as the ordinary white feldspathic glaze. The tzŭ-chin *purée* is first mixed with the feldspathic *purée*, and some of the lime and fern-ash *purée* of the same consistence is afterward added to the mixture. The proportions of the three ingredients depend upon the tint required; it may range from that of 'old gold' to the darkest chocolate color.

"I have been shown this year (1722), for the first time, a species of porcelain which is now in fashion (*à la mode*): Its color approaches that of the olive and is given the name of *lung-ch'uan*. I have heard it called *ch'ing kuo*—the name of a fruit which nearly resembles the olive.† This color is given to porcelain by mixing together seven cups of the tzŭ-chin *purée*, four cups of feldspathic *purée*, two cups of lime and fern-ash *purée*, and one cup of crackle *purée*. The last, named *sui yu*,

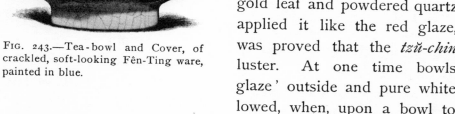

rock, causes a quantity of veins to
is applied alone, the porce-
ring when struck,
with other glazes,
though reticulated
and is not more
The ordinary vari-
over, and cut in every
finity of veins; from
be taken for a broken
ments remaining in
in mosaic. The color is

"They tried lately to mix
with the ordinary glaze, and
but the attempt failed, as it
glaze excelled in grace and
were made with the 'golden
within; another variation fol-

FIG. 243.—Tea-bowl and Cover, of crackled, soft-looking Fên-Ting ware, painted in blue.

which is prepared from a kind of
appear on the porcelain; when it
lain is fragile, and does not
but, when mixed
the porcelain, al-
with veins, rings,
fragile than usual.
ety is marbled all
direction with an in-
a distance it might
piece with the frag-
place; it is like a work
usually grayish.
gold leaf and powdered quartz
applied it like the red glaze,
was proved that the *tzŭ-chin*
luster. At one time bowls
glaze' outside and pure white
lowed, when, upon a bowl to

which they were going to apply the *tzŭ-chin* glaze, they stuck on, in one or two places, a round or square of moistened paper. The paper was taken away when the glaze had been applied, and the space filled in with a painting in red or in azure blue. Sometimes such medallion spaces were colored with a blue or a black ground, and, after having been fired, were penciled in gold and fired anew; a number of such different combinations might be imagined.

"Not long ago a new material was discovered that could enter into the composition of porcelain. This is a stone, or species of chalk, called *hua-shih*,‡ the same which Chinese doctors use to make a draught which they say is detergent, aperient, and refreshing. The potters use it to replace the *kao-lin*. Porcelain fabricated with *hua-shih* is rare, and much dearer than the other; it has an extremely fine grain, and with regard to the work of the brush, if it be compared with ordinary porcelain, it is like vellum compared with paper. Moreover, this porcelain is so light as to surprise one accustomed to handle other kinds of porcelain; it is

---

* The worthy father must be mistaken here, as we extracted a detailed prescription in Chapter VIII from the records of the *Ming* dynasty. The color referred to is the well-known *fond laqué* of French ceramic writers.

† The Chinese olive, so called, is the fruit of a species of canarium.

‡ *Hua-shih* is steatite, which is widely used in China as a febrifuge. But many other substances have been sent to Europe under the same name, so that Salvétat writes that it is sometimes a mixture of steatite and amphibole, at others ferruginous clay, or impure *kao-lin*. Vogt says (*La Porcelaine*, page 225), "It is a natural mixture of two thirds of *kao-lin* and one third of white mica." The peculiar porcelain made of it, as described above, is the *sha t'ai* of the Chinese, the "soft paste" of collectors, described in the last chapter, distinguished by its light weight, its tendency to crackle, and the fine, neat lines of its decoration when painted in cobalt-blue.

also much more fragile than the common sort, and it is difficult to seize the proper moment of its firing. Some, who do not use the *hua-shih* to make the body, content themselves with making a kind of glue of it, in which they immerse the porcelain when it is dry, so that it takes up a layer, on which to receive the colors and the glaze, by which means it acquires a certain degree of beauty. The *hua-shih* is washed when it is taken from the mine and prepared like the *kao-lin.* I am assured that porcelain can be made of it alone without anything else mixed, but one of my converts, who works with it, tells me that he combines eight parts of *hua-shih* with two parts of *pe-tun-tse.* It is five times the price of *kao-lin.* It is also used for painting designs over the glaze in slip.

"There is one secret that the Chinese lament having lost: they once had the art of painting upon a porcelain bowl fish or other animals, which became visible only when the porcelain was filled with some liquid. This kind of porcelain was called *chia-ch'ing*—that is to say, 'azure put in press,' indicating the position of the color. The porcelain to be painted thus must be very thin; when it has been dried, the color is applied with a strong touch, not outside, as usually, but inside, on the sides of the cup; the ordinary decoration is fish, the most natural thing, as it were, to appear when the cup is filled with water. As soon as the painting is dry a light layer of slip is spread over it, which confines the color between two coats of earth. When the slip has dried, the glaze is put on inside the cup, which is afterward put upon the polishing wheel and cut away outside as thin as possible without penetrating to the color, and lastly the outside is glazed by immersion. When everything is dry it is fired in the ordinary furnace. The work is extremely delicate, and demands a skill that the Chinese seem no longer to possess.

FIG. 244.—Ground of mottled blue (*bleu fouetté*), penciled in gold, with white reserves painted in underglaze blue and enamel colors.

"There is another kind of porcelain made here with an outer pierced casing, carved in openwork (*à jour*), so as to inclose the cup which holds the liquid. The cup and the pierced casing form one piece. I have seen other charming pieces in which Chinese and Tartar ladies are painted after life, with the costume, the coloring, and the features, all finished in the most *recherché* style, so that at a distance the work might be taken for an enamel.

"To-day, it may be said, there is a renaissance, and the beautiful azure reappears upon porcelain once more. When it is applied it is of a grayish-black color; when it is dry and it has been coated with glaze it is eclipsed altogether, and the porcelain appears perfectly white; the colors are then buried under the glaze, but the fire brings them out in all their beauty, almost like the heat of the sun as it brings out from a chrysalid a gorgeous butterfly in all its brilliant hues.

"The place where the furnaces are presents another scene. In a kind of vestibule which leads to the furnace are seen piles of cases made of clay, the *seggars* in which the porcelain is incased. The small pieces, like the cups intended for tea or chocolate, are put several in one case; the large pieces have a separate case for each one. The workman copies Nature, which protects fruits within an envelope, so that they may be gradually ripened by the heat of the sun. The cases are placed in columns inside the furnace, the two lowest in each column, imbedded in the gravel floor, being left empty, because the fire has no power so low down. In the middle piles, which are seven feet high, are placed the finest porcelains, at the back of the furnace the coarser kinds, near the entrance the pieces of strong color which are made of materials containing as much *pe-tun-tse* as *kao-lin*, and the glaze of which is prepared from the rocks with blackish or red spots, because this glaze has more body than the other. The cases are made of different colored clays produced in the neighborhood, kneaded together, and are fashioned upon the wheel.

"Some one hundred and eighty loads of pine fuel (of a hundred and thirty-three pounds weight each) are consumed at every firing, and it is surprising that no ashes even are left. It is not surprising that porcelain is so dear in Europe, for, apart from the large gains of the European merchants, and of their Chinese agents, it is rare for a furnace to succeed completely; often everything is lost, and on opening it the porcelain and the cases will be found converted into a solid mass as hard as rock. Moreover, the porcelain that is exported to Europe is fashioned almost always after new models, often of *bizarre* character, and difficult to reproduce; for the least fault they are refused, and remain in the hands of the potters, because they are not in the taste of the Chinese and can not be sold to them. Some of the elaborate designs sent are quite impracticable, although they produce for themselves some things which astonish strangers, who will not believe in their possibility.

Fig. 245.—Tzŭ-chin ground of yellow-brown tint, with reserve medallions in blue and white.

"I will give some examples of these. I have seen here a large porcelain lantern made in one piece, through the sides of which shone a candle, placed inside, so as to light a whole room; this work was ordered seven or eight years ago by the heir-apparent.* The same prince ordered, at the same time, various musical instruments, and among others a kind of little mouth-organ called *tsêng*, which is about a foot high, composed of fourteen pipes, and the melody of which is pleasing enough; but every attempt at making

Fig. 246.—Hexagonal White Vase, of light Fên-Ting type, sparingly crackled, with twigs of prunus winding in open relief round the shoulder.

this failed. They succeeded better with flutes and flageolets, and with another instrument called *yun-lo*, which is composed of a set of little round and slightly concave plaques, each of which has its different note; nine of these are hung in three tiers in a square frame, and played upon with rods, like the tympanum; a little chime is produced to accompany the sound of other instruments, or the voice of singers. It required, they tell me, many trials before they succeeded in finding the proper thickness and density to produce correctly all the notes of the scale. I imagined myself that they had the secret of inserting a little metal in the body of the porcelain, to vary the notes; but have been undeceived, for metal is so ill adapted to combine with porcelain that if a copper 'cash' happened to be put upon the top of a pile of porcelain in the kiln, the coin as it melted would pierce all the cases and porcelain in the column, so that a hole would be found in the middle of every one. To return to the rarer works, the Chinese succeed best in grotesques, and in the representation of animals. The workmen make ducks and tortoises which will swim in water. I have seen a cat painted after life, in the head of which a little lamp had been put to illuminate the eyes, and was assured that in the night the rats were terrified by it. They make here too very many statuettes of Kuan-yin,† a goddess celebrated throughout all China, represented holding an infant in her arms, and worshiped by sterile women who wish to have children.

"There is another kind of porcelain, the execution of which is very difficult, and which has consequently become exceeding rare. The body of this porcelain is extremely thin, and its surface very smooth inside and out; notwithstanding which there can be detected in it, on close

---

* One of these beautiful eggshell lanterns is illustrated in Plate XI. The heir-apparent was the fourth son of the emperor, the prince who reigned afterward as *Yung-chêng*. It is interesting to find him mentioned as patronizing the art so early as 1704 or 1705.

† Refer to Plate LX for a finely decorated figure of the period. Kuan-yin is the Buddhist divinity Avalôkita.

inspection, molded designs, such as a ring of flowers, or other like ornaments.* They are executed in this way: When it has been shaped upon the wheel it is pressed upon a mold carved with the designs which are impressed inside, and then it is pared down outside, as finely and thinly as possible, with the knife on the polishing wheel, to be ultimately glazed and baked in the ordinary furnace.

Fig. 247.—Large Bottle-shaped Vase of K'ang-hsi blue and white of brilliant color, with sprays of prunus spreading upward from the base to cover its surface with white flowers and buds. The slightly everted lip is defined by a light band of triangular fret; no mark.

"European merchants demand sometimes from the Chinese workmen porcelain slabs, to form in one piece the top of a table or bench, or frames for pictures. These works are impossible; the broadest and longest slabs made are only a foot across or thereabouts, and if one goes beyond, whatever may be the thickness, it will be warped in baking. The extra thickness does not facilitate the work, rather the contrary; and this is why the native slabs, instead of being made thick, are formed of two faces, with a hollow interior, traversed by a solid cross-piece; these slabs, used for inlaying carpentry, have two holes pierced at either end, so that they may be inserted in a bed, or in the back of a chair, when they look very effective.

"The mandarins, who know the genius of Europeans for inventions, often ask me to have brought from Europe novel and curious designs, in order that they may present to the emperor something unique. On the other hand, the Christians press me strongly not to get any such models, for the mandarins are not so easy to be convinced as our merchants, when the workmen tell them that a task is impracticable; and the bastinado is liberally administered before the mandarin will abandon a design which may bring him, he hopes, great profit.

"As each profession has its particular idol, and divinity is conferred here as easily as the rank of count or marquis is given in some European countries, it is not surprising that there should be a god of porcelain. The *Pou-sa* † (the name of this idol) owes its origin to these kinds of designs which it is impossible for the workmen to execute. They say that formerly an emperor decreed positively that some porcelain should be made after a model which he gave; it was represented to him several times that the thing was impossible, but all these remonstrances served only to excite more and more his desire. His officers persecuted the workmen incessantly. The poor wretches spent all their money and gave themselves infinite pains, but they got nothing but blows in return. At last one of them in a moment of despair threw himself into the burning furnace and was consumed in an instant. The porcelain which was being baked came out, they say, perfectly beautiful, and pleased the emperor, who demanded nothing more. After his death the unfortunate man was regarded as a hero, and he became in course of time the idol who is now the protector of the workers in porcelain.

"Porcelain having been so highly esteemed through so many centuries, one would wish to know in what respects that of the earlier times differs from that of our own days, and what

* For a striking example of this work, refer to Plate LXVII.

† *Pou-sa* is the Chinese contraction of the Sanskrit *Bôdhisattva*, a personage who has only one more stage of human existence to pass through before he becomes a Buddha. It is applied secondarily to any idol. The Pou-sa, who has become proverbial in Europe as the god of luxurious indolence, often molded in porcelain, is the representation of Mâitrêya, the coming Buddha or Messiah of the present Kalpa.

the Chinese think of it themselves. It must not be doubted that China has its antiquaries, whose predilections are all for ancient works. The Chinaman, indeed, has an innate respect for antiquity, although one finds defenders of modern art; but porcelain is not like ancient medals, which reveal the science of distant ages. Ancient porcelain may be ornamented with Chinese characters, but they mark no point in history, so that the curious could only find something in the style and in the colors which could lead them to prefer it to that of the present day. I believe that I heard it said, when I was in Europe, that porcelain, to have its full perfection, must have been buried for a long time in the ground; this is an absurdity which the Chinese ridicule. The history of King-tê-chên, speaking of the most beautiful porcelain of earlier times, says that it was so *recherché* that the furnace was hardly opened before the merchants were disputing for the first choice. There is no question here of having it buried.

"It is true that in digging up the ruins of old buildings, and especially in cleaning out old abandoned wells, fine pieces of porcelain are sometimes discovered, which have been hidden there in times of revolution; the porcelain is beautiful, because at such times they would only think of hiding what was precious, in order to recover it when the troubles were over. It is esteemed not because it has gained from the moist earth some new beauty, but because its ancient beauty has been preserved, and that alone has its price in China, where they give large sums for the smallest utensils of the ordinary pottery that was used by the Emperors *Yao* and *Shun*, who reigned many centuries before the *T'ang* dynasty, during which porcelain began to be used by the emperors.

"The mandarin of King-tê-chên, who honors me with his friendship, makes to his patrons at the imperial court presents of old porcelain, which he has the talent of making himself. I mean that he has discovered the art of imitating ancient porcelain, or at least that of a medium antiquity; he employs at this work a number of artisans. The material of which these false *ku-t'ung*—that is, ancient counterfeits—are made is a yellowish clay, which is brought from a place not far from King-tê-chên, called Ma-an-shan (Saddle-back Hill). They are very thick; a plate of this kind which the mandarin gave me weighs as much as ten ordinary plates. There is nothing peculiar in the workmanship of this kind of porcelain, except that it is given a glaze prepared from a yellow rock, which is mixed with the ordinary glaze, the latter predominating; this mixture gives to the porcelain a sea-green color. After it has been baked it is immersed in a very strong bouillon made of fowls and other meat; it is stewed in this a while, and is afterward put into the most filthy sewer that can be found, where it is left a month or more. When it comes out of this sewer it passes for being three or four centuries old, or at least for a specimen of the preceding dynasty of the

Fig. 248.—K'ang-hsi Blue and White, a Teacup with carved open-work sides, mounted on a rice-bowl with pierced outer casing.

Ming, when porcelain of this color and thickness was highly esteemed at court. These false antiques are also similar to the genuine things, in that they do not ring when struck, and emit no humming vibrations when held close to the ear.

"They have brought to me from the *débris* of a large shop a little plate which I value much more than the finest porcelain of a thousand years ago. There is painted on the bottom of this plate a crucifix between the Holy Virgin and St. John; they told me that they used formerly to export such porcelain to Japan, but that they had made none of it since sixteen or seventeen years ago. Apparently the Christians of Japan availed themselves of this industry during the persecutions, to have images of our sacred mysteries; the porcelain, mixed in the cases with the rest, might escape the search of the enemies of religion; the pious artifice would have been discovered later and rendered of no avail by a stricter search, and this is why, no doubt, they have left off making things of the kind at King-tê-chên."

FIG. 249.—Two saucer-shaped Dishes: (*a*) with floral decoration, painted in enamel colors; mark, Yung-chêng; (*b*) decorated with peaches and bats, painted in brilliant enamel colors; mark, Ch'ien-lung.

CHAPTER XII.

THE YUNG-CHÊNG PERIOD.

THE Emperor *Yung-chêng*, who succeeded his father *K'ang-hsi*, reigned for only thirteen years (1723–35), a comparatively short interval between the long reign of sixty-one years of his predecessor and the reign of sixty years of his son and successor, the celebrated *Ch'ien-lung*, who resigned the throne after he had reigned a complete cycle, in accordance with a vow that he had made not to outreign his grandfather, if the celestial powers would allow him to reign as long. The ceramic productions of this reign are sometimes grouped with those of the reign of *Ch'ien-lung*, and described under the same heading, but, in my opinion, they are of sufficient interest and importance to deserve a chapter to themselves. It is a transition period in which the strong colors and bold, vigorous decoration of the preceding reign are gradually toned down, until they merge into the half tints and broken colors which mark the more regular and carefully finished designs on the porcelain of the reign of *Ch'ien-lung*. The deep irides- cent greens boldly laid on in thick patches, which character- ize the last reign, are only by gradual degrees replaced by a green of less brilliant tone and more even shade, so that an early *Yung-chêng* piece often retains a touch of the old vigor. If it want something of the pristine brilliancy, the new reign is distinguished for the neat precision of its pencil- ing, the soft purity of its color- ing, and the finished technique of its ceramic productions. They are well illustrated in this col- lection, especially in the deco- rated class, as in the magnificent round dishes in Plate XLVIII and Fig. 101, the pilgrim bot- tle in Plate XLVII, and the Buddhist ecclesiastical vase in Plate XX, all of which are marked in full with the "six- character" mark of the reign. The decorated citron-yellow vase in Plate LXV, the Taoist-Triad vase in Plate XXI, and some of the egg- shell plates, although they do not happen to be marked, are, from their style and coloring, attributable to the same pe- riod. Among the single col- ors, the gray vase illustrated in Plate LXXXV has the

FIG. 250.—Vase invested with a bright copper-red *soufflé* glaze, having a thin or burned-out patch which is deco- rated with a picture in sepia touched with gold.

mark of the reign inscribed underneath, and the pea-green celadon (*tou-ch'ing*) vase in Plate XL, the crackled gray vase in Plate LXXXVI, the etched sea-green celadon (*tung-ch'ing*) vase in Plate XXXVIII, and the pink monochrome vase of "rose Dubarry" in Plate LIII are to be referred, in all probability, to the same period.

Two of the colors especially characteristic of the *Nien Yao*, or " Nien Porcelain," of this epoch are the *clair-de-lune*, or *yueh-pai*, and the bright *soufflé* copper-red. A specimen of the former is given in Plate LI (b); and the color of the new reign is the same, although the fabric of the porcelain is generally more delicate and the form more studied. The latter occurs in a rare combination with painted decoration in the charming little vase of baluster shape seen in Fig. 250, which deserves a word of description:

Nien Yao Vase, exhibiting the characteristic monochrome glaze of bright ruby-red tint and stippled surface. The *soufflé* glaze is applied over the whole surface, with the exception of a panel of irregular outline reserved on one side of the vase, where it is shaded off so that the red fades gradually into a nearly white ground. Within the panel there is painted, over the glaze, the picture of Tung Fang So, a Taoist divinity, in flowing robes, speeding across the clouds with a branch of peaches, the sacred fruit of longevity, on his shoulder. This is lightly etched in sepia and touched with gold, with the addition of a few strokes of pale overglaze cobalt-blue and *rouge d'or* of the *Yung-chêng* period. The foot of the vase is encircled by an ornamental scroll, nearly obliterated, painted over the ruby ground in black and gold. There is no mark underneath.

FIG. 251. — Six-lobed Melon-shaped Vase with a white glaze minutely crackled (*truité*), with a close network of dark lines, giving a gray effect.

The Nien just referred to is, as the reader will recall, Nien Hsi-yao, an official of the Nei Wu Fu, or Imperial Household, who was appointed in the beginning of the reign of *Yung-chêng*, commissioner of customs at Huai-an-fu, with control over the river dues of the three provinces of Kiangsu, Kiangsi, and Anhui, and the superintendency of the imperial porcelain manufactory at Ching-tê-chên, for which he was also required to provide the necessary funds out of the customs dues. He held the post till the first year of the reign of *Ch'ien-lung*, when he was promoted, and replaced in the commissionership by T'ang Ying. He was consequently director of the porcelain works during the whole of the reign of *Yung-chêng*, and some of the peculiar productions of the period are still commonly known as Nien Yao, after him. He seems to have made periodical tours of inspection to Ching-tê-chên, during one of which he repaired the temple of the patron god, and erected a stone tablet in the courtyard to commemorate the fact. The inscription on this monument, which still stands there, records his official visit to the place in the fifth year of the reign of *Yung-chêng* (1727), and his orders that the porcelain made for the use of the emperor should be sent by boat twice every month to be inspected by him at Huai-an-fu, and that he would forward it on to the palace at Peking. We have a long list of the decorative designs and colors of the imperial porcelain made under his inspection, which is derived from official sources, and which is given in full detail in the next chapter. It supplies a fund of exact information, and is, on that account, of the greatest interest.

According to the *Ching-tê-chên T'ao lu*, " the vases made at this time included very many of soft eggshell color and well-rounded form, the glaze of which shone with the luster of pure silver. Some were decorated in blue and white, others in colors, and the various processes of painting, engraving, modeling under the glaze, and carving in pierced work, were all practiced in turn. The reproduction of ancient wares and the invention of novelties were undertaken in the imperial factory under his (Nien's) direction."

The rounded form referred to in this extract is exhibited in the oval, melon-shaped vase of six-lobed outline in Fig. 251, which is coated with a silvery-white glaze, very finely crackled (*truité*) with a close reticulation of dark lines, so as to give a general gray effect; and in the white vase of the period in Fig. 252, the neck of which is encircled with the form of a coiling dragon modeled in openwork relief and enameled in *rouge d'or* of crimson tint, the rest of the surface being pure white, except for an occasional single peach-blossom touched in delicate colors near the foot and on the shoulder of the rippled surface of the vase, which was once marked underneath, but has had the inscription purposely ground away.*

The good form and perfect technique of the period are well shown in two other illustrations. The first is a large baluster vase (*mei-p'ing*), Fig. 253, with gracefully rounded outlines, which is artistically decorated in brilliant enamel colors with fruits and flowers, the branches springing from below on one side and spreading upward in all directions upon the vase, so as to cover it with large pomegranates and peaches and bunches of yellow dragon's eye (*Nephelium longanum*) fruit, mingled with sprays of scarlet pomegranate-flowers and pink peach-blossom. The mark underneath, penciled in underglaze blue within a double ring, is *Ta Ch'ing Yung chêng nien chih*, "Made in the reign of *Yung-chêng*, of the great *Ch'ing* [dynasty]." The other vase (Fig. 257), though unmarked, is a typical piece of the period, in form, style of decoration, and coloring. The peculiarly tall, slender form springing from a spreading foot seems to have been introduced at this time. The scene depicted on the vase is the appearance of the Taoist goddess Hsi Wang Mu coming across the sea, borne upon a floating lotus-petal. The base of the vase is surrounded by scrolled and crested green waves, from which green and blue rocks rise in the background, and a temple with veranda and curling eaves—the abode of the divinity—is seen in the midst of the sea, with a gigantic stork perched on the roof. From a rock behind the temple springs a sacred peach-tree laden with scarlet and pink fruit, the branches mingled with rosy clouds floating across the shoulder of the vase, illuminated by the vermilion disk of the sun. A second stork is flying back to the temple, as the aërial messenger of the goddess, carrying in its beak two scrolls tied by a red band. The frail craft, a scarlet lotus-petal, floating on the sea in the foreground, contains two female figures. The goddess is sitting upon a rustic seat in the stern, dressed in conventional style in long robes and floating scarf with a short cloak of lotus-leaves thrown across her shoulders, and holds a branch of sacred fungus (*ling-chih*). The standing figure in front is her attendant, clad in a similar costume with a deep collar of fig-leaves, holding a rosy peach fringed with green leaves, and having a basket by her side full of flowers and Buddha's-hand citrons.

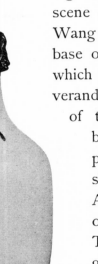

FIG. 252.—Yung-chêng Vase, with a ground of purest white, sprinkled with a few peach-blossoms painted in delicate colors, and having a dragon winding round the neck tinted in *rouge d'or*.

Fig. 56 shows an example of "slip" decoration in partial relief, painted in underglaze cobalt-blue, as well as in the enamel colors, coral-red, yellow, greens of different shade, and black. It has inscribed underneath the usual seal-mark penciled in underglaze blue of the reign of *Yung-chêng*. It is a brush cylinder (*pi-t'ung*), of wide low form with swelling mouth, decorated with an appropriate motive, *Mêng Pi Shêng Hua*—i. e., "The Pencil Blossoming in Dreams." On the right a young man in scholarly dress is reclining asleep upon a couch; his figure, and the rocks and palms which rise in the background, are modeled in salient relief. From the top of his head proceeds a scroll which unrolls to show another scene, in which the same figure is seated at a table, with ink upon the pallet and a brush in his hand, about to dash down upon paper the poem evolved in dreamland, which he had vainly tried to compose during waking hours. The title of the picture, which is given above, is a half stanza from a classical poet. The Chinese artist always presents a dream as an unrolled scroll proceeding from the head of the dreamer in this quaint fashion.

Two little tea-jars are examples of modeling in relief and openwork carving, two distinct processes of work which distinguish some of the largest and most important vases of the time.

* The mark is not infrequently obliterated in China on the lapidary's polishing wheel, and some of the finest pieces of Chinese porcelain are found to have been thus defaced. Such pieces have usually been stolen from the imperial palace by some of the eunuchs, or from some important collection by the servants in charge and treated in this way to avoid detection.

That shown in Fig. 254 has a ring of lotus plants projecting in salient relief round the base, and another lotus encircling the top of the cover. It is painted in enamel colors with gilding, with a temple hung with gold bells rising in the midst of the sea; with swallows flying in the air, and with a border of gilded diapers encircling the shoulder alternating with wavy scrolls painted in black. The other little jar of similar form (Fig. 255), which has the foot surrounded by a pierced openwork scroll, is decorated with lotus-leaf-shaped panels containing sprays of peonies, displayed upon a spiral black ground, sprinkled with blue bamboo-leaves and white plum-blossoms.

The saucer-shaped dish in Fig. happens to have the mark of the encircled by a double ring, the being usually not marked. enamel colors, with a cissus, a spray of roses, stems of *Polyporus* ted fungus of Taoist ite symbolical design lain, which was first reign, is that shown saucer - dish in Fig. ed with branches of ing both flowers and the rim of the dish terior, and with five fly- five happinesses. It is a Chinese that every decora- have some recondite mean- introduced simply for orna- few sprays of simple flow- cient for the ordinary cups tended for more vulgar The Emperor *Yung-* Chinese to have been a ramic art, and some of the distinguished the latter part due directly to the interest apparent, as described by letters. During his reign

FIG. 253.—Baluster Vase richly decorated in enamel colors, with fruits and flowers; mark, Yung-chêng.

249 (*a*) is included here, because it reign penciled underneath in blue, eggshell plates of the period It is decorated inside in flowering bulb of nar- and two branching *lucidus*—the variega- sacred lore. A favor- upon imperial porce- introduced in this upon the *Ch'ien-lung* 249 (*b*), which is paint- sacred peaches bear- fruit, that wind over to decorate the in- ing bats, symbols of the common notion of the tion for imperial use must ing of this kind and not be ment, like a landscape or a ers that are thought suffi- and bowls that are in- use.

chêng is considered by the special patron of the ce- more elaborate work that of the preceding reign was he took in it when heir- Père d'Entrecolles in his he continued to send down

to Ching-tê-chên from the imperial collections at Peking a number of antique objects and specimens of ancient glazes to be reproduced in the imperial manufactory. The reproductions are described to have been often more finished and perfect than the originals, and they figure as such in many a private collection, both in China and abroad. Their variety and character will be enumerated in the next chapter, which is taken directly from the official records of the time.

FIG. 254.—Jar with a girdle of lotus plants in relief;
decorated with enamel colors and gold.

CHAPTER XIII.

OFFICIAL LIST OF THE DESIGNS AND COLORS PRODUCED AT THE IMPERIAL MANUFACTORY IN THE REIGN OF YUNG-CHÊNG.

THIS list was first published in the *Chiang-hsi-t'ung-chih*, the General Description of the Province of Kiangsi, in which Ching-tê-chên, with its Imperial Porcelain Manufactory, is situated. I am translating it from the latest edition of this voluminous compilation (book xciii, folio 11–13). It is given there under the heading, "An Old List of the Different Colors of the Round and Square Porcelain, and of the Vases ordered to be made for the Emperor." The following explanatory note is added by the editors below the title: "With respectful reference to the productions of the imperial porcelain manufactory, among the ornamental vases and jars, the vessels for sacrificial wine and for meat offerings, the dishes, bowls, cups, and platters for ordinary use, ordered to be sent in annual rotation to the palace, there are so many different kind of things, that it would be impossible to attempt to enumerate them all. We will extract from Hsieh's Description (of the province) a list of fifty-seven kinds given there, in order to give a general idea of the porcelain made at the time."

The first edition of the *Chiang-hsi-t'ung-chih*, we are told in the introduction, was published in the *Ming* dynasty, in the reign of *Chia-ching* (1522–66). Two revised editions were issued during the reign of *K'ang-hsi* (1662–1722), and another in the reign of *Yung-chêng*, which was published in the cyclical year *jên-tzŭ* (1732). This last edition is the one referred to above. It was com-

FIG. 255.—Jar with open-work scrolls round the foot; decorated in enamel colors.

piled by Hsieh Min, who was governor of the province of Kiangsi from 1729 to 1732. The list, therefore, can not be later than 1732. It was prepared specially for the official work, and affords an invaluable description of the porcelain made in the reign of *Yung-chêng*, under the superintendence of the director, Nien Hsi-yao, referred to in the last chapter. This is altogether confirmed by the internal evidence of the list itself, as many of the things described are characteristic productions of his time, and are still known to Chinese collectors as *Nien Yao*.

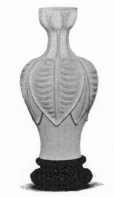

FIG. 256.—Sparsely Crackled White Fên-Ting Vase of rare form, molded with a whorl of palm-leaves encircling the shoulder, connected by ridges with eight foliations on the bulbous mouth.

This list, with some minor variations, is given by Julien (*loc. cit.*, livre vi, page 192), who quotes it from the annals of the city of Fou-liang, under the somewhat misleading title *Catalogue des émaux et des vases anciens qú'on imite à King-te-tchin*. His translation of the Chinese, too, is very inaccurate, probably because he was not familiar with the objects described. I venture to allude to this because his book is so universally accepted as the text-book on the subject; there is no space to notice all the discrepancies, and I will therefore pass on at once to the list:

"1. Glazes of the *Ta-kuan* period, with iron (-colored) paste.* (鐵骨大觀釉). These are of three different colors: (1) pale blue, or *clair-de-lune* (*yueh pai*); (2) pale blue or green (*fên ch'ing*); (3) dark green or *gros vert* (*ta lü*)—all of which are copied from the colors of the glazes of specimens of the *Sung* dynasty sent from the imperial palace."

The specimens which were sent out to be copied must have been examples of the *Kuan Yao*, the "imperial ware" of the *Sung* dynasty, which was described in Chapter V as having been made at the capital of the time, the modern K'ai-fêng-fu. It was not till long afterward that it came to be called *Ta-kuan Yao*, after the name of the period *Ta-kuan* (1107–1110), in which it was invented, to distinguish it from the "imperial ware" of more recent times.

"2. Ko Yao glazes, with iron (-colored) paste. (鐵骨哥釉).

"These are of two kinds—(1) rice-colored, (2) pale blue, or green (celadon), both copied from the colors of the glazes of ancient pieces sent from the imperial palace."

Reproductions of the ancient crackled ware of the *Sung* dynasty made at Liu-t'ien in Lung-ch'üan-hsien, the invention of which was attributed to the elder Chang, from which it derived its name of *Ko Yao*—i. e., "Elder Brother's Ware."

"3. Uncrackled Ju (-chou) glaze, with copper (-colored) paste. (銅骨無紋汝釉).

"Copied from the color of the glaze of two pieces of the *Sung* dynasty—a cat's food-basin (*mao shih p'ên*), and a mask-shaped dish (*jên mien hsi*)."

The traditional tint of the Ju-chou porcelain is sky-blue, and the reproduction of the old glaze forms the *yü kuo t'ien ch'ing*, "the blue of the sky after rain," of modern times. The peculiar shape of the second piece reminds one of the wine-cup (*jên mien pei*), molded in the form of a man's face, of *Sung* imperial ware, which was described in Chapter V. Such a cup would make a convenient dish for washing (*hsi*) pencil-brushes, for which purpose, from its uneven surface, it would be well adapted.

FIG. 257.—Tall, slender Vase painted in enamel colors of the *famille rose*, with a picture of the Taoist divinity Hsi Wang Mu.

"4. Ju (-chou) glaze with fish-roe crackle of copper (-colored) paste. (銅骨魚子紋汝釉).

"Copied from the colors of the glaze of a piece of the *Sung* dynasty sent from the imperial palace."

"5. White Ting (-chou) glaze. (白定釉).

"Only one kind is copied, the *Fên Ting;* the other variety, the *T'u Ting*, is not imitated."

These two varieties of ancient porcelain have been already described and illustrated. The *Fên Ting*, which is composed of fine white material, is enameled with a soft-looking, ivory-white glaze, with a surface either plain or crackled, generally the latter, as in the gourd-shaped vase illustrated in Plate LXXXIX. The little vase in Fig. 256, with foliations molded in slight relief covered by a sparsely crackled glaze, is a piece attributed to this period, fashioned after an ancient model.

"6. Chün (-chou) glazes. (均釉).

* Julien's rendering the first four examples is *Excipient en fer, Excipient en cuivre*, and recent writers have twitted the Chinese, on his authority, for not being able to distinguish enameled iron and copper from porcelain. The last paragraph, again, he translates: "Ces trois sortes d'émaux avaient la couleur et le lustre des vases des *Song* appelés *Nei-fa-song-khi*, c'est-a-dire vases fournis pour l'usage du palais (dans la période *King-te*, 1004–1007)." There is no allusion to this period in the original text.

"Five different colors have been copied from ancient specimens sent from the imperial palace, viz.:

"(1) Rose crimson (*Mei-kuei Tzŭ*).

"(2) Pyrus japonica pink (*Hai-t'ang Hung*).

"(3) Aubergine purple (*Chieh-p'i Tzŭ*).

"(4) Plum-colored blue (*Mei-tzŭ Ch'ing*).

"(5) Mule's liver mingled with horse's lung (*Lo kan ma fei*).

"And besides, in addition to these, the four following varieties have been taken from new acquisitions:

"(6) Dark purple (*Shên Tzŭ*).

"(7) Rice-colored (*Mi-sê*).

"(8) Sky-blue (*T'ien Lan*).

"(9) Furnace-transmutations, or *flambés* (*Yao Pien*)."

This is the most complete list we possess of the colors that were produced at the Chün-chou potteries during the *Sung* dynasty, and the whole empire must have been ransacked in

FIG. 258.—Ovoid Vase with mottled clouds of brilliant *sang-de-bœuf* tones on one side, spreading into a background of translucent celadon tint, which invests the rest of the surface.

order to get together so many treasures to be copied. The colors, it should be noticed, are all those of the *grand feu*, produced by different combinations of oxide of copper and cobaltiferous oxide of manganese, transmuted by the flames, oxidizing or reducing according to circumstances, of the large furnace. The skill of the potters in this line at this particular period has never been rivaled, and their work often figures in collections among the genuine antiques, for the form as well as the color of the original seems generally to have been carefully reproduced. A striking example of a shaped bowl of antique form, exhibiting the "Pyrus japonica glaze"—a pink ground flecked with darker red—was illustrated in Fig. 126. This is marked *Yung-chêng* underneath, indicating that it was an avowed reproduction of this time. An original piece of the *Sung* dynasty is illustrated in colors in Plate XCIV. The names of the colors are generally sufficiently descriptive of the varied shades, but no two pieces of the time are exactly alike, and some of the most brilliant successes in the originals, as well as in the attempts at reproduction, must have often been due to mere hazard.

"7. Reproductions of the copper-red of *Hsüan-tê* porcelain. (仿宣窰霽紅). Two varieties are included:

"(1) The clear red (*Hsien Hung*).

"(2) The ruby red (*Pao-shih Hung*)."

The bright red of ruby tint derived from copper was used in the reign of *Hsüan-tê* as the color of the sacrificial cups which were employed by the emperor in the worship of the sun. Hence the name of *chi hung*, which means "sacrificial red," when it is properly written. The character used above is a borrowed one of the same sound, which means "clear sky," and is properly used only for the next glaze. Other unauthorized characters are sometimes substituted by writers who are ignorant of the derivation of the term, the strangest of which is *chi hung*, "chicken-red," on which M. Grandidier seems to base his term *sang du poulet*.

"8. Reproduction of the deep blue of *Hsüan-tê* porcelain. (仿宣窰霽青).

"The color of this glaze is deep and somewhat reddish; it has an orange-peel texture and palm eyes."

The orange-peel texture refers to its undulatory surface; the "palm eyes" are due to the production of tiny bubbles in the glaze. The color is of purplish tint; it is generally crackled, and the saucer-dishes on which it often occurs are usually found marked underneath with the seal of *Hsüan-tê*, lightly impressed under the glaze.

"9. Reproductions of colored glazes of the Imperial Manufactory. (仿廠官釉).

"These are of three kinds: (1) Eel-yellow (*Shan-yü Huang*). (2) Snake-skin green (*shê-pi Lü*). (3) Variegated yellow (*Huang pan tien*)."

These three glazes, which were invented in the preceding reign of *K'ang-hsi* by Ts'ang Ying-hsüan during his directorship, have been described in Chapter X.

"10. *Lung-ch'üan* glazes. (龍泉釉).

"These are of two shades, pale (*ch'ien*) and deep (*shên*)."

The *Lung-ch'üan* glaze of this time, which derives its name from the place where the old celadons of the *Sung* dynasty were made, is of a pronounced greenish tone, and it is often called *tou-ch'ing*, or "pea-green," for that reason. The color was produced by the addition of a little cobalt to the next glaze, which is the celadon proper. The *Lung-ch'üan* glaze is well represented in Plate LXXI, and in the ground color of the fish-bowl illustrated in Plate XXXVI.

"11. *Tung Ch'ing* glazes. (東青釉).

"These are of two shades, pale (*ch'ien*) and dark (*shên*)."

This color, the sea-green celadon, takes its name, which means "eastern green," from the fact that its celebrated prototype was made at K'ai-fêng-fu, the eastern capital of China in the early part of the *Sung* dynasty. Whatever may have been the materials of the old color, the recent reproductions owe their tint to the addition to the ordinary white glaze of a very small proportion of the ferruginous clay (*huang-t'u*), which produced the "dead-leaf" brown (*tz'ŭ-chin*). The typical celadon color is too well known to need description; it is, according to Salvétat, "un ton pale clair légèrement bleuâtre, analogue au ton de certains verres de gobeletterie." The peculiar clear translucency is difficult to reproduce on paper, but the shade of color is perfectly represented in Plates VII and XXXVIII; the last vase is one attributed to the *Yung-chêng* period.

FIG. 259.—Vase of Coral-red *soufflé* ground, displaying a dragon in translucent white relief etched under the glaze.

"12. Reproduction of rice-colored glaze of the *Sung* dynasty. (仿米色宋釉).

"This has been taken from fragments of broken pottery discovered in the ruins of an ancient manufactory of the *Sung* dynasty at a place called Hsiang-hu, situated twenty *li* to the eastward of Ching-tê-chên, both the colored glaze and the form of which have been reproduced."

"13. Reproduction of pale-blue (or green) glaze of the *Sung* dynasty. (粉青色宋釉).

"The specimens copied here in form and color were obtained at the same time as the rice-colored pieces of the *Sung* dynasty just referred to."

"14. Reproduction of the oil-green glaze. (仿油綠釉).

"This was copied from an ancient piece of the furnace-transmutation (*yao pien*) class sent from the imperial palace, the color of which resembled moss-green jade (*pi yü*), having a brilliant ground variegated with mottled tints of antique rare beauty."

There is a small vase of the "peach-bloom" type illustrated in Plate L, which answers remarkably well to this description, being invested with a green glaze variegated with streaks and mottled clouds of deepest emerald, passing into olive as they run down across the field.

"15. The Chün (-chou) glaze of the muffle stove. (鑪均釉).

"The color of this is between that of the Canton pottery ware and that of the enamel of the Yi-hsing 'boccaro' stoneware,* and it excels these in its markings and in the changing tints of its flowing drops."

This glaze is the "robin's egg" of the American collector, and no better name could be imagined for it. It has greenish-blue dappling and flecking on a reddish ground, the green being subordinate to the blue. The term "muffle" is added to distinguish it from the high-fired Chün-chou glazes which are described above and under No. 6, but in modern usage this is generally omitted, now that the other glazes are no longer prepared, so that the "robin's egg" is the "Chün yu" of the present day. The glaze is prepared, according to the *Ch'ing-*

---

* The references here are, doubtless, to the glazes of these two potteries described in the next two sections.

tê-chên T'ao lu (book iii, folio 12), by combining nitre, rock-crystal, and cobaltiferous manganese with the materials of the ordinary white glaze.

"16. Ou's glazes. (歐 釉)·

"These have been copied from productions of the ancient potter named Ou. There are two varieties made, one with red markings (*hung wên*), the other with blue markings (*lan wên*)."

This potter flourished in the *Ming* dynasty at Yi-hsing-hsien, near Shanghai, in the province of Kiangnan, where he made a red stoneware, the kind known to us from a Portuguese word as boccaro ware, which is still made there.

FIG. 260.—Large K'ang-hsi Vase with bulbous neck of powder blue, edged with white rims.

"17. Glaze flecked with blue. (青 點 釉)·

"This has been copied from the colored glaze of an ancient piece of Kuang Yao sent from the imperial palace."

The "Kuang-Yao" is the brown stoneware made in the province of Kuangtung, at Kiang-yang-hsien, in the prefecture of Chao-ch'ing-fu. An example is illustrated in the statuette of Bodhidharma in Plate XLI.

"18. *Clair-de-lune* glaze. (月 白 釉)·

"The color resembles very closely that of the Ta-kuan glaze (No. 1), but the paste of the porcelain is white. The glaze is not crackled. There are two shades—pale (*ch'ien*) and deep (*shên*)."

This is the pale sky-blue glaze derived from cobalt which is one of the choicest and most characteristic single colors of the period. It is of the monochrome tint of the vase of the preceding reign, which is illustrated in Plate LI.

"19. Copies of *Hsüan* (-*tê*) porcelain decorated in ruby-red. (仿 宣 窰 寶 燒)·

"There are four varieties: (1) With three fishes, (2) with three fruits, (3) with three *ling-chih*, (4) with five bats, symbols of the five happinesses."

The designs were painted *sur biscuit* in copper-red, as described in Chapter VII. The name of *pao-shao*—i. e., "ruby-fired"—comes from an old tradition that powdered rubies were mixed with the glaze; amethystine quartz is really used in the present day, but this has nothing to do with the red color, which is a copper silicate.

"20. Copies of the Lung-ch'üan glaze decorated in ruby-red. (仿 龍 泉 釉 寶 燒)·

"This is a new process, introduced during the reigning dynasty. There are also the following four kinds of decoration: (1) With three fishes, (2) with three fruits, (3) with three *ling-chih*, (4) with five bats."

The color of the ground and the effect of the red decoration may be seen from a glance at the fish-bowl illustrated in Plate XXXVI, which is fashioned in the similitude of a lotus-leaf with the details of the plant picked out in copper-red on the ground of greenish celadon. Of the different decorations given above, the three fruits are most frequently seen on the outside of globular jars, for instance, which are ornamented with peaches, pomegranates, and Buddha's-hand citrons in the shape of three medallions. The outlines and leaves are occasionally touched in cobalt-blue, penciled under the glaze at the same time as the copper-red.

The small ovoid vase in Fig. 258 offers a charming example of the decorative effect of these two colors in combination. The irregular splash that covers one-third of its surface is of the deepest and most brilliantly scintillating ruby color in the middle, and shades off to crimson and pinkish mottled tints, as it gradually fades away into the celadon ground which invests the rest of the vase.

"21. Turquoise glazes. (翡翠釉).

"These are copied from three varieties sent from the imperial palace: (1) Plain turquoise (*su ts'ui*), (2) flecked with blue (*ch'ing tien*), (3) flecked with gold (*chin tien*)."

The turquoise glaze, produced by a combination of oxide of copper with a flux containing nitre, and applied *sur biscuit*, is finely crackled. It is called by the Chinese *fei-ts'ui*, from the

FIG. 261.—Graceful Vase with a floral decoration in colors, relieved by a finely crackled yellow ground.

similarity of its tint to that of the azure plumes of the kingfisher which are extensively used by them in jewelry. It is represented in nearly a hundred shapes in the collection, and some of its different shades may be seen reproduced in Plates XLIV, LXXXIV, XLV, and LXXV. The second variety referred to above, where it is flecked with purple, is not rare, but the third variety, the gold-spotted turquoise glaze, is quite unfamiliar to me.

"22. The *soufflé* red glaze. (吹紅釉)."

The method of application of this glaze has been described by Père d'Entrecolles in the last chapter, and a specimen was exhibited there in Fig. 242, of the kind with a ruby-red ground derived from copper silicate. There is also a *soufflé* iron-red of coral tint, produced by sprinkling the prepared oxide upon the white glaze of porcelain that has been previously fired in the large furnace, and fixed by baking the piece a second time in the muffle stove. There is a charming example of this before us in Fig. 259; a vase with a four-clawed dragon in pursuit of the jewel worked in relief in the paste, finished with the graving tool, and reserved under the translucent white glaze, while the rest of the surface is covered with a coral-red of soft tone, shading off into paler tints as it merges into the irregular edge of the dragon medallion. The stippled texture, displaying an infinity of minute mottled points, indicates its *soufflé* application.

"23. The *soufflé* blue glaze. (吹青釉)."

This was also described in the last chapter. The *ch'ui-ch'ing* glaze, often called "powder-blue," is one of the chief triumphs of the Chinese potter, and shows at its best, perhaps, when left as a single color, neither penciled over with gold nor contrasted with bright enamel colors, as is often the case. Nothing could be more magnificent than the vase, eighteen inches high, illustrated in Fig. 260, in its brilliant blue coat of intense mazarin tint, the ground flecked with darker spots, displaying, as it does, every shade of pure color flashing out from the depths of a translucent medium. The prepared cobalt material is blown upon the raw body of the piece, which is subsequently glazed and fired in the large furnace, so that it gradually penetrates the glaze, liquefied by the heat of the *grand feu*. The glaze must not be of a hard nature, we are told, like that of the white porcelain; it must be liquefied by having a larger proportion of chalk in its composition, otherwise the color will not penetrate.

FIG. 262.—Teapot of "Armorial China," decorated in enamel colors, with gilding of the Yung-chêng or early Ch'ien-lung period.

"24. Copies of *Yung-lo* porcelain, including pieces of eggshell (*t'o-t'ai*), of plain white (*su-pai*), and with engraved (*chui*) and embossed (*kung*) designs. (仿永樂窰脫胎素白錐拱等器皿).

These varieties are all well known to collectors, but very many of the pieces that figure in collections as genuine relics of early *Ming* date are copies, with the original designs and marks carefully reproduced, that came from the workshops of the period we are discussing. They are too perfect in technical finish, and never show the irregularity of shape and pitting of glaze that so frequently mark the ancient porcelain. The quality, in short, is exactly that of the decorated eggshell plates of the same date, and I have heard it argued from this fact that the latter must really date from the reign of *Yung-lo*, even if they were painted in subsequent times; they are really contemporary; it is only that the white eggshell is antedated. For a genuine early specimen of this class, refer to Fig. 70.

"25. Copies of porcelain of the reigns of *Wan-li*, and of *Chêng-tê*, decorated in the five colors. (仿 萬 歷 正 德 窰 五 彩 器 皿)."

The five-colored decoration of the *Wan-li* period was executed in overglaze enamel colors, with the exception of the cobalt-blue, which was previously painted on the raw body before glazing. It is illustrated in Figs. 167 and 106. That of the reign of *Chêng-tê*, of more archaic style, was in colored glazes, which were laid upon the unbaked paste, worked in outline and chiseled, and which were fired in the *grand feu*. A reproduction of this class with the *Chêng-tê* mark impressed underneath the vase, which may date from the time we are considering, has been given in Fig. 162.

"26. Copies of porcelain of the reign of *Ch'êng-hua*, decorated in the five colors. (仿 成 化 窰 五 彩 器 皿)." This has been discussed at sufficient length in Chapter VII.

"27. Copies of porcelain of the reign of *Hsüan-tê*, with painted designs on a yellow ground. (仿 宣 花 黃 地 章 器 皿)."

This refers probably to pieces painted in colored glazes, with the designs relieved by an enameled yellow ground. I have seen bowls and saucer-dishes of the kind, decorated with

FIG. 263.—Twin Vase of the Ch'ien-lung period, decorated with panel pictures, painted in European style, from European originals.

peonies—the flowers violet and the leaves green—surrounded by a yellow ground, which had the mark of *Hsüan-tê* underneath. The finely modeled vase illustrated in Fig. 261, although it has no mark, is an example of a similar technique, which is to be attributed probably to this reign of *Yung-chêng*. It is decorated with peonies, chrysanthemums, and daisies, growing from rocks, with a butterfly or two flying in the intervals. The details of the decoration are all lightly engraved in the paste. The colors are green and purple, with a few touches of white, displayed upon a background of pure bright yellow, which is minutely crackled throughout. The foot is coated with the same *truité* yellow glaze underneath, and has no mark attached.

"28. The *cloisonné* blue glaze. (法 青 釉).

"The combination of this glaze is founded upon recent experiments. Compared with the purplish-blue glaze (described under No. 8), it is deeper and more brilliant, and it has no orange-peel markings or minute bubbles (palm-spots)."

The character *fa* (the first of the three) is used here as a contraction for *fa-lang*, "*cloisonné* enamel." The color referred to is that generally known by the name of *pao-shih lan*, or "sapphire-blue," which was introduced about this time, and which is illustrated in Plate XXIX.

"29. Copies of European figures and models after life executed with carving and embossed work. (仿 西 洋 雕 鏤 像 生 器 皿).

"Sets of the five sacrificial utensils (*wu kung*), dishes (*p'an*), plates (*tieh*), vases (*p'ing*), and boxes (*ho*), and the like, are also decorated with colored pictures painted in the European style."

We saw, in the last chapter, in Père d'Entrecolles's letters, that porcelain was made at Ching-tê-chên for export to Europe, and painted with foreign designs brought there by Cantonese traders; and he also tells us that the mandarin in charge asked him to procure new designs from Europe, so that he might make more novelties for presentation at court. Here we learn that such things were made at the imperial manufactory and sent direct to the emperor at Peking.

On the other hand, many of the sovereigns of Europe sent to China about this time for services of porcelain, to be decorated for them and painted with their coats of arms. Most collections of Oriental porcelain contain specimens of "armorial china," the majority of it dating from this reign and the succeeding one; some from the earlier reign of *K'ang-hsi*. A selection has been published with the pieces illustrated in colors by W. Griggs, London,* and the date

* *Illustrations of Armorial China.* Privately printed. One hundred copies only. 1887.

is often fixed by tracing back the piece to its original owner. The mug, for example, in Part IV of his work, decorated in coral-red, gold, and black, which has the arms, crest, and supporters of Thomas Trevor, created Baron Trevor of Bromham, December 31, 1711, emblazoned upon it, must have been made in this reign, because Lord Trevor died June 19, 1730, the impaled arms being those of his second wife, Anne, daughter of Robert Weldon, Esq.

A teapot of "armorial china," with a ducal coronet upon it, is illustrated in Fig. 262, and a vase painted with copies of European pictures by a Chinese artist in Fig. 263. The vase shown in Fig. 264 is one of the class fashioned in European style, with branches of fruit molded round the pedestal, and a delicate interlacement of wild roses and other flowers filling the hollows of the flowing bandlike handles; it is decorated in gold with phœnixes and dragons, the latter painted on the outside of the handles, with their centipede bodies and winged insect heads, and of very un-Chinese aspect.

"30. Copies of porcelain, painted in monochrome yellow, with chiseled green designs. (仿澆黃錐綠花器皿)."

The porcelain copied here must have belonged to the class decorated in mixed enamel colors, which I have described under the reign of *K'ang-hsi*, at the end of Chapter X. The designs of flowers, dragons, phœnixes, etc., were chiseled in the paste, and filled in with green enamel, while the rest of the surface was enameled yellow, the two colors being laid on with a brush *sur biscuit*.

"31. Copies of monochrome-yellow porcelain. (仿澆黃器皿).

"Two kinds are made: (1) With plain ground (*su ti*), (2) with engraved designs (*chui hua*)."

The word *chiao*, used here, means literally "watered," but it does not imply the idea of "pale," as it is sometimes rendered; this is proved by the fact that in the modern lists it is replaced by another character of the same sound, meaning "bright" or "pretty"; it is used only of single colors. The tint of the "imperial yellow" of the time was orange, due to the presence of iron with the antimony. It is the "prohibited color" of the present day, sacred to the emperor, and is often enameled over imperial five-clawed dragons, disporting in clouds chiseled in the paste under the glaze.

"32. Copies of monochrome purple-brown porcelain. (仿澆紫器皿).

"There are two varieties made: (1) With plain ground (*su ti*), (2) with etched designs (*chui hua*)."

The *Chiao Tzŭ* is the purplish-brown single color, produced by the cobaltiferous ore of manganese (*ch'ing liao*), which shares with the "imperial yellow," and the transparent green of camellia-leaf tint, the distinction of being used for the emperor's services of porcelain.

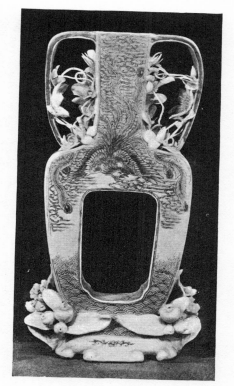

FIG. 264.—White Vase penciled in gold with phœnixes and conventional scrolls, and enveloped with fruit and flowers delicately fashioned in complete open-work relief.

"33. Porcelain with engraved designs. (錐花器皿).

"All the different kinds of glazes may have this decoration."

The engraved designs (*chui hua*) are etched at the point with a graving tool in the paste of the piece before it is quite dry, and it is subsequently glazed by immersion, or by sprinkling.

The white vase (Fig. 265) of the "Fên-Ting" class is an example of this work, having on the front and back of its swelling body the figure of a five-clawed dragon, enveloped in clouds, delicately etched in the paste under the ivory-white glaze.

"34. Porcelain with embossed designs. (堆花器皿).

"These may be associated with all the different kinds of glazes."

The embossed designs (*tui hua*) are worked in relief upon the paste, the outlines having been previously traced with a graver, and any additional paste required is applied by a brush. *Pâte-sur-pâte* reliefs are now executed on porcelain in this way all over the world. The reign of *Yung-chêng* is especially distinguished for this kind of work.

"35. Coral-red porcelain. (抹 紅 器 皿).

"Reproduced from old pieces."

The term *Mo Hung* is applied to the process of painting the coral-red monochrome derived from iron over the glaze with an ordinary brush. The characteristic tones of color are perfectly exhibited in Plates XXXII and XCII.

"36. Porcelain decorated in coral-red. (彩 紅 器 皿).

"Reproduced from old specimens."

The term *Ts'ai Hung* means "Painting in red," just as *Ts'ai Shui-mo* (No. 40) means "Painting in black." It is applied to the art of penciling the decoration in coral-red over the glaze, the piece being fired afterward in the muffle stove. Plate LXVII displays a peerless model.

"37. Porcelain enameled yellow after the European style. (西 洋 黃 色 器 皿)."

The heading leaves it an open question whether it was the form of the pieces, or the enamel color, that was modeled after the European style. In all probability it was the color,

FIG. 265.—Delicate White Vase with looped handles springing from dragons' heads, and dragon designs lightly etched in the paste under the ivory-white glaze.

and the beautiful lemon-yellow, which makes its appearance now for the first time on Chinese porcelain, would be the new shade indicated. The tint is perfectly shown in the ground of the vase which is illustrated in Plate LXV.

"38. Porcelain enameled purple after the European style. (西 洋 紫 色 器 皿)."

"39. Silvered porcelain. (抹 銀 器 皿)."

The term *Mo Yin*, "Painting with silver," refers to the application of the metal in the form of an enamel as a single color. It was not spread upon white porcelain, but over a coat of pale golden tint, lightly colored with the "dead-leaf" or *tzŭ-chin* glaze. The enamel had to be gently fired in the muffle stove on account of the fugitive nature of the silver.

"40. Porcelain decorated in ink black.* (彩 水 墨 器 皿)."

The decoration of porcelain by pictures penciled in black or sepia was a novelty introduced at this time. Père d'Entrecolles describes in the last paragraph of his second letter how attempts had been made to paint vases with the finest Chinese ink, but all in vain, as the porcelain always came out white—a result not very surprising—as the carbon to which the color of Chinese ink is due would be immediately dissipated in the furnace. The ruby-backed eggshell plate shown in Fig. 230 is a fine example of painting in sepia, having the encircling bands of basket-work, diaper, and brocaded patterns, as well as the picture which forms its main decoration, all penciled in that tint. The picture represents the dragon procession of the great midsummer festival, which is celebrated throughout China on the fifth day of the fifth moon. The large barge made in the form of a dragon, attended by a smaller boat with a band of music, is being towed along a river, accompanied by two lines of horsemen. The banks are fringed with willows, and the crenelated wall of a city is seen in the background, which is filled in with the usual details of a Chinese landscape.

"41. Reproductions of pieces of pure white porcelain of the reign of *Hsüan-tê*. (仿 宣 窰 塡 白 器 皿).

"These include many different objects, thick and thin, large and small."

The first word in the compound term *t'ien-pai* used here (the fourth and fifth characters)

* In Julien's list, which is extracted from the *Fou-liang-hsien Chih*, there is an interesting note attached here, which is made, however, into a separate heading. It says that "by the new process the details of landscapes and figure scenes, flowering plants and birds, are all executed with shading, so as to reproduce the light and dark strokes in the original pen-and-ink drawing."

means "filled in," or "fully," but another word having the signification of "pure" is often substituted for it. Few ceramic terms have, however, given rise to so much misunderstanding, owing to a gratuitous assumption that it was glazed white in order to be afterwards "filled in" with enamel colors. So Du Sartel creates a class with the heading of "T'ien Pai," to include a variety of objects painted in colors *sur biscuit*—a class which, as Grandidier justly observes, threatens to remain without a member to represent it. The "pure white" porcelain of the time, which was said to rival the finest and most translucent white jade, has been already sufficiently described in Chapter VII, under the reign of *Hsüan-tê* (1426–35).

"42. Copies of Chia (*-ching*) Porcelain painted in blue. (仿嘉窰青花)."

The blue and white decoration of the *Chia-ching* period (1522–66) was distinguished for its deep, strong coloring. It has been fully described already, and is well illustrated in Plate XLIX.

"43. Copies of *Ch'êng-hua* Blue and White Porcelain with the decorations penciled in pale blue. (仿成化窰淡描青花)."

Reproductions of this period are much more common in collections than the originals, although genuine pieces occasionally occur. They are small in size, boxes for seal vermilion, miniature vases, wine-cups, or tiny saucers, and usually have the mark of *Ch'êng-hua* (1465–87) delicately penciled underneath in the same gray-toned blue with which the decoration is painted. The technique of the drawing in these pieces is remarkable for its clear penciling and miniature-like finish, and a small round box, as well as its cover, will often be found most elaborately painted both inside and outside.

"44. Rice-colored glazes (米色釉).

"These differ from the reproduction of the rice-colored glaze of the *Sung* dynasty (No. 12). They are of two kinds: (1) pale (*ch'ien*); (2) deep (*shên*).

"45. Porcelain decorated with underglaze red. (釉裏紅器皿).

"In one class of pieces (1) the decoration is entirely painted in the underglaze red; another class (2) has green leaves in combination with red flowers."

FIG. 266.—Globular Vase of perfect technique, lightly decorated in maroon, with peony sprays which have the leaves touched with green; mark, K'ang-hsi.

The term *yu-li-hung* (the first three of the group of five Chinese characters immediately above this) means literally "red inside the glaze"; the color, due to copper silicate, ranges from a bright "peach-bloom" tint to a dull maroon. It is a color of the *grand feu* of very ancient origin in China.

The two classes given above may be illustrated by two beautiful vases, both dating from the preceding reign of *K'ang-hsi*:

1. Heavy solid vase (Fig. 229), of finished form and technique, decorated in maroon copper-red, under a white glaze of harmonious translucent tone, with five horizontal bands of dragons and other grotesque monsters in scrolled sea-waves, separated by narrower bands of diaper and lozenge fret, and with two rings of formal foliations encircling the lip. The "six-character mark" of the reign of *K'ang-hsi* (1662–1722) is penciled underneath in cobalt-blue in the style of the "peach-bloom" vases.

2. A small vase (Fig. 266), of globular, bowl-like form, a writer's water-pot (*shui ch'êng*), with the rim of its mouth strengthened by a silver collar. It is decorated soberly and chastely with two little sprigs of peony, which have the blossoms tinted a warm maroon, and the tiny leaves, outlined and veined with the same underglaze red, filled in with a bright green overglaze enamel. The mark is precisely similar to that of Fig. 229.

"46. Copies of coffee-brown glazes. (仿紫金釉).

"Two different shades are produced: (1) reddish (*hung*); (2) yellowish (*huang*)."

The *Tzŭ-chin*, or "burnished gold," glaze is derived from yellow ferruginous clay (*huang-*

t'u) and varies in shade, in proportion to the concentration of the glaze, from the darkest chocolate-brown to the tint of "old gold." It is of ancient origin, and has been referred to many times already under its various names of "fond-laque," "dead-leaf," "coffee-colored," "café-au-lait," "or bruni," etc.

"47. Monochrome yellow porcelain decorated in the five enamel colors. (澆黃五彩器皿)·

"This is a novel decoration founded upon recent experiments."

FIG. 267.—Ch'ien-lung White Vase of quatrefoil section, with embossed designs of floral scrolls and bats; etched seal underneath.

The enameled yellow ground was either plain or etched in the glaze with a close pattern of spiral scrolls. A description of a piece will give an idea of the class. Large bottle-shaped vase with swelling body, twenty-one inches high, rich-ly decorated in enamel colors with gilding, with the ground of yellow enamel engraved in scrolls, interspersed with col-ored flowers, among which stand out, in high embossed relief, vases of flowers, bowls of fruit, incense urns, guitars, chessboard, fans, books, and scroll paintings, the varied ap-paratus of a Chinese library, mingled with emblems and symbols, all painted in the brilliant enamels of the *Yung-chêng* period.

A charming little vase, decorated in colors upon a yellow background, which may also be referred to this period, is shown in Fig. 261. It is painted in green and purple, with a few touches of white with peonies, chrysanthemums, and daisies growing from rocks, and with butterflies flying above. The details of the decoration are all delicately etched in the paste. The yellow ground, of pure tone, is minutely crackled, and the foot is coated under-neath with the same *truité* yellow glaze, and has no mark attached.

"48. Copies of monochrome- green porcelain. (仿澆綠器皿)·

"Two kinds are made: (1) with plain ground (*su ti*); (2) with engraved designs (*chui hua*)."

The green monochrome (*chiao lü*) of this period is a bright, attractive color composed of copper silicate in combination with a lead flux. Bowls and dishes of imperial ware, often etched with dragons under the glaze, are not rare, but vases are less common, and prized accordingly; they are usually pieces that once belonged to temple altar sets.

"49. Porcelain painted in colors in European style. (洋彩器皿)·

"In the new copies of the Western style of painting on enamels (*fa-lang*) the landscapes and figure scenes, the flowering plants and birds, are, without exception, of supernatural beauty and finish."

The class of *Yang Ts'ai*, or "Foreign Coloring," is very extensive and varied, as it includes not only the vases, eggshell plates, and other things painted with foreign designs, but also objects decorated with Chinese scenes in the same class of colors. It represents, more or less, the class that has been called the *famille rose*, on account of the prevalence of a pink among the enamel colors. In addition to the pink and crimson derived from gold we notice a bright lemon-yellow, a pale green, and a general preponderance of soft tints in marked contrast to the bold, vigorous coloring of the *K'ang-hsi* epoch. The colors were those previously in use among enamelers in copper, and were first introduced into China from abroad, probably from India. The art of painting in enamels upon copper flourished in China at the same time, and it would be easy to collect a series of rose-backed and crimson-backed copper dishes decorated in the same characteristic style, and painted in the same colors, as the eggshell porcelain dishes of the period.

"50. Porcelain with embossed designs executed in undercut relief. (拱花器皿)·

"These are applied in combination with all the different colored glazes."

The term *kung-hua*, which means literally "arched designs," is used to convey the idea of more salient relief than that of *tui-hua*, or "embossed designs," of No. 34, although the two terms are occasionally interchanged. The dragon curled round the neck of the celadon vase illustrated in Plate XL is an example of this kind of work which may be referred to the reign of *Yung-chêng.*

"51. Porcelain enameled Red after the European style. (西洋紅色器皿)."

The single colors included in this class would be the crimson (*yen-chih hung*) derived from gold, and the pink (*fên hung*) obtained by an addition of a proportion of the white enamel, obtained from arsenic, to the crimson. A beautiful example of the latter monochrome, a *rose d'or* of the "rose Dubarry" tint, which dates probably from this period, is shown in Plate LIII.

"52. Copies of the Black Glaze. (仿烏金釉).

"There are two varieties of this made: (1) with the decoration reserved in white upon the black ground; (2) with the black ground penciled over in gold."

These would be reproductions of the so-called "mirror-black" monochrome glaze, which was one of the special triumphs of the potters of the preceding reign of *K'ang-hsi,* and which is well illustrated in Plates IX, LXI, and LXII. The copies have an intense lustrous depth, but without the greenish, iridescent tones of the originals.

"53. Porcelain enameled Green after the European style. (西洋綠色器皿)."

This would be the pale-green monochrome, which is occasionally found replacing the pink on the back of eggshell dishes of the time, or applied as a single color on pieces interrupted by painted medallions.

Sometimes it is of palest *eau-de-Nil* tint. It is made by tingeing the white enamel of the muffle stove with a little of the green enamel derived from copper.

"54. Porcelain enameled Black after the European style. (西洋烏金器皿).

"55. Porcelain enameled in Gold—i. e., Gilded. (抹金器皿). After the Japanese (*Tung Yang*).

"56. Porcelain painted in Gold. (描金器皿). After the Japanese.

"57. Porcelain painted in Silver. (描銀器皿). After the Japanese."

The Japanese are commonly called *Tung Yang Jên,* or "Eastern Sea Men," by the Chinese, and Julien is incorrect in translating the term as "l'Indo-Chine," the natives of which would be "southerners," and who, moreover, never had any porcelain to copy. The "old Imari" porcelain of Japan, which was decorated after the pattern of later *Ming* times, and marked with the same Chinese marks, now comes across to be recopied at Ching-tê-chên, just as old Delft plates, copied from older Chinese blue and white, were reproduced later in the same Chinese factory, as is proved by some curious specimens on the shelves of the British Museum. It is not so easy to distinguish the copies of the old Japanese pieces, with a simple decoration of a pair of quails, a straw hedge,

Fig. 268.—Cylindrical Vase, one of a pair, richly decorated in K'ang-hsi enamel colors; European mounts.

and such-like, painted in soft colors, from the originals; they form a subdivision of the class of *Yang Ts'ai* (No. 49). The Chinese are inveterate copyists, and it is fortunate that they usually register the fact, as in the above three cases.

FIG. 269.—Snuff-bottle, decorated in blue and white,
with peach-bloom dragon; mark, Ch'ien-lung.

CHAPTER XIV.

THE CH'IEN-LUNG PERIOD.

AFTER the death of the Emperor *Yung-chêng*, in 1735, he was succeeded by his son, who began his reign with the title of *Ch'ien-lung* on the first day of the following year, and reigned till the end of the year 1795, when he resigned the throne after a long reign of sixty years, in accordance with a vow that his reign should not exceed that of his celebrated grandfather *K'ang-hsi*.

The reign of this last emperor, as we have seen, ranks as by far the most brilliant period in the history of the ceramic art. The reign of *Yung-chêng* was distinguished, as the official annalist has just told us, by many new inventions and by a remarkable success in the reproduction of the colored glazes of olden times, and in the long reign of *Ch'ien-lung* the new inventions introduced in the previous reign were gradually developed, till the porcelain attained a finished technique and a decoration of perfect symmetry, which are among its chief characteristics—so much so, in fact, that one is apt to get tired at last of its conventionality and almost mechanical perfection, and long for the artistic irregularity and the bold, vigorous coloring of the older style, which is so varied as never to be monotonous.

The successes of the early years of *Ch'ien-lung* are due to T'ang Ying, the famous director of the imperial manufactory, who occupies the same position now that Nien Hsi-yao did in the previous reign of *Yung-chêng.* T'ang Ying received his first appointment in the ceramic field of work from the emperor in 1728, and was ordered to proceed at once to Ching-tê-chên, to take charge of the imperial works under Nien Hsi-yao, who was appointed in the following year commissioner of customs at Huai-an-fu, still retaining, however, his post of chief director of the imperial porcelain manufactory. In the first year of the new reign (1736) T'ang Ying succeeded him in these two posts, and he remained at Huai-an-fu till 1739, when he was transferred to Kiukiang-fu, where he lived for the next ten years as Chief Commissioner of Customs of the Provinces of Kiangsi, Kiangsu, and Anhui, and Director of the Imperial Manufactory. He was a voluminous writer, and his writings have been published in a collected form, including disquisitions on his work, as well as the poems composed by him, as he surveyed the surrounding scene from the top of the Jewel Hill, at Ching-tê-chên and on many other occasions. He relates how, for the first three years, he always had his meals with the workmen and slept in the same room with them, so as to gain a familiar knowledge of all the smaller details of their handicraft. A chapter of his autobiography may be quoted

FIG. 270. — Crackled Yao-pien Vase of the Ch'ien-lung period, with transmutation splashes of mingled green, olive-brown, and purple.

here from the *Chiang hsi t'ung chih*, which says that the intimate knowledge that T'ang Ying finally succeeded in acquiring of the creative power of the fire in the development of colors had certainly never been equaled:

"Among the least of crafts, which can yet, however, supply the needs of an emperor as well as afford a means of livelihood for the common people, is the art of the potter in the manufacture of vessels, which, in their highest uses, figure as sacrificial bowls and dishes, in their lowest as articles of daily service for eating and drinking. Porcelain does not date from to-day. Researches show that it was first made during the *Han* dynasty, that the industry has been constantly practiced down through succeeding generations, and that among all the different localities that of Ch'ang-nan (Ching-tê-chên) has prevailed and flourished beyond any other. The preceding *Ming* dynasty built the imperial manufactory at the foot of the Jewel Hill, and appointed officials to superintend the work, but their regulations were bad, the public funds and materials were wasted, and the people were oppressed, so that they were unable to gain a living by their work. Who will dare to say that pottery is a mean thing, and that therefore the superintendents need not be so very careful?

"I (Ying), a native of Shêng-yang, in the province of Kuantung (Chinese Manchuria), whose family has for generations shared in the imperial favor, since they followed the dragon standard to Peking,* had my name en- 'Imperial Household.' In my youth I Yang-hsin-tien, and worked there for that the emperor now reigning came to heaven and earth in acknowledgment of be secretary (*lang*), and only fear my in the autumn of the sixth year (1728) month, the late Prince of Yi conveyed (imperial) orders, appointing me (Ying) facture in the province of Kiangsi, workmen in cases of disease and trade among the merchants. The the emperor's grace is all-pervad- omable. In reverent obedience once from the capital, and, in the arrived at the manufactory at regulate the work of the potters obedience to the decree. With ing a 'cash' of the funds intrust- made according to the indents. statement of accounts, have been

FIG. 271.—Fluted Vase of the Ch'ien-lung period, enameled yellow, with a green dragon coiled round the neck in openwork relief.

rolled at my birth in the Nei-wu-fu, the was employed in the palace in the more than twenty years. In the year the throne (1723) I prostrated myself to the imperial grace in promoting me to inability to deserve such honors. Later, of the reign of *Yung-chêng*, in the eighth to me, by word of mouth, the celestial to superintend the porcelain manu- and instructing me to relieve the trouble, and to encourage the imperial words were truly grand; ing, and his thoughts are unfath- to the order, I (Ying) started at tenth month of the same year, Ching-tê-chên, and hastened to and the trade of the merchants, in care and trembling, without wast- ed to me, I had the porcelain A list of the things sent, and a forwarded by me each month to

the superintendency of the imperial household (Nei-wu-fu). Up to now, the cyclical year, *yi-mao* (1735), I have been seven years engaged in the work. Although but 'a broken-down horse,' I put forth all my strength. My ability is poor, and my faults many, and it is only by the emperor's grace that I have escaped punishment. An annual allowance (in addition to salary) of five hundred taels has been granted me for fuel and water, so my family subsists on the imperial bounty, which a life's poor work could ill requite. The potter's work is a humble one, yet my own life, as well as that of the craftsmen, depend on the favor of the emperor, and I can not but proclaim the imperial grace. The ritual wine-vessels (*tsun*) and the sacrificial bowls (*kuai*) are now all made of clay, so as not to waste the national resources, and the daily wants of the people are also supplied by the potter's craft, so that the work must continue to be carried on by our successors. If the rules of the art be preserved, the labor will be halved, and the gain two-fold; if the rules be forgotten, money will be wasted, and the artisans' labor lost, so, for the use of after times, I have compiled the present epitome. Although I (Ying) dare not profess a complete knowledge of all the minute details of the ceramic art, yet I have prac-

---

* Many of the Chinese on the northern frontier joined the Manchus when they marched on Peking in 1643. They were enrolled afterward, on the Manchu plan, under banners, to form the Han Chün, or "Chinese army," and their descendants are retained to the present day. T'ang Ying was a captain of his banner.

ticed it diligently for a long time, and am familiar with the official lists of the articles produced, with the composition of the glazes used in their decoration, with the designs and dimensions of the pieces, as well as with the wages and food of the workmen, their rewards for diligence, and their fines for negligence. Although naturally stupid, I have learned one or two of these things, which I have collected and written down, and had them cut upon stone tablets, erected on the south side of the Jewel Hill, so that my successors in the directorship may have some materials for further researches, and be encouraged in their careful zeal; to put on record also the emperor's compassion for the people, and his instructions that the funds should not be wasted nor the workman's labor unrecompensed. What I have carefully written, I know personally, and I submit it with deference to the officials that shall succeed me. 'The farmer may learn something from his bondman, and the weaver from the handmaid who holds the thread for her mistress.'"

This scrap of autobiography, written in the high-flown language, bristling with classical quotations, affected by the Chinese *literati*, however feebly rendered in the translation, is sufficient to show the zeal of the worthy T'ang Ying in his work. Although nominally subordinate to Nien Hsi-yao, who was promoted to be commissioner of customs the year after the arrival

FIG. 272.—Bean-shaped Snuff-bottle, with archaic k'i-lin in blue and green on yellow ground; K'ang-hsi period.

of T'ang Ying at Ching-tê-chên, and transferred to his distant post at Huai-an-fu, the work must have owed much to his personal superintendence. In the first year of the reign of *Ch'ien-lung* (1736), T'ang Ying became in his turn commissioner of customs for the viceroyalty, and was himself transferred to Huai-an-fu, where he remained three years, retaining, like his predecessor, the post of director of the porcelain manufactory, but only making, he tells us, one official visit of inspection to Ching-tê-chên during the period.

In 1739 the commissionership was finally transferred to Kiukiang-fu, and the director was, at his new post, within easy reach of the scene of his former labors. His family, who were, as we have seen, originally natives of Manchuria, were enrolled by the new dynasty under the Han Chün, or Chinese Bannermen, and T'ang Ying was captain of his

banner. A full list of his titles, in the year 1741, is inscribed upon the long mark of dedication which has been taken from an altar candlestick, made by him in that year, and reproduced in facsimile in Chapter IV. In addition to his appointments in connection with the Imperial Household at Peking, he was then the imperial commissioner in charge of the customs stations of Huai-an-fu, Hai-chou, and Su-ch'ien-hsien, in the dual province of Kiangnan, and of Kiukiang-fu, in the province of Kiangsi, with the control of all the customs dues of the viceroyalty, made up of these provinces, and was at the same time director of the imperial porcelain manufactory. In the year 1743 he visited Peking, and he brought up with him on that occasion, no doubt, the sacrificial set of utensils, which he had made for the Taoist temple near that city. As soon as he arrived at the palace he was handed an imperial decree, dated the eighth day of the fourth month of that year, directing him to write a detailed description of twenty illustrations of the manufacture of porcelain, which had been found in the imperial library, and to send back the album as soon as he had finished. The pictures were returned in the following month to their former seclusion, and have never been, I believe, published. With regard to the description written by the accomplished director, and submitted at the same time to the imperial glance, no Chinese book on ceramic art is considered to be complete without it, and I will translate it in the next chapter from the pages of the annals of the province of Kiangsi, so often quoted.

T'ang Ying returned to his post at Kiukiang the same year and remained there as director of the porcelain manufactory till 1749.

The writers of the *Ching-tê-chên Tao lu* say, under the heading of "The Porcelain of

T'ang of the Reign of *Ch'ien-lung*": "This heading refers to the porcelain made at the imperial manufactory (at Ching-tê-chên) under the direction of T'ang Ying, Secretary of the Imperial Household. The Honorable T'ang, in the cyclical year *hsü-shên* (1728) of the reign of *Yung-chêng*, first came to reside at the imperial manufactory as assistant to the director Nien, and he acquired a great reputation for his work. In the first year (1736) of the reign of *Ch'ien-*

FIG. 273.—Ch'ien-lung Vase of Ku Yueh Hsüan style, delicately painted in enamel colors.

lung he was placed in charge of the customs at Huai-an-fu. In the eighth year* (1743) he was transferred to be commissioner of customs at Kiukiang-fu. In both these posts he retained the directorship of the porcelain manufacture. He had a profound knowledge of the properties of the different kinds of earth and of the action of fire upon them, and took every care in the proper selection of the materials, so that his productions were all highly finished and perfectly translucent. In the reproductions which he made of the celebrated porcelains of ancient times every piece was perfectly successful; in his copies of famous glazes there was not one that he could not cleverly imitate. His genius and ability were so great that he succeeded in everything he attempted. He also made porcelain decorated with the various colored glazes newly in-vented—viz., foreign purple (*yang tzŭ*), cloisonné blue (*fa ch'ing*), enam-eled silver (*mo yin*), painted in sepia (*ts'ai shui-mo*), foreign black (*yang wu-chin*), painted in the style of *cloisonné* enamels (*fa-lang hua fa*), painted with foreign enamel colors on a black ground (*yang ts'ai wu-chin*), with white designs reserved on the black ground (*hei ti pai hua*), with the black ground penciled over in gold (*hei ti miao chin*), the new sky-blue monochrome (*t'ien-lan*), and the transmutation glazes (*yao-pien*). The paste of the pieces was white, rich, and compact; the fabric, whether thick or thin, was brilliant and lustrous; and the imperial porcelain attained at this period its greatest perfection."

"He also, in obedience to an imperial decree, respectfully described the 'Twenty Illustra-tions of the Manufacture of Porcelain,' arranged them in order, and wrote detailed descriptions of the illustrations, which were presented by him to the emperor."

"The learned Li chü-lai of Lin-ch'üan in his preface to the Collected Works of the Honor-able T'ang, says: 'As results of his genius alone, flowering and producing fruit in his mind, the ancient manufacture of the large dragon fish-bowls and of the Chün-chou porcelain, which had long been lost, was re-established; and turquoise (*fei-ts'ui*) and rose-red (*mei-kuei*) glazes were produced by him of new tints and rare beauty. T'ang was thoroughly de-voted to his work, and the brilliancy of his genius is reflected in the beautiful porcelain made by him.'"

When T'ang Ying was appointed to his new post at Huai-an-fu in 1736, he left behind, for the instruc-tion of his successors, a collection of memoranda en-titled *T'ao ch'eng shih yu k'ao*, "Draughts of Instruc-tion on the Manufacture of Porcelain," which are often quoted in official books. The author writes in his

FIG. 274.—Libation Cup of Ku t'ung ts'ai, being painted in enamel with gold to imitate patinated bronze; mark, Ch'ien-lung.

preface to these drafts, which is quoted in the Fou-liang-hsien Annals: "When I was sent by imperial decree in the sixth year of the reign of *Yung-chêng* (1728) to undertake the super-intendence of the porcelain manufactory, I was unacquainted with the finer details of the porce-lain works of the province of Chiang-yu (Kiangsi), where I had never been before. But the materials are the same as those employed in other art-work and are changed in the fire in accordance with the chemical laws of the five elements, and they are combined after old pre-

---

* This must be an error. The official annals of the province of Kiangsi make his appointment date from 1749, and this is confirmed by the inscription in Chapter IV, which proves that he was commissioner at Kiukiang in 1741.

scriptions, as well as by new experiments. I worked hard with heart and strength, and for three years shared with the workmen their meals and hours of rest, until in the ninth year, *hsin-hai*, of the cycle (1731) I had conquered my ignorance of the materials and processes of firing, and, although I dared not claim familiarity with all the laws of transformation, my knowledge was much increased. After five more hot and cold seasons had passed by, during which 'his pottery vessels were not imperfect and the potter had not asked for sick-leave,' the accounts were made up to the thirteenth year of *Yung-chêng* (1735), and it was found that, for an expenditure of several tens of thousands of taels of treasury silver, no less than between 300,000 and 400,000 pieces of porcelain, comprising all kinds of vases and round ware, had been sent up to the palace at Peking for the use of the emperor. After the sovereign had flown up to heaven on a dragon, in the first year of his successor *Ch'ien-lung* (1736), I received the appointment of Commissioner of Customs at Huai-an and had to leave the immediate superintendence of the porcelain works.   For this drafts of the instructions of the scattered leaflets as have them in order, adding some work during the nine years in

T'ang Ying is the last of anything outside of the pages names of a long line of his other artist is often talked of as years of the reign of *Ch'ien-* a contemporary. This is the adopted the studio name of *Ku* Ancient Moon," by splitting the name, into its two component in Chapter IV. He was, I am palace at Peking, where a manu- superintendence of the Jesuit tioned here only because his been sent down to Ching-tê- celain, which was considered by material than glass. The glass a clear glass of greenish tint

FIG. 275.—Yung-chêng or early Ch'ien-lung White Porcelain of eggshell thinness; purest tone and perfect finish.

reason I have collected the these years, and as many of been preserved, and arranged notes of the progress of the which I have been director." the directors of whom we hear of the annals, on which the successors are registered. One having flourished in the early *lung*, so that he must have been worker in glass named Hu, who *Yueh Hsüan*, "Chamber of the Chinese character *Hu*, his sur- parts, *Ku Yueh*, as explained told, a worker in glass in the factory was founded under the missionaries, and he is men- productions are said to have chên to be reproduced in por- the emperor to be a more noble made by him was of two kinds: with an embossed decoration

executed in colored glasses, and an opaque white glass, which was either engraved with etched designs or decorated in colors. It is the former kind that is most highly valued in the present day, a tiny snuff-bottle being sold for as much as several hundred taels, or even for a thousand dollars; the latter kind was the type that was copied in porcelain. The result was the ware of peculiar vitreous aspect which is technically known as *Fang Ku Yueh Hsüan*, or "copies of Ku Yueh Hsüan." Mr. Hippisley was one of the first to introduce these wares to the outside world, and he has exhibited several choice specimens in his collection at the Smithsonian Institution at Washington. He says (*Catalogue, loc. cit.*, page 423): "Ku Yueh hsüan* introduced about the year 1735 the use of an opaque white vitreous ware for the manufacture of articles of small dimensions, such as snuff-bottles, wine-cups, vessels for washing pencils in, etc. The vitreous nature of the body imparts a tone and brilliancy to the colors used in the decoration which is greatly admired, and the best specimens of this ware will well repay minute study. The choice of groundwork is effective, the grouping of the colors soft and harmonious, the introduction of European figures is interesting, and the arrangement of flowers evidence of the highest artistic skill. The earliest pieces were marked, usually in red, *Ta Ch'ing nien chih*,

---

* Mr. Hippisley seems to take Ku Yueh Hsüan to be the actual name of the man, whom he refers to as being "a subordinate officer, I believe in the directorate of the Ching-tê-chên factories."

'Made during the great Pure (the *Ch'ing* or present) dynasty,' the later pieces had the mark, within a square seal-like border, *Ch'ien lung nien chih,* 'Made during the reign of *Ch'ien-lung,*' engraved in the foot, and filled with a thick, bright blue enamel glaze. T'ang Ying (in his imitations of this vitreous ware in porcelain) appeared to have employed for his purpose a very pure glaze of a highly vitrifiable nature, and to have thereby effected an enamel brilliancy that no other porcelain shows, and to have also secured to a considerable extent the same soft transparency in the decorative colors which was so much appreciated on the Ku Yueh Hsüan vitreous ware. Specimens of this porcelain, which is quite rare, are held in very high esteem by the Chinese, alike for the purity of the paste, the brilliance of the glaze, and the beauty of the decoration, and are considered among the finest productions of the period during which the manufacture attained its highest excellence."

The glass ware referred to here is outside our province. Of the porcelain modeled in the Ku Yueh Hsüan type a beautiful specimen was illustrated in Fig. 68—a teapot with the mark of the *Yung-chêng* period penciled underneath in overglaze blue enamel. Another example is presented here in Fig. 273, which I will briefly describe:

Small bottle-shaped vase, with a globular body and gently tapering neck expanding above into a prominent lip, coated with a lustrous white glaze of vitreous aspect decorated with delicate enamel colors of the Ku Yueh Hsüan type. On the body is a picture suggestive of an autumnal scene, with roses growing by a rockery, trees with autumn-tinted leaves and marguerite daisies, in the foreground of which a pair of quails, beautifully painted with a miniature-like finish, stand out prominently. The neck of the vase is decorated with a ring of formal palmate design, the shoulder is encircled by two bands, a pink scroll worked in relief succeeded by a blue fret, and the lip is defined by a line of gilding.

There is a couplet of verse written at the back:

"Years roll by as we sit at the table, painting pictures in colors;
Charmed by all the happy notes of Nature, listening to the calling quails."

The headpiece is a small oval panel with the seal characters *Jên Ho,* "Benevolence and Harmony," inside; at the foot of the stanza are two small oblong panels with the inscription *Ssŭ Fang Ch'ing Yen,* "Serenity and calm throughout the empire." The motto is declared to be appropriate to the emperor alone, and it is outlined in red, the color of the sacred "vermilion pencil."

The next vase of Ku Yueh Hsüan style, exhibited in Fig. 263, is an example of the class decorated with European pictures. It is a small ovoid vase of broad shape, formed, as it were, of twin coalescing vases, with the line of junction indicated by a vertical groove. The shape is like that of the pair of vases of which one is illustrated in Plate LXXVI, and, like them, it once had a cover, now lost; the bottom has had a piece chipped out so as to remove the date of the four-character seal, penciled underneath in black, leaving only the tail-end *nien chih,* but we can not be far wrong in supplying *Ch'ien-lung* as the missing half. The vase is painted in delicate enamel colors, *rouge d'or* predominating. It is decorated with two large oval medallions and two small round panels with scrolled borders, displayed upon a floral ground, and with bands of ornamental design around the neck and foot, all in the ordinary Chinese style of the period.

FIG. 276.—K'ai-pien Vase with crackled glaze and undulatory surface, painted in subdued blues with touches of maroon red.

The small round medallions contain landscape sketches with European houses. The large oval panels are filled with copies of European pictures, cleverly executed, but betraying in the details the touch of the Chinese artist. In one there is a female figure in pink dress and purple robe with two children, copied, apparently, from a sacred picture representing the Virgin Mother with the Infant Jesus and St. James. The other, similarly shaped, and upon the opposite side, contains a picture of a garden scene with two girls in European costume, one of whom is carrying a basket of flowers.

The enamel colors used in painting these vases are precisely those that had been previously used in the West in enameling upon metal. The working palette of the enamel painter was rich in variety of colors, as metallic oxides readily lend themselves to an infinite number of combinations with glass. The green, blue, red, turquoise, gray, orange, and yellow may be obtained either pure or compound, so as to form shades as gradual as a chromatic scale. The light-red color is called in old English books upon the subject "the chief and paragon of all." It is said to have been discovered by a goldsmith who studied alchemy, and found it one day at the bottom of his crucible in trying to make gold.

This last is the color which suddenly makes its appearance upon Chinese porcelain in the beginning of the eighteenth century, in common with the other new enamel colors which are known collectively to the Chinese potter as *Yang Ts'ai,* or "Foreign Colors." The earliest

FIG. 277.—White Ovoid Vase etched with floral scrolls, and surmounted by a dragon in undercut relief, enameled dark red with touches of gold; mark, Ch'ien-lung.

date-mark found upon the "rose-backed" plates, which are decorated in these colors of the *famille rose,* is that of the cyclical year *hsin-ch'ou* (1721), the last year but one of the reign of *K'ang-hsi.* It was this emperor who was probably the means of introducing these colors into China, through the medium of the Roman Catholic missionaries, of whom he was a great patron. He founded a manufactory of colored glass near the palace at Peking, under their superintendence, where, no doubt, many of the materials were manufactured for the use of the school of enamelers upon copper that was also established at Peking about the same time under their tuition, and produced painted work executed in the style of Battersea enamels. He even tried to introduce the manufacture of porcelain, and had all the materials brought up to Peking for the purpose, as described by Père d'Entrecolles in his letters, but this project failed, partly on account, it is suggested, of the opposition of the porcelain guild. The enamelers in

metal were more successful, and their work was sent to Ching-tê-chên to be reproduced in porcelain. The same designs occur on both, and are associated with the same rose-colored grounds and pink diapers. I have a small mirror, for example, mounted in a copper frame, which is enameled at the back with the same sacred picture that is painted upon the vase that has just been described, and a long series of such identical designs might be collected. European pictures are not an inappropriate decoration for the enameled work, recalling its original source, but there is no excuse for the unseemly scenes which are occasionally associated with them, and which prove that the missionaries of those days were assailed with the same scandalous stories that are put forth about them in the present day.

Actual specimens of old European enamels were also sent at this period to Ching-tê-chên and copied in porcelain. This is proved by an interesting cup of Chinese porcelain from the Marquis collection at Paris,* which is thus described: "A wide shallow cup with two open flowing handles, of fine and light porcelain, an exact imitation, both in form and decoration, of the piece of Limoges enamel which has served as its model in China, so that it might even be mistaken for the original. It has, outside, ornamental designs reserved in white upon a black ground, enhanced by gilding; inside, it is decorated in different colors with flowers and fruit, executed with the enamels of the *famille verte.* Close to the basket of fruit painted in the bottom of the bowl there is found, faithfully reproduced, the monogram I. L. of the Limoges enameler, Jean Laudin."

One of the most remarkable features indeed of the practice of the ceramic art in China at this period was the way the world was ransacked for new objects to copy. Père d'Entrecolles describes how his mandarin friends pressed him to get for them new models from Europe for this purpose. In the last chapter we saw how specimens of ancient ware of all kinds were sent down to Ching-tê-chên to be copied. Pieces of "old Imari" porcelain came from Japan

* This cup is now, I have reason to believe, in the Grandidier collection in the Louvre.

at the same time to be imitated. The author of the *T'ao Shuo* declares that the older designs in chiseled gold, in embossed silver, in carved jade and other hard stones, in lacquer ware, in mother-of-pearl inlaid work, in carvings of rhinoceros horn, bamboo, wood, gourd, and shell, were all, without exception, executed in porcelain, as exact copies of the originals, and that the potters were supplanting the skilled artificers in all these different branches of work. The texture of the ivory, shell, or bamboo is carefully indicated in the porcelain, and the surface colors are reproduced so as to bring out the tints of the variegated marble and pudding-stone, the mottled jade, the striped carnelian and agate, the veined walnut-wood, and the carved cinnabar lac, with such exactitude that it is necessary to handle the piece to convince one's self that it is really made of porcelain. The aspect of gold and silver was given by enamels prepared from the metals themselves; the surface tints of copper and bronze, the rust of iron, and the play of colors upon ancient patinated bronze in which the Chinese antiquarian takes so much delight, were produced by combinations of different glazes, applied either with the brush or by sprinkling over the first ground color.

A characteristic example of the iridescent "iron-rust" (*t'ieh-hsiu*) glaze is illustrated in Plate XIX, showing a deep bronze-colored ground, speckled with lustrous metallic spots, and flecked with red clouds. In Fig. 274 is exhibited a specimen of the class of ancient bronze design which is known as *ku t'ung ts'ai*. It is a libation cup (*chüeh*) of antique style, molded in relief and enameled with color to imitate patinated bronze. The handle is fashioned in the form of a dragon, and the bowl of the cup is encircled by a broad sunken band containing archaic designs in relief, with an ogre's face (*t'ao-t'ieh*) under the lip, and conventional scrolls starting from dragons' heads round the sides. The surface, enameled olive-brown flecked with "tea-dust," is penciled in gold with scrolls and borders of rectangular fret; the ground of the sunken band, which is pitted, is partially filled in with a grayish-blue overglaze of mottled tints passing into green. There is a seal underneath, outlined in gold, *Ch'ien lung nien chih:* "Made in the reign of *Ch'ien-lung.*" Some of the larger objects of this class exhibit a remarkable combination of brilliant colors, such as copper alone is capable of producing, and it is wonderful how the same tints are almost instantaneously brought out artificially by the oxidizing power of the furnace flames, that usually require centuries to develop by gradual oxidation of the metal buried in moist ground.

Fig. 278.—White Beaker of ancient bronze form and archaic design, with nine dragons in undercut relief, painted in delicate enamels.

The technique of the class just described is similar to that of the transmutation, *flambé*, or *yao-pien* glazes, which derive their most brilliant colors from the same protean metal. These flourished abundantly during the *Ch'ien-lung* period, to which three of the vases shown in the colored illustrations may be referred. The egg-shaped vase in Plate XVI is a brilliant example of the kind, with its lightly crackled glaze vertically splashed with all the different tints imprinted by the flames as the liquescent glaze was running down in the furnace, passing from turquoise through purple and other intermediate shades of red to the richest crimson. The vase in Plate LXXXVIII has the same brilliant *flambé* glaze running down over its surface so as to form large tears, only partially covering the crackled surface of mottled olive-brown tint due to iron, which is often used on such pieces in combination with the copper that produces the typical colors. The quadrangular vase in Plate XLVI, with open scroll handles at the sides and relief panels in front and at the back, differs from the other two in having a very fine, compact, and white paste; the shape is one often reproduced in copper-red (*chi-hung*) vases of *flambé* type in the present day, some of which are of very brilliant color, albeit wanting in depth and too glossy.

With regard to the monochrome porcelain of this reign, the colors which distinguished the *Yung-chêng* period continued to be produced under the directorship of T'ang Ying, who had learned his art in the ateliers of the latter period. The soft red derived from gold, passing from the deepest crimson of the rose petals, through "rouge red," or *yen-chih hung*, down to the palest of the pinks called by them *fên-hung*; the lemon-yellow, camellia-leaf, and paler tone of green, the bright blue, the brilliant glossy black, and the other colors of the foreign enameler's palette, were still prepared, although in process of time they gradually lost something of their pristine purity. The same may be said of the *soufflé* copper-red of ruby tone, and the sky-blue or *clair-de-lune*, the two finest shades of the Nien Yao. The coral-red, on the contrary, comes into greater prominence, and is gradually improved in tone till it excels that of any of older times,* as in the beautiful monochrome vase selected for illustration in Plate XCII, and in the vase shown in Plate XXVI, where it forms a pure vermilion ground round a dragon pursuing the magic jewel, enameled green with touches of other colors. The ordinary green, yellow, and manganese brown or purple are common single colors, either plain or investing an etched decoration engraved with a style in the part underneath the glaze. The fine white porcelain, like that of the preceding reign, is of special pellucid purity and soft, pearly tone; the egg-shell vase in Fig. 275, which is modeled on the lines of the pink vase illustrated in Plate LIII, and which is perfectly plain with the exception of faintest rings in the paste defining the rims of the neck and of the foot, is a white vase of this kind, which may be attributed to either of these two reigns. A new shade which now appears among the single colors is the intense deep blue known to the Chinese as *pao-shih lan*, or "sapphire-blue," which is often seen in combination with imperial dragons faintly engraved in the paste, and usually with a square seal of the *Ch'ien-lung* period impressed underneath the piece, the foot being coated with the same glaze. This last glaze, however, is usually finely crackled, as is shown in the vase of rich sapphire-blue color illustrated in Plate XXIX. Many of the single colors of the time are, in fact, distinguished by having this finely crackled reticulation in the glaze, the *truité* of the French, the *yü-tzŭ wên* or "fish-roe" crackle of the Chinese. The colored

FIG. 279.—Large Gourd-shaped Vase decorated with sprays of "The Hundred Flowers," painted in enamel colors; mark, Ch'ien-lung.

glazes in these cases were applied, *sur biscuit*, on porcelain that had been previously fired in an unglazed state. The manganese-purple and the turquoise-blue of the time are among the finest of these, especially the latter, which excels that of any previous period in its mottled shades of purest cerulean hue, exactly resembling those of the plumes of the kingfisher, from which it derives its Chinese name of *fei-ts'ui*, which is contracted sometimes to *ts'ui sê*, *sê* meaning color. The tones of color are perfectly displayed in the two graceful beakers of ancient bronze design in Plates XLIV and XLV, the first of which is modeled with archaic details under the glaze, while the second, left plain, has nothing to detract from the symmetry of its outlines or the beauty of its coloring.

---

* The calcined peroxide of iron was formerly painted on, mixed with a simple flux of white lead; now it is combined with the ordinary vitreous flux of the enameler, and acquires the brilliant tint known to the Chinese as *tsao-'rh hung*, the "red of the jujube," the fruit of the *Zizyphus communis*.

The finely crackled green and yellow monochromes of the same class, which are usually bracketed together, are characteristic colors of the period, the production of which is continued down to the present day. Of the "fish-roe green," or *yü-tzŭ lü*, a typical specimen is seen illustrated in Plate XXVII; this is also called by the Chinese *kua-p'i lü*, or "cucumber-green," a name more appropriate to the color of the vase illustrated in Plate LXXVIII; it is sometimes called "apple-green" by Western collectors, but this term (*p'ing-kuo lü*) is always applied by the Chinese to the green which accompanies their *p'ing-kuo hung*, or "apple-red," on the "peach-bloom" vases of the *K'ang-hsi* period. The yellow crackle of the same type, called *yü-tzŭ huang*, or "fish-roe yellow," is illustrated in Plate LXXXVII; under the name of "mustard-yellow," which indicates its usual shade, it acquired at one time a celebrity which it hardly deserved.

The ordinary crackle of the time, marked by the wider reticulation of lines, which is likened to fissured ice, and hence known by the name of *ping lieh wên*, is sufficiently illustrated by the vase of archaic design shown in Plate LXXVII, which is coated with the grayish-blue glaze called *Ju yu*, from its resemblance in color to that of the ancient Ju-chou porcelain, after which it was modeled; it is marked underneath in blue with the date-mark of *Ch'ien-lung*. Crackled glazes were among the specialties of the period, and were produced at will in any color or combination of colors. The variety of *soufflé* glazes was also very great, and many novel combinations were introduced by the application of a different shade of the same color, or of a new color altogether. The second enamel was sprinkled on in the form of a fine rain by blowing through a bamboo tube with gauze tied over the end, which was lightly dipped in the color, or it was flecked on in larger or smaller tears with a brush dipped in the moist color; or, again, it was painted on in larger patches of overglaze enamel; the effect of each process can be readily distinguished, so that a fuller description is unnecessary.

FIG. 280.—Octagonal Flower-pot decorated in panels, with flowers, fruit, and butterflies painted in enamel colors.

The decorated porcelain produced during this long reign of sixty years is also of almost infinite variety. If it wants something of the artistic freedom of design and brilliancy of coloring which distinguish the *K'ang-hsi* period, it evinces a grace and technical finish of its own. Brilliant greens of different shades predominate in the painted porcelain of the latter reign, which is indicated by the selection for it of the name of *famille verte*. In the new reign the green is paler in tone and occupies a subordinate position among the colors; it is supplanted by reds of crimson and pink shades derived from gold, hence the name of *famille rose* which is often applied to the decoration.

The decorated porcelains may be conveniently classified under the headings of the table in Chapter X:

A. Colors of the *grand feu.*
B. Colors of the *demi-grand feu.*
C. Colors of the muffle stove.

We shall find that the eight classes which were comprised in the table under the above three headings are all abundantly represented in the productions of the reign of *Ch'ien-lung.*

There is nothing special to be noticed in the first two classes which include the pieces painted in cobalt-blue and in copper-red respectively. The blue and white is generally carefully penciled with graceful floral sprays and conventional scrolls, but the blue has lost its pulsating vigor, and the glaze its pellucid depth. The white ground is purer in tint, but it is apt to become almost chalky, and one misses the tinge of blue which seemed to give a note of harmony to the older pictures. Mr. Monkhouse in his appreciative introduction to the catalogue of blue and white, already referred to, asks: "Does this tinge come from the pigment with which the vase is painted? If so, it is, perhaps, one advantage of the Chinese practice of baking the paste, the blue and the glaze, at the same firing. The tinge, whether gray or blue, is always in accord with the quality of the blue."

A typical example of blue and white, with the seal of *Ch'ien-lung* inscribed underneath, may be seen in the ritual wine-pot with Buddhist symbols and floral scrolls in Fig. 90. The

FIG. 281. — Snuff - bottle with brilliant decoration on deep red ground ; mark, Ch'ien-lung.

two pieces now to be mentioned are decorated in mixed underglaze colors, and belong, therefore, to the third class on the table. The pilgrim-bottle (*pao yueh p'ing*) in Fig. 176, outlined in the shape of the full moon, is decorated on each side with a five-clawed imperial dragon coiling round the magic jewel. The dragons, the flames proceeding from their bodies, and the effulgent jewels in the middle, are painted in copper-red of maroon tint; the scrolled clouds which fill in the intervals and the crested sea-waves at the base of the vase are painted in cobalt-blue. The outside of each loop-handle is decorated in blue with a spiral scroll, and the seal of the *Ch'ien - lung* period underneath is penciled in the same underglaze color. The smaller bottle-shaped vase in Fig. 276 is an example of the so-called "soft-paste" class, decorated in the same two colors as the last piece. The crackled (*k'ai-pien*) glaze, which has a slightly undulatory surface, is traversed throughout with a reticulation of fine lines. The monstrous lionlike quadruped, drawn after the unusually grotesque fashion of this time, is standing at the foot of a spreading pine-tree, with a bat flying overhead, all painted in blues of subdued tones: the flames which proceed from the shoulders and hips of the monster are tinged copper-red, and its eyes are lightly touched with rings of the same underglaze color. There is no mark attached.

A representative piece of the fourth class, "decorated in glazes of several colors," is illustrated in Plate XXXI in the magnificent vase, two feet high, decorated with imperial dragons in the midst of clouds, with the details engraved in the paste and enameled green, displayed upon a monochrome yellow ground.

The remaining four classes, including all the different kinds of decoration in enamel colors fired in the muffle stove, are particularly well filled. In the reign of *Ch'ien-lung*, according to Chinese authorities, the highest art was lavished on porcelain-painting in colors, and the dealers thronged round the mouth of the kiln to have the first pick of the things as they were taken out. The "red shops," as the manufactories of colored ware had been commonly called since the introduction of the coral-red derived from iron, one of the earliest of the enamel colors, were now widely patronized, instead of those of the producers of single colors and the decorators in plain blue and white, who had hitherto monopolized attention. The three beautiful specimens selected for illustration in colors are unrivaled examples of the style and coloring of the time. The first, Plate LXIV, is one of a pair of quadrangular vases, with openwork railings projecting from the corners, which are richly decorated in colors with gilding. The large panels are painted with landscape pictures of the four seasons, bordered by scrolls, penciled in gold on a soft coral-red, by bands of gold-brocaded blue or embroidered yellow. The study of the colors on a vase of this kind,

FIG. 282. — Ch'ien - lung Eggshell Vase with panel pictures and floral reliefs, painted in enamel colors, with gilding.

of which the date is certainly known, is an invaluable aid to the correct classification of the enameled single colors which are so often unmarked. The second vase, Plate LXXVI, is a typical member of the *famille rose*, exhibiting broad bands of crimson *rouge d'or* etched with scrolls. Like the foregoing vase the base is enameled pale green underneath, a characteristic of the finest decorated porcelain of this reign which is worthy of notice. The mark is written here in bright overglaze blue, in one horizontal line; in the former case it is in the form of a seal, penciled in red on a white panel reserved in the middle of the pale-green ground. The third of the *Ch'ien-lung* pieces, the hexagonal lantern with pierced openwork sides in Plate XXII, is another striking evidence in its soft, harmonious tone of coloring, in its graceful decorative designs, and in its finished technique, of the artistic skill of the potters of this period.

It is possible to admire the fine productions of this time, and yet to prefer the bolder style and stronger coloring of the decorated porcelain, as well as the brilliancy of the monochromes of the older reign of *K'ang-hsi.* M. Grandidier, a practiced connoisseur of Chinese ceramic art, observes: "Some collectors prefer the delicate porcelains of the *Ch'ien-lung* epoch to any other; I can find no fault with them; others remain cold, dull, and indifferent in the presence of the most perfect of these marvels, and are only enthusiastically attracted by the porcelain of the *Ming* dynasty, so majestic in its barbaric effect; these last are not wrong, and I offer them my approval. Some, again, put in the first rank the productions of the time of *K'ang-hsi*, and they are right. I exclude none of these three periods; each has its special qualities of a different order, and I admire them all sincerely without admitting the superiority of any one over the others. Beauty has always the gift of captivating me, and under all its forms; queen of the world, it reigns an absolute sovereign in the realm of art."

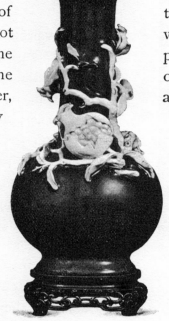

FIG. 283.—Vase of dark olive-green "tea-dust" tint, with a branch of pomegranate winding round in full undercut white relief; mark, Ch'ien-lung.

There is no fixed line of demarcation between the decorated porcelain of the *Yung-chêng* and *Ch'ien-lung* periods. Two pieces, in form and design as well as in smaller technical details, might pass for productions of the former reign had they not the mark of *Ch'ien-lung* inscribed underneath, etched under the glaze in the first case, penciled in cobaltblue in the second. The oval bowl-shaped vase in Fig. 277 in white with scrolls of lotus and peony flowers etched under the clear glaze; the dragon of archaic design, coiled in openwork relief round the rim, is enameled redbrown and touched with gold. The saucer-shaped dish in Fig. 249 is painted in the same brilliant enamels as the large dish illustrated in Plate XLVIII, with branches of peaches springing from the circular rim of the foot and passing over the border of the dish to decorate its interior, as well as its outer surface. The branches bear pink flowers and buds, as well as large peaches, the fruit of long life, and they are accompanied by five flying bats, painted in shaded red, emblems of the five happinesses, three being displayed in the field, two on the outer edge of the saucer. In Fig. 278 is exhibited a charming little vase, modeled as a four-sided beaker (*tsun*), of ancient bronze design, with an archaic scrolled band round the waist, and vertical dentated ridges projecting from the sides and corners; upon it are seen the lizardlike forms of nine dragons, in undercut relief, painted in delicate *Ch'ien-lung* colors, of which a large *Ch'ih-lung*, with four small ones crawling over its body, composes the handle, while four others coil round the neck of the vase.

Two other pieces will serve to give an idea of the great variety of flowers depicted in the naturalistic floral decoration of porcelain at this time. The flower-pot of eight-lobed form in Fig. 280 has eight panels of flowers and fruit, with butterflies and dragonflies, all painted in delicate enamel colors. The front panel displays the fir, bamboo, and prunus, so often associated as emblems of longevity; the next, proceeding from right to left, contains flowering bulbs of narcissus and sprays of roses, followed in order by pomegranates and chrysanthemums; a group of begonias; of hibiscus (*Rosa sinensis*) branches; sprays of *Dielytra spectabilis* and azuretipped marguerite daisies; of yellow jasmine and scarlet *ling-chih* (*Polyporus lucidus*); of redleaved amaranthus and orchids (*Cymbidium ensifolium*). The large double gourd-shaped vase (*hu-lu p'ing*), nearly two feet high, in Fig. 279, displays in its rich floral ground the "hundred flowers" of the Chinese, painted in natural colors, so that each species may be recognized at a glance by one familiar with the garden flora of China. Among them may be distinguished peonies of several kinds, lotus, chrysanthemum, magnolia, roses, hibiscus (both pink and yellow), orchids, iris, lilies (scarlet and white), asters, hydrangea, wistaria, dielytra, pomegranate, begonia, narcissus, convolvulus, syringa (white and lilac), *Pyrus japonica* (*hai-t'ang*) and double peach, *Olea fragrans*, cockscomb, etc. The foot is encircled by a band of formal foliations in shaded blue and green upon a pink monochrome ground, between heavily gilded rims. The base enameled, like the inside of the mouth, pale green, has a reserved panel in the middle in which is penciled in red the seal *Ta ch'ing Ch'ien lung nien chih*—i. e., "Made in the reign of *Ch'ien-lung*, of the great *Ch'ing* [dynasty]." *

Fig. 284.—Articulated Celadon Vase with archaic designs in relief under the glaze of pale shaded pea-green; mark, Ch'ien-lung.

The varied processes of decoration in white slip over colored glazes; of embossing in plain, and in undercut relief; of pierced designs, intended either to be left in openwork or to be subsequently filled in with glaze; and of making composite vases, composed either of articulated pieces or furnished with movable appendages — all these branches of the ceramic art were executed with success at this time, and some examples have been already illustrated in these pages. The vase in Fig. 282 displays the floral embossed work which was so exactly copied at Meissen in early Dresden porcelain that it is, at first sight, difficult to distinguish the copies from the originals, as they are now placed side by side for comparison within the glass cases of the museum at Dresden. It is an ovoid vase of fine eggshell texture, overlaid with a close-set floral decoration composed of chrysanthemums, hai-t'ang (*Pyrus japonica*), and daisies, painted in red, green, and gold. Within this floral ground are reserved two oval panels, painted in delicate enamels with familiar scenes of domestic life, an interior with ladies drinking wine out of tiny gilded cups, and a garden with another group of ladies looking at fighting cocks; scrolled bands penciled in gold round the rims of the vase complete the decoration. The vase in Fig. 283 exhibits a floral decoration in full undercut relief projecting from a background of "tea-dust," or *ch'a-yeh mo*. The "tea-dust" is one of the characteristic *soufflé* glazes of the time, an olive-green monochrome ground thickly flecked with tiny spots of lighter green. The vase, grooved with three vertical lines, has an indented foot and a three-lobed lip. The branches of fruit in white relief are pomegranates, winding round the vase and leaving a small interval on the shoulder, which is filled by a branded stem of sacred fungus (*Polyporus lucidus*) which is also enameled white. The foot, coated underneath with the same "tea-dust" glaze, has the seal, stamped in the paste, *Ta Ch'ing Ch'ien lung nien chih*—i. e., "Made in the reign of *Ch'ien-lung*, of the great *Ch'ing* [dynasty]."

No better examples of pierced work could be found than the lantern with openwork panels, which is illustrated in Plate XXII, and the magnificent vase with pierced trellis-work

---

* A magnificent jar (*kuan*) forty-five centimetres high, of broad, massive form, illustrated by M. Grandidier (*loc. cit.*, Plate XXXVI, 109), is covered with the same floral decoration. The author describes it as "composed of an interlacement of floral sprays in juxtaposition presenting an infinite variety of types and of colors; the Chinese flora is represented upon it with an incredible luxury. It produces the effect of an immense sheaf of flowers—of a colossal bouquet. (From the Summer Palace)." The cover is apparently wanting. Its fellow, which is in the Dana Collection in New York, is, if I remember rightly, complete with the original cover decorated with the same floral ground crowned with a gilded knob.

in the outer casing that is shown in Fig. 185. This last is also provided with a movable appendage in the form of a revolving belt attached to the waist of the double gourd; it is marked underneath with a gold "seal" of the *Ch'ien-lung* period. An articulated specimen is presented in Fig. 284, which represents a celadon vase of bronze form and design, cut across into two parts by a wavy, dovetailed line of four-lobed foliated outline. The designs, worked in relief in the paste, in a broad band encircling the body of the vase, consist of four monstrous ogre (*t'ao-t'ieh*) faces, conventionalized into ornamental scrolls. The varying depth of the investing glaze produces corresponding shades in soft tones of pea-green. The seal of *Ta Ch'ing Ch'ien lung nien chih*, "Made in the reign of *Ch'ien-lung*, of the great *Ch'ing* [dynasty]," is penciled on the foot in cobalt-blue underneath a coat of the same celadon glaze.

The last technical process of decoration to be noticed here is that in which the pierced designs cut in the porcelain are filled in with glaze, producing a charming effect when the piece is looked at as a transparency. This is sometimes known as "rice-grain" decoration. It may either form the sole ornamentation of a piece or be employed in combination either with blue and white or with colored enamels, a few leaves or petals in the latter case, for example, being treated in this way so as to appear transparent when held up to the light. The most usual form is that of bands of diaper or star pattern. The delicate bowls of this reign which display an intricate conventional pattern, like that of lacework, contrasting in its greenish transparency with the pure white ground, are among the most graceful and charming of ceramic triumphs; they are called "lace-bowls" by collectors, and have a tiny seal mark of the reign penciled underneath in blue. Still rarer are vases of which we have one for illustration in Fig. 285, the sides of which are pierced throughout with a lacework pattern of conventional peony-flowers in the midst of leafy scrolls, and which has the pierced floral pattern filled in with glaze. The structure of the vase is of eggshell thinness and undulatory surface, and the decoration imparts a marvelous lightness of effect. The borders of the vase are encircled by rings of conventional ornament molded in slight relief, so as to be picked out in white on a ground of palest celadon tint. There is no mark inscribed, but it could hardly belong to any other epoch, and its peculiar delicacy and beauty make it a fitting type to close this brief sketch of the ceramic art of the reign of *Ch'ien-lung*, the chief charm of which lies in these two qualities.

Fig. 285.—Ch'ien-lung "Lace-work" Vase of eggshell texture, the sides pierced with scrolled designs, being filled in with transparent glaze.

Fig. 286.—Snuff-bottle; twin double gourds with decoration in
brilliant enamels on yellow ground; mark, Ch'ien-lung.

CHAPTER XV.

THE TWENTY ILLUSTRATIONS OF THE MANUFACTURE OF PORCELAIN DESCRIBED BY T'ANG YING.

T'ANG YING, the celebrated director of the imperial porcelain manufactory at Ching-tê-chên, to whom we have already so often referred, came up to Peking in the eighth year of the reign of the Emperor *Ch'ien-lung* (1743). He had been absent for fifteen years, engaged in superintending the ceramic works, and was sent for now by the emperor, who was anxious for personal information about the details of the industry from a professor of the art. On the twenty-second day of the fourth intercalary month he was summoned to the Office of the Board of Works in the Yang-hsin-tien, one of the large halls of the imperial palace, to take part as a member of a commission which had been especially appointed for the purpose of revising some of the classical works on technical subjects. When he arrived there a series of twenty illustrations of the manufacture of porcelain, which had been found in the imperial library, were handed to him, together with an imperial rescript, dated the eighth day of the preceding month, ordering him (T'ang Ying) "to arrange the illustrations in their proper order, and to describe carefully the different processes illustrated in the water-color pictures, specifying the hills from which the porcelain earth was obtained, as well as the sources of the other materials; and finally to return the pictures, with the descriptions which he had written attached, to the imperial library."

The task was completed in twelve days, and the result was "reverentially submitted to the imperial glance for correction" in a memorial by T'ang Ying, who subscribes himself as "Junior Secretary of the Imperial Household (Nei Wu Fu), Tao-t'ai in charge of the Customs at Kiukiang, and *ex-officio* Director of the Imperial Porcelain Manufactory." The pictures have remained in seclusion ever since, and have never, so far as I know, been published. Their description by T'ang Ying, on the contrary, is to be found either in its complete form or in abstract in every Chinese book of any pretensions on ceramics. The most complete form, including copies of the original imperial decree and of T'ang Ying's memorial announcing the completion of his task, is contained in the chapter on porcelain in the *Wên fang ssŭ k'ao*, "Researches on the apparatus of the library," by T'ang Ping-chün, a book published in the reign of *Ch'ien-lung*. The most authentic version is to be found in the official annals of the province of Kiangsi (*Chiang hsi T'ung chih*, book xciii, folio 19–23), where it is published as an appendix to the article on porcelain.

Fig. 287. — Eggshell Vase,
delicately painted in colored
enamels and gold, with illustrations of silk culture and
weaving.

There is, unfortunately, no word of the date of the pictures themselves; it is only stated that they were painted by order of the emperor, but of which particular emperor we are not informed. We know that the Emperor *K'ang-hsi* had two series of pictures painted to illustrate the different processes of rice-cultivation and silk-weaving, which were published, with imperial odes attached, in the thirty-fifth year of his reign (1696), under the title of *Yü chih Kêng chih T'ou*. Each series consists of twenty-three pictures, ending with the worship of the patron deities, and the form resembles that of the *T'ao Yeh T'ou*, the "Illustrations of the Manufacture of Porcelain," which would seem to have been designed after their model. Ordinary albums of pictures of the different processes in the preparation of tea, silk, and porcelain are common enough, but these, which have generally been painted at Canton for foreigners, come under a different category.

There is a beautiful eggshell vase in the collection, shown in Fig. 287, decorated in the delicate enamel colors with gilding of the *Ch'ien-lung* period, which displays in detail the various processes of the cultivation of silk in China. The different steps are exhibited in a succession of scenes with groups of busy women and children represented as gathered either in the interior of houses of elaborate design or in courtyards filled with flowering trees and palms; from the hatching of the tiny eggs, the feeding of the worms in every stage of their growth, in the open baskets ranged on curtained bamboo shelves, with mulberry-leaves, to the winding of the silk from the chrysalides, and the weaving of the spun material in looms of complicated structure. In the first scene a boy is bringing baskets of mulberry-leaves slung from a pole on his shoulder; in the last scene a second is seated at the large hand-loom. A wreath of red and pink roses underneath the upper rim, which is gilded, completes the decorations of the vase.

FIG. 288.—Snuff-bottle; decorated in enamels of the Yung-chêng period.

With regard to the series of twenty illustrations of the manufacture of porcelain, T'ang Ying in his memorial observes that they are not enough to give a complete picture of all the different technical processes, and that still less must an exhaustive account of the ceramic industry be expected in his notes, which are intended only to be descriptive of the illustrations. As far as they go, however, they form a sketch of the art from the hand of a master, which is translated in this chapter as literally as possible, with the addition of a few explanatory notes at the end of each section.

Illustration No. 1 : "Mining for the Stone and Preparation of the Paste."

"In the manufacture of porcelain the body is formed of molded earth. This earth is prepared from stone which must be mined and purified for the purpose. The stone is found in the province of Kiangnan, within the prefecture Hui-chou Fu, at Ch'i-mên-hsien, which is two hundred li distant from the porcelain manufactory. The two mountains called P'ing-li and K'u-k'ou, in this district, both produce the white stone. It is obtained by mining, and when broken exhibits black veins branching like the deer's-horn seaweed. The natives take advantage of the mountain torrents to erect wheels provided with crushers. Having been finely pulverized, it is then purified by washing and levigation, and made up in the form of bricks, which are called *pai-tun* or 'white bricks' (*petuntse*). When the color is uniform, and the texture perfectly fine, it is used for the making of the round pieces and vases of eggshell and of pure white porcelain, and of similar objects decorated in blue.

"Besides this there are several other kinds of earth called Kao-ling, Yü-hung, and Ch'ien-t'an, after their different places of production, which are all situated in the province of Kiangsi, within the bounds of the prefecture Jao-chou Fu. They are dug out and prepared in the same way as the *petuntse*, and can only be used for mixing with this last, or in the making of coarser and thicker ware.

"The picture shows the different processes of mining, of pounding, and of washing, which are comprised in the heading, 'Mining for the stone and preparation of the paste,' and it is not necessary to describe them more fully."

Porcelain consists essentially of two elements—viz., the white clay, or *kaolin*, the unctuous and infusible element, which gives plasticity to the paste, and the feldspathic stone, or *petuntse*, which is fusible at a high temperature, and gives transparency to the porcelain. The feldspathic stone from Ch'i-mên-hsien, alluded to above, has been chemically analyzed by Ebelmen, who describes it as a white rock of slightly grayish tinge, occurring in large fragments, covered with oxide of manganese in dendrites, and having some crystals of quartz imbedded in the mass. It fused completely into a white enamel under the blowpipe. Applied by immersion upon a piece of Sèvres porcelain, and fired in the large furnace, it produced a very fine glaze.

With regard to the other materials used in the preparation of the paste of Chinese porcelain, which varies very widely in composition, their name is legion. Nearer sources of the feldspathic rock have been discovered in Yü-kan-hsien, and at a place called Hsiao-li, not far south of Fou-liang-hsien, specimens of which have also been analyzed. Another kind of compact tough rock, which is pounded in larger mills, yields a yellow material called *huang-tun*, which is used for coarser ware, but is said to be required for the proper development of the colors of certain glazes.

Illustration No. 2: "Washing and Purification of the Paste."

"In porcelain-making the first requisite is that of washing and purifying the materials of the paste, so as to make it of fine homogeneous texture. The presence of stars (i. e., crystals of mica) or of fragments of stone would cause flaws in the porcelain, foreign bodies or loose paste would lead to cracks.

"The method of purifying the paste is to mix the materials with water in large earthenware jars, and to stir the mixture with wooden prongs, so that it remains suspended in the water while the impurities sink to the bottom. The paste is then passed through a fine horse-hair sieve, and next strained through a bag made of a double layer of silk. It is then poured into a series of earthenware jars, from which the water is run off, and the paste is left to become solidified. A wooden box with no bottom having been placed upon a pile composed of several tiers of new bricks, a large cloth of fine cotton is spread inside, and the solidified paste is poured in, wrapped round with the cloth and pressed with more bricks, which absorb all the water. The prepared paste, freed from the superfluous water, is then thrown on to large stone slabs and worked with iron spades until it has become perfectly compact and ductile, and fit for the manufacture of porcelain.

"All the different kinds of paste are prepared in the same way, the various materials having been mixed in definite proportions according to their different properties. The picture contains in detail the various utensils and the different processes of work comprised in this department of preparation of the paste."

Père d'Entrecolles in his letters gives a more detailed account of the washing of the materials of the paste and the proportions of the ingredients. He says that the finest porcelain is made of equal parts of kaolin and petuntse; that the usual proportion is four parts of kaolin to six of petuntse; and that the least amount of kaolin that can be used is one part to three parts of petuntse. The larger proportion of kaolin gives a greater plasticity to the paste, and enables it to be more readily fashioned on the wheel; it also gives strength to the material when fired, so that it will withstand a higher temperature without softening. For this reason the Chinese call it "the bone," while the feldspar, the more fusible ingredient, which gives translucency to the porcelain, is "the flesh." The hard porcelain of Sèvres and of Germany contain a greater proportion of kaolin, and are consequently more aluminous than any Chinese ware. It is found at Sèvres, however, that it was too hard for the proper development, from a decorative point of view, of the colors, and in 1880 MM. Lauth and Vogt began to make a more siliceous porcelain with a calcareous glaze, attempting to imitate as closely as possible Oriental porcelain. This porcelain, which bears the name at Sèvres of *porcelaine nouvelle*, can be ornamented, like that of China, with glazes of single colors, with *flambés*, with decorations under the glaze in colors of the *grand feu*, as well as in the muffle stove with bright and limpid enamels fixed in relief on the surface of the pieces.*

This new porcelain is composed of:

Kaolin	38 parts.
Feldspar.	38 "
Quartz	24 "

It is fired at a temperature of about 1,350° C.; the older hard porcelain at Sèvres is fired at 1,550°; and that of China, according to the recent researches of M. Vogt, at 1,475°.

---

* *La Porcelaine*, par Georges Vogt.

The following table gives the composition of different kinds of porcelain:

Source.	Alumina.	Silica.	Oxide of Iron.	Potash.	Soda.	Lime.	Magnesia.	Authority.
Meissen	35.43	60.0	. . .	2.26	1.55	0.57	. . .	Muller.
Sèvres	34.5	58.0	. . .	3.0	. . .	4.5	. . .	Salvétat.
Vienna (old)	34.2	59.6	0.8	2.0	. . .	1.7	1.4	Laurent.
Sèvres, 1880	32.0	60.75	0.8	3.0	. . .	4.5	. . .	Vogt.
Vienna	31.6	61.5	0.8	2.2	. . .	1.8	1.04	Laurent.
Bayeux	30.0	61.6	1.56	3.26	. . .	3.56	. . .	Salvétat.
Berlin	28.0	66.6	0.7	3.4	. . .	0.3	0.6	A. Laurent.
Foëcy (Berry) . . .	28.0	66.2	0.7	5.1	. . .	. . .	. . .	Salvétat.
Limoges	24.0	70.2	0.7	4.3	. . .	0.7	0.1	Salvétat.
Sèvres, *pâte nouvelle* .	22.6	70.83	. . .	2.32	2.09	1.1	0.46	Vogt.
Paris	22.0	71.2	0.8	4.5	. . .	0.8	. . .	Laurent.
China	22.2	70.0	1.3	3.6	2.7	0.8	. . .	Salvétat.
Bohemia	21.3	74.78	. . .	2.48	0.58	0.64	. . .	Muller.
Japan	20.55	70.77	. . .	3.99	3.16	0.83	0.18	Vogt.
China	20.7	70.5	0.8	. . .	3.9	0.5	0.1	Salvétat.
China	19.3	73.3	2.0	2.5	2.3	0.6	. . .	Salvétat.
Nymphenburg . . .	18.4	72.8	2.5	0.65	1.84	3.3	0.3	Vielguth.

Illustration No. 3: "Burning the Ashes and preparing the Glaze."

"All kinds of porcelain require glaze, and the composition used for glazing can not be prepared without ashes. The ashes for the glaze come from Lo-p'ing-hsien, which is one hundred and forty li to the south of Ching-tê-chên. They are made by burning a gray-colored limestone with ferns piled in alternate layers; the residue, after it has been washed thoroughly with water, forms the ashes for the glaze. The finest kind of petuntse made into a paste with water is added to the liquid glaze ashes, and mixed to form a kind of *purée*, the proportions being varied according to the class of porcelain. Within the large jar, in which the mixture is made, is placed a little iron pot, through the two handles of which a curved stick is passed, to make a ladle for measuring the ingredients. This is called a *p'ên*. For example, ten measures of petuntse paste and one measure of ashes form the glaze for the highest class of porcelain. Seven or eight ladles of paste and two or three ladles of ashes form the glaze for the middle class. If the paste and ashes are mixed in equal proportions, or if the ashes are more than the paste, the glaze is only fit for coarse ware.

"In the picture the little iron pot which is seen floating inside the large jar is the *p'ên*, or 'measure.'"

Specimens of rock from Lo-p'ing-hsien were sent to France by Père Ly, the Chinese Lazarist priest, and examined by M. Salvétat, who describes it as a compact limestone lightly colored by pyrites disseminated throughout the mass. The ashes left after repeated combustion of this rock with ferns are composed mainly of lime, the action of which is to increase the fusibility of the petuntse, the vitrifiable feldspathic rock which gives its peculiar properties to the glaze. This rock is the same that is used in the composition of the porcelain body; only the best pieces are picked out for the glaze, those of uniform greenish tone, which are covered with dendrites in the form of arbor-vitæ leaves. The Chinese call this *Yu-kuo*, "glaze fruit"—i. e., essence of the glaze. A specimen analyzed by Salvétat had the following composition:

Fig. 289. — Snuff-bottle; royal blue double gourd.

Water	2.3
Silica	75.9
Alumina	14.2
Oxide of iron	0.8
Lime	0.5
Oxide of manganese	0.3
Magnesia	a trace
Potash	2.8
Soda	3.2

The analysis of two actual glazes chipped off from pieces of Chinese porcelain by the same authority gave:

Silica	68.0	64.1
Alumina	12.0	10.2
Oxide of iron . . .	a trace	a trace
Lime	14.0	21.0
Potash and soda . . .	6.0	5.1

The glaze of Chinese porcelain is always rich in lime. It is the lime that gives the characteristic tinge of green or blue, but at the same time produces a brilliancy of surface and translucent depth never found in the harder glazes which contain no lime. The glaze of the *nouvelle porcelaine* of Sèvres is prepared with thirty-three per cent of chalk.

Illustration No. 4: "MANUFACTURE OF THE CASES OR SEGGARS."

"The porcelain while being fired in the furnace must be kept perfectly clean; a single spot of dirt makes a colored stain. Moreover, the blast of air and fierce flames of the furnace would injure the delicate paste. For these reasons it is necessary to place the porcelain inside the seggars. The clay used in making these cases comes from the village of Li-ch'un, which is on the northeast of Ching-tê-chên. It is of three different colors—black, red, and white. A kind of blackish-yellow sand, which is found at Pao-shih-shan, is mixed with the clay to form the paste, so that it may be more readily fired. The cases are fashioned on a wheel, which is similar to the wheel used for porcelain. The paste need not be finely levigated. After the cases have been partially dried they are roughly finished off with the knife, put into the furnace, and fired for the first time empty. When baked and ready for use, they are called by the name of *tu-hsia,* or 'finished cases.'

"The workmen who manufacture the seggars are accustomed with the same coarse paste to make, on the same wheel, a supply of earthenware bowls for the daily use of the potters in their native hamlets."

The seggars are made of a common yellow ferruginous clay, which darkens to a brick-red tint when fired. They are in the form of circular trays about six inches high, fitting one upon the other, so as to form the columns seven feet in height, which are ranged inside the large furnace. Intervals to allow free play of the flames are left between the piles. The lower cases, which are partially imbedded in the gravel floor of the furnace, are left empty. The bottom of each tray forms the cover of the case below, only the top case having a cover of its own. If the pieces of porcelain are too high for the case, one or more circular rings of the same size as the trays are substituted, by which means the height of the seggar can be increased indefinitely. In early times, as we saw in the descriptions of the *Ming* dynasty, they had special kilns for firing the seggars; now they are fired empty, together with the older cases which are charged with porcelain in the usual way, the new ones being placed in the middle of the columns. A supply of flat disks (*rondeaux*) made of biscuit porcelain, or of fire-clay, is provided as supports for the pieces of porcelain, which are prevented from adhering to the disks by dusting them over with kaolin.

Illustration No. 5: "PREPARATION OF THE MOLDS FOR THE ROUND WARE."

"In the manufacture of the round ware each several piece has to be repeated hundreds or thousands of times: without molds it would be most difficult to make the pieces all exactly alike. The molds must be made in accordance with the original design, but the size can not be so precisely measured; they must be larger than the model, otherwise the piece will come out smaller than the pattern. The raw paste, which is expanded and loose in texture, becomes during the process of firing contracted and solidified to about seven or eight tenths of its original size, a result following from the natural laws of physics. The proper proportionate size of the unbaked piece is fixed by the mold, and therefore the molders use the term 'prepare' (*hsiu*) instead of 'make' (*tsao*). Each piece must have several molds prepared, and the size and pattern of the contents when taken out of the kiln must be exactly alike. A good practical knowledge of the length of firing required and of the natural properties of the paste is necessary before it is possible to estimate the exact amount of shrinkage, so as to fashion the molds of the proper form. In the whole district of Ching-tê-chên there are only three or four workmen reputed clever at this special handiwork."

The term "round ware," or *yuan-ch'i,* is a general term applied by Chinese potters to all the different kinds of porcelain articles in ordinary use, such as dishes (*p'an*), bowls (*wan*), cups (*chung*), and platters (*tieh*). They are first "thrown" on the wheel, the wheels being of two sizes, managed by different classes of workmen. After having been fashioned on the wheel, they are given to the molders to be pressed in the molds referred to above, which are of rounded form externally, and are composed of two parts, the outside of the piece being molded in the one, and the interior by the other, which is called technically the "core." The use of the mold by Chinese potters can be traced back to very early times. The *K'ao kung chi*, a technical work of the *Chou* dynasty (B. C. 1122–249), which has been already referred to, distinguishes the ordinary potters (*T'ao jên*), who worked with the wheel, from the molders (*Fang jên*), who made the round, tazza-shaped sacrificial dishes called *tou* and the oblong bowls for meat offerings called *kuei.* The *Lun Hêng*, a critical book of the *Han* dynasty by Wang Ch'ung, who lived A. D. 19–90, refers to the molds used by potters of that time under the name of *kuei-lien:* "The potters make molds of earth which fix the size of the pieces so that they can not be enlarged or diminished afterward; correct estimates of the sizes required must be made beforehand, as they are changed during baking."

Illustration No. 6: "FASHIONING THE ROUND WARE ON THE WHEEL."

"There are several different processes of work in the manufacture of this round ware. The square, polygonal, and ribbed pieces, and those with projecting corners, have to be carved, engraved, molded, and finished with the polishing knife, all of which are different branches of work. The plain round pieces are turned on the wheel, being distributed according to their size between two classes of workmen. The first take the large pieces and fashion the round dishes (*p'an*), the bowls (*wan*), the cups (*chung*), and the saucer-plates (*tieh*), from one up to two or three feet in diameter; the second make on the wheel the same kind of pieces which measure less than a foot across. The wheel consists of a disk of wood mounted below upon a perpendicular axle, so as to revolve continuously for a long time, during which the piece must be properly turned, without becoming too thick, too thin, flattened, or otherwise misshapen. There is a carpenter at hand to repair it when necessary.

"Beside the wheel is an attendant workman, who kneads the paste to a proper consistence and puts it on the table. The potter sits upon the border of the framework and turns the wheel with a bamboo staff. While the wheel is spinning round he works the paste with both hands; it follows the hands, lengthening or shortening, contracting or widening, in a succession of shapes. It is in this way that the round ware is fashioned so that it varies not a hair's breadth in size."

The potter's wheel is one of the most ancient instruments of human industry, and the date of its invention is lost in the mists of time. The simplest form is that described above, which is kept in motion by the feet of the workman as he fashions the piece of porcelain with his hands. Just as simple a form is still in use at many manufactories—at Sèvres, for example. In most large factories, however, the wheel is of more elaborate construction, and it is kept in motion by some mechanical means, so that the potter is relieved of a portion of the work. Even in China, as we see in pictures, an assistant is often there, rotating the wheel with a rope passed round it, the ends of which he holds in his hand, or balancing himself by a rope attached to the ceiling while he turns the wheel with his foot. This is the "throwing wheel" by which the soft white clay is fashioned, with the half of the fingers only, into a shape roughly approximating that desired; it is on the polishing wheel, or "jigger," that it is finally "turned" to the exact shape of the model or design.

When the thrower has a piece to fashion on the wheel, he first places on the top a flat disk, which he puts in the middle and moistens with water, and then upon this disk he places the quantity of paste necessary to form the piece, dips his hand into diluted paste or "slip," and puts the apparatus in motion with his feet; then, pressing between his hands the shapeless lump of paste, he raises it, lowers it, makes it into a kind of large lentil, and pierces the lenticular mass with his two thumbs; he lifts it up once more while squeezing the lump between his thumb and fingers into the shape desired. He develops it gradually, keeping it moist all the time with slip, and brings it by degrees to a form which approaches, more or less, that of the perfect piece. The smaller objects are shaped between the thumb and index finger, either of one hand or of both hands. Larger pieces are made by being pressed between the hand and wrist or with the help of a pad or sponge. The workman in this case usually stands, and the size of the pieces that he can make is limited by the length of his arms. If this limit has to be exceeded, he must build up the borders of the cylinder, previously thrown on the wheel, with bits of paste stuck on with slip. The pieces with no mouths and those with very narrow necks are thrown in two halves, which are cemented together with slip.

The precautions to be taken to secure a good result, according to Brongniart, are: 1. The paste must not be too soft; it will be easier to throw, but at the risk of some defect. 2. The workman must have a sure hand and not press unequally on any part of the piece that he is lifting into shape. 3. And specially, it is important that he maintain a perfect accord between the speed of rotation of his wheel and the rate of ascent of his hands, so as to describe a spiral, cylindrical, or conical, in which the steps are the smallest possible. The more plastic and kaolinic the paste the more difficult it is to throw it successfully—not that this paste is harder to throw than a *short* paste, but because any inequalities of molding and pressure are so much more apparent in this than in a thinner paste. The principal defect of a bad throw is 'screwing' (*vissage*). This defect consists of grooves, more or less apparent after firing, which start from the base and rise in spirals like the thread of a screw. These grooves are due to inequalities of the pressure exerted while the piece is in the hands of the workman. If the paste be less plastic, less supple, the pieces to be turned subsequently must be so much the thicker; generally speaking, the thickness of pieces of hard porcelain as they come from the throwing wheel is so great that one can hardly at first sight recognize the form that will be ultimately evolved on the jigger, the turning wheel proper.

Illustration No. 7 : " Manufacture of Vases (*Cho ch'i*)."

"The vases and sacrificial vessels, called *p'ing*, *lei*, *tsun*, and *yi*, are comprised in this general name of *cho c'hi*. The plain round vases are fashioned upon the potter's wheel, in the same manner as the ordinary round ware; they are then dried in the open air and turned on the polishing wheel to be finished with the knife. After the vase has been thus shaped it is washed with a large goat's-hair brush dipped in water, till the surface is perfectly bright and spotlessly clean. After this the glaze is blown on, it is fired in the kiln, and comes out a piece of white porcelain. If painted in cobalt on the paste and then covered with glaze, it is a piece decorated in blue.

"In making the carved polygonal, ribbed, and fluted vases, the paste, wrapped in cotton cloth, is pressed with flat boards into thin slabs, which are cut with a knife into sections. The pieces are joined together by a cement (*barbotine* or slip) made of some of the original paste with water. There is another kind of vase which is made by the process of molding, and which is finished after it is taken from the mold in the same way. The carved polygonal vases and the carved molded vases have to be filled in and washed clean with the brush in the same way as the round vases turned upon the wheel.

"All the varied forms of vases may be engraved with the style, or embossed in relief, or carved in openwork designs, for which purposes, when sufficiently dried, they are given to artificers specially devoted to these several branches of work."

The character *cho*, which means properly "carved jade," is applied in Chinese ceramics to vases generally, which are called *cho ch'i*, in contradistinction to the *yuan ch'i*, or "round pieces," which include the bowls, cups, plates, etc., intended for ordinary use. The *p'ing* was originally a bottle-shaped vase, in which the mouth was less in diameter than the body, but the term is now applied to all kinds of ornamental vases; the *lei* are sacrificial vases with scrolled grounds; the *tsun* are the vases with flaring mouths that we call beaker-shaped, and the *yi* the modern incense urns; the former are modeled after ancient bronze wine-vessels, the latter after the bronze bowls used in olden times for sacrificial offerings of food and corn.

The round (*yuan*) vases are turned upon the wheel, the square (*fang*) vases are made of sections of paste, pressed or molded in various ways, and cemented together by slip. The author of the *Shih wu kan chu*, a miscellany published in 1591, says: "In the manufacture of porcelain it is the square pieces that are the most difficult. They are so difficult because when taken out of the kiln they are so often misshapen or cracked and rarely free from some defect. During their making the corners have to be evenly carved, the fluted parts have to be scooped out with the knife, and the lines of junction of the sections have to be closely cemented; in some unseen corner there may be a want of cohesion, or some slight irregularity, either above or below, in front or behind, to the right or left. Hence the common saying that the square is difficult. The round vases are made at one operation, and follow the movements of the hands, while the wheel does more than half the man's work; not like the square and ribbed vases, which depend wholly upon the manual skill of the artisan."

The different branches of work alluded to above are more fully described in the letters of Père d'Entrecolles, translated in Chapter XI.

Illustration No. 8: "COLLECTION OF THE MATERIAL FOR THE BLUE COLOR."

"All kinds of porcelain, whether round ware or vases, that have to be decorated in blue, whether modeled after that of the reigns of *Hsüan-tê, Ch'êng-hua, Chia-ching*, or *Wan-li*, require this blue color for the painting of their decoration. The deep blue monochrome glaze, *gros bleu*, also requires this blue for its preparation. The material comes from the province of Chekiang, where it is found in several mountains within the prefectures Shao-hsing Fu and Chin-hua Fu. The collectors who go into the hills to dig for it wash away the earth which adheres to it in the water of the mountain streams. The mineral is dark brown in color. The large round pieces furnish the best blue and are called 'best rounds,' distinguished in addition by the name of the place of production. It is brought by merchants to the porcelain manufactory, and is buried by them under the floor of the furnace, roasted for three days, and washed after it is taken out, before it is finally offered for sale, ready for use. The material is also found in different mountains in the provinces of Kiangsi and Kuangtung, but the color produced by these kinds is comparatively pale and thin, and it is unable to support the fire, so that they can be used only in painting coarse ware for sale in the market.

"The picture exhibits only the collection of the material: the processes of preparation and of roasting are not shown."

Blue is the leading decorative color on porcelain, as the learned author of the *T'ao shuo* observes. In the *Chin* dynasty (265–419) blue porcelain was called *p'iao tzŭ*, resembling in color the pale blue shade (*p'iao*) of certain silks. In the *T'ang* dynasty (618–906) it was called the blue color of distant hills; in the *Chou* dynasty (951–960) the blue of the sky after rain; under the *Wu Yueh* the prohibited color, because it was reserved for the sovereign; afterward, under the *Sung* dynasty (960–1279), although other colors were also used, the *Ju-chou* porcelain was baked with a pale blue glaze; the finest imperial porcelain of the time was starch-blue (*fên-ch'ing*), and the crackled Ko yao and the ordinary Lung-ch'üan porcelain of the time were also of bluish shade.

Abundant specimens of the Chinese mineral have reached Europe. Ebelmen, in his book so often quoted (vol. i, page 385), says that he had specimens of the mineral as it comes from the mine, of the same after it had been roasted in closely luted porcelain crucibles placed under the floor of the furnace, and of the powder produced by grinding the roasted material in mortars. The raw mineral had the form of irregular concretions hollow in the interior, of a deep brown color with a slight shade of green, giving a brownish powder which stained the fingers. Heated in a closed tube it gave off twenty per cent of water, and after prolonged calcination acquired a more pronounced greenish shade. It proved to be a complex mineral of cobaltiferous manganese in the form of oxides, which did not, however, constitute all the mass of the fragments, being associated with a variable quantity, up to nearly half the weight, of silicate of alumina.

The analysis of two specimens gave the following result:

	Raw mineral.	Roasted mineral.
Loss in the fire (water and oxygen)	20.00	4.00
Silica (insoluble residue)	37.46	27.00
Oxide of copper	0.44	2.00
Alumina	4.75	
Oxide of manganese	27.50	65.00
Oxide of cobalt	5.50	
Oxide of iron	1.65	
Lime	0.60	1.00
Magnesia	a trace	a trace
Arsenious acid	a trace	1.00
Oxide of nickel, sulphur	a trace	
	97.90	100.00

The complex structure of the mineral explains the minute precautions taken by the Chinese in selecting the best pieces, and also the infinite variety in the shades of blue obtained after firing. The larger the proportion of cobalt the purer the blue; a blackish or grayish tint is said to be due to an excess of nickel or iron, a purplish to an excess of manganese. The vigor of the color is due, however, as much to the limpid purity of the white glaze which it has to penetrate, being painted, as it always is, on the raw body of the porcelain. Penciled *sur biscuit* upon Sèvres porcelain, glazed, and fired *au grand feu*, the thinner strokes came out blue, but the deeper parts were sensibly grayish. Its fugitive nature caused the loss of much of the color, as it was fired at a temperature so much higher than that of the Chinese furnace.

Illustration No. 9: "Selection of the Blue Material."

"The blue material, after it has been roasted, must be specially selected, and there is a particular class of workmen whose duty it is to attend to this. The superior kind selected is that which is dark green in color, of rich translucent tint and brilliant aspect. This is used in the imitation of antiques, for the monochrome blue glaze, and for fine porcelain painted in blue. When of the same dark-green color, but wanting somewhat in richness and luster, it is used for the decoration of the coarser porcelain made for sale. The remainder, that has neither luster nor color, is picked out and thrown away.

"When the material has been selected it is ready for use. The method employed is to paint with it upon the piece that has not been fired, to invest the piece afterward with glaze, and then to fire it in the furnace, from which it comes out with the color uniformly transformed into a brilliant blue. If it has not been invested with glaze the color will be black. Should the piece be overfired, the blue of the painted decoration will "run" into the white ground of the piece.

"There is one kind of blue, commonly called 'onion sprouts,' which makes very clearly defined strokes which do not change in the furnace, and this must be selected for fine painting.

"The picture shows baskets filled with boxes of the color, with an ordinary background; there is no actual reference in it to the selection of the color."

The cobaltiferous manganese mineral, which is collected from the hills, where it occurs either on the surface of the ground or at the depth of a few feet, is of very uncertain composition. One portion of the same concretionary piece may be rich in cobalt, while another is quite inert, consisting of silicate of alumina with perhaps a few crystals of quartz. The pieces are generally about the size of the thumb and flattened in shape, and are known commonly by the name of *shih-tzŭ ch'ing*—i. e., "stone-blue," or "mineral-blue." But the material figures in books under a multitude of synonyms. In the *Sung* dynasty* it was imported from western Asia under the name of *Wu ming yi*—i. e., "nameless rarity"—and there are several specimens of the Chinese mineral under this name in the *Musée d'Histoire Naturelle* at Paris, which were examined by Brongniart. Other names are *T'ao ch'ing*, "ceramic blue"; *Ta ch'ing*, "gros bleu"; *Fo-t'ou ch'ing*, "Buddha's-head blue"; *Pao-shih-lan*, "sapphire-blue," and a number of other names, with the place of production prefixed; the only difficulty of which is the way they are contracted—*chê liao*, literally "*chê* material," being the form usually found in Chinese books for *chêkiang ch'ing liao*, or "blue material of Chêkiang," the province from which the best is obtained. A name which puzzled me for a long time was *Hun-shui ch'ing*, "turbid-water blue," till I found that it referred to the *purée* prepared by mixing a little of the first-class blue with water that had been employed for painting the ground of a piece with the decoration reserved in white, like the celebrated "hawthorn ginger-pots," with their brilliant mottled grounds of pulsating blue, of which one is so beautifully illustrated in Plate II.

The same mineral is employed in the preparation of the black glazes, for which purpose it need not be so good—that is to say, so rich in cobalt, according to the Chinese. Sometimes the decoration of what was intended to be a blue and white piece will come out of the kiln perfectly black, because the glaze was laid on too thin.

Illustration No. 10: "Molding the Porcelain and Grinding the Color."

"After the large and small round pieces have been shaped on the wheel, and have been sufficiently dried in the air, they are put into the molds which have been previously prepared, and are pressed gently with the hands, until the paste becomes of regular form and uniform thickness. The piece is then taken out and dried in a shady place

---

* Cf. *Chinese Porcelain before the Present Dynasty*, by S. W. Bushell (page 52).

till it is ready to be shaped with the polishing knives. The damp paste must not be exposed to the sun, as the heat would crack it.

"With regard to the preparation of the color for the artists, it must be ground perfectly fine in a mortar; if coarse, spots of bad color will appear. Ten ounces of the material are put into each mortar, and it is ground by a special class of workmen for a whole month before it is fit to be used. The mortars used for grinding it are placed upon low benches, and at the sides of the benches are two upright wooden poles supporting cross-pieces of wood, which are pierced to hold the handles of the pestles. The men, seated upon the benches, take hold of the pestles and keep them revolving. Their monthly wage is only three-tenths of an ounce of silver. Some of them grind two mortars, working with both hands. Those who work till midnight are paid double wages. Aged men and young children, as well as the lame and sick, get a living by this work."

The color referred to above is still the cobalt-blue, the predominating color of old Chinese porcelain. The Chinese owe their success in the ceramic art in great measure to their careful and methodical preparation of the materials. Imagine the patience of a man sitting on a bench, as described here, for a whole month, with a pestle in each hand, grinding the same color all the time, and satisfied with monthly wages of less than half a dollar; with the addition, however, it is to be hoped, of an allowance of food! The editor of the official records of the imperial manufactory says that two of the chief criteria of success are perfect dryness and fineness of all the materials: "The furnace must be dry, the porcelain must be dry, and the fuel must be dry; then there will be little breakage, loss of shape, or dullness of color. The clay must be fine, the color must be fine, and the work of the artist must be fine; then the defects of coarse, rough finish, of spoiled coloring, and of stains will be avoided."

Oxide of cobalt is one of the most ancient and widely known of the coloring matters used in the decoration of all kinds of pottery. As M. Deck says in *La Faïence* (*loc. cit.*, page 185): "The beautiful blue color of the oxide of cobalt is persistent at the highest temperature of the porcelain furnace; its coloring power is so strong that the least trace is enough to color the vitreous flux. It has an immense vogue, and is the color most frequently used in ceramic decoration, both in ancient and modern times. It has the great advantage of accommodating itself to all fires, from the most violent to the most feeble. It combines and harmonizes with every kind of medium (*fondant*), and can be applied to all sorts of ceramic bodies, and its blue color is one of the most beautiful and the most solid in our palette. The Egyptians and Assyrians employed it from the highest antiquity; the Persians, Chinese, and Japanese have executed charming decorations with nothing but this blue; it is perhaps the most suitable color to be employed alone in decoration."

Illustration No. 11 : "Painting the Round Ware in Blue."

"The different kinds of round ware painted in blue are each numbered by the hundred and thousand, and if the painted decoration upon every piece be not exactly alike, the set will be irregular and spoiled. For this reason the men who sketch the outlines learn sketching, but not painting; those who paint study only painting, not sketching; by this means their hands acquire skill in their own particular branch of work, and their minds are not distracted. In order to secure a certain uniformity in their work, the sketchers and painters, although kept distinct, occupy the same house.

"As to the other branches of work—embossing, engraving, and carving in openwork—they are treated in the same way, and each is intrusted to its own special workmen. The branch of decorating in underglaze red, although really distinct, is allied to that of painting. With regard to the rings round the borders of the pieces and the encircling blue bands, these are executed by the workmen who finish the pieces on the polishing wheel; while the marks on the foot underneath, and the written inscriptions, are the work of the writers who attach the seals.

"For painting flowers and birds, fishes and water-plants, and living objects generally, the study of Nature is the first requisite; in the imitation of *Ming* dynasty porcelain and of ancient pieces, the sight of many specimens brings skill. The art of painting in blue differs widely from that of decoration in enamel colors."

In this rapid sketch of the art of painting in underglaze cobalt-blue most of the different processes of decoration displayed in collections of Chinese blue and white porcelain are touched upon. The blue is painted upon the white body of the porcelain before it is glazed by immersion or otherwise, and the encircling rings which define the borders of bowls and the shoulders of vases are easily penciled by a light touch of the brush as the object revolves on the jigger; by no other method could they be executed with such perfect regularity. A single line of blue of this kind round the rim is the sole decoration of some of the translucently white eggshell wine-cups of the reign of *Wan-li*, which are among the lightest and most delicate objects ever produced in porcelain. The work of the writer, who outlines the seals and other marks and writes the labels and verses that accompany the pictures, is quite as important as that of the artist, in the estimation of the Chinese, who are great connoisseurs of caligraphy, and distinguish at first sight, from that one criterion, a piece of imperial manufacture (*kuan yao*) from the production of a private kiln (*ssŭ yao*).

Painted decoration in copper-red under the glaze properly finds its place here. The technique is the same, and the pieces, after they have been glazed, are fired in the same furnace as the blue and white. For an illustration, see Fig. 229. It may, of course, be used in combination with the blue in the decoration of the same vase, or with other colors of the *grand feu*, such as celadon, or coffee-brown.

Illustration No. 12: "Fashioning and Painting of Vases."

"The different forms of vases and sacrificial vessels comprised in the general term of *cho ch'i* include the square, the round, the ribbed, and those with prominent angles; there are various styles of decoration executed by painting in colors and carving in openwork. In copies from antiquity artistic models must be followed; in novelty of invention there is a deep spring to draw from. In the decoration of porcelain correct canons of art should be followed; the design should be taken from the patterns of old brocades and embroidery, the colors from a garden as seen in springtime from a pavilion. There is an abundance of specimens of the *Kuan, Ko, Ju, Ting*, and *Chün* (wares of the *Sung* dynasty) at hand to be copied; and water, fire, wood, metal, and earth (the five elements of physics) supply an inexhaustible fund of materials for new combinations of supernatural beauty. Natural objects are modeled, to be fashioned in molds, and painted in appropriate colors; the materials of the potter's art are derived from forests and streams, and ornamental themes are supplied by the same natural sources. The sacrificial wine-vessels, *tsun* and *lei*, are of equal importance; the censers, shaped like the ancient bronzes, *yi* and *ting*, emit flames of brilliant color. In addition to the ancient earthenware drums (*wa fou*), many kinds of musical pipes are now made, and the artistic skill of the color-brush perpetuates on porcelain clever works of genius."

In this paragraph T'ang Ying, instead of describing the illustration, gives a disquisition upon his view of the correct canons of art, as applied to the decoration of porcelain, expressed in high-flown antithetical couplets, which are not so easy to render intelligibly in plain prose. Julien suppresses them altogether as "devoid of interest from the point of view of history and of fabrication," but they give us some insight into the ideas of a Chinese artist and the motives of his decorative work. Antiquity is always the first desideratum; the forms of the objects are taken from productions of the old ceramic factories of the *Sung* dynasty, which were themselves derived from more ancient bronzes; and the decorative designs are often derived from the patterns woven in China from the most ancient times in brocades or worked by the needle in silk embroideries. The prevalence of colored grounds, of medallions, and of all the varieties of diaper, in the decoration of Chinese porcelain, is traced back to the occurrence of similar patterns in these brocaded and embroidered silks.*

Illustration No. 13: "Dipping into the Glaze and Blowing on the Glaze."

"All the different kinds of round ware and vases, including the pieces decorated in blue, as well as the copies of Kuan, Ko, and Ju porcelain, must have the glaze applied before they are fired. The ancient method of putting on the glaze was to apply it to the surface of the vase, whether square, tall, fluted, or ribbed, with a goat's-hair brush filled with the liquid glaze, but it was difficult to distribute it evenly in this way. The round ware, both large and small, and the plain round vases and sacrificial vessels used all to be dipped into the large jar which held the glaze, but they failed by being either too thickly or too thinly covered, and, besides, so many were broken that it was difficult to produce perfect specimens.

"In the present day the small round pieces are still dipped into the large jar of glaze liquid, but the vases and sacrificial vessels and the larger round pieces are glazed by the *soufflé* process. A bamboo tube one inch in diameter and some seven inches long has one of its ends bound round with a fine gauze, which is dipped repeatedly into the glaze and blown through from the other end. The number of times that this process has to be repeated depends partly on the size of the piece, partly on the nature of the glaze, varying from three or four times up to seventeen or eighteen. These are the two distinct methods of glazing: by immersion and by insufflation."

* The names of more than twenty of these brocade patterns that were copied in *Ming* porcelain were enumerated in Chapter VII.

The glaze contains a notable proportion of lime, which aids in the liquefaction of the feldspathic base, and gives the slight greenish tinge to the ground, which is one of the characteristics of Chinese porcelain. It is applied in China upon the raw body of the piece, which has been previously dried in the open air. In other countries the unglazed ware undergoes a preliminary baking to bring it to the condition called *dégourdi,* so that even the largest pieces may be strengthened sufficiently to enable them to be dipped in the water holding the materials of the glaze in suspension. The porous clay absorbs the water, and there is deposited on the surface a uniform layer of the vitrifiable materials suspended in it. Large vases five feet in height are glazed in this way at Sèvres, being placed in open wooden cages and lowered by means of pulleys; they are immersed for thirty or forty seconds, according to the greater or less strength of the preliminary baking, and are then allowed to drain, after which any difference of thickness is corrected as much as possible by hand.

The French consul, M. Scherzer, fully describes the Chinese method of glazing by sprinkling: "Having brought the finely pulverized materials to the consistence of a liquid *bouillie* by mixing them with pure water, the workman takes a tube of bamboo which he covers at one end with fine gauze and dips it into the glaze, which he projects upon the vase by blowing through the opposite end. The number of layers that the workman sprinkles in this way depends upon the nature of the glaze. For the white, three layers are applied successively by blowing, while the fourth and last layer is given with a very soft brush. For the colored glazes the operation is more complicated and comprises nine successive layers; the first three are applied by blowing the glaze upon the piece properly dried, sufficient time being left between each to acquire its original dry condition. The fourth layer is painted on with a very soft brush. The fifth, sixth, and seventh layers are given by blowing. Finally, the eighth and ninth are applied with the brush."

FIG. 290. — Snuff-bottle; blue and white flower-design on brown crackled ground.

M. Vogt says that the qualities required for a perfect glaze are so numerous that its preparation is unquestionably one of the most delicate operations of the ceramic art. A good glaze ought, during firing, to spread uniformly over the piece that is being enameled, without forming either of the defects of "shrinkage" or "bubbling." Its fusibility ought to be adapted to the degree of temperature required for the firing of the paste. If too fusible, it will penetrate the paste, and the glazing will be dull and dry; if too hard to melt, it will be covered all over with little holes, which give to the porcelain the peculiar appearance that is called technically *coque d'œuf.* There must, besides, be a perfect agreement in the coefficient of dilatation between the paste and the glaze. If not, as the porcelain cools the glaze will break, and its surface will be soon furrowed by a network of lines. This crackled condition, which is called technically *tressaillure,* is due solely to a physical cause; it is the result of a difference of dilatation between the paste and the glaze, as the piece is returning to the surrounding temperature. The crackles are started when the glaze, as it is cooling, contracts more than the paste; being fixed to the paste, it must necessarily crack, and the space between the lips of the furrows indicates the difference of contractibility. In the inverse case — that is to say, when the paste contracts more than the glaze — the glaze may be detached in splinters and "scale off"; a piece with this defect is irretrievably lost. It is not so with the defect called *tressaillure.* A perfect master of paste and glazes can produce at will fissures in the glaze, forming more or less close networks, composed of lines joining together with no long straight lines between; in this case a defect is converted into a good quality, and we have the *craquelé* or *truité.* The Chinese make such good use of this quality as to be able to produce on the same piece crackled zones of different dimensions in the midst of uncracked glazes.

The conditions that change the coefficient of dilatation in porcelain are not well ascertained; it is known, however, that alkalies increase it in the glaze, and that silica increases it in the paste. A paste rich in alumina, invested with a non-calcareous glaze, always tends to become crackled, according to M. Vogt. This is confirmed by Chinese accounts. The Ting Yao, the so-called "soft porcelain" of collectors, which is so apt to become crackled, is characterized by a highly kaolinic paste, and the glaze is prepared without lime. The milk of lime, which is an important ingredient of the ordinary Chinese glaze, is replaced in the crackled glazes by a *purée* composed principally of steatite previously ground to a fine powder. Any of the ordinary colored glazes may be crackled by adding this last to their ordinary ingredients. Some glazes are always crackled, without requiring the addition of anything to their ordinary ingredients, like the turquoise and aubergine purple, single colors of the *demi-grand feu*, which are both of *truité* texture; the turquoise glaze is rich in alkali, being prepared with a niter flux, and the aubergine glaze is combined with a minimum amount of lead.

Many of the curious ceramic terms met with in old Chinese books are due to alterations of the glaze during firing, such as "palm-eye" spots, the effect of bubbles, "crab's-claw" and "chicken's-claw" veining in the substance of the unctuous glaze, and "orange-peel" texture of its undulatory surface. These partake really of the nature of small flaws, a recent Chinese writer remarks, and are only particularly noticed as criteria of genuine productions of an early time, when the porcelain was not so perfectly glazed as it is in the present day.

Illustration No. 14: "Turning the Unbaked Ware and Scooping out the Foot."

"The size of the round piece has been fixed in the mold, but the smooth polish of the surface depends on the polisher, whose province is another branch of work, that of 'turning.' He uses in his work the polishing wheel, which in form is like the ordinary potter's wheel, only it has projecting upward in the middle a wooden mandrel, the size of which varies, being proportioned to that of the porcelain which is about to be turned. The top of this mandrel, which is rounded, is wrapped in raw silk to protect the interior of the piece from injury. The piece about to be turned is put upon the mandrel, the wheel is spun round, and it is pared with the knife till both the inside and outside are given the same perfectly smooth polish. The coarser or finer finish of the form depends upon the inferior or superior handiwork of the polisher, whose work is consequently of great importance.

"With regard to the next process, that of scooping out the foot, it is necessary, because each piece, when first fashioned upon the potter's wheel, has a paste handle left under the foot two or three inches long, by which it is held while it is being painted and the glaze blown on. It is only after the glazing and the painting of the decoration are finished that this handle is removed by the polisher, who at the same time scoops out the foot, after which the mark is written underneath.

"In the picture the workmen are seen occupied in the two processes of polishing the surface and scooping out the foot."

To prepare the porcelain for the polishing wheel or "jigger," it has to be dried sufficiently to enable it to be shaved with the knife without being reduced to powder. The tools used by the Chinese workmen are of the simplest kind—thin iron plaques of rectangular or curved outline. The piece is mounted upon the mandrel, so that its axis is a prolongation of the axle-tree of the apparatus, and it is shaved down to the required thickness while the wheel is revolving. Encircling bands or fillets that have to be executed in relief, and rings defining the shoulder or borders of the vase, are carved at the same time with a neatness and regularity that no other process could attain.

The removal of the shapeless lump of clay which has been left projecting underneath the foot is one of the last operations in the fabrication of the piece; the mark is penciled in blue, the glaze is applied over it, and the piece is ready for the furnace. The rim round the edge of the foot is left uncovered with glaze, and exhibits the peculiar character of the paste to the eye of a connoisseur. In older specimens no glaze is applied to the foot, and a portion even of the outside of the bowl or cup is left unglazed, the glaze running down in thick, unctuous masses so as only partially to cover the surface, stopping short in a wavy line of thick drops. During the *Ming* dynasty there were some characteristic differences in the feet of bowls which may be noted in this connection. The shallow spreading eggshell bowls of the reign of *Yung-lo* have a sandlike rim and smoothly glazed bottom; the altar-cups of the reign of *Hsüan-tê* have a conical projection in the middle with a threadlike rim at the edge; the shallow cups painted with fish, of the reign of *Chia-ching*, have a circularly rimmed base with a loaflike prominence inside the bowl. In the present dynasty, too, the foot of the vase is often examined as an aid to the determination of its date, the presence or absence of glaze, its plain or crackled texture, and its particular shade of color affording a valuable criterion for that purpose in different cases.

Illustration No. 15: "Putting the Finished Ware into the Kiln."

"The kiln is long and round, and resembles in shape a tall water-jar (*wêng*) turned over on its side. It measures a little over ten feet in height and breadth, about twice as much in depth. It is covered with a large, tiled building which is called the 'kiln-shed.' The chimney, which is tubular, rises to a height of over twenty feet behind, outside the kiln-shed.

"The porcelain, when finished, is packed in the seggars and sent out to the furnace men. When these men put it in the kiln they arrange the seggars in piles, one above the other, in separate rows, so as to leave an interspace between the rows for the free passage of the flames. The fire is distinguished as front, middle, and back; the front of the fire is fierce, the middle moderate, the back feeble. The different kinds of porcelain are placed in the furnace according to the hard or soft quality of the glaze with which they are coated. After the kiln has been fully charged the fire is lighted, and the entrance is then bricked up, leaving only a square hole, through which billets of pine wood are thrown in without intermission. When the seggars inside the furnace have attained a silvery red color (white heat) the firing is stopped, and after the lapse of another twenty-four hours the kiln is opened."

The form of the furnace has already been fully described, and the changes in its dimensions from ancient to modern times have been alluded to. It has gradually become larger in size, till in the present day, according to M. Scherzer, although the breadth is about the same as that described above, being three and a half meters, the height and length are increased by about one-half to five meters and ten meters respectively. The way in which the Chinese take advantage of the irregularity of the form and of the varied force of the fire in different parts of the furnace has also been described. During the *Ming* dynasty there were different kinds of furnaces in the imperial manufactory—furnaces for the clay seggars, for the large garden fish-bowls, for the blue and white porcelain, and for the colored glazes, etc. In the present day there are none, with the sole exception of the muffle stoves for the second firing of the porcelain painted in enamel colors. Everything is sent out to be fired in the private kilns, called *Pao Ch'ing Yao*, because they guarantee the success of each firing. There are two classes of kilns at Ching-tê-chên. In the first kind the fuel is pine wood; all the imperial porcelain is sent to these. In the second kind, which are intended for the firing of the commoner and coarser porcelain, the fuel is ordinary brushwood, which is brought in by men from the neighboring hills.

Illustration No. 16: "Opening the Kiln when the Porcelain has been Fired."

"The perfection of the porcelain depends upon the firing, which, reckoning from the time of putting in to that of taking out, usually occupies three days. On the fourth day, early in the morning, the furnace is opened, but the seggars inside, which contain the porcelain, are still of a dull-red color, and it is impossible to enter yet. After a time the workmen who open the kiln, with their hands protected by gloves of ten or more folds of cotton soaked in cold water, and with damp cloths wrapped around their heads, shoulders, and backs, are able to go in to take out the porcelain.

"After the porcelain has all been removed and while the furnace is still hot the new charge of ware is arranged in its place. In this way the new porcelain, which is still damp, is more gradually dried, and is rendered less liable to be broken into pieces or cracked by the fire.

"The men in the picture who are leaning on the table wrapped in cloths are those that take the porcelain out of the kiln; the other men who are carrying loads of firewood are waiting to fire the next charge; the actual process of carrying out the contents of the furnace is not clearly indicated."

During each firing the "gentle fire" or *petit feu* is kept up for about twenty-four hours, to heat the porcelain gradually, until the interior is brought from a dull red to a cherry red. Having attained this stage, the period of the "fierce fire" or *grand feu* begins, during which pine billets are thrown in as fast as possible till the furnace is quite full, and it is kept full till the necessary white heat has been attained, and this is continued during the third stage.

This is the general course of the fire, but its effect varies in different parts of the furnace according to the oxidizing or reducing nature of the flames. If air predominates in the products of combustion, the flame will be _oxidizing;_ if, on the contrary, unburned gases are circulating in excess, the flame will be _reducing._ The fireman judges by inspection: if the flames are perfectly clear, he considers them to be oxidizing; if they are thick and loaded with heavy volumes of smoke, he concludes they are reducing. A clever fireman is able at will to make his furnace pass from one to another of these conditions, and ought even to know how to keep the flames neutral, neither oxidizing nor reducing, which will give the maximum temperature without exerting any chemical influence upon the porcelain that is being baked.

All hard porcelain is composed essentially of kaolin, feldspar, and quartz. To give to this mixture the transparency and vitrification which characterize porcelain, it is necessary to reach during the firing at least the temperature required to fuse the feldspar. Feldspar fuses at about 1300° C., and this is the minimum point at which a porcelain rich in feldspar can be successfully fired. For a highly kaolinic porcelain it is necessary to push the heat up to 1500°, or even to 1550°. Submitted to these high temperatures, the elements of the porcelain change their nature; the feldspar in fusion attacks the quartz and the kaolin to form new combinations.

Illustration No. 17: "ROUND WARE AND VASES DECORATED IN FOREIGN STYLE."

"Both round ware and vases of white porcelain are painted in enamel colors in a style imitated from Western foreigners, which is consequently called _Yang ts'ai,_ or 'Foreign Coloring.' Clever artists of proved skill are selected to paint the decoration. The different materials of the colors having been previously finely ground and properly combined, the artist first paints with them upon a slab of white porcelain, which is fired to test the properties of the colors and the length of firing they require. He is gradually promoted from coarse work to fine, and acquires skill by constant practice; a good eye, attentive mind, and exact hand being required to attain excellence.

"The colors which are employed are the same as those used for _cloisonné_ enameling upon copper (_Fa-lang_). They are mixed with three different kinds of medium, the first being turpentine, the second liquid glue, the third pure water. Turpentine is best adapted for free coloring; glue is more suitable for thin washes, water for retouching the colors in relief. While it is being painted the piece is either supported upon a table or held in the hand, or laid upon the ground, according to its size, and it is placed in the position most convenient for the ready use of the brush."

The art of _cloisonné_ enameling upon copper was introduced into China from the West. It was one of the early industrial arts of Byzantium, and is fully described in the writings of the monk Theophilus, who lived in the eleventh century A. D. It was from Byzantium that it must have come to China, as is clearly proved by the Chinese name for the art, _Fa-lan,_ or _Fa-lang,_ which is a corruption of _Fo-lang,_ or _Fo-lin,_* the name of Byzantium in the Chinese historical annals. As explained by the author of the _T'ao Shuo,_ the syllable _lin_ is pronounced _lang_ in the dialect of Canton, and he accounts in this way for the change of _Fo-lin_ to _Fo-lang._ _Fo-lang Ch'ien,_ or "_Fo-lang_ inlaid work," is given by him as the correct form of the full name; but the Chinese shirk trisyllabic locutions as too complicated, so the third syllable was first dropped; the others became gradually corrupted to _Fa-lan,_ in which the second character means "blue," and all trace of the original derivation is lost. Another common name for the art, which is cultivated in Peking in the present day, is _Ching-tai Lan,_ or _Ching-tai_ enamel, and the mark of the reign of _Ching-tai_ is not infrequently found underneath ancient specimens. The emperor of the _Ming_ dynasty who reigned under this title occupied the throne in 1450–56, and he is said to have patronized the art, and to have had sets of sacrificial utensils made

---

* The name of _Fo-lin_ or _Fu-lin_ has given rise to much discussion. It first occurs in the annals of the _Sui_ dynasty (581–621) as the name of a country situated 4,500 li to the northwest of Persia. It often occurs subsequently, applied to the Greek Empire as the successor of the Roman Empire (_Ta Ch'in_), and as rivals of the rising Arabs (_Ta-Shih_). The initial was originally hard in Chinese, and the name is generally supposed to be derived from πόλιν, just as the Turkish name of Constantinople (Stamboul, or Istambúl) seems to be a corruption of εἰς τὴν πόλιν. The Greeks were proud of the title of "citizens" of their great city. Some derive the name from "Frank," but the Chinese could hardly have heard of the Franks so early as the sixth century. Dr. Hirth's valuable paper on _China and the Roman Orient_ may be referred to for a fuller discussion of the question, without adopting, however, his proposed identification of _Fu-lin_ with Bethlehem.

for temples. It was in 1453 that Constantinople was taken by the Turks under Mohammed II, and some of the Greek workmen may possibly have come to China as fugitives about this time.

Julien translates the expression *Fo-lang Ch'ien Yao,* "Porcelaines à incrustations (*ornées d'émaux*) de *Fo-lang (de France).*" Although it is a kiln ware (*yao*), it has certainly nothing to do with porcelain, and there is no probability of its introduction into China having been due to France, although it is adopted by Salvétat, who writes: "This fact presents by itself a very great importance in the history of the industrial progress of nations. It is well known that in China enamels upon copper are made in great perfection. It appears to follow from this passage that the Chinese only made these enamels in imitation of productions that Europe —perhaps France—sent to them by way of exchange."

The old Byzantine enamels were generally worked upon gold. In China the usual excipient is copper, which is gilded after the enamels have been fired and polished, so that the designs appear like a mosaic of colors inclosed in *cloisons,* the outlines of which are defined by a line of gold. Two other processes of enameling are also executed in China: the *champlevé,* in which the pattern is excavated in the solid copper vase, to be filled in with the enamel colors; and the transparent (*à jour*) enameling, in which the colors are inserted in open *cloisons,* having no background; both these methods were employed previously in Byzantium, and may be seen also in old Russian ecclesiastical work. There is yet a fourth process of enameling on copper in China, where the colors are painted on without any previous preparation of the excipient; this is chiefly carried on in the province of Canton, where the art is said to have been introduced from the country of Ku-li—i. e., Calicut, in India; the productions are commonly known under the name of *Yang tz'ŭ,* or "foreign porcelain." The author of the *Wên fang ssŭ k'ao* says of this: "One often sees incense-urns and flower-vases, winecups and saucers, bowls and dishes, wine-ewers and boxes, painted in very brilliant colors; but, although vulgarly called porcelain, they have nothing of the pure translucency of the true material, and are fit only for the service and ornament of the ladies' apartments—not for the chaste decoration of the library of a scholar or mandarin."

FIG. 291.—Snuff-bottle; perforated design in reticulated work upon ground of broken sticks; dark green glaze.

The enamel colors in the present day are manufactured in the glass-works in the province of Shantung, and sent thence to every part of China to be employed in all kinds of enameling upon metal, and in the glazing of common earthenware and *faïence,* as well as in the decoration of porcelain. They are composed of a vitreous flux, colored by a small percentage only of metallic oxide, which is generally kept in solution in the state of silicate. The coloring materials are oxide of copper for the greens and bluish greens; gold for the reds; oxide of cobalt for the blues; oxide of antimony for the yellows; arsenious acid for the whites; peroxide of iron is used for coral-red and other shades of this color, and impure oxide of manganese gives the blacks. The last two materials which give the colors directly are only mixed with the flux, not dissolved. These form the colors of the muffle stove, by the fire of which they are incorporated in the softened white glaze. It is impossible to employ them in the decoration of European porcelain, the hard glaze of which contains no lime, and when the Chinese enamel colors were tested at Sèvres they scaled off in the stove. They have all been thoroughly examined in Europe and chemically analyzed.

Illustration No. 18: "OPEN AND CLOSED MUFFLE STOVES."

"White paste porcelain that has been previously fired in the furnace is first decorated by the artist with painting in colors. When it has been painted in colors it must be again fired to fix the colors. For this purpose two kinds of muffle stoves are used, one kind being open, the other closed.

"The open stove is used for the smaller pieces. This stove is similar to that used for *cloisonné* enamels on copper, and it has a door opening outward. When the charcoal fire has been lighted inside, the porcelain is placed upon an iron wheel, which is supported upon an iron fork, by which the porcelain is passed into the stove, and the fireman holds in his other hand an iron hook, so that he may be able to turn the wheel around in the fire to equalize the action of the heat. When the colors appear clear and bright the firing is reckoned to have been sufficient.

"For large pieces the closed stove is employed. This stove is three feet high and nearly two feet and three-quarters in diameter. It is surrounded by a double wall to hold the charcoal fire, the wall being perforated below for the entrance of air. The porcelain is introduced into the interior of the stove, while the man holds a circular shield to protect himself from the heat of the fire. The top of the stove is then closed by a flat cover of yellow clay and closely luted. The firing takes a period of about twenty-four hours.

"The process of firing the monochrome yellow, green, and purplish brown porcelains is the same as the above."

The open muffle stove is no longer used in China. The author of the *Ching-tê-chên T'ao lu* says (chapter iv, folio 5): "Porcelain painted in colors at Ching-tê-chên was formerly not so highly valued, until the beginning of the reign of *Ch'ien-lung*, when both the mandarins and the common people thronged to buy it, so that the supply had to be day by day increased. The manufactories are commonly called 'red shops,' but the owners style themselves 'stove-men.' They do not, however, use open and closed muffle furnaces made in the ancient style, but only build up a cylinder of bricks on the ground like the mouth of a well, a little over three feet high and between two and three feet broad, leaving holes underneath for the draught. The decorated porcelain is put inside, a cover is fixed over the fire, and that is all. It is called a muffle stove (*shao lu*), and there are fixed rules for the time of firing. If you ask them what the open and close stoves are, they will generally answer that they do not know."

There is a good representation of this modern *shao lu* in Julien (*La Porcelaine Chinoise*, Plate XIV), which is copied from the book just quoted. The open stove which accompanies it is taken from some older Chinese book. There are good illustrations of the open and closed muffle stoves of the forms described above in the Atlas accompanying Brongniart's classical work (*Les Arts Céramiques*, Plate XLIV) taken from a Chinese book of the *Ming* dynasty.

Illustration No. 19 : "Wrapping in Straw and Packing in Cases."

"After the porcelain has been taken out of the furnace it is arranged into four separate classes, which are known by the names of 'first-class color,' 'second-class color,' 'third-class color,' and 'inferior ware,' and the price is fixed accordingly at a high or low rate. The porcelain of 'third-class color' and the 'inferior ware' are kept back for local sale. The round ware of 'first-class color' and the vases and sacrificial vessels of the 'first and second class' are all wrapped up in paper and packed in round cases, there being packers whose duty it is to attend only to this work. With regard to the round ware of 'second-class color,' the dishes and bowls are tied together in bundles, each composed of ten pieces, which are wrapped round with straw and packed in round cases, for convenience of carriage to distant parts.

"The coarser porcelain intended for ordinary use, which is distributed throughout the different provinces, is not packed in cases with straw, but only tied up in bundles with reeds and matting. From thirty or forty pieces up to sixty make a 'load' sufficient for a man to carry at each end of his yoke. The 'loads' are packed inside with reeds and matting and bound round outside with strips of bamboo, ready to be conveyed either by water or by land as may be more convenient.

"The workmen who do the packing are generally known by the name of 'mat-men.'"

The above description refers especially to the productions of the imperial manufactory, only the best pieces of which are picked out to be sent to Peking, while the rest are sold locally. A regular supply is sent to the palace twice every year, an additional amount being requisitioned on any extraordinary occasion, such as an imperial wedding; the lists are generally published at the time in the *Ching Pao*, the official "Peking Gazette." According to T'ang Ying in his "Records of the Porcelain Manufactory," quoted in the *Annals of the Province of Kiangsi:* "After the porcelain made in the imperial manufactory has been finished, every year at the two seasons of autumn and winter, a number of broad flat-bottomed boats and a gang of porters are hired to convey to the capital the six hundred and more casks packed with round pieces and vases. The annual supply required for the palace of round ware of the highest class, including round dishes, bowls, cups and saucer-plates, ranging from between one and two inches up to two and three feet in diameter, amounts to between 16,000 and 17,000 pieces, in addition to 6,000 or 7,000 pieces selected from the best of the second class. These are all packed together in casks and conveyed to Peking, to be ready for imperial presents, and for the emperor's own use. The vases of all kinds intended for ornamental and sacrificial use of the highest class, including ovoid vases with tall, narrow necks, sacrificial vases with scrolled designs, beaker-shaped vases and urns for burning incense, etc., ranging from three and four inches up to three and four feet in height, require a yearly supply of over 2,000 pieces, without reckoning the 2,000 or 3,000 vases selected from the best of the second class. These also are all packed together in casks and conveyed at the same time to Peking."

In addition to the firing of the imperial porcelain, the kilns at Ching-tê-chên, which are numbered by the thousand, practically supply the whole of the Chinese Empire, as well as the porcelain required for export to foreign countries. Boats laden with it are no uncommon sight in the inland waterways of China, and I have even seen a line of large wheelbarrows under full sail, pushed and supported on both sides by running men and drawn in front by donkeys, speeding along the highways

> "Of Sericana, where Chineses drive
> With wind and sail their cany waggons light."
>
> *Paradise Lost,* iii, 437.

Illustration No. 20 : "Worshiping the God and offering Sacrifice."

"Ching-tê-chên, situated within the jurisdiction of Fou-liang Hsien, is only some ten or more *li* in circuit, environed by mountains and rivers, so as to form, as it were, an island, yet on account of its porcelain production merchants throng to it from all quarters. The private kilns, between two and three hundred in number, exhibit a constant succession of flames and smoke the whole year round, and give employment to not less than several hundreds of thousands of workmen and assistants. The porcelain industry gives subsistence to an immense number of people whose life hangs on the success or failure of the furnace fires, and they are all devout in worship and sacrifice.

"Their god, named T'ung, was once himself a potter, a native of the place. Formerly, during the *Ming* dynasty, when they were making the large dragon fish-bowls, they failed in the firing year after year, although the eunuchs in charge inflicted the most severe punishments, and the potters were in bitter trouble. Then it was that one of them, throwing away his life for the rest, leaped into the midst of the furnace, whereupon the dragon bowls came out perfect. His fellow-workmen, pitying him and marveling, built a temple within the precincts of the imperial manufactory, and worshiped him there under the title of 'Genius of Fire and Blast.' Down to the present day the fame of the miracle is cherished, and the potters continue to worship him, not a day passing without reverential sacrificial offerings. Theatrical shows are also instituted in his honor, during which crowds of people fill the temple grounds. He is worshiped here as the tutelary gods of agriculture and land are in other parts of the empire."

The Chinese are devoted to ancestral worship, in the ceremonies connected with which sacrifice is offered to the *manes* or spirits of the deceased. Many of their deities are canonized mortals who have lived among them in historical times. No schoolboy must enter a public school without paying reverence to the picture of the sacred sage, Confucius, who lived B. C. 551–479; and every soldier worships the image of Kuan Ti, the God of War, who lived on earth as Kuan Yü, and was beheaded A. D. 219, after a life of martial prowess. The potter, T'ung, the vicarious sacrifice of whose life is sketched above, was not, however, the first deity of the craft. His predecessor was named Chao, according to the *Ching-tê-chên T'ao lu* (book xiii, folio 10), which says that it was in the reign of *Hung-hsi*, who lived A. D. 1425, that the assistant director of the porcelain manufactory, Chang Shan, was the first to worship the patron god of the potters, and built a temple within the walls of the manufactory. The deity, whose surname was Chao, his name K'ai, and his literary appellation Shu-pêng, is said to have been in charge of the work during the *Chin* dynasty (265–419), to have acquired a wide reputation for the choice productions inspired by his genius, and to have risen afterward to the rank of prince. It was in this dynasty that the famous azure-blue glaze first came into vogue, and we should like to know more of the history of the director Chao, if he be not altogether a legendary character. His temple has long been in ruins, and his cult is now supplanted by that of another patron god. The present temple was rebuilt in the reign of *Yung-chêng* by Nien Hsi-yao, as commemorated by a stone tablet, erected by him in front of the main hall, which is still standing. T'ang Ying, in the next reign, discovered a large fish-bowl, decorated with dragons, of the reign of *Wan-li*, the bottom of which had fallen out in the kiln, and had it installed in the temple courtyard as a specimen of the porcelain "composed of the blood and bones of the deity."

FIG. 292.—Snuff-bottle, with intricate designs in high relief
of lions chasing wheels and fire emblems; Ch'ien-lung.

CHAPTER XVI.

MODERN PERIOD (1796–1895).—IMPERIAL LIST OF THE YEAR 1864.

DURING the long reign of *Ch'ien-lung*, which came to an end in 1795, there was a gradual degeneration in the artistic qualities of the porcelain produced at the imperial manufactory, and this is reflected in a still more marked degree in the ceramic products of the private kilns of *Ching-tê-chên*. The decoration lost by degrees much of its vigor and freedom of execution, and the colors gradually failed in the depth, purity, and brilliancy of tone which distinguished the older period. These defects are not compensated by a certain improvement in technical manipulation and a studied finish of design, which are mechanical rather than artistic. A century has passed since the death of *Ch'ien-lung*, and there has been hardly any check to this steady progress of degeneration in any of the five reigns of his successors. These reigns may be conveniently grouped together to form the modern period of the ceramic art in China, which will consequently comprise about a century, dating back from to-day. They are barely represented in collections, unless perhaps by an occasional imitation, which has been so perfectly reproduced as to deceive the unwary collector. Still, some knowledge of the porcelain of the time is necessary, if only to enable one to distinguish such modern counterfeits from the real antiquities that they are intended to represent. A glance at the designs and processes of decoration in use at the present time is necessary, moreover, to help us to understand the descriptions in the older books, when we have not the actual pieces before us. Chinese art, more perhaps than any other, is essentially reproductive and imitative, and most of the modern designs can be traced back to early periods. The artists seem to have no inventive faculty, and yet it is astonishing to notice how rarely they adopt anything from abroad in recent times.

FIG. 293.—Double Snuff-bottle with coral-red decoration; Ch'ien-lung.

The imperial porcelain of the reign of *Chia-ch'ing* (1796–1820) can hardly be distinguished, except by the mark, from that of *Ch'ien-lung*. It is highly appreciated by the Chinese connoisseurs on account of its finished technique and the perfect regularity of its decorative designs. The figure scenes are carefully painted, and the scrolled borders and lambrequins are finely and neatly penciled. There is a class of vases, characteristic of this reign, which are entirely covered with elaborate scrolls of diverse pattern in underglaze blue, enhanced by a richly gilded background, and which are highly decorative; but this highly ornate style of decoration seems more fitting for enameling on metal than on a fragile material like porcelain. The mark on the imperial porcelain of this reign is usually attached in the form of a seal, impressed in the paste; the foot, as well as the interior of the vase, is often glazed with the same pale-green enamel that was noticed in the official productions of the preceding reign.

The perfect finish of the monochromes of the time is beautifully shown in the finely crackled turquoise vase that has been illustrated in Fig. 8, which is delicately etched under the soft-toned glaze with dragons and bats enveloped in scrolled clouds, and is marked underneath with the seal, also etched in the paste, of *Ta Ch'ing Chia ch'ing nien chih*—i. e., "Made in the reign of *Chia-ch'ing* of the great *Ch'ing* [dynasty]." Of the other single colors the imperial yellow and the coral-red are among the most successful, although not equal to the finest productions of the *Ch'ien-lung* period.

The bowl illustrated in Fig. 294 is an example of the more complicated decoration of the period. It is ornamented with floral emblems of longevity in a threefold series, consisting of blossoming prunus-trees, sprays of bamboo, and fir-trees with Polyporus fungus (*ling-chih*), which are painted in enamel colors inside and outside the bowl in identical designs, and have the foliage and flowers pierced in parts and filled in with glaze so as to be transparent. The decoration is completed by a medallion containing melons painted in the bottom of the bowl. The seal, penciled in blue under the foot, is *Ta Ch'ing Chia ch'ing nien chih*—"Made in the reign of *Chia-ch'ing*, of the great *Ch'ing* [dynasty]."

This emperor, like his accomplished father, *Ch'ien-lung*, was fond of poetry. I have in my possession some pieces of a tea service made for him, which are decorated in soft enamel colors with bands of floral scrolls, relieved by a bright enameled ground, and defined by lines of gilding. These are inscribed with an ode of his own composition, celebrating the virtues of tea, the rhyming verse being signed *Chia-ch'ing* in two small panels of round and square outline, attached at the end of each inscription and penciled in vermilion. The full seal mark of the reign is also penciled underneath in red, within an oblong white panel reserved in the bright

yellow enamel which covers the rest of the ground. The accompanying superscription is taken from the interior of one of the little fluted dishes of this set; and it is followed by an attempt at a literal version of the simple verse, which consists of four stanzas of ten characters, each stanza ending with the same rhyme:

"Finest tribute tea of the first picking
And a bright full moon prompt a line of verse.
A lively fire glows in the bamboo stove,
The water is boiling in the stone griddle,
Small bubbles rise like eyes of fish or crab.
Of rare Ch'i-ch'iang tea, rolled in tiny balls,
One cup is enough to lighten the heart,
And dissipate the early winter chill."

"Written by the emperor in the middle decade of the 'little spring' month (i. e., the first month of winter, the tenth month), of the cyclical year *ting-ssŭ* (1797) of the reign of *Chia-ch'ing*.

(Signed) *Chia-ch'ing*."

The Emperor *Tao-kuang*, who succeeded his father, *Chia-ch'ing*, reigned for thirty years, from 1821 to 1850. Some illustrations of the porcelain of his time have been already given. The finest work was lavished at this time on articles intended for ordinary use, such as soup-basins, rice-bowls, teacups with covers, and miniature wine-cups, and the seal mark of *Tao-kuang* is usually well represented in collections of such things. One of the most attractive of the styles is a plain decoration reserved in white on a soft coral-red ground, which defines the out-line of sprays of bamboo, or other simple floral designs in a charming way. An idea of this may be gained from the flanged bowl in Fig. 63; the floral decoration in this, outlined in

FIG. 294.—Bowl, painted inside and outside with an identical floral decoration, with details in pierced " rice-grain " work filled in with glaze; mark, Chia-ch'ing.

red, has the blossoms of the China rose slightly touched with pale green. The incinerated iron oxide in these cases is very finely pul-verized and intimately mixed with the enameler's plumbo-alkaline flux, and it acquires a brilliancy of tone which is not attainable by the ordinary method of painting it on combined by means of glue with a white-lead flux. This enameled red ground, which dates from the *Yung-chêng* period, is the "jujube-red" of Chinese ceramic art. The "medallion bowls" of this period are perhaps the most general favorites, and in London, at Christie's auction-rooms, where they are wont to figure under the name of "Peking basins," they are seldom sold for less than ten guineas a pair. The name is as mislead-ing as that of "Nanking blue and white," as porcelain was never made at either Peking or Nanking. The bowls are found at Peking to-day, because they were sent there from *Ching-tê-chên* at the time

they were made for the service of the emperor. They are ordinary rice-bowls in shape, as may be seen from a glance at the typical specimen illustrated in Fig. 73. This has an etched crim-son ground brocaded with conventional flowers, and the medallions which are reserved in the *rouge-d'or* ground contain sprays of flowers and fruit, while the interior is painted in under-glaze cobalt-blue with a basket of flowers encircled by floral sprays. In a second set of similar bowls the medallions are filled with landscapes of lake and mountain scenery, repre-senting the four seasons. In a third series, decorated with the same crimson ground, the medallions display the varied paraphernalia of the liberal arts known as the *po ku*, or "hundred antiques."

In addition to the crimson (*rouge-d'or*) ground, the "medallion bowls" display etched grounds of four other colors, viz., pink (*rose d'or*), which is derived also from gold; lavender, a manganese color of a charming tint approaching the shade commonly known as French gray; lemon-yel-low, and blue; this last is the least successful of the colors, although the rarest, being somewhat of greenish tone. The reserved medallions usually contain sprays of prunus, magnolia, chrysanthemum, and lotus, mingled with the sacred longevity fungus and bunches of scarlet nandina berries. The yellow bowls include, in addition, another series with four medallions filled with miniature landscapes of hill scenery dotted with temples and pagodas, and a third set with three medallions containing outdoor scenes with rams, emblems of the universal revivifying power of spring, accord-

FIG. 295.—Melon-shaped Snuff-bottle with deco-ration of vines, in blue and white; mark, Yung-chêng.

ing to the punning motive, *San yang k'ai tai*, in which Yang means "spring" as well as "ram." The blue medallion bowls have the etched ground overlaid with colored clouds, and the four medallions painted with mythological subjects corresponding to the picture in the interior, which is painted in shaded blue. This is a circular medallion containing a picture of a male and female stellar divinity in the midst of clouds, with their constellations above their heads and a flock of birds flying around their feet. The picture suggests a joyous meeting of lovers, *hsi* meaning "joy" as well as "magpie," the "joyous bird" of the Chinese. The stellar divinities in the picture are the cowherd "Ch'ien Niu," riding upon a buffalo, identified with a constellation comprising portions of Capricornus and Sagittarius, and "Chih Nü," the Spinning Damsel, *a* Lyræ.

An ancient legend related by Huai Nan Tzŭ, who died B. C. 122, promulgates the romantic idea that the two are separated all the year round except on the seventh night of the seventh moon, when Magpies fill up the Milky Way to enable the Spinning Damsel to cross over. A legion of poetical allusions have sprung from this passage picturing the separated lovers gazing at each other from afar or celebrating their joyful reunion.* Of the four medallions on the exterior of the bowls, two opposite ones contain separate pictures of the same cowherd and spinster; the other two are filled with outdoor scenes, in one of which the Spinning Damsel is seen walking under a tree with maiden attendants, in the other in amorous dalliance with her lover in a garden pavilion.

Some of the most beautiful bowls and plates of this time, as well as richly decorated vases, have the mark of *Shên-tê-t'ang*—"Hall for the Cultivation of Virtue"—inscribed underneath. It has already been explained that this was the designation given by the emperor to one of the halls of his palace. That the mark really belongs to this reign has been doubted, but it is proved by a small bowl with everted brim in the Hippisley Collection (No. 367 in the catalogue), which is "decorated with a spray of white plum and longevity fungus, beautifully painted, accompanied by a poem from the pen of the Emperor *Tao-kuang*, and bearing his seal attached. The seal is in the form of a little oval panel with the two characters, placed vertically, reserved in white upon a vermilion ground. Nothing is sacred to the fraudulent imitator in China, and this hall-mark is often forged, so that it is found, as Sir A. W. Franks remarks (*loc. cit.*, page 213), "on specimens of different kinds and very varied quality."

FIG. 296.—Snuff-bottle; celadon on modeled decoration; Ch'ien-lung.

Some of the white unglazed porcelain made at this time, reminding one of the Parian ware of European potteries, is finely modeled and of finished technique. It is seen especially in articles intended for the writer's table, such as cylindrical brush-pots, seals, boxes for seal vermilion, and the like.

The Emperor *Hsien-fêng* succeeded to the imperial throne in 1851. During his reign the south of China was ravaged by the "Long-haired Rebels" (the *Tai-pings*), who started from the provinces of Kuangtung and Kuangsi, reached the province of Kiangsi in his third year, and were not finally expelled till the spring of the third year of the reign of his successor, *T'ung-chih* (1864). Ching-tê-chên was besieged and taken by the rebels, the imperial potteries were burned to the ground, and the workmen either massacred or driven away. Imperial porcelain of this period is consequently rare, as it could only have been produced and forwarded to Peking during the early part of the reign. It resembles in character the production of *Tao-kuang*, and is inscribed generally with the six-character mark of the reign, penciled underneath in red in the ordinary script. Among the pieces I have seen that are worthy of special notice are vases of good form decorated with nine five-clawed dragons, painted in soft enamel colors, on a white background which is etched in the paste with scrolled waves; and a dinner service of bowls, cups, and saucer-shaped dishes, painted in colors with processional figures of the eighteen Lohan, or Arhats of early Buddhist history.

In the third year of the reign of the young Emperor *T'ung-chih* (1864), after the expulsion of the rebels from the province of Kiangsi by Li Hung-chang, who was appointed acting viceroy in that year, while Tsêng Kuo-fan, the celebrated viceroy, took command of the imperial army in the field, the imperial manufactory at Ching-tê-chên was rebuilt. A short account of the seventy-two buildings which were erected more or less on the old foundations by the new director, Ts'ai Chin-ch'ing, who was appointed at this time, has already been given in Chapter IX. Some idea will be gained of the porcelain manufactured by a discussion of the official list

* Mayer's *Chinese Reader's Manual*, pp. 97, 98.

of the articles which were requisitioned in this year for the use of the emperor. This is extracted from the Annals of the Province of Kiangsi (*Chiang hsi T'ung chih*, book xciii, folio 13–16), where it comes immediately after the official list of the reign of *Yung-chêng*, the analysis of which has been given already in Chapter XIII. The new list is dated the third year (1864) of the reign of *T'ung-chih*. It is comprised under two headings, of which the first is devoted to the vases and larger pieces (*cho ch'i*), the second to the round ware (*yuan ch'i*).

"A. Vases to be sent to Peking for the Emperor. (大 運 琢 器).

"1. Quadrangular vases with apricot-shaped medallions and two tubular handles enameled with the Chün glaze. (均 釉 四 方 杏 元 雙 瑄 瓶)."

The modern *Chün Yu* is so called because the colors of the glaze are intended to resemble that of the ancient Chün-chou porcelain of the *Sung* dynasty. It is the *soufflé* glaze with a greenish-blue flecking and dappling on a reddish ground, the red being subordinate to the blue, which has been appropriately named "Robin's Egg" by American collectors. The form described here is that of the brilliant *flambé* quadrangular vase illustrated in Plate XLVI, which has an apricot-shaped medallion worked in slight relief in the paste under the glaze, in front and behind, and two wide tubular handles at the sides.

"2. Quadrangular vases with apricot-shaped medallions and two tubular handles invested with Ko Yao glaze. (哥 釉 四 方 杏 元 雙 瑄 瓶)."

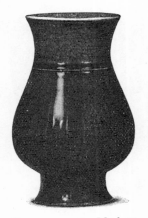

The shape is exactly the same as that just described, and it occurs not infrequently from the reign of *Ch'ien-lung* downward, in the stone-colored crackle traversed by a network of reddish lines, which is known as *Ko Yu*. *Ko* means "elder brother," and the name dates from early in the *Sung* dynasty, when two brothers named Chang are related to have made celadon ware at Lung-ch'üan. The productions of the elder brother, which were distinguished by having a crackled glaze, were called *Ko Yao*, and the name, as applied to crackled porcelain generally, has survived to the present day. It is given especially to the ordinary stone-gray crackle which is seen in every Chinese collection. The crackling is produced by combining with the materials of the glaze a natural stone called *Lan-t'ien shih*, from its place of production, which appears to be a kind of compound magnesia silicate allied to steatite, and which takes the place of the lime that gives solubility to the ordinary glaze.

Fig. 297. — A Modern Crackled *sang-de-bœuf* Vase of intense and brilliant color.

"3. Quadrangular vases with the *pa kua* symbols enameled with the *Ko Yao* glaze. (哥 釉 四 方 八 卦 瓶)."

These are tall oblong vases of square section with the eight trigrams of ancient Chinese mystic lore worked in relief underneath the crackled stone-gray glaze. The eight symbols usually stand out in relief on each of the sides, but sometimes, as in the vase of this kind illustrated in Plate XXIII, there are two displayed on each side, separated by the dual *yin-yang* symbol in the middle. Vases of this form and design stand upon Taoist altars holding the slips of bamboo used in divination; the vase is shaken, and the stated number of slips are selected at each operation to determine the prognostic, which is worked out by the presiding seer with the aid of his divination books, while the worshiper is burning incense before the sacred shrine.

"4. Vases in the form of ancient wine-vessels of jade enameled copper-red. (霽 紅 玉 壺 春 瓶)."

Yü hu ch'un is the common name of a vase with bulging pyriform body poised upon a circularly rimmed foot, contracting gradually upward with a narrow neck and expanding sharply at the orifice to make a wider horizontal lip. The name comes from the modeling of the form on the lines of the graceful wine-vessels that used to be carved out of jade, although these last were generally ewers furnished with a curved spout, an open flowing handle, and a knobbed cover, while the porcelain type is an ornamental flower-vase. The term *chi-hung* used here answers to the bright ruby-red derived from copper, which is the most successful of the modern single colors, and occasionally will almost rival the celebrated *sang-de-bœuf* of the *K'ang-hsi* period in the brilliancy of its flashing tones. The character *chi* employed above is an unauthorized form, that one would hardly expect to find in an official list; it means the color of the sky after rain, and can consequently be combined properly only with *ch'ing*, "blue," to form *chi-ch'ing*, as in No. 42, below, and another character with the same sound, meaning "sacrificial," ought to be substituted, *chi-hung*, or "sacrificial red," being the traditional name of the ruby-red cups which were made in the reign of *Hsüan-tê* for the ritual worship of the emperor on the Altar of the Sun.

"5. Vases in the form of ancient wine-vessels of jade with threads worked in relief decorated in blue. (青花起綾玉壺春瓶)."

I have not seen an example of this kind, but am told that the vases have encircling rings worked in the paste in the form of ropes, so as to divide them into sections for decoration in blue and white.

"6. Vases of the *Yü hu ch'un*, or carved jade type, decorated in blue with garden scenes inclosed by railings. (青花欄杆玉壺春瓶)."

These vases, the form of which has been already described, have an open-rail fence drawn round the lower part of the bulging body, inside which rise clumps of graceful bamboos, shrubs of nandina with bunches of berries and flowering trees of all kinds, with an occasional rockery in the intervals. The design dates from the reign of *Ch'ien-lung*.

"7. Vases in the form of paper-beaters, with the *t'ai-chi* symbol, invested with imperial glaze decorated in colors. (花廠官釉太極紙搥瓶)."

The *chih-ch'ui p'ing*, or "paper-beater vase," has a cylindrical body rounding in above to a straight upright neck, of about the same length as that of the body of the vase. If the body is more bulging and the upright neck proportionally narrower, as in the powder-blue vase which is illustrated in Plate XCIII, we have the *Yu-ch'ui P'ing*, or "oil-beater vase," the shape being that of the mallet commonly used in China for crushing seed to extract the oil. The *t'ai-chi* symbol referred to is the creative monad disk dividing into the dual *yin yang*, "darkness and light," which is displayed in Plate XXIII.

"8. Quadrangular vases, with the elephant symbol of great peace enameled sky-blue. (天青四方太平有象瓶)."

The rebus *T'ai p'ing yu hsiang* (fifth to eighth characters above), "an augury of great peace," was referred to in Chapter V, in the description of an ancient pallet of *Sung* porcelain etched with the figure of an elephant. The vases referred to above have two handles molded in the form of elephants' heads, implying the same happy augury. The modern single color called *t'ien-ch'ing*, or "sky-blue," is derived from cobalt mixed with the feldspathic glaze of the high fire; it is of somewhat darker tone than the *clair de lune* of older times, which was produced by the combination of the same ingredients with a purer and more translucent glaze.

"B. ROUND WARE TO BE SENT TO PEKING FOR THE EMPEROR. (大運圓器)."

"9. Medium-sized bowls decorated in brown with dragons. (紫龍中盌)."

These are the bowls with five-clawed imperial dragons of maroon tint; the decoration was painted on with the copper-red color *sur le cru*, and the piece was subsequently glazed and fired in the large furnace, so that the technique is the same as that of the blue and white.

"10 Medium-sized bowls enameled in copper-red. (霽紅中盌)."

Chi-hung is the ruby-red monochrome derived from copper silicate referred to under No. 4 of this list.

"11. Large bowls painted in blue with the Indian lotus. (青西蓮大盌)."

The Western or Indian lotus (*Hsi Fan lien*) is the most common motive of the conventional floral scrolls with which Chinese porcelain is so often decorated.

"12. Five-inch dishes painted in blue with the Western lotus. (青西蓮五寸盤)."

The dishes and plates of a Chinese service are all round, and what we should call saucer-shaped. In this list those of half a foot in diameter and upward are called *p'an*, "round dishes"; those of less size are called *tieh*, which we may conveniently render as "platters."

"13. Medium-sized bowls painted in blue with the eight mystic trigrams and storks in the midst of clouds. (青雲鶴八卦中盌)."

The bowls are decorated outside with eight flying storks enveloped in scrolled clouds. The stork is the aërial courser of the Taoist immortals, and it is often represented carrying in its beak bamboo slips of fate inscribed with the *pa kua* symbols.

"14. Wine-cups decorated in enamel colors with narcissus-flowers. (五彩水仙花酒盅)."

The wine is served hot at the Chinese banquet, poured into tiny bowl-shaped cups of porcelain. The *Narcissus tazetta*, which has white flowers with yellow cups in the center, is a favorite floral decoration on porcelain; it is the *shui hsien hua*, "the water-fairy flower," of the Chinese.

"15. Wine-cups with expanding rim painted in red with dragons. (彩紅龍撇口酒盅)."

This is the design most frequently seen on these little cups. The dragons, of the imperial five-clawed type, are painted in coral-red over the white glaze; the porcelain, having been previously glazed and fired in the large furnace, is decorated with the iron-red color, and fired a second time in the muffle stove. The bowl illustrated in Plate LXVII may be referred to as a beautiful example of this kind of decoration.

"16. Round dishes a foot in diameter decorated in blue with a pair of dragons. (青雙龍滿尺盤)."

"17. Soup-bowls with dragons incised in the paste under a dark imperial yellow glaze. (嬌深黃暗龍湯盌)."

The soup-bowl (*t'ang wan*) is smaller and shallower than the ordinary rice-bowl (*fan wan*). The first character used here means literally "pretty" or "bright"; it is substituted for another of the same sound meaning "watered," which is technically given to several single-colored glazes applied with a brush. *An lung* means "concealed dragons," but *an* has a special technical meaning in ceramic art, and *an hua* is the expression always used for decorations etched with a style in the paste, which are brought out more strongly by holding the piece up to the light.

"18. Medium-sized bowls of barrel-shaped form with dragons incised in the paste under a bright yellow glaze. (嬌黃暗龍墩式中盌)."

"19. Teacups enameled bright yellow. (嬌黃茶盅)."

The teacup (*ch'a-chung*) referred to here is taller and more upright in form than the *ch'a-wan*, and differs in never being furnished with a cover, but the names are often used indiscriminately; neither has a handle at the side like our teacups. When a teapot is not used, the tea-leaves are infused in cups with covers, which are called *kai-wan, kai* meaning "cover." When the tea is drunk, the cover is manipulated so as to leave only a narrow chink at the rim of the cup, to keep the tea-leaves inside.

"20. Medium-sized bowls with dragons incised in the paste under a bright yellow glaze. (嬌黃暗龍中盌)."

"21. Medium-sized bowls of ringlike outline painted in blue with designs of the three fruits. (青花三果班子中盌)."

The three fruits which are usually represented are the peach, pomegranate, and Buddha's-hand citron, emblems of the three abundances (*san to*) of years, sons, and promotions.

"22. Soup-bowls with expanding rims with dragons incised in the paste under a bright yellow glaze. (嬌黃暗龍撇口湯盌)."

"23. Round dishes six inches in diameter painted in blue with a pair of dragons. (青雙龍六寸盤)."

"24. Round dishes a foot across painted in blue with a decoration of spiral scrolls inclosing longevity characters. (青花蠶紋壽字滿尺盤)."

"25. Teacups (*Ch'a Wan*) painted in blue with sprays of the *Olea fragrans* flower. (青木 樨花茶盌)."

The *Mu-hsi* is a dwarf variety of *Olea fragrans* with reddish flowers, which are even more sweet-scented than those of the ordinary white variety; it is but rarely employed for the decoration of porcelain.

"26. Medium-sized bowls decorated in enamel colors with sprays of precious lotus. (五彩 寶蓮中盌)."

The precious lotus (*pao lien*) is one of the varieties of the *Nelumbium speciosum* held sacred by the Buddhists, who liken the precious jewel of their faith to the limpid drops of pure water that collect upon its broad peltate leaves.

"27. Teacups decorated with white bamboo upon a ground painted red. (彩紅地白 竹茶盌)."

This charming design, with the graceful leafy sprays of the bamboo reserved in white and relieved by a soft coral-red background, was adopted in the imperial manufactory in the *Ch'ien-lung* period, the seal of which is found penciled in blue underneath bowls of almost eggshell thinness and purest color. The red is produced from iron peroxide prepared by the incineration of the green sulphate. The more modern bowls are thicker, and the red tends to become of a brick-dust hue.

FIG. 298.—Vase of semi-egg-shell texture, decorated in underglaze blue, with relief modeling touched with colors, and with panel pictures painted in colors.

"28. Six-inch saucer-dishes painted in blue with the 'three friends' and figure scenes. (青三友人物六寸盤)."

The "three friends" (*san yu*) in ordinary Chinese parlance are the evergreen pine, the bamboo, and the winter-flowering plum, which keep green in cold times of adversity. In the decoration of porcelain they are usually grouped in a landscape scene with the figures of hermits or aged pilgrims. But there is another group of "three friends" in the persons of Confucius, Buddha, and Lao Tzŭ, who are often depicted examining scrolls of ancient lore, or engaged in distilling the *elixir vitæ*.

"29. Tea-dishes (*Ch'a P'an*) painted in blue with a pair of dragons. (青雙龍茶盤)."

There are no porcelain saucers in Chinese tea-sets, their place being taken by boat-shaped saucers of metal, lacquer, or some other material. The tea-dishes referred to here are little trays with upright borders of oblong, four-lobed, or fluted outline, like the one that was described under the reign of *Chia-ch'ing*, with the imperial verse inscribed upon it.

"30. Six-inch saucer-shaped dishes decorated with green dragons on a ground with scrolled waves incised in the paste and painted in colors. (彩暗水綠龍六寸盤)."

"31. Round dishes a foot in diameter, painted in blue with archaic phœnixes. (青夔鳳 滿尺盤)."

The *k'uei fêng* is the peculiar conventional phœnix of ancient bronzes in which the body degenerates into ornamental scrolls.

"32. Round dishes nine-tenths of a foot across, with a blue ground inclosing dragons and clouds painted in yellow. (藍地彩黃雲龍九寸盤)."

This is a very ancient style of decoration, which we noticed in the description of the imperial porcelain of the reign of *Chia-ching* (1522–66). The piece is first treated like an ordinary blue and white specimen, which is to have the decoration reserved in white upon a mottled blue ground, the white parts being subsequently enameled yellow, and the dish being refired to fix the color.

"33. Medium-sized bowls decorated with phœnix medallions painted in ruby-red underneath a pure white ground. (填白釉寶燒紅團鳳中盌)."

The red of the *grand feu*, which is derived from copper, has had the name of *pao shao hung*, literally "ruby-fired red," since the time of *Hsüan-tê* (1426–35), when it was first used in the decoration of porcelain, and there is a widespread conviction in China that the color is actually produced by rubies pulverized and combined with the materials of the glaze. In the present day amethystine quartz (*tzŭ ying shih*) is used in the preparation of the color, but this can act only in modifying its solubility and penetrative power, because, like the ruby, amethyst becomes colorless in the intense heat of the furnace. The expression *t'ien pai yu*, which is used here to distinguish the class from that painted in red under a celadon ground, like No. 39 in this list, has also given rise to much misapprehension both in China and elsewhere. The character *t'ien*, "filled in," is substituted for an older one of the same sound meaning "pure" or "sweet," and the expression can hardly mean "white glaze to be filled in with colors," although Du Sartel, in *La Porcelaine de Chine*, gives it so on Julien's authority, and makes it the heading of a whole class, which, as a critic justly observes, threatens to remain without a member to represent it.

"34. Teacups painted with yellow dragons and clouds relieved by a blue ground. (藍地彩黃雲龍茶盌)."

"35. Six-inch saucer-shaped dishes of copper-red. (霽紅六寸盤)."

"36. Medium-sized bowls of copper-red. (霽紅中盌)."

"37. Seven-inch saucer-shaped dishes of copper-red. (霽紅七寸盤)."

"38. Soup-bowls of depressed barrel-shaped form enameled brown. (紫金釉墩式湯盌)."

This glaze, called *tzŭ chin*, or "burnished gold" (or *bruni*), by the Chinese, is derived by them from a native ferruginous mineral called *tzŭ chin shih*, which is combined with the glaze in the way so fully described in Père d'Entrecolles's Letters.

"39. Medium-sized bowls painted with phœnix medallions in red under a celadon glaze. (冬青釉紅團鳳中盌)."

Tung-ch'ing is the Chinese name of the soft sea-green shade which we call celadon. In modern books it is often written, as it is here, with "winter" as the first character, as if it were "evergreen"; originally it appears to have been written with a character of the same sound (*tung*) meaning "east," the tint being that of the porcelain produced during the *Sung* dynasty at the eastern capital, the modern K'ai-fêng-fu, in the province of Honan. The combination of the decoration in underglaze copper-red of the *grand feu* with the celadon glaze has been already noticed in the description of the porcelain of the reign of *Yung-chêng*.

"40. Seven-inch round dishes decorated in the five enamel colors with spiral scrolls and words of happy augury. (五彩蠶紋如意七寸盤)."

The spiral-scroll design is likened by the Chinese to "silkworm coils"; forms of it occur on the most archaic bronzes. A fitting felicitous inscription, which is often displayed on modern imperial porcelain, is *Wan shou wu chiang*, "A myriad ages never ending!" Several other formulæ were found in the lists of the *Ming* dynasty given in Chapter VII.

"41. Teacups (*Ch'a chung*) decorated in the five enamel colors with mandarin ducks and lotus-flowers. (五彩鴛鴦荷花茶盅)."

The beautiful waterfowl called *Anas galericulata* is commonly known as the "mandarin duck." They exhibit, when paired, a remarkable attachment to each other, and have thus become emblems of connubial love and fidelity in a higher sphere. This decoration is often met with, and it has already been described in the ceramic art of the *Ming* dynasty.

"42. Teacups (*Ch'a Wan*) enameled deep blue. (霽青茶盌)."

The character *chi* is defined in dictionaries as the color of the clear sky after rain, and *chi ch'ing* in ceramic parlance is the deep blue monochrome tint derived from cobalt, which in its deepest shade, approaching that of indigo, becomes the *ta ch'ing* of the Chinese, the *gros bleu* of Sèvres. It may be either blown on to form the "powder-blue" glaze, or painted on with the brush in the ordinary way.

"43. Teacups (*Ch'a Wan*) decorated in colors with the eight precious emblems. (彩八寶茶盌)."

The *Pa Pao* referred to here are the eight precious emblems of the Taoist cult, the several attributes of the eight *genii*, or immortals, which are displayed on the large pilgrim bottle in Fig. 50.

"44. Large bowls decorated with the Pa Hsien painted in blue, and sea-waves penciled in red. (彩紅海水青花八仙大盌)."

The eight Taoist immortals crossing the sea in procession is a favorite subject of decoration for the sides of a bowl, each one holding in his hands his distinguishing attribute. A large bowl of the old *famille verte* is illustrated by the inimitable pencil of Jules Jacquemart in Plate IX of *Histoire de la Porcelaine*, although the author, in his description of the bowl, ingeniously discovered an emperor and empress accompanied by a band of musicians in the procession of figures.

"45. Medium-sized bowls decorated inside in blue and white, and outside in colors with lotus-flowers. (內青花外彩荷花中盌)."

"46. Bowls decorated with the eight symbols of happy augury. (八吉祥盌)."

The *Pa Chi-hsiang*, the well-known set of eight Buddhist symbols that are so often found on porcelain, were figured and described in Chapter IV.

"47. Bowls of peach-yellow porcelain decorated in green. (綠花桃黃瓷盌)."

These are said to be invested with a monochrome ground of the shade referred to, variegated with green mottled clouds, which are overlaid in the style of some of the composite *flambé* glazes.

"48. Round dishes five inches in diameter with purple and green dragons on a monochrome yellow ground. (紫綠龍嬌黃五寸盤)."

This is a very favorite pattern in the imperial palace to-day. It comes under the heading of the "three-colored decoration of the muffle stove." The outlines of the designs are incised in the paste and filled in with manganese-purple and copper-green glazes, so as to be displayed on the enameled yellow background. The bottom is also coated yellow, and the mark underneath is penciled in green.

"49. Three-inch platters (*Tieh*) with purple and green dragons on a monochrome yellow ground. (紫綠龍嬌黃三寸碟)."

"50. Soup-bowls of the fourth size enameled bright yellow. (四號嬌黃湯盌)."

"51. Round dishes five inches in diameter, decorated with phœnixes and clouds. (雲鳳五寸盤)."

"52. Medium-sized bowls decorated in the five colors, with dragons and phœnixes in the midst of flowers. (五彩龍鳳串花中盌)."

"53. Four-inch platters with purple and green dragons on a monochrome yellow ground. (紫綠龍嬌黃四寸碟)."

"54. Round dishes nine-tenths of a foot in diameter, decorated in colors with the eight Buddhist symbols of happy augury in the midst of a floral ground. (彩八吉祥串花九寸盤)."

"55. Large bowls decorated in colors, with phœnixes of archaic design flying through flowers. (彩夔鳳串花大盌)."

There is a certain amount of repetition in this somewhat lengthy catalogue, but it is hoped that it may be a useful contribution to the terminology of the ceramic art, and it is with this view that the Chinese characters in the original have been inserted under each heading. Actual specimens of the articles described are not rare in collections, and it is always safest to go back from the known to the unknown, and it is more especially so in China, where nothing modern is acceptable unless it be modeled after the antique. Chinese decorative art in its present phase is highly conventionalized. It has never been distinguished for originality, and some of its most prominent motives, like the dragons and phœnixes that occur so frequently in the lists, have been adopted from India through Buddhist channels, and may be traced back to the *nagas* and *garudas* of Indian mythology.

Another aspect of modern porcelain manufacture is the direct and studied reproduction of older pieces. The correct date is certainly inscribed upon the porcelain of the imperial factory, but it is rarely, if ever, found upon the productions of the private kilns. The most ambitious efforts of the private potters are carefully copied from ancient pieces, and the original marks, as well as every detail of the ornamental designs, are exactly reproduced. For the rest, the general rule is that the commoner the ware the more ancient the mark; and a visit to any ordinary crockery shop in China will show that nearly every blue and white cup on the shelves is marked *Hsüan-tê*, and that most of the colored ware is inscribed *Ch'êng-hua*, although everything in the shop is avowedly modern, and the pieces have not the slightest pretensions even in style to such an early date as the *Ming* dynasty.

Some of the colorable imitations of celadons and other single colors come from Japan, but Japanese porcelain rings with a different note when tested, being made of other materials than

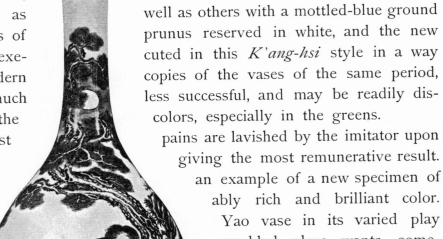

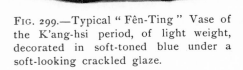

that of China. The Chinese are in these the fabrication of fraudulent counterfeits, vases decorated with figure scenes, as overspread with sprays and blossoms of pieces are occasionally brilliantly exe- to deceive the unwary. The modern decorated in enamel colors, are much tinguished by the want of luster in the

For the single colors the greatest the rarest and most expensive, as The vase shown in Fig. 297 is *sang-de-bœuf* glaze of remark- It rivals a genuine old Lang of crimson shades, albeit the thing in depth of tint. The perfect; the thick, grayish, mi- which the interior is coated is the foot of the vase has had remove drops of glaze that firing. It is impossible to drops, which usually occur in never on the old, when the tributed throughout, always line of mathematical regular- exhibits no marks of the pol- the new pieces is much more

latter days also coming to the front in and have lately exported blue and white well as others with a mottled-blue ground prunus reserved in white, and the new cuted in this *K'ang-hsi* style in a way copies of the vases of the same period, less successful, and may be readily dis- colors, especially in the greens.

pains are lavished by the imitator upon giving the most remunerative result. an example of a new specimen of ably rich and brilliant color. Yao vase in its varied play crackled glaze wants some- technique, however, is less nutely crackled glaze with deeply fissured in places, and to be ground on the wheel to have "run" down during the remove all traces of such modern pieces of the kind— glaze, which is uniformly dis- terminates below in a straight ity, and the foot of the vase ishing wheel. The glaze in fluescent, so that the color

FIG. 299.—Typical "Fên-Ting" Vase of the K'ang-hsi period, of light weight, decorated in soft-toned blue under a soft-looking crackled glaze.

tends to run down, and the upper rim of the vase is often left perfectly white. I may perhaps be excused a personal reminiscence to express my meaning: On a visit to a curio-shop in Peking one day this year, I was ᴗwn a small *sang-de-bœuf* vase, the lower part of which displayed the richest color, but the upper two inches of the neck were a glassy white, and I remarked that, were it not for the neck, it might well pass for an old piece. A month later I was invited to see a collection that a traveler was making, and in the most prominent position was exhibited the same little vase, neatly mounted in a case, lined with pale blue silk, to throw out its color. Two inches of the neck had been sawn off, and the place had been so carefully rounded and polished that no suspicion of the fact had occurred to the purchaser, who fondly imagined that he possessed a genuine antique of the first water. I must confess that I did not expose the ingenious fraud of the "heathen Chinee" at the time, but am driven to do penance now as *particeps criminis*.

For cutting porcelain the jade-carver's wheel is the means commonly employed. The apparatus, which is worked by a treadle, is fitted with flat disks of soft iron of different sizes. The disk selected, when it has been fitted for use, is kept moistened at the edge with a paste made of garnet or ruby powder mixed with water. It is astonishing to see how readily a large porcelain vase can be cut horizontally in two, or the rim of a chipped piece trimmed perfectly even, by a simple machine like this. Many a neat ovoid vase has been carved in this way out of the lower part of a broken beaker; and, by the same means, originally oblong tiles, intended to be inlaid in woodwork, are often found to have been bisected longitudinally, so that the two faces may be framed and mounted separately as companion pictures.

The imperial porcelain of the present reign of *Kuang-hsü* continues to be decorated in the same lines, and it does not call for any special notice. There has been some attempt at a revival of the ceramic art under the patronage of the empress dowager, who has ruled China during two long minorities. In addition to her other accomplishments, she is a professed artist and calligraphist, and a picture from her pencil with her autograph signature is often seen occupying the place of honor among the birthday gifts of a high mandarin. The special seals attached to the porcelain made for her palace have been already given in Chapter IV.

Quite recently Ching-tê-chên has been devastated by floods brought down by the mountain torrents, and a sad account of ruin and desolation is related by Rev. Virgil C. Hart, D.D., one of the latest missionary visitors to the place. It is to be hoped that better times are in store for China, and for the porcelain industry, which was once one of her chief glories. As M. Grandidier says, in concluding his work (*La Céramique Chinoise*, page 224): "The modern period, up to the present day at least, is little worthy of our attention; the art is dormant, and holds itself aloof, disowned, abandoned, dishonored. Cheapness attracts the buyer. The fatal consequence is a common product; quality is incessantly sacrificed to quantity. The hour of decadence struck a hundred years back, and there is no sign by which to foresee any serious renaissance near at hand."

FIG. 300.—Snuff-bottle; blue and white,
of Ch'ien-lung period.

FIG. 301.—Snuff-bottle, modeled in high relief, and
decorated in brilliant colors; Ch'ien-lung.

CHAPTER XVII.

THE FORMS OF PORCELAIN OBJECTS AND THEIR USES IN CHINA.

THIS is a wide subject, on which there is opportunity here for only a few desultory remarks. An extensive collection of Chinese porcelain exhibits a long series of objects of multitudinous shapes and sizes, removed from their original habitat, and far from their usual surroundings, so that the proper use of some of the things can hardly be guessed by the uninitiated. Images of Buddhist and Taoist divinities, torn from their temple shrines, are grouped with profane figures, and sacred ritual vessels, intended for ancestral offerings of food and wine, are mingled promiscuously with common utensils of daily life. A seated representation, for instance, of Maitreya, the Buddhist Messiah, with rosary in hand, whose smiling features and luxuriant figure have earned for him in France the traditional title of the Pousa or god of content and sensuality, is placed close to the reclining figure of Li T'ai-po, the celebrated poet, who has fallen, overcome with wine, and is embracing his capacious wine-jar, designed to hold water for the ink-pallet of a modern emulator of his genius. An ecclesiastical vase from a Buddhist altar, like the one of a pair, illustrated in Plate XX, should be distinguished from an ornamental flower-vase or a perfume-sprinkler; and a sacred libation-cup, or a cup designed for use during the marriage ceremony, from an ordinary wine-cup. Sweet-smelling flowers are highly appreciated by the Chinese, and we see perforated baskets of porcelain in which they are suspended before Buddhist altars, pierced cylinders and boxes for the table, and openwork flasks, fashioned in the form of scent-sachets, intended to be strung upon a lady's girdle, filled with blossoms of the scented jasmine or of the *Olea fragrans*. So one ought to be able to diagnose the use of an incense-urn or a joss-stick holder, to recognize a bowl for goldfish, a flowerpot, or a dish for flowering bulbs, an arrow-receptacle (*chien-t'ung*), or a brush-cylinder (*pi-t'ung*), the apparatus for a game of gobang, or a dice-box. The dice-box is a little round tray with a raised circular rim, within which fits the dome-shaped cover in which the dice are shaken; this is taken off to show the result of the throw. Cricket-fighting is another favorite pastime with the Chinese, and the curved hollow cellules with movable covers, in which the tiny champions are brought to the fray and incited to combat, are sometimes molded out of white biscuit porcelain, although ordinary *faïence*, being more absorbent of water, is a better material for the purpose. The cricket naturally lives in damp places, and, in solitary captivity, is kept in an earthenware jar with a cover like an old-fashioned tobacco-jar, the lid of which is excavated to hold water. The cricket-bowls of ancient porcelain that we read of are of wide, shallow form, and are used as the arena of the fight.

The author of the *T'ao Shuo*, in the first chapter of his book, gives a brief sketch of the various kinds of objects made during the present dynasty, the outlines of which may be followed here with some amplification by the way. He begins with a list of the sacrificial vessels of bronze, dating from the Three Ancient Dynasties, that are now all made in porcelain, including the large vessels of varied form called *tsun*, the smaller vases called *lei*, from their scrolled designs, the tripod or four-legged bowls called *ting*, the bowls without feet (*yi*) for offerings of corn, the wine-jars (*yu*), and the libation-cups (*chüeh*). The forms of the ancient vessels are not, however, always exactly copied, nor are the uses necessarily the same in modern times. The *ting* and *yi*, for example, which used to contain rice and millet, are now employed for burning incense, which was unknown in ancient China before the introduction of Buddhism; and the ancient vessels of bronze, fashioned in the form of an elephant or of a rhinoceros, in which the hollow body contained the wine, are now represented by the same animals, molded of solid porcelain, carrying on their backs capacious vases with movable covers. The forms of these are figured in the illustrated ritual books, and accompanied by a minute description of the different designs and dimensions.

Some idea of the variety of the sacrificial vessels may be gathered from an account of the tables set out for the ceremonial worship of the emperor at the T'ai Miao, the Ancestral Temple in the Prohibited City at Peking, to which he proceeds in state four times every year, to officiate as chief priest and preside over a banquet prepared for the spirits of his ancestors. A row of six libation-cups (*chüeh*) filled with wine is placed in front, followed by four tureens of yellow porcelain containing soup and broth, which include a pair of *têng*, tazza-shaped, with solid stem and spreading foot, and a pair of *hsing* with mask handles and three scrolled legs, all of which are provided with covers. In the center are four deep dishes, with spreading feet and shaped covers, made of wood, lacquered and gilded, filled with boiled rice and three kinds of millet, a pair of *fu* of oblong shape, and a pair of oval *kuei*.* These are flanked on either side by twelve stemmed bowls with covers containing all kinds of cooked dishes, sturgeon and minced carp, deer's sinews, minced hare and minced deer, sweetbread, pickled pork, etc., with cakes of different sorts, and fruit, including hazelnuts, water caltrops, the prickly water-lily (*Euryale ferox*), jujubes, and chestnuts; the twelve bowls (*pien*) on the right being made of closely woven slips of bamboo, lacquered yellow, the twelve (*tou*) on the left of carved wood, gilded. Next come three large oblong metal trays on separate stands with the meat offerings of a bullock, a sheep, and a pig. A box of woven bamboo, in front of all, holds rolls of undyed silk stuffs, which are burned so that the spirits of the deceased may be clothed as well as fed.

FIG. 302.—Small Censer with openwork sides, on tripod of ivory-white Fu-chien porcelain.

The *Wu Kung*, or set of five sacrificial utensils, which is never absent, is displayed in the foreground on a separate table, consisting of an incense urn in the center, with two pricket candlesticks and two side pieces. The last are changed at each season, a pair of rhinoceros vases (*hsi tsun*) being set out in the spring, a pair of elephant vases (*hsiang tsun*) in the summer, a cup-shaped pair of vessels (*chu tsun*) in the autumn, and a pair of plain ovoid vases with spreading lips (*hu tsun*) in the winter.

The ritual vessels for the Ancestral Temple are enameled yellow, that being the imperial color. It is also, in accordance with notions upon color symbolism, which the Chinese share with other ancient Oriental nations, the color of earth, so that the porcelain vessels for the Altar of Earth in Peking are also enameled yellow, as well as those used by the emperor in his worship of the patron god of agriculture, and by the empress in her worship of the patron goddess of silk, at their respective temples. Blue is the color of heaven, and its temple is roofed with tiles of sapphire tint, and the ritual vessels used upon the Altar of Heaven have to be enameled blue, as well as those used in the Temple of the Land and Grain, where the emperor offers annual sacrifices for a favorable harvest. Red is the symbolical color of the sun, and the ritual vessels of porcelain displayed upon its altar are still invested with that color, as they used to be in the days of *Hsüan-tê*, when the famous ruby-red, derived from copper, was first introduced for the altar-cups to hold the wine offered up by that emperor in the worship of the sun. White is the color of Jupiter, the Year Star of the Chinese, and is reserved for the sacred vessels used upon its altar.

* One of these dishes, made of yellow porcelain, is figured by Grandidier (*La Céramique Chinoise*, Plate II, 7).

Some of the Buddhist altar sets of five pieces (*wu kung*) that have just been referred to are noble specimens of the ceramic art. A similar set is often seen on Taoist altars, like that made by T'ang Ying for presentation to the Temple of Tungpa, near Peking, of which the inscription was given in Chapter IV.

The same sacrificial set of five pieces is displayed upon the domestic altar of larger Chinese houses, but in smaller houses one sees perhaps only a single censer, like the specimen of ivory-white Fuchien porcelain, illustrated in Fig. 302, which is inscribed underneath with the sacred *svastika* symbol. In other cases a tazza-shaped cup is placed before the sacred shrine, to hold a daily offering of fresh flowers, flanked by a pair of lions mounted upon pedestals, from which spring little tubes to hold the molded rods of fragrant sawdust, which are commonly called "joss-sticks" by foreigners, "joss" being the pigeon-English corruption of the Portuguese *Dios*. The burning of incense is an indispensable accompaniment of every act of worship. One of these lions (*shih-tzŭ*) is exhibited in Fig. 303, and the tube which holds the stick of incense is seen in the picture rising from the pedestal at the back. The lion figures in Buddhism as a protector of the faith. The tazza-cup is called *ch'ing shui wan*, or "pure-water bowl"; it may be replaced by a plain white bowl of ordinary form, and the beautiful "lace-bowls" of the reign of *Ch'ien-lung* are specially prized for the purpose.

FIG. 303.—Figure of a Lion mounted upon a pedestal, with a tube at the side for a joss-stick; ivory-white Fuchien porcelain.

Two other Buddhist vessels may be noticed here, the alms-bowl (Chinese *po*, Sanskrit *pâtra*), and the lustration vase (Chinese *tsao-p'ing*, Sanskrit *kuṇḍikâ*), which every mendicant monk carried in olden times. The alms-bowl is of flattened globular form rounding into a small circular mouth. The lustration vase, intended for ceremonial ablution, is of more varied form; one of them is presented in Fig. 304 with a tall, curved spout springing from the monstrous head of a dragon, which is richly decorated with floral diapers and bands of conventional ornament, painted in colors of the *K'ang-hsi* period, relieved by a *tzŭ-chin* ground of "old-gold" tint. The older lustration vases are larger and of plainer form; sometimes they are elaborately worked in the paste, under a crackled glaze of the *Sung* dynasty, with dragons, frogs, fish, crabs, and all kinds of water plants—antitypes of the famous Palissy ware, which is ornamented in similar style.

There is another incense apparatus with no religious significance, which is provided as part of the furniture of every Chinese reception-room or library of any pretensions. The emperor is always represented as having one on the table before his throne, and it is a necessary part of the equipment of a scholar's study. This is the *San Shê*, or "Set of Three," which is so often seen mounted on stands in Chinese collections, carved in jade, rock-crystal, turquoise, *lapis lazuli*, and other precious materials, molded in bronze or silver, enameled in painted or *cloisonné* work upon metal, as well as in *faïence* and porcelain. The three pieces of this set comprise an urn (*lu*) for burning the chips of sandalwood or other scented material with the fumes of which the room is to be impregnated; a box (*ho*) with a cover to store the fragrant fuel ready for use; and a vase (*p'ing*) to hold the miniature tongs, poker, and shovel, made usually of gilded copper, with which the fire is kept up.

The Chinese *literati* are very particular in selecting their library apparatus and writing-tools, and a long series of scholars have published at different times a small library of books on the subject. For the writing-table there are porcelain pallets (*yen*); rests for the cake of ink (*mo chuang*); water-pots (*shui ch'êng*) of varied form, with tiny ladles of gilt metal or coral inside; water-droppers (*t'i-tzŭ*) of quaint designs, such as a tortoise or a three-legged toad distilling drops from its mouth, a lotus-pod, or a miniature wine-ewer; paper-weights (*chên chih*), a coil of dragons, a scantily clad urchin or gayly dressed girl reclining upon a leaf, or such like; hand-rests (*pi ko*) of oblong shape, with convex surface, to support the wrist when writing.

The pencil-brush (*pi*) of the writer or artist may be mounted in a porcelain handle (*pi kuan*); it has a bath (*pi hsi*), a dish in which it may be dipped and washed, which is often a specimen of ancient celadon, or of some other celebrated production of the older dynasties; "there is," according to our Chinese authority, "a bed (*pi chuang*) for it to lie down in, a rest (*pi ko*) for its support, the orthodox form of which is a miniature range of hills, and a cylinder (*pi t'ung*) for it to stand up in when not in use." The ancient seals (*yin*) of the *Han* dynasty, which used to be carved in jade or molded in copper, are now all copied in porcelain; they are of oblong form, surmounted by handles, fashioned in the form of a camel, a tortoise, an archaic dragon or tiger, a curved tile or two interlacing rings. Some of these seals have been dug up in Irish bogs, supposed to be of great antiquity, and a volume has been published on the subject.*

There are oblong plaques of porcelain, covered with written inscriptions, or decorated with pictures, in blue or white, or in colors, prepared to be mounted as panels in large leaf screens, framed in carved and lacquered wood; decorated porcelain panels for inlaying in an oblong wooden pillow, to provide a cool rest for the head in the hot season; hollow slabs of circular and oblong shape, with pictures painted on both front and back, to be inserted in the wood-work of beds, a round slab being placed at the head of the bed in the middle, succeeded by a series of oblong slabs, extending down the sides, and triangular mounts for the legs. Then there are porcelain mounts for the two ends of the wooden rollers attached to scroll pictures; porcelain handles for walking-sticks; sets of chessmen with boards, and other games, including a pair of bowls, of the traditional form of the Buddhist alms-bowl, for holding the black and white men for the game of *wei-ch'i*, the "miniature war practice" of the Chinese.

With regard to vases adapted for the display of cut flowers to decorate the reception-room or library, it would require a volume to describe all the varied shapes and designs. Archaic bronze forms alone, in which China is so rich, afford an inexhaustible series of models, as may be seen by a glance at the voluminous illustrated books on the subject, such as the *Po ku t'ou*, and the *Hsi ch'ing ku chien* catalogue of the imperial collection of the Emperor *Ch'ien-lung*, which have already been referred to. The older ceramic productions supply another suggestive source of inspiration, and according to the *T'ao Shuo*, select specimens of the Ting-chou, Ju-chou, crackled Ko Yao, and imperial porcelains (Kuan Yao) of the *Sung* dynasty, as well as porcelain vases of the celebrated reigns of *Hsüan-tê*, *Ch'êng-hua*, and *Chia-ching*, and *cloisonné* enamels on copper, of the reign of *Ching-tai*, of the *Ming* dynasty, are sent down from the palace, and gathered, besides, into the workshops at Ching-tê-chên from all parts of the empire for the purpose.

FIG. 304.—Lustration Ewer of Buddhist ecclesiastical form, painted in K'ang-hsi colors, relieved by an "old-gold" (*tzŭ-chin*) ground.

The same book describes porcelain vases generally as ranging in size from a height of two to three inches up to between five and six feet. In shape the *hu* are round, like the ancient earthenware vessels of that name; the *tan* are round and swelling below like the gall-bladder, from which their name is derived; the *tsun* are broad and round in section, with low body and expanding mouth, the *ku* of slender hornlike form, with vertical ridges on the body and trumpet-shaped mouth; these last two are archaic bronze forms, being varieties of what we, for some unexplained reason, call beakers.

There are two special works before us on flower-vases, both of which were published toward the end of the *Ming* dynasty in the beginning of the seventeenth century. The first, entitled *P'ing shih*, "History of Vases," is by Yuan Hung-tao, a famous scholar and high official who died in 1624, and whose biography, together with that of his two brothers, "The Three Yuan," as they were called by their contemporaries, is recorded in the *Ming shih* (or Annals). In his description of the forms he says:

---

* *Notices of Chinese Seals found in Ireland*, by Edmund Getty, Dublin, 1850.

"Among the vases in private collections in the province of Kiangnan, the finest are the ancient beakers (*ku*) with trumpet-shaped mouths, invested with a bright azure-blue penetrating into the paste marked with patches of vermilion tint rising in slight relief; these may be termed golden halls for flowers. Next in rank come select specimens of the imperial potteries of the *Sung* dynasty, of the crackled Ko Yao, of the crackled white porcelain of Hsiang-shan, near Ningpo, and of the ivory-white Ting-chou ware; these, when slender and graceful in form and of rich luster, all make elegant cots for the fairy blossoms. Vases for the decoration of the scholar's study ought not to be large and heavy, and any of the porcelain productions of the above factories, such as the vases shaped like paper-beaters, those with goose-necks, those fashioned in the shape of aubergine fruit, the flower bags or baskets (*hua nang*), the flower-beakers (*hua tsun*), the receptacles for divining-rods, and the bulrush-shaped—any of these that are short and small are suitable for chaste decoration."

The other book, called *P'ing hua p'u*, is a treatise on vases and the methods of arranging flowers in them, by Chang Ch'ien-tê, a son of the author of the *Ch'ing pi tsang*, an antiquarian work that has already been quoted, and for which he wrote a preface dated 1595. He says:

"In the art of floral decoration the first requisite is the selection of the vases. In spring and winter they should be of bronze, in summer and autumn of porcelain, on account of the variations of temperature. The larger ones are placed in the reception-hall, the smaller in the library, on account of exigency of space. Bronze and porcelain are preferred to gold and silver, as harmonizing better with the simple tastes of a scholar. Rings and pairs are to be avoided, and special attention is to be given to rarity and beauty. The mouth of a vase should be small and the foot thick, so that it may stand firmly and not emit unpleasant vapor."

The last paragraph recalls a favorite shape of the *Ming* dynasty, slender below, enlarging upward to a wide, bulging shoulder, and finally rounding into a small, narrow neck; this is the *mei p'ing* or "prunus vase" of the Chinese, who consider the form appropriate for the display of blossoming branches of the *mei hua*, the winter plum; in American auction catalogues it is often called a "gallipot," for some reason not clear to the uninitiated. Gourds are considered most suitable for the display of lotus-flowers, bulrush-shaped vases for peony-blossoms. The Chinese never arrange flowers in mixed bouquets; a spray or two of bamboo may be put with orchids, or a few blades of reed or other water-plant with lotus-blossoms, that is all. The festivals of the four seasons must be celebrated by a lavish exhibition of their floral emblems, the spring peony, the summer lotus, the autumn chrysanthemum, and the winter prunus. Each month of the year, too, has its distinctive flower, which the florist is expected to produce for his patrons in due rotation, as well as to provide a supply of cut flowers for other calendar holidays and festive occasions.

FIG. 305.—Snuff-bottle. Gray-blue crackle of the K'ang-hsi period. Mark, Ch'êng-hua nien chi.

Next to vases for cut flowers we come to flowerpots for growing plants, which are always pierced in the bottom with one or more holes, and are often provided with saucers. Some of the smaller ones, intended for interior decoration, are finely modeled and elaborately painted in colors. The ancient Chün-chou flowerpots, in their brilliant red coats of richly varied transmutation tints, rank as the most valued treasures of the Chinese connoisseur. The larger flowerpots, which are intended for the veranda and balcony, are also of varied form and design, being round, square, or polygonal, barrel-shaped, or like a miniature tank with rolled sides, and in other cases simulating the trunk of a tree or some grotesque monster. The large dragon fish-bowls (*lung kang*) that are placed on wooden stands in Chinese gardens or courtyards and filled with lotus-plants or with goldfish have been often referred to. Smaller bowls (*yü kang*) of the same shape are made for keeping goldfish in rooms, and are often decorated in the traditional way with dragons; others are made in the shape of the Buddhist alms-bowl as flattened globes with small circular mouths, the most attractive of which, perhaps, are the white bowls in which the sides have been pierced on geometrical lacework patterns and filled in with transparent glaze, giving a charmingly light effect as they stand on a side-table in front of the window. The shaped dishes of foliated outline mounted upon low, scrolled feet are for the cultivation of narcissus-flowers, which it is the ambition of every Chinese householder to have in full blossom upon New Year's day; the bulbs are supported in the dish by a layer of pebbles and kept watered. A circular dish of plainer form is generally seen upon one of the tables at the same time piled up with a heap of Buddha's-hand citrons or fragrant melons to perfume the air; the large *Yung-chêng* dishes, of which one is illustrated in Plate XLVIII, are used in the palace for this purpose, and a still more choice receptacle for the fragrant fruit is a dish of old Lung-ch'üan celadon, or of some other kind of ancient porcelain of the *Sung* dynasty.

Many other objects are made of porcelain for the reception-room: Barrel-shaped seats (*Tso-tun*); slabs of rectangular or circular shape for insertion in the tops of tables and benches; hanging baskets with pierced sides for flowers, hanging lamps (*kua-têng*) of eggshell thinness, or with openwork panels, like the two beautiful ex- amples illustrated on these pages; and all kinds of boxes and cabinets of varied shape and design.

Three characteristic forms of the floral receptacles with pierced open- work sides through which the fragrance of the flowers is diffused through- out the room, are shown here. Fig. 306 is a hanging basket decorated in enamel colors, with gilding of the *K'ang-hsi* period, with floral band near the rims, and the sides painted in black, green, and yellow to simulate wicker. The cylinder which fits inside is painted in coral-red with scrolls of lotus and a ring of spiral fret.

Fig. 307 shows a basket-shaped bowl, with a cover surmounted by a lion, decorated in *K'ang-hsi* colors. The handle is painted in black lines upon a yellow ground to imitate basket-work. The sides are pierced in six panels of hexagonal trellis interrupted by chrysanthemum-flowers alternately red and light purple, and the cover has a similar openwork design. The borders are painted with scrolls in red. The perfume globe, *hsiang ch'iu*, in Fig. 308, is of light biscuit porcelain inlaid with *K'ang-hsi* colors, a brilliant green in combination with the usual enam- els of the old *famille rose*. The pierced medallions contain alternately

FIG. 306.—Hanging Basket with pierced sides, paint- ed in enamel colors, with gilding of the K'ang-hsi period.

peony and lotus flowers. It has a tiny round cover for the introduction of the flowers, and is strung with a silk cord, although it would usually stand on the table. It is fashioned in the likeness of one of the globular gourds which are often carved in openwork as receptacles for fragrant flowers, as cages for singing cicadas, or to carry fighting crickets in safe custody inside.

There must always be a pair of hat-stands (*mao chia*) on one of the side-tables for visitors' hats, which are kept on the head during calls of ceremony, but are allowed to be taken off on less formal occasions; these are often made of porcelain and vary very much in form. M. Grandidier describes an elaborate *porte-calotte* exhibited in his collection in the Louvre, consist- ing of a sphere supported by a long tube, to which it is buttressed by branches of foliage, mounted upon a lobed stand with trefoil feet, the globe being hollow so as to hold fire or ice, according to the season, for the purpose of warming or cooling the hat. Another not uncommon design has a little box supported upon long, curved spindle legs with a perforated lid, adapted to hold a scent *sachet* or a few chips of sandalwood.

Having disposed of objects of utility, we come to those intended solely for decorative pur- poses. To this class belongs the great majority of the vases and jars seen in Oriental collec- tions. Their function is purely ornamental, although in form they are lineal descendants of the flower-vases, the wine-receptacles, and the jars with covers for storing preserved fruits and dried tea-leaves, that were made for actual use in earlier times.

An ornamental group or set of five pieces is often seen arranged in line on one of the long side-tables of the Chinese reception-hall. This is the *Wu Shê*, or "Five Set," and it may be either of a single color, or decorated in one or several enamel colors, or painted in blue and white. It consists of a vase (*p'ing*), in which the mouth is less in diameter than the body, placed in the middle, a pair of jars (*kuan*) with covers on each side of the central vase, and a pair of beaker-shaped vases (*ku*), with flaring mouths wider than the bodies, at the two ends of the line. This arrangement differs from that of the *garniture de cheminée*, or "mantelpiece set," of European collections, which is also composed of five pieces of similar design displayed in line, but the central vase of the Chinese set is missing, its place being usurped by a third covered jar; two other jars are placed at the ends of the line, and the pair of beakers between the jars. This was the conventional "garniture" of the Dutch in their interiors of the sixteenth and seventeenth centuries, in which the Oriental porcelain lighted up the old oak furniture, and gathered an added brilliancy contrasted with its dark setting. These were ideal surroundings for the lustrous blue and white porcelain of the *K'ang-hsi* epoch, and it could hardly be exhibited anywhere under greater advantages.

One of these *garnitures de cheminée* has been photographed for Fig. 213. It is decorated in bands and panels of varied form painted in bright enamel colors with gilding, relieved by a monochrome *tzŭ-chin* ground of coffee-brown tint. The ground is interrupted by encircling bands and lambrequins of floral brocade, by blossoms of peony, aster, peach, and plum, and by scrolled and foliated panels filled with pictures of landscape scenes with temples and pagodas. The covers of the jars, enameled with the same brown ground, have leaf-shaped reserves painted with peony-flowers. The peculiar style of decoration is commonly known in Europe as "Batavian," the Dutch having imported it so largely in the last century, during the time that they were the chief merchant-carriers from the far East.

FIG. 307.—Covered Bowl with pierced panels on the sides; decorated in colored enamels of early K'ang-hsi date.

The magnificent ovoid vases, five feet in height, with bell-shaped covers on the top, which made their first appearance toward the end of the reign of *K'ang-hsi*, gorgeously decorated in colors of the *famille rose*, are called by the Chinese *ti p'ing*, or "ground vases," their place being on the ground at the sides of the entrance of the hall, mounted upon low stands of carved wood. In Europe they are seen occasionally on the grand staircase of a palace, supporting branched chandeliers of ormolu.

A peculiar shape of the reign of *K'ang-hsi* is the *chien t'ung*, or "arrow cylinder." The Manchu Tartars have always been famous for their skill in archery, and even in the present day the military officer depends on it for his promotion. The arrow receptacles are either tall cylinders, or of square tubular form, and are mounted in socketed pedestals of the same material surrounded by an openwork railing. They are very richly decorated in the brilliant enamel colors of the period, combined with relief molding and chiseled openwork, as exemplified in the characteristic specimen in Fig. 313.

The small vases with thin necks tapering upward to a contracted orifice, like the pair of which one is presented in Fig. 309, are perfume sprinklers (*hsiang shui p'ing*). This pair, which came from the collection of a Persian prince, uncle of the Shah, had been mounted in that country with metal, and doubtless used there for sprinkling rose-water, the favorite scent of the Persians. The porcelain is, of course, Chinese, and it is decorated in the characteristic style of the *K'ang-hsi* period with a powder-blue ground, interrupted by three reserved medallions of quatrefoil, pomegranate, and fan shape, which are lightly penciled in underglaze blue upon a white ground with wild flowers growing from rocks.

The smallest vases of all are the snuff-bottles (*yen hu*), one or two of which are generally laid upon the small table that stands on the divan of a Chinese reception-room, with little ivory spoons attached to the stoppers inside, to ladle out the contents. The tobacco plant is indigenous to America, and there is no reason for doubting that it was introduced into the Far East by Spanish or Portuguese ships at about the same time that it reached Europe. In fact, the Chinese Emperor *Wan-li* (1573–1619) vied with his contemporary, James I of England, in fulminating edicts which he issued against the new weed, that was then just coming into vogue in China. It flourished, notwithstanding, and in the present day it is cultivated throughout the empire and smoked alike by man, woman, and child. But the little bottles seem to have been made in China before the introduction of snuff, and the apparent anachronism is due to the fact that they were originally intended to hold valuable aromatics or rare drugs, which is proved by their old name of *yao p'ing*, or "medicine-bottles." Glass bottles are now gradually coming into use for the purpose, but old-fashioned druggists still send out their pills in the little porcelain flasks. The itinerant medicine-venders often have a supply of these little flasks made to order, with their professional name inscribed on one side, and perhaps a quaint superscription on the other, like *ch'i tai* or *pa tai*, "seven generations" or "eight generations," to indicate that the secret formula has been a hereditary possession for so long a period. Before the Portuguese ships appeared in the Indian Ocean and interrupted the traffic, Chinese junks visited the coasts of Africa and Arabia, and seem to have taken a quantity of these medicine-bottles of coarse fabric and rough manufacture to store the precious aromatics which formed the most valuable part of their cargo. Little bottles of the kind are found to-day in Cairo, and their fraudulent introduction into ancient tombs by the Arab workmen has led some to claim for them a fabulous antiquity, after Rosellini,* who describes one as having been "found by him in an Egyptian tomb which had never been opened before, and the date of which belonged to a Pharaoh reigning not later than the eighteenth century before Christ." Their false pretensions have been long ago exposed by Sir Walter Medhurst and Sir Harry Parkes, in the Transactions of the China Branch of the Royal Asiatic Society, and need hardly have been alluded to here, had one not seen a row of the so-called snuff-bottles exhibited among true Egyptian antiquities in the Abbott Collection in New York, and found Dr. Prime boldly claiming, in his book on the *Pottery of all Times and Nations* published in 1879, an age of a thousand years for three snuff-bottles in his own collection, obtained by him from Arabs at Thebes and Cairo.

FIG. 308.—Pierced Globe of delicate K'ang-hsi porcelain, decorated *sur biscuit* in enamel colors.

There is a peculiar attraction in Chinese snuff-bottles, and I have seen three envoys of great European powers at Peking vying with each other in the acquisition of rare specimens. They are made of many other materials besides porcelain, such, for example, as cameo-glass, jade, rock-crystal, amethyst, carnelian, chalcedony, heliotrope, sardonyx, chrysoprase, turquoise, agate, *niellé* bronze, damascened iron, painted and *cloisonné* enamels, carved cinnabar lac, etc. Several pamphlets have been written on the subject, the latest of which is the beautifully illustrated contribution, under the title of *Chinese Snuff-Bottles* by Mr. M. B. Huish to the Opuscula of the Odd Volumes Sette, of which, unfortunately, only one hundred and forty-nine copies have been printed, the circulation being limited to Odd-Volume members.

Of the porcelain snuff-bottles several of quaint form and cunning device have been selected for some of the head-pieces for these pages, and Plate XXXVII is specially devoted to their illustration. The collection exhibits, in epitome, many of the different processes of decoration, including single colors plain and crackled, painting in blue, red, and in many colors, relief modeling and openwork carving in those provided with a pierced outer casing. The different forms of larger vases are reproduced in miniature, single or bijugate; there are flasks upright and recumbent, gourds of all kinds, trellis designs, and basket wickerwork. One little bottle simulates a bursting cob of maize, another the fruit of the eggplant, a third is fashioned, as it were, of two lotus-leaves joined together, a fourth of a pair of butterflies. A quaint form is that of a Chinese damsel whose inverted body is the receptacle for the snuff, while one leg is hollowed for the spoon, which is cemented to the tiny porcelain foot that is made to officiate as the stopper of the strange bottle.

The civil mandarin may have the one hundred and eighth bead of his official rosary, or the clasp of his girdle, made of porcelain; the military mandarin, the broad ring which protects his thumb against the bowstring, or the little tube which is attached to the top of his hat to hold

* *I Monumenti dell' Egitto*, etc., vol. ii, p. 337. Pisa, 1834.

the streaming peacock's feather. Chinese ladies are said to possess in their inner apartments boxes, large and small, for holding powder, rouge, and other cosmetics, in which they indulge so freely, as well as bottles for liquid scents; they occasionally wear in their headdress elaborate hairpins of porcelain, they adorn themselves with earrings and bracelets, fasten their robes with porcelain rings and buttons, and attach ornamental pendants to their girdles. Some of these things are very delicately decorated. There is a certain badge worn at religious ceremonies which often finds its way into collections; it has inscribed on one side the Chinese characters *chai chieh*, "fasting and abstinence," inclosed within an ornamental frame, and on the other side the same motto in the Manchu script; it may be of oblong or oval form, or shaped like a double gourd.

The pretty little vase-shaped receptacle in Fig. 314, with globular body and wide-spreading neck, is an imperial hand-spittoon (*cha-tou*). It is decorated in two shades of coral-red with a pair of five-clawed dragons pursuing pearls in the midst of clouds, a band of conventional flowers, and rings of gadroon and spiral fret. It may be referred confidently to the *Ch'ien-lung* period, although there is no mark underneath. A pair of taller vessels of the same form are usually seen on the toilet-table in a Chinese room, perhaps with a toothbrush standing up in one; they take the place of glass tumblers with us.

Our Chinese guide proceeds next in the *T'ao Shuo* to give a brief enumeration of the porcelain services and other things made for the dining-room. He begins with rice-spoons,

FIG. 309. — Perfume Sprinkler, powder-blue ground with reserve panels, penciled in underglaze blue; Persian metal mounts.

teaspoons, and the chop-stick service. The latter consists of a pair of chopsticks for each guest (which he uses in lieu of knife and fork) and a number of little saucer-shaped dishes of varied form, some empty, for the guests to lay their chop-sticks on, or to use as they help themselves from the bowls that are being constantly brought in courses of four or eight plats; others dotted about the table filled with melon-seeds, peach-kernels, nuts, and sweetmeats. The "drageoirs," or comfit-dishes, are sometimes modeled in the form of a large lotus-flower or plum-blossom in movable compartments, so that they can be taken to pieces to form separate little dishes for the dining-table. Comfit dishes of this floral or geometrical design, dating from the reign of *K'ang-hsi*, are often very richly decorated, being enameled *sur biscuit* with graceful scrolls of the same flower, displayed upon a bright green or buff-colored ground.

The different kinds of bowls, teacups, wine-cups, dishes and platters have been already referred to, and it is not necessary to describe all the various forms of teapots and wine-ewers. The tall ewers of cylindrical shape with tiara-fronted tops, like that in Fig. 168, are used by the Chinese for iced fruit-sirups; the Mongols are fond of the same design for their *koumis* or milk-wine ewers, which are made of bronze or silver. The ordinary wine-cups of the Chinese are small, sometimes not larger than thimbles; marriage wine-cups are of more elaborate design; sacrificial libation-cups are molded in the form of bronze ritual-vessels with hieratic designs. For the dining-table there are also vinegar-cruets, oil-lamps, pricket candlesticks, and square receptacles for the snuff from the candles (*la tou*), made of porcelain. For daily use there are wash-basins, pots, and pans, and jars of manifold form and capacity, which need not be minutely described.

Some of the dinner services used for sending out dinners from restaurants are of very elaborate character, the covered dishes being molded in the form of ducks, fishes, and the like, so as to indicate the nature of their contents.

White services, decorated with arabesques and other designs incised in the paste under the glaze, are intended for use during mourning. Imperial mourning-bowls are etched with five-clawed dragons under the white glaze.

FIG. 310.—Ivory-white Vase of Fuchien ware, with a dragon
molded on the surface in salient relief.

CHAPTER XVIII.

PECULIAR TECHNICAL PROCESSES.—CRACKLE PORCELAIN.—FURNACE TRANSMUTATIONS.—SOUFFLÉS.—
LAQUE BURGAUTÉE.—PIERCED AND "RICE-GRAIN" DESIGNS.—WHITE SLIP, ETC.

BEFORE proceeding to a consideration of the colors and the motives of decoration of Chinese porcelain, a few words may be said on certain characteristic technical processes of their ceramic art. Some of the peculiar methods referred to have been successfully imitated in Japan, as well as, more recently, in Western countries, but they were all first invented in China, the original country of the art.

Crackle porcelain is one of the most peculiar productions of the Oriental potter, and has not been successfully imitated elsewhere. Several of the most ancient wares are distinguished by their crackled glazes. There lies on the table before me at the present moment a collection of potsherd fragments of bowls and dishes dating from the *Sung* and *Yuan* dynasties, recently dug up within the precincts of the city of Peking, which are all crackled. The glaze has been laid on so thickly in some of these ancient pieces that it is actually thicker than the underlying paste, accounting so far for the hackneyed native simile of "massed lard." It ranges in color through all shades of purple to the pale cerulean tint known as *yueh pai*, or *clair de lune*, and has its lustrous depth traversed by an infinity of lines so as to look like fissured ice. The Chinese collect such fragments of old vessels, when the color is sufficiently attractive, to mount them in girdle clasps, or to frame them in gilded metal for use on the study-table as rests for the wrist of the writer, etc. An old legend declares that the azure-tinted porcelain of the ancient Imperial House of Ch'ai, which flourished in the tenth century, was so brilliant that a fragment placed in front of the helmet of a warrior would even deflect the course of an arrow.

There are two varieties of the old celadon porcelain made at Lung-ch'üan during the *Sung* dynasty which differ in the glaze, one being uncrackled, while that of the other was crackled. The invention of this last was attributed, as we have seen in Chapter V, to an elder brother of a family of potters named Chang, and it was from this fact that it first came to be known as *Ko Yao, ko* meaning "elder brother." Another common name for crackled porcelain is *sui ch'i, sui* meaning "broken," or "shattered in pieces." This name, derived from the mosaiclike aspect of the glaze, looking, it was said, as if the porcelain

FIG. 311.—Snuff-bottle with green and white dragon; mark, Tao-kuang.

were made of a thousand separate pieces cemented together, also dates from the *Sung* dynasty, when it was applied to the crackled porcelain produced at Chi-chou, in the province of Kiangsi. This is described in the old books as resembling the ancient *ko yao*, both in color and in being reticulated with lines like fissured ice. Descriptive names of crackle that are often met with are *ping-lieh*, "fissured ice," which is applied to the coarser variety, and *yü tzŭ*, "fish-roe," which is applied to the variety with a closer crackled network that is called by French ceramic writers *truitée*, on account of its fancied resemblance to the fine scales of the trout.

Crackling, as has been explained in Chapter XV, is due to a physical cause. It may happen accidentally in some pieces during the firing of a European furnace, although it is then considered to be a defect. Its production in China even was doubtless originally accidental; but it had to be produced artificially in the imitation of the old glazes which exhibited this peculiarity, until finally the Chinese potter was enabled to produce it at will. The crackled glaze in the present day, according to the *Ching-tê-chên T'ao lu*, is prepared from a natural rock found at San-pao-p'êng, from which place it is brought to the manufactory in the form of prepared bricklets called *sui ch'i tun*, or "crackled-ware bricklets." These, when finely levigated,

FIG. 312.—Vase decorated with a landscape in blue under a white glaze, overlaid with variegated splashes of *flambé* glaze.

produce the ordinary crackled glaze; when they are roughly washed the crackled lines appear at larger and wider intervals. In the old crackle of the *Sung* dynasty, made at Chi-chou, the porcelain, which was heavy, thick, and of strong, coarse texture, was coated with glazes of two colors, either rice-gray or light blue. The mosaic-like crackled lines were produced by the addition of *hua-shih*, or steatite, to the materials of the glaze. When ink or vermilion was rubbed in, and the superfluity rubbed off after the piece was finished, a charming network of fissured lines appeared of subdued black or red tint.

There was another variety of crackled porcelain produced at the same manufactory in which a decoration in blue was added to the grayish-white crackled ground, being painted on the raw body before the application of the glaze. Specimens of archaic-looking crackle roughly decorated in blue, generally with dragons, are found in the present day in Borneo and other islands of the Eastern Archipelago. They are highly prized by the Dayaks and handed down in families as heirlooms. Some of them may date from the *Sung* or *Yuan* dynasties, like the plain crackled ware with which they are associated. The little tripod censer in Fig. 66, although it may not perhaps be so old, is a good illustration of the style.

There is another kind of crackled porcelain of more modern date than the last, in which the surface, originally white, is tinted pink or crimson. It is represented by comparatively small pieces, such as vases a few inches high, teacups, and the like, and the surface is usually finely crackled, or *truitée*. The color is produced by *yen-chih hung*, or *rouge d'or*, combined with a flux, and is the same as that employed for the celebrated ruby-backed dishes. The crackled piece, after it has been fired, is placed in a little cage or netting made of iron wire and heated strongly in a coal fire; it is then removed, and the color, suspended in water, is blown on the heated surface with the usual bamboo tube covered with gauze; it produces immediately the effect desired, and requires no further firing.

Crackled porcelain may also be decorated in enamel colors, which are fixed in the ordinary way by a second firing in the muffle stove, and some very beautiful bowls of the *K'ang-hsi* period illustrate this combination. The style and technique of the colors fix the date, if the bowl be not marked, with a certainty that could hardly be attained by an examination of the crackled glaze alone. A striking example in the present collection is the statuette of Kuan Yin, the Goddess of Mercy, which is reproduced in colors in Plate LX.

With regard to the crackled glaze in single colors, which include some of the most attractive of Chinese monochromes, they are well represented in the colored plates. The Chinese potter claims to be able to crackle any one of the monochrome glazes by introducing some of the *sui-ch'i tun*, or "crackle petuntse," into the ingredients. Some of the single colors, however, such as the coral-red produced by iron, and the *rouges d'or* of pink and ruby shades, are never in actual practice so treated. These colors are so delicate as to require no extrinsic adornment to add to their charm. Some others of the monochromes, on the contrary, are always crackled, such as the turquoise-blue derived from copper, and the aubergine purple of cobaltiferous manganese, both *couleurs du demi-grand feu*. Turquoise crackle in its varied shades is fully illustrated in Plates XCIII, LXXXIV, XLV, and LXXV; and a magnificent vase of finely crackled purple blue of deepest and richest tone is presented in Plate XXIX.

Several of the early ceramic productions of the *Sung* and *Yuan* dynasties are distinguished by their crackled glazes, like the two pieces illustrated in Plate XII. It was during his repeated attempts at the reproduction of such ancient pieces that the modern Chinese potter acquired his skill in the management of crackle. The modern representation of the old *clair-de-lune* crackled glaze of Ju-chou is the vase illustrated in Plate LXXVII, with its glaze of the color technically known as *ju yu*—i. e., "Juchou glaze"—varying from pale blue to gray, traversed by a reticulation of reddish lines; the representative of the purple-colored imperial ware (*kuan yao*) of the southern *Sung* dynasty is the crackled lavender vase in Plate XLIII, with its brown-tinted mouth and its foot artificially coated to simulate the brown paste of the original model. In a similar fashion the crackled white *Fên Ting* vases exhibited in Plates LXXXIX and XCI, both of which date from early in the present dynasty, are the representatives of the ancient ivory-white crackled porcelain made at Ting-chou in the *Sung* dynasty, from which they take their name; and the crackled grayish-green vase in Plate LXXXVI is a representative of an ancient celadon.

The most brilliant of all the crackles is the celebrated Lang-yao of the reign of *K'ang-hsi*, already described in Chapter X, the original *sang-de-bœuf* of ceramic connoisseurs, which ranks deservedly among the highest achievements of the Oriental potter. Its gorgeous mottled dress of mingled tones of crimson and ruby shade can be seen in the four vases, selected from the series in the collection, to be illustrated in Plates LIX, LVII, I, and LVI. The largest and most characteristic example, perhaps, is the vase in Plate LIX, which shows the crackled texture of the glaze, the stippled ground, and the vertically streaked play of rich colors, passing from the deepest crimson through all intermediate shades to pale apple-green toward the rim. The tall, graceful vase in Plate LVI and the beaker in Plate I both exhibit rich, full tones of red, deepening in the latter case almost to black upon the shoulder of the vase. But a more perfect example than the bottle-shaped vase in Plate LVII, in its rich coloring and finished technique, could hardly be imagined, and it displays near the base the typical patch of apple-green which is so often associated with the ox-blood red. An occasional vase of the Lang yao type is seen, in which the crackled glaze is entirely apple-green (*p'ing-kuo ch'ing*), with perhaps a patch of red near the lower rim.

FIG. 313.—Tall, Rectangular Arrow Receptacle, mounted in a socket pedestal, exhibiting relief and openwork modeling, and a rich decoration in enamel colors of the K'ang-hsi period.

The green monochromes of Chinese porcelain are generally produced by copper, the exceptions being the celadon proper, or *tung-ch'ing*, the sea-green tint of which is due to ferruginous clay, and the modern representatives of the old Lung-ch'üan celadons, which are brought to a more pronounced grass-green or olive-green hue by the addition of a small dose of cobalt to the ingredients of the former glaze; any of these celadon glazes may be purposely crackled. A brilliant green derived from copper is the leading note in the decoration with colored enamels of the *K'ang-hsi* period, and the same color appears naturally in the foreground among the monochromes of the time. It is distinguished by its marked iridescence, a quality which is displayed in a high degree by the vase illustrated in Plate LXXIX. The vases in Plates LXXXI and LXXVIII are invested with crackled green enamels of two of the shades comprised by the Chinese under the name of *kua-p'i lü*, or "cucumber-green," which is fairly distinctive, although other names are used in European books, such as "camellia-leaf green," or "apple-green." The last term ought, I think, to be confined to the pale green so often found upon porcelain, associated with the "apple-red," which is also due to copper; the same dual combination that occurs curiously on the rind of a ripe apple. The fourth vase of green crackle, illustrated in Plate XXVII, is a typical example of the "fish-roe green" (*yü-tzŭ-ch'ing*) of the Chinese, which, like its congener, the *truitée* yellow or mustard crackle, was a favorite glaze of the *Ch'ien-lung* period. A fine specimen of this *yü-tzŭ huang*, or "fish-roe yellow," of the Chinese, is displayed in Plate LXXXVII.

The discussion of transmutation colors succeeds that of the ordinary crackled porcelain by natural transition, because they attain their most brilliant effect in combination with a crackled glaze. The name of "furnace transmutation" is a literal rendering of the Chinese term *yao pien*, which is applied especially to the *flambée* porcelain of variegated coloring, due to different degrees of oxidation of the copper silicates to which it owes its brilliant hues, passing from the warmest crimson through all intermediate shades to turquoise-blue. It is difficult to depict in words the gorgeous effect of the varied play of colors in this decoration, which is justly considered to be one of the most marvelous products of the Orient. The cause of this transmutation is well known. Copper in its first degree of oxidation gives to the vitrified glaze the bright ruby-red tint known to the Chinese as *chi hung*, or "sacrificial red"; with more oxygen it produces a brilliant green, and at its highest degree of oxidation a turquoise-blue. Any of these effects may be produced in the chemical laboratory. In the furnace the various modifications are produced suddenly by the manipulation of the fire. In a clear fire with a strong draught all the oxygen is not consumed, and is free to combine with the metal in fusion. If, on the other hand, the fire be loaded with thick smoke, the carbonaceous mass will greedily absorb all the free oxygen, and the metal will attain its minimum degree of oxidation. So, when placed in a given moment in these various conditions by the rapid and simultaneous introduction of currents of air and sooty vapors, the glaze assumes a most picturesque appearance; the surface of the piece becomes diapered with veined and streaked colorations, changing and capricious as the flames of spirits; the red oxide passes through violet and green to the pale blue peroxide, and is even dissipated completely upon certain projections, which become white, and thus furnish another happy fortuitous combination.

FIG. 314.—Small Vase of Ch'ien-lung imperial porcelain, decorated in two shades of coral-red.

The transmutation glazes are of ancient date in China, some of the Chün-chou porcelains of the *Sung* dynasty being of this class. The name of *Lo kan ma fei*—i. e., "mule's liver and horse's lung"—was, in fact, invented as descriptive of the mingled colors of one of the varieties of Chün-chou vases which was sent down from the palace in the reign of *Yung-chêng* to be copied at Ching-tê-chên. The name was well chosen, suggesting, as it does, what has been described by an expert * as the mixture of red, blue, violet, and yellowish green, flowing over the porcelain like a kind of lava of blood, lungs, and liver, chopped up and melted into enamels. The idea of liver-colored would suggest brown as well, and we often, indeed, found this color present in the old *flambé* glazes, due doubtless to the presence of iron. The occurrence of yellow and brown spots on certain *flambés* is always a sure indication of the existence of iron.

Père d'Entrecolles, in his second letter dated in 1722, the last year of the long reign of the Emperor *K'ang-hsi*, writes: "There has just been brought to me one of those pieces of porcelain that are called *yao-pien*, or 'transmutation.' This transmutation occurs in the furnace, and is caused either by some defect or excess in the firing, or perhaps by some other causes which are not easy to conjecture. This piece, which was a failure, according to the workman,

* *La Porcelaine*, par Georges Vogt, p. 23.

and which was the effect of pure chance, was none the less beautiful nor the less highly prized. The workman had designed to make vases of red *soufflé*. A hundred pieces had been entirely lost; the one alone of which I am speaking had come out of the furnace resembling a kind of agate. If one were willing to run the risk and the expense of repeated trials, one might discover, as the result, the art of making with certainty what chance had produced a single time." The words of the worthy Father are prophetic, for it was early in the succeeding reign of *Yung-chêng* that the art was verily discovered and rapidly brought to perfection; the best pieces of this class are rarely marked, but the rare marks are seals of *Yung-chêng* and *Ch'ien-lung*, which are sometimes impressed in the paste underneath.

The process described above may be characterized as the academic transmutation method. In actual practice the result is often aimed at in a more artificial way. The piece, coated with a grayish crackle glaze, or with a ferruginous enamel of yellowish-brown

FIG. 315.—Cylindrical Beaker of *laque bur-gautée* of the K'ang-hsi period.

FIG. 316.—Vase, coated *sur biscuit* with parti-colored splashes of yellow, green, and olive-brown, associated with a white glaze of soft ivory tone.

tone, has the transmutation glaze applied at the same time as a kind of overcoat. It is put on with the brush in various ways, in thick dashes not completely covering the surface of the piece, or flecked on from the point of the brush in a rain of drops, etc. The piece is finally fired in a reducing atmosphere, and the air, let in at the critical moment when the materials are fully fused, imparts atoms of oxygen to the copper, and speckles the red base with points of green and turquoise-blue, so that the glaze becomes vitrified into the characteristic variegated hues as it gradually cools. An inspection of the pieces will indicate the various methods of application. The hexagonal vase, for example, illustrated in Plate LXXXVIII, has a crackled glaze of olive-brown tint overlaid with thick splashes of *flambé* glaze, which have run down in the kiln in massive drops, so as to stand out on the surface of the vase in marked relief. The receptacle for divining rods in Plate XXIII, which is a more modern piece, with a thinner glaze, also indicates, from the association of olive-brown with the mottled grays and purples which bedizen its sides, the presence of iron as well as of copper.

A curious combination of the transmutation glaze with blue and white decoration is presented in the vase, attributed to the early *Ch'ien-lung* period, that is shown in Fig. 312. It is painted in underglaze blue with a landscape scene, hills with temples and pavilions, and a lake with boats upon it, and with bands of rectangular fret round the rims. This is overspread with splashes of *flambé* glaze, so as nearly to conceal the picture under variegated clouds of purple, crimson, and olive-brown tints, which become crackled where the glaze is thin. The interior of the vase is coated with the same crackled and variegated glaze.

The next special technical process to be noticed is that of the application of *soufflés*. The bamboo tube with gauze tied over one end that is used by the potter has already been described. With that the Chinese blow on the ordinary white glaze in repeated layers, as well as many of the single colors, such as the cobalt-blue, the high-fired reds derived from copper, the coral-red produced by iron, the pinks and carmines of gold, and the pure metals, gold and silver combined with a lead flux. The colors applied in this way can generally be recognized by the stippled aspect of the glaze, which is well marked in the *sang-de-bœuf* glaze of the Lang Yao, and in the ruby-red monochrome of the succeeding reign of *Yung-chêng*, which is one of the most characteristic glazes of the class of porcelain known as Nien Yao. What we have especially to notice now are the compound glazes in which a second color is blown upon a monochrome previously prepared. Such is the "Robin's Egg," or *Chün Yu*, which was alluded to in Chapter XIII as a *soufflé* glaze with a greenish-blue flecking and dappling on a reddish ground, the red being subordinate to the blue. The second color in these compound glazes is either blown on so as to cover the entire surface of the first with a delicate stippling, combining with and modifying the original tint, such as red upon a green or yellow ground, or green upon yellow; or it is projected in layer drops, which dapple the surface or run down over the piece in regular veins, leaving traces' like tears.

One of the best-known glazes of this class is the *Ch'a-yeh-mo*, or "Tea-dust" glaze, produced by the insufflation of green enamel upon a yellowish-brown ground, which owes its

color to iron. The combination produces a peculiarly soft tint of greenish tone, which was highly prized in the reign of *Ch'ien-lung*, when it was invented, so that a sumptuary law was made, according to M. Billequin, restricting the use of this color to the emperor, to evade which collectors used to paint their specimens with imaginary cracks, and even to put in actual rivets, to make them appear to be broken.

Another *soufflé* combination of the same time produced the *T'ieh-hsiu-hua*, or "Iron-Rust Decoration," which has been described in Chapter XIV, and is well illustrated in colors in Plate XIX. The *Ku-t'ung-ts'ai*, or "Ancient Bronze Coloring," which is one of the chief triumphs of the same reign of *Ch'ien-lung*, offers some analogies to the iron-rust decoration. There is a specimen in the *Musée du Louvre* (No. 248) which, according to M. Jacquemart, when placed among bronze objects can not be distinguished from them; it is necessary to examine it

Fig. 317.—Snuff-bottle with foliations in soft paste, white on dark blue ground. Ch'ien-lung.

closely and to touch it to recognize the work of the potter. The ground of the piece is bronze-colored, some of the salient parts being gold-tinted; while the decorations impressed upon the sides, in the style of metal casting, have received in the hollow parts a greenish-blue enamel, which simulates perfectly the natural oxidation of an ancient copper object. A smaller specimen of similar character is shown in Fig. 274.

Some of the many imitations of natural materials on which the Chinese pride themselves were referred to in the same chapter. There are cups simulating walnut-wood, with the grain so perfectly rendered in painted enamels that it is difficult to believe, without handling them, that it is not the actual veining of wood. The vase in Fig. 316 is enameled inside and outside in colors of the *K'ang-hsi* period, laid on *sur biscuit*, to look like tortoise-shell.

The carved cinnabar lac, of which a specimen was illustrated in Plate XXXVII, 4, is sometimes laid and worked upon a porcelain base, such as a vase or cup. It is also perfectly imitated in porcelain, with the designs modeled in the paste in similar relief and enameled vermilion. There is another peculiar combination of the incrusted lacquerwork with porcelain, which has been named *porcelaine laquée burgautée*, after *burgau*, the French name of the shell of the turbo. This was first noticed and described by Jacquemart, but he erroneously attributes it to Japan, although the style of art and the nature of the porcelain both prove it to be Chinese. The Chinese call it *Lo-tien Tz'ŭ*—i. e., "Porcelain inlaid with shellwork"—and the technique is the same as that of the incrusted cabinet work of Canton, only worked upon porcelain instead of wood. The porcelain is comparatively thick, with solid rims, and the ground of the piece is usually left unglazed, so that the lacquer may adhere more firmly to the surface. The finest vases date from the reign of *K'ang-hsi*, and it seems to have been first worked on porcelain at this time, in spite of the fact that the mark of *Ch'êng-hua* of the *Ming* dynasty is occasionally found inscribed underneath.

The decoration of the *laque burgautée* class is generally of a landscape character, executed in a mosaic mother-of-pearl, varied sometimes by thin plaques of beaten gold and silver, displayed upon a velvety background of ink-black lac. The pieces of shell, extremely thin, are tinted artificially, shaped with the knife, and combined cleverly by the artist to form the details of the picture. The patience of the workman is almost incredible, shaping one by one the leaves of a willow-tree, or of a clump of bamboos, the feathers of a bird, the glittering morsels designed to represent the pebbly bank of a river, or the faults of a rock, and carving silhouettes for clouds and waves, fine and supple as the strokes of a pencil. There is a large bowl in the Sèvres Museum, covered with a lake scene, with lotus-flowers, reeds, and waterfowl, which is a *chef-d'œuvre* of naturalistic art. I have seen a large vase of the kind nearly three feet high, of the *K'ang-hsi* period, with the neck and swelling body filled in with black lac, exhibiting in delicately tinted mosaic the varied scenes of Chinese lily life, in their minutest details, each scene being labeled in tiny characters; the gilded disk of the sun was shining over all in its pristine brightness; but the silver walls of the houses had become quite black from age. The little cylindrical beaker illustrated in Fig. 315 is a less important example.

The next peculiar technical processes in the short list that forms the heading of this chapter are those of ornamental pierced work of the ordinary kind, and pierced work filled in with glaze, so as to form the transparencies which are known from their usual shape as "rice-grain" designs. These methods have been already described. They are now well known, and are practiced all over the world, at Sèvres and Worcester, as well as in Japan. Fig. 318 is a Japanese vase of this description that was exhibited at the Chicago Exposition. They may be used in combination with all kinds of decoration, but are most charming and effective in pure white porcelain, such as the little white cups of design similar to the one illustrated in Fig. 138, which are lined with beaten gold or silver when used, and the white bowls with lacework transparencies of the *Ch'ien-lung* period, which are the lightest and most delicate of all the triumphs of the ceramic art. A white cup of the kind just referred to is presented in Fig. 319. The sides are carved with a trelliswork of *svastika* pattern, in the intervals between five circular solid medallions, from which stand out in salient relief figures of the longevity god, alone in his glory, and of the eight Taoist genii, associated in pairs. The figures, modeled in "biscuit," project from the glazed ground of velvety aspect. Their background of clouds, and the light scrolls which wind round the borders of the cup, are worked in white slip, contrasting in its cloudy opacity with the underlying glaze. The delicate little cup in Fig. 322 is carved in openwork with a broad trellis band composed of five medallions of pierced floral pattern, connected by a ground of interlacing circles, reminding one of the open tilework of Chinese architecture. A narrow pierced band encircles the upper rim.

FIG. 318.—Beaker-shaped Vase of Hirado porcelain, with the decoration partly painted in shaded blue, and partly pierced and filled in with glaze so as to appear as a transparency.

The little flower cylinder in Fig. 333 shows the combination of pierced work with painted decoration. It is a receptacle for scented blossoms like the fragrant jasmine, the *mo-li-hua* of the Chinese, which is closed at the top, but has a hole in the bottom for the introduction of the flowers, shaped for a screw cover. The top and sides are painted in delicate enamel colors of the *Ch'ien-lung* period, upon a ground molded in relief, and pierced in the intervals of the decoration, so that the scent of the flowers may penetrate. The figures, which are grouped under a tall pine, represent the Taoist Triad of star gods. Lu Hsing stands in the middle, holding a *ju-i* scepter; Shou Hsing, upon his right, is leaning upon a long, gnarled staff, with a scroll tied to the top, a peach in his hand, his robes brocaded with longevity characters; Fu Hsing, upon his left, holding a baby boy in his arms, while two sprites dance in the foreground, clapping their hands. On the cover is a representation of a Taoist figure speeding across the clouds, with a branch of sacred peach on his shoulder.

The "rice-grain" decoration, in which the pierced ornamentation is filled in with glaze, seems to be of comparatively modern introduction in China. No marks anterior to the reign of *Ch'ien-lung* have been noticed, and the majority of the marked pieces bear the date of his successor, *Chia-ch'ing* (1796–1820). The white bowls and saucer-shaped dishes of the soft, fritty material made in Persia, which were known as Gombroon ware, have rude decorations of the same nature, but, as Sir A. W. Franks observes, "there is no evidence to show in which country this mode of ornamentation originated." In addition to the ordinary rice-grain work, which is usually associated with conventional designs, painted in blue of grayish tone, this process supplies a means of varying the usual colored designs by making the dragons, storks, or other details transparent, or by picking out some of the leaves in the foliage or the petals of a flower. The mug of European form in Fig. 321 displays the typical mode, the sides being pierced with a broad band of rice-grain transparencies arranged in a formal star pattern. The handle, composed of two interlacing bands, is studded at their four points of junction with flowers worked in relief, which are tinted in underglaze cobalt-blue, touched with gold, and the bands of conventional design, which are painted in the same grayish blue round the borders, are also picked out with gilding. The upper rim is stained brown; the bottom is unglazed, and there is no mark attached.

The class of porcelain with white slip decoration includes those specimens in which the white decoration appears to have been applied in a semi-liquid state, technically called "slip,"

FIG. 319.—White Cup, with pierced trellis-work inclosing solid panels, studded with projecting Taoist figures, which are partially unglazed.

or *engobe*, on a colored ground. Designs are also modeled in relief in the same slip in the paste of porcelain before it is glazed, and have been referred to in the description of celadons and *flambés*, as well as in that of decorated vases, but these would be excluded. The white slip decoration is used in China in combination with one of the dark-brown coffee-colored monochromes of the *tzŭ-chin* glazes, or with the dark and pale blue and the lavender-tinted glazes derived from cobaltiferous manganese. Some of the soft, siliceous wares of Persia are ornamented on a blue ground with white designs of this kind applied in relief, and they have been imitated in the Italian potteries, at Nevers, Rouen, and elsewhere. For this reason Jacquemart has attributed the vases of hard porcelain with white slip decoration on a brown ground to Persia, and he figures one, which is undoubtedly Chinese, in Plate XIX, No. 1, of his book, as a production of Shiraz. There is no reason, however, to suppose that hard porcelain was ever made in Persia, although it appears from their style and designs that some of the specimens were made in China for the Indian or Persian market. The gourd-shaped vase shown in Fig. 323, which has a copper rim and cork-like stopper engraved with figures and birds of Persian workmanship, is a fair illustration of the style, dating from the *K'ang-hsi* period. It is enameled with an iridescent *tzŭ-chin* ground of dark-brown color. The white decoration over the glaze, roughly modeled in low relief and lightly touched with the graving tool, consists of four sprays of conventional flowers, two on each half of the gourd. The three circles from which the lower sprays seem to sprout would be rocks in more finished work; in Jacquemart's vase, which is almost as roughly decorated as this one, there is a somewhat similar design, which is taken for an articulated cactus-stem; in addition to the floral decoration there is an ornamental border round the bulbous enlargement of the neck of this vase of scroll design with beaded pendants, which is often met with upon Chinese vases of this type.

The other illustration exhibits, in Fig. 324, a small vase of baluster form, also attributed to the *K'ang-hsi* period, invested with a pale-blue glaze of the tint called by the Chinese *t'ien-ch'ing*, or "sky-blue," sparsely crackled with a few brown lines. It is decorated in slight relief with a spray of blossoming prunus carefully modeled in white slip and finished with the graving tool. The foot, coated with the same pale-blue glaze underneath, has the prominent rim artificially colored iron-gray.

Fig. 320.—Tazza-shaped Cup, with conventional decoration
in enamel colors of the Ch'ien-lung period.

CHAPTER XIX.

CHINESE CERAMIC COLORS.

THE principal colors used by the Chinese in the decoration of their porcelain and the chemical composition of some of them have been already alluded to. A list of the colored glazes employed during the *Ming* dynasty was included in Chapter VIII, together with a number of the prescriptions used in their preparation. Still, a short chapter on the special subject of ceramic colors may not be superfluous.

The most striking point in Chinese ceramic art is the paucity and simplicity of the materials with which they produce so many brilliant effects. They have no chemical knowledge, and their methods are entirely empirical, depending on the varied effects produced by the admixture of the simple coloring materials, on the different results obtained by their combination with different glazes, and on the degree of oxidation of the minerals due to the manipulation of the fire. Take, for example, the native mineral which, after calcination and pulverization, is used for painting in blue and white, and in the preparation of blue glazes. It is found on the hillsides in several parts of China, occurring, not far from the surface of the ground, in small, irregular nodules of concretionary formation, and is essentially a cobaltiferous peroxide of manganese, mixed with oxides of iron and nickel, with traces of arsenic, bound together by a variable proportion of silica. But the composition of this complicated ore seems to vary indefinitely, not only in the productions of different provinces, but even in specimens dug up from the same hillside. The purity of the blue depends upon the richness of the mineral in cobalt; an excess of manganese will give it a purplish tinge; it will be darkened by too much nickel or iron. So the presence of an expert is required at the imperial manufactory, whose sole duty it is to pick out the best pieces, judging from their color and aspect, to supply the coloring material for the painted decoration in blue and the powder-blue grounds, and for the monochromes ranging from the darkest blue *chi ch'ing* down to the palest *clair de lune*, which are obtained by mixing the calcined mineral in different proportions with the ordinary feldspathic white glaze of the *grand feu*. The blue enamel of the muffle stove, used in overglaze decoration in colors, is also formed of the same cobaltiferous material, combined with a vitreous flux; it varies very much in tone, and is often of purplish tint. The same mineral is used in the preparation of the ordinary black glaze of the painted wares, and of the aubergine purple glaze

Fig. 321.—Mug, with a star-pattern band of pierced "rice-grain" work, and painted borders of blue picked out with gold.

of the *demi-grand feu*, but in these cases the colors are due mainly to manganese, and the Chinese expressly say that the poorer ores are available for these two glazes. The cobaltiferous ore is used, again, to modify the tint of other single colors, to give a pea-green hue to the ordinary celadon glaze due to the protoxide of iron, or to convert the carmine (*yen-chih hung*) of gold purple of Cassius into amaranth, the color of the blue lotus-blossom (*ch'ing-lien*) of Chinese ceramic art.

The influence of different glazes and of the reducing or oxidizing powers of the flames in changing the colors of the same material is well illustrated in the case of copper. When this element is maintained in a highly siliceous medium in the minimum condition of oxidation in a reducing fire, it develops, as a suboxide, a brilliant red of ruby tone, the typical red of the *grand feu*. When fired with a lead flux it becomes fixed as a protoxide, and develops a brilliant green, ranging from pale apple-green to the deepest emerald in the *gros vert*, according to the concentration of the glaze; it becomes in this way the source of all the greens of the muffle stove, as well as of the finely crackled cucumber-green of the *demi-grand feu*, which is applied generally *sur biscuit*. Finally, when fired with niter, or with a lead flux containing an excess of alkalies, the silicate of copper is still more highly oxidized, and develops a beautiful turquoise-blue. Similar changes may even be made to appear upon the same piece. A Lang-

FIG. 322.—Cup of White Porcelain, pierced with medallions and bands of delicate trellis-work.

Yao vase, for example, often displays a patch of apple-green toward the edge of its rich mantle of *sang de bœuf*, and the peach-bloom glaze owes its charm to the peculiarly soft combinations produced by the fortuitous mingling of the two colors. The three colors are all seen together in the mottled garb of a *flambé* specimen, brought out by the oxidation of the glaze while still fluescent by a current of fresh air suddenly introduced into the furnace.

So iron, when fired in a reducing atmosphere in the large furnace, in the presence of a large excess of silicates, develops, as a protoxide, the peculiar sea-green tint known to us as celadon, deepening to an olive shade, or to a dark bottle-green, as the proportion of iron increases. The same element develops, as a peroxide, a graduated series of browns, ranging, according to the concentration of the glaze and the "warming" influence upon the color of the oxidizing flames, from pale buff, through *café au lait*, dead leaf, chocolate, and bronze, to the blackish shade of the darkest *fond laque*. The peroxide mixed with a simple flux of white lead painted on the porcelain over the white glaze, and fired in the muffle stove, produces the beautiful red which, in its purest tone, reminds one of coral, and is usually called coral-red. This is the *mo hung*, or "painted red," *par excellence*, of the Chinese. When it is combined with a silico-alkaline vitreous flux it takes on a brighter hue of the same vermilion color, which suggests to the Chinese the red cheeks of the ripe jujube, one of their favorite fruits, so that they call the glaze now *tsao-erh hung*, or "jujube-red."

The above shades of red differ completely in tone from those of the other red of the muffle stove, which is obtained from gold precipitate, the compound of tin and gold which is commonly known as purple of Cassius. This produces the tints of the underneath borders of the rose-backed dishes, which are enameled with glazes of single color ranging from deep carmine, the *yen-chih hung*, or "cosmetic rouge" of the Chinese, down to *fên hung*, or pink, the "rose Pompadour," or "rose Du Barry," of French ceramic writers.

There is occasionally, on the other hand, a remarkable resemblance in the shade of coloring of glazes produced from different elements, so that a pale cobalt monochrome of sky-blue (*t'ien ch'ing*) tint may be confused for a moment with an azure-tinted glaze of turquoise shade derived from copper. On closer inspection, however, the latter will be seen to have a minutely crackled texture, being one of the glazes of the *demi-grand feu*, while the former is one of the single colors of the *grand feu*.

These few introductory remarks are intended to show that some knowledge of the chemistry of colors is absolutely necessary as an aid to their distinction and classification. Their proper distinction is often of great assistance in the correct chronological arrangement of the specimens in which they occur. The presence of any of the *rouges d'or*, for example, would prove that the piece could not be earlier than the seventeenth century, in the first quarter of which these colors were introduced.

The coloring materials used by the Chinese in the decoration of porcelain are few and simple when compared with those employed in Europe. They comprise oxide of cobalt for the ordinary blues; oxide of copper for certain reds and greens and for turquoise-blue; oxide of antimony for the yellows; gold for carmines and pinks; arsenious acid for opaque whites; oxides of iron for celadon, coral-red, and browns; and peroxide of manganese less rich in cobalt for the blacks and purples. "In Europe," as M. Ebelmen observes,* "they make use of the different oxides that have just been enumerated, and take advantage also of many other substances unknown to the Chinese. The tint of the oxide of cobalt is modified by combining it with oxide of zinc or alumina, sometimes with alumina and oxide of chrome; pure oxide of iron furnishes a dozen shades of red, from orange-red to the deepest violet-red; ochres, pale or dark, yellow or brown, are obtained by the combination of different proportions of oxide of iron, oxide of zinc, and oxides of cobalt or nickel; the browns are prepared by increasing the dosage of oxide of cobalt in the prescriptions for the ochres; the blacks, by the suppression of the oxide of zinc in the same preparations. We vary the shades of our yellows by the addition of oxide of zinc or of tin to clear them, and of oxide of iron to deepen their tone. Oxide of chrome, either pure or combined with oxide of cobalt or the oxides of cobalt and zinc, gives yellowish greens and bluish greens, which can be made to range from pure green to almost pure blue. Metallic gold furnishes for us the purple of Cassius, which we can afterward transform at will into violet, into purple, and into carmine. We may cite also the oxide of uranium, and the chromates of iron, baryta, and cadmium, which give useful colors, and will conclude by mentioning the recent application of metals unoxidizable by fire, the discovery and preparation of which require a knowledge of chemistry that the Chinese are far from possessing."

The poverty of the Chinese palette, however, is more apparent than real, as they produce by different combinations of the colors an infinite variety of shades, so that the color scale is almost exhausted in their series of monochromes. Some colors may have escaped their incessant researches, like the abnormal pigments extracted from petroleum and coal-tar, such as Magenta and Solferino, the fruits of recent scientific investigation, broken and fugitive tints of uncertain shade that can well be spared.

Fig. 323.—Gourd-shaped Vase with conventional decoration in white slip upon a dark-brown iridescent ground, and Persian chased metal mount and cap.

Ceramic colors are simple or compound, pure or broken; red, yellow, and blue are simple colors. Red and yellow form orange, yellow and blue form green, blue and red form violet; these are compound colors.

The intensity of the coloring can be attenuated by white, the colors can be deepened by black. It is by this means, by the addition of white or black to other colors, that all the different grades of tone are produced. M. Grandidier gives a list of about eighty different shades of color represented by select specimens in his own collection of Chinese porcelain, now worthily installed in the Louvre at Paris under his own official curatorship. They occur there not only as monochromes, but also as backgrounds for painted decoration in blue or in different colors, relieving and enhancing the brilliancy of the effect in an infinite series of combinations, several of which have been illustrated and referred to in our own pages. Porcelain is conveniently divided into monochrome and polychrome, but in actual practice the same colors are used for both kinds, the only essential requisite being that they will withstand the degree of temperature required for the firing. The same gold pink (*rose d'or*), for example, that is used for enameling the monochrome black of an eggshell dish, serves for penciling the diapered bands that decorate the interior; and the same cobaltiferous material that is blown on to form a powder-blue ground is used for painting the blue lines of the pictures in the medallions reserved for the purpose. In another class of pieces that have been already decorated in colors of the *grand feu,* the white ground may be subsequently filled in with soft enamels such as yellow or coral-red, or, again, any of the singly-colored grounds may be stippled with *soufflés* of other enamel, to be subsequently fixed in the muffle stove.

The decoration of Chinese porcelain becomes more interesting when their methods of applying the colors are compared with those employed in Europe. As M. Ebelmen explains, the processes employed in Europe are very varied: sometimes pastes of different colors are used

FIG. 324.—Small Vase with a pale-blue cobalt glaze, sparsely crackled, decorated with a floral spray executed in white slip.

for the body; sometimes the coloring material is incorporated with the glaze; sometimes, again, the colors are applied upon the surface of white porcelain. The first two methods of decoration require a degree of temperature as high as that necessary for the firing of the porcelain itself. The colors employed are called *de grand feu.* For painting, on the contrary, upon the surface of porcelain, only such colors are used as can be vitrified at a much lower temperature than the preceding; these are the colors called *de moufle,* the only ones that afford, up to this time, resources for painting upon porcelain pictures that can be compared with oil paintings of the old masters on canvas.

The Chinese coloring materials can be classed in the same way as those used in Europe into two main divisions: those that can be compared with the colors of the *grand feu,* and those that have more analogy with the muffled colors. These last differ, however, from the European muffle colors in being mostly true vitreous enamels, the same that are used for enameling on metal. There is an intermediate division in China, known as the colors of the *demi-grand feu,* which differ from those of the first division in being combined with a lead flux, and fuse at a lower temperature, although practically they are generally fired in the same furnace. We will attempt a cursory classification of the colors under these three divisions, adding a few notes on the principal tones of color as we proceed.

I. HIGH-FIRED COLORS OF THE GRAND FEU.

The principal colors that come under this division are: the whites derived from the ordinary feldspathic glaze; the series of reds and a grayish celadon-green obtained from copper; the ordinary celadons, olive-greens, and different shades of brown, which owe their coloring to iron; the blues and purples of the cobaltiferous oxide of manganese, and the blacks derived from the same complex mineral. The coloring materials referred to above are occasionally used in combination; the sea-green celadon of iron is darkened by the addition of a dosage of the cobalt mineral, and the black monochrome ground of the cobaltiferous manganese is rendered lustrous and iridescent by the addition of *tzŭ-chin shih,* the ferruginous material of the *fond-laque* glazes. The work of the Chinese potters is mainly empirical, and some of their principal successes, the despair of European imitators, are due to mixtures, in different proportions, of the cobaltiferous, in manganesian and ferruginous minerals, with the fusible white glaze. The result will depend not only upon the richness of the materials in these ingredients, but also upon the atmosphere of the furnace, in its reducing or oxidizing effect.

The colors of this division are combined with a feldspathic glaze, rendered more soluble by a notable addition of lime. This distinguishes them at once from the colors of the next two classes, in the flux of which oxide of lead is an indispensable element. The coloring materials are usually mixed with the white glaze, and applied upon the white surface of the unbaked porcelain by immersion, by insufflation, or with the brush. Occasionally the color is projected by the *soufflé* method upon the body of the piece and invested afterward with the white glaze in successive coats. The porcelain in China is rarely submitted to a preliminary baking as in Europe, but some of the ancient celadon glazes are described as having been applied *sur biscuit.*

The white glazes may be noticed first. In every collection of Chinese porcelain there are two varieties of white that ought to be carefully set apart from the ordinary productions of the Ching-tê-chên potteries. These are the products of Ting-chou in the province of Chihli, and of Tê-hua in the province of Fuchien. The Ting-chou ware dates from the *Sung* dynasty; it has been described in Chapter V, under its two varieties, the *Fên Ting*, with the paste white like flour, and the *T'u Ting*, with a less pure yellowish body. The glaze, which is either uncrackled or crackled, has in both varieties an ivory-white tone, and a texture resembling in surface that of soft-paste porcelain, to which it is frequently likened. The decoration, which is often of very intricate floral design finished off with bands of geometrical scroll-work, is either molded in relief or chiseled at the point in the paste under the glaze. The ornamentation of the *Ming* dynasty is less elaborate in character. During the present dynasty the old potteries are closed, but fine reproductions of the Fên Ting class have been made at Ching-tê-chên, especially in the reigns of *K'ang-hsi* and *Ch'ien-lung*.

The ceramic production of Tê-hua is the *Chien Tz'ŭ*, or Fuchien porcelain of the *Ming* and *Ch'ing* dynasties, which will be described in a later chapter. It is the typical *blanc de Chine* of collectors, with a rich satiny glaze of siliceous aspect closely blending with the paste underneath, either creamy white in color, or of a more opaque tone approaching that of ivory; it is represented chiefly by well-modeled statuettes of Buddhist divinities, such as those of the Goddess of Mercy, of Maitreya the Coming Buddha, figures of lions and mythological animals, incense-burners, tea-pots and libation-cups, the latter of oval or octagonal shape, made to imitate the cups carved out of rhinoceros horn, with *appliqué* ornaments of archaic character.

FIG. 325.—Vase, painted in enamel colors of the early *famille rose*, with the star-gods of happiness, rank, and longevity, and the goddess Hsi Wang Mu with female attendant. The central decoration nearly covers the Chinese character *Shou,* "longevity."

After the specimens of these two potteries have been grouped upon separate shelves, there will remain a varied assortment of plain white porcelain to represent the potteries of Ching-tê-chên. White, when pure in tint, has always been highly esteemed in China, where the earliest porcelain was made to simulate the precious cups and bowls of translucent white jade. The reign of *Yung-lo*, the third of the *Ming* emperors, is distinguished for its fragile white porcelain ornamented with impressed designs giving transparent effect like the water-mark in paper, and the reign of *Wan-li*, toward the end of the same dynasty, is marked by the renaissance of pure white jadelike wine-cups of eggshell thinness and incredible lightness. White is the mourning color in China, and a relic of an imperial mourning dinner service is often seen on a foreign shelf in the shape of a rice-bowl etched with five-clawed dragons under a pellucid white glaze. The delicate white cups carved in openwork and the charming lacework bowls with pierced designs filled in with glaze were described in the last chapter.

Plain white porcelain is generally enameled, but there is a special variety which is purposely left in the state of biscuit without any coating of glaze, like the Parian ware of the West. The special Chinese name for this is *fan tz'ŭ*—i. e., "turned porcelain," as if the vase were inverted, so that the unglazed interior appeared outside, and the fiction is occasionally kept up by applying a touch of glaze inside the mouth. Flower-vases molded with a string network in relief, brush-cylinders, boxes for seal-color, and water-pots for the writing-table with landscapes in salient relief, snuff-bottles, and many other small objects, are met with of this kind. The covered cylindrical pots in which fighting crickets are kept, the open cellules in which they are brought to the fray, and the trays on which they fight, are usually made of brown earthenware, because it absorbs water more readily, but they are sometimes seen molded out of unglazed white porcelain.

In addition to the glazed white porcelain intended to remain plain white, a quantity is turned out to be subsequently decorated with enamel colors. Most of it is finished at the manufactory; some is sent to Canton and painted in the peculiar style which characterized the old porcelain of the East India Company commonly known as "India China." An occasional piece has found its way abroad and been afterward painted in surface colors with European designs at Meissen or Chelsea.

The reds of the *grand feu* are derived from copper. The copper is generally applied in China in a metallic form, the molten metal, derived from the cupellation of silver, or from other sources, being granulated by being thrown into water, finely pulverized, and fused with a large excess of silica in a reducing fire, so as to be converted into a protosilicate. The firing is a most delicate operation, and must be stopped at the critical moment to attain a bright uniform color: if it be pushed too high, the metal will be dissipated, and the vase will come out wholly or partially colorless; if it be insufficient, the piece will be dull or liver-colored; if the flames be allowed to become oxidizing for a moment, it will be transformed into a persilicate, and be converted to green or even to turquoise-blue, this last color representing the maximum amount of oxidation. Copper is the protean metal which gives rise in this way to the varied changes of color known as furnace-transmutation, or *yao-pien*, which were described in the last chapter.

Red is a favorite color with the Chinese in the decoration of their porcelain, but this copper-red of the high fire is easily distinguishable at a glance from the reds of the muffle stove, which are derived from iron or gold. It shines out from the depth of the translucent glaze with tones approaching that of the ruby, so that the Chinese call it *pao-shih hung*, or "ruby-red"; the iron-reds (*fan hung*), on the contrary, are more superficial and of coral or brickdust hue; the *rouges d'or* (*yen-chih hung*), which are also surface enamels, are carmine or pink.

Copper-red is one of the most ancient of Chinese ceramic colors, being met with in some of the most brilliant monochromes among the productions of the Chün-chou potteries in the *Sung* dynasty. The reign of *Hsüan-tê* (1426–35) of the *Ming* dynasty was especially distinguished for its ruby-red, which was used at this time either as a single color or in painted decorations. The wine-cups used by the Emperor *Hsüan-tê* at the ritual services at the Temple of the Sun were made

Fig. 326.—Libation Cup of antique Kuang Yao, with a mottled purple overglaze on a crackled yellow ground; dark grayish-brown paste.

of this color. Later in the *Ming* dynasty, in the reigns of *Chia-ching* and *Wan-li*, we are told that the firing of the copper-red was found to be too difficult, and that its place was usurped by the iron-red, which was much cheaper, and easier of application. In the reign of *K'ang-hsi* it reappeared as the *Yu-li hung*, or "glaze-inclosed red," described at the time by Père d'Entrecolles, and the brilliant *sang-de-bœuf* of the *Lang Yao*, together with the attractive peach-blooms of this period, were both discovered in attempts at reproducing the sacrificial red of *Hsüan-tê*. The attempts culminated early in the next reign in the production of the well-known monochrome red of the *Nien Yao*, a stippled color of bright uniform tint, which continued to be successfully produced during the reign of *Ch'ien-lung*. There is a marked renaissance of the copper-red as a single color in quite recent times, and a piece is occasionally seen rivaling the finest old *sang-de-bœuf* in its brilliant tones of color, although inferior in technical finish.

It may be useful to add a few points of distinction between these different reds. The Lang Yao of the reign of *K'ang-hsi,* which may be considered as the *sang-de-bœuf* proper, displays a brilliant red of crimson tone, permeating the vitreous enamel, which is crackled throughout, and strewn under the surface with innumerable little points. These points have been justly compared to the tiny bubbles of carbonic acid that are continually rising to burst on the surface of gaseous water in a thermal spring. The vases are glazed underneath, and exhibit three typical bottoms, according to Chinese connoisseurs, a plain white enamel, a grayish celadon crackle, or an apple-green crackle. The red of these vases is rarely uniform; their chief charm is in the mingling modulated tints of their mottled texture and streaked depths, varied, perhaps, by an occasional patch of apple-green near the rim. Some are wanting in limpid depth and become brownish or even liver-colored; these are failures in baking.

Fig. 327.—Butterfly-shaped Snuff-bottle; imperial yellow glaze.

The *Lü Lang Yao,* or "Green Lang Yao," of the Chinese is much rarer than the *sang-de-bœuf,* and it is not certain that the pieces which exist were not accidentally produced in the firing of vases that were originally intended to be red. On careful examination a spot or two of red will generally be found lurking in places where the glaze is deepest. M. Ebelmen (*loc. cit.,* page 445) refers to several examples of celadon coloration as obtained by him in his experimental researches upon the copper-red. He explains how a reducing atmosphere is necessary to maintain the coloring material at a minimum of oxidation for the production of the red, and how, in an oxidizing atmosphere, on the contrary, the color would totally disappear if the volatilization of the metal were possible, or would become green if the coloring material survived in appreciable quantity. According to this hypothesis, some specimens of so-called celadons would be either abortive reds or copper-greens of sufficiently poor color. He places in his class of *céladon de cuivre* all the vases, barrel-shaped garden-seats, and balustrade fittings that the Chinese make in stoneware. He quotes also a very remarkable fact of a fragment of sea-green or grayish celadon porcelain, showing clearly in the fracture an opaque-red layer, looking like sealing-wax, in immediate contact with the paste. The oxidizing atmosphere, in this case, had acted only on the surface, which it had changed from red to a pale greenish tint.

Another glaze that owes its charming tints to copper is the peach-bloom, or *peau de pêche,* which has been already described and fully illustrated in these pages.

The *Chi-hung* was brought to perfection by Nien Hsi-yao, the director of the imperial potteries in the reign of *Yung-chêng.* The name, which means "sacrificial red," dates from the reign of *Hsüan-tê* of the preceding dynasty, as already explained. The red vases of the *Nien Yao,* as this porcelain is called after its inventor, are coated with a deep, uniform glaze of ruby tone, the stippled texture of which indicates the method of application of the color by insufflation. In the next reign of *Ch'ien-lung* this single color loses something of its purity and transparency and becomes brownish, so that it has been compared to that of the skin of a medlar (*peau de nèfle*). The modern *chi-hung* vases are less uniform in tint, developing purplish or crimson mottled shades like the old *sang-de-bœuf,* or changing to the variegated *flambé* tints described in the last chapter. But they are improving daily under the stimulus of high prices, and I have a new vase now before me, clothed in as brilliant a garb as any ancient Lang Yao specimen.

The next colors of the high fire for consideration are those due to iron, which range, according to the degree of oxidation of the metal, from the palest sea-green to the deepest brown. It is to the paler green shades that the term celadon is properly confined; the darker shades, which are due to the peroxide, are the yellow-browns and browns of the *fond-laque* division. Some French ceramic writers use the term celadon in a much wider sense, to include the pale blue derived from cobalt, which is the *yueh pai,* or *clair de lune* of the Chinese, and hardly needs a second name of "starch-blue" celadon (*céladon bleu d'empois*), as well as the *soufflé* tea-dust (*ch'a-yeh mo*), and some even group the crackled turquoise and purple of the *demi-grand feu* in the same division. We use it here as generally synonymous with the Chinese ceramic color *tou-ch'ing*, literally "pea-green," which includes the two varieties of *Tung ch'ing*, the color of the old celadon ware made at the Eastern Capital of the *Sung* dynasty, and the *Lung-ch'üan yu*, the glaze of the ancient Lung-ch'üan celadons of contemporary date. The prescription for the *tou-ch'ing* glaze, which was applied to the celadons of the *Ming* dynasty,

FIG. 328. — Tall Vase, thirty inches high, decorated with a battle scene in enamel colors, of early K'ang-hsi date.

made at Ching-tê-chên, was coloring material was derived and the color was explained lime and iron developing a influence of a reducing atmosphere of oxidation. A similar prescripdons of the present dynasty, whereis made by the addition of a small oxide of manganese, the effect of it approaches that of the Chiditional color of the ancient

The celadons comprise some of which approach blue; the tones vary with the depth effect of the incised and relief pany it. The old celadons of sometimes darkening almost coming in exceptional cases this is explained by the chem"What would happen if the oxidizing atmosphere? The if the iron were in sufficient hardly any green in it should are found in Chinese producof iron be increased a little, dons to a deep lac-brown in olive-green or a bottle-green

The browns, in fact, owe rial as the celadons, the comcalled *tzŭ chin shih*, literally

given in Chapter VIII. The from a yellow ferruginous clay, to be due to the silicates of light greenish shade under the maintaining the iron at a minimum tion produces the *Tung-ch'ing* celaas the Lung-ch'üan glaze of to-day dosage of calcined cobaltiferous which is to darken the shade till nese olive, which is the traLung-ch'üan wares.

many shades of clear green, others tend to become gray; of the glaze, enhancing the designs which often accomthe *Sung* dynasty are found to bottle-green, or even bebrownish. The *rationale* of ist M. Ebelmen, who asks: celadon glaze were fired in an tint would pass into red, and proportion a warm tone with be obtained. All these shades tions, and if only the oxide one can pass from the celaan oxidizing atmosphere, to an in a reducing atmosphere." their color to the same matepact ferruginous clay, which is "brown gold stone," because

it is the mineral source of the ceramic golden browns. Its preparation and mode of application were fully described in Père d'Entrecolles's Letters. When mixed with a large excess of feldspar and lime it produces a clear buff, or an "old-gold" tint. The Chinese tell how the potters tried to produce a yellow monochrome by mixing actual gold with the glaze of the high fire, but found that the metal was all evaporated in the furnace, so that they returned to the *or bruni* as a graceful and efficient substitute. Among other monochrome shades of this class, found on highly fired Chinese porcelain, are brown ochre, *café au lait*, chestnut, capuchin, maroon, deadleaf (*feuille morte*), chocolate, bronze, lac-colored (almost black), etc. The darker shades are often highly iridescent.

The blues of the *grand feu* owe their color to cobalt, which resists the highest temperature of the furnace. The Chinese coloring material is a native cobaltiferous mineral of very variable composition, which has been already sufficiently described. The best pieces having been selected by an expert, they are first calcined in porcelain capsules, and then pulverized in hand-mortars for a whole month before the material is considered fit for use. The purest and most brilliant blues are produced when the material is applied immediately upon the raw white body of the unbaked piece, and covered with the white feldspathic glaze which it penetrates under the solving influence of the fire. The magnificent blue and white decoration, and the powdered blue grounds of *lapis lazuli* tint that distinguish the reign of *K'ang-hsi* were all executed in this way, giving an undulating intensity and pulsating depth to the color, and preserving it, moreover, indefinitely, so that a vase two hundred years old will look as if just fresh from the kiln. If the ore be not sufficiently rich in cobalt, the color will be grayish; if the glaze be too thin, or the piece be overfired, so that the color comes to the surface, it will be turned black by the oxidation of the manganese, which is always present in the ore. The *soufflé* blue may be crackled by the addition of the proper ingredients to the white glaze, bringing out a clear color quite different in tone from the more finely crackled deep sapphire-blue of the *demi-grand feu*, illustrated in Plate XXIX, in which the cobaltiferous material is combined with a lead flux.

When mixed with the feldspathic glaze and applied in the fashion of the ordinary single colors the effect of the cobalt is different. There is no longer the same intensity and depth of color, but we have in compensation a peculiar purity of tint and softness of tone in the series of charming single colors which the Chinese potter has achieved in this way. The most delicate of all ceramic colors, the *yueh pai*, or *clair de lune*, displayed in Plate LI, is produced by the smallest addition of cobalt. Added in larger quantity the ordinary *t'ien ch'ing*, or "sky-blue," glaze of the vase shown in Plate LXXIV is developed in the furnace. A still larger proportion is required to bring out the *chi-ch'ing*, the "blue of the sky after rain," which is defined as the deep azure of the clear rifts between the clouds.

We possess many specimens dating from the *Sung* and *Yuan* dynasties, like the two illustrated in Plate XII, which derive their color from cobalt-tinged glazes of the *grand feu*, crackled or uncrackled in texture. They often display shades of lavender or pale purple, indicating the presence of manganese in the coloring material. The celebrated ancient ware of Ju-chou was purer in tint than any other of the *Sung* porcelains, being described as a *clair de lune* of the color of the blossoms of the *Vitex incisa*, the "sky-blue flower" of the Chinese.

The same cobaltiferous mineral is utilized in the production of the black grounds of the *grand feu*, for which purpose the pieces of ore that are less rich in cobalt will suffice. Père d'Entrecolles describes two kinds of black glaze. The first, which is duller in aspect, is obtained by combining three parts of the blue coloring material with seven parts by weight of the ordinary feldspathic glaze, but the proportions may be varied in accordance with the tint required; the mixture is applied to the unbaked piece, which is afterward fired in the big furnace. It forms an effective background for a decoration in gold, which is penciled on after the first baking, and fixed by refiring in the muffle. The second black glaze, called *wu chin*, or "metallic black," which is more lustrous and iridescent in aspect, is formed by adding

FIG. 329.—Libation Cup of archaic form and design, painted in enamel colors of the K'ang-hsi period.

some of the *tzŭ-chin shih*, the ferruginous mineral which produces the coffee-brown glazes, to a liquid mixture composed of the above ingredients, in which the porcelain is plunged, and baked in an oxidizing fire. If the firing be carelessly managed the color will be brown instead of black, as we often see in modern pieces.

The colors of the high fire are used in combination with each other in the decoration of Chinese porcelain, as well as singly for monochrome glazes. The essential point is that all the associated colors should be able to be brought out properly by the same fire. The underglaze cobalt-blue seems to be developed with any kind of fire if only it be buried in the depths of the glaze in the presence of an excess of silica, so that we see blue and white painting, with touches, perhaps, of bright copper-red, associated on one vase with broad bands of palest sea-green celadon and zones of grayish crackle, and on another find zones of warm dead-leaf brown encircling the shoulder and rims and separating pictures penciled in blue. The blue seems to acquire additional brilliancy when enhanced, as it occasionally is, by a background of ox-blood or peach-bloom of the same mottled tones as characterize the single-colored vases of the period. Many of these different combinations have been already referred to; one of the most effective is that of copper-red with pale celadon, as illustrated in Plate XXXVI; in such

FIG. 330.—Snuff-bottle; imperial yellow crackle.

pieces the red coloring material is painted with a brush upon the unbaked surface before the celadon glaze is applied; it gradually infiltrates under the solving action of the reducing fire till it penetrates to the surface. There is always a certain lack of clearness of definition in designs produced in this way, which is often combated by tooling the outlines in the paste, or working them into low relief.

Another common combination of high-fired colors upon vases is that where the decoration is executed in blue and maroon with touches of celadon. The cobalt and copper colors are painted on under the glaze, while the celadon is inlaid, as it were, in the white enamel, filling in the outline of a rockery, for example, or some other detail of the picture. In other styles of decoration we see lustrous black grounds with reserve medallions containing cameo pictures in blue, and powder-blue vases with panels of mirror-black displaying pictures in gold that have been penciled on subsequently to the first firing. The dead-leaf and coffee-colored grounds of the *grand feu* furnish in the same way a long series of combinations. Finally come an infinite variety, designed for additional decoration in enamel colors, which can be fired in the muffle stove at a comparatively low temperature without injury to the original highly fired colors, on which the enamels are overlaid, or with which they are intermingled.

2. COLORS OF THE DEMI-GRAND FEU.

Among the monochromes peculiar to Oriental porcelain there are some which appear to have been applied *sur biscuit*—that is to say, upon porcelain that has already been fired in the furnace. On close examination they are seen to be *truité*, to have a minutely crackled texture, a characteristic which is rarely seen in glazes fired at a very high temperature. On being tested with hydrofluoric acid by M. Ebelmen, they proved to contain, in addition to the blue, yellow, and green coloring agents, a notable proportion of oxide of lead. This approaches them to the enamel colors of the muffle stove included in the next class. They are fired by the Chinese in the deepest part of the large furnace, and are placed below the level of the vent-hole opening into the chimney, where the temperature is much lower than it is in the body of the kiln.

The colors of this class are not numerous; they comprise turquoise-blue, aubergine-violet, yellow, and green. Their composition is sufficiently well known, as they are all included in the list of colored glazes of which the prescriptions were given in Chapter VIII, extracted from technical books of the *Ming* dynasty, and the Chinese accounts have been confirmed by a qualitative analysis of actual specimens.

The mode of application of these glazes is described by Père d'Entrecolles. The bowls, for example, are first fired unglazed in the large furnace, from which they come out quite white but lusterless; if they are to be single-colored, they are immersed in a crock containing the coloring materials made into a kind of cream with water; if they are to be party-colored, like the bowls known to the Chinese as "tiger-spotted," which are daubed all over, inside and outside, with irregular blotches of purple, green, yellow, and white, the colors are laid on with a brush. The piece is finally fired again in the most temperate part of the large furnace, as a fierce fire would destroy the colors.

These were the earliest vitreous colors used in China, and they were employed centuries before the enamel colors of the muffle stove were introduced. Fusing as they do at a comparatively low degree of heat, they are available for the decoration of common pottery or earthenware, as well as of porcelain, and they are widely utilized for this purpose throughout the East, more especially for architectural decoration. In the celebrated porcelain pagoda of Nanking, which was rebuilt in the beginning of the fifteenth century (but is now destroyed), only the white bricks were made of porcelain; the colored tiers, panels, and antefixal ornaments were all of enameled earthenware. The roofs of the palaces and imperial temples in Peking are covered with yellow tiles; those of the princes with bright green; the Temple of Heaven shines in the sun as intensely purple as the vase in Plate XXIX; and broken ornaments in all the soft tones of crackled turquoise are to be picked up in the ruins of the summer palaces which were burned in 1860. All the four colors are represented also in the grotesque monsters of European form, and in the helmets and trophies of arms that were designed by the Jesuit Frère Attiret for the fountains and other decorations of the Versailles that was built under his superintendence at Yuan-ming-yuan in the last century for the Emperor *Ch'ien-lung.* These were made at the potteries near Peking. I allude to them here because at these very potteries they are now busily engaged in making a quantity of vases and bowls glazed with the same beautiful colors, to which the soft excipient seems to impart an added softness, which are destined for exportation to supply the increasing demands of enthusiastic collectors of "single colors." The fact that yellow clay used often to be mixed with the porcelain earth in the old fabrics, to enhance the brilliancy of the glaze colors, gives a certain *vraisemblance* to the fraudulent reproductions which I have seen sold for as many dollars as they would cost in cents to produce.

3. Enamel Colors of the Muffle Stove.

The materials used by the Chinese in their ordinary decoration in colors fuse at a much lower temperature than that required for baking porcelain, and they are painted over the glaze on pieces that have been previously fired, and which must be refired in the muffle to fix the colors. They may be compared to our own muffle colors, but they differ in some essential points, in their composition as well as in their mode of application.

There is, to begin with, a radical difference in the first principles of Chinese art, shown in the want of perspective, the absence of shading, and the studied avoidance of mixed tints. The highest aim of the artist at Sèvres is to copy an oil-painting on canvas of one of the old masters, to reproduce exactly every varied shade of color in the original, and to take care that, after baking, the picture shall appear uniformly glazed. The Chinese artist is attempting to reproduce on porcelain a water-color on silk or paper of one of his old masters, limned in pure, soft colors, with no broken tints and no mixed tones. The Chinese colors are far from presenting the uniformity of thickness and glazing that is considered to be *de rigueur* in Europe in a painting on porcelain. Some are brilliant, perfectly fused, and laid on so thickly as to stand out in tangible relief on the surface of the porcelain; the carmines obtained from gold, the purple-blues, the greens, and the yellows are examples; others, such as the iron-reds and the blacks, present generally a dull surface, and are only glazed in the thinner parts; their depth is always less than that of the vitrified colors. In the Chinese pictures there is no

Fig. 331. — Blue and white Snuff-bottle with red dragon.

shading in the figures or other details; the outlines are sharply defined by single lines of red or black; there is no gradation in the different tints; the colors are laid on in broad strokes, to which the artist returns occasionally to execute a damask, either with the same color, with other colors, or with metals; he rarely mixes on his palette powders of different coloring materials. The aspect of their pictures, when examined closely, reminds one of the glass mosaics that were so artistically executed in Europe during the thirteenth century, and in which all the details of the design and modeling of the figures were produced simply by red or brown lines upon the mosaic work executed in fragments of white or colored glass.

These enamels are colored by a small percentage only of the metallic oxide dissolved in the vitreous mass, and they require to be laid on thickly to give the proper intensity of tone; this gives a relief which is impossible to obtain by any other method, and imparts a certain *cachet* to Chinese productions. The general harmony of the coloring is due to the nature and composition of their enamels. The flux, in China, is composed of silica and oxide of lead combined with a greater or less proportion of alkalies. It holds in solution, in the state of silicates, a few hundredths only of the coloring oxides, the number of which is extremely limited. The coloring materials are *oxide of copper* for the greens and the bluish greens, *gold* for the reds, *oxide of cobalt* for the blues, *oxide of antimony* for the yellows, *arsenious acid*, and more

rarely stannic acid, for the whites. Oxide of iron and the impure oxides of manganese, which give the first *red*, the second *black*, are the sole exceptions, and this is, no doubt, because it is impossible to obtain these colors in solutions by means of the oxides that have just been mentioned.

M. Ebelmen gives the following *résumé* of his researches:

"1. The colors called muffle *colors*—that is to say, baking at a very low temperature compared with that at which porcelain is baked—are essentially few in number.

"2. The palette is composed not of colors, properly so called, but of enamels—that is to say, of plumbo-alkaline glasses, variously colored by a few hundredths of dissolved oxides.

"3. The composition of the vitreous flux is generally very uniform; its tint is always light, and it is this lightness of tone, as well as the vivacity of the coloring, which gives Chinese porcelain its harmonious effect and characteristic richness.

FIG. 332.—Artistic Vase of the Yung-chêng period, beautifully painted in enamel colors on a ground of purest white; neck strengthened by European mounting.

"4. The enamels are colored by oxide of cobalt, by oxide of copper in the state of binoxide, and by gold—all substances easily soluble in a vitreous flux, and of very simple preparation.

"To these shades the Chinese add a yellow derived from antimony, and an opaque white, the base of which is sometimes tin, sometimes arsenious acid, both of which they mix with the other enamels, as they combine these last with each other to obtain a nearly infinite variety of shades, which, however, it is always possible to decompose and to reduce to the five following elements: Blue from oxide of cobalt, blue or green from oxide of copper, carmine from gold, and yellow from oxide of antimony.

"If we add to these enamels the very impure oxide of cobalt, which, under the glaze, will always develop into blue, the same oxide mixed with white lead to make it adhere to the glaze becomes black; and the calcined oxide of iron, which, combined with white lead and with flux, produces a series of iron-reds, dull or brilliant, light or dark; and finally gold, which is made adhesive by the addition of a tenth part of white lead, we shall be able to gain a complete idea of the means that form all the resources of the Chinese decorator."

The enamel painting in colors of the next period, which came in after the new Manchu dynasty was firmly established, is commonly known as *K'ang-hsi Wu ts'ai*—i. e., "Decoration in colors of the reign of *K'ang-hsi.*" The pictures are usually executed entirely in enamels, the underglaze blue being replaced by a surface cobalt silicate of vitreous composition, which accompanies the old purple enamel color derived from the same native manganese ore less rich in cobalt. The full, strong red of coral tint continues and improves in purity of tone, and the greens become more and more prevalent and brilliant, so that the class has been called by the distinctive name of *famille verte.* This class, the coloring of which is perfectly shown in the vase illustrated in Plate VI, is also known in China by the name of *ying ts'ai*, or "hard colors," to distinguish it from a different style of coloring which was introduced toward the end of the same reign, executed in pale tints of pure tone and broken colors, among which carmines, pinks, and an amaranth purple, all derived from precipitated gold, appeared for the first time in ceramic art. This constitutes the decoration in *juan ts'ai*, or "soft colors," which is known also by the name of *fên ts'ai*, or "pale colors." Plate LXIII is a fine example of the style.

FIG. 333.—Cylinder with pierced openwork sides, decorated in enamel colors of the Ch'ien-lung period.

But it is time to examine the enamel colors in detail. They are brought to Ching-tê-chên in the shape of irregularly broken fragments of vitreous composition from the glass-works in the province of Shantung. A collection of Chinese glass will exhibit all the different single colors in their primitive state, simply molded into shape to form various kinds of utensils and ornaments. The pieces as they come from the glass manufactory, composed of a plumbo-alkaline flux of very uniform composition tinged by the metallic oxide which gives the color, have first to be pounded and finely pulverized, and at the same time a variable proportion of white lead is added if it be necessary to increase the fusibility, and some siliceous sand if the color be too soft. The color is finally worked on the palette, either with turpentine, with weak glue or with pure water, and painted on over the glaze with the brush.

In addition to their use in the decoration of painted porcelain, these enamel colors are all used singly to produce monochromes. The class of monochrome enamels, all of which are fired in the muffle, will include: the reds of vermilion and coral tint derived from iron, exemplified by a typical example in Plate XCII; the carmines and pinks derived from gold, of which one is represented in Plate LIII; the yellows, ranging from the pale canary of Plate LXV to the deep imperial yellow of Plate V, which are derived from antimony, tinged more or less by the presence of iron; the plain, uncrackled greens of varied tone and sheen, often iridescent, which owe their color to copper binoxide; the uncrackled sapphire-blue of intense tone known as *pao-shih lan*, due to cobalt silicate; the deep grayish purple (*tzŭ*) manganese monochrome, and a brilliant glossy black of vitreous composition.

The white enamel colors owe the opacity of their tint to arsenic, of which they generally contain about five per cent. The vitreous compound is widely used also in combination with other colors, being mixed with them, to modify their tint and make them opalescent. The various white enamels known to the Chinese by the names of *ya pai*, "ivory-white," *hsüeh pai*, "snow-white," and *po-li pai*, "glass-white," differ but slightly in composition. The *yueh pai*, "moon-white," of the enameler's palette, which has a pale greenish tinge, is prepared by adding a small amount of one of the transparent greens to the white.

The blacks, of varied composition, all owe their color to cobaltiferous manganese not rich in cobalt. The calcined mineral is sometimes painted on combined with white lead as a flux and mixed with glue, when the surface will be a dead black, and only partially vitrified at the edges by combining with some of the silica of the white glaze. The *wu chin*, or "metallic black" of the enameler's palette contains an additional quantity of oxide of copper, which imparts a greenish tone. The same coloring material, when mixed with the ordinary vitreous flux, produces the brilliant color known as *liang hei*, or "glossy black," which contains a smaller proportion of oxide of manganese than the other blacks.

FIG. 334.—Blue and white Snuff-bottle. Mark, Ch'ien-lung.

The blue of the enamel painter, like that of the *grand feu*, owes its color to cobalt. There are many shades, differing in fusibility, but all made by the same method, and consisting of oxide of cobalt, more or less impure, dissolved in a more or less fusible plumbo-alkaline glass. The color is very intense in the state of silicate, so that the deepest sapphire-blue does not contain more than one and a half per cent of oxide of cobalt, and the lighter azure-blue, called *fên ch'ing*, yields only one-third as much on an analysis of the flux. The presence of oxide of manganese gives a violet tint. The enamel fuses on the surface of the porcelain in salient relief so that it can be distinguished at once from the underglaze blue; its brittleness causes it to be easily injured, and it is occasionally found broken and scaled off in patches, the result of wear.

The green enamels used for the surface decoration of porcelain are all colored by oxide of copper, being either pure, or changed to a yellowish tone by the addition of prepared yellow, or to a bluish tone by the addition of arsenical white or the use of a harder flux. The flux is varied according to the tint de-

FIG. 335.—Snuff-bottle, with foliations in relief. Mark, Tao-kuang nien chih.

sired. Oxide of lead in excess deepens the green; soda communicates a tint less blue than that developed by potash under similar circumstances. The pale sea-green tint used for filling in distant mountains is called for that reason *shan lü*, or "mountain green"; this is the pure binoxide of copper, and it is converted into turquoise-blue of darker or lighter shade by being mixed with different proportions of white enamel containing arsenic. The color called *ku lü*, or *vert passé*, is made by the combination of antimonial yellow with the copper green. The deepest shade of camellia-leaf green,

FIG. 336.—Snuff-bottle, dark, lustrous brown glaze over dark blue decoration. Ch'ien-lung.

called *ta lü*, or *gros vert*, is brought out in the firing of the pure copper oxide dissolved in a highly plumbiferous flux combined with the smallest possible proportion of alkalies.

The yellows of the muffle stove are colored by antimony. Antimony alone is colorless, but in combination with oxide of lead it gives a bright canary-yellow when pure. When contaminated with iron a reddish or orange tone is produced. The purest tint is exhibited in the yellow ground of the vase illustrated in Plate LXV, and the same yellow characterizes the finest painted decoration of the period. The imperial yellow, which is specially reserved in China for the use of the sovereign, is of fuller, deeper tone, approaching orange. Peroxide of iron is purposely mixed with the pulverized yellow enamel to produce the surface color of dull aspect which is known by the name of *ku t'ung*, or "old bronze."

The deep purplish brown monochrome enamel, approaching a dark claret color, which is known to the Chinese as *tzŭ*, is produced by manganese. The oxide of manganese communicates to alkaline glazes, as we saw in the colors of the *demi-grand feu*, a beautiful *violet d'évêque* (bishop's purple), or aubergine purple; to lead glazes it gives the brownish or grayish purple of the muffle stove, which we find in imperial ware in combination usually with dragons and other ornamental designs, etched at the point in the paste underneath.

FIG. 337.—Snuff-bottle in the form of a bud; yellow glaze.

The reds of the enameler's palette remain for consideration. They consist of two distinct and well-defined classes, viz., the *rouges de fer*, which owe their color to iron peroxide, and the *rouges d'or*, which owe their color to gold precipitate, the purple of Cassius. The former are of brick-dust or bright coral hue; the latter are rose-colored, carmine, or pink. Peroxide of iron is self-colored, and does not require to unite chemically with any other substance to bring out its tint. In this it resembles the peroxide of manganese, which produces the black, and the technical application of the two colors is consequently the same. The peroxide of iron requires only a simple flux to cause it to adhere and to glaze its surface. It is prepared in China by the incineration of crystals of green vitriol (sulphate of iron). The peroxide is combined with five times its weight of white lead, the two materials being passed through a fine sieve and triturated together; a little glue must be dissolved in the water when it is used on the palette, and it must be painted on with a light brush. The color applied in this way is of deep, full tone, but of dull aspect, as it depends for vitrification on the small proportion of silica that it is able to absorb from the underlying glaze; it differs from the ordinary enamel colors in not being in appreciable relief. This is the *ta hung*, or *gros rouge* of the Chinese, also known as *mo hung*, or "painted red," being the ordinary red of decorative painting on porcelain. The iron peroxide, like the peroxide of manganese, is also employed in combination with the ordinary plumbo-alkaline vitreous flux when the color is required to be more brilliant and glossy. The bright coral-red single color, known to the Chinese by the name of *tsao-'rh hung*, or "jujube red," is produced by this means; it differs from the other in being completely vitrified, even when laid on thickly, and excels it in translucency and luster, although not so deep and full in tone. The vase illustrated in Plate XXVI displays this ground in combination with a decoration in enamel colors; in other cases it is employed with the best effect to form a rich ground for ornamental designs reserved in white, as in the charming little bowls of the *Ch'ien-lung* period, which are so gracefully decorated with white sprays of bamboo, thrown out in crisp outline by the lustrous vermilion background.

FIG. 338.—Beaker-shaped Vase of the K'ang-hsi period, decorated in brilliant enamel colors.

The *rouges d'or* are of com- into the Chinese ceramic field, unknown until the latter part of are not mentioned by Père d'En- corresponding to the year 1721 cer-dishes of Chinese porcelain class, and they occur among the style known as *juan ts'ai*, or attributed to the reign of K'ang- hung, from its likeness to the is brought to Ching-tê-chên in of ruby-colored glass, the pre- ing been previously combined finely pulverized, worked up on pentine, and painted on without deep carmine of the rose-backed blossoms of a flower on a deco- also as *hua hung*, or "flower frequent use in coloring petals. the usual plumbo-alkaline flux, per cent of metallic gold. A "rose Du Barry" type, is pre-

paratively modern introduction and seem to have been quite the reign of K'ang-hsi. They trecolles, but the cyclical date has been found on several sau- decorated with enamels of this colors of vases painted in the "soft coloring" that are credibly *hsi*. The color called *yen-chih* cosmetic rouge of the Chinese, the shape of irregular fragments cipitated purple of Cassius hav- with a vitreous flux. This is the palette with water or tur- further addition to produce the eggshell dishes, or the crimson rated piece. The color is known red," on account, probably, of its Analysis shows it to consist of tinged with about one-quarter pink called *fên hung*, of the pared by mixing the materials

of the carmine color with those of the ordinary white enamel. The third color of this class, which is called by the name of *ch'ing lien*, or "blue lotus," is prepared by mixing together three enamels—the carmine, colored ruby-red by dissolved gold; the ivory-white, made opaque by arsenious acid; and the deep blue derived from cobalt; the result when fired is a deep amaranth of purplish tone.

Gold is also used in its ordinary metallic form in gilding porcelain and in penciling upon it decorative designs, which are fixed by being fired in the muffle. Père d'Entrecolles has described fully its method of preparation and its application, mixed with one-tenth of its weight of white lead, by means of weak glue. It is singular that exactly the same proportions are employed in Europe in mixing the gold with the flux which makes it adhere to the porcelain, although the flux used at Sèvres is subnitrate of bismuth. Silver is also employed in China in its metallic form, combined with white lead, whether as a *soufflé* overglaze or as an effective decoration penciled upon a dead-leaf ground.

FIG. 339.—Eggshell Dish, decorated in soft enamel tints with gold,
the Taoist divinity Hsi Wang Mu, with female attendant.

CHAPTER XX.

MOTIVES OF DECORATION OF CHINESE PORCELAIN.

THE principal modes of decoration have been casually alluded to already in the description of particular pieces and of the style of different periods, but a short *résumé* of the more usual motives selected by the Chinese artist may be attempted in a separate chapter. A complete account of the varied phases of an art the principles of which differ so completely from our own, or of the alien religions and strange philosophy which furnish its chief subjects, is hardly to be expected. The first impression is apt to be that of the grotesque, and we notice the absence of perspective in the landscapes, the want of drawing in the figures, and the strange forms of the weird monsters that are so often introduced. It is necessary to get accustomed to these peculiarities to appreciate the full effect of the vivid and harmonious coloring in which the brush of the Oriental decorator of porcelain has never been surpassed. The same effect is aimed at whether he be painting on the raw body with a single color, such as cobalt-blue, so that the picture may be imbibed in the fire in the translucent depths of the white overglaze, or whether he be working with the vitreous colors of the enameler's palette, which are applied over the glaze and fixed in the lesser heat of the muffle stove. It is brilliancy which is the leading note in the decoration of porcelain, and it is produced in its perfection in the vivid greens of the polychrome pictures of the old *famille verte*, as well as in the pulsating vigor which distinguishes the best "blue and white" of the same reign of *K'ang-hsi*. These two achievements mark the culminating point of the ceramic art of China, and they have never been surpassed in any other country.

FIG. 340.—Snuff-bottle; shape of a gourd overgrown by a gourd vine.

The earliest prehistoric pottery that is dug up from the ground in all parts of Eastern Asia, specimens of which are so highly prized by the Chinese as relics of the time of their sacred emperors, *Yao* and *Shun*, whose virtues are extolled by Confucius, is made of coarse, yellowish clay. It is roughly ornamented with indented dots and scored lines arranged in geometrical patterns, or with string marks, impressed while the clay was still moist, and has generally a remarkable similarity to the archaic pottery discovered in other parts of the world. In the *Han* dynasty it begins to be marked with inscriptions in the same way as the bricks and tiles of the period, which indeed it exactly resembles in material and structure. An example of this is a roughly shaped globular vessel, six and a quarter inches high, six inches in diameter, with an expanding mouth strengthened by a prominent lip, which has been added to my collection since the chapter on Marks was written. The form is precisely that of some of the Anglo-Saxon urns dug up in England. The mark, which is stamped under the foot of the vase, so that the characters stand out in low relief, is *Wu fêng êrh nien*—i. e., "second year of the *Wu-fêng* period," which corresponds to B. C. 56, the eighteenth year of the reign (B. C. 73–49) of the Emperor *Hsüan Ti* of the *Han* dynasty.

The more finely finished pieces of the *Han* dynasty are composed of a kind of gray faïence coated with a brilliant green glaze derived from copper, the tint of which is fitly compared by the Chinese to that of the rind of a cucumber. The vases, modeled in the form of the sacrificial bronze vessels of the period, have usually mask handles fashioned in the shape of monsters' heads, and are ornamented with encircling bands worked in relief in the paste under the glaze. These bands are generally filled with the forms of grotesque dragons and other monstrous creatures traversing a frieze of clouds. The designs are identical with those

employed at this period in
carved in bas-relief on stone
duce into Europe by the ex-
at the Oriental Congress at
graphs of these rubbings are in-
volume † lately published by my
Professor of Chinese at the *Collège*
sulted by every student of early
so strikingly in these mural sculp-
acter, and are especially inter-
ancient myths of the Chinese,
the introduction of Buddhism
tronomical star-gods, headed
throned in the Great Bear,
lites continually circle in token
the midst of clouds shaping
dragons and winged horses,
and rain, and the dreaded god
bow, the latter being depicted
arched body. There are battle
with chariots and spearmen,
men of mythical times with
pageants, such as Confucius
the meeting of Confucius and
from classical times follow, a
sins of tyrannical sovereigns,
feudal devotion, the virtuous
the paragons of filial piety,
motives for the decoration of

FIG. 341.—Showing the other side of the vase illustrated in Figure 328.

the mural sculptures of tombs
which I was the first to intro-
hibition of a series of rubbings
Berlin in 1881.* The photo-
cluded in the beautifully illustrated
friend M. Chavannes, the learned
de France, which should be con-
Chinese art. The scenes displayed
tures are of the most varied char-
esting as indications of the
before they were modified by
from India. We see the as-
by the Supreme Deity en-
round which the lesser satel-
of homage, the storm-gods in
themselves into the forms of
the elemental gods of wind
of thunder canopied by a rain-
as a two-headed dragon with
scenes and warlike processions
representations of the early
serpent bodies, and peaceful
attended by his disciples, or
Lao Tzŭ. Historical scenes
series of pictures of the assas-
and of the noted examples of
heroines of ancient story and
that have so often supplied
porcelain in more modern days.

One of the stone slabs figures the felicitous omens that herald the rule of a virtuous sovereign; the well of pure water that appeared spontaneously without digging; the miraculous bronze tripod in which food could be cooked without fire; the spotted unicorn called *lin* (*k'i-lin*); the yellow dragons that appeared swimming in the lakes; the calendar plant of the time of the Emperor *Yao*, that indicated the day of the month by throwing out a sprout on each successive day of the waxing moon, till there were fifteen, and by dropping one by one these sprouts each day of the waning moon; the six-legged monster: the white tiger that harmed no man; the jade horse; jade growing up miraculously from the ground; the red bear; the twin tree with two trunks united above; the crystal gem (*pi-liu-li*), disk-shaped, with a round hole in the middle; the deep-green tablet (*hsüan kuei*) of jade, of oblong shape, with pointed top, an ancient badge of rank; two-headed quadrupeds, birds, and fishes; the white carp that appeared to *Wu Wang*, the founder of the *Chou* dynasty, as he was crossing

* *Inscriptions from the Tombs of the Wu Family from the Neighborhood of the City Chia-hsiang-hsien in the Province of Shantung* By Dr. S. W. Bushell.

† *La Sculpture sur Pierre en Chine au temps des deux Dynasties Han.* Par Edouard Chavannes, Paris, 1893.

the ford at Mêng-chin; the white deer on which foreign envoys from the south are said to have ridden to the court of the ancient Emperor *Huang Ti;* the silver wine-jar (*yin wêng*), and the jade symbol of victory (*yü shêng*), the form of which resembled that of a weaver's spindle, or of two disks united by a central bar.

Bronze has been one of the principal materials for artistic work in China from the most remote times, and the collections of bronze antiquities that have been published in the many illustrated books that are referred to in the chapter on Bibliography have furnished a mine of wealth for the potter in supplying forms as well as decorative designs. The circular mirrors of bronze, for example, which go back to the *Han* dynasty (B. C. 206–A. D. 220), are molded and engraved on the back with varied designs, accompanied often by written inscriptions, and form by themselves a suggestive chapter of Chinese art. The round mirror is a sacred article in the Taoist cult, being supposed to have the power of detecting evil spirits masquerading in

FIG. 342.—One of the square ends of the Summer Pillow exhibited in Fig. 16, decorated with a scene from a comedy.

human guise by reflecting their true form, and the back is usually covered with pictures of mythological and astrological character. In the *Han* dynasty we have winged figures of the celestial deities, four-horse chariots, and grotesque monsters in the style of the mural sculptures of the time, lions and phœnixes in the midst of arabesquelike scrolls of flowers, dragons, and sea-horses in festoons of grapes. The divinity Hsi Wang Mu, "Royal Mother of the West," with kneeling attendants bearing offerings, and bands of musicians, is seated, either enthroned alone, or in association with Tung Wang Fu, "Royal Father of the East"; the legends connected with these two deities are supposed to be partly borrowed from Hindu sources, being arranged like those relating to Indra and his consort, and the Buddhistic aspect of the figures, posed as

they are occasionally on lotus thalami, lends some color to the supposition. The astrological figures on the *Han* mirrors are those of the four quadrants of the uranoscope, viz., the azure dragon of the eastern quadrant, the somber tortoise and serpent of the north, the white tiger of the west, and the red bird of the south. The bronze mirrors of the *T'ang* dynasty (618–906) display a further series of astrological figures, including the twelve animals of the solar zodiac, the twenty-eight animals of the lunar zodiac, the asterisms to which they correspond, etc. The list of the animals of the solar zodiac has been already given in Chapter III, in connection with the duodenary cycle. They are represented on the backs of the mirrors in rings, which are sometimes filled in with sprays of flowers or leafy scrolls. On porcelain of more modern times the animals are occasionally grouped in a landscape scene filled in with ordinary details. They are also found molded in porcelain, either in a series of small animal forms, or as statuettes with human bodies and animal heads.

One of the large bronze mirrors of this period, fifteen inches in diameter, with the usual boss in the middle, perforated for a silk cord, has round the boss a ring of the four quadrants enumerated above, followed by a succession of concentric rings. The second of these rings has the *pa kua*, the eight trigrams of broken and unbroken lines, used in divination; the third ring contains the twelve animals of the solar zodiac; the fourth, the ancient names of the lunar asterisms in archaic script; the fifth, the figures of the twenty-eight animals of the lunar zodiac, followed by their names, the names of the constellations over which they rule, and those of the planets to which they correspond. The planets are arranged in the same order as in our days of the week, and the Chinese are supposed to have derived their first knowledge of the division of the periods of the moon's diurnal path among the stars into weeks of seven days about the eighth century, when they obtained also the animal cycles, which had been previously unknown to them. Their knowledge of the twenty-eight lunar mansions is, however, far more ancient, and long discussions have taken place as to whether they were invented in Chaldea, India, or China, or derived from some common source in central Asia. Professor W. D. Whitney, in his studies on the Indian *Nakshatras,* or Lunar Stations, sums up the discussion by the conclusion that, "considering the concordances existing among the three systems of the Hindus, Chinese, and Arabians, it can enter into the mind of no man to doubt that all have a common origin, and are but different forms of one and the same system."

In addition to the astrological and hieratic devices on these old bronze mirrors, which are mostly of Taoist character, with wild animals, such as the deer and hare, bringing herbs in their mouths to the hermit, or sacred birds, such as the swallow and crane, carrying in their beaks scroll messages from the gods or fateful talismans for the religious recluse, there is another kind with purely ornamental decoration. These are covered with sprays of natural flowers and butterflies, with conventional garlands of idealized flowers, such as are called by the Chinese *pao hsiang hua,* or "flowers of paradise," with fish swimming in waves among moss and water-weeds, with boys circling round the field waving flowers, with dragons and phœnixes disporting in the midst of floral arabesques, and with many others of the designs that we find so often repeated later as art motives for ceramic decoration.

FIG. 343.—Seated Figure of Kuan-Ti, the national god of war, painted in brilliant enamels with gilding of the K'ang-hsi period.

In Buddhism, bronze objects of the same circular form, looking like large medallions with the face polished to a mirrorlike surface, represented the sacred wheel (*fa lun*), and are molded on the back with Sanskrit *dharani.* One of these is sometimes placed in the hand of a Buddhist divinity, or suggests the decoration of a porcelain dish penciled with concentric rings of Sanskrit writing.

The ancient bronze moldings, in connection with the carvings in jade of the *Han* dynasty, which were executed in a similar style, furnished in fact the first models for the porcelain manufacture. The old crackled wares of the *Sung* dynasty, the grass-green celadons, and the ivory-white Tingchou porcelain of the same period (960–1279), all have the decorative designs molded in relief or engraved in the paste underneath the glaze, which was applied subsequently. We know nothing from actual experience of the older fabrics, but are told in the books that they were made in imitation of white and green jade, and that they owed their chief beauty to the brilliant tints of their single colors, emulating the emerald hue of moss-green jade, or the clear blue of the sky after rain. Specimens of the *Sung* dynasty are not so uncommon; the vases are seen to have been molded with the designs of the character that has been described, outside, so as to cover their surface; the bowls, cups, and dishes have had the interior ornamented by being pressed upon the mold and finished afterward with the graving tool. Among the most frequent of the molded designs are phœnixes flying among flowers, and brocaded grounds composed of interlacing sprays of Moutan peonies and lilies, the rims being defined by encircling bands of fret of varied pattern. A pair of fishes is occasionally seen in bold relief in the bottom of a circular dish of old celadon porcelain, and the same design is found on the older copper basins of the *Han* dynasty; other dishes are lightly engraved under the glaze with a spray of lotus or of peony, or with grounds of checkered and fluted pattern. There is no reference to painted decoration till toward the end of the *Sung* dynasty, and even then only in the case of some of the coarser productions, which seem to have been occasionally roughly ornamented with a few strokes of brown derived from some ferruginous material, or with touches of a dull blue composed of impure manganiferous cobalt laid on over the glaze and incorporated with it at the same firing. The blue and white of the *Yuan* dynasty (1280–1367) was probably of the same type, and perhaps some of the crackled jars roughly painted in blue with dragons, that are cherished as heirlooms by the Dayaks of Borneo and in other islands of the Eastern Archipelago, may date from this period.

China has never been so isolated from the outer world as some have supposed. The oldest writings and traditions have so much in common with those of the ancient Accadians and

FIG. 344.—Snuff-bottle with soft enamel decoration of Ch'ien-lung period. Mark, Ch'êng-hua.

Babylonians as to suggest the theory of a joint origin for both.* Many of the philosophical ideas of the early Taoist writers are evidently inspired from a Hindu source, and the Buddhist missionaries, when they came to China in the first century A. D., brought with them carved images and sacred pictures, and besides exercised subsequently a considerable influence on Chinese art, as is freely confessed by native writers on the subject. Even before the Christian era the Emperor *Wu Ti* of the *Han* dynasty had opened up intercourse with western Asia, sent envoys who penetrated as far as the Persian Gulf, followed by a large army, which conquered the Greek kingdom of Ferghana, enthroned a new king there, and exacted a tribute of Nisæan horses, so famous in classical history, which were, indeed, the avowed object of the expedition. Herodotus describes these horses, which "sweated blood," as coming from Nisa in Media; and Ssŭ-ma Ch'ien, the author of the *Shih Chi*, the first of the official Chinese histories, who has been called "the Chinese Herodotus," describes them in similar terms under the name of *Ni-ssŭ* horses; while Li Kuang-li, the commander-in-chief of the expedition, who was appointed in the year B. C. 102, was given the honorary title of Nisæan General. The Greeks are described in the Chinese history under the name of *Yuan*, which is equivalent to Iaon, the name they have always borne in Asia; and the influence of Greek art is betrayed by several details in the mural sculptures of Chinese tombs dating from the *Han* dynasty as well as in early Buddhist sculpture.

During the succeeding centuries there was occasional intercourse both by land and by sea until the thirteenth century, when nearly the whole of Asia was under the dominion of the Mongol descendants of Genghis Khan, who occupied the thrones of both China and Persia, overran Russia, and reached nearly to the walls of Vienna. Marco Polo in his well-known *Travels* describes his journeys about this time between Europe and Cathay both by sea and by land. Rubruquis, the envoy of Saint Louis of France to Mangu Khan, who arrived at Karakorum in the year 1252, found there a Parisian goldsmith named Guillaume Boucher, who was specially attached to the court and had made for the Khan's palace a wonderful fountain of silver, which he describes minutely. It was in the form of a tall tree surmounted by an angel with a trumpet, having four large receptacles concealed

FIG. 345.—Blue and white Snuff-bottle.

in its trunk, from which started four pipes, emerging in the form of gilded serpents, and terminating in the mouths of four silver lions which surrounded the foot of the tree, and furnished a supply of wine, cosmos made from mare's milk; mead made from honey, or rice-water, whenever either of these four beverages was required. It was toward the close of this dynasty that the Byzantine art of *cloisonné* enameling in copper seems to have been first introduced into China, as the *nien-hao* of *Chih-chêng* (1341–67) is found underneath the foot of pieces which there is no reason to doubt are actual productions of the time, although the art was not officially adopted until the reign of *Ching-tai* (1450–56) of the next dynasty.

* *Western Origin of the Early Chinese Civilization. From 2300 B. C. to 200 A. D.* By Terrien de Lacouperie. London, 1894.

We are told by Sir John Malcolm, in his History of Persia (volume i, page 422), that a hundred families of Chinese artisans and engineers came to Persia with Hulagu Khan about the year 1256, and it has been surmised that there were some potters among the number. If there had been they would have found many processes of decoration in use there in the fabrication of faïence and fine earthenware (for no true porcelain has ever been made in Persia) such as would seem hitherto to have been unknown in their own country, and it seems natural to conclude that these would have been introduced into China about this time rather than invented *de novo.* The reign of *Hsüan-tê* (1426–35) was the first to become celebrated for its blue and white, and the Chinese attribute its excellence to the quality of the cobalt mineral which was imported by them at the time from Western Asia under the name of "Mohammedan blue." The process of decoration in enamel colors combined with a lead flux, which were painted on over the white glaze and fixed by a second firing in the muffle stove, came in later.

Blue was the leading color in the decoration of porcelain throughout the *Ming* dynasty (1368–1643). The other colors were at first principally used as grounds to relieve the blue designs, or to fill in ornamental details that had been previously reserved in white on a blue ground. Even in the reign of *Wan-li* (1573–1619), when painting in enamel colors had come into wider vogue, the blue was still sketched in first on the raw body, while the other enamel colors were filled in afterward over the glaze. A complete palette of overglaze enamel colors appears later as a characteristic of the reign of *K'ang-hsi* (1662–1722), and the large vases of this class decorated in brilliant enamels of the *famille verte*, that are so often classified as *Ming* pieces because they are inscribed with the mark of *Ch'êng-hua*, are really productions of the *K'ang-hsi* period.

FIG. 346.—The Twin Merry Genii of Taoist mythological lore, decorated in enamel colors with gilding of early Ch'ien-lung date.

Next to bronze designs and antique carving, the patterns of old silk brocades and woven stuffs afforded frequent motives for the decoration of porcelain, as we have already seen in Chapter VII. China is the original country of silk, and it has been celebrated for its woven productions from the most remote times. The twelfth book of the *Po wu yao lan,* an excellent work on objects of art which has often been quoted, and which was published in the beginning of the seventeenth century, is devoted to ancient silks under the heading of *chin,* "brocades," and *hsiu,* "embroideries," the former of which were woven on the loom, the latter worked by hand with the needle. It includes an account of the designs used in different dynasties, in which there occurs a curious notice of five rolls of brocade with dragons woven upon a crimson ground that were presented, in the second year of the *Ching-ch'u* period (238), by the Emperor *Ming Ti* of the *Wei* dynasty to the Empress of Japan, who is recorded to have sent an embassy to the Chinese court in that year. Under the *Sung* dynasty (960–1279) is given a list of about fifty brocade patterns of the same general character as those enumerated on page 136; and this is followed by another long list of figured silk handkerchiefs of the time, which were woven with designs similar to those of the brocades, and used for head wrappers and for carrying things in. This list of handkerchiefs ends with a reference to the white wool kerchiefs of the Kitan Tartars, the arabesque designs used by the Nüchih Tartars, and the white kerchiefs of the Koreans of the period, which were woven with figures of eagles, vultures, and flowers, with pheasants and other birds.

All the different designs enumerated in both these lists have been constantly used in later times in the decoration of porcelain.

The painter on porcelain claims for himself only a subordinate position in the school of Chinese art, and his greatest triumph is a colorable imitation of one of the old painters on silk and paper, whose pictures are kept mounted upon rollers in Chinese cabinets. These pictures are either graphically sketched in black ink, or delicately tinted in water-colors, painting in oil being unknown to the Chinese. The Chinese artist is first a writer, and he acquires his skill in outline as a calligraphist of the written script, which was often originally a picture of the object. He has always possessed, as M. Paléologue observes in *L'Art Chinois* (page 246), the sentiment of color, and has acquired by intuition, as it were, a perfect skill and finished delicacy in its application. It is mainly in the advantage they have taken of the vibration of

FIG. 347.—Snuff-bottle. Shou Lao and a deer in brilliant enamels on a *sang-de-bœuf* ground. Ch'ien-lung.

colors that the Chinese have revealed their power as colorists. Instinct and observation have taught them that by shading the tints upon themselves a singular depth and intense power can be brought out. In painting on porcelain, even more perhaps than in painting on silk, they have made the colors vibrate and pulsate by putting blue upon blue, red upon red, yellow upon yellow, in every shade from the lightest to the darkest. The defects of want of perspective and absence of relief modeling are less noticeable on porcelain than in pictures executed on a larger scale.

With regard to the different branches of his art there is nothing that the artist on silk or paper, followed in his turn by the painter on porcelain, has not attempted. He treats in succession religious and historical subjects, scenes of actual daily life, illustrations of poetry, romance, and the drama, landscapes and copies of Nature, animals real and mythical, flowers natural and symbolical, etc. The Chinese generally recognize four *genres*, viz.: (1) Figures (*Jên Wu*); (2) Landscape (*Shan Shui*), the name meaning literally "hill and water"; (3) Nature (*Hua Niao*), literally "flowers and birds"; and (4) Miscellaneous (*Tsa Hua*).

As a striking example of the first class of decoration with figures, the large vase, thirty inches high, that is illustrated in Figs. 328 and 341, may be presented. It is painted with a battle scene, sketched with a certain amount of life and energy, so that the picture covers the whole surface of the vase, extending over the neck as well as the body. The colors used are the brilliant overglaze enamels of the *K'ang-hsi* period (1662–1722), greens of different shade predominating, and the dark cucumber-green, the pale apple-green, and rich purple exhibit the finely crackled texture which distinguishes some of the monochrome glazes of the period. The names of the generals that are written on their banners show that the scene is taken from the *Hsü Shui Hu*, a well-known collection of stories of brigands of the reign of *Hui Tsung* of the *Sung* dynasty, in the beginning of the twelfth century, and we must turn to the book for a short explanation:

The general, Sung Chiang, had been sent by the emperor with an army to recover the city of Ch'in-chou in the province of Shensi, which had been captured by brigands. The brigands, led by Lei Ying-ch'un, accompanied by his wife P'o-p'o Niang, who was called Pai Fu-jên, "The White Lady," a noted swordswoman, whose charger was a lion that vomited flames, had taken refuge in the Hung-tao Mountain, which was over one hundred miles round. Sung Chiang had advanced his troops, massed in three divisions, to the attack, and Lei Ying-ch'un had been killed by Lin Ch'ung in the first battle. The White Lady, when told the news of the death of her husband, had wept bitterly, but had hastened to the front, and had defeated the two generals Hua Jung and Ch'in Ming, whose horses had fled affrighted by the lion, and alarmed by the power of the enemy's magicians over the elements.

Sung Chiang, the imperial general, afterward had a number of imitation lions made with moving eyes and heads filled with sulphur, which could be lighted at the critical moment. This is the moment chosen for illustration. The White Lady, wielding a long-handled sword, is seen in the foreground mounted upon a grotesque lion, and her charger is just turning back, frightened by the dummy lions which are grouped on the other bank of a river, as if being driven in a team by an attendant. She is attended by two of her generals on horseback, whose names are inscribed on their banners, Chang Ying-kao and Ching Ch'ên-pao, and the large, waving triangular banner displays the constellation of the Great Bear and the archaic dual symbol in token of her occult art. The loyal generals are gathered on the other bank of the river, the large square flag which is carried by one of the horsemen being inscribed *Ta Sung*, "Great Sung," the name of the reigning dynasty. The smaller group depicted on the neck of the vase represents the commander-in-chief of the imperial army and his staff, the waving banner being inscribed *Shuai*, the title of his rank. His commands are rendered by the man below, who is beating a drum. They are all gazing upward, looking at an apparition in the sky in the guise of a martial figure, which is approaching with each foot poised upon a fiery wheel. This is Kuan Ti, the national god of war, who appears in China at critical occasions as an omen of victory, and animates the fray, just as the gods of ancient Greece were related to have done in Homeric times.

We are told in the story that afterward the White Lady returned riding a chestnut horse, to be killed by Hu Yen-sho, and that her two generals, whose names are given above, were slain at the same time by the great general Ch'in Ming and by Kuan Shêng the "long-sworded," whose devices are to be seen inscribed among the rest upon the vase. The background of the picture is a mountain scene with large pines growing from precipitous rocks.

The next illustration (Fig. 16) exhibits a "cool pillow" of porcelain for summer use, which is also painted in brilliant enamels of early *K'ang-hsi* date, laid on over the white glaze, including manganese purple, coral-red, black, and a few touches of gold, relieved by bright emerald-green and pale primrose-yellow grounds. It is covered in the middle with a foliated panel of floral brocade, with peony scrolls painted in colors on a yellow ground, so as to extend over three of the sides. The fourth side has a round hole in the middle of a painted flower, which is fitted with a screw cover, so that fragrant flowers or scented herbs may be introduced into the hollow interior of the pillow. The borders are surrounded by bands of diaper and spiral fret. The square ends, of which one is shown in Fig. 342, are decorated with scenes from some comedy. A traveler of mature years, with an attendant carrying baskets of fruits or flowers, is standing in the courtyard of a house at the porch of which stands a lady, bowing politely as she listens to him talking. The wine-cups placed side by side on the table inside suggest an approaching wedding, which is perhaps the subject of the discussion.

Porcelain is often molded after sacred designs in the form of images and the like, or illustrated with themes derived from some one of the religious cults followed in China, and a word of introduction on the subject may be attempted here. There are in China three systems commonly spoken of by foreigners as "religions," and known as Confucianism, Taoism, and Buddhism. The first is the cult of the *literati*, of which Confucius, who lived B. C. 551–479, is the prophet, and the reigning emperor, as the Son of Heaven and the vice-regent of the Supreme Deity on earth, is the great high priest, and he has the sole right of offering sacrifice, unless he deputes the duty to one of the princes or high mandarins. It is really a system of state philosophy rather than a religion, as Confucius was himself a professed agnostic, and was wont to refuse to discuss the supernatural with his disciples, but the practice of ancestral worship is inextricably interwoven with its tenets. The state gods, like Kuan Ti, the God of War, are deified mortals, and subject to promotion or degradation by the emperor, who rules the celestial hierarchy on the same lines as the earthly mandarinate, and may even adopt into it any deity from the other cults.

Fig. 348.—Standing Figure of Shou Lao, the deity of longevity, painted in enamel colors.

The God of War has already been noticed as appearing in the air as an omen of victory in a battle scene depicted on the large vase illustrated in Figs. 328 and 341. Kuan Yü, a well-known historical character, rose into celebrity in the troublous times at the close of the *Han* dynasty. He is reputed to have been in early life a seller of bean-curd, but to have subsequently devoted himself to study, until in the year 184 he casually encountered Liu Pei, when the latter was about to take up arms against the rebellion of the Yellow Turbans, and a solemn compact was sworn in a peach orchard. The fidelity of Kuan Yü to his adopted leader remained unshaken in despite of many trials. At an early period in his career he was created a baron by the notorious regent Ts'ao Ts'ao, who tried to turn the hero from his fealty to Liu Pei, whose two wives had fallen into his power, by shutting up Kuan Yü at night in the same house with the two imprisoned ladies; but the trusty warrior preserved their reputation from innuendo, and proved his own fidelity by mounting guard in an antechamber the livelong night with a lighted lantern in his hand. His martial prowess was proved in many campaigns with Liu Pei, before the throne of his chief as sovereign of Shu became assured, but he fell a victim at last to the superior force and strategy of Sun Ch'üan, the founder of another of the Three Kingdoms into which the empire then became subdivided, and was taken prisoner and beheaded in the year 219. Although always celebrated as one of the most renowned of China's heroes, it was not till early in the twelfth century that he was canonized by the Emperor *Hui Tsung* of the *Sung* dynasty. By the Emperor *Wan-li* of the *Ming* dynasty he was raised, in 1594, to the rank of *Ti*, the highest in the hierarchy, and since that date, and especially since the accession of the reigning Manchu dynasty, his worship as the God of War has been firmly established.

The porcelain figure presented in Fig. 343 is Kuan Ti, the Chinese God of War, as he sits enshrined upon the altar in the gateway or front hall of most of the temples in China. It represents a mail-clad warrior seated, in a speaking attitude, with one hand uplifted, in a wooden chair which has dragons' heads projecting from its arms, one of his legs resting on rocks, the other placed on a lion footstool. The figure is molded in one piece, with the exception of the hands, which can be detached.

FIG. 349.—Dâgaba Shrine, decorated in enamel colors, with gilding of the Ch'ien-lung period.

The principal God of Literature Ti Chün, whose constellation is one Ursa Major. He is represented in darin dress and a broad-brimmed accompanied by attendants carrying nalia. His superior claims have his satellites known as K'uei Hsing, star *k'uei*, and who is by far the the present day, although he was teenth century. Tradition says attained by his literary genius examinations, but was re- was entitled on account of precipitated himself in his River, and was borne to the in the firmament by the ette reproduced in Fig. 86, glaze enamel colors, shows one leg upon the head of a from the waves. His face pulsive features, projecting eyes, and two budding legs are encircled by and the cloak waving with long, floating ends of movement. A pen- his uplifted right hand, cup of ink in his other

is the stellar divinity, Wên Chang of the smaller groups of stars in pictures as a dignified figure in man- hat of antique style, riding a mule, banner-screens and other parapher- been ousted, however, by one of who is the personification of the most popular God of Literature in not formally canonized till the four- that he once lived on earth, and the highest grade at the official fused the post to which he his ugliness, whereupon he despair into the Yellow place which he now occupies dragon. The porcelain statu- which is decorated in over- K'uei Hsing standing with fish-dragon, which is rising is that of a demon, with re- canine teeth, protuberant horns; the bare arms and bracelets and anklets, loosely above the head conveys the impression cil-brush is wielded in and he holds a square hand, or a cake of ink

molded in the form of a silver ingot. The fish-dragon (*yü-lung*), which is his special attribute, is the emblem of literary perseverance and success, and is often used alone in symbolical decoration, as in the blue and white piece shown in Plate LXIX. The Yellow River passes in its course through a famous defile known as Lung-Mên, or "Dragon-Gate," and according to old legends, when the salmon ascend the stream in the third moon of each year, any that succeeded in passing through the precipitous rapids at this point become transformed into dragons. The list of successful candidates is called the "dragon list" in allusion to this.

Taoism is the second of the three great religions of China. Lao Tzŭ, the founder of the occult philosophy of the Taoists, is said to have been born in the year 604 B.C., and to have been a keeper of the official records at Lo, the capital of the *Chou* dynasty, in the province of Honan, till near the close of the fifth century B.C., when he was visited by Confucius. The meeting of the two sages is one of the scenes on the mural tomb sculptures of the second century that have been already alluded to, and it forms occasionally the motive of the decoration of a porcelain vase. After a long period of service Lao Tzŭ retired from office, foreseeing the decadence of the suzerain house of *Chou*, and traveled away to the west. The governor of the frontier pass of Han Ku besought him to write a book before retiring from the world, and was intrusted with the *Tao Tê Ching*, before the author disappeared from mortal ken. This work, the Bible of Taoism, has been translated into several European languages. Later legends have assigned to its author a period of fabulous antiquity, and a miraculous conception through the influence of a star, alleging him to have been the incarnation of the supreme celestial entity, which they called the "Venerable Prince of the Great Supreme," whence he is also termed Lao Chün, or "Venerable Prince." Shou Lao, the "Ancient of Ages," the stellar god of longevity, whose celestial seat is near the south pole, is supposed to be the disembodied spirit of the venerable philosopher. The mystic elements of his teaching were progressively developed by his early disciples in their search after an elixir to preserve the body from decay and death, and in their efforts to discover the *lapis divinus*, and to transmute metals into gold, which gave rise to the ancient study of alchemy, in its two leading branches. Their first great patron was the Emperor *Wu Ti* (B. C. 140–87) of the *Han* dynasty, and from his period onward the reverence paid to Lao Tzŭ began to assume a divine character. In A. D. 666 the emperor of the *T'ang* dynasty canonized him with the title of "Imperial God of the Dark First Cause," and other titles were added subsequently, till it has become difficult to distinguish his attributes from those of Shang Ti, the supreme god of the celestial hierarchy. Shang Ti is identified with the northern pole star, his chariot is the Great Bear, and the stars of the circumpolar space constitute his court — the Taoist kingdom of heaven — under appropriate titles. Shou Lao is established at the opposite pole of the heavens, and only appears on auspicious occasions. He is represented (Fig. 348) as a venerable man of benevolent aspect, with bald head, protuberant forehead, and long, flowing white beard, dressed in robes brocaded with the character *shou*, "longevity," and carrying a sacred peach in his hand. Sometimes he is mounted upon a deer, or speeding through the air on a stork, or he may be depicted as a mortal sage in a rocky landscape riding an ox on his long journey to the west.

FIG. 350.—Blue and white Snuff-bottle.

The old "Nature gods" of the Chinese, the devouring ogre of the wilderness, called T'ao-tieh, whose features are delineated on archaic bronzes, the rain- and storm-gods, which appear dimly outlined in the dark clouds before the tempest, and the dreaded thunder-god, whose bolts are the prehistoric stone axes and celts that are often found in ground washed away by the torrent after a thunderstorm, have all been adopted by the Taoists, but they are rarely seen on porcelain, and need not detain us here.

Much more popular is the Taoist Triad of Happiness, Rank, and Longevity, "Fu, Lu, Shou," which is depicted in Fig. 325. The vase is decorated in delicate enamel colors with gilding of the *Yung-chêng* period, with scattered scrolls of clouds and flying storks bringing branches of peaches in their beaks. On one side the strokes of the character *shou*, "longevity," filled in with a brocaded ground, are interrupted in the middle by a peach-shaped medallion containing a picture of a group of figures gathered under a spreading pine. The three principal figures represent the Taoist Triad, the others being only attendant sprites. The Star God of Rank, Lu Hsing, stands in the middle, dressed in mandarin robes, with a winged official hat of ancient style, and holding a *ju-i* scepter; the Star God of Longevity, Shou Hsing, stands on his right, leaning upon a long staff, to the top of which is slung a scroll, and holding in his left hand a peach, the sacred fruit of life; the Star God of Happiness, Fu Hsing, on the other side, has a babe in his arms, who is reaching out his hand for the peach. The boy dancing at the side holds up a lotus-flower, the one standing at the back a hand-organ (*tsêng*). On the other side of the vase the strokes of the companion character *fu*, "happiness," are interrupted in the middle by a circular medallion containing a picture of the Taoist goddess, Hsi Wang Mu, accompanied by two female attendants, crossing the sea on a raft.

The goddess is represented again in the saucer-shaped dish of eggshell porcelain painted in soft enamel colors with gilding, which is shown in Fig. 339. The central panel is designed in the shape of a peony-petal, and sprays of peony-flowers and buds are displayed upon the lilac diaper which surrounds it. It is painted in sepia tints, touched with gold, with the picture of two graceful female figures, representing the Taoist divinity, Hsi Wang Mu, with a youthful attendant standing upon branches of equisetum moss, as if floating on water, with their scarfs flowing in the breeze. The goddess, dressed in dragon-brocaded robes, holds a gilded scepter; the attendant carries a dish of peaches, the "fruit of life" of Taoist story. The rim of the dish is encircled by a band of pink diaper, interrupted by medallions containing sprays of peony, the floral attribute of the goddess.

FIG. 351. — Snuff-bottle; dark apple-green crackle; K'ang-hsi.

Hsi Wang Mu, the queen of the genii, is the ruler of the Taoist paradise in the K'un-lun Mountains, which is celebrated in ancient myth and fable. Legends in the old books record the visit of the Emperor *Mu Wang* in his journey to the west in B. C. 985, and relate how he was entertained by the goddess in her fairy abode, where she lives, surrounded by troops of genii, on the shores of the "Lake of Gems," where grow all kinds of trees bearing fruit of jewels and precious jade, and the peach-tree whose magic fruit confers the gift of immortality. The goddess bestows this fruit upon the favored beings admitted to her presence, or dispatches it by the azure-winged birds who serve, like the doves of Venus, as her messengers. The magnificence of her mountain palace is described in glowing terms by Lieh Tzŭ, a Taoist allegorical writer of the fifth century B. C. In later times the Emperor *Wu Ti* of the *Han* dynasty is alleged to have been favored with visits by Hsi Wang Mu and her fairy troop, and his regal entertainment of his supernatural guests is a well-worn theme of old picture and story.

The snuff-bottle shown in Fig. 347 exhibits Shou Lao again, in the guise of an aged pilgrim, leaning upon a long staff to the gnarled head of which is tied a double gourd, the traditional pilgrim's bottle. The deer at his side has a branch of the sacred Polyporus fungus in its mouth, and the bats flying round are introduced as symbols of happiness. At other times he is seen as a venerable figure seated on the rocks in a mountain landscape under a pine-tree, with the bamboo, flowering plum, and sacred fungus growing near, and his familiar animals, the deer, tortoise, and stork, near at hand, while the motley crowd of immortals and genii gather round in homage, distinguished by their various attributes. The best known of these is the group of Taoist *rishi*, or hermit immortals, that constitute the *Pa Hsien*, the "Eight Genii," of the Chinese, whose emblems were given in the chapter on Marks. The individual members of the eight have long been venerated among the Taoist saints, although they do not seem to have formed into a defined group before the thirteenth century. They are regarded as the patron saints of different arts and industries, and are found separately as porcelain statuettes, or united in the decoration of porcelain bowls and dishes, especially on those intended to hold sacrificial offerings. Their names and attributes are as follows:

1. *Chung-li Ch'üan*, who lived during the *Chou* dynasty, and was one of the discoverers of the elixir of life. He is represented as a fat man, with bare, pendulous abdomen, holding a sacred fungus, or a peach, in one hand, and in the other a fly-brush, or a fan, with which he is said to revive the spirits of the dead. He is also known as Han Chung-li.

2. *Lü Tung-pin*, born in 755, was one of the most prominent among the later Taoist patriarchs, who held office as magistrate of Tê-hua, and studied the mysteries of alchemy in the recesses of the hills called Lu Shan in the province of Kiangsi. A personage of martial aspect, he is armed with the sword of supernatural power, with which he traversed the empire for upward of four hundred years, slaying dragons and ridding the earth of divers evil things. He is also known by his personal name of Lü Yen, and is worshiped everywhere as the special patron of the sick, who hang up the magic sword by their bedside to exorcise maleficent spirits. Under the designation of Lü Tsu, or the "Patriarch Lü," he is the patron saint of the fraternity of barbers.

3. *Li T'ieh-kuai*—that is to say, "Li with the Iron Crutch"—presents himself in the guise of a lame and crooked beggar dressed in rags. No precise period is assigned to his existence on earth, but he is said to have been of commanding stature and dignified mien, and devoted to the study of Taoist lore, in which he was instructed

by Lao Tzŭ himself, who used to summon his pupil to the celestial spheres. When his spirit mounted on high, the care of his body, which remained on earth, was confided to one of his disciples. On one occasion, unhappily, the watcher was called away to the deathbed of his mother, and his trust being neglected, when the disembodied spirit returned it found its earthly habitation no longer vitalized. The first available refuge was the body of a lame beggar, whose spirit had at that moment been exhaled, and in this shape the sage continued his existence, supported by an iron crutch, and carrying a pilgrim's gourd, from which clouds and magic apparitions are often seen to be issuing. He is the special patron of astrologers and magicians.

4. *Ts'ao Kuo-ch'iu* is said to have been the son of a famous general of the tenth century, and brother of an empress regent of the *Sung* dynasty. He is dressed in official robes, wears a winged hat, and carries a pair of castanets. He is the patron of mummers and actors.

5. *Lan Ts'ai-ho*, a legendary being of whom little is known, the sex even being uncertain. One story says that it was a weird woman dressed in a tattered blue gown, with a cloak of leaves, who used to beg a livelihood in the streets, chanting a doggerel verse denunciatory of fleeting life and its delusive pleasures. She carries a spade and a basket of flowers, and is worshiped by gardeners and florists as their tutelary saint.

6. *Chang Kuo Lao*, a celebrated necromancer, who is said to have flourished in the seventh and eighth centuries, and to have possessed a wonderful white mule which carried him thousands of miles at a stretch. He used to carry the picture of his mule folded and hidden away in his wallet, and made the beast resume its proper shape by spurting water on the picture. At other times he would conjure it out of his magic gourd. He is recognized by the peculiar musical instrument which he carries, a kind of drum of bamboo, with a pair of rods. He is the patron of artists and calligraphists, and of scholars generally.

7. *Han Hsiang Tzŭ* is reputed to have been a great-nephew of the celebrated statesman Han Yü, who lived 768–824, and was an ardent lover of transcendental study. As a pupil of the patriarch Lü Tung-pin, he gained admission into the Taoist paradise and climbed the tree of life, the sacred peach-tree, from which he fell to the ground, and, in descending, entered into the state of immortality. He is represented as a young man playing upon a flute, and is specially worshiped by musicians.

8. *Ho Hsien Ku*, the maiden immortal of the group, is said to have been a native of the neighborhood of Canton. At the age of fourteen a spirit visited her in a dream, and instructed her in the art of attaining immortality by eating powdered jade and mother-of-pearl. She followed these instructions implicitly, vowed herself to a life of virginity, gradually renounced ordinary human food, and acquired the faculty of traversing the hills in spiritualistic fashion, as if endowed with wings. She used to return at night with the herbs she had gathered during her solitary wanderings. She still appears occasionally to her favored votaries, floating upon a cloud of many colors, as depicted on the charming eggshell dish illustrated in Plate LXIII, where she is represented as carrying in her hands a large jar of the elixir of life. She is usually clad in a cloak of mugwort-leaves, carries a lotus, and is the tutelary genius of housewifery.

The oblong porcelain plaque which is exhibited, mounted in its frame of carved wood, in Fig. 352, is painted in enamel colors of the *Ch'ien-lung* period, with a picture of the eight immortals (*Pa Hsien*) crossing the sea on their way to the immortal realms on the far bank. The shore to which they are proceeding is a conventional mountain scene, with tall pines in the foreground, representing the Elysian fields of the Taoist cult.

Tung Fang So, who lived in the second century B. C., was one of the favorite associates of the Emperor *Wu Ti* of the *Han* dynasty, into whose service he entered B. C. 138, when the young sovereign summoned the most gifted scholars and men of genius. He encouraged the emperor's leaning to the superstitious and marvelous, and was soon after his death adopted as a Taoist saint and endowed with all kinds of miraculous qualities. He was declared to be an embodiment of the planet Venus, and to have been incarnate many times in the course of Chinese history. The goddess Hsi Wang Mu, who saw him during her visit to the court, is said to have exclaimed, "That is the boy who once stole three of my sacred peaches, and acquired thereby a longevity of nine thousand years!" He is always represented holding a gigantic peach in his hand, or speeding across the clouds with a branch of the fruit of life thrown over his shoulder.

The list of Taoist genii is nearly endless,* for every vocation has its tutelary saint, who is often a deified mortal who once worked at the craft, as in the case of the patron Pousa of the potters, the story of whose vicarious sacrifice has been related in the chapter on Ching-tê-chên.

---

* There are several books on the subject, one of the earliest being the *Shên Hsien Chuan*, by Ko Hung, written in the fourth century A. D., which gives a series of biographical notices of eighty-four immortals. Cf. Harlez, *Le Livre des Esprits et des Immortels. Essai de mythologie Chinoise d'après les textes originaux.* Bruxelles, 1893.

Sailors worship the goddess Ma Ku, and build temples at the seaports, where she is enshrined under the title of T'ien Hou, "Empress of Heaven"; she appears riding upon the storm-clouds, or floating on the rough sea-waves, to direct her votaries in times of danger, and is liberally propitiated by *ex voto* offerings when they are once more safe on shore. The complaisant Taoists have even dedicated an altar for thieves, and supplied them with a deity of their own, to whom they devote a portion of their ill-gotten gains after a successful raid. Some

FIG. 352.—Oblong Plaque painted in enamel colors, with a picture of the Eight Genii crossing the Sea.

of the genii are connected with folk-lore rather than religion, and partake of the nature of the fairies of Western story, like the mischievous elf who hides away in the thorny recess of the jujube-tree, or the tiny peachling whose abode is in the kernel of the fruit.

Among other genii often represented in the decoration of porcelain are: Liu Han, whose familiar is the three-legged toad from the moon, which reveals to him secrets of immortality and hidden treasures, and who holds up a coin or jewel between finger and thumb, or waves a string of cash in the air; Wang Ch'iao, the philosopher prince of the sixth century B. C., who is seen playing upon the flute as he rides through the air upon the white crane, from whose back he waved a final adieu to the world as he ascended to the immortal realms; and the scantily clothed hermit, Huang An, who sits cross-legged upon the back of a tortoise swimming across the sea. The twin genii, called Ho Ho Erh Hsien— that is to say, "Two Genii of Union and Harmony"—are perhaps the most popular of any. They are two cronies, *Arcades ambo*, who take many forms, being represented sometimes as ragged mendicants, with staff and besom, in friendly converse, as they approach a priest who is ringing a monastery bell; sometimes as a couple of hermits with smiling, boyish faces, one carrying a lotus-flower, the other a box from underneath the cover of which a cloud may be seen issuing which is shaping itself into the form of bats as emblems of happiness. The twin merry genii are presented in Fig. 346, with the arm of one encircling the neck of the other. They have gold bracelets and anklets, and their robes are richly brocaded in enamel colors with gilding of the *Ch'ien-lung* period, so that they have altogether a very mundane aspect, and their supernatural character might hardly be suspected were it not for the cloud-enveloped pedestal of celadon tint on which they are posed, which mark them as celestial beings. These smiling features pervade domestic life in China: they are printed on the wall-paper, and woven in silk as appropriate hangings for the marriage couch, and even towels imported from abroad are seen stamped in fugitive ink with the effigies of the two merry genii. Should there be an estrangement between lovers or friends, one of them must go to a temple, burn incense at the shrine consecrated to the two genii, and bring away a pinch of ashes from the censer, and if this be surreptitiously put into a cup of tea and the decoction be drunk by the estranged one unknowingly, it will infallibly bring about a complete reconciliation.

Buddhism, the third great religion of China, was introduced from India. The earliest missionaries came overland to the southwest of the Chinese Empire, the modern province of Ssŭ-chuan, and arrived in the second century B. C., but gained few converts. It was not till the year 61 A. D. that the Emperor *Ming Ti*, in consequence of a dream of a golden figure of supernatural proportions, whose head was encircled by a shining halo, sent an embassy to India, which brought back with them many sacred books and images. Two Indian priests, Matanga and Gobharana, accompanied the mission on its return to China, and the emperor built a temple for their residence at Loyang, then the capital. It was called Pai Ma Ssŭ, "White Horse Monastery," in commemoration of their having brought the Sanskrit books on a white horse, and they forthwith proceeded to translate those books into Chinese. Buddhism penetrated subsequently to Korea, and through that country into Japan, which, however, it did not reach till the middle of the sixth century.

FIG. 353.— Blue and white Snuff - bottle; mark, Ch'ien-lung.

Buddhism is well known, in comparison with Taoism, and there is a vast literature on the subject available for reference, so that it need not detain us so long. One of the most recent works on the subject is that written by Dr. Waddell,* on the borders of Tibet. It is well illustrated, and will be found a mine of myth and symbolism, the author having, he tells us, purchased a Buddhist temple, with all its ritual fittings, and obtained much of his information on obscure points from learned lamas on the spot.

Sâkyamuni, the historical Buddha, is rarely molded in porcelain, more precious materials, such as jade, rock-crystal, amethyst, or turquoise, being considered more suitable for his exalted dignity when represented on a small scale. His principal representations are:

1. *His Birth.* A figure of a child standing erect upon a lotus-thalamus, pointing upward to heaven with his right hand, downward to earth with his left, according to the tradition which tells us that he cried out at the moment, "I the only, most exalted one!"

2. *Sâkya returning from the Mountains.* Of ascetic aspect, with beard and shaven poll, attired in flowing garments and holding his hands in a position of prayer. The ear-lobes are enlarged, a sign of wisdom, and the brow bears the *ûrna*, the luminous mark that distinguishes a Buddha, or a Bôdhisattva.

3. *The All-wise Sâkya.* A Buddha seated cross-legged upon a lotus throne, resting the left hand upon the knee, the right hand raised in the mystic preaching pose. The hair is generally represented as a blue mass composed of short, close curls, and a jewel is placed about midway between the crown and forehead.

4. *The Nirvâna.* A recumbent figure lying upon a raised bench, with the head pillowed upon a lotus.

5. *In the Sâkyamuni Trinity.* Either erect, or seated in the attitude of meditation, with the alms-bowl in his hands, between his spiritual sons, the Bôdhisattvas Manjusrî and Samantabhadra, the three forming a mystic triad.

Manjusrî, or Manjughosha, "The sweet-voiced," the Buddhist Apollo or God of Wisdom, is the great dispeller of ignorance. With the bright sword of divine knowledge, which he wields in his right hand, he cuts all knotty points, and he carries in his left hand the bible of transcendental wisdom placed upon a lotus-flower. He is often represented mounted on a lion.

Samantabhadra, "The All-good," the other celestial Bôdhisat of the Buddhist Trinity, is always seated upon an elephant, and usually holds a book.

Gigantic images of the above triad occupy the center of the large hall of a Chinese temple, while the walls are lined with figures of the eighteen Lohan (*Sanskrit*, Arhat), representing the chief of the early apostles or missionaries of the faith, each provided with its own particular shrine and altar. The number was originally sixteen, and the Japanese still keep to the original group, not having adopted the two saints which have been more recently added in China. Each of these " eighteen Arhats " is figured in a fixed attitude, and each has his distinctive symbol or badge, in the same way as our apostles are represented—Mark with a lion, Luke with a book, etc. The group is sometimes painted on a porcelain vase or snuff-bottle, or is seen passing in procession round the sides of a bowl or cup intended for sacrificial use.

The two best-known members of the group are perhaps the seventeenth and eighteenth: *Dharmatrâta*, born, like the original sixteen, in India, and *Ho-shang*, "The Monk," the only one that has a Chinese name. Dharmatrâta, as a lay devotee, wears long hair. He holds a vase

* *The Buddhism of Tibet, or Lamaism, with its Mystic Cults, Symbolism, and Mythology, and in its Relation to Indian Buddhism.* By L. A. Waddell, M. B., etc., London, 1895.

and fly-whisk, carries on his back a bundle of books, and gazes at a small image of the mystic celestial Buddha Amitâbha. He wrote seven works, of which the chief, *Udânavarga*, a collection of verses from the Buddhist Canon, has been translated into English by Mr. W. W. Rockhill.

Ho-shang, "The Monk," is the familiar Pu-tai Ho-shang, "the Priest with the Hempen Bag," whom the Japanese call *Ho-tei*, that being their pronunciation of the first two syllables of his name, which mean "hempen bag." They describe him as a Chinese bonze or monk, who lived about a thousand years ago, and was remarkable for his fatness, his love of children, and especially for always carrying a large hempen sack, from which his name was derived. The

bag, which has always a bolsterlike roundness, is put to many uses; it may be a bed on which the owner is reclining, a receptacle for the hundred precious things, or a trap for the little boys and girls who cluster round and are enticed inside to see the wonderful things it contains; whatever it may be, it is as inseparable from Ho-tei as are his fair, round stomach and double chin. In China he represents the last incarnation of *Maitreya*, "The Loving One," the coming Buddha or Buddhist Messiah, and his obese image, with a loosened girdle in one hand and a rosary in the other, is enshrined by them in the front hall of every temple, under the name of Mi-lo Fo—i. e., Maitreya Buddha. He ranks as a Bôdhisat, having only once more to pass through human existence to attain Buddhahood, and under this title, contracted to *pou-sa*, or *poussah*, has become proverbial in French as an emblem of contentment and sensuality. His image is very frequently molded in porcelain, and it has often been erroneously considered to be that of the martyr patron of the potters, and labeled as *le dieu de la porcelaine*. Maitreya is supposed now to be enthroned in the Tushita heaven, and he is a favorite deity of the Tibetans.

The most popular of all the Buddhist divinities in China, as well as in Japan, is Kuan Yin, the Goddess of Mercy, whose figure is illustrated here in Plate LX. She also ranks as a Bôdhisat, and is identified with Avalokita, "The Keen-seeing Lord," the spiritual son of the celestial Buddha Amitâbha, who shares with him the dominion of the Paradise in the West. This is the most powerful of all the Bôdhisats, and the one of which the Dalai Lamas of Tibet pretend to be the incarnation. Avalokita, being a pure mythological creation, is seldom, like Buddha, represented as a mere man, but is invested with all kinds of supernatural forms and attributes. The four-handed form figures him as a prince sitting in the Buddha posture, with the front pair of hands joined in devotional attitude, while the other hands hold a rosary and a long-stemmed lotus-flower. Another form has eleven heads, piled up in the shape of a cone, and eighteen, or even forty hands, grasping symbols and weapons, and stretched out in all directions to defend and rescue the wretched and the lost; and some of the manifestations are endowed with a thousand eyes, ever on the lookout to perceive distress. The Chinese Buddhists relate that Avalokita once appeared on earth as a daughter of a king of the *Chou* dynasty in 696 B. C., although Buddhism was not introduced into the country till long after that date. The princess was sentenced to death by her father for refusing to marry, but the executioner's sword broke without harming her. When her spirit went down to hell, hell was changed into paradise, until Yama, the ruler of the realms below, sent her back to life, and she was miraculously conveyed upon a lotus-petal to the island of Potala. Hers is the image that is worshiped throughout the far East to-day as the personification of love and charity. In one of its shapes, Kuan Yin the Maternal, the Goddess of Mercy has a child in her arms, and is specially sacrificed to by women desirous of offspring, who load her altar with *ex-voto* offerings of doll-like babes made of silk or molded in porcelain. These are the images that have been occasionally mistaken for representations of the "Virgin and Child."

Bôdhidharma is a Buddhist saint frequently represented in Chinese and Japanese art, and he is seen molded in stoneware in Plate XLI. He was the twenty-eighth and last of the line of Indian patriarchs, and the first Chinese patriarch. The son of a king in southern India, he came to China by sea in the year 520, and was the first to bring the palm called patra (*Borassus flabelliformis*). He settled in Loyang, where he was called "The Wall-gazing Brahman," because he remained perfectly still the whole time engaged in silent meditation. He died about the year 529, and was buried in the monastery grounds, but was met, the legend says, soon after, enveloped in his shroud, on his way back to his native land, holding one shoe in his hand, saying, when questioned, that he had forgotten to bring the other. The grave was afterward opened; the corpse had disappeared, and only a single shoe was found. Bôdhidharma is often pictured crossing the water standing upon a reed, which he had plucked from the bank. The Chinese form of his name is Tamo, and some of the more credulous of the early Roman Catholic missionaries in China were inclined to believe, from the similarity in the names, that he might be identified with St. Thomas, who is supposed to have gone as an apostle to India, and might well, they argued, have extended his journeyings to China.

The influence of Buddhism on Chinese art was of the most profound and far-reaching nature, and extended to building and sculpture, as well as to the carving of images in precious stones, the casting of ritual vessels of novel design in metals, and the painting of sacred pictures on paper and silk. In all these arts the Hindu monks are said to have been skilled, and they imposed their canons on the Chinese, so that down to the present day the sacred images are modeled on the old lines, and exhibit a marked Aryan type and physiognomy. Monasteries were soon founded throughout China in the most picturesque spots in the hills, with tall pagodas to enshrine sacred relics and *chaityas* of varied form as funeral monuments, such as now make a necessary adjunct to every Chinese landscape. One of the ordinary forms of the *chaitya*, or *dâgaba*, is seen molded in porcelain in Fig. 349. It is a microcosm of the universe according to Buddhist ideas. The plinth is square, the form of earth; the hollow shrine, with open door, has the vaulted form of heaven; and the spire is horizontally ridged to represent the thirteen celestial spheres in superimposed tiers; the umbrella-shaped top is crowned with the "jeweled vase," bound with waving fillets. The painted decoration of strings of colored beads and gilded rings hanging from grotesque monstrous heads, and of arabesque scrolls of conventional flowers, is also of Buddhist type.

Among Buddhist mythological animals, the dragon (*nâga*) and the golden-winged bird (*garuda*) are the chief. The former had a serpent form like the cobra, and the latter had something in common with the adjutant-bird, the enemy of the serpent tribe, but the Chinese have modified both after their previous conceptions of the dragon (*lung*) and phœnix (*fêng*). The lion is an animal that occupied an important place in Hindustan as one of the insignia of royalty and a supporter of the throne, and it is often figured also as a guardian of the jewel of the law. It was new to China, not being a native of the country, and even now, although a pair of bronze or stone lions stands before the gateway of every palace and large temple in China, and another is often molded in porcelain in miniature, as we

FIG. 355.—Brown Stoneware (Kuang Yao) Vase of archaic form, enameled with a thick glaze of pale greenish-blue crackle.

have seen, for ritual use, they are always of grotesque form, and have flames issuing from the hips and shoulders, the attributes of mythological animals. The lion in ordinary Chinese art is a tame beast, sporting with a brocaded ball; their own king of beasts is the dreaded tiger, which contends with the dragon as the prince of the powers of the air.

The elephant, the horse, and the hare are sometimes seen in a picture on a porcelain vase, crossing the dark sea which leads to paradise, the only animals that have obtained admittance to Nirvana by their own merit. The elephant is also molded in porcelain for the Buddhist altar as the bearer of the jeweled vase, and the horse as carrying on his back sacred books; the hare, which now lives in the moon, was exalted after it had offered itself a willing sacrifice as food for Buddha when he was starving. When horses form the decoration of a vase, it is generally the team of eight famous horses of the ancient Emperor *Mu Wang*, which were driven by his charioteer Tsao Fu, on his expedition to the K'un-lun Mountains to visit Hsi Wang Mu, the Queen of the Genii.

The four supernatural or spiritually endowed creatures (*Ssǔ Ling*) of the Chinese are the dragon, the phœnix, the tortoise, and the unicorn. Sometimes the tiger is associated, making a group of "Five Ling."

1. The dragon (*Lung*), the chief among the scaly reptiles, is conventionally depicted as a four-footed monster, resembling some of the huge saurians that have recently been discovered by paleontologists, and the fossil bones of such, it may be added, really figure as "dragon's bones" in the Chinese pharmacopœia. It is conventionally represented with a bearded, scowling head, straight horns, a scaly, serpentine body, with four feet armed with formidable claws, a line of bristling dorsal spines, and flames proceeding from the hips and shoulders. The claws, originally three in number on each foot, were afterward increased to four and five, the last number being restricted to the imperial dragon of the last and present dynasties, as brocaded on imperial robes and painted on porcelain made for the use of the palace. The dragon, in ancient philosophy, corresponds to the East, to spring, etc., and " Azure Dragon " is the name of the eastern quadrant of the uranosphere. It has the power of transformation, and the gift of rendering itself visible or invisible at pleasure. Kuan Tzǔ (seventh century B. C.) declares that "the dragon becomes at will reduced to the size of a silkworm, or swollen till it fills the universe; it desires to mount, and it rises until it affronts the clouds; to sink, and it descends until hidden below the fountains of the deep." The early cosmogonists described four kinds of dragons: the celestial dragons (*t'ien lung*), which support and guard the mansions of the gods; the spiritual dragons (*shên lung*), which rule the winds and produce rain for the benefit of mankind; the earth dragons (*ti lung*), which direct the flow of rivers and springs; and the dragons of hidden treasures (*fu ts'ang*), which watch over buried wealth concealed from mortals. The Buddhist dragon of the law (*fa lung*) is represented as tightly grasping the jewel of the faith in one of its outstretched paws; originally hostile, it has become submissive to Buddha and a trusty guardian of the faith. The celestial dragons in Chinese art, as they ascend and descend, are usually represented in pursuit of effulgent jewels that appear to be whirling in space, and that are supposed to be of magic efficacy, granting every wish. The congener of the celestial dragon is the *chiao lung*, the dragon of lakes and marshes, who is figured in the lunar zodiac, already referred to, as a dragon-headed serpent without feet. The *p'an lung* is the dragon coiled in a circle, hibernating in the watery depths, that often forms medallions on bowls and dishes; some say it is the dragon which does not mount to heaven. The *ch'ih lung* is the archaic dragon of ancient bronzes, a clinging, lizardlike reptile with clawless feet and spiral bifid tail, that is often molded in relief on libation wine-cups and other porcelain vessels of antique design. The Chinese dragon is sometimes hornless; occasionally, but very rarely, it is provided with a pair of wings. The fish dragon has already been alluded to as the chosen emblem of literary success; and there is also the yellow dragon, or dragon horse, the most honored of its tribe, which rose out of the river Lo, in the time of the fabulous *Fu-hi*, the legendary founder of the Chinese polity, with a scroll upon its back inscribed with the eight mystic trigrams (*pa kua*). The dragon is peculiarly symbolical of all that pertains to the Son of Heaven, the emperor's throne being styled the dragon-seat, and his face described as the dragon-countenance; his banner is the dragon flag, and after his death he is borne aloft by dragons to the regions of the blessed.

2. *Fêng* is the name of the male, *huang* the name of the female, of a fabulous bird of wondrous form and mystic nature, the second of the four supernatural creatures. The compound of the two (*fêng-huang*) is the generic name of the bird which has many symbolical analogies with the phœnix of the Greeks, and, like it, is immortal, has its dwelling in the highest regions of the air, and only appears to mortals as a presage of the advent of virtuous rulers, or an emblem of an auspicious reign. In the fabulous times of *Huang Ti* the phœnix made its nest in the palace, and the ancient *Book of History* records that they came with measured gambolings to add splendor to the musical ceremonies of the great *Shun*. In the eastern gateway of the palace of to-day a huge bronze phœnix hovers under the roof of the great hall, over its nest, which is also fashioned of bronze in the shape of a circlet of clouds. The phœnix has always been taken as the presage and emblem of a virtuous sovereign, and it figures still as the special emblem of the Mikado in Japan. In China it used to rank above the dragon, which was the emblem of a good minister. In the present day it has become the special emblem of the empress, and the dragon that of the emperor. In poetry the inseparable *fêng* and *huang* are models of conjugal love. The phœnix is usually depicted with the head of a pheasant and the beak of a swallow, a long flexible neck, plumage of many gorgeous colors, a flowing tail, between that of an argus pheasant and a peacock, and long claws pointed backward as it flies. They are seen flying in the midst of scrolled clouds mingled with forked flames, or wending their way through a close floral ground, which is preferably made up of sprays of the tree-peony. Three times three is the lucky number for the decoration of a vase, just as we find nine dragons on another vase in pursuit of whirling jewels, or nine lions sporting with as many brocaded balls. If there be ten, one is certain to be much larger than the rest, and it will be the parent dragon or phœnix, with nine young ones.

3. The tortoise (*Kuei*) is the third of the supernaturally endowed creatures. The greatest of the tribe is the divine tortoise, which rose out of the river Lo, and presented to the gaze of *Yü* the Great a mystic plan of numerals inscribed upon its back, which he deciphered and adopted as the basis of moral teaching and a clew to the philosophy of the unseen. The shell of the tortoise was used in divination by the ancient Chinese, who augured

from the lines on the scorched shell, in the same way as other ancient tribes used to augur from the roasted blade-bone of a sheep. Like the rest of the sacred group, the tortoise is given a marvelous longevity, even a span of five thousand years, and after a certain age it bears the sign of its patriarchal dignity in the shape of a hairy tail. As an emblem of strength it appears in Hindu legends, supporting an elephant, which in turn bears the world; in China it is represented as bearing on its back P'êng Lai Shan, the sea-girt abode of immortal genii.

4. The unicorn (*Ch'i-lin*), the fourth of the group of supernatural creatures, has its generic designation compounded of the names of the male (*ch'i*) and of the female (*lin*). It is usually written *k'i-lin*, and this name, under the form of *kylin*, is often erroneously applied in European ceramic books to lions, and generally to other lionlike grotesque creatures with which the Chinese fill in rocky landscapes under the generic name of *hai-shou*, or "sea-monsters," the *chimères* of old French catalogues. The Chinese unicorn has the body of a deer, with slender legs and divided hoofs, the head resembles that of the dragon, the tail is curled and bushy, like that of the conventional lion, and the shoulders are adorned with the flamelike attributes of its divine nature. Its appearance is a happy portent, and it used to grace the palaces of the ancient emperors of fabulous times. It is said to attain the age of a thousand years, to be the noblest form of the animal creation, and the emblem of perfect good; and to tread so lightly as to leave no footprints, and so carefully as to crush no living creature.

Other supernatural animals occur occasionally. They are usually composite creations, like the dragon-horse of ancient fable, lionlike monsters with the heads of wolves, and the like. The fox is a beast whose nature is deeply tinged with supernatural qualities, and it bears a worse reputation in China than its brother does in. European fairy tale. It is a spirit of mischief, of supernatural cunning, with the power of assuming various forms, its favorite and most baneful transformation being into the semblance of a young and beautiful girl, in which shape it lures its victim to destruction. The fox is the courser upon which ghostly beings ride, and when it reaches the term of a thousand years it becomes a Celestial Fox, characterized by a golden color and nine tails, and serves in the halls of the Sun and Moon. The hare has already been alluded to as living in the moon, where it sits under the shade of the *Olea fragrans* tree, pounding the elixir of life with pestle and mortar. Its companion in the moon is the toad (*ch'an-ch'u*), into which the lady Ch'ang-ngo was changed, after she had stolen from her husband the drug of immortality which had been given to him by the goddess Hsi Wang Mu, and taken flight with her precious booty to find refuge with the moon. These legends appear to be of Taoist origin, and the animals are those that the solitary hermit was accustomed to see in his mountain retreat. He was wont to gather his herbs in the light of the full moon, and this luminary was an important power in his alchemistic speculations. The deer is another of his sacred animals; it is represented bringing the Polyporus fungus (*ling-chih*) in its mouth, and is always placed near the deity of longevity as one of his peculiar attributes.

The other animal attributes of Taoist divinities are the tortoise and stork, whence comes the usual birthday greeting, "May your years be those of the tortoise and stork!" The stork (*ho*) is the sacred bird *par excellence*, and is supposed to attain a fabulous longevity. The variety usually

Fig. 356.—Eggshell Plate, with a richly enameled *rouge-d'or* ground interrupted by panels and floral designs painted in colors on a white ground.

represented is the Manchurian crane (*Grus viridirostris*), which is characterized by a plumage of white and black, and by a bare crimson patch upon the crown. It must not be confounded with the egret, which is often found in the decoration of porcelain in combination with the lotus, and which has no mythological attachments. The stork is the aërial steed of some of the genii, and it brings the talismanic rods of fate in its beak from the other world. In pictures of the Taoist paradise it is often seen swimming round the rock on which the sacred peach-tree is growing, or gathering in large flocks upon the pine-clad shores of the Mount of the Immortals.

There are also a number of emblems of longevity selected from the vegetable kingdom, which supply frequent motives of decoration. Among fruits the most prominent place is given to the peach (*t'ao*). It is an emblem of marriage, as well as a symbol of longevity; the early odes liken a bride in her graceful elegance and promise to a blossoming peach-tree, and the most ancient superstitions of the Chinese attribute magic virtue to its twigs, which were brought in the beaks of sacred birds. The peach is the tree of life in the mystical dreams of the Taoists; it grows in the grounds of the palace of the goddess Hsi Wang Mu, bearing fruit that ripens but once in three thousand years, and conferring that period of life upon those that are fortunate enough to taste it. The peach figures with the pomegranate and the Buddha's-hand citron, as "the three fruits" (*san kuo*) symbolical of the three abundances (*san to*), viz., abundance of years, abundance of sons, and abundance of happiness.

The fungus of longevity (*chih*), usually called *ling-chih*, *ling* meaning "miraculous," is a branched woody fungus of brightly variegated coloring, known to botanists as *Polyporus lucidus*, as determined by Sir Joseph Hooker from a dried specimen taken by me from a Taoist temple at Peking to the herbarium at Kew. Chinese myth dilates upon its rapid growth, its vivid coloring, and its durability. It sometimes incloses curiously a growing plant, so that blades of grass appear to be sprouting out of its substance, a combination of good omen; more propitious still is a branching stem bearing seven or nine heads, and this sometimes forms the motive of the shape of a *flambé* vase, the gorgeous coloring of which is intended to represent the natural tints of the variegated fungus. A branch of this fungus is placed as a magic wand in the hand of Taoist genii, and the peculiar shape of the head of the jeweled *ju-i* scepter, which has been frequently referred to, betrays its original derivation from the same fungus form.

FIG. 357.—Globular " Hawthorn Ginger-Pot " (*mei-hua-kuan*), of the K'ang-hsi period, with the blossoms, originally in white reserve, filled in alternately with enamels of pale-green and brickdust-red tints.

The Chinese gourd is another of the chosen emblems of longevity on account of the durability of its dried fruit, as well as a symbol of fertility from the quantity of seeds it produces. There are single and double gourds of varied form, cultivated varieties of *Lagenaria vulgaris*, the calabash or bottle-gourd. Bottles and drinking-cups have been made of its dried shell from the most ancient times, and it is still used in temples for libation-cups and ladles for sacrificial wine. The variety of the bottle-gourd called *hu-lu*, the "double gourd," which is naturally contracted into a waist in the middle, is the pilgrim's gourd *par excellence*. The Taoist hermit carries one strung upon his girdle, and occasionally conjures spirits and apparitions from its interior, like the magician in the stories of the Arabian Nights.

The pine, bamboo, and winter-blossoming plum (*sung, chu, mei*) are constantly grouped together as a threefold symbol of longevity. The first two figure as evergreens, emblems of a green old age; the last as a tree which throws out blossoming twigs from its gnarled, worn, and leafless trunk before the winter is over. The three may form the sole decoration of a vase, or be combined in Taoist pictures to form sacred groves in their mountain paradise, or a canopy for the God of Longevity, as he sits enthroned on the "rock of ages" (*shou shan*), worshiped by the motley crowd of immortals.

The plum (*Prunus domestica*) is sacred to Lao Tzŭ, who is said to have been born under its branches, and three of its purple fruit form his special attribute. This fruit, called *li* in Chinese, is to be distinguished from the smaller and sourer fruit called *mei* (*Prunus mume*), the blossoming twigs of which make such an effective floral decoration, as in the so-called "hawthorn" jars and vases.

This charming variety of prunus is the typical flower of winter, the tree-peony (*Pæonia moutan*) being the typical flower of spring, the lotus (*Nelumbium speciosum*) of summer, and the chrysanthemum of autumn. These "Flowers of the Four Seasons" (*Ssŭ Chi Hua*) are a frequent motive for the decoration of the four faces of a quadrangular vase, or the four side panels of a bowl. The amateur of the chrysanthemum is T'ao Yuan-ming; the lover of the lotus, the poet Li T'ai-po; and a pair of large round dishes or bowls are often decorated with companion pictures of these two worthies surrounded by their favorite flowers. T'ao Yuan-ming was a noted scholar and poet of the fifth century, who resigned the seals of office in preference to "bending his back" to a superior functionary, remarking that it was not worth while to "crook the loins for the sake of five measures of rice." After he had retired he passed his days drinking, playing upon the lyre, and making verses amid the chrysanthemums that embellished the garden of his retreat, until he died, 427 A. D., at the age of sixty-two. Li T'ai-po, the most famous of the poets of China for his erratic genius, romantic career, and devotion to the wine-cup, as well as for his powers of verse, has already been often referred to. The scene in which the emperor himself is handing dishes to him at a banquet, while his favorite and haughty concubine attends with the poet's brush and ink-pallet, and the chief privy counselor, Kao Li-ssŭ, pulls off his boots, is often pictured on porcelain as the *ne plus ultra* of success of literary genius.

The Chinese artist excels in flowers and birds. The four plants to which he devotes the most attention are the prunus (*mei*), the bamboo (*chu*), the orchid (*lan*), and the chrysanthemum (*chü*), and most art books contain a series of studies of these, some of which, published over two centuries ago, are curious examples of the technique of printing in different colors. Among the other flowers used in decoration the following may be mentioned: Shao-yao, the *Pæonia albiflora;* T'u-mi, the *Rosa rugosa;* Jui-hsiang, the *Viburnum odoratissimum;* Mo-li, the *Jasminum sambac;* Lien-hua, the *Nelumbium speciosum;* Kuei-hua, the *Olea fragrans;* Hai-t'ang, the *Pyrus spectabilis;* Chih-hua, the *Gardenia florida;* Ting-hsiang, the *Syringa sinensis;* Ch'iang-wei, the *Rosa indica;* Mou-tan, or *Pæonia moutan;* Yü-lan, or *Magnolia yulan;* Chi-kuan, the *Celosia cristata;* Hu-tieh-hua, the *Iris japonica;* Hsiu-ch'iu, the hydrangea; K'uei-hua, the hibiscus; Chiu-hai-t'ang, the *Begonia discolor;* Ho-pao moutan, the *Dielytra spectabilis;* Shih-chu, the Dianthus or pink; and the Shui-hsien-hua, the "Water-fairy" flower, or *Narcissus tazetta.* Some of these may be combined to form a floral rebus, or they may be massed together with sprays, as in the vase shown in Fig. 279. Particular birds also are commonly associated with particular trees and flowers, such as phœnixes, peacocks, or pheasants with the Moutan peony; partridges or quails with millet; swallows with the willow; storks with the pine, etc. The composition called *Po Niao Ch'ao Fêng,* or "The Hundred Birds paying Court to the Phœnix," represents all the different kinds of birds coming in pairs to gather round a couple of phœnixes which are seen strutting proudly in the foreground.

FIG. 358.—Wine-Pot of the K'ang-hsi period, decorated in colors relieved by a brown ground overlaid with gilded designs.

Painters of figure subjects (*jên-wu*) have a wider range of selection, as may be gathered from a glance at the catalogue of the Anderson Collection which is now in the British Museum.* The kind of pictures chosen for the decoration of porcelain is often a reflex of the manners and customs of the times. The close of the *Ming* dynasty was a period of luxury and indolence, and the decorated porcelain is painted with pictures of court life, with bands of gayly dressed damsels playing instruments of music, and with all phases of processional pomp. Magistrates are represented seated in state at the justice-table, and parties of scholars and poets are grouped in garden pavilions, drinking wine and making verses. The Emperor *Lung-ch'ing* (1567–72) was notorious for his profligacy and for his devotion to the pleasures of the harem, and we find some of the imperial porcelain of his reign so defaced with erotic scenes that there is no place for it in a decent collection. After the Manchu con-

* *Descriptive and Historical Catalogue of a Collection of Japanese and Chinese Paintings in the British Museum.* By W. Anderson, F. R. C. S., London, 1886.

quest of China in 1644, when the Emperor *K'ang-hsi* was firmly established on the throne, and the imperial porcelain manufactory was once more at work, the decoration reflects a changed scene. Pitched battles, single combats of spearmen mounted on party-colored horses, and military processions with men in armor, are the new order of the day. The ladies of the court even are often seen mounted on horseback and engaged in equestrian sports, which the emperor watches seated in a raised pavilion. The heroes most frequently pictured are the military commanders of the troubled times of the "Three Kingdoms," and the historical drama supplants for the moment scenes of comedy. There is a certain crude vigor in the art of the earlier half of this reign, which has led many to attribute the productions to a more archaic period. Before the end of the long reign of sixty years a more finished style has come into vogue, and the strong, brilliant colors that distinguish the older style are gradually being replaced by shades of softer tint, such as seem to befit the new themes, which are illustrations of the processes of agriculture and silk-weaving, pictures of the liberal arts, and scenes from the tales of the popular drama.

Themes from the classical times of the ancient *Book of History* are popular subjects of illustration; such as the story of *Shun*, the model emperor of ancient times, who was chosen to succeed to the throne on account of his filial piety by the Emperor *Yao*, who is pictured approaching with a cavalcade bearing presents to *Shun* as he is plowing in the fields with an ox; or that of Kiang Tzŭ-ya, the trusted counselor of Si Po, the prince of *Chou*, in the twelfth century B. C., who is sitting on the rock, fishing with a rod, when the prince comes to offer him the minister's badge of office and a state chariot for him to ride in. Among literary subjects may be mentioned The Seven Worthies of the Bamboo Grove (*Chu Lin Ch'i Hsien*), a famous association of learned men who used to meet, about the year 275, for discussion and jovial relaxation in a grove of bamboos; and the "Orchid Pavilion" (*Lan T'ing*), the rendezvous in the fourth century of a party of distinguished scholars, whose compositions in prose and verse have survived to the present day in the handwriting of the celebrated calligrapher, Wang Hsi Chih, who was one of their number. A pattern for poor scholars is the high mandarin of the *Han* dynasty, who is seen in the picture reading a book while carrying bundles of fagots, as the humble seller of firewood used to do when his thirst for knowledge led him to read incessantly, until the fame of the wood-seller's learning was noised abroad, reached at last the ears of the emperor, and led to his appointment to office.

The "Twenty-four Paragons of Filial Piety" and the "Virtuous Heroines," whose stories as models of chastity and wifely devotion are recorded in the old annals, are familiar to all students of Chinese lore. The Chinese standard of female beauty is seen in the "Pretty Girls" (*Mei Jên*), with long, graceful figures, which the old Dutch collector used to call "*lange lijsen.*" The artist occasionally poses the figures with slender bamboos waving in the background, or willow-branches drooping overhead, as accessory suggestions of airy grace and willowy elegance. Others are scattered in a garden picking flowers, or again collected in four groups practicing the four liberal accomplishments of "writing, painting, music, and chess." Familiar life is not neglected by the artist, and ladies and children are seen in the midst of ordinary household surroundings, embellishing the interior of an eggshell dish, or decorating a charming vase of the *famille rose*. Children are sympathetically shown, either masquerading in mock procession, or flying kites and playing games, such as hobby-horse and blindman's buff. Stories of clever children are also pictured, like that of the rescue of the little eleventh-century boy who had fallen into a large porcelain fish-bowl as he was trying to reach a frog, by one of his playmates, who had the presence of mind to seize a stone and break a hole in the side of the bowl to let out the water, while the rest of the children were running away affrighted, leaving their comrade to drown. The rescuer was Ssŭ-ma Kuang (1009–86), who afterward became one of the most distinguished statesmen and historians of the *Sung* dynasty.

FIG. 359.—Bowl of the K'ang-hsi period, painted in blue inside, enameled brown outside, and pierced through the glaze with an ornamental band of birds and flowers.

CHAPTER XXI.

PORCELAIN MADE FOR EXPORTATION.—SPECIAL FORMS AND DESIGNS.—INDIAN CHINA.—ARMORIAL CHINA.—JESUIT CHINA.—HINDU STYLE.—ORIENTAL PORCELAIN DECORATED IN EUROPE.—IMITATIONS.

DOWN to the end of the *Ming* dynasty the Chinese seem to have carried on the porcelain manufacture on their own lines, and decorated it after their own taste; we hear nothing of novel forms or special designs made for exportation to foreign countries. There had been a large quantity of Chinese porcelain exported to Western countries from early Mohammedan times, when the Arabs first came to Canton by sea, and were permitted to establish a colony there under the control of their own magistrates. Chinese fleets rode in the Persian Gulf, as related in their own annals of the ninth century, and confirmed by Mohammedan writers of the time. During the *Yuan* dynasty (1280–1367), when the same Mongolian house ruled Persia and China, the relations between the two countries became still more intimate, and there was constant traffic by land as well as by sea, for an account of which the celebrated Travels of Marco Polo may be consulted. In the *Ming* dynasty the overland route was barred by the Mongolian Timur (the great Tamerlane), but Chinese ships continued to go west, touched at Ceylon and Ormuz, passed the Straits of Babelmandeb into the Red Sea, to land cargo at Jidda, the port of Mecca, and coasted the shore of Africa as far southward as Magadoxu and Zanzibar. The voyages are described in detail in the Chinese annals of the reigns of *Yung-lo* (1403–25) and *Hsüan-tê* (1426–35). Early in the next century the Portuguese made their appearance in these seas, and from this time no more Chinese junks were seen in the Indian Ocean. The great mart was in the Persian Gulf, and any porcelain that reached Europe before the discovery of the voyage round the Cape of Good Hope would have come by caravan to Cairo or to Aleppo. Ancient Chinese porcelain has been found in the present day at many stations of the route that has been thus briefly sketched. Collections have been gathered from Kandy, and from other parts of the interior of Ceylon; many of the older specimens in the South Kensington Museum were purchased in Persia by Major Murdoch Smith; and the greater part of the old celadon dishes in European possession are described as having

FIG. 360.—Teapot of "Armorial China," richly decorated in enamel colors with gilding.

been obtained in Cairo. Chinese celadon has also been discovered by Sir John Kirk in ruins at Zanzibar, together with Chinese "cash" of the tenth and eleventh centuries. Potsherds of the same peculiar sea-green ware have even been dug up, we are told, on the African mainland farther south, on the sites of ruined cities in Mashonaland.

In the year of the Hejira 567 (A. D. 1188) we find the first distinct mention of porcelain, out of China, in the record of a present of forty pieces having been sent to Nureddin, the Caliph of Syria, by his lieutenant Saladin, afterward the celebrated hero of the Crusades, on the occasion of his conquest of Egypt. It penetrated subsequently to the principal countries of

Europe, and is classed in court inventories of the thirteenth and fourteenth centuries among the most precious possessions of sovereigns, being mounted in gold and silver and inlaid with jewels. It was about 1440 that the Sultan of Babylonia (i. e., Cairo, which was often called Babylonia in the middle ages) sent a present of three bowls and a dish of Chinese porcelain (*porcelaine de Sinant*) to Charles VII, King of France. In 1487 an ambassador arrived at Florence from Egypt with valuable presents, including some large vases of celadon porcelain for Lorenzo de' Medici. In the same year porcelain is enumerated in the Maritime Laws of Barce-lona among the imports from Egypt into Spain.

The earliest piece of Ori-ental porcelain that can be referred to as having been brought to Eng-land before the Refor-mation is a pale sea-green bowl mounted in silver gilt, which is pre-served in New College, Oxford, under the name of Archbishop Warham's cup, and which is said to have belonged to that prelate (1504–32). In the year 1506, Philip and Joan, of Austria, who had taken the title of King and Queen of Castile, left the Low Coun-tries for Spain, but were driven by a storm into Weymouth, where they were entertained by the high sheriff, Sir Thomas Trenchard. When the king took his leave he presented his host with some bowls of blue and white porcelain, one of which was inclosed in massive silver gilt, Moresco pattern, and one of them is said to be still kept in the Trenchard family.

FIG. 361.—Eggshell Saucer Dish of "Armorial China," decorated in soft delicate enamels, with gilding, for Holland.

Mounted specimens of Elizabethan date are not so uncommon. In the Blue and White Catalogue of the Burlington Fine Arts Club (*loc. cit.*, page 3), a basin decorated in four panels with vases of lotus-flowers and birds, mounted in English silver gilt (Elizabethan hall-mark), and lent by Sir Wollaston Franks, is described. At the same time there were exhibited four cele-brated pieces, mounted in the same style, from the Burghley House collection, which are be-lieved to have been in the Cecil family from the time of Queen Elizabeth. One of the pieces, painted in brilliant blue with phœnixes and chrysanthemums, was marked with the date of the contemporary Chinese Emperor *Wan-li* (1573–1619). Mr. Cosmo Monkhouse, the learned editor of the catalogue, says in his Introduction: "Perhaps it was out of the same 'parcel' of china that the Lord Treasurer Burghley offered to Queen Elizabeth one porringer of 'white porselyn' garnished with gold, and Mr. Robert Cecill a 'cup of green pursselyne,' as New Year's gifts in 1587–88."

After the discovery of the route by the Cape of Good Hope, porcelain became better known in Europe. The Portuguese navigators appeared on the shores of the far East in the begin-ning of the sixteenth century, and arrived at Canton in the year 1517, where they were at once admitted to trade. Japan was opened to them in 1542 by the shipwreck of a Portuguese vessel on the shore of the island of Kyushu, where they were well treated by the Japanese, and allowed to set up a trading establishment at Nagasaki. During the time that the Por-tuguese enjoyed the monopoly of the East Indian trade they imported splendid collections of porcelain, including vases of the largest size, like those that used to be installed in the Royal Palace of Alcantara, now unfortunately dispersed. The Dutch succeeded the Portuguese in the control of the trade with the far East. Van Neck established a factory at Batavia in 1602, the Dutch East India Company was formed in the same year, and under its auspices vast quantities of porcelain were imported into Holland and the north of Europe. A fine selection, made 1698–1722, is still to be seen in the Johanneum at Dresden, and another is preserved in the palace at The Hague.

The English East India Company, which was established in the reign of Queen Eliza-beth, did not for a long period after its foundation succeed in opening a direct trade with

China, being excluded by the Portuguese and Dutch. The port of Gombron, opposite to Ormuz, in the Persian Gulf, was for a long time the chief entrepôt of the British trade, and the earliest "China ware" introduced into England derived its name of "Gombron ware" from this place. In 1631, among the wares and merchandise allowed to be imported from India, a catalogue includes "China dishes and *puslanes* of all sorts." In 1640 a factory was established at Canton, and direct trade has been carried on, with occasional interruptions, since that date.

With regard to the kinds of porcelain imported, a fund of interesting information has been gathered by Du Sartel (*loc. cit.*, pages 112–148) from French catalogues of the eighteenth century, of which that of the Fonspertuis Sale * is one of the most important, containing notes by Gersaint, a celebrated expert of the time. The earliest porcelain imported was of single color, principally celadon or white; blue and white followed, as confirmed by Père d'Entrecolles, writing in 1712, who says that up to that date this was almost the only kind exported from China to Europe. Gersaint also writes in the same strain in 1747.

The porcelain imported seems to have been generally a selection from the ordinary contemporary productions of the private potters of Ching-tê-chên. The work of the imperial manufactory could only have been exceptionally represented, as it is reserved for the service of the emperor. The private collections of Chinese connoisseurs were not ransacked, as they are in these later days, so that we can hardly expect to find any important examples of ancient ceramic art among the piles of dishes, plates, and tea services that were imported, as we gather from old bills of lading, by the hundred thousand. Among the larger decorated vases of the reign of *K'ang-hsi*, a certain number are usually set aside in European collections because they happen to be inscribed with old marks, and are supposed, moreover, to have an archaic aspect. Representative cabinets of so-called *Hsüan-tê* and *Ch'êng-hua* porcelains are filled in this way, although genuine *Ming* dynasty porcelain, which is rare even in China, is conspicuous by its absence.

It was in the reign of *K'ang-hsi* (1662–1722) that porcelain seems to have been first made at Ching-tê-chên in new forms and special designs for the European market. These were often executed after European models and designs taken there for the purpose by native agents from Canton. The earliest pieces with foreign designs were made for Persia and the Mohammedan market, and were decorated with scrolls of Arabic writing, generally texts from the Koran, the incorrect lettering of which, apart from the character of the floral designs with which they were associated, betrayed the Chinese hand. Next came Chinese copies of the

FIG. 362.—Teapot, with Cup and Saucer, of eggshell porcelain, decorated with floral sprays and brocade designs in Ch'ien-lung colors.

old Imari ware of Japan, which were so perfectly executed during the reign of *K'ang-hsi* that it would be sometimes difficult to distinguish the copy from the original were it not for the different quality and ring of the paste. In later days Delft ware has been copied in a similar way, one of the faïence plates, originally painted in blue after Chinese lines, having been repro-

---

* *Catalogue de la vente des tableaux, bijoux, porcelaines,* etc., de M. Angram, Vicomte de Fonspertuis. Paris, 1747.

duced in porcelain, so that it might have been mistaken for the first model, if the Chinaman had not tried to copy the initials of the signature of the Dutch decorator.

Porcelain has also been decorated in China for the Hindustan market in the form of quadrangular sweetmeat trays, oblong boxes with covers, and the like, painted with copies of Indian miniatures, such as nautch girls dancing before men of rank, holding up swords and flowers, or potentates seated on marble terraces with attendants standing behind holding fans, and a line of slender arches of palace architecture rising in the background. The cover of a betel-nut box of this class is illustrated by Jacquemart (*loc. cit.*, Plate XVII, Fig. 3), as an example, however, of his class of *porcelaine hindoue*, the existence of which is highly problematical. A label is occasionally attached to these pictures, penciled in gold; but the Arabic inscriptions are always very incorrectly written, evidently by persons unacquainted with the language, and

FIG. 363.—Bowl of Chinese porcelain, decorated in enamel colors of the eighteenth century, in the Siamese style.

the unaccustomed hand is detected as readily as when the Chinese artist is trying to form European letters.

The usual style of Arabic inscriptions on Chinese porcelain is shown in Fig. 103, an eggshell saucer-shaped dish, with designs penciled in black and filled in with gold, which is to be attributed, from its technique, to about the middle of the eighteenth century. It has a medallion in the middle with a dentated border from which four projections extend inward, which is filled with Arabic writing, and a broad belt of the same script on a gold ground encircles the border of the dish. The rim is surrounded by a narrow band of floral scrolls consisting of alternate sprays of peony and chrysanthemum of purely Chinese design. Two dishes of the same shape, size, and technique are now in the British Museum.*

The name of "porcelaine des Indes" in France, of "India china" in England, was applied generally in the eighteenth century to the decorated Chinese porcelain which was imported in such large quantities, and eagerly sought after, until the time came when a similar material could be produced in Europe. Although the art of making hard porcelain was discovered in Saxony by Böttger in 1708, it was not till 1760 that it was made at Sèvres, and it hardly came into domestic use before the end of the eighteenth century. Meanwhile it was made and specially painted in China for exportation, and often from designs furnished by Europeans. In the sale catalogue of the collection of Vicomte de Fonspertuis by Gersaint, which has just been referred to, the Chinese and Japanese are generally referred to as "Indiens." Some confusion would have been avoided if the term "porcelain of the East India Company" had been adopted instead of "India china." Jacquemart has ascribed the porcelain of this class to Japan, but on very slender grounds. Others by a still more singular hallucination have attributed it to Lowestoft in England, although there are many dated specimens anterior to 1777, the date of the so-called invention of hard paste at Lowestoft. Sir A. W. Franks has exposed these fallacies and proved its Chinese origin. A large proportion of it was evidently painted in Canton by Chinese artists, the porcelain being brought for the purpose overland from Ching-tê-

* See the Franks Catalogue, *loc. cit.*, Nos. 619, 620.

chên, glazed in the ordinary white state, with the addition perhaps of a few rings or outlines in underglaze blue defining the spaces intended to be filled in with colors. The style was similar, and the colors employed were the same that were used in the *ateliers* of Canton in the decoration of painted enamels on copper, which are a specialty of the place, under the name of *yang tz'ŭ*, or "foreign porcelain," so called, we are told, because the art was originally introduced from Calicut in India. Precisely similar designs occur on the copper and porcelain objects of the period, which were molded in identical forms, and fired in the same muffle kilns to fix the colors. The porcelain of this class is known to the Chinese by the name of *yang ts'ai*, or "foreign colors." It is comparatively rare, however, in China, having been principally made for exportation and sent abroad at the time it was made.

Many of the services have on them the armorial bearings of the persons for whom they were made. The collection in the British Museum is very rich in this class of "armorial china," including portions of services made for Frederick the Great, and for the royal families of Denmark and France, as well as many pieces with the arms of European families of rank, and of merchants who are known to have traded with China. A large service was made for the palace of the Swedish kings at Gripsholm, the name of which is inscribed on the pieces.

The large, deep plate illustrated in Fig. 52, which is nearly nineteen inches across, is an earlier specimen of armorial china than the above. The decoration is partly in underglaze blue, partly in overglaze muffle colors of the *K'ang-hsi* period, blue, green, yellow, and red, with touches of gold, and the rim is gilded.

Some of the earlier pieces decorated with foreign designs were painted entirely in blue. The tall cups with covers called "Keyser cups," which are illustrated in Sir Henry Thompson's Catalogue, and also by Jacquemart, are painted with a broad panel containing St. Louis of France and his queen on a canopied throne, and narrower alternate panels with kneeling figures and birds, and have inscribed round the top, L'EMPIRE DE LA VERTU EST ETABLI JUSQU'AU BOUT DE L'UNIVERS. The inscription is occasionally misspelled in a way that at once betrays the Chinese hand (see page 59). A second well-known series of tall cups and saucers is painted in blue with a Dutch design known as *Kockock in het Huisje* (the cuckoo in the house); a sketch of a small building on a platform with trees and plants and two birds above.

The decoration was sometimes copied from European pictures brought to China for the purpose, so that we find in collections of Chinese porcelain sea views with Dutch vessels, punch-bowls with pictures of English harvesting and of the harvest feast inscribed underneath HARVEST HOME, and grotesque copies of the famous pictures of the elements by Francesco Albani, now in the gallery at Turin. One would hardly expect to see an English political cartoon on Chinese porcelain, but refer to Franks Catalogue, *loc. cit.*, No. 625:

"PUNCH-BOWL. Chinese porcelain, painted in colors with gilding; on each side are a pair of medallions exactly similar, each forming a satirical coat of arms. No. 1, Bust of John Wilkes; crest, a lion passant; supporters, Sergeant Glyn and Lord Temple; motto, ALWAYS READY IN A GOOD CAUSE; above is inscribed, WILKES AND LIBERTY. No. 2, Bust of Lord Mansfield, with a hydra below; crest, a viper; supporters, Lord Bute and the Devil; motto, JUSTICE SANS PITIE. The devices on this bowl appear on the heading to an address by John Wilkes, 'To the Gentlemen, Clergy, and Freeholders of the County of Middlesex,' dated from King's Bench Prison, Saturday, June 18, 1768. They are entitled 'ARMS OF LIBERTY AND SLAVERY.'"

A Dutch skipper, detained in harbor after a voyage to China, would have a picture of his ship painted on porcelain, as shown by the service noticed by Jacquemart and Le Blant (*loc. cit.*, page 384), which was decorated in colors with gilding, with a vessel under full sail, flying the Dutch flag, and inscribed underneath, T: SCHIP. VRYBURG CEVOERT: DOOR: CAPITEYN JACOB. RYZIK IN: CHINA. INT IAAR. 1756 (The ship Vryburg, conducted by Captain Jacob Ryzik, in China, in the year 1756). A plate of similar decoration, described in the Franks Catalogue (*loc. cit.*, No. 598), has the inscription, written in a medallion, CHRIST SCHOONEMAN OPP^R. STUERMAN OP T'SCHIP VRYBURG: TER REEDE WANPHO IN CHINA INT IAAR: 1756 (Christopher Schooneman, chief mate of the ship Vryburg, in the roads off Whampoa, in China, in the year 1756). Whampoa is the harbor of Canton, and the plates were doubtless painted in that city while the ship was in port. There would be hardly time to send the order on the long overland journey to Ching-tê-chên, and it is still less likely that the artists of Nippon had anything to do with them, although M. Jacquemart argues so at some length.

Occasionally the decoration is of more familiar character. Fig. 361 represents a saucer-shaped eggshell dish in the Walters Collection, painted in brilliant enamel colors with gilding. The design that decorates the interior, composed of waving foliations mingled with paneled bands, has the shape of a coat of arms, and it is surmounted by the figure of a white goose, the Chinese emblem of marriage, standing upon a gilded visor of grotesque form, looking somewhat like a crest. The two oval shields displayed side by side in the middle contain the monograms I. V. E. and I. B. upon blue grounds of different shade. These are no doubt the initials of the Dutch bridal pair whose names are penciled in full below within a blue band in

FIG. 364.—Rose-backed Eggshell Plate, decorated in enamel colors, with a landscape picture and diapered border enclosing panels with fruits and flowers.

gold letters, IAN: VAN: ENS and IOANNA BOCHOUTE. The band of scrolled foliations that encircles the above designs is etched in gold. The border of the dish is decorated with a gilded diaper interrupted by four foliated medallions. Two of these contain miniature portraits of the happy couple, the other two are filled with symbols of good omen, a heart between two pairs of clasped hands, tied by ribbons to musical stones, hung with beaded tassels and waving fillets.

The porcelain made to order for the European market, with which the Dutch inundated Europe for more than a hundred years, is generally overdecorated, in accordance with the foreign taste. Jacquemart justly distinguishes the objects made at the same time which were decorated according to Chinese taste by classifying them under the title of " porcelaine artistique." A single spray of flowers, a sacred or mythological figure encircled by a lightly etched floral scroll or a key border, or a dramatic scene with the personages in antique costume, forms the whole decoration, following the canons of Chinese art. The result is more attractive than the most gayly decorated scenes of familiar life framed in as many rings of different floral diaper as it is possible to get into the space ; such, for instance, as surround the seven-bordered eggshell plate illustrated in Plate X, fascinating as this is from its minute finish. The vases of the same style and period being covered with richly dressed officials in their robes of office, have been sometimes classed apart under the title of " mandarin porcelaine." This style is a favorite one with the Cantonese artist to the present day, when he is working for his foreign patron, although the native school of art, following always the canons of the old masters, disdains the modern costume of everyday life.

Among the objects made for Europe are found wash-basins and ewers of elaborate form completely covered with floral brocaded grounds of diverse pattern, interrupted in the middle by a medallion with a coat of arms. The tea services which were imported consisted generally of a teapot with a hexagonal or octagonal tray, a pair of ovoid jars with covers as tea-caddies, a graceful cream-jug with cover, one large bowl, a variable number of teacups with or without handles, sometimes furnished with saucers, often without, and a plate or two for cakes, or a couple of saucer-shaped dishes. Few perfect sets remain, but several separate pieces of the class have already been figured. Fig. 362 shows a typical teapot with a cup and saucer of the same pattern, which are not so elaborately decorated as some of the services of the period, but still somewhat overloaded with floral ornaments, as the sprays of prunus with birds perched upon them seem to be a little cramped for want of space, in the intervals between the foliated panels displaying *ch'i-lin* in the midst of brocaded flowers, with which the rest of the surface is covered.

There is one class of Chinese porcelain which has been dignified with the name of "Jesuit china," as it was supposed to have been made under the influence of the Jesuit missionaries. The pieces are usually painted in blue and white, and date from the earlier part of the reign of *K'ang-hsi* (1662–1722). They are characterized by having the crucifix and other sacred symbols of the Roman Catholic faith introduced in the intervals of the decoration, which is usually of the ordinary Chinese style, as may be seen in the jar illustrated in Plate XIV, which has the cross and three nails with the Christian monogram I. H. S., inclosed in a quatrefoil panel. The symbols in these specimens are penciled on the paste under the glaze, and must have been put on at the same time as the other part of the decoration, before the firing.

Jacquemart in his several works on ceramic subjects has tried to establish the existence of both Hindu and Siamese porcelain, but on very insufficient grounds; and I am strongly inclined to agree with Sir Wollaston Franks that there is no evidence that true kaolinic pottery was ever produced either in Hindustan or in any of the countries of the peninsula of Farther India. They have, on the contrary, always depended on China and Japan for their supply of porcelain until quite recent times, when a few factories have been established there on European lines. The class of pieces on which Jacquemart principally relied is well exemplified in the bowl illustrated in Fig. 363.

It is necessary to say a few words here on the subject of the decoration of Oriental porcelain in Europe. This was first attempted in Holland, as is shown by M. Havard in his researches into the annals of the corporation of Delft potters.* It was about 1700 that these potters are said to have discovered the secret of the preparation of a certain number of the colors of the muffle stove. These enamel colors, which were of the same class as those employed by the Chinese, were used not only for their own soft faïence, but also in the decoration of hard porcelain imported from the far East, being applied on white pieces, or on pieces spaced with a few blue lines, as prepared at Ching-tê-chên for the artists of Canton, which were passed on to Europe for the purpose. Other pieces, in which the decoration appeared to Dutch taste to be sparse, had the white ground filled in with various accessories and details of semi-Oriental style, the result being a curious hybrid combination of colors as well as of styles. Some of these may be seen illustrated by Du Sartel, with the piece in its original state placed side by side with the *sur-décoration*. Gersaint, the "expert" of Paris, in his catalogue published in 1747, describes two square bottles of porcelain of this kind painted in colors with figures of men and tigers, and adds that "the figures, animals, and other ornaments on these bottles have been painted in Holland, as is done there, often *mal à propos*, on pieces of fine white porcelain."

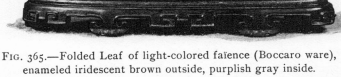

FIG. 365.—Folded Leaf of light-colored faïence (Boccaro ware), enameled iridescent brown outside, purplish gray inside.

It is not difficult to distinguish the work of the Dutch decorator by the aspect of the colors, apart from the style; the Dutch palette comprised black, red derived from iron, a dull blue, and a pale green; the four enamels are applied in strong relief, but are wanting in vivacity and transparency, and look as if the coloring oxides were not sufficiently developed. The red is especially distinctive, being always of deep brick-red tint, imperfectly glazed, and standing out in tangible mass, piled on, as it were, with a thick brush. The Chinese iron-red, on the contrary, is of coral tint, is perfectly incorporated with the glaze, and affords no appreciable relief even when most intense in tone.

Several of the other European manufacturers of porcelain of the eighteenth century tried their skill in the decoration of Oriental porcelain. The work of Saxon artists is seen in the Dresden Museum placed beside the primitive pieces of old Japanese porcelain; the work of French artists is preserved in the Musée at Sèvres; and there are in the British Museum several examples of color painting from Bow and Chelsea, and of transfer printing from

* *Histoire de la faïence de Delft.* Par Henri Havard. Paris, 1877.

Worcester, all executed on Oriental porcelain. The Musée de Limoges contains an interesting series of specimens, including some of rare Venetian work, like the Japanese vase illustrated by Du Sartel (*loc. cit.*, Fig. 117), which was originally an artistic production of an Oriental artist of the seventeenth century, simply ornamented with a narrow scroll border round the shoulder, and with light sprays of flowers repeated at the base and round the neck, penciled in coral-red and gold. The Venetian artist, in his task of filling in this chaste and graceful decoration, had

FIG. 366.—Celadon Vase of the K'ang-hsi period, of typical tint, with floral scrolls worked in slight relief under the glaze.

at his disposal only the black enamel which was used in his country for enameling upon glass. Treating the porcelain vase as if he were decorating one of the feathery glass cups that he was accustomed to handle, he first completed the floral scrolls on the neck with an elaborate band of birds and flowers of charming design, and then painted on the body of the piece two large vases with Japanese flowers springing from their interior. The rest of the space was filled in with a garden scene, enlivened by the figures of two mandarins with strange birds and insects flying round them, painted according to the fancies, more brilliant than exact, which the Italian artist fondly imagined about the things of the far East. At a later date much Oriental porcelain, principally blue and white, according to Sir Wollaston Franks, has been spoiled by painting it in tawdry colors, with gilding — a detestable process which, he says, was carried on not long ago in London. There are also quite modern forgeries on which coats of arms have been added to old pieces of porcelain painted in colors, where the sparseness of the original decoration left room for such additions; these can be detected by the different conditions of the old and new enameled colors, the former being somewhat altered by passing twice through the fire.

Sur-décoration in all its phases is also practiced in China. It may be contemporary with the original decoration, as in the case when a blue and white piece has come out of the kiln with some defect of the glaze, and a spray of flowers has been deftly painted on in enamel colors to conceal the defect and fixed in the muffle. On the other hand, it may be quite modern, and an attempt may be made, for example, to increase the value of a blue and white vase by plastering on a fusible enamel of some other color, such as the yellow of antimony, which is easily refired, and so present the original blue designs with a new livery. The "ginger-pot" illustrated in Fig. 357 was originally an ordinary example of the reign of *K'ang-hsi* (1662–1722), marked underneath in blue with a double ring, and had the scattered prunus-blossoms reserved in white, on a blue ground of poor color, traversed in the usual way by a reticulation of darker lines. It has been varied by having the petals of the alternate flowers filled in with bright-green and dull-red enamels, so as to present a kind of formal diaper studded with blossoms of these two shades. The red might pass, as the buds of the prunus are naturally tipped with red, but the glaring inconsistency of green flowers stamps the production at once as a forgery, apart from the coloring, which is certainly not that of the *K'ang-hsi* period, if it be Chinese at all.

Another kind of subsequent decoration is shown in Fig. 359. It is a strongly made porcelain bowl of the *K'ang-hsi* period (1662–1722), with the interior painted in blue under a white glaze with chrysanthemum scrolls spreading over the field, and with a floral border round the rim, while the exterior is enameled with a dark-brown monochrome glaze of "dead-leaf" type. The chocolate-colored glaze has been pierced through to the white paste underneath, so as to decorate the bowl outside in *intaglio* with a broad band of floral sprays and birds, executed in European style. This has been worked on the lapidary's wheel, probably in Austria.

The Chinese cut porcelain, hard as it is, is cut with the utmost facility on the jade-cutter's lathe, which is provided with cutting disks and piercing tools of soft iron that, when in work, are kept constantly moistened with corundum paste. The top of a chipped vase or bowl will be shaved off evenly—"barbered" as they call it—or the jagged edges of a fracture will be neatly rounded, for a new piece of porcelain to be fitted in the holes and cemented round the rim. A reproduction of the original design is then painted over *à froid* in common oil colors. The Chinese collector has a horror of a *mao ping* (crack or other small defect), and infinite trouble is taken to conceal one by carrying sprays of flowers along the fissures, or even by investing the whole of the white ground of the vase with an inky coat of lampblack hardened by cement, or by applying a uniform coat of lacquer. The *sur-décoration à froid* will become discolored in time, and it may be detected at once by a wash of weak acid, which should always be sponged on in

FIG. 367.—Large Beaker, brilliantly decorated in cobalt blue, with magnolias standing out in white relief upon a blue background; mark, K'ang-hsi.

The question of the cient wares is a burning would-be connoisseur of perience while he educates his less. Where the demand is so come unlimited. At the Kioto triumphs of the Japanese in the lain were exhibited on long ters are daily improving in their de-bœuf and blue and white of the tile works of Peking are days in the manufacture of single United States. In Europe the Chinese porcelain with marks ware was an exact copy of the and the pride they take at Chinese eggshell is proved by the original plate and its copy, defy the visitor to distinguish known shop of Samson at Paris "Oriental porcelain" made in there as avowed imitations. the same French things, as back room of a curio-dealer grimed with real Oriental tiquity, and the casual be deceived under such al- ever it may be, many of way into cabinets, and

case of doubt. modern reproduction of an- one. *Caveat emptor!* The porcelain must buy his ex- eye. Any other test is worth- great the supply threatens to be- Exposition of 1895 the latest imitation of old Chinese porce- shelves; the Ching-tê-Chên pot- reproductions of the finest *sang-* the *K'ang-hsi* period, and even busily occupied in these latter colors for the markets of the old Chelsea potters turned out complete; the earliest Meissen ancient artistic sort of Japan; Sèvres in the reproduction of the display in the museum of placed side by side, as if to between the two. The well- is full of all the varieties of France, but one views them It is different when one sees I have seen them, in the at Shanghai, purposely be- dirt to give an air of an- globe-trotter is more apt to tered circumstances. How- these forgeries find their flaunt for a brief while their

borrowed plumes, until they are detected as impostors and banished to another sphere. The Walters Collection is happily free from such unauthorized intruders, so the question need not detain us further. But it has been laid down on good authority that doubt is one of the first requisites of the scientific inquirer, and it is certainly required in China for things Chinese almost more than in other parts of the globe.

FIG. 368.—Cream Jug of European form, decorated in
soft enamel colors with gilding.

CHAPTER XXII.

PORCELAIN PRODUCTION IN THE OTHER PROVINCES OF CHINA.—THE WHITE PORCELAIN OF THE
PROVINCE OF FUCHIEN.—THE YI-HSING BOCCARO WARE OF THE PROVINCE OF KIANGSU.—
THE POTTERIES OF THE PROVINCE OF KUANGTUNG.

THE province of Kiangsi has been the one great center of the porcelain manufacture during the present dynasty, and it may be said generally that nothing of any artistic value is produced elsewhere in China in the present day. In earlier times a certain amount of porcelain was made in other provinces for local consumption, and some of the fabrics attained special excellence and even acquired a wider vogue under some of the past dynasties when directly patronized by the emperor reigning at the time, or temporarily stimulated by demands for export abroad, but most of the different manufactories have failed, either from want of support or from exhaustion of the materials, and those that still remain produce now nothing worthy of their old renown.

A list of these potteries, ancient and modern, has been compiled by Julien (*loc. cit.*, pages li–lxvi), and the different localities referred to have been indicated upon a map of China prepared by him for the purpose. Thirteen out of the eighteen provinces of China are represented in this list, but many of the potteries, included because they have been mentioned only once perhaps in some ancient book, have long been extinct, and some of the others, like that of Sin-p'ing, in the province of Honan, the reputed place of the invention of porcelain, are, as we have endeavored to prove, purely hypothetical.

The principal potteries that were still working toward the end of the *Ming* dynasty, in the beginning of the seventeenth century, are briefly enumerated in the *T'ien kung k'ai wu*, a little manual of industrial work which was published at that time. It says (Book II, folio 10):

" The white plastic clay called *ê-t'u* is required for the fabrication of porcelain, and the finest and most beautiful pieces can not be made without it. Throughout the whole of China there are only a very few places in which it is found—viz., in the north: (1) at Ting-chou, in the prefecture of Chên-ting-fu (province of Chihli); (2) at Hua-t'ing-hsien, in the prefecture of P'ing-liang-fu (province of Shensi); (3) at P'ing-ting-chou, in the prefecture of T'ai-yuan-fu (province of Shansi); (4) at Yu-chou, in the prefecture of K'ai-fêng-fu (province of Honan). In the south it is produced (1) at Tê-hua-hsien, in the prefecture of Ch'üan-chou-fu (province of Fuchien); (2) at Wu-Yuan-hsien and at Ch'i-mên-hsien—both situated in the prefecture of Hui-chou-fu (province of Anhui).

" In the potteries of Tê-hua there are fabricated only the figures of divinities and statuettes of famous persons artistically modeled and various ornamental objects of fantastic form not intended for actual use. The porcelain which comes from the districts of Chên-ting-fu and K'ai-fêng-fu is occasionally of yellowish shade. The productions of all the other districts are far from equaling that of Jao-chou-fu (in the province of Kiangsi).

" The two kinds of porcelain that were made at Li-shui and at Lung-ch'üan, in the prefecture of Ch'u-chou-fu, in the province of Chekiang, had the enamel applied after the pieces had been fired. The cups and bowls (from these two districts) which range from sea-green, or celadon, up to a dark-green color approaching that of lacquer, are called *Ch'u Yao*—i. e., 'Ch'u Ware,' after the name of the prefecture.

" With regard to the porcelain which is so eagerly sought after by foreigners from all the four quarters of the world, this is all fabricated at Ching-tê-chên, in the district of Fou-liang-hsien, and the prefecture of Jao-chou-fu. Porcelain has been constantly produced there from the period *Ching-tê-chên* (1004–07), when the imperial manufactory was founded, down to our own days, although neither of the two materials of which the paste is made is produced in the district."

The porcelain of the province of Chekiang acquired some renown as early as the *Chin* dynasty (265–419), when it was made at Wên-chou-fu, and in the *T'ang* dynasty (618–906) the cups of Yueh-chou, the modern Shao-hsing-fu, were esteemed above all others for tea services, and the famous ware of "prohibited color" reserved for imperial use was produced in the same district. Now there remains in this province only a small local manufactory at Chapu, a port on the northern shore of Hangchou Bay. When the Emperor *Ch'ien-lung* visited the province of Chekiang in the year 1780, a series of illustrations of the handicrafts of the people was presented to him, which was afterward published under the title of *T'ai p'ing huan lo t'ou*—"Illustrations of the Vocations of Peaceful Times"—and which has been lately republished. The fifty-eighth of the one hundred pictures is that of the porcelain-seller carrying his fragile wares in a couple of baskets slung upon a pole. The artist says in his description:

"In the province of Chekiang they have made porcelain from ancient times. The prohibited color (*pi sê yao*) of Yueh-chou, the Lung-ch'üan ware (old celadon), and the *Ko Yao*, or crackled celadon, are among the most celebrated of its productions of olden time. With regard to the different ceramic productions of the present day the porcelain that is most highly valued by the people for eating and drinking purposes all comes from Ching-tê-chên in the adjoining province of Kiangsi. Potteries have been recently established in Chekiang at Chapu, where they make vases, basins, wine-cups, rice-bowls, and the like. The porcelain is white, with designs painted in blue, and the potters strive to emulate their rivals of Jao-chou-fu."

Hangchou is one of the places thrown open in September, 1896, to foreign residence and trade, as a result of the recent war between China and Japan; and it will be interesting to inquire whether the potteries at Chapu (the port of Hangchou) are still working, and, if so, what is the quality of the production.

The potteries at Ting-chou in the province of Chihli ceased to work at the close of the *Ming* dynasty, when we found Chou Tan-chu'an making at Ching-tê-chên reproductions of ancient four-legged censers of the peculiar ivory-white finely crackled ware that used to be produced at Ting-chou, and astonishing his contemporaries by his imitative skill. During the present dynasty all the Fên Ting ware, the so-called "soft paste" porcelain, whether plain white or decorated in soft underglaze cobalt-blue, has continued to be made in Kiangsi. It is the same with many of the other old wares; the *Ju Yao* and the imperial porcelain (*Kuan Yao*) of the *Sung* dynasty, the old celadons, plain and crackled, and the *flambé* glazes of ancient Chün-chou among the rest. These were all attempted to be reproduced by T'ang Ying in the reign of *Yung-chêng* (1723–35), in the imperial manufactory at Ching-tê-chên. Their original localities know them no longer.

FIG. 369.—Kuang Yao Vase with ringed mask handles, invested with a deep crackled glaze of bright green mottled with other tints.

The potteries at Tz'ŭ-chou in the province of Chihli are indeed the only representatives of the better known manufactories of the *Sung* dynasty that have continued to turn out porcelain down to the present day. Their productions were not much esteemed in former days, when they were described as a kind of inferior "Ting-Yao," and the modern work is still less valued, its only recommendation being a certain archaic simplicity of form and design. The paste is very white, but it is opaque and imperfectly vitrified. This Tz'ŭ-chou ware is well known in Peking and throughout northern China, as it supplies the domestic needs of the common people. Among the more curious objects are pillows made in the shape of scantily clothed urchins and hollow in the interior, so that they can be filled, if it be desired, with hot water in cold weather. Rudely molded idols and figures of Buddhist and Taoist saints are also produced here, roughly painted in different shades of brown (*tzŭ-chin*) derived from iron peroxide, or penciled in a dull blue with manganiferous cobalt applied over the glaze.

The province of Fuchien, in the south, has long been noted for its production of porcelain. The *Chien Tz'ŭ*, or *Chien Yao*—i. e., "Fuchien porcelain"—of the *Sung* dynasty, was originally fabricated at Chien-an-hsien, in the prefecture of Chien-ning-fu, although the potteries were moved later in the same dynasty to Chien-yang-hsien, which is within the bounds of the same prefecture farther north. The porcelain of Chien-an is referred to by the author of the *Ch'a Lu*, a book on tea written in the eleventh century, in which he speaks of the teacups of Chien-an under the name of "leveret-fur cups," and describes them as being of thick material invested with a soft black glaze flecked with lighter spots like the fur of a hare. Other authors of the time speak of the black glaze being sprinkled with yellowish tears. These cups were the most highly prized of all by the enthusiasts of the competitive tea parties of the time. When tea clubs were started in Japan these were the cups that were valued by the Japanese at a hundred ounces of silver each, and they supplied models for some of the early tea-jars made in that country, the dark, speckled glaze of which might be described in the very words of the old Chinese writers of the *Sung* dynasty in their description of this fabric.* The manufacture of porcelain in this district continued to flourish during the *Yuan* dynasty (1280–1367), but after that we hear of it no more.

Early in the *Ming* dynasty, if not before, potteries were established at Tê-hua-hsien, in the same province of Fuchien, which was then subject to Ch'üan-chou-fu, but was afterward placed under the jurisdiction of Yung-ch'un-

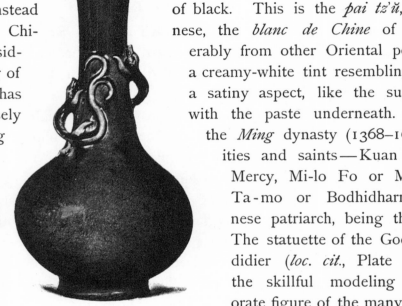

FIG. 370.—Kuang Yao Vase with crackled transmutation glaze of variegated green and purple.

ing, and are the sole source of the is different from the older ware that "Fuchien porcelain," being white instead porcelain," *par excellence*, of the Chi- ceramic writers. It differs consid- the paste of smooth texture being of while the rich, thick glaze, which has soft paste porcelain, blends closely potteries became renowned during their figures of Buddhist divin- Avalokita, as the Goddess of as the Buddhist Messiah, and last Indian and the first Chi- most frequently represented. Mercy, illustrated by M. Gran- furnishes a striking example of Fuchien potters. A more elab- form of the same Pusa is illus- moges by M. du Sartel (*loc. cit.*, vinity is seated upon a lotus

chou. These potteries are still work- well-known Chien Tz'ŭ of to-day, which was described under the same name of of black. This is the *pai tz'ŭ*, "white nese, the *blanc de Chine* of French erably from other Oriental porcelain, a creamy-white tint resembling ivory, a satiny aspect, like the surface of with the paste underneath. These the *Ming* dynasty (1368–1643) for ities and saints—Kuan Yin or Mercy, Mi-lo Fo or Maitreya, Ta-mo or Bodhidharma, the nese patriarch, being the three The statuette of the Goddess of didier (*loc. cit.*, Plate X, 28), the skillful modeling of the orate figure of the many-handed trated from the Musée de Li- Plate XVII, Fig. 60). The di- thalamus, with one pair of arms

folded in front with the fingers raised in mystic fashion, while eight other pairs of arms are extended in every direction, to display to the whole world, as it were, the various sacred symbols grasped in the hands. In the same plate are illustrated two groups of three figures gathered under a pine-tree, with a rocky background, two of whom are playing chess, molded in the same ivory-white porcelain. These are scenes from the legend of Wang Chi, one of the Taoist patriarchs, who is said to have flourished under the *Chin* dynasty (265–419). While wandering in the hills one day to collect firewood, he found two aged men playing chess, and laid down his axe to watch the game. One of the players gave him a fruit-stone, which he swallowed. After a while they exclaimed, "It is long since you came, and time to go home." He found that the handle of his axe had moldered into dust, and when he reached home many generations had passed away and he was clean forgotten, so he retired again to the mountains and devoted himself to Taoism, till he was finally enrolled among the immortals.

The natives of this province are among the most superstitious of the Chinese,† and their religious temperament seems to be reflected in the character of their ceramic productions. The rice-bowls are molded with figures in relief of the eight Taoist genii worshiping the Longevity

* A recent letter from Japan says that the potter Takemoto, of Tokyo, is making a specialty of black glazes, with the aim of rivaling the Chien Yao of the *Sung* dynasty, and has succeeded in producing many varieties of mirror-black and raven's-wing-green glazes, of leveret-fur streaking and of russet moss dappling; more varieties, by the way, than I suspect were ever turned out from the original kilns in China.

† See *Social Life of the Chinese.* By the Rev. Justus Doolittle. New York, 1867.

God, and the ordinary wine-cups have the air of sacrificial libation-cups, being shaped like the old carved cups of rhinoceros horn, and impressed outside with all kinds of Taoist sacred emblems. When a mark is attached it is a religious symbol like the *swastika*, or simply the name of the potter, stamped somewhere underneath the foot or on the reverse side of the piece. They were not, however, above working for the European market, as is proved by whole shelves of European figures and designs molded in this peculiar white porcelain, which are exhibited in the Johanneum at Dresden, dating from the seventeenth and the beginning of the eighteenth centuries.

Three pieces of Chien Tz'ǔ have been selected from the Walters Collection for illustration here. The censer (*hsiang lu*) in Fig. 371, which is of depressed, rounded shape, with the body bulging in the middle, is molded with a floral decoration on one side composed of sprays of bamboo and peony-flowers growing from rocks, worked in relief under the ivory-white translucent glaze with which it is invested. There is a circular panel stamped underneath, with four archaic characters in the middle, *Hsüan tê nien chih*—i. e., "Made in the reign of *Hsüan-tê* (1426–35)"—but the piece does not look so old.

The vase in Fig. 372, of solid make, has the globular body ornamented with four identical sprays of prunus (*mei hua*) modeled in strong relief, and the neck, which has a wide ring projecting horizontally below, is encircled above by a line of fret succeeded by a band of triangular foliations, while a similar band defines the shoulder of the vase. The glaze is of pure ivory-white tint, and the technique generally is that of the *Ming* dynasty.

The third, a small vase illustrated in Fig. 373, with wide circular base and short cylindrical body rounding in at the shoulder to a straight tubular neck, is an example of the form known to the Chinese as hoof-shaped vases (*ma t'i p'ing*). It is molded in sharp relief with the eight Buddhist symbols of good augury (*pa chi-hsiang*) enveloped in waving fillets and leafy scrolls, and the rims are defined by light conventional foliations. The rich, satiny glaze is ivory-white with a slight creamy tinge. There is no mark, but the style of execution points to the reign of *Ch'ien-lung* (1736–95), or somewhat earlier.

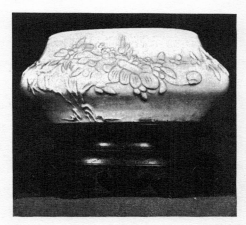

FIG. 371.—Incense Burner of Fuchien porcelain, with floral decoration in relief under the ivory-white glaze; mark, Hsuan-tê.

Two typical pieces of Chien Tz'ǔ are illustrated in Plate XIII. In the little wine-pot molded in the form of a pomegranate the artist has reproduced remarkably well the characteristic tone of the white glaze. In the teapot the glaze is somewhat grayer in shade, but very rich and lustrous, and the unglazed base exhibits the peculiarly smooth texture of the paste. A picked specimen of the white porcelain of Ching-tê-chên of the finest quality is illustrated in Plate XC, and it will be seen, on comparison, to have a slight tinge of blue, although the glaze is of perfect purity and translucency; this shade is due to lime, which is always added by the Chinese in appreciable quantity to give fluidity to the glaze when the porcelain is being fired. The white *Fên-Ting* glaze is quite different from either of the other two, as may be seen by turning to Plate LXXXIX, an admirable specimen, to be referred probably to the *K'ang-hsi* period. The glaze here looks thinner, and it has a wavy or undulatory surface, as it seems to sink into and blend intimately with the siliceous paste underneath; the ivory-white, which is the prevailing tone, has a creamy tinge, and it is delicately crackled with an infinity of fine lines.

There is a crackled variety of the Chien-Tz'ǔ, which, however, I have met with only in quite modern vases of no particular merit or beauty, having the glaze deeply fissured by a wide reticulation of colorless lines; so that it ought not to be confounded with the delicately crackled Fên-Ting porcelain.

In addition to the ivory-white porcelain, which has given the Fuchien potters their chief reputation, they also make a quantity of ordinary domestic ware for local consumption. Missionaries penetrate to all parts of the interior of China in these days, and one of them* gives a pleasing sketch of the potters at work in this district which is worth quoting:

"Tek-kwa [the local pronunciation of the *Tê-hua* of the mandarin dialect] is the most extensive manufactory of china in the Fuhkien province. The valley is broad, and clothed over a considerable area with very pretty houses, in many cases resembling Swiss chalets. Pottery, pottery everywhere, in the fields, in the streets, in the shops. In the open air children are painting the cups. Each artist paints with his own color, or his own few strokes, whether a leaf, a tree, a man's dress or beard, and passes it over to his neighbor, who in turn applies his brush to paint what is his share in the decoration. I have seldom received a more courteous and cordial welcome than from these artists in earthenware at Tek-kwa."

The writer is somewhat vague in his use of the terms "china," "pottery," and "earthenware" in this short paragraph, and we wish that he had looked at the ware with a technical eye and told us the exact nature of the material. The Chinese themselves are apt to be just as vague in their definition of *tz'ŭ* (porcelain), and to find their ultimate criterion in the clear ring that they can produce by striking the object with their long finger-nails. This test is not infallible, as a perfectly vitrified stoneware of colored opaque body, if it be not too thick, will give as musical a ring as the most snowy and translucent pottery of pure kaolinic structure. The two ceramic wares of China that still remain for a word of notice would nevertheless always be rejected by a Chinese connoisseur from his porcelain class, although, strangely, we find specimens of the first, the faïence of the province of Kuangtung, so often figuring with porcelain vases on the shelves of the Occidental connoisseur.

FIG. 372.—Fuchien porcelain of pure ivory-white tone, with an embossed decoration of floral sprays under the glaze.

This is the *Kuang-Yao* of the Chinese, the "Pottery of Kuangtung." It is in material a colored stoneware, the fabric passing from pale yellowish-gray through buff and various intermediate shades of yellow and red to deep brown. All kinds of things are made of it, architectural antefixal ornaments, cisterns, fish-bowls, and flower-pots for gardens, religious images, sacred figures, and grotesque animals, tubs and jars for storage, domestic utensils, and vessels for eating and drinking, and many objects of ornament and fantasy—the various articles, in fact, that are made in other parts of China of porcelain. The ware is exported to all parts of the world, and piles of it are to be seen in the commoner stores in China Town at San Francisco.

There are two principal centers of manufacture in the province. The first is in the vicinity of the treaty port of Amoy, from which it is exported by sea. Dr. S. W. Williams, in his description of the principal articles of export from China,† says, under Chinaware:

"The largest part of the export at present consists of coarse blue ware to India and the archipelago. Large manufactories of it exist at Pakwoh, a village near Shih-ma, between Amoy and Changchou, and the common articles of domestic use find their way from Amoy to India and the archipelago, Siam, and over the southern provinces. Its fantastic figures and uniformity of coloring and design have impressed themselves on the popular mind of Asiatics. . . . Of the fine ware, which is made at King-tê-chên in Jao-chou-fu, not so much is exported. Some of it is brought to Canton in its plain state, and the pieces are painted according to demand. The figures are sketched in Indian ink, and then painted with water-colors mixed with strong glue; the pieces are then placed in a reverberating furnace about half an hour, and taken out and washed when sufficiently cooled. The division of labor in the preparation and painting of chinaware is carried to a minuteness not often seen in other branches of native art."

The second manufactory is in the extreme south of the province of Yang-chiang-hsien. The author of the *Ching-tê-chên T'ao lu* says, under the heading of *Kuang-Yao*:

"This was first made in the province of Kuangtung, in the district of Yang-chiang-hsien, in the prefecture of Chao-ch'ing-fu. It was probably fired in the same way as the foreign painted enamels on copper (which, the author tells us in another part of his book, had been copied from those made at Calicut in Hindustan), so that porcelain is included in the official description of the province among the productions of Yang-chiang-hsien. I have seen censers for burning incense, vases, cups and platters, bowls and round dishes, gourd-shaped bottles and boxes with covers, and the like, made of this ware, which were finely decorated in the most brilliant colors; but in style, finish, and artistic treatment it is not to be compared with real porcelain, and it is never free from unsightly fissures in some part of the glaze in which the body of the piece is exposed to view. Nevertheless, the reproductions that have been made at Ching-tê-chên, under the superintendence of the director T'ang Ying, are worthy of attention for the beauty of their coloring, which exceeds by far that of the original Kuang-Yao."

The particular glaze referred to in this last paragraph was a *soufflé* blue. It figures as No. 17 in the list given in Chapter XIII, where it is described as having been copied by T'ang Ying from an ancient specimen of Kuang-Yao which had been sent down from the imperial palace at Peking for the purpose. The glazes of the Kuang-Yao are often, indeed, of the mottled and variegated class, the prevailing ground being blue, which may be streaked and flecked with green and pass into olive-brown toward the rim. But many other colors occur, such as purple, camellia-leaf green, and stone-colored crackle; they are usually colors of the *demi-grand feu*, and may develop the most brilliant reds of *sang-de-bœuf* tone, as in the figure of the Buddhist patriarch Bôdhidharma, illustrated in Plate XLI, which is invested in a robe of lustrous crimson. This statuette is a typical example of Kuang-Yao, and exhibits the reddish-gray color of the dense, hard material in the parts uncovered by glaze. On the vases of more ancient date the surface is often only partially enameled, the glaze stopping in an irregular line as it runs down and congeals in drops, so that a third part of the piece may be left bare. In this it resembles some of the ancient wares of the *Sung* dynasty, with which it may be confounded if special attention be not paid to the *pâte*, which is peculiarly dense and opaque, although it may occasionally be of a pale grayish tint approaching white.

The vase in Fig. 369 is a characteristic production of the potteries of Kuangtung. Molded of solid form, with two ring handles in relief springing from grotesque lions' heads, it is invested with a thick, translucent glaze of bright green tint, mottled with dark brown, and becoming grayish blue at the edges. This does not quite reach the bottom of the vase, ending below in an undulatory line, so that the brown stoneware body is exposed to view at this spot.

FIG. 373.—Fuchien Vase of white porcelain, with a bluish tinge, molded with Buddhist symbols inclosed in floral scrolls.

The bottle-shaped vase in Fig. 370, with a pair of lizardlike dragons (*ch'ih-lung*) of archaic shape projecting in openwork relief from the neck, is made of light but hard stoneware of brown color. It is covered with a translucent crackled glaze of rich emerald-green tint, passing into purplish gray at the rim of the vase and over the more prominent parts of the accessory modeling.

In Fig. 374 is illustrated one of the quaint little receptacles for water (*shui ch'êng*) designed for the desk of a Chinese writer. An ancient specimen of Kuang-Yao, judging from the texture of the paste, which is of pale buff color, and the celadon hue of the glaze, it is molded in the form of a sacrificial ox, with a small oval bowl attached to the mouth, into which the pencil-brush may be dipped. A channel leads from this through the mouth of the ox, the body of which is hollowed to hold water, and the back is pierced with a circularly rimmed aperture. The design is adopted from one of the ancient sacrificial wine-vessels of bronze, which, however, were usually modeled in the form of a rhinoceros, and this is suggested by the spiral folds on the skin, the thick legs, and the grotesque outline of the miniature monster before us.

The Chinese ceramic ware that remains for our consideration is the *Yi-hsing Yao*, which derives its name from its place of production—Yi-hsing-hsien, in the prefecture of Chang-chou-fu, in the province of Kiangsu. It has been cursorily referred to already in Chapter VII, in a notice of some of its earlier productions during the *Ming* dynasty. The pottery produced here is a fine kind of stoneware of various tints—buff, red, brown, and chocolate-colored, red predominating. The Portuguese called it *boccaro*, and the name has remained. Böttger, the inventor of Saxon porcelain, first tried his hand in the imitation of this material in 1708, with some success, although his essays hardly deserved the epithet of *porcelaine rouge*, with which they were baptized. The Elers, who established a pottery in Staffordshire, England, also copied the red varieties with great exactness, so that it is not always easy, according to Sir Wollaston Franks, to distinguish their productions from Oriental examples.

The Chinese prefer this fine stoneware to any other, even to true porcelain, for the infusion of tea, and for keeping delicate sweetmeats. There is a special book which is often quoted (but I have not seen the original), called *Yang-hsien ming hu hsi*, written by Chou Kao-ch'i, an author of the seventeenth century, who gives an account of the teapots (*ming hu*) made here (Yang-hsien being an old name of Yi-hsing). These teapots are made in the most varied and fantastic forms, such as a dragon rising from waves, a phœnix or other bird, a section of bamboo, the gnarled trunk of a pine, or a branch of blossoming prunus, a fruit such as a peach, a pomegranate, or a finger-citron, or a flower like the nelumbium, the Chinese lotus.

Many of the pieces derive their sole charm from the simple elegance of the form and the soft self-coloring of the fine, close faïence in which it is modeled. Others are ornamented with designs molded in relief, impressed with delicate diapers, or engraved with decorative designs. Others, again, are painted in enamel colors, applied with a brush so as to come out in sensible relief, or inlaid, as it were, in a ground previously prepared for the purpose, the technique being that of *champlevé* enamel on copper. The enamel colors may be either single or multiple. The material makes a charming background for a spray of flowers worked in clear cobalt-blue combined with a vitreous flux, or for a landscape lightly penciled in the soft grayish white afforded by arsenic. The decoration in multiple colors is almost too elaborate, especially when the piece is completely covered, so that none of the ground is visible, in

FIG. 374.—Small Kuang Yao Water Receptacle of celadon, for the writing table.

which case the nature of the excipient can be detected only by examining the rim of the foot underneath.

All kinds of things have been made at Yi-hsing-hsien of this peculiar faïence, and out of the multitude of objects of use and ornament that are usually made in China of porcelain, there is hardly one that is not also to be found in *boccaro* ware. This last material is, however, considered most suitable for small *objets de luxe*, and these are often very cunningly and minutely finished. Miniature teapots and fruit and flowers of charming design are made to hold water for the writer's pallet; perfume-bottles, rouge-pots, powder-boxes, trays, saucers, and other nameless accessories for the toilet-table of the harem; small vases for flowers, comfit-dishes, chopstick-trays, and miniature wine-cups for the dinner-table. The mandarin wears a thumb-ring, a tube for the peacock's feather in his hat, and has enameled beads and other ornaments for his rosary made of this material; the Chinese exquisite carries a snuff-bottle, the tobacco-smoker has his water-pipe, and the opium devotee the bowl of his bamboo pipe artistically inlaid in soft vitrified colors.

Two of these small pieces have been selected for illustration. The first (Fig. 23) is a snuff-bottle of brown Yi-hsing ware, decorated with a miniature mountain landscape of temples, pavilions, and bridges, painted in soft-toned enamel colors. The second is a little receptacle for water, fashioned out of pale buff-colored faïence in the form of a folded leaf, and imbued with autumnal tints, the outer aspect being covered with a roughened brown enamel, while the interior is coated purplish gray. The ivory stand, carved in openwork with bamboos and flowers and mounted upon a second rosewood stand, shows how it was once appreciated in China.

Glazed stoneware is made in the other provinces of China, but nothing of artistic value or interest seems to be produced that can be compared with the fine-grained *boccaro* of Yi-hsing. Potteries near Peking have been referred to as producing a kind of archaic-looking ware, which is occasionally enameled in brilliant single colors so as to cover the ground and conceal the material. This is a kind of glazed earthenware or terra-cotta, and can be easily scratched with a steel point. The ordinary glaze is a reddish brown of marked iridescence, shining with an infinity of metallic specks, an effective background to the molded decoration which covers the surface. The designs are generally of hieratic character.

This terra-cotta is largely used in China for architectural purposes. The ruins of Wan-shou-shan and the other imperial summer palaces near Peking that were burned in 1860, have furnished large images of Kuan-Yin enameled with turquoise-blue and other soft colors, smaller Buddhist images that were inlaid by the thousand in the brick walls of their temples, and dragons, k'i-lins, phœnixes, and other figures, that formed the antefixal ornaments of the roofs. Not the least interesting of these relics are the shields and trophies of arms of European design, and the classical figures for the fountains of the Italian palace which was built in the Yuan-Ming-Yuen for the Emperor *Ch'ien-lung* under the superintendence of the Jesuit missionaries. These were all made in the encaustic tile-works near Peking.

It has been imagined by some that porcelain was so common in China that it usurped the place of all other ceramic wares, but this is not the case. From true kaolinic pottery, or true porcelain, we pass through all the different grades of faïence and stoneware, in which the material becomes gradually coarser and less perfectly vitrified, till we come to ordinary glazed earthenware, and finally to unglazed terra-cotta, which is roughly fired in an open kiln. These should be set apart in collections, and an attempt be made to classify them according to the different places of production, as well as in chronological sequence. The study is not without interest, as the development of some of the minor potteries that have been working for centuries in their own lines occasionally throws a side-light on the gradual progress of the decoration of porcelain. Although this is essentially a Chinese art, it has been more modified by external influences than some of its humbler sisters, which I would venture to bring into more prominent notice for that reason.

Fig. 375.—Three boys rolling a snowball.

CHAPTER XXIII.

CHINESE BIBLIOGRAPHY IN RELATION TO THE CERAMIC ART.

A SHORT excursion in the vast field of Chinese bibliography is undertaken here, in order to give some of the principal sources of information that have been availed of, and to indicate the ground that is open for further research. In the course of it the Chinese names of most of the books that have been quoted in the preceding pages will be given, with a reference to the dates of their publication, and a brief sketch of the nature of their contents.

Of works on the ceramic art that have been published out of China, two special books* are available for reference, in addition to more partial bibliographical lists which accompany some of the general works on pottery, such as the one of which the title is quoted below.†

Some idea of the vast extent of Chinese literature may be gathered from the scholarly work of the late Alexander Wylie, agent of the British and Foreign Bible Society in China,‡ which, extensive as it is, is only a short epitome of the 欽定四庫全書總目, *Ch'in ting Ssŭ k'u chüan shu tsung mu*, the voluminous descriptive catalogue of the Imperial Library of the present dynasty, which was drawn up by command of the Emperor *Ch'ien-lung*, and completed in 1790. The library is arranged, as indicated by the title of the catalogue, in *Ssŭ k'u*, or "Four Divisions," viz., Classics, History, Philosophy, and *Belles-Lettres*, and the catalogue alone consists of two hundred books.

The Five Classics or Canonical Books in the first division, which have been occasionally referred to in our text, include:

1. The 易經, *Yi Ching*, "Book of Changes," which is so highly reverenced by the Chinese on account of its antiquity and the unfathomable wisdom which is supposed by them to lie concealed under its mystic symbols. These are the *pa kua*, the eight trigrams of ancient divination, which are often represented on porcelain of all periods, especially on ritual vessels of the Taoist cult.

2. The 書經, *Shu Ching*, "Book of History," a collection of state documents of the "Three Ancient Dynasties," ranging from the time of *Yao* and *Shun* in the third millennium B.C., down to the reign of *P'ing Wang* of the *Chou* dynasty, which ended in the year B.C. 720.

3. The 詩經, *Shih Ching*, "Book of Odes," a collection of songs of homage and popular ballads, three hundred and eleven in number, selected by Confucius from among those current in ancient times in the various petty states into which China used to be divided.

4. The 三禮, *San Li*, "Three Rituals," comprising the *Chou Li*, the Ritual of the *Chou* dynasty, the *Yi Li*, "Decorum Ritual," and the official *Li Chi*, "Book of Rites." The first of the three, the "Ritual of the Chou," is the most interesting to us in the present connection, because it contains a short notice of the government potters of the period under the two headings of *t'ao jên*, "potters," who worked on the wheel, and *fang jên*, "molders," showing that these two branches of the handicraft were already distinguished at this early period. The cooking utensils and sacrificial utensils that they made seem to have been of common clay, and were directed to be sold in the market under certain official regulations. The particulars are contained in the 考工記, *K'ao kung chi*, "Artificer's Record," which forms the sixth section of the classic. The names and dimensions of the vessels are given in the original, but little else is known about them, and Chinese authorities even differ as to whether the pottery of the time was glazed or not. The figures in the 三禮圖, *San Li Tou*, "Illustrations of the Three Rituals," in

---

* *Bibliographie céramique. Nomenclature analytique de toutes les Publications faites en Europe et en Orient sur les arts et l'industrie céramiques, depuis le XVIᵉ siècle jusqu'à nos jours*, par Champfleury, conservateur du Musée de Sèvres. Paris, 1881.

A List of Works on Pottery and Porcelain in the National Art Library, compiled for the use of students and visitors, by R. H. Soden Smith, Science and Art, Department of the Committee of Council on Education, South Kensington Museum. The first edition was published in 1875, but revised and enlarged editions, incorporating later additions to the art library, have since been issued.

† *Pottery: How it is made; its Shape and Decoration. Practical Instructions for Painting on Porcelain and all Kinds of Pottery with Vitrifiable and Common Oil Colors*. With a full bibliography of standard works upon the ceramic art, and forty-two illustrations. By George Ward Nichols. New York, 1878.

‡ *Notes on Chinese Literature*. By A. Wylie. Shanghae, 1867.

twenty books, by Nieh Tsung-yi, who lived in the tenth century A. D., and in the other illustrated commentaries of more modern date, are generally imaginary and more or less fanciful.

5. The 春秋, *Ch'un Ch'iu*, "Spring and Autumn Annals," is the only one of the five canonical books that was actually compiled by Confucius. It is the history of his native state of Lu (in the present province of Shan-tung), from 722 to 484 B. C., derived from the official records of the *Chou* dynasty.

In Chinese bibliography the dictionaries are placed after the classics. The most ancient of them is the *Êrh Ya,* 爾雅, a relic of the *Chou* dynasty, which at one time used to rank as one of the canonical books. The commentary which is always associated with the text was written by Kuo P'u of the third century A. D., but the accompanying illustrations date only from the *Sung* dynasty, about the tenth century. The next dictionary is the 說文, *Shuo Wên*, which is devoted to an explanation of the ancient characters in which the classics were origi-nally written; it was compiled by Hsü Shên at the close of the first century A. D., and was presented by him to the Emperor *An Ti* in the year 121. The largest of the dictionaries, and the one that is invaluable for special research, is the 佩文韻府, *P'ei wên yun fu*, which was compiled under the special superintendence of the Emperor *K'ang-hsi*, and published in 1711 in 110 thick octavo volumes. The foreign Chinese-English dictionaries need hardly be alluded to here; those by Williams and Giles are the best.

The second great division of Chinese bibliography includes the works on history, geog-raphy, and kindred subjects. The "Twenty-four Dynastic Histories" form the first class. Con-temporary records are written day by day by the state historiographers in China, and one of the first duties of a new dynasty, when it is firmly established on the dragon throne, is to appoint an imperial commission to compile an official history of the preceding dynasty from the archives preserved in the historiographers' office. These histories are therefore practically contemporary. They are all framed on a nearly uniform model, the general arrangement being in three sections, as follows:

1. *Imperial Records*, containing a succinct chronicle of the several emperors of the dynasty. 2. *Memoirs*, consist-ing of a succession of articles on Mathematical Chronology, Rites, Music, Jurisprudence, Political Economy, State Sacrifices, Astronomy, Natural Phenomena, Geography, and Literature. 3. *Narratives*, comprising official biographies of all persons of eminence, and ending with a short description of any foreign nations that happen to have sent em-bassies to China during the period.

The official histories commence with the 史記, *Shih Chi*, by Ssǔ-ma Ch'ien, who lived B. C. 163–85, and who has been termed the Herodotus of China. His *Historical Records*, in 130 books, start from the most remote antiquity and extend down to the year B. C. 122. The other dynastic histories that have been occasionally referred to, generally by quotations from individual biographies, are the 隋書, *Sui Shu*, "Book of the *Sui* [dynasty]," covering the years 581–617; the voluminous, 唐書, *T'ang Shu*, 'Book of the *T'ang*" (618–906); the 宋史, *Sung Shih*, "History of the *Sung*" (960–1279), the most extensive of all, comprising as it does 496 books; and the 明史, *Ming Shih*, "History of the *Ming*" (1368–1643), which is the last of the series of twenty-four.

Works on geography and topography follow next in order. The series of topographical writings in China is justly pronounced by Mr. Wylie (*loc. cit.,* page 35) to be unrivaled in any nation for extent and systematic comprehensiveness. Leaving out of account the sections devoted to geography in the several dynastic histories, there are separate official works on every part of the empire. At the head of these may be placed the 大清一統志, *Ta Ch'ing Yi t'ung chih*, in 500 books, which is a geography of the whole empire, published about the middle of the eighteenth century under imperial patronage. This takes up the various prov-inces *seriatim*, giving under each an account of the astrological divisions, limits, configuration of the country, officers, population, taxes, and renowned statesmen. Under each prefecture and department is a more detailed description of the various districts, giving, in addition to the above, the cities, educational institutes, hills and rivers, antiquities, passes, bridges, defenses, tombs, temples, men of note, travelers, female worthies, religious devotees, and productions of the soil. Besides the above general compilation there are separate topographical accounts of each of the eighteen 省 (*shêng*) "provinces," of every 府 (*fu*) "prefecture" and 州 (*chou*) "department," of almost every 縣 (*hsien*) "district" or "county," and, in many cases, of smaller towns included in the district.

The province, for example, of Kiangsi, which interests us more particularly, containing as it does the great center of the manufacture of porcelain, has a general description called 江西 通志, *Chiang hsi t'ung chih*, which has been very often quoted. This was first published in the reign of *Chia-ching* (1522–66) of the *Ming* dynasty; two new and revised editions were issued during the reign of *K'ang-hsi*, and another, much enlarged, was completed in 162 books in the next reign (1732), under the superintendence of Hsieh Min, who was then governor of the province. In the reign of *T'ung-chih*, after the Taiping rebellion had been put down, an imperial commission, whose names and titles fill six folios of the book, was appointed, under

FIG. 376.—Double-fish Vase, one of a pair, of blue-green celadon, mounted in metal as jugs.

the presidency of the viceroy, Tsêng Kuo-fan, to make a new revision. It was completed in 1882, and the result is the bulky work in 180 books which is now before us. The account of the imperial porcelain manufacture forms part of the ninety-second book, under the heading of *T'ao Chêng*, "Porcelain Administration."

There were other descriptive works on the province in circulation before the publication of the above, of which the 豫章大事記, *Yü chang ta shih chi*, or "Record of Important Affairs of the Province," under its ancient name of Yü-chang, is the most important. This was written by Kuo Tzŭ-chang, a president of the Board of War in the *Ming* dynasty.

The 饒州府志, *Jao chou fu chih*, is the official description of the prefecture Jao-chou-fu, in the province of Kiangsi, which has Fou-liang-hsien as one of the seven districts or counties under its jurisdiction. The edition before me is dated the eleventh year of the reign of *T'ung-chih* (1872); it reprints several of the prefaces of the older editions, the first of which is dated in the cyclical year *hsin-wei* (1511) of the reign of *Chêng-tê* of the *Ming* dynasty. There are thirty-two books, the third of which, devoted to "Bridges, Antiquities, Customs of the People,

and Natural Productions," includes an article on the porcelain industry, which is appended to the last section, under the heading of 陶廠, *T'ao Ch'ang*, "Imperial Porcelain Manufactory."

A still more complete account of the ceramic industry is the one that is included in the 浮梁縣志, *Fou liang hsien chih*, "The Description of Fou-liang-hsien," which has been so often quoted in these pages, and which is referred to in some detail in the introductory chapter of this work as one of our chief authorities on the subject. The earliest edition of this work was published during the *Sung* dynasty, in the year 1270; the edition at our disposal was the official revision issued in the reign of *Tao-kuang* (1821–50). The eighth book contains a memoir on porcelain from the official standpoint, entitled 陶政, *T'ao Chêng*, "Porcelain Administration."

There is no official description of Ching-tê-chên itself in the regular series, but the place of one is fairly well filled by the 景德鎮陶錄, *Ching tê chên T'ao lu*, "Description of the Porcelain of Ching-tê-chên." This was published under direct official sanction, as described in the preface by Liu Ping, the chief magistrate of the district, and is dated 1815. It contains a good map of the town, a plan of the imperial potteries, and fourteen woodcuts illustrating the different processes of manufacture, sketched by an artist on the spot.

Gigantic encyclopædias made up of extracts from existing works, classified under different headings according to the subject-matter, form one of the most remarkable features of Chinese literature. The 太平御覽, *T'ai p'ing yü lan*, which is very often referred to, was compiled in 1,000 books, divided into fifty-five sections, after a mandate issued by the second emperor of the *Sung* dynasty in the year 977. The largest of all is the 永樂大典, *Yung lo ta tien*, the vast cyclopædia of the Emperor *Yung-lo* of the *Ming* dynasty, who appointed a commission of scholars in 1403 to collect in one body the substance of all the classical, historical, philosophic, and literary works hitherto published, embracing astronomy, geography, the occult sciences, medicine, Buddhism, Taoism, and the arts. Their work was completed in 1407, and the result was 22,877 books, besides the table of contents, which occupied sixty books. It was ordered by the emperor to be transcribed for printing, but the expense was too great, and it still remains in manuscript, although many ancient and rare works, that would otherwise have been irretrievably lost, have been pieced together again from the extensive quotations in the manuscript columns and reprinted separately. From this we may pass on to the 欽定古今圖書集成, *Ch'in ting ku chin t'ou shu chi ch'êng*, the huge cyclopædia of the Emperor *K'ang-hsi*, the second of the present dynasty, which contains 10,000 *ch'üan* or "books." It gives 426,304 extracts, long and short, from older books, which are arranged under 6,109 headings, distributed among thirty-two classes, and the full-page illustrations number 8,041. These illustrations are executed in the style of the *Ming* dynasty, which is celebrated for its woodcuts, and the printing was done with movable copper type cast expressly for the purpose, ordinary Chinese books being printed from wood-blocks. There is a complete example of the original quarto edition, which was limited to about 100 copies, in the British Museum, and a new edition has been recently published in octavo form at Shanghai by the aid of the photolithographic process. There are some curious illustrations in this encyclopædia under the heading Porcelain, but of importance from a literary and antiquarian point of view only.

Books on art come next for a word of notice. The Chinese have methodical treatises of more than a thousand years' standing on writing, painting, engraving, music, and the kindred subjects that are grouped together under the name of liberal arts. An elaborate treatise on painting, in ten books, appeared during the *T'ang* dynasty (618–906), entitled 歷代名畫記, *Li tai ming hua chi*, "Records of the Celebrated Pictures of Different Dynasties," by Chang Yen-yuan, with descriptive and historical details regarding the art, having reference particularly to a hereditary collection of paintings in the family of the author, and accompanied by biographical sketches of the artists. The 宣和畫譜, *Hsüan ho hua p'u*, is a description, in twenty books, of the pictures in the imperial collection during the *Hsüan-ho* period (1119–25). There is a companion publication called 宣和書譜, *Hsüan ho shu p'u*, containing specimens of the calligraphy of successive ages gathered from the imperial archives of the same time. But all the older books have been supplanted by the large compilation which was referred to in Chapter V under the title of *Imperial Cyclopædia of Celebrated Writers and Painters*, the 欽定佩文齋書畫譜, *Ch'in ting P'ei wên chai shu hua p'u*. This was drawn up by a commission appointed by the Emperor *K'ang-hsi*, who wrote the preface himself when the book was published, in the forty-seventh year of his reign (1708). The titles of the principal authorities, which are cited in the introduction, number 1,844. The cyclopædia comprises 100 *chüan*, or books, and it is divided usually, in Chinese fashion, into sixty-four *pên*, or volumes. It is a perfect mine of information, giving instructions in the arts of writing and painting, descriptions of manuscripts and pictures, notices of celebrated collections and collectors, and of the certificates of authenticity which they are in the habit of writing on the scrolls, biographical notices of writers and artists, etc. None of the artists on porcelain, however, seem to be mentioned by name, although there are occasional references to the designs used in ceramic decorations, as in book xii, folio 24, which gives a long list from official sources of the motives of decoration employed in the eighth year of the reign of *Chia-ching* (1528).

The Chinese, it is well known, have the greatest reverence for antiquity, and the study of ancient relics and of the inscriptions upon them forms another important branch of literature. Archæologists classify the specimens, which are constantly being dug up from the ground, under the two headings of *Chin*, "Metal," and *Shih*, "Stone." The former class includes sacrificial vessels, musical instruments, and ordinary utensils of bronze, bronze mirrors, bronze weapons, and coins; the latter class comprises stone sculptures in bas-relief, carved inscriptions, Buddhist images and other figures, prehistoric stone weapons, vessels and utensils of nephrite or other kinds of jade, archaic pottery, inscribed bricks and tiles, etc. There are separate works on ancient bronze vessels and on swords dating from the fifth and sixth centuries A. D., but they include much that is legendary. The most important of the old books on ancient bronzes now in circulation is the 宣和博古圖錄, *Hsüan ho Po ku t'ou lu*, "Illustrated Description of Antiquities published in the *Hsüan-ho* Period," in thirty books,

FIG. 377.—Bottle of pale blue soufflé ground pencilled with darker blue; European mounts.

which was compiled by Wang Fu in the beginning of the twelfth century, and has been frequently reprinted since. It is usually printed together with the 考古圖, *K'ao ku t'ou*, "Illustrated Examination of Antiquities," the description of a similar collection of older date written by Lü Ta-lin in 1092, in ten books; and with a smaller work in two books entitled 古玉圖, *Ku yü t'ou*, "Illustrations of Ancient Jade." Another collection of the *Sung* dynasty is the 紹興鑑古圖, *Shao hsing chien ku t'ou*, "Illustrated Mirror of Antiquities of the *Shao-hsing* Period" (1131–62), which furnished a model for the porcelain censer with fish handles of the reign of *Hsüan-tê* of the *Ming* dynasty, referred to in Chapter VII. The most magnificent work of this class of more recent times is the illustrated descriptive catalogue of the imperial collections at Peking, entitled 西清古鑑, *Hsi ch'ing ku chien*, which was published by the Emperor *Ch'ien-lung* in 1751 in forty-two folio volumes; the 西清續鑑, *Hsi ch'ing hsü chien*, in fourteen folio volumes, is a supplement to the above catalogue, still unpublished, and circulating in a few manuscripts only; and the 寧壽古鑑, *Ning shou ku chien*, is another work similar to the preceding, also as yet unpublished, which is written and illustrated in the same superb style, twenty-eight volumes in folio, being the description of the collection of antiquities in the Ning-shou Kung, another of the palaces within the prohibited city at Peking. The original edition of the *Hsi ch'ing ku chien* costs several hundreds of dollars in China, but it has been lately so perfectly reproduced at Shanghai by photographic process, in small octavo, that it is within the reach of every collector, and it ought to be at hand, for the study of bronze forms and designs.

The 淑清院陳設檔, *Shu ch'ing yuan chên shu tang*, which was quoted in Chapter V (page 98), is very different from the above, being merely an ordinary official inventory in manuscript of the furniture and specimens of art work on daily exhibition in the Shu-ch'ing Yuan, one of the palaces in the Western Gardens (*Hsi Yuan*) on the northern shore of the large lake in the imperial city, corrected to the thirteenth year of *Chia-ch'ing* (1808).

The standard work on ancient jade is the 古玉圖譜, *Ku yü t'ou p'u*, "Illustrated Description of Ancient Jade," in 100 books, with more than 700 full-page woodcuts. It was compiled by an imperial commission, composed of the notorious Lung Ta-yuan and eighteen other members, including one writer and four artists, appointed by the second emperor of the Southern *Sung* dynasty, and it was completed in the year 1176. A manuscript copy was purchased for the Imperial Library in 1773; the Emperor *Ch'ien-lung* ordered it to be printed in the palace, and it appeared in 1779, with a preface dedicating it to the emperor. Some doubts have been expressed by native scholars as to the authenticity of the book, but on more or less slender grounds, and we may accept the imperial imprimatur as a sufficient warrant. The genuine character of many of the objects figured may be more justly criticised; there is certainly no ground for the remote antiquity that is ascribed to some of the inscribed pieces.

In addition to these special works there are several books of a wider scope devoted to the general subject of antiquities and objects of art. The *Ming* dynasty was distinguished for this kind of research, and the authors of the four following books, which have been quoted more than once in our pages, all belong to that time; each one gives a short chapter on porcelain. They are all before me now, and, arranged in the order of their publication, are:

    1. The 格古要論, *Ko ku yao lun*, "Discussion of the Principal Criteria of Antiquities,"

in thirteen books, by Tsao Ch'ao, published in the reign of *Hung-wu,* the founder of the *Ming* dynasty, in the year 1387. A revised and enlarged edition was prepared by Wang Tso and issued in 1459. The new editor always carefully marks the additions made by him, so that the text of the original edition may be easily distinguished. The following table of contents will give some idea of the scope of the work, which is interesting from its early date:

Book I. Ancient Lyres, and other stringed musical instruments.

Book II. Old Manuscripts, with a discussion of the distinctive characteristics of the paper and ink.

Book III. Inscriptions from ancient stone tablets and other monuments, classified according to the provinces from which the rubbings were obtained.

Book IV. Select Extracts from Previous Authors on the subject.

Book V. Old Pictures, with a discussion of the peculiar water-colors employed, and other marks of authenticity.

Book VI. Precious Stones and Jewels, including jade, agate, moss-agate, rock-crystal, glass, cat's-eyes, emeralds, pearls of different kinds, garnets, rubies, sapphires, lapis lazuli, coral, and amber; rhinoceros horn and ivory, with reference to concentric openwork spheres, libation-cups, and other carvings; gold, silver, steel and inlaid iron-work, white metal; sacred figures occurring in natural stones; ancient bronzes and methods of distinguishing false antiques, etc.

Book VII. Ancient Ink Pallets, with an account of the natural stones suitable for their fabrication, references to pottery pallets, and to pallets made of ancient tiles and potsherds. Curious Stones; jet and variegated stones used for inlaying furniture, minerals resembling jade, agate, or mother-of-pearl used for carving, etc. Ancient Pottery and Porcelain; with notes on the productions of different manufactories, commencing with the ancient azure-tinted products of the Ch'ai potteries, and ending with the contemporary wares of the imperial potteries of Fou-liang-hsien. There are brief references to Korean pottery, and to the introduction of the process of painting in enamels on copper from the Arabs (*Ta-shih*), in which the editor tells us that the same coloring materials were employed as in the *cloisonné* enameling on copper (*Fo-lang Ch'ien*), which was so called because it originally came from Byzantium.

Book VIII. Lacquered Work; painted lac, carved cinnabar lac, lac inlaid with gold, lacquered furniture inlaid with mother-of-pearl, etc. Brocaded and embroidered silks, silk stuffs woven on the loom with threads of different colors. Asbestos cloth, carpets of silk and wool. Foreign Woods, sandalwood, rosewood, ebony, and other fragrant or variegated kinds. Varieties of Bamboo.

Book IX. Description of Objects for the Study and Library. Brushes, cakes of ink from different parts, principal paper factories, seal vermilion, books and their care, etc.

Book X. Collections of Essays and Prefaces of old authors on the subject.

Book XI. Miscellaneous Researches, Part I. On Jade Seals. On Iron Tablets of Authority.

Book XII. Miscellanies, Part II. Wording of Imperial Edicts. Official Girdles, with a description of the jade, gold, silver, and other appendages that were worn upon them at different times as tokens of rank.

Book XIII. Miscellanies, Part III. On a series of illustrations depicting the process of rice-culture and of silk-weaving. Researches on the old palaces of the *Sung* and *Yuan* dynasties.

2. The 妮古錄, *Ni ku lu*, "Description of Antiquarian Inquiries," is a work of the same character as the last, but smaller, being an account in four books of old manuscripts, pictures, antiquities, and other objects of art and curiosity, etc., by Ch'en Chi-ju, an author of the *Ming* dynasty, which was published in the middle of the sixteenth century.

3. The 清秘藏, *Ch'ing pi ts'ang*, "Collection of Artistic Rarities," is another little work in two books on antiquities, pictures, brocaded silks, ancient bronzes, porcelain, seals, jewels, and miscellaneous objects of art, by Chang Ying-wên, who wrote the last page on the day he died. It was published by his son Chang Ch'ien-tê, the author of a book on flowers, vases, and the art of arranging flowers in them, which will be alluded to presently, and who wrote the preface for his father's work, which is dated 1595. There is a curious notice in the second book of a visit to an exhibition, called *Ch'ing Wan Hui*—i. e., "Exposition of Art Treasures"—which was held in the province of Kiangsu in the third month of the fourth year of the reign of *Lung-ch'ing* (1570), the objects being loaned for the purpose by four of the principal families of the province.

4. The 博物要覽, *Po wu yao lan*, "General Survey of Art Objects," which was referred to in Chapter V, is perhaps the best work of the class that is under consideration. It was written by Ku Ying-t'ai, in the reign of *T'ien-ch'i* (1621-27) of the *Ming*, but remained in manuscript till the beginning of the present dynasty, when it was printed by Li Tiao-yun, with a preface signed by himself as editor. It comprises sixteen books, which make two octavo volumes bound in Chinese style. The second book is devoted to porcelain, under the several headings:

1. The Ju-chou, Imperial, and Ko potteries, of the *Sung* dynasty, with lists of the different objects made in the last two potteries arranged in three classes according to their artistic value.   2. The Ting-chou potteries, with a list of the most important objects produced there in the *Sung* dynasty.   3. The ancient Lung-ch'üan potteries, with an account of the grass-green celadon porcelain made there in the *Sung* dynasty, and a list of the objects that are considered most worthy of notice.   4. Ancient potteries of the province of Fuchien.   5. Description of the ceramic production of Chün-chou during the *Sung* dynasty.   6. The Arabian enamels on copper.   7. Glassware.   8. Ancient and modern productions of Jao-chou, referring to the porcelain made at Ching-tê-chên.

There is only the briefest notice in this last section of the older porcelain of the *Sung* and *Yuan* dynasties, but the productions of the writer's own dynasty (the *Ming*) are described at greater length, under the several reigns of *Yung-lo* (1403–24), *Hsüan-tê* (1426–35), *Ch'êng-hua* (1465–87), and *Chia-ching* (1522–66), and Ku Ying-t'ai is constantly quoted by connoisseurs as the best authority for this period.

Literature is, as it were, a religious cult for the Chinese scholar, and he cherishes the tools of his craft as almost sacred.   There is a small class of books written in this connection on the furniture and literary apparatus of the study, among which certain articles of porcelain find a place.   One of the earliest of the books of this class is the 筆 經, *Pi Ching*, "Canon of the Pencil Brush," by Wang Hsi-chih, a celebrated calligrapher who lived 321–379; he wrote down the poems of the club that used to meet in the Lan T'ing or "Orchid Pavilion," and down to the present time these poems, as written by Wang, continue to be cut in stone all over China as models of handwriting.   The 文 房 四 譜, *Wên fang ssŭ p'u*, is one of the older books on the materials of the study, which was compiled by Su Yi-chien in 986.   It consists of four parts, which treat respectively of pencils, ink-pallets, ink, and paper, with remarks on the various descriptions and characteristics, historical memoranda, and essays and stanzas appended to each section.

The 考 槃 餘 事, *K'ao p'an yü shih*, by T'u Lung, a writer of the sixteenth century, is another general handbook for the man of learning and culture, of somewhat wider scope, discussing, as it does, in order :

Printed Books, Ancient Inscriptions, Manuscripts and Calligraphy, Painting and Artists, Paper, Ink, Brushes, Pallets, Music and the Lyre, Perfumes and Incense-burning Apparatus; Tea, its choice brands, preparation, tea-drinking utensils; Flowers, their cultivation in pots and their display in vases; Storks for the garden and the different varieties of goldfish; the Country House in the Hills, its library, medicine-room, summer-house, Taoist and Buddhist shrines, and outdoor pavilion for drinking tea; Furniture, materials for the study, traveling apparatus, etc.

It is a curious epitome of antiquarian information, extending to boats and fishing-rods, as well as describing the forms of vases, etc., and ends with the pictures of two double and single gourds, which are recommended as the lightest and most elegant of wine-flasks for the pilgrim to carry on his girdle when traveling.

The work of the present dynasty of this class that is the most frequently referred to is the 文 房 肆 考, *Wên fang ssŭ k'ao*, an examination of the belongings of the scholar by T'ang Ping-chün, which was published in eight books in the forty-seventh year of the reign of *Ch'ien-lung* (1782).   It is illustrated with a portrait of the author and a picture of his study, with palms, dryandra-trees, and bamboos growing from rocks in the background of the pavilion in which he is seated with an open volume on the table.

The first two books are devoted to ink-pallets of carved stone, illustrated by forty-six full-page woodcuts of appropriate designs.   Book III contains an account of paper, ink, and brushes, and an investigation of ancient pottery and porcelain.   This last is mostly a medley of quotations from older writers, strung together somewhat loosely, and generally without acknowledgment of the sources from which they are derived, and it contains little that can not be found under better auspices in the *T'ao Shuo.*   Book IV is on ancient bronzes and the means of distinguishing modern imitations; on jade, ancient and modern, its history and characteristics, with notes on the minerals that resemble it; on lyres, ancient and modern.   Book V treats of the history of the written character, books, and paintings, and Book VI of the art of literary composition.   Books VII and VIII give an account of the drug ginseng, and a collection of essays and miscellaneous inquiries.

The special books on tea and its preparation occasionally throw some light on the porcelain of the corresponding time in their description of the cups and other utensils employed in its infusion.   We should know nothing of the early fabrics of the *T'ang* dynasty (618–

906) were it not for the 茶經, *Ch'a Ching,* the "Tea Classic," written by Lu Yü in the middle of the eighth century, the contents of which have been briefly sketched in Chapter I (page 14). The author discusses the colors of the different glazes, and gives the palm to the pale-blue cups from Yueh-chou, as imparting an agreeable greenish tinge to the yellow liquid. The writers of the *Sung* dynasty (960–1279), on the contrary, such as Ts'ai Hsiang, who wrote the 茶錄, *Ch'a Lu,* "Description of Tea," in the eleventh century, prefer the black cups mottled like hare's fur, which came from Chien-an (Chien-chou), as showing the last trace of the whitish tea-dust that remained in the bottom in the course of their competitive trials. The earliest book on the subject is the *Ch'uan Fu,* "Odes on Tea," by Tu Yu, a poet of the *Chin* dynasty (265–419), and he, as well as many of the other old versifiers, is often quoted when the ceramic productions of the time happen to be touched upon by them. Some of the *Sung* dynasty books on tea are illustrated with woodcuts, like the 茶譜, *Ch'a P'u,* by Ku Yuan-ch'ing, published in 1269, which gives curious pictures of the little copper roller, the miniature stone grinding-mill, the gauze sieve, the little "tea-jar" for the dust, made of carved vermilion lac, the teacup with its vertically striated bowl and widening mouth, the graceful ewer for boiling water, of which the best, the author tells us, were made at this time of gold, the bamboo whisk, and the napkin, or duster of brocaded silk. No teapot was used at this period; the hot water was poured on a carefully weighed quantity of tea-dust put into the cup, and stirred with the whisk, which is exactly like that used to-day in other countries in the preparation of more inebriating "drinks." The winner in the "tea-fight" was he whose tea withstood the most "waters," and whose sediment-trace lasted longest on the bottom of the bowl. For teapots we must consequently refer to more modern works, like the 陽羨茗壺系, *Yang hsien Ming hu hsi,* "Account of Celebrated Teapots of Yang-hsien (an old name of Yi-hsing)," by Chou Kao-ch'i, which is a disquisition on those of the peculiar brown boccaro ware which is still made at Yi-hsing-hsien, near Shanghai. Two special books on vases were published toward the close of the *Ming* dynasty, in the beginning of the seventeenth century, which have been quoted in Chapter XVII, viz., the 瓶史, *P'ing shih,* "History of Vases," by Yuan Hung-tao, and the 瓶花譜, *P'ing hua p'u,* a small treatise, in one book, on vases (*p'ing*) and the art of arranging cut flowers (*hua*) in them, by Chang Ch'ien-tê, already alluded to as the author of an introduction to his father's book on antiquities entitled *Ch'ing pi ts'ang,* which was dated 1595.

The forms of the ritual vases used by the emperor in the various sacrificial ceremonies at which he officiates are all figured and minutely described in the various official books, such as the 欽定大清會典圖, *Ch'in ting Ta Ch'ing Hui tien t'ou,* the imperial illustrated edition of the statutes of the reigning dynasty, a voluminous compilation in eighty books, accompanied by 102 books of plates. For Buddhist and Taoist ritual vessels reference must be made to the canonical books of the two religions. The principal Taoist writer, who has been quoted once, is Chuang Chou, who lived in the fourth century B. C., and left the work in ten books called 莊子, *Chuang Tzŭ,* which has been translated into English.

FIG. 378.—Small Tray, from the same set as the teapot in Fig. 360, painted in colors, with a similar crestlike badge in the middle.

The most important manual industries of the Chinese are rice-cultivation and silk-weaving, the former being the work of the men, the latter of the women. There is an annual ceremony celebrated at the Temple of Agriculture at Peking, during which the emperor plows a furrow, followed by the chief officers of state; and the empress picks mulberry-leaves and feeds silkworms on a stated occasion each year, accompanied by the ladies of the court, before worshiping the tutelary Goddess of Sericulture at the temple which is consecrated to her inside the palace. The different processes of work have been favorite subjects for artists of all periods. The Emperor *K'ang-hsi,* the second of the reigning dynasty, wrote a preface and composed a series of verses to illustrate the two sets of drawings executed by Chiao Ping-chên, an official of the Astronomical Board, which are published in the 御製耕織圖, *Yü chih Kêng Chih T'ou*, "Imperial Edition of Illustrations of Agriculture (*Kêng*) and Weaving (*Chih*)," which has been referred to already, and which was published in the thirty-fifth year of his reign (1696). The plates, twenty-three in each set, are engraved in the finest style of Chinese art, and have the imperial verses on the page opposite each picture inclosed in a broad frame containing a pair of imperial dragons represented rising from the sea in pursuit of the flaming jewel of omnipotence. Apart from their artistic value they afford naturalistic scenes of ordinary Chinese life, and it would be interesting to compare them with the twenty illustrations of the ceramic industry described in Chapter XV, which seem to have been drawn up on the same model, should these last ever be recovered from their hiding-place in the palace libraries.

There is a little manual of Chinese industry called 天工開悟, *T'ien kung k'ai wu,** illustrated with pictures, which was compiled by Sung Ying-shêng and published in the year 1637, toward the close of the *Ming* dynasty, and which gives a brief account of the various industrial processes, arranged in three books in the following order:

Book I notices agriculture, different kinds of cultivated corn, and processes of irrigation; culture of silkworms, silk-winding, and silk-weaving; dyeing of stuffs, manufacture of the colors employed, including indigo-blue, safflower-red, and yellow extracted from the flowers of the *Sophora japonica;* winnowing-machines and mills for grinding corn; salt from sea- and river-water, rock-salt obtained by mining; sugar, honey, and methods of preserving fruit. Book II refers to the work of the potter, to tile- and brick-making, and to porcelain; the metals and their different alloys used in the casting of sacrificial utensils, images, cannon, mirrors, and money; boats and carts; axes, spades, files, knives, saws, anchors, needles, and gongs; mineral lime, lime from oyster-shells, coal; crystallized products, alum, iron-sulphate, copper-sulphate; sulphur, arsenic; mineral and vegetable oils; the manufacture of paper, paper from the mulberry (*Broussonetia papyrifera*), paper from bamboo. Book III describes such metals as: Gold, silver, copper, including bronze, brass, and white metal, tin, iron, zinc, lead, white lead, and red lead. Arms: Bows, shields, gunpowder, saltpeter, cannon, fowling-pieces; mines, cinnabar, vermilion, ink, coloring materials; spirit distilled from corn; precious stones, pearls, diamonds, jade, agates, rock-crystal, and glass.

Some of the books that come under the class of miscellanies have occasionally been quoted when they touch on the ceramic art—for example, the 事物紺珠, *Shih wu kan chu*, a general miscellany of affairs and things, by Huang Yi-chêng, which was published in forty-one books in the year 1591; and the 長物志, *Ch'ang wu chih*, a somewhat similar miscellany of rather later date. The 論衡, *Lun Hêng*, referred to in Chapter XV, is a much earlier work, being a critical disquisition by Wang Ch'ung, one of the most philosophical writers of the *Han* dynasty, who lived A. D. 19–90.

Collected works of individual authors form one of the principal divisions of the fourth and largest class of Chinese literature, which is usually known as *belles-lettres*. The titles chosen for these works are often of a fanciful nature, so as to give the uninitiated no clew to the name of the author. In the account in Chapter VII of the porcelain of the reign of *Chê'ng-hua*, for example, two authors are referred to. The first is Kao Shih-ch'i, a miscellaneous writer who lived 1645–1704; he is quoted under his literary appellation of *T'an-jên*, "The Tranquil," as Kao T'an-jên; his collected works are entitled 高江村集, *Kao Chiang-ts'un chi*, Chiang-ts'un chi being a favorite *nom-de-plume* of the author. The collected works of the second author are quoted under their title of 曝書亭集, *P'u-shu t'ing chi*, "Memoirs of the Pavilion for Sunning Books," which was the "hall-name," or library-name, of Chu Yi-tsun (1629–97), a celebrated scholar and poet. He was the author of the *Jih hsia chiu wên*, a fine historical and archæological description of Peking in many volumes, and was altogether a most voluminous writer, his literary works, which were published under the above *nom-de-plume*, filling no less than eighty books.

There are two illustrated books on the making of ink which should have been noticed before, as the woodcuts which were originally designed as models for the molds in which the cakes of ink were pressed are very finely executed, and supply a rich fund of information on Chinese art motives. The authors, according to the editors of the Imperial Library Catalogue,

---

* There is a copy of this book, which is very rare, in the Bibliothèque National at Paris. Some of the articles in it have been translated by Stanislas Julien and published in the proceedings of L'Académie des Sciences and in the *Journal Asiatique*.

who notice both books at some length, were both good scholars and cultivated artists, clever in writing all the ancient and modern styles of character, and their works are full of antiquarian and symbolical lore.   For this reason they are most useful to the foreign inquirer into such subjects.   The first of these two books is the 程氏墨苑, *Ch'êng shih mo yuan,* "Collection of Ink of the Ch'êng Factory," in twelve books, by Ch'êng Chün-fang, of Hi-Hsien, in the province of Anhui.   This is a large collection of cuts, exhibiting artistic designs for cakes of ink, drawn from many different sources, sacred and profane.   There is a series of eulogistic prefaces at the beginning, one of which is by the celebrated Italian Jesuit priest Matteo Ricci, the founder of Roman Catholic missions in China.   His preface, dated the thirty-third year of *Wanli* (1605), is signed with his Chinese name, "Li Ma-t'ou, of Ou-lo-pa (Europa), composed and written with a quill by himself."   It includes a complete syllabary written in the Italian hand and reproduced in facsimile, and the worthy father has contributed, besides, three European woodcuts as designs for ink, one of which depicts the "Destruction of Sodom and Gomorrah," by way of inculcating a moral lesson on heathen readers.   The second work is the 方氏墨譜, *Fang shih mo p'u,* "Description of Ink of the Fang Factory," in six books, by Fang Yü-lu, a fellow-townsman and trade rival of Ch'êng, who was the imperial maker of the time, and accused Fang of stealing his secrets and pirating his ink.   The work of the latter, however, is a fine specimen of xylography executed in the finished style of the *Ming* dynasty.   It was published in six books, in the year 1588, and contains 385 cuts of cakes of ink of all sizes and shapes, exhibiting a large number of antiquarian, symbolical, and mythical designs, the same as those which are often used in the painted decoration of porcelain.   Although fairly eclectic in his religious views, the author shows a certain predilection for Buddhism, and he gives in the fifth book, which is devoted to the Buddhist cult, an interesting collection of emblems and pictures, as well as a series of circular mirrors and amulets containing inscriptions in ancient Sanskrit and representations of old manuscripts written on palm-leaves tied together in bundles.   One or two of the most sacred are inscribed with the quaint label *Pu k'o mo,* "Not to be rubbed," as if it were expected that the ink should be treated as a relic and not used in the ordinary way.   The cakes of ink molded with his signature are cherished as works of art by collectors of the present day.

Having disposed briefly of the writers on other subjects who touch more or less cursorily on the ceramic art, or who throw indirectly some light on the question, we come at last to the special authors on pottery and porcelain.   These are, unfortunately, very few in number.   The subject is looked upon by the *literati* of the high school from two points of view: either that the ordinary bowls, cups, and dishes of every day are too common for their notice, or that porcelain vases and the like of elaborate form and brilliant decoration are too meretricious, and therefore unsuited to the simple tastes of a scholar.   There is always a censor ready to remonstrate with an emperor who is inclined to patronize the art, on the ground of expense; calling his attention to the ancient kings, whose sacrificial vessels were recorded to have been of plain pottery, and who are said to have deemed glaze too great a luxury for their earthenware.   The ancient sages, according to some modern commentators, knew everything, and they explain away the primitive character of rudimentary art, as shown by relics recovered from the ground, by such theories of voluntary abnegation on their part; they were only afraid of exacting too much from the people.

The earliest memoir that we have on the ceramic industry treats it from an economic point of view, deprecates the exactions of the mandarins of the *Yuan* or Mongol dynasty, who looked at it only as a source of revenue, and remonstrates with them as squeezing the poor Chinese potters so remorselessly that they were driving away the industry from its old seat at Ching-tê-chên.   This memoir, under the title of 陶記略, *T'ao Chi Lüo,* "Abstract of Ceramic Records," by 蔣祁, Chiang Ch'i, has been preserved in the annals of the district of Fou-liang ever since it was first printed there in the edition that was published in the year 1322. It has been translated in Chapter VI, and therefore requires no further notice here.

There is no special writer, as far as I know, during the *Ming* dynasty, and we have derived most of our information from the accounts of the imperial manufactory detailed in the official geographical works, in connection with what has been gathered from contemporary writers on art subjects. These accounts are strikingly elucidated by the water-color drawings of the illustrated album 歷代名瓷圖譜, *Li Tai Ming T'zŭ T'ou Pu*, "Illustrated Description of the Celebrated Porcelain of Different Dynasties," by Hsiang Yuan-p'ien, which dates from the latter part of the sixteenth century, and which has been fully described in Chapter V.

T'ang Ying, 唐英, the most celebrated of the superintendents of the imperial manufactory during the present dynasty, is the author of the 陶冶圖說, *T'ao Yeh T'ou Shuo*, the description of the twenty illustrations of the manufacture of porcelain, which was translated in Chapter XV. The other articles from his pen which have been referred to were mostly written as introductory to or as part of the accounts of the work of the imperial factory in the official books. The articles are entitled 陶成記, *T'ao ch'êng chi*, "Records of the Ceramic Manufacture," or 陶成示諭稿, *T'ao ch'êng shih yü k'ao*, "Leaflets of the Regulations of the Ceramic Manufacture." They are doubtless included in the collected works of

FIG. 379.—Gourd of K'ang-hsi period, decorated in blue with bands of gray crackle and buff mono-chrome; European silver mounts.

T'ang Ying, which the author of the *Ching-tê-chên T'ao lu* (Book VI, folio 3) refers to as having been issued with an introductory eulogistic preface by Li Chü-lai of Lin-ch'uan, in the province of Kiangsi, but which I have not had an opportunity of consulting.

The special work on the ceramic art that is always referred to when the subject is discussed by the learned in China is the 陶說, *T'ao Shuo*, a comprehensive description of pottery and porcelain by Chu Yen, which was first published in the thirty-ninth year of the reign of the Emperor *Ch'ien-lung* (1774). The author 朱琰, Chu Yen, whose literary appellation was 桐川, T'ung-ch'uan, was also known as 笠亭, Li-t'ing, the latter being his "hall-name" or *nom-de-plume*, under which a selection of his writings was published. He was a native of Hai-yen, in the province of Chekiang, and was a voluminous writer, judging from a long list of his works given in the preface, which was composed by a relative of the author to introduce a new edition of the *T'ao Shuo*

issued in the year 1787, which is the best edition. This list comprises twelve different works besides the present one, which is characterized as being the most important of all, and includes "A Commentary on the *Shuo Wên*," the ancient dictionary of the second century A. D., "Selections from old Prose Authors and Poets of the *T'ang* and other Dynasties," "Instruction for Playing the Lyre," "On the Art of Versification," etc., winding up with a "Collection of Verses of his own [Li T'ing's] Composition." He is described by his contemporaries as a learned scholar and antiquarian, and when he was appointed in the year 1767 to a post in the secretariat of Wu Shao-shih, who was the governor of the province of Kiangsi from 1766 to 1771, he at once proceeded to study the history of the ceramic industry, the porcelain of Ching-tê-chên being the most important product of the province of Kiangsi.

The title *T'ao Shuo* means literally "Discussion of Pottery," the word *t'ao* being equivalent to "pottery" (*la céramique*) in its widest sense, and made to comprise all kinds of clay objects fired in the kiln, so as to include the different varieties of earthenware, glazed and unglazed, faïence and stoneware (*grès*), as well as porcelain. The form of the book consists of a series of extracts bearing on the subject gathered from the wide field of native literature, in the course of which nearly a hundred and fifty different authors are quoted. This is accomplished by a running commentary in the form of notes, which are distinguished by having the character *an* prefixed to each paragraph, and by having the columns of type printed on a lower level, so as to leave a wider interspace at the top of the page. The general scope of the work will be indicated by a glance at the table of contents which follows:

Book I. Discussion of Modern Times. An account of the porcelain made at Jao-chou-fu during the present dynasty. The description of the twenty illustrations of the porcelain manufacture from the Imperial Library, written in 1743 by T'ang Ying, director of the imperial manufactory.

Book II. Discussion of Ancient Times. The invention and early history of pottery. Researches on the productions of the different potteries, from the beginning of the *T'ang* dynasty, in 618, to the close of the *Yuan* dynasty, in 1367.

Book III. Discussion of the *Ming* Period. The Jao-chou-fu potteries and the porcelain produced at the imperial manufactory there during the *Ming* dynasty (1368–1643). The processes of manufacture during this dynasty under the headings: 1. Materials and Colors. 2. Departments of Work. 3. Coloring Materials and their Preparation. 4. Painted Decoration in Underglaze Cobalt - Blue. 5. Embossed Work, Incised Designs, Decoration in Gold and in Overglaze Enamel Colors. 6. The making of the Cases or Seggars. 7. Furnaces and the Methods of Charging them. 8. Rules for Firing the Porcelain.

Book IV. Discussion of Particular Ceramic Objects, Part I. 1. Objects of the *T'ang* and *Yü* (third millennium B. C.), referred to in old books. 2. Objects of the *Chou* dynasty (B. C. 1122–249). 3. Objects of the *Han* dynasty (B. C. 206, A. D. 224). 4. Objects of the *Wei* dynasty (A. D. 221–264). 5. Objects of the *Chin* dynasty (A. D. 265–419). 6. Objects of the contemporary Southern and Northern dynasties (420–588). 7. Objects of the *Sui* dynasty (589–617).

Book V. Discussion of Particular Ceramic Objects, Part II. 8. Objects of the *T'ang* dynasty (618–906). 9. Objects of the five dynasties (907–959). 10. Objects of the *Sung* dynasty (960–1279). 11. Objects of the *Yuan* dynasty (1280–1367).

Book VI. Discussion of Particular Ceramic Objects, Part III. 12. Objects of the *Ming* dynasty (1368–1643). Description of some sacrificial utensils made for imperial worship. Porcelain of the reign of *Yung-lo*. Porcelain of the reign of *Hsüan-tê*. Porcelain of the reign of *Ch'êng-hua*. Porcelain of the reign of *Chia-ching*, under the headings: (1) Specimens painted in blue on a white ground. (2) Blue specimens; being either decorated in white reserve on a blue ground, or coated with single - colored glazes, viz., in cobalt - blue of lighter or darker shade, or in turquoise-blue derived from copper. (3) Specimens decorated in blue outside, with the interior of the bowl or cup glazed white. (4) White porcelain; either plain, or with decoration incised at the point in the paste under the white glaze. (5) Brown porcelain of the *fond-laque* or "dead-leaf" type; in two shades of dark brown or "old gold" tint, either plain or engraved, under the glaze. (6) Single colors, such as coral-red, green, and imperial yellow, and mixed decorations, not included in the other classes. Porcelain of the reign of *Lung-ch'ing*. Porcelain of the reign of *Wan-li*, including: (*a*) Specimens in blue and white; (*b*) Specimens decorated in enamel colors; (*c*) Specimens of single colors, and of complicated decoration not included in the other two classes. Reproductions of the ivory-white Ting-chou porcelain. The dawn-red wine-cups and the eggshell cups of Hao Shih-chiu, a celebrated potter of the reign of *Wan-li*.

In the 1787 edition of the *T'ao Shuo*, which is now before me, there are no less than four eulogistic prefaces and appendices from different hands. One of them, dated in the cyclical year *chia-wu* (1774), is by Pao T'ing-po, the learned editor and publisher of the large collection of reprints issued in the eighteenth century under the title of 知不足齋叢書, *Chih pu tsu chai ts'ung shu*. Some Chinese books are to be found only in these vast collections of reprints, which are analogous to Bohn's Miscellany, only that all the works are published at the same time instead of being issued at intervals.*

The work that has just been described is mainly literary and antiquarian in its character, and it is, besides, more than a century old. For a more recent account of the ceramic art in China we must turn to the 景德鎮陶錄, *Ching tê chên T'ao lu*, "History of the Ceramic Industry at Ching-tê-chên," which has been partially and somewhat imperfectly translated into French.† In the professed translation there is a complete rearrangement of the order of the books, and a short analysis of the plan of the original may not be out of place here. The author, Lan P'u, whose literary appellation was Pin-nan, was a native of Ching-tê-chên, who lived, he tells us, in the midst of the porcelain works, and was constantly taking notes of the various technical details with a view to publishing a book on the subject. But he died toward the end of the reign of *Ch'ien-lung*, at the close of the eighteenth century, and his manuscript was put by for twenty years, his widow lacking funds to publish it. In the sixteenth year of the reign of *Chia-ch'ing* (1811) a new governor, or chief magistrate, named Liu Ping, was appointed to Fou-liang-hsien, and he happened to engage, as teacher for one of his sons, Chêng T'ing-kuei, who had been educated as a scholar by Lan P'u. The professor introduced his old master's book to the notice of the new governor, who requested

---

* See Wylie's *Notes on Chinese Literature*. The Appendix, pages 205–224, contains the titles of some of these collections and lists of their contents.

† *Histoire et Fabrication de la Porcelaine Chinoise.* Ouvrage traduit du Chinois, par M. Stanislas Julien, Membre de l'Institut. Paris, 1856.

him to edit it, and it was finally published in the year 1815, with a preface by Liu Ping, and a post-face by the editor, Chêng T'ing-kuei. As explained in the appendix, the editor re-arranged the manuscript and divided it into eight sections, which form Books II to IX of the printed work. Book I contains a map of the district, a plan of the imperial manufactory, and a series of fourteen illustrations of the different processes of work, which were sketched on the spot by Chêng Hsiu, a brother of the editor, and offer a fairly complete picture of the industry as it is carried on in the present day. The plates in the French translation differ considerably from these, being squeezed laterally into half the space, and being, besides, occa-sionally combined together, so as to confuse some of the details of the work, and they have even been completed, when thought necessary, by the insertion of parts of pictures taken from Chinese albums of much older date. The descriptions of the fourteen illustrations are mostly abridged, as is avowed by the editor, from those of the famous twenty illustrations described for the Emperor *Ch'ien-lung* by T'ang Ying. Book X, entitled "Supplementary Observations," is mainly the work of the new editor, assisted by a string of *collaborateurs*, some with techni-cal knowledge of the art derived from personal experience, whose names he gives at the end of the book.

The following is the original table of contents:

Book I. Illustrations of Technical Processes with Descriptions.

Book II. Records of the Imperial Porcelain Manufactory under the reigning dynasty. Origin of the various kinds of porcelain made at Ching-tê-chên.

Book III. Technical Catalogue, enumerating the different furnaces and the classes of firemen employed, the various branches of manual decorative and artistic work, the auxiliary branches of work, the forms and designs of objects, the various kinds of glazes and the coloring materials used in their preparation, etc.

Book IV. General Account of the Porcelain Manufacture as it is carried on in the present day.

Book V. Examination of the porcelain made at Ching-tê-chên during successive dynasties, beginning with the first year (583) of the period *Chih-tê*, in the reign of the last sovereign of the *Ch'ên* dynasty, and ending with the reign of *Ch'ien-lung* of the present dynasty (1736–95).

Book VI. Examination of the different kinds of ancient porcelain that are now imitated at Ching-tê-chên.

Book VII. Investigation of ancient ceramic wares. Examination of the ceramic productions of the different provinces and districts, including those of the present day. Investigation of foreign productions, referring cursorily to Korean ceramic ware, and to painted and *cloisonné* enamels on copper introduced into China from the West.

Book VIII. Miscellaneous quotations on the ceramic subject from different authors, Part I.

Book IX. Miscellaneous quotations on the ceramic subject, Part II.

Book X. Supplementary observations on some points in the foregoing work by the editor, Chêng T'ing-kuei.

The first and last books are the additions of the new editor, who tells us that the other eight represent the original work, in his own words, of his old master Lan P'u.

The *T'ao Lu* is indispensable for an inquirer into the technology of the ceramic industry in China, and its statements may be relied upon as being generally taken from actual personal knowledge, but in the historical and critical accounts of the ancient productions it is decidedly inferior to the *T'ao Shuo*. The author relies mainly on the *Wên Fang Ssŭ K'ao*, which has already been referred to as one of the least critical of those which relate to the apparatus of the scholar's study.

With the exception of mere manuals for the use of the curio-dealer, I have seen nothing of later date, so that we have no more recent work of authority on the subject, and, in truth, the decadence of the ceramic art in modern times is so rapid that it scarcely deserves a chronicler.

FIG. 380.—Mishima Bowl of dark stoneware, enameled with a white glaze with incised designs filled in with encaustic black clay; (2) Conical Archaic Bowl of Korean faïence, of yellowish color stippled with darker spots; from an old tomb.

CHAPTER XXIV.

KOREA.

Korea an intermediary between China and Japan. A class of early Japanese decorated porcelain wrongly attributed to Korea. Questionable existence of an indigenous ceramic art in the country. Notices in Chinese literature of early Korean productions. Ancient crackled and celadon examples in Korea. Korean Mishima ware and other early encaustic decorations. Relics dug up from tombs. Modern ceramic manufactures.

KOREA is situated midway between China and Japan, and derives its chief importance from having been the medium of the introduction of the arts and sciences from the mainland of Asia into the Japanese islands. The earlier ceramic relations of the three countries have been cursorily summed up in Chapter II, and it was noticed there how the Japanese traced back the source of each successive step in their practice of the ceramic art either to Korea or to China. Korea would seem, however, merely to have played the part of an intermediary, and to have carried on to Japan the knowledge of technical points which it had derived from China in the course of its traffic with the latter country. This traffic has been principally carried on by sea from the ports of the province of Shantung. Korea has only recently been thrown open, but the country has been thoroughly explored during the last few years, and it is now known that no artistic pottery is produced there in the present day, and no indisputable evidence of any original skill in former times has been discovered.

Before the poverty of the land was laid bare it was possible, with some show of probability, to attribute to it the possession of unknown art treasures, and Jacquemart accordingly endowed Korea with a class of decorated porcelain of artistic beauty and perfect finish, which he styled *Famille archaïque de Corée*, under the mistaken idea that the mixed Japanese and Chinese character of the designs indicated an intermediate origin. We are indebted, however, to his artistic faculty for the separation of this class from other Oriental porcelains, and for its correct designation as "archaic," for it seems really to have been one of the earliest productions in enamel colors of the Arita kilns of Japan. The porcelain of this class was among the first brought to Europe from Japan by the Dutch, whose original trading establishment was at Hirado, not far from the Arita kilns. The importation of the artistic ware appears to have ceased before the end of the seventeenth century, so that specimens were eagerly sought for by the earlier collectors in Europe, who gave them a prominent place in their cabinets under the name of *première qualité coloriée du Japon*. The description of several pieces may be found in the *Catalogue de la vente de M. Randon de Boisset*, which was compiled by the French expert Julliot in 1777, who writes:

"The late collector, endowed with a delicate and severe taste, gathered together important examples of several kinds, and most particularly of the ancient Japanese porcelain called *première qualité coloriée*, for which, as a true connoisseur, he had a special predilection. This porcelain, of which the composition is now entirely lost, has always captivated the attention of amateurs by the fine grain of its beautifully white paste, the charming tints of its soft reds, the velvety tones of its clear greens, and its intense sky-blue. The merits of this class of porcelain are perfectly recognized, so that some of the best collections are, or have been, composed of it, which alone is its sufficient eulogy."

This peculiar class, in fact, is readily identified by its fine compact paste of ivory-white tone, which has been justly likened to that of the Hirado blue and white porcelain, invested with a thin non-vitreous glaze, and simply decorated, in soft enamels, with a few formal flowers symmetrically posed, or a clump of bamboos rising from behind a trellis fence of straw. The flowers are usually the iris, chrysanthemum, pink, or peony; the light ornamental borders are triangular or rectangular frets or zigzags; birds or symbolical animals are rarely seen, still more rarely figures. The designs, sketched either in black or in red, are lightly touched with soft colors, combined with the perfect harmony that distinguishes old Japanese art; the decoration being sparingly applied, as if to display as much as possible of the perfectly white ground. The dominating color is a well-glazed iron-red of rich tone; the other colors, applied in enamels so as to stand out in relief upon the surface, are a pale clear green, a pure sky-blue, a light yellow, and a brilliant black; the gold is applied more solidly than usual; blue under the glaze is excluded. The vases and jars are generally small and of polygonal outline, of molded forms, and not fashioned upon the wheel; the bowls and cups are fluted and flanged, and often provided with socketed stands. A typical example of this charming class is represented by the saké-bottle of square section illustrated in colors in Plate XCVII, Fig. 1, which is reasonably attributed to the middle of the seventeenth century.

Some other specimens are illustrated in colors by Du Sartel, in *La Porcelaine de Chine*, to which reference has often been made.

Pieces of this peculiar type supplied the first models for many of the early porcelain works of Europe. At Meissen the imitations were very close, as may be seen in the Dresden Museum, where the originals and the copies are purposely exhibited side by side. They were also copied at St. Cloud; at Chelsea, on pieces bearing the earliest mark—the raised anchor; at Bow, on the plates decorated with quails, and elsewhere. There is a bowl of Bow porcelain in the British Museum decorated in the same style as the plates with quails, having an inscription upon it stating that it was "painted by Thomas Croft in 1760 in the old Japan taste"; which shows, as Sir Wollaston Franks remarks, "that both in England and France this porcelain was recognized to be Japanese, and of some antiquity." So it was in China, for it was exactly reproduced in the factories at Ching-tê-chên during the second half of the reign of *K'ang-hsi* (1662–1722), under the name of *Tung Yang Ts'ai* or Japanese colors, so that some care must be taken not to confound these early Chinese copies with the originals, the main criterion being the different quality of the *pâte*, besides the frequent occurrence of "spur-marks"* underneath the foot of the Japanese pieces.

This appears to have been the earliest decorated porcelain brought in any considerable quantity to Europe from the East. It was imported into Holland in the ships of the Dutch East India Company and distributed by them under the title of *porcelaine des Indes*. The Dutch seem also to have exercised some influence over its decoration in Japan, according to an interesting passage quoted by Jacquemart from the account of the embassy of the Dutch Governor who was sent by the company to Yedo in the year 1634, and who was rewarded afterward for the success of his mission by being given the monopoly of the valuable traffic in porcelain. We are told there: †

"While the Sieur Wagenaar was preparing for his return voyage to Batavia, he received 21,567 pieces of white porcelain; and a month previously a very large quantity had arrived at Disma [that is Desima or Deshima], which, however, had not had a great sale because there were not flowers enough upon it. For some years past the Japanese have applied themselves to this kind of work with much industry, and they have become so skillful at it that not only the Dutch, but even the Chinese buy of them. The best porcelain is that which is made at Fisen (Hizen), the earth at no other place being so white or so fine as it is here. The Sieur Wagenaar, a great connoisseur, and very clever himself at this kind of work, invented a flower design upon a blue ground which was found to be

---

* The slender projections of the paste designed to support the piece and prevent contact with the floor of the kiln are technically known as "cock-spurs." They are broken off afterward, and leave small rough marks on the glaze. They are found occasionally, although rarely, on Chinese pieces. The Chinese technical term is *t'o-chih*, or "supporting twigs."

† *Ambassades Mémorables de la Compagnie des Indes Orientales des Provinces Unies vers les Empereurs du Japon.* Amsterdam, 1680, folio; IIe partie, p. 102.

so pretty that out of two hundred pieces on which he had it painted not a single one remained unsold, so that there was not a shop without some of it on display."

The first porcelain manufactory in the province of Hizen was founded in the beginning of the seventeenth century near Arita by Li Sanpei (or Risampei), a Korean potter who was brought over in 1598 in the suite of Prince Nabeshima. He discovered the necessary materials in the neighborhood in the Idzumi Mountains, and initiated the Japanese workmen in the new art. The earliest decoration is said to have been penciled in cobalt-blue under the glaze after the fashion of the faïence that previously had been made there. The honor of acquiring for Japan the art of painting in enamel colors applied over the glaze is generally attributed to Tokuzayemon, a native of Imari in the same province, who is supposed to have learned it from a Chinese resident at Nagasaki about the middle of the century. But the

clear vitreous enamel colors of the muffle stove which distinguish this class of porcelain were not known at this time in Chinese ceramic decoration, and when they were introduced into China, in the latter half of the reign of *K'ang-hsi*, their source was acknowledged to be foreign. In India they had been previously used for centuries in enamel painting upon metal. Their introduction into Japan seems to have been due to the Dutch, at a time when the factories at Ching-tê-chên were closed on account of the wars at the end of the *Ming* dynasty, and their usual supplies of porcelain from that source had failed. The influence of the Dutch in the further development of the ceramic art in Japan is shown in a more marked degree in the polychromatic "old Imari ware," which gradually supplanted the more artistic and simply decorated porcelain that has just been referred to.

FIG. 381.—Shaped Dish of "Old Japan" Imari ware, richly decorated in brilliant colors with gilding.

This porcelain, decorated in the style of the many-colored Chinese production of the *Wan-li* period with blue under the glaze in combination with overglaze enamel colors and gilding, became the established ware of the Hizen potteries by the year 1680.

Fig. 381 shows a typical example of one of the more finely decorated pieces of the period. The foliated border and the interior of the dish, divided into panels by lines of underglaze blue, are filled with diapers of varied design, and the slope is encircled by a broad band with four-clawed dragons of Chinese type disporting in clouds. The overglaze colors are a full iron-red, brilliant green, yellow, and manganese-purple, the last three being in strong relief. The under surface of the rim is roughly painted in dark blue under the glaze with sprays of flowers and symbols in panels. There are several spur-marks underneath.

This is a choice specimen of the richly ornamented ware known in Europe *par excellence* as "Old Japan," which was fashioned and decorated expressly for the European market, and was imported in large quantities into Europe toward the end of the seventeenth century, when Augustus the Strong filled his Japanese Palace with the magnificent jars and beakers and the huge dishes which are still displayed in the museum at Dresden. There is no longer any question here of sparse decoration such as we are told made the older porcelain unsalable, the surface being covered with mythological monsters and gorgeously plumaged birds in the midst of profuse floral sprays of chrysanthemum and peony. There is no space in a modest Japanese interior for such monstrosities, and the native connoisseur can hardly be brought to acknowledge them as genuine productions of his own country, any more than he will accept the large vases decorated with armies of mail-clad figures or legions of saints that are painted in Yokohama to-day for the foreign market, and which figure in the West as fair representatives of the modern ceramic art of Japan.

This long digression is preparatory to the introduction of the vexed question of the existence of polychromatic decoration in Korea before the date of its introduction into Japan. The description of three remarkable specimens may be quoted from the catalogue* of the Brinkley Collection, which was exhibited at the Boston Museum of Arts in 1884, where they are described as " Korean Ware."

" ELEPHANT, on stand. Height, five and a half inches; length, seven inches. Heavy stoneware, covered with a cream-colored glaze slightly crackled. The trappings of the elephant are black; his feet, ears, mouth, and howdah-cloth are of a reddish brown. Date, 1260."

" VASE, with narrow base and swelling body. Height, thirteen inches; diameter, twelve inches. Stoneware cream-colored glaze finely crackled. Round the base and shoulder are lines and a band of diaper. On the sides are three large medallions bordered by broad black lines. One medallion contains the figure of an old man seated; behind him is a fir-tree with a gourd hanging from its branches; before him, conventional waves and a design intended to represent the constellation of *ursa major* (*Sh'chiya no hoshi*). The second medallion contains a stork flying down toward reeds and lotus-plants. The third, an open lily, surrounded by leaves. All the decoration is in very dark brown, and the inside is covered with a glaze of that color. Date, 1300."

" VASE, with narrow base and swelling body. Height, eleven and a half inches; diameter, twelve inches. Stoneware, covered inside and outside with a cream-colored glaze. Round the neck are two bands of floral scroll in red and green enamels. Round the base a band of conventional leaves. Round the body are three large medallions. In one is a man seated on a fish swimming in green waves; in the distance are mountains and a castle. In another are two figures with trees, a hill, etc., in green and red. Date, 1300. [This is a very remarkable specimen. Korean ware decorated with colored enamels is exceedingly rare—so much so, indeed, that its very existence has been doubted. The present specimen has been preserved in the province of Kaga, in Japan, since 1598.] "

There is another archaic-looking ware often attributed by Japanese experts to Korea, which has crude designs lightly penciled in dull blue overlaid with a deeply crackled glaze of grayish tone. The paste is of open porous texture, like the old Tingchou productions of China, and the general aspect of the pieces reminds one of the ancient crackled wares of Chinese origin treasured by the Dayaks in Borneo and in other islands of the Eastern Archipelago. A specimen which was brought from Japan as a piece of ancient Korean ware is presented in Fig. 134. It is a small globular vase roughly decorated in dark blue with a broad band round the body containing two lions sporting with filleted balls, and a narrow band of conventional ornament encircling the shoulder. The thick glaze, of ivory-white tone, is crackled with deeply fissured lines, and covers the base, only leaving the foot-rim exposed, which is white, of porous texture, but intensely hard; there is no mark inscribed underneath.

With regard to the porcelain objects sent from Japan as old Korean, it is necessary, first, to show that the particular piece is not a modern reproduction; secondly, that it is not an old piece of one of the less known Chinese wares which may have been brought to Japan through Korea. There are two Chinese wares, for instance, which often figure as Korean upon the shelves of museums. The first is the Tz'ŭ-chou ceramic ware of the Chihli province, which is decorated in shades of brown, and like the peculiar class of Satsuma known as "Sunkoroku," to which reference will presently be made. The second is the ivory-white porcelain of the province of Fuchien. Ten pieces of so-called Korean ivory-white porcelain were exhibited at the Boston Museum of Arts in 1884. Captain Brinkley says, in regard to this ivory-white porcelain, that " it is often exceedingly difficult to distinguish it from Chinese ware, and, indeed, the question is still open whether the so-called Korean ivory-white is not porcelain of Chinese manufacture, which found its way to Japan through Korea. Japanese experts maintain obstinately that such is not the case. They profess to recognize without difficulty a difference between the Chinese and Korean paste, and by way of historical confirmation adduce

* *Collection of Japanese, Chinese, and Korean Porcelain, Pottery, and Faïence, illustrating all the Best-known Wares of the Three Countries*, p. 111, Nos. 779–781.

the authenticated fact that from the time of her invasion by Taiko's armies (1596), and the consequent paralysis of all her art industries, Korea entirely ceased to send Japan any specimens of the beautiful ivory-white porcelain, though its great value to the latter country, as well as Korea's intimate relations with China, rendered such a traffic more than ever probable."

There is also an ancient brown stoneware attributed to Korea coated with a thick crackled glaze resembling very closely the old Chinese crackle of the *Yuan* dynasty (1280–1367), which has been illustrated in Fig. 3.

The only certain information that we have about old Korean porcelain is derived from Chinese sources. The first Chinese author who alludes to it at any length is Hsü Ching, who wrote the *Hsüan-ho fêng shih Kao-li t'ou ching,* * an illustrated description of the country, customs, and institutions of Korea (*Kao-li*), in forty books, after his return from a mission to the country on the occasion of an accession of a new king, in 1125. The maps and illustrations which originally accompanied the manuscript were unfortunately lost before the book was printed for the first time, in the year 1167. The following is a literal translation of his notes upon the subject:

" There is a ceramic ware made in Korea of green color, which is called by the natives of the country 'kingfisher green.' In these latter years the pieces have been more skillfully fashioned, and the color of the glaze has also been much improved. There are wine-pots (*chiu tsun*) molded in the shape of melons, with small lids at the top surmounted by ducks squatting in the midst of lotus-flowers. The Koreans are clever also in the making of bowls and dishes (*wan, tieh*), wine-cups and teacups (*pei, ou*), flower vases (*hua p'ing*), and hot-water vessels for tea-drinkers (*t'ang chan*), which are all, generally speaking, copied from the forms of the Ting-chou wares (of China), so that I need only allude to them and not illustrate them by figures, only giving the wine-pots, as being of novel and original design.

" In Korea the table vessels used at entertainments for eating and drinking are usually made of gilded metal or of silver, although they esteem green porcelain ware more highly than either of these two materials. They have incense-burners (*hsiang lu*) shaped like lions, which are also of 'kingfisher green' color, the four-footed monster being represented seated upon a lotus-leaf with tilted margin, which forms the stand of the urn. This is one of the most ingenious and striking of their ceramic designs; the other forms are for the most part modeled after the shapes of the ancient imperial porcelain of Yueh-chou, or from the modern productions of the kilns of Ju-chou.

" The pottery made by the Koreans includes also large water-jars (*wêng*), with broad bellies and contracted necks ending in very small mouths, which are as much as six feet high and four and a half feet in diameter, and hold between fifty and one hundred gallons of water each. These are used for storing water on the boats passing upon the sea between islands when water is difficult to procure, so as to carry on board a sufficient supply."

The term "kingfisher green," used here, is intended to indicate the light blue-green tint of the plumes of the kingfisher's feathers, which are much used in the East for inlaying gold and silver ornaments of jewelry. The clear emerald-green color of jadeite, which is so highly prized by the Chinese, has earned for it a similar title of "kingfisher stone" (*fei-ts'ui*).

In ceramic parlance the term indicates the translucent emerald-green hue of the old celadon glazes, which approach sometimes an olive tint. The color was obtained in China by the mixture of an iron mineral with the ordinary white glaze of the *grand feu*, darkened by the addition of a variable proportion of the cobaltiferous ore of manganese, and the term was adopted to distinguish the new color from the deeper camellia-leaf green of the older wares, which was derived from copper. The most ancient Korean porcelain of which we have any certain knowledge is really a celadon monochrome of the characteristic tint of this beautiful variety of jadeite. A pair of bowls of this kind were presented by the King of Korea to President Carnot, of France, as "the most valuable of the ancient productions of his poor country," and are now preserved in the museum at Sèvres. There is a similar bowl, gadrooned below with a border of lotus-petal design, in the Dana collection at New York, which was, I believe, originally given by the King of Korea as a present to an American physician who had been consulted by him.

The next notice of Korean ceramic ware is in the *Ko ku yao lun*, the well-known book on objects of art by Ts'ao chao, published in 1387, which has been so often quoted. The short paragraph on "Korean Ceramic Manufacture" (*Kao-li Yao*), in Book VII, folio 22, says:

---

* See *Notes on Chinese Literature*, by A. Wylie, *loc. cit.*, p. 46.

" The ceramic objects produced in the ancient Korean kilns were of a grayish-green color resembling that of the celadon ware of Lung-ch'üan (in China). There was one kind overlaid with white sprays of flowers, but this was not valued so very highly."

These are the conclusions of a Chinese connoisseur of the fourteenth century. The second class which he refers to is a faïence inlaid with encaustic designs in white clay, like the so-called *Henri Deux* faïence in Europe, and it was, on the contrary, most highly valued in Japan, and formed the model of some of the early Japanese manufactures, like the Yatsu-shiro faïence of the province of Higo, which was decorated with storks flying among clouds, in the Korean style, or with simple combinations of lines and diapers, the designs being traced in the paste and filled in with white clay before glazing. A typical vase of ancient Korean work of this kind is illustrated in Plate CXVI. The decoration was occasionally varied by the execution of a portion of the encaustic designs in black.

The vogue attained in Japan by the tea ceremonies known as the *cha-no-yu* under the Ashikaga Shoguns was the chief cause of the great popularity of Korean pottery in that coun-

Fig. 382.—Old Korean Bowl, with a lightly incised decoration under a buff-tinted celadon glaze, sparsely and superficially crackled.

try. The first fixed rules for the cult seem to have been made under the patronage of the Shogun Yoshimasa (1443–73), after he had retired to private life in this last year. The famous Taiko Hideyoshi in 1594 appointed Sen-no-Rikyu, a celebrated virtuoso, to revise the old statutes of the cult, and the elaborate code of etiquette drawn up by him has hardly been varied since his day. Up to this time utensils of Korean pottery had been preferred to any others for the tea ceremonial, and the Korean experts of the craft who were brought over to Japan at the end of the sixteenth century, after the expedition to Korea in 1592–96, introduced their technique into several of the Japanese manufac-tories. Nearly all Japan's chief potteries are said to have dated from that time, her teachers in the art of porcelain-making being

Korean captives. In the following century a number of Korean potters settled at Yatsushiro, in the province of Higo, and the Japanese pottery produced there still preserves unmistakable char-acteristics of its Korean origin, the fine reddish *pâte* being enameled with a diaphanous, pearl-gray glaze, uniform, lustrous, and finely crackled, overlying encaustic decoration in white slip.

One class of Korean tea-bowls is known to the Japanese by the name of Mishima ware, because the formal lines of its decoration resemble at a distance the printed columns of the almanac which is issued from a famous temple at Mishima on the Tokaido, the great route from Kioto to Yedo. There is a Mishima basin in the Franks collection in the British Museum, which was sent from Japan as Korean, but is considered by the learned curator to be more probably a production of the Yatsushiro kiln, and is described by him as follows:

" BASIN. Gray glazed Japanese stoneware, with engraved designs, filled in with white clay. Inside, a chrysan-themum surrounded by similar flowers; and inside and out, borders of zigzag pattern with hatched lines. Mishima ware. Diameter, five and a half inches. No. 1185."

The shallow bowl illustrated in Fig. 380 (1), which is of the same diameter as the above, was also sent from Japan as an example of Korean Mishima ware, but is pronounced by Mr. H. Shugio to be a Japanese reproduction of the old Korean style, judging from the peculiarities of the *pâte*. This is of dark reddish-gray color, and is enameled with a white glaze of soft aspect, decorated in geometrical patterns with formal bands of vertical lines and encircling rings of diaper, which are lightly etched with a graving-tool, and filled in with black.

Among the other ancient Korean bowls in the collection is the one illustrated in Fig. 382, which is of rounded conical shape with upright edge, and has a solid circular rim round the foot. It is coated with a smooth celadon glaze of buff tone, sparsely crackled, and is roughly scored in the paste underneath with ornamental lines both outside and inside, the pattern in the interior simulating a flower. The foot, and a portion of the exterior surface, where the glaze does not reach the bottom, show a light-red paste, which is roughened in crêpe-like fashion. The bowl, broken into fragments, has been pieced together and cemented with gold lacquer in Japan.

In former times it was the custom in Korea, as well as in China, to bury pottery with the dead, the pottery vessels employed for the purpose being a flask filled with wine and a set of

bowls containing a provision In more recent times it has tries to place the funeral the grave. It is a capital up this pottery, but speci- way into collections, not-

The bowl illustrated in was brought from Seul, the Walter C. Hillier, H. B. M. gether with a small saucer- ware dug up from an old conical shape, two inches inches in diameter, pale-colored faïence, yellowish glaze with darker spots. glazed, exhibits points of mica, perfectly tritu-

There is no rean pottery, so any more modern and, in truth, the of the present time worthy of notice, kind possible, and any artistic interest. specimens in the and The Hague are mon description, elers confirm the lequin, who collect-

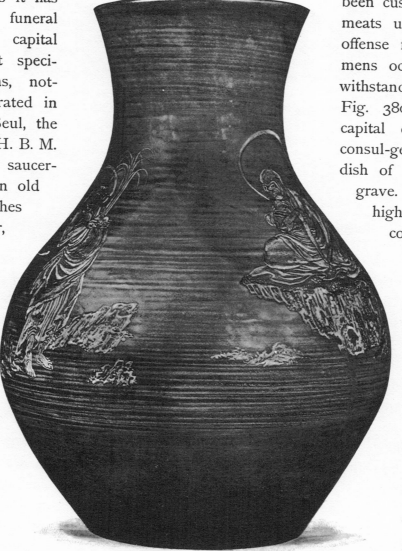

FIG. 383.—Temple Vase of Takatori pottery, enameled with a crackled green glaze of mottled tint, decorated in slip in low relief with Buddhist figures.

of cooked millet and rice. been customary in both coun- meats upon an altar above offense for a Korean to dig mens occasionally find their withstanding.

Fig. 380 (2), for example, capital of Korea, by Mr. consul-general in Korea, to- dish of Korean ivory-white grave. It is of archaic high, five and a half composed of a hard coated with a thin thickly flecked The foot, un- many glistening marks of an im- rated clay.

mention of Ko- far as I know, by Chinese writer, ceramic productions seem to be hardly being of the crudest quite devoid of The few authentic museum at Leyden of the most com- and all recent trav- accounts of M. Bil- ed some pieces at

Peking for the museum at Sèvres, and recorded his experiences in the *Gazette des Beaux-Arts*, 1877, page 230. Japan certainly owes many of the technical methods of the different varieties of the old Satsuma faïence to Korea, and Korean potters were the first instructors in the early productions of most of its porcelain kilns, but the stroke of genius which converted a manual handicraft into a new branch of art was due entirely to the innate artistic faculty of the Japanese themselves. There is no evidence of anything of the kind in Korea.

FIG. 384.—Ornament (Okimono) of Hirado porcelain, molded in the shape of a white colza turnip with blue-tinted leaves, with a rat crouched upon the bulb.

CHAPTER XXV.

CERAMIC ART OF JAPAN.

Introduction. Bibliography. Table of the principal centers of the ceramic industry.

IT is with some diffidence that I approach the subject of the ceramic art of Japan, not being so intimately acquainted with it as with that of China, and having, moreover, a very superficial knowledge of the language and literature. I have been fortunate in having had the opportunity of referring any doubtful points as to the date of a piece, or its origin, to Mr. Henry Walters and to Mr. Shugio. At the outset I acknowledge my indebtedness to them. Much more has been written in Europe upon Japanese porcelain and pottery than upon Chinese, and the former is, consequently, far better and more generally known, so that a lengthy disquisition is not necessary here, even did space allow. There are several books, both English and French, available for further reference.

The early relations of Chinese and Japanese ceramics have already been alluded to, and it has been shown how the Japanese acknowledge their debt to China at every step. Chinese is the classical language of the Japanese, and many of the technical books of the latter are written almost entirely in the Chinese script, only the order of the characters being changed, in obedience to the new construction and grammar of a different language. Most of the ceramic terms have been adopted directly from those current in China, and are employed in the same sense, differing only in pronunciation; a few have become obsolete, being used only in books, and being replaced in ordinary parlance by colloquial equivalents. This last is the case with the Chinese *tz'ŭ*, "porcelain," which occurs constantly in the text of Ninagawa Noritane's work, and is used by him to include the ancient fine white kaolinic potteries coated with camellia-leaf green and ash-colored glazes, of which he figures two fragments, in the same way as it is by the Chinese, although we should question the right of such wares to be called "porcelain," on account of their want of translucence. It survives also in the Japanese name of celadon porcelain, which has always been highly esteemed by them under the name of *seiji*,* according to their peculiar pronunciation of the Chinese *ch'ing tz'ŭ*, literally "green porcelain." The ordinary term for porcelain in Japan is *Setomono*, "Seto-ware," Seto being the place in the province of Owari where the first fine glazed pottery was made after a Chinese model, in

---

* With regard to the pronunciation of Japanese letters, in the system of orthography which has been generally followed here, the vowels are to be pronounced as in Italian, the consonants as in English: e. g., *a* as in father; *e* as in prey; *i* as in machine; *o* as in no; *u* as in rule; when a horizontal line is over *o* or *u* the sound is prolonged; diphthongs are *ai*, as in aisle; *au*, with the sound of *ow* in now. Care must be taken to pronounce the vowels separately; in *cha-ire*, "tea-jar," the second word is read ee-ray, and is consequently sometimes written *iré*; in *Ninsei*, the name of the celebrated Kyōto potter, the second syllable, pronounced *say-ee*, may be written *seï*. *N* at the end of a word has the sound of final *n* in French; in the middle, when followed by *b*, *m*, or *p*, it is *m*; and *t*, in combination, is *d*. Consonants often become soft, *chi* or *shi* becoming *ji*; *ho*, bo; *tsu*, dzu; *su*, zu; *ku*, gu, etc. The native dialectal variations and the different orthographical systems of foreigners make consistency difficult, if not impossible, and the efforts of the Romajikwai, a society founded in Japan for the purpose of securing a uniform system of transliteration, have not yet met with the success they deserve.

the thirteenth century of our era, and the term is now used in Japan in the same way as chinaware or china is commonly used by us.

The classical term for "pottery" in its widest sense is *tōki*, the Chinese *t'ao-ch'i* [t'ao-k'i], which comprises in Japan, as it does in China, all kinds of ceramic ware, common earthenware (Japanese *tsuchiyaki*), and the different varieties of stoneware (Japanese *ishiyaki*), as well as true porcelain. *Yaki* means "baked," and *yakimono*, "baked ware," is more commonly used in Japan as the general term for pottery, including all kinds of ware fired in a kiln. The productions of the province of Hizen, for instance, are grouped under the term *Imari-yaki*; those of Kyōto are known as *Kyō-yaki*, and the fine faïence of the province of Satsuma, *Satsuma-yaki*, is so called, as well as the worse stoneware of the province of Bizen, *Bizen-yaki* or *Imbe-yaki*. In this sense "yaki" generally takes the place of the Chinese *yao*, although the latter character occasionally occurs among Japanese marks upon porcelain in the compound *kwan-ko* (Chinese *kuan-yao*), "imperial ware," and *kin-ko* (Chinese *chin-yao*), "brocaded porcelain," as it does also, rarely, in its primitive sense of "kiln" in the potters' mark of *Fu-ji-yo*,* i. e., "Matchless Kiln." The Japanese name of the brocaded silk that has just been referred to under the name of *chin* is *nishiki*, and this is given, by an analogy, to porcelain decorated in enamel colors, which is, however, known also as *go-sai*, the equivalent of *wu-ts'ai*, "five-colored," the technical Chinese name. "Blue and white" is commonly known in Japan as *sometsuke*, which means simply "figured"; "crackled porcelain" is called *hibiyaki*, "hibi" being the equivalent of the Chinese *wên*, "a crack in crockery."

The ceramic wares of Japan exhibit great differences in their composition, texture, and appearance, but may be roughly classed under three principal heads: 1. Common pottery and stoneware, coarse or fine, ornamented by engraving the surface, inlaying with colored clays, and coating it with glazes. 2. A cream-colored faïence, with a glaze, often crackled, and delicately painted in enamel colors. 3. Hard porcelain.

To the first of these classes belong the wares of Bizen and Takatori, old Seto, Shigaraki, and other small fabrics, and it includes the Raku wares of Kyōto. The texture varies from that of the ancient wares of Shigaraki and Iga, which are fashioned in an earth almost as coarse as fine gravel, to that of the Banko-yaki, made in the province of Isé, which has been compared to Wedgwood, the material being a fine brown clay of remarkable toughness, so that it can be molded into extremely light and thin forms. The Raku ware of Kyōto is somewhat soft and tender, while the products of the Bizen province have an almost metallic hardness. The Japanese take advantage of the different qualities of the paste in the fabrication of objects according to the use to which they are intended to be put. The soft paste of the Raku bowls makes them feeble conductors of heat, so that they are preferred by the votaries of the Cha-no-yu to bowls of porcelain or any other material, as they retain the heat in the tea for a longer period, and, moreover, do not burn the hands, as they are clasped in both palms when the tea is sipped in the orthodox way. The remarkable hardness and refractory quality of the Bizen stoneware make it especially suitable for incense-burners, hand braziers, and charcoal stoves, and its fineness and toughness render it a good medium for modeling, to which use it has been put with great success, so that in the pottery of Bizen are to be found the choicest masterpieces of Japanese plastic skill.

The principal factories of the second class are those of Satsuma and Awata, and the more modern establishments at Ota, near Yokohama, and elsewhere, where the recent imitations of the Satsuma ware are produced. Both the Satsuma and the Awata wares, the latter of which are made in one of the suburbs of Kyōto, are made of a kind of porcelain clay of very refractory nature, which does not undergo a partial fusion like the genuine porcelain mixture, or, at any rate, not to the same degree. The glaze is composed of feldspathic materials and lixiviated wood-ash, without any addition of lead or borax; when cooled it is always crackled with a fine network of superficial lines. The final simultaneous baking of the body and the glaze

---

* See the *Franks Catalogue, loc. cit.*, Japanese marks, Plate XIV, Fig. 175.

takes place in a temperature much higher than that to which the so-called biscuit is submitted in the preliminary firing. The soft-looking glaze of ivory-white tone forms an admirable background for the decoration in enamel colors, which is painted on subsequently and fixed by a third firing in the muffle stove. This last is an easy process, so that Satsuma ware is often imported in a plain state, to be painted by artists in the ateliers of Kyōto or Tōkio. The Awata ware is distinguished from the slightly buff-colored Satsuma ware by a more marked yellow tint, which has earned for it the name of *tamago-yaki*, or "egg pottery." The material of both these wares may be considered to be a kind of semi-porcelain.

The third class comprises the true porcelain wares, of which the coarsest are included in the productions of Kutani and Awaji, while the most celebrated fabrics are in the province of Hizen, at Seto in Owari, and Kiyomidzu near Kyōto. A full and detailed account of the materials and technique is given in the second part of *Le Japon à l'Exposition Universelle de 1878*, published at Paris under the authority of the Imperial Japanese Commission, which has been reprinted in Japan under the title *Les Laques et La Céramique du Japon*, Yokohama, 1879. The processes, in the main, are very similar to those followed in China, with the exception of the temperature to which Japanese porcelain is submitted before it is either painted or glazed, which is often conducted in an ordinary malt oven. The clays are evidently less tenacious than the ordinary Chinese kaolins of Ching-tê-chên, hence Japanese specimens are frequently slightly out of shape, and they seem to require numerous supports in the kiln, which have left the scars on the glaze known as "spur-marks," which are rarely found on Chinese pieces.

FIG. 385.—Vase of Kyōto faïence, with a grayish sparsely crackled glaze decorated in enamel colors and gilding, with flowers and insects in the "Nishiki" or brocaded style.

One of the chief charms in the simplicity and marked of Japanese pottery consists originality of the old potter, who was not content with a slavish imitation of the Korean or Chinese model on which the technique of his art was professedly based, but always succeeded in imparting a peculiar *cachet* to his productions, which are not to be confounded with their prototypes. He was truly, in his palmiest days, an artist-potter, and not a mere machine working for the glorification of his brother of the brush. This is shown in the pleasing quaintness of form in which he fashioned the pieces intended for the personal use of his daimyo patron, and in the loving care which he devoted to their finish, rude as they look at first sight to an untrained eye. The Japanese artist is not ashamed of his hands or his tools, and just as he delights to show the marks of the brush in a rapid sketch or a line of bold calligraphy, so does he prefer to retain the natural prints of the fingers impressed on the soft clay as the piece is being molded, or even to accentuate the marks of the spatula with which it is being roughly shaped and decorated. The simpler the decoration of this rustic pottery the better, and the greatest triumph of the artist is to suggest a pine wood on the seashore or a silhouette of the sacred volcano of Fujisan (Fuji-no-yama), in a single curved line. As a people, the Japanese are singularly free from ostentation, and their homes exhibit a simplicity and refinement in all their surroundings which render them unique. They are devoted admirers of Nature's art. As in woodwork the ornamental value of the natural grain or the rugosities of the bark are considered of such high interest that remarkable specimens are accorded the most honorable place in the house; as in metal-work the natural patina is looked upon as its chief beauty; so in earthenware the earthiness of earth has to them a charm which should not be hidden, but developed by the work of the artist. The art of it lies in the eloquence it displays of its earthy nature, just as the art of old Venetian glass lies in the witness it bears of its vitreous nature.

I am following here the argument of Mr. Charles Holme, the author of the sympathetic chapter on *Pottery and Porcelain*, in the excellent work on *Japan and its Art* by Mr. M. B. Huish, the well-known editor of *The Art Journal*, in which periodical the articles first appeared that are now collected into a small volume that ought to be in the hands of every student of the subject. Mr. Holme speaks with some authority, having devoted much time to the question both in England and in Japan, and from the producer's as well as the artistic point of view. He is defending the simple taste of the native school of connoisseurs and of those who follow them against the views of the European collectors, who reserve their highest admiration for such examples of the ceramic as display a more florid and elaborate style of decoration painted in rich colors with a profuse use of gold and silver.

Mr. Holme's account of the colored glazes used in decoration may also be quoted with advantage : *

"Toshiro, a Japanese potter of the early thirteenth century, made a special visit to China to perfect himself in his art, and on his return to his native town of Seto, in Owari, he introduced great improvement in the character of the wares made there. Although the glazing of pottery may have been practiced in Japan at a much earlier date than the time of Toshiro, there is no doubt that it was owing to his exertions that a great impetus was given to the art. He not only improved the quality of vitreous enamels, but he introduced new and artistic methods of their application. From his time onward great attention was paid to this branch of the potter's art, of which it soon became one of the most important and interesting features. To know something of Japanese glazes is to be familiar with the soft greenish grays of the Sanda Seiji ware, the dull leaden blue or the metallic sheen of the brown glaze of Bizen, iridescent blacks, reds, browns, and bottle-greens of the Raku wares, the lustrous yellow-brown of Ohi, the splashed Oribé wares, the thick opaque overglazes of Shigaraki, the delicate grays and salmon shades of Hagi, the heavy brown and yellow glazes of Tamba, or the speckled grays and browns of Soma. These and many others of like interest and beauty, as they are better known and their characteristics better understood, have an ever-increasing charm to the earnest and sympathetic student, who soon ceases to wonder, as perchance he may at first have done, at the artistic value in which they are held by the Japanese connoisseur."

There has been much discussion as to whether the rustic simplicity of the Japanese pottery was due to the innate taste of the people or to the artificial cult of the *Cha-no-yu* affected by the feudal nobles, who were the special patrons of the industry in its early days. In these discussions it has been usual to assume that the tea clubs were a peculiar institution of Japan. But we have seen that the cult was practiced in all its details in China, and that there are illustrated books on the subject dating from the early part of the *Sung* dynasty (960–1279), with pictures of the apparatus, and a full account of the proceedings at the competitive tea meetings at which the comparative virtues of decoctions made from the powdered leaves of various brands of tea, as well as of the fragrant fumes of the different kinds of incense imported from the shores of Arabia and Africa, were tested with the same ceremonial rules that we find afterward adopted in Japan. Prose authors and poets of this dynasty in China descant alike on the merits of the speckled black cups which they liken to the plumage of the gray partridge (*Perdrix cinerea*) and the "leveret-streaked" or "hare's-fur" glazes of the productions of the kilns of Chien-chou, which were dark brown or black streaked with lighter spots of yellowish tinge. There are the kilns at which Toshiro, the "father of pottery" in Japan, acquired the rudiments of the art toward the close of the *Sung* dynasty, and his productions and those of his immediate successors, figured by Ninagawa Noritane, seem to be exact copies of the Chinese originals as described above. The archaic shapes are similar, and the primitive technique is the same, the way in which the glaze runs down outside and gutters below, so as only partially to cover the bowl, leaving the lower margin, as well as the foot, bare. The Japanese in their estimation of the different kinds of pottery place the Chinese or Korean specimens first, and their own early reproductions next; the tea-jars and tea-bowls are wrapped in padded bags of silk brocade, inclosed in lacquer boxes protected by outer cotton covers,

* *Japan and its Art.* By Marcus B. Huish, LL. B. Second edition. London, 1892. Chapter XIV, p. 230.

and are brought out by their owners only on special occasions, to be handled with the greatest care.

The shapes and uses of Japanese vases are well described by Sir Wollaston Franks in his introduction to the native report on Japanese pottery which forms one of the art handbooks of the South Kensington Museum. The pottery utensils used in the tea ceremonies are a furnace, water-vessels, jars to hold powdered tea, a pan for ashes, and a tea-bowl. The furnace (*furo*) is generally a globular vessel on three legs, with openings in the upper part to create a draught. Into this upper part fits the vessel in which the water is boiled, a smaller repetition of the same form, with two handles and a lid. The water-vessels comprise a vase or pitcher (*midzu-sashi*), with a supply of fresh water for washing the utensils, and a slop-basin (*midzu-koboshi*); they are usually rudely made, and often with lacquer covers. The tea-jars (*cha-iré*), of which specimens are illustrated in Plates CXIV and CXV, are generally small oviform vases of hard pottery, with no decoration beyond the mottled glaze, and with flat lids of ivory; they are all of small size, as the green tea is powdered and very strong, besides being very costly. The tea-bowl (*cha-wan*) is purposely very rudely made, and varies in shape. Some tea-bowls are round shallow dishes, others tall and nearly cylindrical; the tea is not only made in the bowl, but drunk out of it, and great care is taken to make the edge smooth to the lips. The ash-pan (*horoku*) is a shallow pan of unglazed ware, with incurved rim. It holds the charcoal ashes with which the brazier or furnace is partly filled, as well as the urn in which the incense is burned.

FIG. 386.—Kŏro, or Incense-Burner of Hirado blue and white porcelain, with a picture in the inner cylinder, seen through the openwork trellis, of five children playing in a garden, under a pine-tree which spreads over the pierced cover.

Incense-burning formed part of the tea ceremony, and it was also a favorite pastime among the Japanese nobles of old times, the incense game consisting of guesses of the names of the perfumes that were being burned, with forfeits, etc. The incense-boxes (*kōgo*) are of the most varied shapes, generally small in size. The incense-burner (*kŏro*) also varies considerably. Some incense-burners are modeled after old Chinese forms, others quaintly fashioned as men, animals, or birds, like the urn of Hirado porcelain illustrated in Plate CX, which represents a pup squatted on the ground, the head of which, detached, forms the cover of the censer; others are intended to be hung from the ceiling, like the old Imari censer decorated in red and gold which is figured in Plate CVI. The lower part of the censer is filled with fine white ashes, with a piece of lighted charcoal on the top on which the tablet of incense is placed; on this account the old incense-burners in collections show no marks of fire on the lower part, although begrimed with smoke above and underneath the lids. They are used occasionally as clove-boilers (*chōji-buro*) to perfume the room with the aromatic odor of cloves.

A small earthenware hand brazier (*shiu-ro*) is used for warming the hands, which is usually pear-shaped, with an aperture in the side, and is modeled in many quaint forms. A small charcoal burner of pottery is fitted inside the *tabaku-bon*, or portable tobacco-box, from which the smoker lights his pipe, a miniature jar of cylindrical shape.

The objects intended for use on the writing-table are generally fashioned after Chinese models, and we find similar cylinders for holding the brushes, vases for water to dip them in, brush-rests and ink-rests, paper-weights of varied design, and small screen pictures mounted on stands, miniature water-droppers for the ink-pallet, boxes for the vermilion used for seals, small flower-vases, etc.

The flower-vases (*hana-ike*) form a large class. Some are adapted to stand upon the shelves of the recessed alcove of the living-room, known as the *tokonoma*, others to hang against one of the pillars, or to be suspended by cords from the ceiling. These last are fashioned in all kinds of designs, a gnarled branch of a fir-tree or a jointed section of bamboo, a bunch of wistaria-blossom, an old pine-cone, a gourd, a firefly, or a swallow beating against the wall. Among ornamental pieces (*okimono*) made by the artist potters there is another long series of figures of men and animals and other forms generally taken from Nature.

Teapots and cups for ordinary tea-drinking, saké kettles, bottles, and cups, water-bottles, and other domestic articles, were also made by celebrated artist potters; but, as a rule, such articles as these, being for general use, have been produced in the way of trade by less renowned potters; the great majority of domestic utensils for table use are made of lacquered wood.

With regard to the multitudinous modes of decoration of Japanese porcelain, the subject motives of the pictures, sacred and profane, and their relations to the art of China and of the farther west, the works on Japanese art are so many, and generally so well illustrated, that a short sketch of the bibliography may be the best way of directing inquirers to the available sources of information. The expedition of Commodore Perry in 1853, and the treaty negotiated by him on behalf of the United States, opened Japan to foreign intercourse, but it was mainly by means of the great international expositions that its wealth in art treasures was made known to the outer world. The first collection was made for the London International Exhibition of 1862 by Sir Rutherford Alcock, who was then British minister to Japan, the author of the *Capital of the Tycoon*, an illustrated narrative of a three years' residence in Japan (two volumes, 1863), and also of a small volume on Japanese art industries.* More comprehensive collections were sent to Paris in 1867, and to Vienna in 1873, under the direction of the Japanese Government, who appointed special commissioners to represent them. Mr. W. T. Walters was officially connected with the Vienna Exposition, and availed himself of this occasion of acquiring an interesting series of objects of Oriental porcelain sent from Persia by Prince Ehtezadesaltanet, an uncle of the Shah, of which some of the Chinese pieces with Persian mounts of chased metal have been illustrated in these pages.

FIG. 387.—Censer of white Hirado porcelain molded in the form of a grotesque unicorn lion, with a movable head as a lid, with the details modeled in relief in the paste and lightly chased under the glaze.

A still more important display of Japanese ceramic art appeared in 1876 at the Great Centennial Exposition at Philadelphia, and there is a certain amount of authentic information on the ceramic industry to be gathered from the catalogue,† although the details are not so full as in the official catalogue of the *Exposition Universelle* of 1878 at Paris, which was also published under the direction of the Imperial Japanese Commission, and to which reference has already been made. It gives a sketch of the history and technique, with lists of the various materials with their Japanese names, that are used at the different factories, and is a fund of exact knowledge. The display of Japanese porcelain in the Chicago Exposition of 1893 that was admitted into the fine-art section was chiefly remarkable for showing some indications of a recent renaissance in the art. The chief representatives of the new school, according to the official catalogue, are Seifu, Kozan, and Takemoto. Seifu Yohei of Kyōto is placed in the very foremost rank of Japanese potters, whether of ancient or modern times, and called the Yeiraku of the *Meiji* era. His chief specialties are celadons, ivory-white and coral, but he also produces jewelry ware showing vitrifiable enamels as pure and brilliant and as perfectly applied as the best work of

---

* *Art and Art Industries in Japan.* By Sir R. Alcock, K. C. B. 8vo. London, 1878.
† *International Exhibition, 1876. Official Catalogue of the Japanese Section and Notes on the Industry of Japan.* Philadelphia: Published by the Japanese Commission, 1876.

former days, and canary-yellow glazes with reserved designs in rich blue of the *K'ang-hsi* type. Miyakawa Kozan, better known as Makuzu, has his kiln at Ota, in the suburbs of Yokohama, and there is hardly anything in old Chinese ware that he can not reproduce. The astute Chinese dealer is said to inclose Kozan's peach-blooms, for example, in the traditional silk-lined box of his country, and to sell them to trustful Occidentals at figures commensurate with the magnitude of the deception. The greatest success of the third potter, Takemoto Hayata, a resident of Tokyo, is declared to have been his copies of the ancient *Chien Yao*, of the *Sung* dynasty, characterized by a glossy black glaze, sometimes showing tints of raven's-wing green, striated with hairlike lines of silver and dappled with golden brown, which he mounted with silver rims in traditional fashion, but which, judging from the description, must have far outshone the originals. In addition to these three, Higuchi Haruzane is easily first among the Hirado potters of the present day. He is distinguished especially for his success in the Chinese "rice-grain" perforated work of the last century.

The vase which was exhibited at the time as his masterpiece is now in the Walters Collection, and is illustrated in Fig. 318. It is a beaker-shaped vase (*hana-ike*), nine and a half inches high, with a bulging body of depressed globular form on a circularly rimmed foot, and a wide neck spreading in a graceful curve into a slightly flaring mouth. The decoration is painted in three shades of underglaze cobalt-blue of soft tones, contrasting admirably with the milk-white surface of the piece, and this again throws out effectively the pale-green, waxlike translucency of the glaze with which the pierced designs on the neck of the vase are filled. Three kylin (*ch'i-lin*) are displayed on the body in darker and lighter shades of blue, drawn in the traditional Chinese style, with the bodies of deer, unicorn dragon heads and flowing tails, and with flames proceeding from their shoulders indicative of their supernatural origin. A ring of ornamental fret encircles the foot of the vase, and a band of paulownia sprays of conventional design winds round the base of the neck. The pierced designs on the neck represent two phœnixes coiled in medallions underneath a fringe of scrolled clouds. The mark penciled underneath in blue in two columns of the tiniest characters reads, *Bai-kwa dō Go Hei sei*— i. e., "Made by Go Hei of the Plum Blossom Hall."

To the Centennial Exhibition at Philadelphia we owe the representative series of the olden ceramic wares of Japan which is now in the South Kensington Museum, having been transferred at the close of the exhibition in accordance with an arrangement previously made with the Japanese authorities, as explained in the catalogue * which forms one of the museum art handbooks. A still more valuable selection is contained in the special Franks Collection, which was first exhibited on loan for some years at the Bethnal Green Branch Museum, when the catalogue † which has been so often quoted was issued. The collection, with many additions made since the publication of the catalogue, is now in the British Museum, having been presented by Sir Wollaston Franks, K. C. B., the accomplished collector and curator.

The first large special work on the subject published in Europe was the ponderous and gorgeously illustrated *Keramic Art of Japan*, ‡ in which the more ornate varieties of the decorated wares are reproduced in colors. But in this, as the authors confess afterward, "some quite modern works of Ota ware and Shiba decoration were described as old Satsuma," although some of the errors were corrected in the large octavo edition of the book which was published later. Uniform with this is the volume on *Marks and Seals*, # by one of the joint authors of the *Keramic Art*, which is a valuable compilation, as the marks are given in exact facsimile, although not always correctly deciphered. The same industrious author has also published a special work on *Enamels*, ‖ and, more recently, another large illustrated volume of 576 pages

---

* *Japanese Pottery. Being a Native Report, with an Introduction and Catalogue.* By A. W. Franks. 8vo. London, 1880.

† *Catalogue of a Collection of Oriental Porcelain and Pottery lent for Exhibition* by A. W. Franks. Second edition. 8vo. London, 1878.

‡ *Keramic Art of Japan.* By G. A. Audsley and J. L. Bowes. Folio, 1878, 1879. Imperial 8vo. London, 1881.

Japanese Marks and Seals. By J. L. Bowes. London, 1882.

‖ *Japanese Enamels.* By J. L. Bowes, printed for private circulation, 1884, and published in London, 1886.

on *Japanese Pottery,* * with a detailed description of the productions of the different kilns, followed by interesting notes on the chief motives of decoration.

The art of Japan has been studied with much success during recent years in America as well as in Europe, its chief exponents being M. Louis Gonse in France, Mr. William Anderson in England, and Professor Fenallosa in the United States. The large work † of M. Gonse, which is a veritable *édition de luxe,* is enriched by a chapter entitled *Étude sur La Céramique,* by M. J. Bing, a well-known authority on the subject, who was good enough to go through the Walters Collection with me one day, with much profit to myself. A small handbook by M. Gonse was issued in Paris in the following year, under the same title of *L'Art Japonais,* as one of the volumes of the *Bibliothèque de l'Enseignement des Beaux-Arts,* with a section on *La Céramique* which gives such an excellent and succinct view of the artistic side of the industry that it has been translated and reproduced in the next chapter.

The excellent work of the German Professor J. J. Rein may also be referred to for notes on the technique of the ceramic industry taken on the spot. An English edition ‡ has been published in London, as well as one of the general work by the same author on *Japan.* These two works are the result of several years of travels and researches in the country undertaken on behalf of the Prussian Government.

FIG. 388.—Okimono (or ornament) of white Hirado porcelain, with the figure of a Shōjō with smiling face and long hair sweeping the ground, standing beside a tripod wine-jar with a bamboo ladle in his hand.

The native literature of Japan upon the subject of ceramic art is not so extensive as of China, partly because in the latter country it has been more directly fostered by the state, since the imperial manufactory was founded at Ching-tê-chên in the beginning of the eleventh century, whereas in Japan the development of the industry was left to private potters under the patronage of the feudal nobles, who were wont to keep their methods to themselves with the utmost secrecy. The first precise details of the porcelain manufacture in Japan were published in 1856, as an appendix to Julien's book on Chinese Porcelain, in a short article on Imari-yaki, translated by Professor J. Hoffmann, of Leyden, from an encyclopædia of the productions of the country printed in five volumes at Osaka in 1799. Among the older books the one most frequently quoted is the *Man-pō zen-sho,* a general book on art subjects in fourteen volumes, published in 1694. A valuable recent record of the arts is the *Kōgei Shirio,* a compilation from older works by Kurokawa Mayori and Murayama, published in 1878, which is said to have formed the basis for the government reports issued by the commissioners of the international expositions already referred to, and of most of the essays published in Europe. Mr. Bowes says, in the preface to his *Japanese Pottery:*

"I have availed myself of this work for much of what I have written about the earlier wares, with which it chiefly deals; but it is singularly deficient in information about the brilliant development of the artistic taste of the country which occurred under the rule of the Tokugawa family during the seventeenth and eighteenth centuries, when, without a doubt, the most exquisite examples of Japanese art were produced."

The same strictures might be applied to the illustrated work on pottery (*tōki*) by Ninagawa Noritane, the late archæologist of the museum at Tokyo, which has been quoted as the special native work on the subject, and which has been partially and somewhat imperfectly translated into French. This forms Parts II to V of the *Kwan ko dzu setsu,* "Illustrations of Antiquity, with Plates and Descriptions," Part I being devoted to city walls and fortifications, accompanied by photographs, and it was published in the tenth year of *Meiji* (1877). If one turns, for example, to the section on Satsuma Yaki in Part III, one finds three speci-

---

* *Japanese Pottery.* With Notes on its Decoration and Illustrations from the Bowes Collection. By J. L. Bowes. Liverpool, 1890.

† *L'Art Japonais.* Par Louis Gonse. 2 vols. gr. in 4to. Paris, 1885.

‡ *The Industries of Japan.* By J. J. Rein, Professor of Geography in the University of Bonn. London, 1889.

mens illustrated; one of these three (Fig. 25) is a narrow-necked vase (*tsubo*) of archaic form, ornamented with only a few parallel rings round the globular body, and coated with a green glaze, guttering below so as to leave an inch or more of russet-colored paste exposed; the other two (Figs. 26, 27) are plain tea-jars (*cha-ire*) with small loop handles, invested with yellowish-brown and dark-brown glazes, the copper-colored feet of which are figured separately to show different forms of the *itoguiri* or concentric thread-marks. One would think that decorated Satsuma hardly existed for the Japanese archæologist, who, however, figures an interesting rice-bowl of old Kutani ware in Part V, Fig. 74, and a more modern teacup of decorated Awaji crackled ware in Fig. 30, the last plate of his work.

The latest book* from a Japanese hand has recently been published in Paris, as one of the volumes of the *Petite Bibliothèque d'Art et d'Archéologie, publiée sous la direction de M. Kaempfen, Directeur des Musées nationaux et de l'École du Louvre.* It is a compilation from native sources, with the names of the authorities generally appended to the quotations, and more care has been taken with the dates than is the case with some other Japanese books— the native report on which the South Kensington Catalogue is based, for example. The ceramic wares are arranged in tabular form according to the places of production in the different provinces, with the names of the first makers, when known, their dates, and a sketch of their principal productions. The table, with a few modifications of what seemed to be misprints, and slight changes in transliteration, is given here (see the next page), as a most useful summary of the industry. The book takes the form of notes attached to the headings of the table. The author's methods may be gathered from a translation of his account of the Raku ware of Kyōto:

"RAKU-YAKI.—The Raku-Yaki, one of the varieties of the Kyō-Yaki, owed their origin to a Korean, a naturalized Japanese, of the name of Ameya Yeisei (1504–1520). After his death his widow continued his industry, becoming at the same time Ama ('bonzesse' or Buddhist nun), and her ware was consequently given the name of Ama-Yaki. Choyu, their son, made here, after a model given to him by Senno Rikiu (1517–1591), the celebrated *chajin* who reformed the code of the tea ceremonies, some cups with a black glaze for Ota Nobunaga (1533–1582), who was then the real head of the Shogun's Government. In the sixteenth year of *Tensho* (1588), Hideyoshi, who had become dictator at the death of Nobunaga, and is better known under the name of Taiko-Sama, ordered him to make a set of cups of a reddish-black color, with which he was so thoroughly pleased that he gave him a gold seal inscribed with the character *Raku*, part of the name of the palace of Ju-Raku at Kyōto, where Hideyoshi was then residing. Choyu marked with it afterward all his pieces. It is starting from this period that the name of Raku was given to the ware made by him and by his descendants. His cups were called Raku-cha-wan. In the period *Keicho* (1596–1614) the gold seal was replaced with a common seal.

"The Raku-Yaki are composed of a white clay without resistance; it appears red when it is coated exteriorly with a yellow earth which becomes red in the kiln; it appears black when a glaze is used in the composition of which enter pebbles from the Kamogawa (Kyōto) reduced to powder. The Raku-Yaki consist only of Tezukuné (articles fashioned by hand), and were all made without the help of the potter's wheel or of the mold. This is why one finds among the pieces that infinite variety of form which justly constitutes their superiority over similar articles derived from other sources."

The following is the genealogy of the Raku. They are all called by the personal name of Kichizayemon:

1. Chojiro choyu († 1592). 2. Chokei († 1642). 3. Doniu († 1657). 4. Ichiniu († 1696). 5. Soniu († 1716). 6. Saniu († 1739). 7. Choniu († 1759). 8. Seitoku († 1778). 9. Riyoniu (end of eighteenth century). 10. Tanniu (beginning of nineteenth century). 11. Keiniu. 12. Kichizayemon, our contemporary.

The interest that has constantly been taken by the ruling classes of Japan in the ceramic art is proved by an appendix attached to M. Ouéda's work, which is entitled "Mæcenases and Grand Personages who are cited in the Foregoing Notes as having patronized the Ceramic Industry." It is a chronological list extending over eleven pages, beginning with the Emperor Yuriaku (A. D. 457–476), who is recorded to have had earthenware vases made for his own use at Fushimi near Kyōto, and ending with Senno Sohitsu, a master of the "Cha-no-yu," who ordered, in 1864, services of utensils for the tea ceremonies from Zoroku, a celebrated potter of Kyōto, and rewarded him with a new name beginning with the same initial as his own.

---

* *La Céramique Japonaise. Les principaux centres de fabrication céramique au Japon.* Par Ouéda Tokounosouke; avec une préface par E. Deshayes, conservateur-adjoint au Musée Guimet. Paris, 1895.

TABLE OF THE PRINCIPAL CENTERS OF THE CERAMIC INDUSTRY IN JAPAN.

POTTERY, FAÏENCE, OR PORCELAIN.	PLACE OF MANUFACTURE.	FIRST MAKER.	DATE OF FIRST MAKING. JAPANESE EPOCH.	DATE OF FIRST MAKING. CHRISTIAN ERA.	PRODUCTIONS.
OWARI:					
SETO: Ko-Seto	Seto (Owari Province)	Toshiro I, continuer	Antei	1227–28	Jars for powdered tea.
Ki-Seto	" "	Toshiro II	Yeinin	1293–98	Tea-jars, incense-pots, flower-vases, cups, etc.
Modern Seto	" "	Kato-Tamikichi	1st Kiowa	1801	Porcelain of most varied use and shape.
Shino	" "		Bummei	1469–86	Cha-no-yu services.
Oribé	" "		Tensho	1573–91	Kōgo (incense-boxes), cups, plates, flower-vases.
Ofukei	Nagoya "		Kwanyei	1624–43	Tea-jars and various objects.
Gempin	" "	Chin-Gempin	Manji	1658–60	Divers objects.
Kuro	" "	Hirazawa-Kuro	Bunkwa	1804–17	Amateur work.
Toyosuke-Raku-yaki	Aichi District (Owari)	Toyosuke	Bunsei	1818–29	Table services coated with lacquer decorated in gold.
Tokonabe	Tokonabe "		Tensho (re-established)	1573–91	Saké-bottles, dishes, cups, flower-vases, etc.
Inuyama or Maruyama	Near Inuyama "		Bunsei	1818–29	Varied.
Mino	Kujiri-Tajimi (Mino)	Kato Yosobei Kagemitsu	2d Tensho	1574	All kinds of pottery.
KYŌTO:					
KYŌ-YAKI: Awata	Awata (Kyōto)	Continued by Ninsei	Kwanyei	1624–43	Tea-jars, cups, dishes, plates, figures of men and animals.
Omuro	Omuro	" " "	" "	"	Midzu-sashi (water-vases), midzu-koboshi (slop-basins), kōro (incense-burners), and objects of varied forms.
Mizoro	Mizoro	" " "	" "	"	Do.
Seikanji Otowa or Kyomidzu	Kyomidzu	" " "	" "	"	Kama (saucepans), midzu-koboshi, kōgo, flower-vases, dishes, plates, etc.
Raku	Ju-Raku	Ameya or Sokei	Yeisho	1504–20	Cups, tea-jars, flower-vases, bowls, kōro, kōgo, midzu-sashi, midzu-koboshi, etc.
Kenzan	Narutaki	Ogata Shinsei	Genroku	1688–1703	Objects fashioned by hand (Tezukune).
Yeiraku	Okazaki (Mikawa)	Zengoro X (Riozen)	Bunkwa	1804–17	Furo (furnaces), reproductions of ancient pieces.
Fushimi	Fushimi (near Kyōto)	Re-established by Ikaruga Koyemon	1st Genwa	1615	Children's toys, statuettes, animals, birds, jars, and dishes for Shintō ceremonies.
Asahi	Uji (near Kyōto)	Established by order of Kobori Masakazu	Shoho	1644–47	Cups, kōgo, bowls.
Shigaraki	Nakano (Shigaraki, Omi)		Koan	1278–87	Tea-jars, midzu-sashi, midzu-koboshi, flower-vases.
Zeze	Zeze (Omi)		Kwanyei	1624–43	Do.
Akahada	Koriyama (Yamato)	Ninsei	Shoho	1644–47	Saké services.
Iga	Marubashira (Iga)		Kenmu	1334–35	Cha-no-yu services.
Banko	Obuke (Ise)	Numanami Gozayemon	Gembun	1736–40	Teapots, cups.
Minato	Minato (Idzumi Province)	Giogi?	Gembun	1736–40	Horoku (ash-pans). Imitations of Kochi or Annam ware.
Kaseyama	Kaseyama (near Yamato)	Morimoto Sukezayemon	Bunsei	1818–29	Dobin (earthenware teapots), Donabe (saucepans).
Kishiu	Wakayama (Kii)	Yeiraku Zengoro X, named Riozen	Tempo	1830–43	Cha-no-yu services.
Sanda	Miwa (Setsu)		Genroku	1688–1703	Imitations of Ko-Seiji (old celadons) of the Chinese *Ming* dynasty.
Tamba	Tachikui (Tamba)		Yeiroku	1558–69	Jars, dishes, Cha-no-yu vessels.
Tozan	Himeji (Harima)		Tempo	1830–43	Pricket candlesticks, cups, table services of ancient style; ordinary household ware of the present day.
Bizen	Imbe (Bizen)		Oyei	1394–1427	Kōro, tea-jars, midzu-sashi, midzu-koboshi, jars, dishes, saké-bottles and large saké-jars, suribachi (mortars).
Idzumo	Matsuye (Idzumo)	Kurasaki Gombei, continuer	Keian	1648–51	Cha-no-yu services, dishes, plates, flower-vases.
Hagi	Hagi (Nagato)	Korai Sayemon, continuer (1598)	Yeisho	1504–20	Cups, plates, dishes, midzu-sashi, midzu-koboshi, kōro, kōgo.
Awaji	Igano (Awaji)	Kashiu Minpei	Tempo	1830–43	Small pieces and various utensils.
Odo (Oto)	Odo (Tosa)	Shohaku	Manji	1658–60	Cha-no-yu services, dishes, and plates.
HIZEN:					
Karatsu	Karatsu (Hizen)		Taikwa-Hakuchi	645–54	
IMARI-YAKI: Arita	Arita	Li Sanpei	Keicho	1596–1614	
Okawaji	Okawaji		Kioho	1716–35	
Shida			Jō-ō-Manji	1652–60	
Odashi	Near Ureshino (Hizen).				Articles of every kind and shape, and of the most varied use.
Yoshida					
Matsugatani	Matsugatani	Arita workmen	Kioho	1716–35	
Shira-ishi	Shira-ishi	Soha, continuer	Ansei	1854–59	
Mikawaji (Hirado)	Oriose	Korean potter	Keicho	1596–1614	
Kameyama	Near Nagasaki.				
Agano	Agano (Buzen)	Sonkai	Keicho	1596–1614	Different pieces, tea-jars, cups.
Yatsushiro	Yatsushiro (Higo)	Sonkai	9th Kwanyei	1632	Tea-jars, cups, ordinary jars.
Satsuma	Nawashirogawa (Satsuma)	Korean workmen	Keicho	1596–1614	Cha-no-yu services, kōro, kōgo, cups.
Koshiro	Minaminoseki (Higo)	Korean workmen	Keicho	1596–1614	
Nakano	Nakano (Chikuzen)	Arita workmen	2d Tenwa	1682	Divers.
Takatori	Takatori "	Hachizo	Keicho	1596–1614	Tea-jars.
Yanagawa	Yanagawa (Chikugo)				Objects in terra-cotta, earthenware saucepans.
Shiga	Shiga (Tsushima)	Yoshida Mataichi	Bunkwa	1804–17	Pieces in Sometsuke (blue and white).
Shidoro	Shidoro (Totomi)		Taiyei	1521–27	Tea-jars, flower-vases.
Kutani	Yamashiro (Kaga)	Goto Saijiro and Tamura Gonzayemon	Kwanyei	1624–43	Tea-jars, midzu-sashi, bowls, etc.
Ōhi	Ōhi (Kaga)	Chozayemon	Tenwa	1681–83	Cups, kōgo.
Imado	Imado (Yedo)		Tensho	1573–91	Furnaces, statuettes, animals, cups, sacrificial utensils of terra-cotta, etc.
Kenya	Yedo	Miura Kenya	Tempo	1830–43	Articles fashioned by hand (Tezukune).
Soma	Nakamura (Iwaki)		Keian	1648–51	Teapots, cups, dishes.
Wakamatsu or Aizo	Hongo (Iwashiro)	Midzuno Genzayemon	Shoho	1644–47	Different pieces of Sometsuke (blue and white).

FIG. 389.—Incense-Burner of Imari ware, fashioned in the shape of a cock
perched upon a stump of wood and painted in enamel colors, black,
brown, and red, with touches of gold and silver. Date, about 1700.

CHAPTER XXVI.

A GENERAL SKETCH OF THE CERAMIC ART OF JAPAN.*

I.

AMONG all the arts of Japan, the ceramic art remained, down to the most recent times, the least known to Europeans, and the one on the subject of which the most erroneous ideas had become current. It can not be said that this was because it had not already attracted much attention. Considerably before the first and timid essays of Albert Jacquemart there had been long discussions about its history and about its productions. Since the early part of the eighteenth century collectors of Chinese porcelain have eagerly sought for what was called in the language of the dealers the *vieilles qualités du' Japon.* But, having started from the outset upon a wrong track, it seemed that criticism was bound to be involved for an indefinite period in its own errors. It required the thorough opening up of Japan after the revolution of 1868, the points of contact brought about by the great exhibitions of Paris, Vienna, and Philadelphia, and the perseverance of two or three collectors, to throw some light upon the real facts of the ceramic history.

It is to M. Bing, the great Parisian importer of Japanese objects, a scholar and at the same time one of the most distinguished of collectors—it is to the rigor of his methods, to the patience of his investigations begun at Paris in 1878, pursued in Japan itself, and continued without intermission during the formation of one of the most beautiful and most curious collections that could possibly be seen—that we owe the first and true clearing up of the question. To-day, thanks to him, one can say that the history of Japanese ceramics is made, the canvas is sketched in solid outline ; it will be possible certainly to fill in details, but not to modify essential lines.

The study of the questions which touch on the history and on the classification of the ceramic productions of Japan would demand developments which neither the nature nor the extent of this volume allow. I shall content myself with a rapid sketch of the question, and shall refer those who are more specially interested in the subject to the fine and very complete study by M. Bing, which I have published in full in my large work. †

As I have said elsewhere, Japanese pottery occupies, in the family of the ceramic art, one of the first places, if not the first. I say purposely "pottery," for it is principally by their work in earthy clays, upon which the varied play of enamel colors produces the liveliest, the most sumptuous, and the most unexpected effects, that the artists of Nippon have proved their superiority. It is sufficient to remark in general terms that hard porcelain occupies a second-

---

* This chapter is a literal but slightly abridged translation of the article on *La Céramique* in the manual of the *Bibliothèque des Beaux-Arts*, entitled *L'Art Japonais*, by M. Louis Gonse, the author of the larger book with the same title referred to in the preceding chapter. It gives the latest views of the accomplished author, and is a charming compendium of the subject from an artistic point of view.

† *L'Art Japonais.* Par M. Louis Gonse. Paris: Quantin. 2 vols. gr. in 4to.

ary rank in Japan when compared with that of the soft clays, the faïence, and the ordinary pottery. The kaolinic productions of the Japanese, perfect as they are occasionally as examples of successful kiln-work, are only in reality more or less clever imitations of the admirable porcelains of China. The Chinese are the *porcelainiers par excellence*, the uncontested masters of kaolin. The Japanese are *potiers* without rivals. With the former the interest of the decoration is often subordinated to the beauty of the materials or to the excellence of the workmanship; with the latter, on the contrary, it remains always the dominant aim. The picturesque effect, the advantage to be gained from the splendor, the transparency, and the vivacity of the enameled glazes: these are the preoccupations of the Japanese potter. A marvelous instinct for the laws of decoration has revealed to the Japanese the fact that pottery, with its forms, its resources, its infinite methods, offered an incomparable field for the development of their imagination.

A disregard of this fundamental character of the ceramic art of Nippon has been one of the most serious obstacles to Europeans in their study of its history. On no other question has there been a greater number of prejudices to be uprooted; *a priori*, it has been necessary on almost every point to take a stand against preconceived views. The Japanese porcelains which had been the delight of our fathers, the dishes and the jars from the factories of Imari and Arita, decorated in blue, or with a decoration in blue, red, and gold—all those pieces called old Hizen, with which the Dutch had inundated Europe during the course of the seventeenth century—were in the eyes of the pure Japanese only second-rate productions intended for commercial export. Down to these later years, the true ceramic art of Japan, that I shall call the national ceramic art, has remained absolutely unknown to Europeans. It was with difficulty that a few rare pieces from Kyōto, known to collectors as *vieux truité*, were brought over with the lacquer that came from that city. Among the centers of the ceramic industry we knew only the least interesting, those least appreciated by the natives of the country, and those least endowed with any personal characteristics. It will be sufficient

FIG. 390.—Saké-Bottle of Oka-waji ware, with a crackled celadon glaze decorated in soft enamel colors and gold.

for me to remark that the vast collections at Leyden, The Hague, and Dresden, where Hizen pieces are to be counted by thousands, do not offer for the visitor's notice a solitary specimen from Kutani, from Kyōto, from Satsuma, from Bizen, or from Owari—that is to say, not a single piece to give him a glimpse of the originality of Japanese taste in ceramic matters. It is hardly credible, but it is so notwithstanding. A stranger who knew nothing of Rouen, of Nevers, or of Moustiers, or of the soft *pâtes* of Sèvres, would be in the same situation *vis-à-vis* France. The worst of it is that these false opinions have the resistance of the most obstinate prejudices; it will require many years still to make amateurs and dealers of the old school understand that their empirical admirations have no value from the Japanese point of view.

II.

The ceramic industry of Japan is divided, therefore, into two thoroughly distinct branches: porcelain and pottery.

The principal center of the porcelain manufacture is the province of Hizen, where important deposits of kaolin are found, especially on the skirts of the mountain of Karatsu, which has in consequence given its name to the primitive ceramic production of this province. The pieces of Karatsu ware, dating back to the thirteenth and fourteenth centuries, that I have had before me for inspection, were of a barbarous type; they were uniformly coated with a gray enamel, rather coarse, thick and always crackled, after the fashion of the Korean pottery of which they are simply an imitation.

It was a potter of the name of Gorodayu Shonsui who brought from China, about 1520, the elements of the making of porcelain. The village which rose up round his first kiln took the name of Arita. There is every reason to suppose that the pieces that came from the hand of Shonsui were timid copies of Chinese porcelain, probably of small dimensions and of blue and white. His two pupils, Gorohichi and Gorohachi, were already more skillful. The pieces of theirs that I have seen, and notably a bowl decorated with sprays, after the Persian style, in blue upon a finely crackled gray ground, testify to progress in the art, which was already at its highest point at the close of the seventeenth century. Kakiyemon introduced at Imari, in 1647, the art of decorating porcelains by means of vitrifiable colors relieved with gold (Fig. 389). The Dutch, established at Nagasaki, gave a vigorous impulse to the new productions; the exportation rapidly increased and created an almost inexhaustible source of riches for the Prince of Hizen; the town of Imari became the principal center of the manufacture, and Europe was literally inundated with its productions. The finer pieces of Imari may possibly rival in technical execution the works of the Chinese ceramic artists, but their decoration is a little monotonous. They are generally mere productions of the workshop, on which, with rare exceptions, the personal invention of the artist is not apparent. The best known type, with a decoration of chrysanthemums and peonies, in blue, red, and gold, has been classed by Albert Jacquemart under the name of *famille chrysanthémo-pœonienne.* This is essentially an article of commerce, exempt from any element of the unforeseen. The potters of Delft, in Holland, devoted themselves to the imitation of its general characteristics. Another type, the peculiar invention of Kakiyemon, is of a more delicate order. The creamy and soft white of the enamel plays the principal rôle here. The decoration, fired in

FIG. 391.—Small Censer of Hirado porcelain, with a pierced outer trellised casing overspread with three sprays of chrysanthemum - flowers modeled in slight relief; silver openwork cover.

the muffle stove, is composed generally of scattered blossoms, painted on sparingly, of graceful birds, and of gardens with flowers, which bring out in its full value the exquisite finish of the glaze. The paste is of the finest grain. It is from the study of this type that the productions of Saxony and of Chantilly were started. The pieces of this sort have always been eagerly sought for by the aristocracy of Japan.

In the course of the eighteenth century the same province gave birth to the porcelain centers of Okawaji, of Hirado, and of Mikawaji. The last two were particularly devoted to the making of objects in pure white without any decoration, or in blue and white (Fig. 391). Fine pieces of Hirado are very highly esteemed. Their white enamels have never, however, been able to attain to the incomparable softness of the old white porcelains of China. On the other hand, they excel the similar Chinese things in the finish, variety, and grace of their form. The incense-burners, fashioned in the shape of birds, pigeons, mandarin ducks, and other animals, or of persons, are objects fit to figure in the most select of collections.

Many potters of the other provinces have tried their hands in kaolinic productions; pieces of high artistic interest and of great technical perfection have come from the workshops of Kutani and of Kyōto; but it is only in the ceramic centers of Hizen that the art attained a complete and continuous development.

III.

It is certain that the origin of pottery reaches back in Japan to the highest antiquity. Japanese authors admit generally that it was the ancient Korean productions of Shiraki, Kudara, and Koma that supplied the first models for their own indigenous productions. It is, on the other hand, no less certain that the primitive pottery of Japan preserved during long centuries an absolutely embryonic and barbarous character, approximating somewhat to the archaic pottery of the Troad and of Mexico. In the fifth century kilns were established in different provinces;

but it is not till the seventh that we can arrive at any precise indications. A Buddhist priest of the name of Gyogi who had come from Korea and is celebrated for the foundation of the temple of Todaiji, where the treasures of the ancient emperors of Nara are to be found preserved to the present day, gave a great impulse to the ceramic industry; he passes as having been the inventor of the potter's wheel. A certain number of pieces made under his direction exist among the treasures of the temple, and would give an idea of the progress realized. One can also see in my work *l'Art Japonais* (tome ii, page 249) the reproduction of a Gyogi piece belonging to the magnificent collection of M. Bing.

The knowledge of the process of enameling dates in Japan only from the ninth century. The first enameled pieces called *Seiji*, with a glaze of neutral gray, recall the ancient celadons. It is starting from this epoch that the direct influence of China intervenes.

A curious fact to be noted is that the development and progress of the ceramic industry in Japan coincide precisely with the introduction of the use of tea. The necessity of obtaining vases well adapted for the preservation of the powdered tea led the potters to decisive researches. It is to a potter of the village of Seto, in the province of Owari, that one owes the first tea-jars called *cha-ire*, those little vases coated with beautiful thick enamel colors, with ivory stoppers, which Japanese amateurs keep tenderly wrapped up in silken cases inclosed in double boxes. Toshiro had made the voyage to China in the beginning of the thirteenth century. His works, so ardently sought by collectors, justify their reputation by the remarkably fine grain of their paste and by their warm and harmonious glazes. The immediate successor of Toshiro was Tojiro.

In reality, all Japanese pottery is derived, when its origin is traced back, from the first workshops of Seto. Hence the consecration of the term *setomono* (Seto articles or objects) to denote ceramic ware generally. The productions of Seto dominate the ceramic industry down to the beginning of the seventeenth century, the moment of the appearance of Ninsei, an artist of genius, who was the veritable creator of the national ceramic art, and who even down to the present day remains the greatest *céramiste* that Japan has ever produced.

The three elements, Chinese, Korean, and Japanese, are blended together in him; and from their union springs an original art armed at every point, the national art, in one word. An admirable logic, a powerfully inventive spirit, a refined and exquisite taste preside over the work of Ninsei. Not only does he invent and bring to perfection the technical details, but he frees the decoration little by little from Chinese conventionalities and endows it with grand ornamental laws after the Japanese genius. He creates, so to speak, fundamental forms of objects so perfectly adapted to their destination that they have remained in current use ever since. The work of Ninsei is marked with a popular character; it flows from an inexhaustible and charming fancy. His researches opened up for his successors the boundless field of polychrome decoration by means of vitrifiable colors.

FIG. 392.—Satsuma figure of Chinese boy (Kara-Ko) holding a palm-leaf fan, richly decorated in enamel colors and gilding.

Ninsei was a native of Kyōto. The date of his birth, as I have already said, is not known precisely, but it must have been during the last quarter of the sixteenth century. He worked during the whole of the first half of the seventeenth century, and died about 1660. Before he devoted himself to the ceramic art he had already acquired great renown as a painter. He traveled in succession through different provinces of Japan, and visited the principal ceramic centers; but it was at Kyōto that he established his domain and founded there, in the suburbs of Kyomidzu, Awata, Mizoro, Seikanji, Otawa, etc., his kilns, the chief of which exists down to the present day, and still carries on his traditions. It is to Ninsei, and to Ninsei alone, that the glory belongs of having made of the ancient capital the most energetic and the most brilliant center of the ceramic art.

The works of Ninsei offer examples of the most varied styles; it seems as if each piece which came from his hand were the fruit of a particular stroke of invention, of a careful study of the art. The most popular creation of Ninsei is that of a pottery with a fawn-colored, finely crackled glaze, decorated with flowers in which blue and green enamels enhanced by gold predominate. This industry, which is carried on at the present time in the suburbs of Kyōto, principally at Awata, at Kyomidzu, and at Iwakura, is known to us under the general name of "old Kyōto" ware. There are no ceramic productions that I prefer to it; only the superb faïences of Persia appear to us capable of rivaling these pieces in harmony and brilliancy. It is hardly necessary for me to remark that authentic works of the great ceramic artist are of extreme rarity. Care must be taken not to confound with them the many pieces of later date which bear his seal, and which are only the productions of his workshop. The ancient specimens are recognized by the fine texture of the paste, by the neatness and suppleness of the outline, by the warm transparency of the glaze, and by the opalescent reflections of the enamels.

The teachings of Ninsei had the most fruitful results. Two artists of great renown, Kinkozan and Kenzan, made Kyōto illustrious at the close of the seventeenth century.

The type created by Kinkozan is very remarkable; it is a nearly black "biscuit" of a very close and very homogeneous texture, which serves as a ground for enamels laid on in regular designs of marked relief, the prevailing color being a dark blue, discreetly interspersed with yellow, white, and green.

Ogata Kenzan, who lived from 1663 to 1743, was the younger brother and pupil of the celebrated lacquer-painter Kōrin. His works are distinguished by an extraordinary freedom in the decorations, laid on in large masses, of powerful tone, among which emerald greens give nearly always the predominant note with their glowing reflections. They show well all the advantage that can be gained from a simplification of the decoration. With Kenzan this apparent artlessness is only the result of profound technical skill. His fine pieces are able to compete in the eyes of amateurs with those of Ninsei. The originality of the forms, of the methods, and of the designs is no less great. The sense of color is even superior in Kenzan. From the standpoint of a full, vibrating, and harmonious richness of enamel coloring, he still remains without a peer. The material of Kenzan's pieces is usually rather coarse, or at any rate light and friable, and is consequently very inferior to that of Ninsei's; their value consists in the splendid vesture with which the artist envelops them. The originals can be distinguished at a glance by a transparency and delicacy in the enamels which no copyist has been able to imitate.

At the close of his life Kenzan migrated to Yedo, where he founded the kiln of Imado. As M. Bing has very justly observed, this ware presents beauties of a different order, and constitutes a very marked evolution in the research of color effects. In the place of the neutral grounds on which his brilliant sketches were first displayed, we have here luminous glazes of a highly vitreous composition which enhanced the bold freedom of the coloring.

Parisian collections contain very beautiful and very numerous examples of the different styles of Kenzan's work.

The history of the Kyōto factories gives us next the names of Ogata Shuhei, who distinguished himself in the modeling of little figures full of life and spirit; of Mokubei and Rokubei, skillful in the finish of small miniature objects, of boxes in the shape of animals for perfumes or unguents; of Dohachi; and lastly of Yeiraku, the most astonishing *pasticheur* that the ceramic art has produced. Yeiraku is in truth a surprising practitioner. His bowls for the preparation of tea are marvels of decorative ingenuity and of technical perfection. He is the last of the great ceramists whose works are worthy of exciting the passion of collectors.

Let us cite, in conclusion, among the special productions which have remained apart, away from the influence of Ninsei or of Kenzan, the pottery of Raku, with monochrome glazes becoming generally red or orange, blending with very friable *pâtes*, and the miniature figures in terra-cotta of Ikakura Goyemon which are the Tanagra of Japan.

Outside the province of Hizen, the only kilns in which porcelain, properly so called, has been produced in at all ancient times are those of Kaga. The center of the industry, founded in the middle of the seventeenth century by a potter named Goto Saijiro, who had gone and found out the secrets of the manufacture at Arita, is found in a locality called Kutani. But the productions of Kutani have never had, like those of Arita, a commercial character; they were destined for the Prince of Kaga, for the Shogun, or for some of the celebrated *chajin*. This is what explains their great rarity and the high price that they have always retained. They deserve, moreover, in all regards, their celebrity. An artist of the school of Kano, of the name of. Morikagé, was the inventor of the artistic decoration at Kutani, and freed it from archaic imitations.

At the end of the seventeenth century the art had acquired a definite character which it has never since lost. The type is well known; its beauty resides in the almost exclusive play of three tones of enamel color, the effect of which in combination is admirable—green, yellow, and violet. Fine pieces of Kutani, with their thick and trans-lucid glazes, have a brilliancy which can vie with that of real jewels. The association of these three colors, the intensity of which is multiplied by the transparency of the glaze, produces upon the eyes a voluptuous sensation, as it were, at least equal to that of certain pieces of old Kyōto. Even the *flambés* of China would almost pale before picked specimens of Kutani.

FIG. 393.—Saké-Bottle of Satsuma faïence, decorated in soft enamel colors and gold with sprays of *Paulownia imperialis*; silver kiku stopper. Satsuma Vase, decorated in enamel colors with a selection from the precious objects called "Takara-mono."

But of all the branches of the ceramic art of Japan, the most celebrated, perhaps, is that of the faïence of Satsuma; it is the one best known in Europe, thanks to the productions imitated or painted with overglaze decorations at Tōkyo which have flooded our markets fraudulently ticketed as Satsuma. All of those large vases, flower-receptacles, and dishes of gorgeous aspect, loaded with gold in relief, were for a long time taken for authentic Satsuma. At first the dealers all became enriched by this easy commerce, selling for a thousand francs at Paris what they had paid fifty for at Yokohama. The secret has been pretty well kept, so that even to-day a number of people allow themselves to be taken in. The pieces that came out of the Tōkyo workshops are at the same time extremely brilliant, and lend themselves with marvelous effect as adjuncts in the furnishing of our rooms. The best are made at Satsuma and decorated at Tōkyo; these have a certain value in themselves.

One can lay down the general rule that all the pieces that have come out of the prince's factory at Satsuma are of small dimensions. One of the largest that is known is the incense-burner in the form of a cat, executed about 1780, presented by the Prince of Satsuma to the Princess Tayasu-Tokugawa, and acquired since and brought to Paris by M. Wakai. This classic specimen of Satsuma presents to us, like all the other pieces made for the use of the Daimyos and of the Shoguns, a very dense *pâte* of extremely fine texture. The glaze, in play of color, ranges from creamy white to the gilded tones of old ivory; upon this harmonious and soft ground, lightly crackled, stand out enamels of tender and airy color, in marked relief, in the midst of which shades of dead gold marble blend with the most delicious effect. As M. Bing has remarked, old Satsuma has the properties of jewelry fully as much as of ceramic ware.

This artistic pottery owes its origin to the expedition which the famous Taiko Hideyoshi made in Korea. It is Prince Shimadsu Yoshihisa who brought back from that country, in 1598, seventeen families of ceramic workmen whom he established in the village of Nawashiragawa. At first they contented themselves with copying the Korean productions with a gray glaze, ornamented with regular designs in black or brown. It is only from the beginning of the eighteenth century that the delicately and minutely crackled faïence that has become so renowned under the name of Satsuma dates, and the first decoration of this was designed by potters summoned from Kyōto for the purpose.

Apart from the production of this type the kilns of this province attempted also monochrome pieces, which present no decoration other than the exquisite colors of their glazes. These exceptional productions are of the greatest beauty and of the greatest rarity.

Among the other centers formed by the Korean potters of 1598, or sprung directly from their influence, it is necessary to mention the kilns of Yatsushiro, Agano, Takatori, Odo, Hagi, Idzumo, Tamba, and Zeze, each of which, in its own style, has produced some remarkable types.

The potteries of Owari, illustrated by the ancient kiln of Seto, had little by little fallen into decadence; we see them rise again for a moment in the seventeenth century under the influence of two eminent artists, Shino and Oribé. Their works present a character of remarkable grandeur and simplicity. Shino has modeled statuettes decorated in enamels of the *grand feu* which attest his profound knowledge of sculpture.

The stoneware (*grès*) of Bizen are productions apart, and their special character does not attach them to any of the types of which I have just been speaking. The origin of these productions is purely Japanese, without any trace of foreign influence, and appears to mount up to the highest antiquity. The fine productions of this princely fabric, especially those of the seventeenth and eighteenth centuries, are particularly appreciated by European amateurs. The baking of the paste of the Bizen ware is effected by a very violent fire, which imparts to it a beautiful brownish red and covers it, by the fusion of the vitreous particles, with a sort of metallic glaze. Bizen pieces bear no other decoration; they are generally personages or animals modeled with singular power. The center of this industry has been for centuries past fixed at Imbé.

Fig. 394.—Chinese Lion (Kara Shishi) of Hirado porcelain of the eighteenth century, with its left forefoot upon an openwork ball of quatrefoil brocade pattern. The details are lightly etched under the white glaze, which is of pale greenish tone.

It is necessary to add to the list of these principal centers of the industry the names of those of less antiquity, or less importance, of Soma (province of Iwaki), of Akahada (province of Yamato), of Minato (province of Idzumi), of Awaji, made illustrious in the last quarter of the eighteenth century by a skillful and ingenious artist of the name of Mimpei.

Some potters have practiced their art in an altogether independent fashion, and have created kilns which have disappeared immediately after their death. Such a one is the old Banko, a pupil of Kenzan, who established himself at Kuwana, in the province of Ise, and produced there works of masterly skill and originality, often rivaling those of his preceptor. Such, again, is the celebrated lacquer-painter Ritsuo, whose incrustations of faïence upon lacquer rank among the rarest and most precious objects that Japan has ever produced. Such, finally, is Koren, the lady modeler in clay, who is still living, and whose works, instinct with spirit, are highly esteemed in Europe.

Toshiro, Gorodayu Shonsui, Kakiyemon, Ninsei, Shino, Kenzan, Banko, Kinkozan, Yeiraku, and Mimpei, these are the names it is important to remember as dominating the whole history of the ceramic art in Japan.

Modern productions are only a more or less adroit imitation of the types created by those great artists. The technical skill is always extremely high, of which the elegant pottery wares of Kyōto, and the Kutani, Satsuma, and Imari pieces of modern days are a proof. The current industry yields still to commerce some charming productions, of exceptional cheapness when compared with our own; but it creates and invents no longer anything that is worthy of comparison with the art-work of the finest epochs.

Fig. 395.—Satsuma Figure of Hotei, the Monk of the Hempen Bag,
painted in enamel colors and gold.

CHAPTER XXVII.

THE PRINCIPAL CERAMIC WARES OF JAPAN.—OWARI POTTERY AND PORCELAIN.—KYŌTO WARES.—
HIZEN PRODUCTIONS: OLD IMARI PORCELAINS, HIRADO BLUE AND WHITE, ETC.—SATSUMA
FAÏENCES, KUTANI OR KAGA WARES.

I. OWARI.

THE collectors of Japanese ceramic wares and the writers on the ceramic art of
Japan may be divided broadly into two schools. The one school is devoted to
the archaic and rustic potteries, coinciding in their views with native connoisseurs, who prefer antique simplicity and quaint originality of design to any
other qualities. Their claims have been ably urged by an enthusiastic advocate
in the preceding chapter. The other school is more attracted by the artistic decoration and
harmonious coloring of some of the old Hizen porcelains, by the subdued tones and technical finish of the Hirado blue and white, and by the soft shades of the enamel colors of
decorated Satsuma faïence enhanced by the finely crackled background on which they are displayed. The latter school is fully justified by the beautiful specimens of these classes exhibited
on the shelves of the cabinets in the Walters collection, as may be seen by the examples
which have been selected for colored illustration in these pages.

The wares will be noticed in the order of the "Table of the Principal Centers of the Ceramic Industry" given on page 349. The list is too long to allow of a discussion of all the
different kilns in the limited space available here, so that reference will only
be made to those represented in the illustrations. For the rest, one may
refer to the books the titles of which have been given in the bibliographical
section of Chapter XXV.

The first province in the list is that of Owari, which is one of the
earliest seats of the industry, and which was so noted in early times that the
name of its productions—"Setomono"—has become a synonym for all kinds
of ceramic wares in Japan, in the same way as china with us has become a
common synonym for porcelains. It is recorded in the official annals that
three potteries of this province were attached to the court of the Mikado in
816, and there are lists, under the years 905 and 1114, of the articles of
earthenware which were furnished at the time for the use of the emperor.
The first real progress in the art is attributed to Kato Shirozayemon, a native
of the village of Seto, whose name is generally abbreviated to Toshiro. He
traveled to China in 1223, with a Buddhist monk named Dogen, and stayed
there five years, studying the Chinese processes of manufacture. The most highly appreciated
ware at the tea-testing parties which were very fashionable in China at this time, as we have
seen, was the dark-colored pottery of the province of Fuchien (*Chien Tz'ŭ*) flecked or dappled
with lighter spots, the tea-bowls of which were known to Chinese virtuosos as "hare's-fur

Fig. 396.—Small
Cylinder with per-
forated side, of
Hizen blue and
white porcelain
inscribed with the
mark of Shonsui.

bowls " or "gray partridge bowls," from the spotted aspect of the glaze. These were the manufactories, no doubt, that Toshiro visited, and the tea-bowls and jars for powdered tea made in the kiln which he set up in his native village after his return were fashioned, after the pattern of the old Chinese pottery of the *Sung* dynasty, of a reddish-brown stoneware coated with dark chestnut-colored mottled glazes, sometimes sprinkled, we are told, with flying yellow spots. His successors lightened up the russet and bronze-colored grounds with a translucent overglaze of golden yellow, or with viscid enamels of transmutation type which became streaked with brilliant *flambé* tints as they guttered down in the kiln over the surface of the jar, but they always left part of the surface of the piece bare, so that the perfect potting of the material might be appreciated. Tea-jars (*cha-ire*) of a similar type were produced in turn

at the other kilns through-
tions are made in the present
classify them with infinite
and shade of coloring of the
microscopic structure of the
examined with a magnifying

Specimens of these tea-
to be found in Plates CXIV
illustrations give an excel-
different forms, with their
varied coloring of the
the soft shades of the
in which the little jars
jar in Plate CXIV, 3,
Seto kilns in Owari
cussing. The water-
side it (Plate CXIV, 1),
brown stoneware of
an olive-brown glaze
low spots and overlaid
orange-yellow, is a more
Fujina kilns in the prov-
to the beginning of the
marked improvement in
due to a skillful potter
cording to Ouéda To-
91), established himself
An-yei (1772–80), after
dairo Harusato, the dai-

FIG. 397.—Vase of Kyōto porcelain, decorated in rich enamel colors with gilding, with elaborate floral scrolls and panel pictures of Buddhist figures.

out Japan, and large collec-
day by the initiated, who
pains according to the texture
glazes, and according to the
paste from different localities
lens.
jars from different kilns are
and CXV, and the colored
lent idea of some of the
ivory lids, and of the
glazes, contrasted with
old brocaded silk bags
are wrapped. The tea-
is a production of the
which we are now dis-
bottle (*shaku-date*) be-
made of a similar
fine grain, coated with
flecked with lustrous yel-
with splashes of crackled
recent production of the
ince of Idzumo, attributed
nineteenth century. A
the manufacture here was
named Zenshiro, who, ac-
kounosouke (*loc. cit.*, page
at Fujina in the period
an invitation from Matsu-
myo of the province of

Idzumo, and made for him, after his designs, pottery for the *cha-no-yu*, of which cult this prince was a great amateur. He was succeeded here in turn by Zenshiro II, Zenroku III, and Zenroku IV, and the fifth of the line, whose personal name is Dentaro, is mentioned as still carrying on the work in the present day. A tea-jar from the same kilns of somewhat earlier date is exhibited in Plate CXV, 3, and is described there.

The two tea-jars which are illustrated in the same plate come from two other kilns, being specimens of Shigaraki ware from the province of Omi, and of Takatori ware from the province of Chikuzen. The Shigaraki potteries date from the *Ko-an* period (1278–87), but at first only jars for storing grain and ordinary domestic utensils were made, of a very hard, dense stoneware of grayish color with a large admixture of sand, which is known as *Ko-Shigaraki*, *ko* meaning ancient. The first articles for the *cha-no-yu* were made in the period *Yei-sho* (1504–20), and the names of several of the celebrated masters of the tea cult have been attached to varieties of this gray stoneware made under their instructions. In 1828, according to the Franks Catalogue (*loc. cit.*, page 41), the Shogun of the Tokugawa family ordered the manufacture of tea-jars called *Koshishiro-Tsukemimi*, since which the factory has become still more noted for its jars, which are said to preserve the flavor of the tea remarkably well on account of the peculiarly hard, impervious quality of the *pâte*.

The Takatori-yaki is yet more famous. In Captain Brinkley's words:

" If popularity be any criterion of excellence, the first place among the achievements of Taiko's imported artisans belongs to the ware made by Shinkuro and Hachizo (natives of the ceramic district of Ido in Korea) at Takatori in the province of Chikuzen. Their earliest productions were after the Korean style, having only one thin coat of diaphanous glaze, but subsequently, with the assistance of Igarashi Jizayemon, a skillful potter of Seto, they began to imitate the Chinese *flambé* glazes, and succeeded so admirably that their pieces were unanimously pronounced the *chefs-d'œuvres* of their times (1624-44). Something of this esteem was no doubt won for them by the patronage of the celebrated art critic Kobori Masakadzu, Earl of Yenshiu, who at the request of Tadayuki, Duke of Chikuzen, instructed * Shinkuro and Hachizo in the shapes and technical details of the pottery which best accorded with the æsthetic code of the Tea Clubs, and afterward, selecting certain of their best productions, gave them names indicative of their peculiar merits. It is scarcely possible to overestimate the value attaching to pieces distinguished by the approval of such an amateur."

At a subsequent period of its history cleverly modeled figures of mythological personages and imaginary animals were turned out by the Takatori workshops for use as incense-burners, alcove ornaments, and so forth, which were coated with a thick, lustrous glaze of a *flambé* character, the general color being gray or buff passing into green, chocolate, brown, or sometimes blue. The large temple vase (*hana-ike*), eighteen inches high, shown in Fig. 383, is of a more archaic type, being enameled with a pale-green crackled glaze mottled with clouds of olive tint, which only partially covers the surface, so that the paste, of light-red color, is left unglazed round the base. Outside the vase, modeled in slip in slight relief, are the figures of three Buddhist saints, with halos in the form of wide rings encircling their brows. One is seated upon a rock in the attitude of meditation; another is elevating with both hands an alms-bowl, from which a spiral column of water is ascending—the special attribute of Nâgasena; the third, apparently Vajrabuddha, is leaning upon a long and knotted pilgrim's staff. The mark stamped in an oblong panel is inscribed *Taka* (short for Takatori), in a circle, and *Arashi Tanemune*, the name of the potter.

To return to the province of Owari: One of the minor productions of the kilns of Nagoya is tabulated as *Gempin-yaki*, the name being that of a Chinaman who became naturalized as a Japanese and established himself there. He is wrongly called a Korean in most Japanese books, even in the official reports of the Philadelphia Exposition. Indeed, one of the difficulties in the discussion of ceramic art is the loose way in which the Japanese writers on the subject apply the term *Korai*, properly Korea, to northern China, and *Kochi*, properly Kochin-China or Annam, to southern China, so that the influence of China on the industry is often apt to be lost sight of for the moment. In this connection the story of Gempin is worth relating, as told by Captain Brinkley. In the year 1640, when the *Ming* dynasty of China was on the point of overthrow by the Manchu Tartars, four Chinese nobles came to Japan to pray for aid against the northern invaders. The Japanese were at first disposed to entertain the request, but reflecting that they would be supporting rulers who fifty years before had sent an army to oppose Hideyoshi's generals in Korea, they ultimately decided to let the *Ming* fight their own battles. The fugitive nobles were, however, treated with all courtesy. Confided to the hospitable care of Japanese barons, three of them seem to have passed the remainder of their lives in uneventful seclusion, while the fourth, Gempin, residing at Nagoya, devoted his leisure to painting and pottery-making. As an artist he possessed considerable ability, but his ceramic efforts are not very creditable, though much valued by the Tea Clubs. His pieces consist of a crackled faïence, decorated sometimes with archaic designs in blue under the glaze, and some-

---

* Hachizo figures in our table as the founder of the Takatori factory. He was the son-in-law of Shinkuro, according to Mr. Ouéda, who says that it was Hachizo and his son Hachiyemon who were sent by the daimyo to receive the orders of Masakazu in the period *Kwanyei* (1624-43). According to him, the principal glazes of the Takatori-yaki were white, light blue, and ash-colored.

times with arabesques in relief. Genuine specimens are generally marked with his name in blue under the glaze.

Down to the beginning of the nineteenth century nothing but faïence was made in the province of Owari, although it is to-day the principal center of porcelain manufacture in Japan. The introduction of porcelain was the work of Kato Tamikichi, a descendant of the celebrated Kato Shirozayemon, the "father of pottery," who went to China in 1223. Tamikichi was sent to Hizen in 1804 to study the processes of fabrication there. It is said that he found the secrets of the manufacture so jealously guarded at the various potteries, that it was not until his marriage with the widow of an Arita potter and the birth of his child seemed to afford a sufficient guarantee of good faith, that his new connections consented to instruct him. After he had learned all he could, Tamikichi left his wife and child to shift for themselves, and

FIG. 398.—Large Dish of "old Imari ware," painted in underglaze blue in combination with enamels and gilding in the typical *chrysanthemo-péonienne* style.

hastened back to Seto to impart his knowledge to his old comrades, whom he rejoined in 1807, after nearly four years' absence. He was rewarded with a hereditary title of nobility by the Prince of Owari, who belonged to the Tokugawa family, and given the privilege of wearing two swords, a rare distinction for a plain potter. The new industry flourished apace, and within fourteen years some two hundred potters had abandoned their old work to take up porcelain. From the first, decoration in blue under the glaze (*sometsuke*) has been a specialty of this province, and its blue and white production fifty years ago is said to have been second to none in Japan. It is famed to-day for colossal dishes over five feet in diameter, slabs for tables mounted upon baluster stands, and temple lamps nine feet high; but the cheaper smalt imported from Europe has usurped the place of the old cobaltiferous ores of China, and scarcely a memory remains of the pure, rich blue of former times, blending so softly with the fluescent paste.

The decorators of Owari porcelain, however, have not confined themselves to the use of blue under the glaze. Since 1820 enameled ware has been made at Inazi in the old Chinese style of the *Ming* dynasty, a white porcelain painted with designs roughly executed in red and green enamels with an occasional addition of blue under the glaze. Another variety is decorated with figure subjects in red and gold upon a white ground, so as to resemble in general effect modern Kaga porcelain. Of late years the Owari potters have developed considerable skill in the use of colors of the *grand feu*, and many pieces decorated in sea-green, maroon, and blue are exported. Celadon monochromes are also made, and a species of *flambé* ware in which chocolate color predominates. There is hardly anything that is not attempted in the present day, but the methods are rough, and it would not be a great loss to art if the potters confined themselves to the making of household utensils, which seems to be their proper field. A large quantity of their ware is taken to Tōkyo to be decorated in enamel colors, so that the two places in combination have been fitly styled the Stoke-upon-Trent of Japan.

Seto itself produces all the materials necessary for the making of ordinary pottery, but most of the ingredients required for porcelain have to be brought from Kamo, in the adjoining province of Mikawa.

The Toyosuke ware was first made by a potter of this name at Aichi, in Owari, about 1825. It is a crackled faïence thinly coated outside with lacquer delicately painted in gold. Of less, if any, artistic value is the *cloisonné* enameling upon porcelain as a base, which discredited the workshops of Nagoya for a few years subsequent to 1870, before the happy renaissance of the ceramic art which has since appeared.

II. KYŌTO.

The origin of the potteries of Kyōto, the old capital of Japan, is lost in antiquity. Tradition ascribes to the celebrated priest Gyogi, about the *Tembiō* period (729–748), the fabrication of earthenware vases at Chawan-saka (Hill of Cups), where the present village of Seikanji, near Kyōto, is situated, which is still the principal center of the manufacture of the Kyomidzu wares. There were gradual improvements in the technique of the ware as time went on, but it was the celebrated potter Ninsei, in the seventeenth century, whose work brought it to the prominent position, from an artistic point of view, which it has since enjoyed. He has been justly given the same place in Japanese ceramics as that occupied by Bernard Palissy in Europe, and a short sketch of his career, as given by Ouéda Tokounosouké, may not be out of place here.

Nonomura Ninsei, whose proper name was Seibei, later Seizayemon, was a native of the province of Tamba. In his youth he learned the ceramic art from a naturalized Korean potter of the name of Butsuami. Having come to Kyōto in the *Genwa* period (1615–23), he continued his apprenticeship at the atelier of an artist of Seikanji. He was attached afterward as potter to the imperial Prince of Ninwaji, who authorized him to adopt his own initial, Nin. Hence the name of Ninsei, which is composed of this initial (*Nin*) and of the initial of his own proper name (*Sei*). Ninsei received later from the same prince the honorary title of Harima no Daijo (a high official grade of the province of Harima). He died at Omuro in the period *Manji* (1658–60).

Ninsei established a succession of kilns in the vicinity of Kyōto, at Mizoro, Omuro, Iwakura, Awata, Seikanji, etc., where he adopted the different processes of Seto, of Hagi and Matsumoto, in the province of Nagano, of Shigaraki, in the province of Omi, etc., as well as the methods imported by the first Korean potters. He excelled especially in making objects for use in the Tea Ceremonies, of *midzu-sashi* (water-bowls), dishes, plates, and such like; a great number of his pieces were painted, and their designs are the work of the celebrated painters Kano Taniu and Kano Yeishin, his contemporaries.

This celebrated potter, who enjoyed a very great renown, had numerous imitators even during his own lifetime. In his later years, during the *Meireki* period (1655–57), he succeeded in producing pieces decorated in several colors (*Nishikide*), which were much admired, thanks to secrets of technique revealed to him by a merchant of Kyōto named Chawanya Kiubei, who had learned them himself from Aoyama Koyemon, a native of Arita. The Arita potter was afterward prosecuted, and, it is said, crucified in his own province for having divulged the secrets of the Hizen kilns, and the Kyōto dealer became a lunatic at the news of the execution of his friend.

After the death of Ninsei the Kyō-yaki was divided into two main branches, the *Awata-yaki* and the *Kyomidzu-yaki.* The names of his principal successors have been given in the preceding chapter.

One of the cleverest of the Kyōto potters, in the estimation of his own countrymen at least, was Mokubei, who flourished at the beginning of the nineteenth century. This is said to be an abridgment of the name of Aoki Yasohachi, a native of the province of Owari. In his later years he became deaf, and took the name of Robei, *ro* meaning deaf. From his youth he showed a great taste for art and antiquity, and his imitative ability procured for him the title of the best artist of modern times. He afterward embraced the career of a potter, and succeeded in rivaling by his talent the works of Ninsei and Kenzan. He is credited with the introduction of molds into Japan, and of many other novel processes derived from a study of Chinese works on the ceramic industry, and he also published a work of his own on the subject. There was nothing that he did not succeed in reproducing, and so perfectly as to deceive the greatest ceramic experts of his time. The enameled stonewares of southern China, the ordinary decorated porcelains and celadons of China, the encaustic inlaid pottery and the ivory-white porcelain of Korea, are said to have been copied by him with success. In the fifth year of the period *Bunsei* (1822) he constructed private kilns Seiren-in, and made sets for the imperial Prince of utensils for the personal use of the princes of Kii of the Tokugawa house. He died in the year 1832.

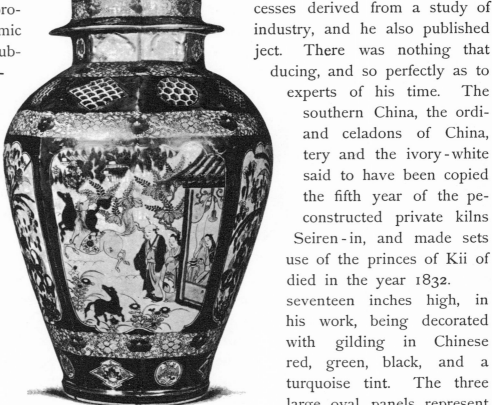

FIG. 399.—Large Covered Jar of "old Imari ware," decorated in colors and gold with pictures of outdoor scenes, and brocaded bands with pierced trellis-work panels.

The vase (*hana-ike*), Fig. 397, is an example of seventeen inches high, in his work, being decorated in bright enamel colors, with gilding in Chinese style. The colors comprise red, green, black, and a light translucent blue of turquoise tint. The three figures inclosed in three large oval panels represent the Buddhist Trinity, Sâkyamuni, Samantabhadra, and Manjusrî, displayed upon a background of variegated clouds, their heads encircled by golden halos. The Buddha is seated on a mat of leaves upon a rock, his forehead marked with the sacred *ûrna*, and a gilded *ushnisha* projecting in the midst of the close black curls of his hair, his hands folded under his robe, which is brocaded with lotus-flowers. Samantabhadra, as seen in the picture, is seated upon an elephant, reading from an open book. Manjusrî, upon a grotesque lion, holds a rolled scroll in one hand, a coral scepter (*ju-i*) in the other.

The panels are framed by green bands of fret, and bands of similar design encircle the upper and lower rims of the vase. The space between the panels is filled with a close reticulation of floral scrolls of lotus pattern, extending up to the middle of the neck, which is marked by a sunk ring containing panels of lotus-blossoms penciled in gold. The upper part of the neck is decorated with three conventional phœnixes displayed in colors on the same red background as the lotus scrolls below.

The mark, written underneath in red within a double red ring in two columns, is *Ko-ki-kwan Moku-bei tsukuru,* "Made by Mokubei at the Hall of Ancient Ware."

III. HIZEN.

The province of Hizen contains many porcelain manufactories, and has from the first occupied the foremost rank in Japan for its artistic productions in that material, Kyōto being more famous for its art work in ordinary pottery than for its porcelain. Tradition carries back the origin of the ceramic industry in this province to the time of the Emperor *Kotoku,* who reigned from 645 to 654.* A few specimens of the primitive pieces made here have been preserved, vases made of an intensely hard refractory clay, uncoated with glaze. The earliest kilns were in the vicinity of the harbor of Karatsu, where the first glazed pottery was made in Japan, and where gradual improvements were introduced into the manufacture under the influence of the early Korean teachers. The first of them was naturalized under the name of Kojiro Kwanja, and there is a temple dedicated to him in one of the adjoining mountains at which the potters still offer incense. In the beginning of the *Keichō* period (1596–1614) the daimyo of Karatsu transferred the workshops, which had previously been within the walls of his castle, to a locality called Karabori ("Chinese canal"), in a quarter of the town named Tojin-machi ("Chinese quarters"), where he established a number of potters who were brought over at that time from Korea. Many kinds of Karatsu-yaki are described, but they are all stonewares of primitive type, comprising principally articles of ordinary domestic use and utensils for the tea ceremonies. The factory is now in a state of decay.

The other ceramic productions of the province of Hizen are all grouped together under the heading of Imari-Yaki, Imari being the name of the seaport at which they are shipped to be distributed to other parts of the empire. There are many different factories, but the three principal productions from an artistic point of view are those of Arita, Okawaji, and Mikawaji (Hirado). Arita is the most important center of porcelain manufacture in Japan. It is about fifty miles to the north of Nagasaki, and its potteries were the source of the "old Japan" porcelain which the Dutch imported into Europe in such large quantities during the seventeenth and eighteenth centuries; the first export of pieces ornamented with colored enamels, in gold and silver, etc., having been, according to the official Japanese report, in the second year of *Shō-hō* (1645). Okawaji is about eight miles to the north of Arita. It was the seat of the private factory of the princes of Nabeshima, established there in the middle of the eighteenth century, their previous locality, close to Arita, having been found to be unfavorable to the maintenance of the required secrecy. The porcelain made here was intended for presentation to the Shogun or to the friends of the daimyo, the rest being reserved for his own personal use, so that specimens are comparatively rare in private collections. The third factory at Mika-waji was under the special patronage of the house of Hirado, and produced the plain white ware of finest texture and the soft-toned blue and white of perfect technique, which are usually given the first place among the porcelains of Japan.

The introduction of real porcelain-making into Japan is attributed to Gorodayu Shonsui, who went to China to study the art, and returned to his own country in the year 1513. After his return he settled in Hizen, and succeeded in making a ceramic ware decorated in the Chinese fashion with cobalt under the glaze, although authorities differ as to the kaolinic structure of the material. A specimen of porcelain said to have been made by him in China and marked with his name, as inscribed below, is preserved in Japan at Nara. The small brush cylinder in the Walters Collection which is inscribed with his mark is shown in Fig. 396, although it would be rash to guarantee its authenticity. It is a little cylinder, five inches high, with a serrated rim, painted under the glaze in dull blue with flowering trees and storks. Through

---

* It was in the reign of this monarch that the old method of counting years by the reigns of the emperors was abandoned in Japan, and the Chinese system of counting by periods called *Nien-hao* (in Japanese *Nen-gō*) was adopted. The first period (645–49) was called *Tai-kwa.*—EDITOR'S NOTE.

the large oval perforation which is pierced in one side is seen the mark, penciled in blue, of *Go-ro-da-yu go Shon-sui tsukuru*, "Made by the honorable Gorodayu Shonsui." *

The first of the Arita kilns was founded in the period *Kei-chō* (1596–1614) by the Korean Li-Sanpei, one of the many potters brought over to Japan by Nabeshima Naoshige on his return from the expedition to Korea. After many researches he discovered the necessary materials in the Idzumi Mountains near the village of Tanaka, which was afterward called Arita. Damaged pieces of his fabrication found on the sites of the old kilns, and preserved in collections under the name of *horidashite*, "dug up from the ground," have a white kaolinic paste. Li-Sanpei, after his naturalization, took the name of Kané, the Japanese pronunciation of Kin-Ko, the name of the place where he was born. Several branches of his descendants are still living, and carry on the same industry, having changed their name from Kané to Kanegae.

FIG. 400.—Water-Pot of Hizen porcelain molded in the shape of a fish-dragon, and painted in underglaze blue with touches of black enamel and gold.

We may follow Ouéda Tokounosouké again in his account of the Arita kilns. In the seventeenth century the development of the ceramic industry in the domains of the princes of Nabeshima was very considerable. One consequence of this was the destruction of the forests round all the centers of the industry, and about 1610 orders were issued by the prince prohibiting eight hundred workmen from carrying on their business as potters, and giving the monopoly of the industry to the Koreans. In spite of this prohibition, however, a certain number of Japanese potters succeeded in getting the permission of the authorities to continue their work. The interdict, instead of arresting the progress of the industry, contributed to its prosperity by giving the monopoly of the manufacture to a certain number of families. Skillful artists appeared in succession, who distinguished themselves by the production of true objects of art. It was not, however, till the *Shō-hō* period (1644–47) that a native of Imari, Toshima Tokuzayemon, learned from a Chinese traveler at Nagasaki the method of decorating porcelain with metal.† The process was indicated to Sakaida Kakiyemon of Nan-kawarayama (who had, it is said, served his apprenticeship in the workshops of Goroshichi, a potter of the house of Hideyoshi), but he failed in his first attempts. It was not till the aid of Gosu Gombei had been enlisted, and after many years of research and repeated experimental trials, that Kakiyemon succeeded. The productions of this novel fabrication, very similar to those of the same class made in China, were exported afterward in their turn into this last country from the port of Nagasaki.

In the period *Kuam-bun* (1661–72) a Prince Daté, of Sendai, sent to Arita a porcelain dealer of Yedo, of the name of Imariya Gorobei, to order some things to be made there. He took back with him, after two years' stay in this place, some articles made by Tsuji Kizaye-mon, who had the reputation of being a clever potter. The articles were offered by Prince Daté at the court of the emperor, and Kizayemon was afterward appointed imperial purveyor and commissioned to send an annual supply to the court. The vases sent to Kyōto for the personal use of the sovereign were painted with chrysanthemum-flowers, the arms of his house, and decorated with flying storks, emblems of longevity according to Japanese symbolism. The grandson of Kizayemon, Kiheiji, who became in his turn court potter, was honored with the official title of "Hidachi no Daijo." It was he who is said to have accidentally discovered the use of seggars. He employed two kinds, the ordinary cylindrical cases piled in columns, in which the more common pieces were fired, and separate seggars covered with lids, the joints of which were luted so as to be hermetically sealed, and which had to be broken when the

---

* No Japanese collection seems to be complete without a specimen with this mark. *Cf. Franks's Collection of Oriental Porcelain* (Plate XIV, Fig. 183), and Bowes's *Japanese Marks and Seals* (Hizen Pottery, No. 81). In the latter case it is strangely deciphered *Go-ro-ta-narabini Sho-zui sin-zo*, "Made by Gorota and Sho-zui together."

† It is uncertain whether the term "metals" (*kane*) used here refers to gold and silver only. or comprises other metal oxides as well, so as to denote enamel color generally.

baking was completed. Tsuji Katsuzo, a descendant of Kiheiji, is one of the cleverest manufacturers of the present day, and is specially skilled in pierced work, specimens of which have been shown by him in the international exhibitions. He is also one of the court purveyors, and is besides a leading member of the "Koransha," a company recently founded at Arita to encourage foreign export. There is now a technical school at Arita, which was established in 1880, to teach the ceramic art in all its branches, and to foster the so-called modern improvements, which threaten to replace the individual touch which has always been the chief charm of Japanese art, by mechanical perfections of machinery and plaster-of-Paris molds, and by the use of the most recondite chemical colors of the *grand feu* of Sèvres.

The situation of the province of Hizen, immediately opposite the coast of Korea, made it the chief medium of the introduction of improvements in the ceramic art of Japan at a time when direct intercourse between Japan and China was interrupted. Its ports have, at the same time, been the means of its export from Japan to the outer world. The Portuguese made their first appearance there in the year 1542, but we hear nothing of the import of porcelain into Europe by them, or by the Spaniards. The Dutch came in 1609, sent a deputation to Yedo to the Shogun Iyeyasu, and were given authority by him to trade. They established their first factory at Hirado in the following year, and after the expulsion of the Portuguese a few years later the monopoly of the foreign trade remained in their hands, with occasional interruptions, until Commodore Perry's expedition in 1853. The Dutch were established at Nagasaki in 1640, when they occupied the small island of Deshima, and were allowed some minor facilities for trade. This, together with a like limited arrangement with the Chinese, was the sole foreign intercourse allowed by Japan for more than two centuries.

FIG. 401.—Saké-Pot of Hizen porcelain, decorated with dragons in the midst of flower-strewn waves, painted in dark green and other enamel colors.

China was devastated by the invasion of the Manchu Tartars in the middle of the seventeenth century, and the porcelain factories at Ching-tê-chên were practically closed for more than fifty years, which cut off the supplies which the Dutch wanted for Europe. This led them to foster the new industry in Japan, and Imari became the chief source of the export of porcelain till the Ching-tê-chên factories were opened again in the early part of the reign of *K'ang-hsi* (1662–1722). The porcelain made under their auspices in Chinese style was decorated with Chinese subjects and inscribed very often with marks of the *Ming* dynasty of China.

Typical specimens of this "old Japan" Imari class have been illustrated in colors in Plates XCV, XCVII, XCVIII, XCIX, and CV, and need not be further described. Two more examples are shown in Fig. 398, a large circular dish with a floral decoration of the kind that has earned for the class the name of *famille chrysanthémo-péonienne*, and a tall jar (Fig. 399) decorated with figure subjects and panels of pierced trellis-work.

ROUND DISH, twenty-two inches in diameter (Fig. 398), decorated with underglaze cobalt-blue in combination with enamel color and gilding. The center is filled with a basket standing upon a railed balcony containing a formal bouquet of peonies and cherry-blossom flanked by two birds. The border is decorated with sprays of chrysanthemums, interrupted by lambrequins containing alternately peonies and butterflies displayed in colors upon backgrounds of mottled blue. The under edge is decorated with three sprigs of plum-blossom. There is no date inscribed underneath, but a number of large "spur-marks" are visible on the glaze.

JAR, with COVER, thirty-one inches high (Fig. 399), of ovoid form with rounded octagonal section, painted in underglaze cobalt-blue of full tone filled in with enamel colors and gilding. The shoulder of the jar and the vault of the cover are pierced with alternated lozenges and medallions of trellis-work, interrupting mottled blue bands, overlaid with scrolls penciled in gold. The rims are encircled by similar bands of blue and gold, three in number, interrupted by smaller panels of the same shape painted alternately with sprays of peony and storks. The blue bands are succeeded by narrower bands of floral sprays upon a white ground. The floral bands inclose the main decoration of the jar, which consists of four panel pictures of Japanese execution in Chinese style. Two of these panels contain outdoor scenes, with figures standing on a balcony and horses in a meadow; the other two are filled with formal vases of flowers.

The two smaller pieces shown in Figs. 400 and 401 are still more markedly inspired by Chinese models, the first being shaped in the form of the fish-dragon (*yü-lung*), the well-known symbol of literary genius and success; while the second, although of more modern date, might almost be mistaken for a specimen of the old *famille verte* of the *K'ang-hsi* epoch.

WATER-VESSEL for the writer's table (Fig. 400), seven and a quarter inches high, molded in the shape of a fish with a two-horned dragon's head, its tail curved as if leaping from the water. Additional support is afforded by one of the posterior fins, and by a tassel suspended from a cord which passes through the dragon's mouth. The details are painted in dark cobalt-blue; the projecting fins of the fish-body, as well as the bullock-like horns and the long mustachios of the dragon head, are enameled black overlaid with gold. There is a mark written in the same under-glaze blue within the throat with the inscription *Ta Ming Chia-ching nien chih*—i. e., "Made in the reign of *Chia-ching* (1522–66) of the Great *Ming* [dynasty]," but this piece is evidently a Japanese production of the fifteenth century.

SAKÉ-POT, of quadrangular section (Fig. 401), eight inches high, enameled in colors. It is covered with a scrolled ground of dark green penciled with black lines inclosing *ch'i-lin*, conch-shells, and scattered plum-blossoms, filled in with deep red, pale yellow, and manganese purple. A border of crested waves extends in white reserve round the bottom, and the rims are touched with yellow-brown. There is a mark penciled in blue underneath in Japanese style, with the inscription *Fu ki chō mei*, "Riches, rank, and long life!" a reproduction of the common Chinese mark *Fu kuei ch'ang ming*.

The next kilns to be noticed in the province of Hizen are those of Okawaji (or Okochi). This was the private factory of the princes of Nabeshima. The kilns were first established at Iwayagawa, close to the Arita, in the period *Kio-hio* (1716–35), but were moved afterward to their present site, and their productions were ordered to be reserved entirely for the prince's own use or for presentation purposes, their sale being strictly prohibited. Great care was taken in the refining of the clay and in the enamel decoration, which is distinguished by the prevalence of clear pale tones contrasting excellently with the pure white paste, a light red color, almost orange, being especially characteristic. There is never an excess of ornament, and the style closely resembles that of the earlier Imari productions which have been referred to under the name of *famille artistique*, and are sometimes known as the *genre Kakiyemon*. The designs are generally somewhat stiff and conventional, but charming medallions are found with well-drawn birds and animals and delicately executed floral sprays. Among the productions of this factory selected for especial notice are a variety of tea-bowls and saké-cups of delicate texture known as *kushité*, "comb-teeth," because they were ornamented with decorative borders composed of closely set parallel lines resembling the teeth of a comb.

FIG. 402.—Cake-Dish of Hirado porcelain, painted in blue with a group of seven Chinese boys playing under a pine-tree.

The example of Okawaji ware shown in Fig. 390 is of rough type and more rustic aspect. It is a saké-bottle (*tokuri*) nine inches high, of oval bladder-like form with irregularly compressed sides, coated with a glaze of greenish celadon color, deeply crackled throughout with a network of dark-brown lines. The foot-rim is iron-gray of a reddish tint. It is decorated in enamel colors of subdued tone in combination with touches of gold, with a maple-tree in autumn-tinted foliage, and an old man standing on a walk underneath, holding in his hand a screen fan mounted upon a long handle. The date is said to be about 1750.

The celebrated Hirado ware ranks as another of the ceramic productions of the province of Hizen. It is also known as Mikawaji-yaki, from the name of the district where it is made, some fifteen miles south of Arita. The kilns, which are still working to-day in the village of Oriosé, were originally called *Hirado-gama*, or "Hirado kilns." They were founded by Sannojo and his son Jo-en, who established themselves at Oriosé, in the *Keicho* period (1596–1614). Sannojo was a son of one of the Koreans who followed the Prince of Hirado of the house of Matsura on his return from the Korean expedition, and who had previously set up kilns at Nakano, in the district of Matsura, under the patronage of this prince. Jo-en made a " blue and white " (*sometsuké*) faïence from materials which he discovered at Egami. Several of his descendants moved afterward to Kiwara and Enaga, which became known, with Oriosé, as the "Three Porcelain Hills" of Hirado.

The industry made great progress in the period *Shotoku* (1711–15), thanks to a native of the locality named Yokoishi Toshichibei, who made the first fine porcelain by mixing the earth previously used with another kind obtained by him from Amakusa.

FIG. 403.—Hirado Censer of pale celadon tint, with openwork cover and trellis casing displaying the badge of the Tokugawa house.

It took a new stride in advance after the establishment in the period *Horeki* (1751–63) of new kilns, which the Prince of Matsura reserved exclusively for the making of articles intended for his own use, or for presents to the Shogun at Yedo, or to his daimyo friends. Among the pieces made at these private kilns, a favorite decoration was a sketch of *Karako* ("Chinese boys") playing around pine-trees. These are described by Japanese connoisseurs as real works of art, the finest representing a group of seven children, the others either five or three. Another class of pieces decorated with relief work of marvelously delicate execution are not less appreciated by Japanese collectors.

An illustration of the Karako decoration is presented in Fig. 402. It is a cake-dish (*Kashizara*), nine and a half inches across, of quadrangular outline with the corners beveled off, and a nearly flat surface gently sloping from the straight rim, painted in soft tones of grayish-blue, with the sketch of a garden scene displaying a group of seven boys, in Chinese dress, quarreling over an interrupted game of *gō* under the shade of a spreading pine. Fig. 386 may be referred to as another instance of the same decoration. It represents a small incense-burner with a pierced outer casing, through the interstices of which can be seen a picture of five children playing in a garden, painted in blue upon the inner cylinder, while a pine-tree spreads its branches in solid relief across the open grating of the cover.

The blue of the Hirado porcelain is a soft grayish-blue, specially attractive from the purity and perfect harmony of its shaded tones. It excels in these respects the productions of all the other Japanese kilns, in which European smalt is often used, the result being a darker and more solid color, but one with little gradation of tone. The Chinese mineral, a cobaltiferous ore of manganese, was imported for use in the Hirado kilns, that found in the province of Chekiang being preferred by the Japanese, as it is by the Chinese, to any other. The nodules, imported in the raw state, were roasted in the furnace, and much depended upon the skill of the expert whose duty it was to pick out the best pieces after roasting. Although the same material is used in Japan as in China, there is generally a peculiar difference in tone in the blue of old Japanese porcelain, which seems to be partly absorbed *into* the glaze instead of being *under* it, while the glaze itself looks softer. The blue, though put on, as in China, before the glaze, was painted in Japan on the clay after it had received a preliminary firing, the principal firing taking place after the glaze had been added. The different appearance, distinguishing it from the Chinese, is probably caused by the materials being less hard and more absorbent, the same cause necessitating the first slight firing, which Japanese porcelain always undergoes.

Hirado porcelain and its different processes of decoration are well represented in our colored plates. The ordinary blue and white is illustrated in Plate CX, Fig. 1, and Plates CXI and CXIII; in combination with relief work in slip in Plate CX, Fig. 2; in combination with more salient molding in relief and with delicate pierced work in the beautiful censer on Plate CXII. This last piece exhibits the ordinary style of the mark, being inscribed underneath in minute script with the potter's name and that of the locality, "Made at Mikawaji in Hirado." The quaint originality of Japanese fancy is seen in some of the forms. The wide-mouthed beaker, for example, in Plate CXIII, is a molded version of the familiar fable of the frog, the Japanese emblem of perseverance and success, its two handles being fashioned in relief as frogs leaping up from the waves which curl round the bowl of the vase, into the branches of willow which sweep down from its upper rim. Who but a Japanese would make a censer in the shape of a puppy with a movable head for the introduction of the incense, as shown on Plate CX?

He has substituted this lion, which figures as a guardian of which leads him so often to carica-

An example of white Hirado a gourd-shaped saké-bottle with slight relief in the paste, and fin- soft-looking glaze. Among the most are the small globular incense-burn- openwork covers, of which one is iature *kōro* two and three quarter trellis pattern of charming design ship, enameled with a pale celadon in a trellis-work are two circular three converging mallow-leaves, gawa family which ruled Japan title of Shogun, and, besides, the feudal principalities. The surmounted by a tiny bow. A is illustrated in Fig. 391, has the three sprays of chrysanthemum- instead of crests, and an open-

The statuette of Sâkyamuni

FIG. 404.—Figure of Buddha standing upon a lotus pedestal, modeled in Hirado porcelain, and painted in blue with touches of brown and black.

for the Buddhist canonical form of a the law, in the spirit of ridicule ture his deities in pictorial art. porcelain is presented in Plate CIX, chrysanthemum sprays worked in ished with the graving tool under cherished productions of these kilns ers, with pierced outer casings and illustrated in Fig. 403. It is a min- inches high, delicately carved in a and wonderfully minute workman- glaze of gray-green tones. Inclosed medallions containing a crest of the badge of the famous Toku- from 1603 to 1868, under the supplied daimyos for many of porcelain trellis-work cover is companion incense-burner, which trellised casing interrupted by flowers modeled in slight relief, work lid of silver.

Buddha, which is illustrated in

Fig. 404, is a production of the Hirado kilns of the close of the eighteenth century, and is painted in blue with touches of brown and black. It is a standing figure, eleven inches high, modeled in the traditional lines, dressed in long, flowing robes with wide hanging sleeves which are painted in blue of lighter and darker shades, with the head encircled by a sweeping halo which is colored yellow-brown, and holding an alms-bowl of the same tint. The face, the neck, and the bare feet are reserved *en biscuit*, the ears are characteristically enlarged, and the forehead has the *ûrna* mark of a Bôdhisattva. The hair, which is arranged in close spiral curls, is gray-black, while the *ushnisha* which projects in the middle of the hair is enameled white. The pedestal is molded in two pieces in the form of a lotus thalamus, surrounded by rings of petals worked in relief, and marked above with a circlet of seeds, and is coated with a whiter glaze of slightly greenish tone. The story is told in Nagasaki that one of the hereditary daimyos of Hirado, who lived over a hundred years ago, was cured of a malady by a pilgrimage to a shrine at the top of Fujiyama, and that each year for the rest of his life he sent a party of his retainers to the sacred volcano with an *ex-voto* offering of one of these figures, which he ordered to be made for the purpose at his porcelain factory at Mikawaji.

Colored enamels were occasionally employed in the decoration of Hirado porcelain, either in combination with the blue, or by themselves. The usual colors are of subdued rather than brilliant tints, comprising a russet-brown, a pale clear green, and a straw-yellow. The vase shown in Fig. 405 is a production of these potteries, and is referred to their palmy period, the second half of the eighteenth century. It is a flower-vase (*hana-ike*), eleven inches high, with a floral decoration relieved by a russet ground broken by a broad band of white round the middle. This band, which is enameled white of greenish tone, extends round the lower half of the wide cylindrical neck, and from the two sides project loop handles springing from the mouths of grotesque unicorn dragons, the parts of the neck to which the handles are attached being modeled in slight relief under the glaze with a wavy pattern mingled with scrolls of clouds. The floral decoration consists of foliated scrolls starting from two large conventional flowers, one of which is displayed upon the front, the other upon the back, of the globular body of the vase. The idealized blossoms represent those of the sacred Indian lotus (*Hsi Fan lien*) of Chinese art, which the Japanese call *Kara-kusa*—i. e., "Chinese plant." Light chains of rectangular fret define the borders of the floral bands and complete the decoration. The bottom is overlaid with a black silver plate; the mark, if there be any, is concealed.

IV. SATSUMA.

Whatever title to ceramic celebrity Japan may base upon her porcelain productions, it is for her pottery she will be longest remembered, and of that pottery the first place belongs incontestably to the Satsuma faïence. The word Satsuma is nearly as well known to us as the word Japan, and it is familiar not so much for its brilliant achievements in the past, for the grand part it took in the war of restoration, or for its tragic rebellion afterward, as for the peculiar type of faïence which it produces. Its soft-looking ivory-colored glaze with its delicately crazed surface provides the most charming background for decoration in enamel colors that can be conceived, while the texture of the *pâte* is so close and fine that it can hardly be distinguished from ivory. No collection is considered complete without a shelf of "old Satsuma," but the pieces commonly seen abroad differ essentially from the beautiful faïence which is so highly prized by Japanese connoisseurs. The latter consists generally of small pieces, cups, incense-burners, tea-jars, figures, and the like, richly but chastely decorated with a spray of flowers or foliage, occasionally with a phœnix, Chinese lion or unicorn, in combination with delicate diapers and lightly penciled fret borders. The materials were carefully selected and prepared, the potting of each piece was perfect, and its decoration was executed with skill and precision, so that the ware has been justly called "jeweled." The ordinary "old Satsuma," on the contrary, is usually of indifferent manufacture, it rings with a dull note, and although all the resources of ingenuity and patience may be lavished upon its decoration, the pains are often lost, as the imperfectly enameled pigments do not last, and the thin wash of alloy which is substituted for pure gold soon becomes tarnished. Elaborate combinations of diapers, bouquets of brilliant flowers, armies of gorgeously appareled saints, peacocks with spreading tails, and dragons environed by golden clouds—all subjects, in fact, that can help to achieve gaud and glitter—are employed by painters who have long since abjured the æsthetic creeds of their country. The Japanese themselves scorn the preposterous jars and huge beakers which find no purchasers in their own country. They represent neither the spirit nor fashion of true Japanese art; but simply the wonderfully adaptive genius of Japanese artists. Just as in the seventeenth century the Arita potters covered the "old Japan" ware of that time with Chinese figures and mythological monsters, interwoven with garlands of peonies and chrysanthemums, when their patrons complained that their own artistically decorated vases had not flowers enough for the Dutch taste, so do the Satsuma decorators to-day crowd their "old Satsuma" with mail-

FIG. 405.—Vase of Hirado porcelain, decorated in three sections, the middle lightly chased with scrolls enameled white, the other two decorated in colors relieved by a russet-red ground.

clad warriors and long Buddhist processions to satisfy the taste of the American and European collector.

But much of this "old Satsuma" is not even Satsuma at all. It is Awata faïence from Kyōto painted in conventional Satsuma style, or some other modern ware, fraudulently painted at the Shiba kilns in Tokyo, at the Ota kilns near Yokohama, or elsewhere. If it is a piece of real old Satsuma, decorated subsequently in enameled colors at one of these kilns, the deception is not so transparent. One of the most daring frauds of recent times was attempted in London in 1879, when a heterogeneous collection of modern Ota and Shiba pieces, vases, *kŏro*, and so forth, were sold by auction under the description of "rarest old Satsuma." A group of some fifty, described as "The Papal Pieces," were stated to have been "prepared for

Fig. 406. — Small Jar of Satsuma faïence, with conventional floral scrolls in enamel colors and gold. Old-silver cover, a lotus-leaf.

the Jesuit priests' expedition from Japan to the Holy City, under special auspices of the Prince of Bungo, in 1582. Francis Xavier himself assisted in the selection of these papal offerings, but it is well known that the collection never left Japan, but was retained by the Prince of Bungo in his fortress during the mission slaughter, after which it was publicly shown as relics of Catholic devoteeship." Some of the pieces were stained to give an appearance of age; others, which had been broken and mended, were catalogued as "bearing evidence of having undergone much vicissitude and hiding," and so on.

It would be tedious to refer further to the many misconceptions that have arisen on the subject. For the first exact information we are indebted to Sir Ernest Satow, K. C. M. G., now H. B. M. minister at Tokyo, who visited the kilns in 1877,* and whose conclusions on the vexed question of the period of introduction of the *nishiki* style of decoration in enamel colors are worth quoting. Speaking of the discovery of white clay in 1624–40, he says that the manufacture of white Satsuma crackled ware dates from then, but for a long time, he adds, the wares appear to have been ornamented very sparingly with color, and he considers that the *nishiki* style of decoration was originated in the period of *Kwan-sei* (1789–1800) by Narinobu, who is reported to have sent two of his artists to Kyōto to learn the art of painting figures, landscapes, and set patterns in this particular style. Another view is that the use of vitrifiable enamels and gold was commenced shortly after the discovery of the white clay, about 1630, that the manufacture subsequently deteriorated for want of patronage, and that its revival at the end of the eighteenth century, although often erroneously described as the origin, was in reality only the *renaissance* of Satsuma enameled faïence.

The history of Satsuma faïence is an epitome of that of the ceramic industry of Japan generally, beginning with the introduction of Korean potters, who discovered the necessary raw materials and taught the technical elements of a handicraft which only gradually became artistic under the inspiration of Japanese genius. Mr. Ouéda (*loc. cit.*, pages 62–74) gives a summary account of it, which we will follow. The kilns of the Satsuma-yaki are dispersed at different points throughout the province. The largest center of fabrication is at Nawashiro, where there is to-day a very considerable production. Like the productions of other factories which abound in the island of Kyusiu (the southernmost island of Japan, of which the provinces of Satsuma and Osumi form the southernmost extremity), the Satsuma wares date from the time of the Japanese expedition to Korea (*Bunroku*, 1592–95). Shimazu Yoshihiro, daimyo of Satsuma, brought back with his army seventeen Korean potters, two of whom were named Hochu and Boku-Heii. Some of the potters established themselves with the first named in the quarter Korai-Machi (Korean Street), at Kagoshima, the capital of the province; the others at Kushi-kino, under the direction of the second. They all came afterward to settle at Chosa, in the adjoining province of Osumi, having been summoned to this place by Shimazu Yoshihiro, who

---

* *The Corean Potters in Satsuma*, by E. Satow, a paper read February 20, 1878. Transactions of the Asiatic Society of Japan, vol. vi, part ii, Yokohama.

had his residence there. This prince, a devoted amateur of the Cha-no-yu, ordered from the Korean potters a large number of pieces to be made after his taste. They were composed of a fine-grained clay, with a glaze colored in shades of blue, yellow, and black; the most precious had a variegated glaze, called "Jakatsu," which is defined in the "Man-po-zen-sho," published in 1694, as a lizard-colored enamel. The pieces are called *Gohondé* (articles with the honorable seal), which Yoshihiro appreciated most, and which he marked with his personal seal. When the daimyo changed his residence to Kajiki, in another part of the province of Osumi, he sent for Hochu to come to Tatsu no Kuchi, built a factory for him there, and charged him to train the workmen. Kihei, the son of this potter, adopted by order of the prince the surname of Kawara (i. e., bank), from the situation of Tatsu no Kuchi on the bank of the Kuro-Kawa. After the death of Yoshihiro, which occurred in the *Genwa* period (1615–23), Hochu continued to carry on the work and to superintend the potters. His family divided into two branches—Tobei, the younger son of Kihei, surnamed Kawara; and Kozayemon, his elder son, Yamamoto. Both established themselves in the second year of *Kwambun* (1662) at Tatsumonji. The Yamamoto are to-day represented by only a single family, while the Kawara count as many as twenty-four.

Tobei had a son named Juzayemon, who settled at Oyamada. His son, who called himself Juzayemon Hoko, was a potter of great merit. In the fifth year of *Meiwa* (1768) he worked in the private factory of the princes of Shimazu at Tateno, in Kagoshima, which he left ten years later. Commissioned by the prince of this house to go to Arita to finish his studies there, he resumed his industry on his return to Oyamada in the eighth year of *Anyei* (1779) with great success. In the fifth year of *Kwansei* (1793), after having visited in succession the principal ceramic districts of the provinces of Hizen and Chikuzen, he went to Kyōto, and from there to the province of Owari, where he studied the fabrication at Ofukei in Nagoya. Returning again to Kyōto, he formed an intimate friendship with Kinkozan Sobei, and studied with him the processes of manufacture of the Kyō-yaki, especially of the Raku wares. The travels of Juzayemon resulted in an immense progress in the industry at Oyamada. The origin of the fabrics called *Samé-yaki* (Sharkskin ware) dates from the time of this celebrated artist.

FIG. 407.—Satsuma Figure of Chinese Boy (Kara-ko) holding up a jewel; richly decorated in enamel colors and gilding.

Boku-Heii and his companions, who settled at first, as we have seen, at Kushikino, moved their workshops in the eighth year of *Keicho* (1603) to Nawashiro. In the nineteenth year of the same period (1614) Boku-Heii explored by order of Yoshihiro his territories in Satsuma and Osumi and discovered new materials required for the fabrication. The kilns of Nawashiro produced thenceforward articles resembling the work of Komogawa, in Korea, which acquired great renown. While Boku-Heii was the director of the factories, Yoshihiro showed a vivid interest in the industry, and he frequently visited the works, which under his patronage rapidly became important. Here, as at Chosa, he marked with his personal seal those pieces which he found to his taste, and they are also called *Gohondé*. The artisan population of Nawashiro rapidly increased, and they turned out successfully their novel vases of white translucent materials and reproductions of the *genres* known as Hakémé, Mishima, and Sunkoroku.*

The factory of Nawashiro, when it was first founded, included in its *personnel* the Korean

* In 1878, according to the official report of the Paris Exposition, the Korean potters at Nawashiro numbered five hundred families, including fourteen hundred and fifty individuals, all carrying on the industry of their ancestors. Never having married any but Korean women, they are said to have retained their distinctive type and language and many of their old manners and customs. The Hakémé and Mishima wares are of Korean origin, and both are of the *pâte sur pâte* class. In the Hakémé the designs, usually in white slip upon a gray body, look as if executed with a brush (*hake*). The Mishima, which has already been referred to, was chased and inlaid with encaustic sprays of white, gray, or black color, and was so called because it reminded the Japanese of the lines of idiographs in one of their printed almanacs. The *Sunkoroku* decoration was painted in browns of different shades in simple floral and diapered patterns. The origin of the name is obscure.

Chin-Tokitsu, a potter full of talent. His son and successor, Toju, had a son Tokitsu, the second of the name, who earned by his great merit the name of Tō-ichi (the first of potters) and a pension bestowed by one of the Shimazu princes. The present fabricator, Chin-Jukwan, is a descendant in the twelfth generation of Tokitsu I. He was appointed in 1857 the director of the factories at Nawashiro, with several hundred workmen under his orders, and the establishment prospered under his direction. The loss of its domains by the house of Shimazu, after the fall of the feudal *régime* in 1869, paralyzed the industry for the moment and threw the workmen into misery. Chin-Jukwan succeeded by his praiseworthy efforts in rescuing them from their difficulties, and in assuring independence for the enterprise and regular work for the potters. The name of Gyoku Kozan is that which he has adopted since this epoch.

The factory of Tateno, at Kagoshima, was founded in the period *Kwanyei* (1624–43). This was another private establishment of the princes of Shimazu. The most skillful artist of this factory was Kono-Sanyemon, who lived in the period *Meiwa* (1764–71). His processes of manufacture were those of Hochu. His productions were crackled, the glaze being either white or of different colors. In the *Kwansei* period (1789–1800), Narinobu, prince of the house of Shimazu, had gold employed in the decoration, and the new productions obtained a great success under the name of "Nishikidé," or "brocaded ware." They were superior to those of Hochu, which are valued only from an antiquarian point of view. It was the artists of Tateno who taught, in the eleventh year of the period *Tempo* (1840), the fabrication of the Nishikidé to Boku-Sokuan, son of Boku-Shoki, of Nawashiro, where this decoration was heretofore unknown. Sokuan was appointed afterward by his prince, in the first year of *Kokwa* (1844), the director of the new factory of Iso, which owes its beautiful productions to this artist. He spent one year there, and then returned to Nawashiro, where he continued to carry on with success the fabrication of the "brocade-painted wares."

Fig. 408.—Satsuma Censer fashioned as a bowl on a tripod stand, pierced with three medallions, and delicately painted in enamel colors and gold.

The decorated Satsuma was never made in large quantities. It was from the first an *article de luxe*, intended for the personal use of the daimyo, or as presents to those he wished to honor. The finest enameled pieces were the work of the artists of the Tateno factory.

The productions of the Satsuma kilns are represented in the colored illustrations in Plates C, CI, CII, CVII, and CVIII, where nine specimens are figured. The comparatively small size of the finer and older pieces is shown by the fact that there is room for two side by side upon each page, except in Plate CII, and this last vase, decorated with storks flying among clouds in enamel colors with touches of gold and silver, relieved by an intensely black ground, is certainly the most recent of the series. The pictures give a good general idea of the soft, creamy tones of the finely crazed grounds, ranging from old ivory to vellum; of the artistic style of the chaste decoration with graceful floral sprays and lightly penciled borders of conventional ornament; of the harmony of coloring and technical finish which distinguish the productions of the artists who worked for the princes of Shimazu at the end of the eighteenth century and the beginning of the nineteenth. Not a single figure is to be seen, and there is no sign of the mail-clad warriors and Buddhist pilgrims, or of the profusion of gorgeous colors, such as mark the "old Satsuma" which is painted in the present day in Japan in such quantities for the export trade.

The earliest piece is the archaic-looking teapot in Plate CI, where the crackled ground is left undecorated, only clouded and stained by use in a way that reminds one, it has been aptly said, of a tobacco-stained meerschaum pipe, and which the Japanese collector is fond of bringing out and polishing with a soft cloth which he keeps for the purpose. The teacup on Plate C is also undecorated, except for a splashed line of overglaze round the rim, of deep amber tint, laid on in one of the monochrome enamels used at Nawashiro in the eighteenth century. The rest of the pieces, which are decorated in the *Nishiki* or brocade-painted style, are sufficiently described. They all belong to the palmy period of the Satsuma factories.

The other Satsuma pieces shown in Figs. 392, 393, 395, 406, 407, 408, and 410 are all of a type similar to the above, and are generally referred to the same period—*circa* A. D. 1800.

1. SAKÉ-BOTTLE (*Tokuri*), eight and a half inches high (Fig. 393), of cylindrico-ovoid form, tapering to a thin neck with a prominent rounded lip. Decorated in subdued enamel colors with formal sprays of the *kiri* flower (*Paulownia imperialis*) with gracefully waved tendrils. A ring of slender foliations spreads down from the neck, alternately greenish-blue and coral-red touched with gold. The flowers are of the imperial type, with a spike of seven florets rising in the middle flanked by two spikes of five florets; and the stopper, which is of silver, is molded in the shape of a *kiku* flower (chrysanthemum), the imperial crest of Japan.

2. TEA-JAR (*Cha-tsubo*), three and a quarter inches high (Fig. 406), of regular oval form with rounded lip, painted in enamel colors and gilding, with a floral brocade ground of checker pattern interrupted by two foliated medallions containing bunches of scarlet cherry or *Pyrus japonica* blossoms enveloped in conventional scrolls, a gadroon band round the foot, and a light floral scroll round the neck completing the decoration. The old cover of oxidized silver is fashioned in the shape of a peltate lotus-leaf with the stalk at the top.

3. SMALL FIGURE (*Okimono*), two and a half inches high (Fig. 395), of Hotei, one of the seven beneficent beings of the Japanese Pantheon, decorated in enamel colors with gilding. Hotei, the Japanese transcription of the Chinese Putai, represents Putai Hoshang, the "Monk with the Hempen Bag," of Chinese Buddhist lore, who is to reappear as the Buddha of the coming age, so that he may be styled the Buddhist Messiah. With shaven head, broad, smiling face, and large pendulous ear-lobes, his cloak loosely thrown back so as to leave the abdomen as well as the right shoulder bare, he is modeled here in the traditional Chinese lines, holding the jewel of the law in his left hand, and seated beside the capacious bag which is his special attribute. His robes are richly embroidered with gold brocade, and his bag is emblazoned with the *takara-mono*, or "precious things," as symbols of the gifts he has to bestow upon his votaries.

These symbols are as frequent in Japanese art as the *po ku*, or hundred antiques, are in Chinese art, and many objects are common to the two lists. The things which occur most often in Japan are: The anchor, an emblem of safety; a branch of coral in a vase, symbol of rank and honor; rolls (*makimono*), either a crossed "pair" rolled up, or one partially unrolled to show the writing; a couple of bridges for the lyre, emblems of harmony; the hammer of Daikoku, which, wielded diligently, produces wealth; the spindle-shaped weight with which the tradesman weighs his silver; a pair of keys of the godown in which precious possessions are stored; two rolls of brocaded silk, or *nishiki*; an orange, on a leafy twig, emblem of fruitfulness; manifold symbols of wealth, such as the cowry, or ancient shell-money, the copper cash with a hole in the middle, the *kotsubo*, a jar full of precious things to be buried for security, a pile of gold *koban*, a chest labeled "a thousand gold pieces," bag-purses of money, etc. Articles of fairy lore are the invisible rain cloak, the wide hat which also renders its wearer invisible, and the feather robe of supernatural beings. Buddhist symbols include the three precious jewels of the law emitting effulgent rays, a pile of sacred jewels heaped upon a stand, a lion with its forepaw upon a jewel (*Shishidama*) as guardian of the faith, and the palm-leaf fan of the pilgrim saint. The rhinoceros horn libation-cups of Chinese symbolism have become in Japan *choji*, or "cloves," although their shape often belies their new name.

4. MINIATURE FIGURE (*Okimono*) of Chinese boy (*Karako*), with partly shaven head (Fig. 407), the hair left in a topknot and two side tufts, in a richly brocaded dress, holding up a sacred jewel. A companion FIGURE, with a palm-leaf fan in one hand, is shown in Fig. 392.

5. VASE (*Hana-ike*), six and a quarter inches high (Fig. 393), decorated in enamel colors and gold, with borders of conventional ornament round the rims, inclosing a selection of the *takara-mono* enumerated above in the description of Hotei, mingled with floral sprays of chrysanthemum and plum blossom, and with branches with twin peaches, the symbolical fruit of long life.

6. Small INCENSE-BURNER (*Kōro*), two and one eighth inches high (Fig. 408), of bowl-shaped outline mounted upon three scrolled feet, with an outer casing painted with a minute diaper of flowers inclosed in interlacing circles, interrupted by three pierced medallions containing a spray of bamboo, a stork, and a bear supporting a leaf-shaped shield, and with a dentated rim molded as three tiers of leaves.

7. INCENSE-BURNER (*Kōro*), six and a half inches broad (Fig. 410), of flattened form, with a large cover modeled in the shape of an ancient Japanese court hat. The "base" is encircled with a diaper of triangular fret pattern; the "cover" is pierced with floral designs and decorated in the intervals with sprays of scrolled flowers enameled in colors with gilding.

V. KUTANI.

The last ware which remains for consideration is that of Kutani, a name almost as familiar to collectors as those of Imari, Hirado, and Satsuma. Kutani is in the province of Kaga, on the west coast of the main island of Japan, and its ceramic productions are called Kaga-yaki and Kutani-yaki indifferently. The exact date of the origin of the factory is not known. Mr. Ouéda gives in the table (see page 349) the period *Kwanyei* (1624–43), although in his notes, which we will follow, he says that the origin of the Kutani-yaki dates back to the period *Keian* (1648–51). It was Mayeda Toshiharu, daimyo of the town of Daishoji, who had the first kilns constructed in the village of Kutani by two of his vassal Samurai named Goto Saijiro and Tamura Gonzayemon. The materials employed in the early wares resembled those of the stoneware productions of Seto, in Owari, but the objects, crude and ungraceful in form, were far from equaling those of this great ceramic center.

Toshiaki, the son and successor of Toshiharu, with a view to developing the industry in his territory, sent Goto Saijiro to Arita, in Hizen, in the period *Manji* (1658–60) to study

FIG. 409.—Tripod Censer with mask handles, of Kutani porcelain, decorated in enamel colors. Cover of lacquered metal.

the processes of manufacture in use there. The Arita workmen were very loath to impart their secrets to a stranger, but he served as a hired menial in the house of a potter for more than three years, and became initiated in all the details of the art. As soon as he had learned all he could he fled by night, and his return made a new era for the ceramic industry of Kutani. The materials found at Suizuka were used by him in the fabrication of his finest vases, and there is still to be seen in that village a porcelain pedestal in the form of a lotus thalamus, with a seated statue of Buddha upon it, which is one of the objects modeled by the artist at this time.

The celebrated painter of Kyōto, Hisazumi Morikagé, happened at this time to be on a visit to Kanazawa, the chief city of the province of Kaga, and he was intrusted with the execution of the designs, and contributed materially to their beauty and renown. Hence the name of *Morikagé-shitaye*—i. e., "Morikagé Sketches"—by which they are still known.

The early wares, known afterward as *Ko Kutani* (ancient Kutani), are of two almost distinct varieties. The first, of a grayish *pâte*, faïence rather than porcelain, was coated with lustrous, full-bodied glazes of the *demi-grand feu*, green, yellow, and purple, the former predominating; the decoration usually consisting of large flowers, in the midst of fret grounds and diaper of archaic pattern, which are penciled in black so as to show through the green or yellow enameled surface. This style is compared by the Japanese to the productions of China and Kochi (Annam), and it was evidently inspired by the former country. The second variety of old Kutani is a milk-white porcelain which is compared to old Imari ware, and may almost be mistaken for it sometimes. The most characteristic examples are to be distinguished, however, by the prevalence of a peculiarly soft russet-red, which differs essentially from the hard, full, brick-dust red of the old Imari ware. The Kaga potters used silver much more freely for decorative purposes than the Hizen potters, while they relegated underglaze blue, on the contrary, to a more subordinate position.

Tradition says that the perfection of their results was due mainly to the great care and patience devoted to the preliminary preparation of the materials, that the mixing and braying of the coloring materials was the daily task of the women and children at the Kutani potteries, and that the rich deep red of the older periods was ground for six months under the pestle before it passed into the hands of the painter.

Although the early Kaga productions were so highly appreciated, the manufacture fell into decay afterward, and the kilns of Kutani were abandoned some sixty or seventy years after their foundation. The industry was revived in the seventh year of *Bunkwa* (1810), by Yoshidaya Hachiyemon, a merchant of Daishoji, who rebuilt the ancient factories and reproduced the different varieties of the old productions. This was the renaissance of the ceramic industry of Kutani. In the eleventh year of the same period (1814) the kilns were moved to Yamashiro, a locality which offered greater facilities of transport; but the necessary materials were still brought there from Kutani and Suizuka. The new fabrications are called Yoshidaya-yaki, after the name of the merchant who revived the industry that had almost disappeared. They rank in quality immediately after the *Ko Kutani*.

Yoshidaya was succeeded by Miyamotoya Riyemon in the sixth year of *Tempo* (1835). The new director was assisted by the painter Iidaya Hachiroyemon, who revived the art of decorating in gold upon the red ground in the characteristic Kutani style. He was the first to introduce the *Nishiki* style of decoration into these potteries. The porcelain made to-day in the district of Nomi and at Kanazawa is, generally speaking, very similar to Iidaya's.

During the last years of the feudal period the house of Mayeda, of Daishoji, encouraged the local industry by large grants of money, and engaged Yeiraku Zengoro, the twelfth of the famous family of hereditary potters of Kyōto, to come to Yamashiro to superintend the work. This potter, whose personal name was Hozen, arrived in 1863, and during the five years that he remained a number of objects were made in the *kinrandé*, or "gold-brocaded," style, of finished form and decoration, and fired in the kilns that were called after him, Yeiraku-gama. But the Yeiraku kilns were closed at the time of the revolution in 1868.

Porcelain commonly known under the name of Kutani-yaki is made in several other localities of the province of Kaga, within the districts of Enuma and Nomi. The ceramic productions of these two districts are generally classified under the headings of Enuma Kutani and Nomi Kutani. The names of many celebrated potters are recorded who have worked in these factories, but there is no space for them here. Potteries exist in the present day at more than twenty localities in the district of Nomi alone. It is in these that the porcelain so well known abroad as *Kaga-Ware* is made. It is painted with a profusion of designs of the red and gold type, often executed with the delicacy and accuracy of a miniature painting, but the gaudy glitter of gilding and massing of red pigment pall after a time upon the least fastidious taste. The Japanese themselves have never appreciated it, and the potters, fearing the inevitable consequences of the monotony, are now reviving with some success the

Fig. 410.—Satsuma Censer modeled in the shape of a Court Hat, with pierced work and painted decoration of floral scrolls.

richer and more varied methods of the older Kutani decorations in polychrome enamels. One of the Kaga potters, Watano Kichiji sent to the Chicago Exposition in 1893 a pair of large vases illustrating this revival. They were covered with an elaborate and boldly designed decoration of hydrangea flowers and leaves in full-toned and brilliant enamels, purple, blue, and green on a yellow ground. Their decorative effect was fine, and they were highly praised.

Kutani porcelain is illustrated in Plates CIII and CIV, and the pictures give a good idea of the peculiarly soft tone of the red ground in the old pieces, which forms such an effective background for the decorative scrolls painted upon it in gold and silver. This is the *kinrande* or "gold brocade" decoration of ceramic writers, and it is evidently inspired by the silk stuffs interwoven with designs in gold and silver thread, which have been made on the looms of the far East from time immemorial, and of which one of the favorite grounds is a soft vermilion. The ceramic designs, too, are those of the old silk brocades of China and

Japan: dragons winding through crested waves, phœnixes traversing scrolls of the tree-peony, conventional bands of sacred lotus, and medallions of formal flowers, with borders of fret pattern, encircling rings of lotus-petals, chains of beads with tassels, and the like.

No large vases nor purely ornamental pieces seem to have been made in the Kutani kilns in the early days, only incense-burners and incense-boxes, saké-bottles and wine-cups, bowls and dishes, and other articles of daily use. The small censer in Plate CIII and the first rice-bowl in Plate CIV are dec- orated in the typ- ical style, with gild- ed and silvered de- signs upon the red ground; the rice- bowl in Plate CIII is decorated besides with touches of en- amel colors of sub- dued tone, including a pale green. The three pieces are referred to the same period, about the middle of the last century; they have a buff-colored or grayish *pâte*, and are enameled red underneath the feet as well, one of the bowls being so com- pletely coated that none of the *pâte* is visible. The third bowl (Plate CIV, Fig. 2) is some- what older, being at- tributed to the begin- ning of the century. It is of thinner, more translucent material, and is molded in the interior with intricate floral scrolls and fret borders, after the tech- nique of some of the ancient Chinese porce-

FIG. 411.—Bowl of Kutani porcelain, artistically deco- rated in brilliant enamel colors with sprays of iris painted upon a soft, milk-white ground.

lains, while the rim is mounted with a silver collar in the fashion of ancient Chinese bowls of the *Sung* dynasty. The ground between the red medallions with which it is decorated outside is filled in with the so-called *yōrakude* or "necklace" designs of the Japanese painted in enamels.

Two other specimens of Kutani ware have been selected for illustration. The censer (Fig. 409), which is decorated in enamel colors, is attributed to the middle of the eighteenth cen- tury. The bowl (Fig. 411), which is artistically decorated in brilliant harmonious colors upon a characteristically milk-white ground, is of earlier date, and may well be ascribed to Morikagé, who, we have seen, was working at these kilns toward the close of the seventeenth century.

INCENSE-BURNER (*Kōro*), five inches high, seven and a quarter inches broad, with a rounded body, bulging below, mounted upon three short legs with scrolled feet, and with two handles projecting from the sides molded in the shape of grotesque lions' heads with gilded tongues protruded and curled at the tips. The surface of the bowl is painted in red, green, and gold, with tiers of mallow-leaves (*aoi*) spreading alternately upward and down- ward so as to cover the ground. The upper rim is defined by a line of pale green, succeeded by a band of curved scrolls in colors, and the lower border is encircled by a ring of rectangular fret. The base is unglazed, with no marks inscribed. The cover is made of lacquered metal.

LARGE BOWL (*Domburi*), six and a half inches high, six and three-quarter inches in diameter, shaped with tall, upright sides slightly swelling at the rim, and a bandlike foot gently spreading outward. It is boldly and artistically decorated with sprays of iris (*shaga*) springing from the base outside and sweeping upward to extend over the rim and ornament the interior as well as the exterior of the bowl with large, brilliant blossoms and broad purple-tinted green leaves. The decoration is completed by a ring of lozenge fret of *svastika* pattern penciled in red round the foot. Mark, *Fuku*, "Happiness," in black, in a small square panel, overlaid with a patch of translucent purple enamel.

The painting, sketched in black outline, is executed in overglaze enamel colors of finely crackled texture, wonderfully intense in tone and of marked iridescent luster. They include a brilliant green, a purplish blue approaching turquoise in some of its translucid tints, and a soft red derived from iron peroxide, in combination with a few touches of black. The general effect of the coloring is magnificent, and one is almost inclined to enshrine this beautiful bowl as a perfect flower of the ceramic art of Japan.

FIG. 412.—A Group of Snuff-Bottles of different dates and styles of decoration.

APPENDIX.

DESCRIPTIVE LIST OF THE ILLUSTRATIONS.

I. COLORED PLATES.

The original water-color drawings from which the lithographic plates were reproduced were executed by Messrs. James and J. C. Callowhill, of Boston, artists whose experience as color-designers in one of the great English potteries gave them special qualifications for the work.

BEAKER-SHAPED VASE (*Hua Ku*), 16½ inches high, enameled with the crackled glaze of the *sang-de-bœuf* mottled tints of the celebrated *Lang Yao*. It exhibits the rich, full tones of the copper-red, deepening almost to black upon the shoulder of the vase. The interior is coated with the same rich red glaze. The lip is defined by a prominent line of white, and the foot by a rounded rim of purest white, projecting beyond the " biscuit " edge below.

The base is invested with an apple-green enamel, mottled with clouds of typical " ox-blood " color. Period *K'ang-hsi* (1662–1722). I.

PLUM-BLOSSOM JAR (*Mei Hua Kuan*), of globular form, with a bell-shaped cover, decorated in brilliant cobalt-blue of the *K'ang-hsi* period (1662–1722), with blossoming branches and twigs of the floral emblem of the New Year. The branches spread alternately upward and downward on the four sides of the jar, so as to display their white blossoms and buds, reserved upon a mottled background of pellucid blue, which is covered with a reticulation of darker blue lines to represent cracking ice, a symbol of the coming spring. The rim is ornamented by a castellated border ; a plain band of white defines the edge of the overlapping cover. The outer surface of the lip surrounding the mouth is unglazed, showing the fine white " biscuit," and its inner side is only partially glazed—one of the " points " of the best " hawthorn jars " of this period. The Chinese offer presents of fragrant tea and preserved fruits at the New Year in jars of this kind, and the plum is the floral emblem of the season. II.

FLOWER-VASE (*Hua P'ing*), enameled with the typical " peach-bloom " glaze, and displaying a characteristic play of color, so as to resemble as far as possible the velvety hues of the bloom of the rind of the ripening peach. A perfect idea of the charming contrast of soft shades of red is given by the artist, who has reproduced the vase in the size of the original, and has attempted to represent the finished polish of the surface as it reflects the picture of an outside scene. The reverse of the vase exhibits a splash of apple-green in the midst of the other colors.

The " mark " underneath, beautifully written in underglaze cobalt-blue, consists of six characters in three columns, *Ta Ch'ing K'ang-hsi nien chih* — i. e., " Made in the reign of K'ang-hsi (1662–1722), of the Great Ch'ing [dynasty]." III.

VASE (*P'ing*), 10½ inches high, with solid spreading foot and tapering above to a slender tubular neck, enameled with a monochrome glaze of darkest green color, the *gros vert* of the French, the *ta lü* of Chinese ceramists. This intense ground color is mottled with clouds of varying shade. The texture of the glaze is " bubbly," and the surface is pitted at places, especially round the base, where it has collected in superfluous drops which have been ground down on the lathe after the piece had been fired. The base is coated underneath with the pure white enamel distinctive of the *K'ang-hsi* period (1662–1722), and this peculiarly strong green occupies a foremost rank among the ceramic productions of this unrivaled reign. IV.

JAR (*Kuan*), nine inches high without the cover, enameled with a monochrome glaze of imperial yellow. The faint horizontal line in the middle indicates that the jar was originally fashioned upon the wheel in two pieces. There is a mark underneath, written in underglaze cobalt-blue in large, bold characters, *Ta Ch'ing K'ang-hsi nien chih*—i. e., " Made in the reign of K'ang-hsi (1662–1722), of the Great Ch'ing [dynasty]." V.

CLUB-SHAPED VASE (*Pang-chih P'ing*), 18½ inches high, richly decorated with the most brilliant enamel colors of the K'ang-hsi period (1662–1722).

The decoration is arranged in four panels, the two upper oblong with rounded indented corners, the lower shaped like ficus-leaves, displayed upon a ground profusely brocaded with flowers. The front panels contain pictures of a pomegranate-tree with a couple of birds perched upon it, labeled *Tan Hua*, " The Vermilion Flower," with the artist's studio seal, *Wan shih chü*, " The Myriad Rock Retreat," appended ; and of a spray of chrysanthemum labeled *Chiao Hua*, " Fresh Flowers." The two panels behind contain pictures of the tree-peony, with birds and butterflies, and a similar floral spray with appropriate stanzas of verse signed with the same seal.

The floral ground is composed of lotus-flowers, with coral-red blossoms, purple buds, and green leaves, mingled with leaves of other water-plants, on a pale-green background dotted with black. This ground is overlaid below with grotesque figures of a lion guarding the wheel of the Buddhist law, and an elephant laden with sacred books ; above, the characters *fu* (" happiness ") and *lu* (" rank "), in black, relieved by sprays of prunus flowers in shaded red. The character *shou* (" longevity ") is penciled in red on the two sides of the neck.

A band of diaper, interrupted by foliated panels containing censers, and a light spiral scroll in red round the lip, complete the decoration. VI.

FLOWER-VASE (*Hua P'ing*), fashioned on the lines of the peach-bloom vases (see Plate III), with the same two white rings in relief round the base of the neck, and a similar mark underneath. It is covered with a celadon monochrome glaze of purest sea-green tint varying in tone according to the depth, so as to bring out the decorative details underneath, which are worked in low relief in the paste. This decoration consists of a fringe of scrolled and crested waves round the lower part of the vase, from which project the tails and a pair of three-clawed feet of two dragons, the remainder of the bodies of the " seaserpents " being concealed, as it were, under the surface of the rough water. The mark written underneath in cobalt-blue, in three columns, is *Ta Ch'ing K'ang-hsi nien chih* —" Made in the reign of K'ang-hsi (1662–1722) of the Great Ch'ing [dynasty]." VII.

PLATE-SHAPED DISH (*Kuo P'an*), 14 inches in diameter, with a broad rim and a prominent boss in the middle, painted in brilliant shaded cobalt-blue of the *K'ang-hsi* period (1662–1722).

The raised medallion in the center is painted with a summer scene, a group of four ladies on a terraced veranda, gathering lotus-flowers from the lake below. This is surrounded by a rocky landscape, with the fir, bamboo, and blossoming prunus on one side, palms and jasmine-flowers on the other, canopied by a bank of clouds above, with the sun, moon, and stars, including the constellation of the Great Bear.

The border of the plate is filled with four garden scenes separated by rockeries, representing the four seasons, with their appropriate floral emblems. Spring is figured by two damsels with book and fan, under the shade of a weeping willow ; summer, by a party in a boat culling lotus-flowers ; autumn, by ladies gathering *Olea fragrans* ; winter, by its special emblem, the flowering prunus.

Underneath, the foot is encircled by a ring of conventional foliations, and the rim is painted with the eight Buddhist symbols of happy augury. VIII.

QUADRANGULAR VASE (*Fang P'ing*), one of a pair, 19¼ inches high, with the oblong sides rounded above and gently tapering downward, decorated with the typical flowers of the four seasons ; the shoulders with four medallions of fruit, and the neck with mythical monsters in two foliated panels. The decoration, sketched in black, and filled in with green, yellow, and manganese purple, is relieved by a background of brilliant black, with a purplish iridescent surface, passing into olive-brown at the edges.

The Moutan peony, emblem of spring, is accompanied by a *Magnolia yulan* tree, with birds in the branches ; the lotus of summer with other water plants, storks, and mandarin ducks ; the chrysanthemum of autumn with birds and butterflies ; and the flowering plum of winter has a couple of birds in its branches. The sprays of fruit include peaches, melons, persimmons, and Buddha's-hand citrons. The *ch'i-lin* on the neck of the vase, with scaly bodies, horned dragon-heads, lions' tails, and deer's hoofs, seated upon a rocky floor, are relieved by a yellow background.

The vase is modeled after a form of the *Ming* dynasty, but is probably not earlier than *K'ang-hsi* (1662–1722). IX.

DEEP SEVEN-BORDERED PLATE (*Tieh*), of eggshell porcelain, decorated in brilliant enamel colors with gilding, and enameled of a ruby tint in *rouge d'or* at the back. In the center is a large leaf-shaped panel, surrounded by a floral diaper, displayed upon a gold ground ; it contains a picture of family life—a lady seated in a chair, with two small boys playing beside her, one holding a lotus-flower, the other a gilded *ju-i* scepter ; two large jars stand on the ground, and there is a table behind hid with vases, books, and pictures upon it, the accessories of a cultured Chinese interior. The slope of the plate is encircled by three borders, a band of pink with dragon scrolls, interrupted by medallions of floral scrolls in blue, between narrower diapered bands of green and yellow ground. Upon the border is another pink diaper, studded with four dragon medallions, and

interrupted by four trellis-bordered panels of white ground painted with sprays of peony, aster, chrysanthemum, and *Rosa sinensis* ; this is succeeded inside by a foliated diaper of pale lilac, outside by a gilded belt of lotus sprays encircling the rim of the plate.

This beautiful plate is known as the " plate with the seven borders," the gold brocade round the leaf being counted as one. X.

OCTAGONAL LANTERN (*Têng*), of elongated oval outline, molded of eggshell porcelain, enameled over the glaze with the brilliant colors and gilding of the best *K'ang-hsi* period (1662–1722).

The lantern is decorated with a procession of the eight Taoist Immortals crossing the ocean (*Pa Hsien kuo hai*), and with symbols of longevity round the borders. The pieced openwork railing at the top and bottom is carved with cloud scrolls inclosing circular *shou* characters, worked in slight relief in the paste under the celadon glaze. The sloping edges are painted with large *shou* characters, alternately green and gold, enveloped in clouds ; and the receding shoulders are also covered with clouded scrolls upon a background dotted with black.

The floor of the lantern is covered with rolling crested sea-waves, painted green ; the top is studded with constellations of gilded stars, a flying stork, and the gilded solar disk. The Taoist figures occupy the eight panels, represented, with their various attributes, floating across the sea. Beginning with the principal and proceeding from right to left, we see :

1. *Chung li ch'üan*, standing upon a large gourd and holding up a monstrous peach.

2. *Lü Tung-pin*, dressed in official robes, with a scroll picture in his hand, and his supernatural sword slung upon his back, standing upon a gnarled willow with its green branches waving overhead.

3. *Lan Ts'ai-ho*, on a floating lotus-leaf, carrying a wicker basket filled with lotus-blossoms and reeds.

4. *Han Hsiang Tzŭ*, playing upon his flute, mounted upon the head of a gigantic shrimp.

5. *Chang Kuo*, riding upon his famous mule, with the magic double gourd slung to his girdle, and a bamboo drum and sticks in his hand.

6. *Ts'ao Kuo-ch'iu*, standing upon a carp, holding a pair of castanets.

7. *Li T'ieh-kuai*, standing upon a panicled reed supported by his " iron crutch," a gourd in his left hand, with the smoke issuing from it unfolding to show the lame and crooked beggar into which his spirit passed.

8. *Ho Hsien-ku*, a slender damsel with a short cloak of leaves, supported upon a lotus-petal and carrying a lotus-leaf.

The last four figures are seen in Fig. 2 in the text, from a photograph of the opposite side of the lantern. XI.

1. TEACUP (*Ch'a Wan*), of the Hang-chou imperial ware (*Kuan Yao*) of the *Southern Sung* dynasty (1127–1279), of semiglobular form, curving in at the lip, with a circularly rimmed, slightly spreading foot, which has a pointed projection in the middle underneath ; invested with a minutely but deeply crackled glaze of grayish-blue color, becoming of more pronounced lavender tint inside the cup. The rim of the foot, where it is not covered by the glaze, shows the characteristic brownish iron-gray color of the paste, and the lip is reddish gray at the edge, where the glaze is thin. It is mounted on a carved stand of dark wood, and is of thick, solid material, in order to retain heat, as prescribed in the ceremonial of the tea clubs of the period. XII.

2. VASE FOR FLOWERS (*Hua Tsun*), of typical *Yuan* dynasty porcelain (*Yuan Tz'ŭ, 1280–1367*), of rounded quadrangular form, with two tubular handles, modeled after an archaic bronze sacrificial design. The glaze, which is spread on thickly, runs down in an unctuous mass, which does not completely cover the foot, and shows a grayish buff-colored paste of intense hardness ; inside the mouth of the vase it runs down for about an inch, and ends also in

an irregularly convoluted line. It is of grayish-blue color, with a shade of lavender, crackled with an irregular reticulation of deep lines, becoming pale brick-red round the upper rims of the vase and handles where the glaze is thin. The surface is stained in two places with mottled clouds of warm red passing into purple at the edges.

Clouds of this kind, the result of some fortuitous oxidation during a firing, are highly valued by Chinese collectors; sometimes they are fancied to take the form of a bird or butterfly, or of some other natural object.　XII.

1. WINE-POT (*Chiu Hu*), of ivory-white Fuchien porcelain (*Chien Tz'ŭ*), modeled in the shape of an inverted pomegranate, and of about the natural size of the fruit, the dentated apex of which forms the foot. The handle is modeled as a branch which sends off two twigs to supply a relief decoration for the bowl as it winds up to make a loop on the cover, which it envelops in a crown of leaves. A line of verse is engraved on the back of the bowl.　XIII.

2. CYLINDRICAL TEAPOT (*Ch'a Hu*), of the same ivory-white porcelain, in the form of a joint of bamboo bound around with a knotted cord, with a pair of bearded dragons of archaic lizardlike design with spreading bifid tails attached to it; the one crawling downward with its back bowed to make the handle, the other lifting up its gaping mouth as the spout. The round cover is surmounted by the tiny figure of a grotesque lion. The design, freely and artistically treated, is clothed with a soft-looking lustrous glaze of the characteristic ivory-white tone of the finest old porcelain of the province of Fuchien, and the base, unglazed, shows the smooth, even texture of the paste. XIII.

1. TALL TWO-HANDLED CUP AND COVER (*Kai Wan*), with each loop handle fashioned in the form of two dragons' heads grasping a round jewel between their gaping jaws, and a bulging cover surmounted by a metal knob shaped like an acorn of European design. The cover, as well as the cup, is decorated in pale blue of pure color, with conventional borders of foliated panels brocaded with white flowers on a blue ground. The intervals on the cup are filled with groups of the paraphernalia of the scholar and artist, books on tables, brushes in vases, water receptacles, and scroll pictures, all enveloped with waving fillets, and mixed with tasseled wands and double diamonds, symbols of literary success.　XIV.

2. SMALL JAR (*Hsiao Kuan*), painted in bright blue in the early *K'ang-hsi* style (1662–1722), with lotus-flowers and reeds growing in water, flying insects, and lightly sketched floral sprays. The front of the vase displays, in an interval left in the floral decoration, a quatrefoil medallion containing the sacred Christian monogram I. H. S., with a cross above, and three nails meeting in a point below.　XIV.

BRUSH CYLINDER (*Pi T'ung*), 9 inches high, of tall, slender form, modeled in the shape of a section of bamboo, with a double ring worked in relief in the paste near the foot, between two lightly etched bands of scrolled design. A *Ch'ih-lung*, the dragon of archaic bronzes, is represented in salient relief as coiled around the tube, with scowling head and bristling mane, having flames proceeding from the shoulders and flanks. The cylinder is enameled with a celadon glaze of grayish-green tint, contrasting with the dragon, which is invested with a white enamel. The bottom is also celadon, leaving a wide encircling rim where the grayish *biscuit* is visible. Period *K'ang-hsi* (1662–1722).　XV.

TRANSMUTATION SPLASH VASE (*P'ing*), of regular ovoid form, slightly tapering below, where it is excavated to make a circularly rimmed foot, and rounding in above toward the mouth, which is surmounted by the form of a coiling dragon. The *Ch'ih-lung*, of three-clawed archaic design, is modeled in salient openwork relief so as to grasp the rim with its claws, and nearly to envelop it with its serpentine body and long, clinging bifid tail. The vase is enameled with a grayish superficially crackled glaze, exhibiting a rich *flambé* investment vertically splashed with mottled stripes of varied changing tint, passing from light

blue through purple and intermediate shades of red into brilliant crimson where the glaze is thickest. The dragon is colored red, and partially splashed with the same *flambé* glaze. The foot is enameled olive-green, with no mark inscribed. The technique and style of decoration indicate the *Ch'ien-lung* period (1736–95), during which this *Yao-pien* or "furnace-transmuted" glaze was much in vogue. XVI.

CLUB-SHAPED VASE (*Pang-chih P'ing*), 17½ inches high, decorated in the brilliant enamel colors, with touches of gold, of the best period of the reign of *K'ang-hsi* (1662–1722). The decoration is arranged in two large oblong panels and four larger circular panels, displayed upon a ground of floral brocade. The scrolled coral-red ground is studded with chrysanthemum-blossoms, alternately tinted apple-green and celadon. The large panel in front has a picture of a gayly plumaged bird perched upon a branch of blossoming prunus, penciled in brown, with red flowers touched with gold, mingled with sprays of bamboo having the leaves filled in with bright green and overglaze blue. The disk of the rising sun is seen above, partly hidden by the clouds of dawn tint, indicated in pale coral-red. The corresponding panel at the back has a bird on a branch of hydrangea shrub, interwoven with sprays of *Hibiscus rosa sinensis*. The circular panels contain landscapes below, insects above, the *Mantis religiosa*, with millet and wild pinks in front, the grasshopper perched on a spear of grass with trifid panicles, and single chrysanthemums behind.

The shoulder slope of the vase is decorated above with a band of scrolled chrysanthemum, with large red flowers and green leaves studding a purple ground, which is interrupted with four foliated medallions containing butterflies. The colors of the gadroon border around the foot, and of the diverse rings of conventional fret and diaper which encircle the upper part of the vase, are perfectly shown in the illustration.　XVII.

CLUB-SHAPED VASE (*Pang-chih P'ing*), 18½ inches high, with a ground of *soufflé* cobalt-blue, in which are reserved panels, decorated, on a white ground, in enamel colors of the *K'ang-hsi* period (1662–1722), including emerald-green, buff, vermilion, red, and black. The blue ground was originally overlaid with a rich decoration in gold of conventional floral scrolls and hanging chains of symbols, of which only traces now remain.

The reserves are outlined in the shape of the Chinese characters for happiness and longevity, interrupted in the middle by medallions containing the figures of the corresponding Taoist divinities. The character *Fu* in front, with a diapered ground, has a circular medallion in the middle, with *Fu Hsing*, the star-god of happiness, an aged personage leaning upon a gnarled staff, attended by two sprites carrying a palm-leaf and a fly whisk. The character *Shou* at the back, filled in with a similarly colored diaper, is interrupted by a peach-shaped panel, with a picture of *Shou Hsing*, the star-god of longevity, inside, in the guise of an aged figure with wrinkled forehead and long beard, a branch of his miraculous peaches over his shoulder, speeding across a rocky landscape, with a conspicuous spreading pine on one side of the picture.　XVIII.

IRIDESCENT IRON-RUST VASE (*P'ing*), egg-shaped, with a small round mouth and a circularly rimmed foot, enameled with a dark-brown monochrome glaze, thickly speckled with minute points of deep metallic lustrous aspect, and irregularly flecked all over with clouds of vermilion color, the lip being covered with a ring of the same red.

It is a striking example of the *t'ieh-hsiu yu*, or "iron-rust glaze," of naturalistic color and inimitable metallic luster. The foot is enameled underneath with a dark olive-brown monochrome glaze of rugose "bubbly" appearance. There is no mark inscribed, although it is evidently an early *Ch'ien-lung* piece (1736–95).　XIX.

BUDDHIST ECCLESIASTICAL VASE (*P'ing*), one of a pair, 16¾ inches high, of hexagonal section and complicated outline, elaborately decorated in brilliant enamel colors with gilding, for the altar set of a Buddhist temple; each altar set consisting of a tripod censer and two pricket candle-sticks, flanked by a pair of vases, five pieces in all.

The body of the vase, of reversed conical form, is modeled in the shape of a *dágaba*, or relic shrine, with a sunk panel in each of the six sides containing a vase, which stands out in relief from the floral background, displaying the sacred wheel of the law surmounted by the *trisula* symbol. The edges and borders are filled with floral brocades and bands of conventional flowers, sprays of fruit, and birds, relieved by grounds of different color. The neck of the vase, channeled externally, and correspondingly fluted inside, is painted with pendant chains of flowers and jewels, relieved by a red ground. The foot is painted in green, with rings of palmetto foliations on a yellow ground, and with gilded chrysanthemum sprays upon a red ground around the rim. The interior of the vase and the under surface of the foot are enameled pale green. A small panel is reserved in the middle, underneath, in which is inscribed the seal in underglaze blue, *Ta Ch'ing Yung-chêng nien chih* —i. e., "Made in the reign of Yung-chêng (1723–35), of the Great Ch'ing [dynasty]." XX.

VASE (*P'ing*), 17 inches high, of cylindrical form, slightly enlarging upward and receding at the neck, painted in the brilliant enamel colors of the *Yung-chêng* period (1723–35).

There is a group of figures on the vase, the three principal of which represent the Triad of the Taoist cult, called *Fu Lu Shou San Hsing*, or "The Three Star-Gods of Happiness, Rank, and Longevity," the other smaller figures being attendant sprites. *Lu Hsing*, the "Star-God of Rank," has the place of honor in the middle, clad in imperial robes, representing *Shang Ti*, the superior ruler of the Taoist pantheon, whose throne is the Great Bear, round which all the other stars revolve in homage; he holds a baton of rank, and has a peony, the "mandarin's flower," stuck in his winged hat. On his right is *Shou Hsing*, the "Divinity of Longevity," an aged, bent figure, with wrinkled, smiling face and bald, protuberant brow, leaning upon a gnarled staff, dressed in robes brocaded with sprays of peach-blossoms, and carrying a peach, the "fruit of life," in his hand. A stork is flying overhead, and a tall pine, another of his emblems, covered with flowering bignonia, rises in the background. He is attended by three playful sprites, dancing under the flowers and striving to reach the peach. On the left stands *Fu Hsing*, the personified "Star of Happiness," his head covered with a blue hood, his girdle embroidered with the sacred fungus and bat, while two other bats, his special attributes, are flying in the air above; he holds a child in his arms, and another is dancing behind. The neck of the vase is decorated in front with a group of fruit, composed of a little branch with twin peaches upon it, surrounded by twigs of water-caltrop, Buddha's-hand citron, pomegranate, olive, melon, and lotus. The foot, excavated to make a circular rim, is unglazed. XXI.

OPENWORK LANTERN (*Têng*), of oval hexagonal form, 10½ inches high, with panels carved in openwork designs, decorated in brilliant colored enamels of the *famille rose*, belonging to the *Ch'ien-lung* period (1736–95).

The six sides of the lantern have oblong panels pierced with trelliswork of two different patterns, surrounding solid circular medallions in the middle, which are painted with pictures of Taoist saints or hermits, each accompanied by an attendant sprite. They are figured in landscapes filled in with appropriate surroundings, pines, dryandra-trees, the sacred fungus, and spotted deer, and carry the usual attributes, such as *ling-chih*, peaches, baskets of flowers and herbs, hoes, or pilgrims' gourds; one of the attendants holds up a double gourd from which a cloud of smoke is issuing at his master's behest, which unfolds above to display a flying crane. The upper and lower receding rims are also pierced with six smaller panels. The borders and edges are all richly decorated with painted diapers of diverse pattern with floral grounds.

A similar lamp is figured by Du Sartel in *La Porcelaine de Chine*, Plate XXXI. XXII.

OBLONG CRACKLED VASE (*Fang P'ing*), 10½ inches high, of square section, with a circular rim at the base, culminating in a short neck leading to a round mouth, and having the corners projected in the form of broken, dentated ridges. The sides are molded in relief, with the creative monad symbol (*yin-yang*) four times repeated in the middle, and the series of eight mystic trigrams (*pa kua*) above and below. The glaze which invests the whole surface is superficially crackled, and colored with thin splashes of grayish mottled purple and olive-brown tints. The foot, somewhat roughly plastered with grayish-purple and olive-brown, has a rim showing a gray paste of comparatively coarse texture. XXIII.

DEEP EGGSHELL PLATE (*Tieh*), decorated in brilliant enamel colors of the *famille rose* with gilding. Of the same eggshell texture and artistic style as the "rose-back" plates, it is decorated, instead, underneath the rim, with three floral sprays, boldly painted in overglaze cobalt-blue. The plate is painted inside with a garden scene containing a group of figures, representing an emperor and empress surrounded by courtiers. The emperor, identified by his robes brocaded with dragons, by the tassels of red silk on the trappings of his white horse, and by the oval banner screens embroidered with gold dragons held up by attendants behind him, has just mounted upon horseback; the empress, followed by court ladies holding dragon-centered processional fans of peacocks' feathers, is in the act of mounting a piebald horse with the aid of a stool, supported by a lady attendant, while a courtier holds the gilded stirrup hanging on the off side of the saddle.

The borders of the plate are filled with ornamental diapers of different pattern; that on the slope inside is interrupted by blue dragon-scrolls, and the broad blue band that succeeds is overlaid with dragon-scrolls in gold; the rim is encircled by a gilded quatrefoil diaper upon a black ground. XXIV.

TRIPOD CENSER (*Ting Lu*), of depressed globular form, rounding in to a wide, circular mouth, supported upon three feet of scrolled outline, which spring from the gaping mouths of grotesque lions' heads projecting from the lower surface of the bowl. It is invested with a glaze of brownish-yellow color, mottled with clouds of darker brown toward the bottom; the glaze, extended over the molded feet, is paler in the relief parts, deep brown in the recesses where it is thicker. The base is unglazed, with the exception of a round patch of the *café-au-lait* enamel in the middle.

The censer dates, doubtless, from the *Ming* dynasty. Vessels of this form are used in Chinese temples for burning "joss-sticks," made of fragrant woods, before the images of the deities. This one must have come from some Taoist temple, as the openwork cover of rosewood is surmounted by a Taoist figure carved out of red agate, representing an acolyte of the god of longevity, with a peach in his hand, leaning upon a deer. XXV.

CORAL-RED VASE (*Hua P'ing*), with globular body and slightly spreading neck, decorated in enamel colors, with an imperial dragon pursuing the jewel of omnipotence, relieved by a monochrome iron-red ground of pure vermilion tint, of the *Ch'ien-lung* period (1736–95). The outlines of the decoration are penciled in underglaze blue. The five-clawed dragon coiled round the neck of the vase is colored green, with the enamel laid on thickly, so as to stand out in slight relief, the jewel being depicted on the shoulder as a yellow disk with a green spiral coil inside emitting bluish flames. The rim of the foot shows a paste of grayish tint; the glaze underneath, of pale-green color, is crackled. XXVI.

CRACKLED GREEN VASE (*P'ing*), 16½ inches high, bottle-shaped, with globular body and wide tubular neck, invested with a monochrome glaze of pale "camellia-leaf green" color, minutely crackled throughout. The foot is enameled underneath with the same glaze, which is also partially spread on inside the mouth so as to leave some of the buff-colored paste visible. The rim of the mouth is lightly touched with a ring of brown tint. The fine crackle is sometimes known as *truitée*, from its resemblance to the scales of the trout; the Chinese call it *yü tzŭ wên*, or "fish-roe crackle," as distinguished from the coarser reticulation of the *ping lieh wên*, or "fissured ice crackle." The color approaches "apple-green." The period is *Ch'ien-lung* (1736–95); it is enameled *sur biscuit* like the finely crackled turquoise vases of the time, and the paste is of similar character. XXVII.

CLUB SHAPED VASE (*Pang-chih P'ing*), 17¾ inches high, painted in overglaze iron-red of darker and lighter shade, with touches of gold and spots of black to define the eyes of the dragons, executed in the vigorous style and coloring of the reign of *K'ang-hsi* (1662–1722).

The body of the vase is decorated in panels of different shape, surrounded by a red ground diapered with chrysanthemum scrolls. Two large oblong panels contain four-clawed dragons disporting among clouds, in pursuit of the jewel of omnipotence, which is depicted as a gilded disk with spiral center, as if whirling in the air. At the sides there are two rectangular panels with flowers and flying insects, branches of pomegranate fruit and blossoming peach and sprays of bamboo, and two panels of foliated outline below, with carp swimming in the midst of water plants. The shoulder is encircled by a brocaded ground of diamond pattern studded with peach-blossoms and broken by four foliated medallions with chrysanthemum-flowers inside; the neck is painted with four circular *shou* characters in a graceful floral scroll; the elaborate decoration being completed by a band of false gadroons round the foot, a ring of spiral scroll on the upright lip, and a castellated border at the base of the neck. XXVIII.

VASE (*P'ing*), 12¾ inches high, covered with a monochrome glaze of an intense and rich sapphire-blue color, minutely and uniformly crackled throughout. It is a cobalt-blue, the *gros bleu* of French ceramists, the *pao-shih lan*, or "sapphire-blue," of the Chinese.

It invests a buff-colored paste, exhibited under the foot, which is unglazed. The vase is probably not older than the *Ch'ien-lung* period (1736–95). XXIX.

FLOWER-VASE (*Hua P'ing*), 10¼ inches high, of solid make, bottle-shaped, with a slightly tapering neck, enveloped in the folds of a dragon modeled in salient relief with openwork. The vase is enameled with a mottled glaze of gray ground streaked with pale purple. The dragon, a three-clawed monster of archaic design, with a spirally curved tail, is enameled crimson with a *rouge-d'or* glaze; one of its long horns, accidentally broken off, has been replaced in gold. It is marked underneath, below the coat of purplish-gray glaze, with a seal, very lightly etched in the paste, containing the inscription *Ta Ch'ing Ch'ien-lung nien chih*, "Made in the reign of Ch'ien-lung (1736–95) of the Great Ch'ing [dynasty]." XXX.

LARGE VASE (*P'ing*), 23½ inches high, decorated with a pair of five-clawed imperial dragons in the midst of clouds, enameled green, displayed upon a monochrome ground of yellow. The details of the design are etched in the paste with a style under the green enamel. One of the dragons is emerging from the sea, the rolling waves of which surround the base of the vase; the other is descending, its tail reaching to the top of the neck. They are enveloped by scrolls of clouds, the rifts of which are occupied by flying bats. A formal band of foliations pointing downward encircles the foot, and a ring of spiral ornament surrounds the upper rim. The foot is enameled yellow underneath, with no mark; the period would be that of *Ch'ien-lung* (1736–95); the design is of imperial character, and the yellow ground of the typical shade reserved for the use of the emperor, known as "imperial yellow." XXXI.

FLOWER-VASE (*Hua P'ing*), with a wide circular mouth, the upright rim of which is surmounted by the head of a five-clawed dragon, its body, projected in salient relief, being modeled in openwork upon the shoulder of the vase. The surface of the vase is covered with a deep monochrome glaze of "iron-red" of dark coral tint and undulating aspect. The dragon is enameled green, the details are touched in black. The mouth is covered inside with a greenish-white glaze partially crackled with brown lines, and the same glaze covers the base, underneath, inside the rim, which exhibits a paste of grayish tone. It is not older than the reign of *Ch'ien-lung* (1736–95). XXXII.

VASE (*P'ing*), 11 inches high, of bottle-shaped outline, with a tall neck, enameled with a thick opaque glaze of grayish tone, mottled and streaked with amethyst, passing into splashes of deep purple shade. The glaze is extended over the lip and for about an inch downward inside the mouth. Underneath the foot it is coated with an opaque ivory-white glaze, slightly crackled. The rim exhibits a rather coarse buff-colored paste resembling that of stoneware, but paler than that of the ordinary *Kuang Yao*, the production of the province of Kuangtung, which is illustrated in Plate XLI. XXXIII.

PLUM-BLOSSOM JAR (*Mei Hua Kuan*) 10½ inches high, of globular outline, with rounded cover, decorated with an interlacement of floral sprays, springing upward from a rockery on one side, and downward from the rim of the jar on the other, so as to cover its surface as well as that of the cover. Two pairs of magpies are perched among the branches. The intervals are studded with single flowers and buds. The colors are manganese-brown of purplish tinge, green, and yellow, relieved by an enameled ground of intense black, which becomes shaded with a greenish tone at the edges. The interior of the jar and the foot are glazed with a greenish-white enamel, and the paste is of somewhat gray porous texture, differing from the perfect technique of the blue and white "ginger jar" of Plate II, but resembling the well-known large vases of the *K'ang-hsi* period, painted with the same colors relieved by a similar black ground. XXXIV.

VASE (*P'ing*), 14½ inches high, of somewhat thick, solid structure, with the neck buttressed with two vertical ribs, encircled above by six tubular handles, and the shoulder studded with a ring of six prominent bosses. It is enameled with a crackled glaze of grayish celadon color, reticulated with fine lines of reddish brown, mottled all over with clouds of copper-red of strawberry hue, flecked with darker shades of brown. The inside of the mouth and the under aspect of the foot are also crackled, but of plain celadon color without mottling. The circular rim of the foot is touched with a coating of iron-gray, to cover the rather coarse buff-colored paste, which is accidentally left bare at one point where one of the handles springs from the neck. It belongs, probably, to the *Ch'ien-lung* period (1736–95). XXXV.

BOWL FOR GOLDFISH (*Yü Kang*), 7 inches high, 10 inches across, modeled in the form of a large lotus-leaf turned up at the edge, so that the folded margin of the peltate leaf makes the irregularly convoluted rim of the bowl, which is etched inside and out to represent the natural venation of the leaf. The two handles which project at the sides are fashioned in full relief in the shape of lotus-flowers, one of which, fully expanded, shows the cup-shaped fruit in the middle. These blossoms, which are colored maroon, are each flanked by two buds of the same color in similar relief. Two more flowers are painted in maroon to decorate the front and back of the bowl; all the tuberculated flower-stems are represented curving up from below. The rest of the surface of the bowl is enameled inside and out with a celadon glaze of greenish tint, which darkens in the etched parts of the design and becomes nearly white over the relief parts. The bottom is unglazed, only superficially coated with a thin wash of brown color. Period *Ch'ien-lung* (1736–95). XXXVI.

SIX SNUFF-BOTTLES (*Pi yen Hu*). 1. Of cylindrical form, decorated with a dragon pursuing the jewel in the midst of clouds, painted in black upon a ground of deep mottled yellow; sea-waves at the foot, lambrequin round the upper rim. Mark underneath, in blue, *Yung-chêng nien chih*, "Made in the reign of Yung-chêng" (1723-35).

2. Of flattened globular form, decorated with landscapes in maroon-red, with the distant hills and water shaded in the same copper-red of greenish tint. The stopper, with gilded rim, is enameled of a crackled apple-green to simulate turquoise. Mark underneath, in one line of "seal" characters, *Ta Ch'ing Tao-kuang nien chih*, "Made in the reign of Tao-kuang (1821-50) of the Great Ch'ing [dynasty]."

3. Of baluster shape, enameled with a crackled monochrome glaze of purplish-gray color. No mark. The spoon is mounted on metal stopper inlaid with coral.

4. Of pilgrim-bottle shape, made of copper invested with Soochow cinnabar lac, carved with scrolls of peonies, fret borders, and dragon-head handles. Intaglio mark underneath, a monogram meaning "myriad-fold longevity and happiness."

5. Of flattened oval form, decorated in enamel colors with a mountain landscape extending all round, with a figure in the foreground standing in front of a pavilion, an old fisherman on a rock angling, a rustic behind carrying a plow, and a boy with brushwood. Stopper, with gilded rim, enameled to represent coral and turquoise. No mark.

6. Carved out of clouded agate, showing the natural veining of the stone, supposed to resemble a dragon concealed by clouds. The stopper, with a rim of turquoise, is mounted with a coral bead. XXXVII.

ETCHED CELADON VASE (*P'ing*), 17 inches high, bottle-shaped, with a bulging body of globular outline, ornamented with bats flying among scrolled clouds, worked in slight relief in the paste and etched so as to cover the body and neck of the vase, the intervals being filled in with ornamental borders. Plainly paneled borders encircle the body above and below, a broad chain of rectangular fret defines the base of the neck, and a band of diamond-pattern fret encircles the mouth, interrupted by four floral studs, and succeeded by a ring of trefoil foliations. The whole surface is invested with a celadon glaze of typical color, which varies in shade according to its depth, thereby enhancing the effect of the etched decoration underneath. The base is enameled white underneath, without any inscription. The period would be *Yung-chêng* (1723-35) or *Ch'ien-lung* (1736-95), the vase being a fine example of the celadon tone of this period called by the Chinese *tung-ch'ing*. The tint resembles that of the vase of the preceding reign, illustrated in Plate VII, but the glaze is not quite so rich and translucid. XXXVIII.

WHITE BOTTLE-SHAPED VASE (*P'ing*), with double ring worked in slight relief in the middle of the long neck under the thick white glaze tinged with a shade of green, which covers the whole surface, reserving the decoration, which is etched in the paste with a graving-tool and left *en biscuit*, showing the natural color of the material after it has been fired. It consists of a four-clawed dragon, winding round the shoulder of the vase in pursuit of the jewel of omnipotence enveloped in flames of effulgence. The mark underneath, penciled in underglaze cobalt-blue, is *Ta Ming Ch'êng-hua nien chih*, "Made in the reign of Ch'êng-hua of the Great Ming [dynasty]," but the form, style of decoration, and technical details, seem to be those of the reign of *K'ang-hsi* (1662-1722). XXXIX.

PEA-GREEN CELADON VASE (*Tsun*), of antique form and design, modeled with a band of lotus-petals rising in slight relief round the foot, and with three prominent ribs encircling the upper part. Upon the shoulder is crouched the monstrous form of a dragon, worked in salient relief and undercut, so as nearly to envelop the circumference of the vase within its massive folds, the interval being occupied by the jewel, with its effulgent halo, which the dragon is pursuing. Of the usual conventional form, it has two branched horns and a bristling mane, the feet are five-clawed, and flaming processes issuing from the shoulders indicate its supernatural character. It is boldly modeled

and finished with engraving. The glaze with which the whole surface is enameled is of *tou-ch'ing*, or pea-green celadon color, and is not crackled. It darkens somewhat in the recesses of the molded decoration.

The foot is coated underneath with the same celadon glaze, and has no mark attached. The piece may perhaps be referred to the reign of *Yung-chêng* (1723-35). XL.

KUANG YAO FIGURE OF BODHIDHARMA (*Ta-mo Hsiang*), the famous Buddhist pilgrim, who came from India to China in the year 520, and was the first of the Chinese Buddhist patriarchs. The statuette, 13½ inches high, is fashioned in the peculiar reddish-gray stoneware of the province of Kuangtung (*Kuang Yao*), exhibited at the base and in the hollow of the figure, which are unglazed. He is standing in the attitude of religious meditation, dressed in flowing robes, with the hands folded in the sleeves; the poll is shaven, and the ears have the traditional large lobes of the Buddhist saint. The breast and face show the natural red color of the fired clay; the hair, left long behind so as to fall over the shoulders in curls, is colored dark brown; the rest of the figure is invested with a thick, lustrous crimson glaze of mottled *flambé* character, overspread with a reticulated cloud of olive-brown tint. XLI.

BLUE AND WHITE BROCADED VASE (*P'ing*), of Persian form, with bulging body and slender, tapering neck, decorated in pale blue of pure tint with floral grounds and foliated panels of floral brocade.

There are four lozenge-shaped panels on the body, of foliated outline, filled with floral designs in white on a blue ground, connected by straps and linked chains. Leaf-shaped panels of similar design spread upward and downward; the intervals are studded with tiny blossoms. The neck has two leaf shaped panels spreading up from the base, and two narrow foliations at the lip; the rest is covered with an overlapping floral pattern. Bands of angular fret round the rim and a ring of conventional ornament to define the shoulder complete the decoration, which is of arabesque character. The mark inscribed underneath is a leaf, outlined in blue, a common sign of the *K'ang-hsi* period (1662-1722), to which this little vase is to be attributed. XLII.

POMEGRANATE VASE (*Shih-liu P'ing*), being fashioned of a curious shape simulating a pomegranate crowned with its permanent calyx. The body, of six-lobed section, is alternately ribbed and fluted, and drawn in above to a short, slender neck, which flares into a recurved mouth with an irregularly indented rim. The lip is tinted with a line of dark-brown color, and the foot is invested underneath with a dark-brown glaze, so that the material might be mistaken for a dark stoneware, did not a slight flaw in the glaze at one point lay bare the whitish paste. The vase is coated outside with a mottled glaze of dull purplish or lavender color, crackled with a network of dark lines. The interior of the mouth is enameled with a lustrous glaze of grayish white more superficially crackled. It appears to be a reproduction, to be attributed to the *Yung-chêng* period, of the famous *Kuan Yao* of the *Sung* dynasty, which is described as having had an "iron-colored foot" and "copper-red mouth." XLIII.

BEAKER-SHAPED VASE (*Hua Ku*), of slender, graceful form, modeled after an ancient sacrificial bronze, with a prominent band round the middle, a spreading foot, and a trumpet-shaped mouth. The surface is covered with molded and etched designs of archaic bronze character, with an ornamental band of scrolls, proceeding from dragons' heads, round the middle, between two rings of interrupted rectangular fret, and with palmations, spreading upward and downward, outlined in spiral curves. It is entirely covered with a minutely crackled glaze of pure turquoise tint, which changes in tone according to its depth, thereby enhancing the effect of the relief and chiseled work. There is no mark underneath, but a similar piece in the collection is engraved with the seal *Ta Ch'ing Ch'ien-lung nien chih*, and this vase must be referred to the same reign of Ch'ien-lung (1736-95). XLIV.

BEAKER-SHAPED VASE (*Hua Ku*), of slender, graceful form, with slightly spreading foot and trumpet-shaped mouth, modeled after an ancient bronze design on lines similar to those of the vase figured in Plate XLIV, but differing in having a perfectly plain surface. It is enameled with the same finely crackled glaze of mottled tones of the purest turquoise tint, which extends over the rim inside the mouth, and invests the base of the foot, with the exception of the circular rim, which is unglazed, and shows the grayish texture of the paste. It must be referred to the same period, the reign of *Ch'ien-lung* (1736–95). It is a pale bluish variety of the glaze which Chinese ceramists call *k'ung-chüo-lü*, or "peacock-green." XLV.

BRILLIANT FLAMBÉ QUADRANGULAR VASE (*Fang Tsun*), 12 inches high, of antique design, with two wide-open scroll handles projecting from the sides of the neck. The mouth has the rounded corners indented, and the indentations are continued downward as grooves, which gradually disappear about the middle of the vase. A pointed ovoid panel is outlined in slight relief on the front and back, to break the uniformity of the surface. The vase is enameled outside with a gray, superficially crackled glaze, overlaid with vertical streaks and mottled clouds, so as to exhibit splashes of brilliant transformation colors of varied tints, passing through brilliant shades of crimson and purple into deep olive-brown. The upper rim and the interior of the mouth are coated with the same *yao-pien*, or "furnace transmuted" glaze. The enamel under the foot is yellow, and not crackled; the paste is very white, as shown by a slight accidental chip. Period, *Ch'ien-lung* (1736–95). XLVI.

LARGE "PILGRIM-BOTTLE" VASE, or *Pao-yueh P'ing*, literally "full-moon vase," 16 inches high, with floral decoration in enamel colors of the *Yung-chêng* period (1723–35).

The scrolled openwork handles, which connect the neck and shoulders, are fashioned in the form of grotesque dragons. The base of the neck is encircled by a band of fret, succeeded above by a formal palmate ring of foliations, below by a scroll border, and a ring of scroll ornament surrounds the foot. The body of the vase is decorated on both sides with flowering branches springing from a point near the foot and spreading over the surface. On the side illustrated we see scarlet pomegranate-flowers and branches of the white prunus and pink *Pyrus japonica*, mingled with twigs of bamboo and sacred fungus. On the other side narcissus-flowers, with white petals and yellow bells in the middle, spring from rocks clad with fungus, with bamboo sprays, and there is a bunch of red nandina berries waving above. A pair of butterflies is flying across the field, and bees are hovering around the plum-blossoms. The seal penciled underneath in underglaze blue is *Ta Ch'ing Yung-chêng nien chih*—i. e., "Made in the reign of Yung-chêng, of the Great Ch'ing [dynasty]." XLVII.

LARGE ROUND DISH (*Ta Kuo P'an*), 20 inches in diameter, with a floral decoration, painted in the brilliant enamel colors of the *Yung-chêng* period, extending from the base over the rim and along the sides, as well as filling the interior of the saucer-shaped dish. The decoration consists of branches of the blossoming plum (*mei-hua*) mingled with sprays of pomegranate (*shih-liu*), both of which send off twigs before they wind over the rim to ornament the under border of the dish with the same white and red flowers. A clump of the branching sacred fungus (*ling-chih*), with its scrolled heads of diverse colors, is sprouting from the branch of the prunus. The mark penciled underneath in cobalt-blue inside a double ring of the same color is *Ta Ch'ing Yung-chêng nien chih*—i. e., "Made in the reign of Yung-chêng (1723–35), of the Great Ch'ing [dynasty]."

The companion dish, of the same size, style, and mark, is decorated, still more effectively, with branches of the tree-peony (*mou-tan*), *Magnolia yulan*, and *Pyrus japonica* (*hai-t'ang*), and has trailing sprays of the three flowers extending round three fourths of the lower border. The large, conspicuous blossoms of the peony are nearly white, tipped with pink, and the magnolia-petals are filled in with the same white enamel. XLVIII.

LARGE GLOBULAR JAR (*Kang*), painted in deep brilliant blue, of the tone of coloring and archaic decorative style characteristic of the *Chia-ching* period of the *Ming* dynasty. The body is divided into four panels of foliated outline, which are filled with landscape pictures of familiar life in China. In front, a poet is seated in a pavilion composing, while a boy attendant holds up his ink-pallet, and two others carry wine-pot and cup. Two men are working in the garden below, the trees of which are the symbolical pine, bamboo, and plum. The scene on the left depicts a scholar on horseback riding to visit a friend in his mountain retreat, at the door of which an attendant is knocking to announce his arrival. Similar scenes occupy the other two panels. The recesses are filled with alternate sprays of peony and chrysanthemum, and the decoration is completed by a band of sacred fungus round the shoulder of the jar, and another of beaded gadroon pattern round the base. Underneath, boldly written in dark underglaze cobalt-blue, is the mark *Ta Ming Chia ching nien chih*—i. e., "Made in the reign of Chia-ching (1522–66), of the Great Ming [dynasty]." XLIX.

TWO VASES (*Hua P'ing*), of the "peach-bloom" type. The first is invested with a grayish-green glaze variegated with streaks and mottled clouds of intense emerald-green, passing into olive at the lower edges as they "run" down over the field. A blush of "crushed-strawberry" tint is seen near the rim at the base. The magnificent coloring seems to be an accidental success of the potter, due to prolonged firing of a glaze unusually rich in copper. The usual mark of *Ta Ch'ing K'ang-hsi nien chih*, "Made in the reign of K'ang-hsi, of the Great Ch'ing [dynasty]," penciled underneath in cobalt-blue, has also "run," the characters being much blurred. The lip has been replaced in gold.

The second piece is clad in a rich, smooth glaze of charmingly uniform color, a pinkish pearl-gray, reminding one of the hue of the opening bud of the lavender. It is flecked with a few olive-brown spots in the receding hollow of the neck. It is of perfect technique, with the lip defined by a rounded edge, and the foot enameled pure white underneath, but not inscribed. The interior of the mouth exhibits a mottled glaze, displaying the most beautiful "peach-bloom" tints. Period, *K'ang-hsi* (1662–1722). L.

FLOWER-VASE (*Hua P'ing*), of graceful shape, exhibiting in typical form the mottled play of colors characteristic of the celebrated "peach-bloom" glaze. The three tints distinguished by the Chinese connoisseur are all seen in the illustration—viz., the *chiang tou hung*, or "haricot-red," of the ground, the *mei kuei pan*, or "rose spots," and the clouds of *p'ing-kuo ch'ing*, or "apple-green." The glaze ends below in the usual sharply cut straight line, so as to leave a rim of biscuit round the foot, which is deeply hollowed out underneath. The mark penciled in brilliant underglaze blue is composed of six minute characters arranged in two columns, reading, *Ta Ch'ing K'ang-hsi nien chih*, "Made in the reign of K'ang-hsi (1662–1722), of the Great Ch'ing [dynasty]." LI.

OVOID VASE (*Hua P'ing*), one of a pair, of the same period as the last, and with the same mark underneath written in still more minute blue characters, covered with a monochrome glaze of pale sky-blue tint, a charming example of the rare *yueh pai*, literally "moonlight white," or *clair-de-lune* glaze. LI.

FLOWER-VASE (*Hua P'ing*), 7½ inches high, with a ring of upright foliated panels molded in slight relief in the paste round the base. The upper part of the neck, which had a slightly flaring mouth, has been ground down and mounted with a silver collar of Japanese workmanship. The vase is enameled with a "peach-bloom" glaze of "crushed-strawberry" tint, flecked with spots of darker red, and mottled with clouds of apple-green passing into a bright grass-green in the middle. The mark written underneath in cobalt-blue under a white glaze is *Ta Ch'ing K'ang-hsi nien chih*, "Made in the reign of K'ang-hsi (1662–1722), of the Great Ch'ing [dynasty]."

The companion vase in the collection, 8 inches high, of a similar form, and with the same mark underneath, has a "crushed-strawberry" ground, flecked with reddish-brown spots, and only slightly clouded, at one spot, with apple-green. The glaze has run down in thick drops and partially enfoliated, leaving bare places, which have been filled in with tiny petals of gold lacquer. The upper rim is capped with a silver mount etched with a floral pattern, and the neck is encircled by scrolled clouds and a gold dragon of Japanese design. LII.

FLOWER-VASE (*Hua P'ing*), 9 inches high, of eggshell thinness, invested with a soft monochrome glaze of pink color, belonging to the *Yung-chêng* (1722–35) or early *Ch'ien-lung* (1736–95) period. This beautiful and rare tint is the same as that with which the backs of some of the delicate eggshell dishes of the time are enameled. It is a variety of the *rose d'or*, being derived from gold; different shades of pink were produced by combining the "purple of Cassius," which gives a pure crimson tint, with graduated doses of white. The pink, illustrated here, is called *hai-t'ang hung*, or "*Pyrus japonica* red," by the Chinese, from its resemblance to the petals of that flower; the deeper crimson of the "ruby-backed" dishes, one of which is illustrated in Plate X, they call *yen-chih hung*, or "rouge-red." LIII.

FLOWER-VASE (*Hua P'ing*), with the "peach-bloom" glaze of the *K'ang-hsi* period (1662–1722). The illustration, in the size of the original, shows the gracefully curved lines of the form and the perfect technique of the piece. The swelling lip is defined by a line of white, and two white rings in slight relief encircle the neck as it springs from the shoulder. The rest of the surface is covered with a rich glaze of velvety aspect, exhibiting the beautiful play of colors which distinguishes the "peach-bloom" or "crushed-strawberry" vases. The neck is coated inside with a glaze of bright apple-green tint, sprinkled with a few dark-red spots, and tipped at the edge with a ring of mottled "peach-bloom." The mark underneath, *Ta Ch'ing K'ang-hsi nien chih*, "Made in the reign of K'ang-hsi, of the Great Ch'ing [dynasty]," is beautifully written in underglaze cobalt-blue, the six characters arranged in three columns. LIV.

WINE-POT (*Chiu Hu*), of somewhat rough paste and antique style, enameled with colors and touches of gold, of the *K'ang-hsi* period (1662–1722). Of oblong form, with the corners rounding inward, it has an upright arched handle which is painted with black lines on a yellow ground, to simulate basketwork. The decoration is in panels, with the typical flowers of the seasons on the four sides; the plum of winter, with a bird perched in the branches, and an evergreen bamboo growing from the rocks beneath; the tree-peony of spring, with butterflies flying around; the lotus of summer; and the chrysanthemum of autumn. The intervals are filled with bands of floral diaper, interrupted on the shoulder by two medallions containing sprays of peony, and formal sprigs of the same flower are painted on the curved spout. The foot is glazed white underneath, with no mark attached. LV.

BOTTLE-SHAPED VASE (*P'ing*), 16½ inches high, of good form and finished technique, enameled with the celebrated red glaze of the *Lang Yao* of the reign of *K'ang-hsi* (1662–1722). The surface of the glaze exhibits a superficial network of crackled lines, and its depth reflects the richly mottled tints of *sang-de-bœuf* type, streaked with lighter shades below. The upper edge of the tall neck is defined by a rounded rim of white. The foot is apple-green underneath, not crackled, mottled with undefined rings of pale red. LVI.

VASE (*P'ing*), 18 inches high, of the celebrated *Lang Yao* of the reign of *K'ang-hsi* (1662–1722). Bottle-shaped, with swelling body and tall, wide, cylindrical neck; the rich, deep glaze, crackled throughout, exhibits the characteristic crimson tints of *sang de bœuf* in its darkest mottling. The base is covered underneath with a gray, "rice-colored" glaze, slightly mottled with brown. LVII.

FLOWER-VASE (*Hua P'ing*), 8½ inches high, covered with the crackled *sang-de-bœuf* glaze, the characteristic colors of which are well represented in the lithograph. The mottling of apple-green crackle exhibited near the foot is still more marked on the opposite side of the vase. The base underneath is coated with a crackled white glaze, barely tinted with green. It belongs to the reign of *K'ang-hsi* (1662–1722). LVIII.

LARGE VASE (*P'ing*), 21 inches high, of the celebrated *Lang Yao* of the reign of *K'ang-hsi* (1662–1722), covered with the characteristic crackled monochrome glaze of *sang-de-bœuf* color. The colors, of varied tone, pass from apple-green to deepest crimson, through all intermediate shades, according to the degree of oxidation of the copper silicates in the glaze. The vase is green toward the edges, where the network of crackles is most clearly visible; red on the body, where the glaze runs down toward the foot in richly mottled streaks; and of dark, sanguineous tint on the shoulder, where the glaze is thickest. The rims are defined by lines of white glaze; the base is covered underneath with a crackled glaze of pale apple-green color. The plate shows well the vertical play of colors, the crackled texture, and the stippled ground which mark this glaze—one of the most brilliant achievements of the Chinese potter. The reflections give a touch of contrast to the tone, and indicate the finished radiance of the surface lit up by the sun. LIX.

STATUETTE OF KUAN YIN (*Kuan Yin Hsiang*), 17 inches high, mounted upon a pedestal, representing the Chinese goddess of Mercy, a Buddhist divinity, the special "hearer of prayers," as the name signifies. Modeled in a dignified pose, she stands upright with braceleted hands crossed in front, her robes, with broad and loose sleeves, hanging gracefully down so as to cover all but the tips of her bare feet. The face, with calm, complacent features, is marked between the eyebrows with the illuminating *ûrna*, characteristic mark of a Buddha, and the ears have the traditional pendulous lobes of a Buddhist saint. The hair is crowned with a tiara of lotus design; a lotus-flower is suspended upon the breast by a jeweled necklace, and another hangs down from the girdle. A short brocaded cloak covers the shoulders and forms a hood, which projects forward in a point above the head-dress. The pedestal is fashioned in scrolled outlines to represent the waves of the sea, with the two-horned bristling head of a dragon emerging in front, flanked by two four-clawed feet, the hinder part of its serpentine form being seen behind.

The figure is enameled with a crackled glaze of soft grayish tone with reticulating brown lines. The decorated parts are painted in the brilliant colors of the old *famille verte*; the hair is jet-black, the eyebrows are outlined in black, and the lips touched with coral-red. The hood is brocaded with scrolls of lotus-flowers; the upper border of the robe is encircled by *shou* characters alternating with flowers. Period *K'ang-hsi* (1662–1722). LX.

TALL VASE (*Hu-lu P'ing*), 28 inches high, of threefold outline, fashioned in the form of a double gourd with broad, swelling waist, and decorated in enameled colors of the *K'ang-hsi* period (1662–1722).

The middle section is decorated on a white ground with two grotesque lions enveloped in flames, and brocaded balls, looking like wheels, surrounded by waving fillets. The balls, outlined in underglaze blue, are painted partly in the same blue, partly in colors, coral-red and green predominating; the lions, painted in similar colors, have the curly manes and spreading tails touched with an overglaze blue enamel. The borders are filled in with a band of floral diaper in colors. The upper and lower segments of the vase are glazed with a monochrome ground of brilliant "mirror-black." This was once profusely painted in gold, and traces remain on the lower part of the vase of floral and diapered grounds, inclosing panels containing rocky scenes with deer, *k'ilin*, and monstrous quadrupeds, surmounted by a ring of symbols, including the double fish, lozenges, and "cash"; and of panels containing landscapes with temples on the upper segment.   LXI.

FLOWER-VASE (*Hua P'ing*), 10½ inches high, of the reign of *K'ang-hsi* (1662–1722), decorated in panels with cobalt-blue of brilliant mottled tone, and in the intervals with floral sprays on an enameled black ground. The body of the vase is decorated with three quatrefoil panels containing vases filled with bouquets of lotus-flowers and reeds, pots of sword-grass, and writing apparatus set on low tables; the neck, with two leaf-shaped panels below, having sprays of chrysanthemum inside, with alternate *svastika* and jewel symbols round the bulb, and with rings of formal foliations round the base and rim. The ground between the panels is filled in with sprays of plum-blossom, painted in delicate green and yellow, relieved by a background of intense iridescent black. There is no mark underneath.   LXII.

SAUCER-SHAPED DISH (*Tieh*), of delicate eggshell porcelain, decorated with brilliant enamel colors of the *Yung-chêng* period (1723–35). The graceful figure, supported by a scrolled bank of many-colored clouds, represents one of the female divinities of the Taoist cult, as shown by her attributes, and seems to be *Ho Hsien-ku*, the virgin member of the band of immortals who, the story says, occasionally appears to her worshipers in a cloud of diverse colors. The goddess is dressed in long, flowing robes, with a short cloak of lotus-leaves thrown across her shoulders and a long black scarf with the ends floating loosely down, and has her jet-black hair ornamented with a pink flower; a pilgrim's gourd hangs suspended from her girdle, and she carries in her hands a large blue jar, tied round with pink silk, containing, doubtless, the beverage of immortality—the magic *elixir vitæ*.   LXIII.

QUADRANGULAR VASE (*Fang P'ing*), 13 inches high, with vertical openwork railings of scrolled outline projecting from the four corners, richly decorated in enamel colors, with gilding, of the *Ch'ien-lung* period (1736–95).

The vase is decorated with foliated panels framed in a blue ground brocaded with bats in gold. The large oblong panels on the body are painted on a white ground with landscape pictures of the four seasons. The picture representing spring is a mountain scene, with temples half hidden by trees, and a river spanned by a plank bridge on which a traveler is standing, admiring the peach-trees with their pink blossoms; a *Pyrus japonica* is flowering near a temple, and the willows on the river-bank are clad in the rich verdure of spring. The summer scene is a similar picture, with pines and poplars in full foliage and reeds waving over the water. The picture of autumn, seen in the illustration, has also a mountain background, with temples and pillared pavilions on the shore of a river swollen by the torrents of the rainy season, and foliage showing bright autumnal tints. A snow scene follows for winter, even the fisherman seated in his boat in the foreground being covered with snow, and showing out white upon the sepia-tinted water. A grove of pines surrounds the temple buildings; all the other trees are bare, sketched in the same neutral shades that darken sky and water.

The neck of the vase has four small square panels filled with colored clouds. The shoulder is decorated with bands of conventional floral scrolls issuing from the mouths of two bats displayed upon a yellow ground. The borders and the openwork railing are enameled of soft coral-red, overlaid with gilded scrolls, succeeded by bands of blue with scrolls of gold peonies round the upper and lower rims. The seal underneath, penciled in red on a white panel reserved in the middle of the pale-green enameled grounds, which characterizes the finest imperial porcelain of this period, is *Ta Ch'ing Ch'ien lung nien chih* —i. e., "Made in the reign of Ch'ien-lung (1736–95), of the Great Ch'ing [dynasty]."   LXIV.

FLOWER-VASE (*Hua P'ing*), of graceful ovoid shape, with tapering neck and expanded rim, enameled with a pure monochrome glaze of delicate citron-yellow tint. The yellow ground is interrupted on both sides of the

vase, to be decorated by little pictures sketched in sepia upon a white ground. The pictures are represented as if painted upon scrolls, partially unrolled so as to show the brocaded mounts at the sides; one is a mountain landscape with a pilgrim in the foreground on the bridge leaning upon his staff, the other a rustic scene with a cottage in front. The rim of the lip and the interior of the mouth are white, with a tinge of green, and the foot of the same color, underneath, with no inscription. It is a choice specimen of a monochrome glaze which seems to have been produced in such perfection only in the reign of *Yung-chêng* (1723–35).   LXV.

SAUCER SHAPED DISH (*Tieh*), of eggshell porcelain decorated with brilliant enamel colors of the *famille rose* and gilding. The motive of the decoration is a screen fan, laid down, as it were, in the dish upon a bed of flowers. The screen is painted with the picture of a pheasant perched upon a rockery, with daisies and grass and a branch of *shan-li-hung* berries in the background. It has a curved bamboo handle tinted red, gilded mounts, and black tassels attached by silken cords. The flowers are sprays of peony and chrysanthemum, displayed in bright colors upon the sepia ground of diapered pattern, which is seen lining the rest of the interior of the dish. The rim is encircled by a wavy band of conventional floral sprays studded with alternate peony and chrysanthemum flowers, penciled in sepia and filled in with gold. Period, *Yung-chêng* or *Ch'ien lung* (1723–95).   LXVI.

BOWL (*Wan*), molded after a characteristic design of the reign of *Yung-lo*, with spreading sides and a gently everted rim nicked at regular intervals in six places. Of eggshell texture and marvelous transparence, it has yet, in addition to the painted decoration, a complicated pattern molded in relief in the paste inside, consisting of an interlacing scroll of lotus lifting up eight blossoms to support the eight Buddhist emblems of happy augury (*pa chi hsiang*), which form a circle round the rim of the bowl, surrounded by waving fillets; this ornamentation, too fugitive to be illustrated, has the effect, under transmitted light, of watered satin or water-marked paper. The decoration, painted in coral-red over the glaze, consists of nine four-clawed dragons—two pairs inside and two outside—speeding round the sides in pursuit of whirling jewels, all enveloped in forked flames, and the ninth coiled in a ring in the bottom of the bowl. This is one of the exclusive designs sacred to the emperor, and the dragons are all four-clawed, a special mark of the *K'ang-hsi* period (1662–1722), to which this bowl belongs. It is thinner and more perfect in technique than a *Ch'ien-lung* bowl, with a glaze of softer tone, although not so brilliant nor so vitreous in aspect, and is of the same style and date as the vase figured in Plate XXVIII.   LXVII.

1. RICE-BOWL (*Fan Wan*), 7¾ inches in diameter, of the *K'ang-hsi* period (1662–1722), artistically decorated in shaded blues, with a lake scene, a group of storks standing in a clump of lotus, rocks and panicled reeds in the background; a medallion of lotus-flowers is painted inside in the bottom of the bowl, and a band of sprays of the same flower round the inner rim. The mark underneath is a six-spoked wheel encircled by a waving fillet with dots, simulating a flower; an identical mark occurs on a brilliant "hawthorn-spray" plate in the collection dating from the same period.

2. WATER RECEPTACLE (*Shui Ch'êng*), 2½ inches high, for the writing-table, in the form of an ordinary teapot, decorated in soft-toned blue under a crackled, soft-looking *fên-ting* glaze of ivory-white tint. It is decorated with the paraphernalia of the scholar: a censer, a book, and a water-pot with ladle inside on a palm-leaf, in front; a lyre in its brocaded case and a *ju-i* scepter tied with fillets, behind; and with four symbols on top—a musical stone, a Buddhist wheel, a lozenge, and a "cash"—and two on the cover, with cloud scrolls between the symbols. The mark underneath is *yü*, "jade," the period that of *K'ang-hsi*.   LXVIII.

3. MINIATURE VASE (*Hsiao P'ing*), 3 inches high, delicately painted in blue, the depressed bulging body covered with interlacing scrolls of Indian lotus, the neck, which is marked near the base by a prominent white ring, encircled by conventional bands of spiral and triangular fret and foliated design respectively. The mark underneath, in well-written characters, penciled inside a double ring, is *Ta Ming Hsüan tê nien chih*—i. e., "Made in the reign of Hsüan-tê (1426–35), of the Great Ming [dynasty]." LXVIII.

PLATE (*P'an tzŭ*), 10½ inches in diameter, painted in underglaze cobalt-blue of lighter and darker shades, in the free, artistic style and tone of coloring characteristic of the *K'ang-hsi* period (1662–1722). The interior of the plate is decorated with a four-clawed dragon emerging from the waves with flames proceeding from its shoulders and flanks, while two fishes, one a carp, are swimming in the water which covers the ground with curling crest, dotted with foam. The border of the plate is encircled by scrolled waves; its under surface is ornamented round the rim with six emblems tied with fillets, including a couple of books, a round jewel, a diamond (*fang shêng*), an umbrella, a conch-shell, and a palm-leaf. The mark underneath, inscribed within a double ring, is *Ta Ming Ch'êng-hua nien chih*, "Made in the reign of Ch'êng hua, of the Great Ming [dynasty]," but the form and style of decoration indicate certainly the reign of *K'ang-hsi*. The fabled metamorphosis of the "Fish Dragon" (*Yü Lung*) is symbolical of the scholar's success at the state competitive examinations. LXIX.

BEAKER-SHAPED VASE (*Hua Ku*), 17½ inches high, of solid material and somewhat archaic form, with a flat base not glazed; decorated with etched borders and painted blue designs, executed in the style of the *Wan-li* period (1573–1619). Three bands of wavy conventional scrolls, lightly etched in the paste under the glaze, encircle the vase so as to divide its surface into two parts, which are decorated in brilliant cobalt-blue of shaded tones. The body represents a combat between a tiger, the king of land animals, and a dragon, prince of the powers of the air. The tiger is in the foreground, crouching upon the reedy bank of a lake, from the waves of which a dragon has just emerged and is seen approaching on the right, with its huge scaly form half hidden by clouds; rocks and clouds fill in the background. The neck of the vase is painted with a rocky landscape with palms rising in the background; a *k'i lin* is seated in front, with flames issuing from its throat and body, indicative of its supernatural attributes; it has a scaly skin, a two-horned dragon's head, the hoofs of a deer, and the spreading tail of a lion. A phœnix is flying in the air above. LXX.

OVOID VASE, of the Buddhist form, called *Kuan Yin Tsun*, because it resembles the ritual vase carried by the goddess of Mercy, 18 inches high, decorated in shaded tones of brilliant blue, in the characteristic style and coloring of the *K'ang-hsi* period (1662–1722).

The body of the vase displays the grotesque forms of three lions of the traditional Chinese type, sporting with brocaded balls, the wheel-like balls being tied with broad fillets, which fill in all the intervals with their spirally waving folds. The neck of the vase, marked with three ribs faintly worked in the paste, is painted in blue with an encircling band of "scepter-head" ornament above a light ring of spiral fret. The mark underneath is a large double ring, penciled in blue, such as frequently occurs at the time referred to, when the potters were forbidden to use the imperial title. This decorative motive is always called *Shih-tzŭ k'un hsiu chiu*, "Lions sporting with brocaded balls," and the lions, by a pun on the word *shih*, which also means "generation," are often said to be symbolical of three generations of the same family. The original ecclesiastical signification of lions guarding the sacred wheel of the Buddhist law seems to be quite forgotten, although one can almost detect the spokes of the wheel in the picture before us. LXXI.

TALL VASE (*Hua-Ku*), 33 inches high, of archaic form, with six prominent serrated ridges projecting vertically from the bulging center, and extending down to the gently spreading foot, and two handles fashioned in the shape of grotesque lions' heads, channeled for rings, on the neck. It is painted in cobalt-blue of characteristic tone, under a rich lustrous white glaze slightly tinged with blue. The decoration consists of conventional scrolls of peonies arranged in vertical panels. A band of sea-waves stretches round the base, two undulating rings of foliated scrolls define the borders of the body, a band of sacred *ling-chih* fungus winds round the shoulder, and two horizontal bands of conventional ornament mark the borders of the neck. Inside the mouth there are two encircling bands of formal flowers, succeeded by a ring of palmated design pointing downward. The mark, inscribed in a framed panel near the upper border, is *Ta Ming Wan li nien chih*—i. e., "Made in the reign of Wan-li (1573–1619), of the Great Ming [dynasty]." The bottom is unglazed. LXXII.

VASE (*P'ing*), of gracefully elongated ovoid form, decorated in brilliant blue, in the style and coloring of the best *K'ang-hsi* period (1662–1722). The picture represents, apparently, a dramatic scene. A traveler in official dress is kneeling in the foreground on a river-bank, to which the boat is moored from which he has just landed, his umbrella and bundle thrown on the ground near. A martial figure stands in front with his hand upon the hilt of his sword, the hero of the piece, indicated by the long pheasant-plumes in his helmet, who is attended by two soldiers armed with long halberds. The background is filled in with rocks and waving willows, enveloped in clouds of mottled blue. The neck of the vase is painted with a few light sprays of bamboo. The mark underneath, penciled in blue within a double ring, of *Ta Ming Chia ching nien chih*, "Made in the reign of Chia-ching, of the Great Ming [dynasty]," is evidently fictitious. LXXIII.

VASE (*P'ing*), 10 inches high, with a decoration of floral bands and ornamental borders, worked in slight relief in the paste, under a monochrome glaze of pale grayish-blue color, derived from the native cobaltiferous ore of manganese. This is the *t'ien-ch'ing*, or "sky-blue," of Chinese ceramists, which resembles somewhat in tint the turquoise glaze illustrated in Plate XLV, although this is, on the other hand, derived from copper, and differs from the cobalt glaze in being minutely crackled. The decoration consists of conventional scrolls of peonies round the body, with a band of false gadroons below and a border of scrolled "scepter heads" above. The rim of the foot is encircled by a continuous rectangular fret, and the shoulder is defined by a chain of similar design. The neck has a ring of palmations, alternately longer and shorter, ascending from the base. The rim of the lip is marked with a line of brownish-yellow color. The foot is enameled underneath with the same grayish-blue glaze as the vase, without any inscription. It may be attributed to the early part of the *K'ang-hsi* period (1662–1722). LXXIV.

CRACKLED TURQUOISE FLOWER-POT (*Hua P'ên*), of rectangular outline and oblong section, with the rim incurved, resting upon four scrolled feet. The interior is strengthened by six vertical ribs; the bottom is perforated by two round holes. It is enameled outside with a rich translucent glaze of deep turquoise tint, which is minutely crackled throughout with a network of well-defined lines. The interior and the under surface, both for the most part unglazed, exhibit a paste of whitish texture resembling that of the vase figured in Plate LXXXIV, and this flower-pot is also to be referred to the *Ming* dynasty. It is probably a production of the reign of *Wan-li* (1573–1619). LXXV.

VASE, WITH COVER (*Kai P'ing*), one of a pair, of broad ovoid shape, composed, as it were, of two vases coalesced into one, with the line of junction indicated by vertical grooves, surmounted by a double composite cover crowned by two gilded knobs. It is painted in the finest enamel colors with gilding of the *Ch'ien-lung* period, tones of red predominating, and is a brilliant example of the *famille rose*. The body of the vase is filled with groups of playing boys painted upon a translucently white ground. On one side there is a group of children playing upon musical instruments, and carrying branches of peach-blossom, gathered round three goats, the special emblem of the creative energies of spring, indicated by the punning name of the design, "*San yang k'ai tai.*" On the other side the boys surround a central figure holding a vase from which a cloud is issuing as it unfolds to display five flying bats, symbols of the five kinds of happiness. The receding neck and the hollow of the foot are filled with broad bands of ruby-red, with the *rose-d'or* ground etched with scrolls and overlaid with chains of symbols painted in colors, fringed with narrower bands of yellow and sepia color diapered with flowers. The cover has a similar scrolled ground, with foliated rings round the knobs. The base, enameled pale green, is inscribed, in overglaze blue, with one line of antique "seal" characters, reading *Ta Ch'ing Ch'ien lung nien chih*, "Made in the reign of Ch'ien-lung (1736–95). of the Great Ch'ing [dynasty]." LXXVI.

VASE (*Tsun*), modeled in the form of an ancient sacrificial wine-vessel of the *Han* dynasty, with encircling bands worked in slight relief in the paste, and three solid handles fashioned in the shape of rams' heads projecting on the shoulder. The glaze with which it is enameled is of grayish tint, crackled throughout with a close network of reddish-brown lines. Upon the shoulder of the vase, where the glaze is thicker, it is pale blue, and the crackled reticulation becomes almost colorless; also upon the spreading rim of the foot, where the conditions are similar. The same crackled glaze extends into the interior of the vase, and invests the base, which is marked in the middle, under the glaze, with the "seal" in dark cobalt-blue, inscribed *Ta Ch'ing Ch'ien lung nien chih*—i. e., "Made in the reign of Ch'ien-lung (1736–95), of the Great Ch'ing [dynasty]." LXXVII.

VASE (*P'ing*), enameled with a monochrome glaze of green of the color of cucumber-rind (the *kua-p'i lü* of Chinese ceramists), minutely and uniformly crackled throughout. The glaze exhibits an undulating surface, and the green color takes on a mottled aspect in places, becoming slightly paler on the shoulder in one spot which happens to be more thinly covered. The finely crackled or *truité* surface of this bottle offers a typical example of the *yü tzŭ wên*, or "fish-roe crackle." The foot is invested underneath with a similar crackled green enamel. The upper rim is touched with brown, which is concealed in the illustration by the ebony stopper. Period, *Ch'ien-lung* (1736–95). LXXVIII.

VASE (*Tsun*), modeled after an archaic bronze form, with bulging body, upright rim, and two tubular handles. Composed of grayish paste, it is invested with a thick brilliant enamel of translucent emerald-green, uniformly crackled with a network of brown lines. Reflected light produces a marked iridescent effect, which the artist has indicated in the illustration. The enamel, which thins to a straight edge toward the foot, is stained below by a line of olive-brown at the point of junction with the ferruginous paste. The foot, unglazed underneath, and showing the circular marks of the wheel, is of dark color, almost black. LXXIX.

TALL VASE (*P'ing*), 18½ inches high, enameled with a monochrome glaze of very dark olive color, becoming black in some parts where the glaze is thickest, as it collects, for instance, upon the shoulder and round the edge of the foot. It was originally richly decorated in gold, with a pair of dragons rising into the air from the sea, traces being still visible, on close inspection, of sea-waves below, and of the forms of large four-clawed dragons pursuing jewels in the midst of clouds, extending over the bulging body and slender neck of the vase. Although there is no mark inscribed underneath, the characteristic shape, coloring, and decorative style all indicate the reign of *K'ang-hsi* (1662–1722). LXXX.

VASE (*P'ing*), 12 inches high, with a bulging body and a solid circularly rimmed foot enameled with a brilliant *Kua-p'i lü*, or "cucumber-green" glaze, minutely crackled throughout. The color ranges from apple-green to dark olive, the surface of the vase being vertically streaked with deep mottled tints of olive, where the glaze has collected as it ran down in the furnace. The same glaze extends down inside the mouth, but the foot is unglazed and has no mark inscribed underneath. If not older, it is an early specimen of the reign of *Ch'ien-lung* (1736–95). The lip is mounted with a silver collar. LXXXI.

VASE (*P'ing*), 17 inches high, bottle-shaped, with bulging body and wide neck, painted with a floral decoration of shaded black, invested with a monochrome iridescent glaze of deep camellia-leaf green. The decoration consists of a boldly designed picture of peonies, with sprays of other plants, growing from rocks in the foreground, and a single leafy spray behind. It has run in some parts so as to be hardly visible under the overglaze, which, paler above, collects as it flows down the vase in unctuous masses, becoming of wonderfully deep, metallic-like luster where it absorbs and mingles with the black underneath. The rim, which has been broken, has been mended in Japan with gold lacquer. The foot is enameled pale green underneath, with no mark attached. The specimen belongs to the reign of *K'ang-hsi* (1662–1722), which is famous for the variety of its green glazes, one of which is called *shê-p'i lü*, or "snake-skin green," because it resembled, in its deep luster, the beautiful iridescent hue which distinguishes the scaly skin of some serpents. LXXXII.

VASE (*P'ing*), 15 inches high, with a globular body poised upon a swelling recurved foot, having a pair of dragons incised in the paste under a monochrome glaze of "eel-skin yellow" (*shan-yü huang*), of the reign of *K'ang-hsi* (1662–1722). The dragons, of the typical four-clawed design of the period, are represented in pursuit of the jewel of omnipotence, a disk with spiral center emitting rays of effulgence; the form of one is half concealed by the rolling waves which are engraved round the base of the vase; the other is fully displayed in the midst of etched scrolls of clouds and forked flames, filling in all the intervals. The investing glaze, of yellowish-brown tint, deepens into olive-brown to enhance the effect of the incised decoration, and collects in brown drops as it runs down over the rim of the foot. The base is coated underneath with the same glaze. The tints resemble precisely those of the *shan yü*, the common brown eel of north China; the glaze was introduced into the imperial manufactory by Ts'ang Ying-hsüan, who was sent to *Ching-tê-chên* by the Board of Works in the year 1683. LXXXIII.

VASE (*Tsun*), 9½ inches high, of somewhat archaic form and design, with the details of the decoration worked in relief in the paste and finished with the graving tool.

The body is encircled by a belt of rings connected by double links, between two lines of rope pattern; a ring of studs surrounds the base between similar lines of rope, and there is another ring of studs at the top above a single rope line. An interrupted chain of rectangular fret defines the base of the neck, and the everted lip is ornamented with a chain of the same fret; the lower part of the neck has a band of spiral foliations embossed with studs. The vase is enameled with a crackled glaze of the deep turquoise tint that is called by Chinese ceramists *k'ung-chüo lü*, or "peacock-green," which enhances the effect of the relief decoration by the brilliant play of its richly mottled tints, varying according to the depth of the glaze. The interior of the mouth, and the foot underneath, are invested with the same turquoise glaze. There is no mark, but the solid, very white paste and the general technique resemble those of the imperial turquoise bowls and plates of the *Ming* dynasty, which are usually marked, so that this vase must be referred to the same period. LXXXIV.

ROBIN'S-EGG GRAY VASE (*P'ing*), 10 inches high, of egg-shaped outline, with an archaic dragon modeled in full relief, with openwork, upon the shoulder of the vase, so as to envelop half of the rim of the circular mouth with its coils. It is two-horned, with indistinct claws and a bifid, spirally curved tail, like the *ch'ih-lung* of ancient bronzes. The dragon is colored maroon on a gray ground; the vase is invested with a thick glaze of bluish-gray tone, flecked with copper-red spots and streaks of mottled maroon tints.

The rim of the foot is iron-gray; the middle is plastered with a yellowish-brown enamel, covering the seal, which is impressed underneath the paste, inscribed *Ta Ch'ing Yung chêng nien chih*, "Made in the reign of Yung-chêng (1723–35), of the Great Ch'ing [dynasty]."   LXXXV.

VASE (*P'ing*), 7¾ inches high, of depressed, bulging form, with a pair of handles projecting from the shoulder fashioned in the shape of lions' heads with rings in their mouths. It is enameled all over with a pellucid glaze of grayish celadon color, crackled with a wide reticulation of brownish-red lines, connected by a few superficial colorless lines within the meshes. The foot is invested underneath with the same crackled glaze, so as to leave the rim uncovered, which is tinted iron-gray. The upper rim and the handles are touched with brownish-red.

There is no mark. It is probably a production of the *Yung-chêng* period (1723–35), emulating the ancient *Ko Yao* of the *Sung* dynasty, which is described as having had iron-colored feet and copper-red mouths.   LXXXVI.

VASE (*P'ing*), of ovoid form, swelling toward the shoulder, which is defined by a line in slight relief as it recedes into the neck. The thin lip of the gently flaring mouth is encircled by a ring of black enamel, and the two solid handles which project from the sides of the vase, modeled as grotesque lions' heads and perforated for rings, are invested with a brilliant bronze-black glaze of metallic aspect. The rest of the surface is enameled with a bright yellow monochrome glaze of slightly greenish tone, crackled throughout with a fine network of superficial lines (*truitée*). The foot is invested with the same glaze. Period, *Ch'ien-lung* (1736–95).   LXXXVII.

FURNACE-TRANSMUTATION VASE (*Yao Pien P'ing*), of hexagonal section, with two open looped handles projecting from the neck, roughly fashioned in the shape of elephants' heads. The enameled surface, superficially crackled with a wide reticulation, exhibits a mottled investment of olive-brown, overlaid with thick splashes of brilliant crimson shades streaked with purplish grays, produced by varied oxidation of the copper silicates of the glaze as it ran down in the kiln in massive drops. The inside of the mouth shows the substratum of pale-green tint, flecked with a few *flambé* spots. The foot is of mottled olive-color, leaving a broad rim unglazed, where the dark, yellowish color of the paste is exposed. Period, *Ch'ien-lung* (1736–95).   LXXXVIII.

DOUBLE-GOURD VASE (*Hu-lu P'ing*), of *Fên-Ting* porcelain, with a grayish-white paste of fine texture, and an ivory-white glaze of purest translucence, delicately crackled throughout with a wavy network of light-brown lines. The decoration, worked in the paste in slight relief, consists of two broad bands of floral scrolls, composed of sprays of the lotus, peony, and lily, designed in a conventional or idealized style, with formal borders of gadroon bands and "scepter-head" scrolls, and a girdle of rectangular, interrupted fret round the waist. The base is invested with a similar crackled glaze. It is an admirable specimen of perfect beauty and finish, to be referred, probably, to the *K'ang-hsi* period, when the potters of Ching-tê-Chên emulated, and surpassed, the makers of the ancient *Ting-chou* ware of the *Sung* dynasty.   LXXXIX.

FLOWER VASE (*Hua P'ing*), of fine form and finished technique, with molded and chiseled designs invested with a white glaze of perfect purity and translucence. The body is ornamented with a broad band worked in relief, composed of a pair of the archaic, one-horned, lizardlike dragons called *ch'ih-lung*, winding through interlacing scrolls of the miraculous fungus of longevity (*ling-chih*). This is

succeeded above and below by an etched band containing symbols encircled by waving fillets, with cloud scrolls in the intervals, the symbols represented being a pair of rhinoceros-horn cups, and the *fang-shêng*, or double lozenge, above, the conch-shell and the palm-leaf below. Round the lip a ring of triangular fret is lightly etched. There is a mark of the *Sung* dynasty penciled on the foot in underglaze blue—*Hsüan ho nien chih*—i. e., "Made in the period Hsüan-ho (1119–25)," a time when the productions of Ching-tê-chên are said to have rivaled the finest white jade. This piece, however, is a reproduction, and, from its perfect technique, is to be attributed to the reign of *K'ang-hsi* (1662–1722).   XC.

VASE (*P'ing*), of white Fên-Ting porcelain of the *K'ang-hsi* period (1662–1772), with a rich, pellucid glaze of pure tone, crackled with a wide network of superficial, colorless lines. The characteristic translucence of the surface is well represented in the illustration. The foot is enameled underneath with a similarly crackled glaze, and has no mark attached.   XCI.

BOTTLE-SHAPED VASE (*Hua P'ing*), enameled with a monochrome coral-red glaze of perfect purity, displaying a remarkably uniform vermilion tint. The lip is defined by a line of white. The foot is coated underneath with a white glaze of greenish tone, leaving exposed a ring of paste of grayish color. There is no mark attached; it belongs, probably, to the *Ch'ien-lung* period (1736–95).   XCII.

VASE (*P'ing*) 15¾ inches high, with a bulging body and slender cylindrical neck, exhibiting the *soufflé* cobalt-blue glaze of mazarin tint in its most brilliant tone of coloring.

There is no mark underneath, but the vase, without doubt, is to be referred to the reign of *K'ang-hsi* (1662–1722). The process of *ch'ui ch'ing*, or "insufflation of the blue," on the unburned clay before glazing is fully described by Père d'Entrecolles in his second letter written from Ching-tê-chên in the year 1722.   XCIII.

ANCIENT CHÜN-CHOU FLOWER-POT (*Hua-P'ên*), 8 inches across, of depressed globular form, with slightly spreading feet, perforated at the bottom with five holes. The bowl is enameled with a rich glaze of finely mottled aspect, in which the prevailing tone of bluish gray is flecked with purple and crimson spots; it becomes stone-gray on the upper rim, and is broadly splashed with crimson at the back near the foot, where it has run down more thickly. In the hollow of the foot is a brown of olive tint. The paste, where it is exposed at the top, shows the material to be a dense, hard stoneware of yellowish tint. The upper rim is mounted with a wooden collar, and the stand is also elaborately carved in rosewood, and incised underneath with the cyclical character *chia*, indicating that it came from the imperial collection at Peking, where the stands are marked in this way. There is a companion flower-pot in the collection, of the same size and shape, enameled with a glaze of darker tint, and more thickly flecked with crimson, passing into purple. They are both specimens of *Chün Yao* from the Chün-chou potteries of the *Sung* dynasty. Modern reproductions of the *Ch'ien-lung* period are distinguished by the finer and whiter texture of their paste and by a more finished technique.   XCIV.

TALL IMARI VASE (*Hana-ike*), 23 inches high, of cylindrical, beaker-shaped form, swelling into a prominent ridge near the foot, and flaring above at the mouth. It is decorated in blue and white in combination with enamel colors and gilding. The floral ground, painted in blue with interlacing sprays of peonies, is interrupted by two long panels of foliated outline, which contain flowers growing from rocks, painted in enamel colors upon a white ground. The blue floral ground is overlaid with fillets of deep vermilion-red tied in bows which inclose flowers, and the foot of the vase is encircled by a ring of foliations filled with stiff upright flowers. The inner rim of the mouth is decorated in plain blue with a band of peony sprays; the foot is glazed white underneath, with no mark inscribed. Period, 1650–1700.   XCV.

Statuette, of Tokyo porcelain invested in white enamel, with the face and right hand reserved *en biscuit*, representing the famous general and statesman, Takenouchi no Sukune, who was the leading spirit in the celebrated Korean expedition under the Empress Jingo, and prime minister under three succeeding emperors, and who is said to have attained the great age of two hundred and fifty years. The figure is boldly modeled, with bearded face and beetling eyebrows, the furrowed brow surmounted by a winged hat of ancient Chinese style. The flowing robes are brocaded with dragon scrolls and ornamental borders worked in relief under the glaze, and the figure of a stork flying among clouds is emblazoned on the breast. The right hand is lifted up as if grasping the official badge of his high rank. The mark incised underneath is *Dai Nippon Tokyo Enouye Riosai tsukuru*—i. e., " Made in Great Japan at Tokyo by Enouye Riosai." It is said to have been specially made for the Philadelphia Centenary Exposition. XCVI.

1. "Old Japan" Imari Saké-Bottle (*Tokuri*), of square section, with a bulging body gracefully tapering upward to a slender neck, ending in a square thin-rimmed mouth. Invested with a glaze of pure ivory-white tone, it is decorated in a formal archaic style with floral designs painted in delicate enamel colors with gilding; the four sides of the body with a gnarled plum-tree bearing red and gilded blossoms, alternating with a conventional spray displaying three bunches of starlike flowers; the neck with long, foliated panels of floral scrolls relieved by coral-red and white grounds. The base is flat and unglazed underneath, showing a fine paste of finished technique; the date would be *circa* 1650.

2. "Old Japan" Imari Saké-Bottle (*Tokuri*), of circular section, with an ovoid body and a long, slender neck with everted lip, decorated in a bold, free hand, after the Chinese style of the *Wan-li* period, partly in cobalt-blue of two shades, painted *sur biscuit* partly in overglaze enamel colors, with profuse gilding. A rocky outdoor scene is represented with two aged figures in Chinese costume in the foreground, one carrying a crooked staff, standing under the trees; the rocks are clad with bamboos, and there are palms rising in the background, and an open rockery with peony shrubs beside it. No mark underneath. Period, about 1700. XCVII.

Tall "Old Japan" Imari Vase (*P'ing*), 25 inches high, painted partly in cobalt-blue, partly in enamel colors with lavish gilding. It is decorated with panels containing pictures painted upon a white ground, irregularly distributed upon a blue ground richly brocaded with flowers. Two large panels, of indented oval outline, contain identical pictures of landscapes, executed in conventional Chinese style, with lake scenes and waterfalls, temples and pagodas; two minor panels, which they partly hide, are filled with drooping wistaria-flowers; and the two indented panels below display the same outdoor scene, with a traveler in Chinese dress attended by two boys, one holding a gilded umbrella over his head, the other pointing to a waterfall. The blue ground which covers the remainder of the vase, with the exception of a few floral reserves and a band of white around the shoulder, a deep cobalt color of mottled brilliant sheen, is overlaid with gilded sprays of chrysanthemum-flowers, an occasional blossom of which is penciled in red; the neck is decorated in gold with a pair of three-clawed dragons among clouds and flames; the shoulder is gilded with a band of conventional flowers on white; and chains of spiral and rectangular fret and heavily gilded rims complete the decoration, with small square patches of gold-leaf applied at irregular intervals inside the mouth.

There is no mark underneath. The vase dates from the middle of the seventeenth century, and is a fine example of the richly ornamented porcelain produced in Japan at this time for export to Europe. XCVIII.

"Old Japan" Imari Saké-Pot (*Choshi*), of hexagonal form with rounded top, the handle of which is the over-arching scaly body of a dragon, which protrudes its head through the side of the pot to form the spout. The dragon, which has a two-horned head and four-clawed feet, with red flames proceeding from its flanks, is modeled after the Chinese type. The enamel colors used in the decoration are deep "iron-red," overglaze blue of greenish tint, pale green, and gold. The top of the saké-pot, being the firmament in which the dragon is disporting, is gilded with cloud scrolls and flames upon a red ground; the cover is painted with similar designs and crowned with a floral knob. The six panels are enameled with grounds of different color; the central panels at the front and back have a circular medallion reserved in the middle of the red ground, which contains a gilded floral crest; the side panels display the three jewels of Buddhistic lore enveloped in flames, and two identical pictures of crested sea-waves and distant hills. The feet are three floral buttons. There is no mark, but the date would be about 1750. XCIX.

1. Teacup (*Cha-wan*), of Satsuma faïence, covered with a finely crackled glaze of pale, mottled-brown tint, invested round the upper rim with a line of light olive-brown, which runs down inside the lip in deep, colored drops, becoming almost black. This rare example of Satsuma decorative treatment is referred to the middle of the eighteenth century.

2. Flower-Vase (*Hana-ike*), of Satsuma faïence, modeled in the form of a four-lobed beaker, and chastely decorated in soft colors with gilding. It is molded with a prominent ring encircling the base of the neck above four panels bordered in spiral relief, which spread downward and are painted inside with red peony-flowers encircled by green leaves, all outlined in gold. The rest of the decoration consists of three narrow bands of conventional ornament, filled in with the same three colors—red, green, and gold. Date, about 1800. C.

1. Incense-burner (*Kōro*), of Satsuma faïence, finely decorated in delicate enamel colors with gilding. The body is divided by bands of spiral fret into three broad panels, which are filled with formal sprays of peonies; conventional foliations surround the shoulder and spread down over the three feet; the neck is encircled by the eight mystic trigrams (*pa kua*) of Chinese philosophy. The dome-shaped cover, decorated with an ornamental band round the rim, is perforated by six round holes, and surmounted by the figure of the Chinese lion couchant. The rims, both of the censer and of the cover, are strengthened by a silver casing. Date, close of the eighteenth century.

2. Teapot (*Choshi*), of Satsuma faïence, of somewhat archaic design, four-lobed in outline, with a short spout, and overarching handle, invested with a minutely crackled glaze of ivory-white tone. It has been used for saké, and the surface is dulled by wear and stained brownish in some places by the liquid. Period, 1700–1750. CI.

Vase (*Hana-ike*), 11½ inches high, of Satsuma faïence, ovoid in form, bulging above, with two handles fashioned in the shape of lions' heads projecting from the shoulder. It is decorated with storks flying among clouds, relieved by an intensely black ground, which fills in all the intervals of the decoration. The details are painted with red and green enamel colors in combination with gilding and silvering, some portion of the cloud scrolls being left untouched, so as to show the natural finely crackled surface of the ivory-white glaze. The borders are encircled by ornamental bands of geometrical design, defined by lines of gold. The base is enameled plain black underneath, with no mark affixed. Date, 1800–1850. CII.

1. Japanese Kutani Incense-burner (*Kōro*), of circular section, with three small feet, enameled with an iron-red glaze of deep vermilion tint, overlaid with gilded and silvered decoration. On the body a three-clawed dragon outlined in gold is winding round the side, above a floor of crested waves painted in silver; a band of lotus-petals, touched in silver with gilded outlines encircles the upper rim. The paste, buff inside, is enameled white round the edge and underneath the foot. CIII.

2. RICE-BOWL (*Meshi-wan*), of Japanese Kutani ware, enameled with the same deep vermilion glaze, and decorated in colors, including a pale green, in combination with the gold and silver. A conventional scroll of the sacred lotus extends round the bowl, studding it with four formal flowers, bordered above by a broad band of ornamental fret, alternately gilded and silvered below, with a ring of lotus-petals. The foot is red underneath, as well as the lower rim, leaving none of the paste visible; the interior of the bowl is coated with a white enamel of pitted texture. Period of both pieces, about 1750.   CIII.

1. JAPANESE KUTANI RICE-BOWL (*Meshi-wan*), enameled with a monochrome iron-red glaze of deep vermilion tint, with gilded rings to define the borders, and decorated in gold and silver, with a pair of phœnixes with long, trailing tails, traversing scrolls of the moutan peony wound round a paling, indicated conventionally in the intervals. The rim of the foot is painted with lozenge-shaped symbols, separated by light scrolls of clouds. The foot is red underneath, the interior of the bowl a greenish white. Date, about 1750.

2. JAPANESE KUTANI RICE-BOWL (*Meshi-wan*), of thin, translucent porcelain, with the interior molded in the style of ancient Chinese *Tingchou* ware, with sprays of lotus, chrysanthemum, aster, and other flowers inclosed in panels, six of foliated outline surrounding the circular panel beneath, and with an encircling chain of rectangular fret—all molded in slight relief under a glaze of pale celadon color. The exterior of the bowl is decorated in enamel colors, with gilding, with four round medallions containing peonies, alternately green and gilded, in a red ground, and with floral designs in the intervals, connected by a network of beaded strings hung with symbols and tassels. The foot is enameled red underneath, with a white rim; the lip is strengthened by a silver collar. Period, 1700–1750.   CIV.

"OLD JAPAN" IMARI INCENSE-BURNER (*Kōro*), modeled in the form of a rounded bowl, mounted upon three small scrolled feet, with two molded handles projecting from the shoulder, fashioned in the shape of grotesque lions, and a cover fitting inside the rim of the bowl, surmounted by an elaborate superstructure, delicately modeled in openwork relief, consisting of a hollow chestnut-tree with prickly fruit upon it, burst open so as to show the gilded nuts inside, and having a spray of chrysanthemum and a bunch of scarlet-berried fruit attached. The rim of the bowl is encircled by a band of fret; the surface, as well as that of the neck, is ornamented with floral scrolls on a vermilion-red ground. This floral ground is interrupted, on the bowl, by panels of dentated outline, which are painted in delicate enamel colors, green, buff, pale purple, red, and gold; a broad panel in front with the picture of a mountain scene, with two aged figures in Chinese costume resting under a spreading pine; two panels, side by side, at the back, one containing peonies growing behind a reed fence, the other a rockery and a blossoming plum-tree. The foot is only partially glazed underneath, with no mark attached. Period, about 1700.   CV.

JAPANESE IMARI HANGING CENSER (*Kōro*), of regular oval form, with a gilded loop-handle at the top for suspension, and an opening of indented oval outline in front for the introduction of the incense, which is closed by a movable silver lid, pierced in the middle with a *kiri-mon*, or Paulownia crest. The censer is decorated outside, in shaded vermilion-red and gold, with panels of brocaded design, both on the front and back, which are decorated with jewels emitting effulgent rays poised upon clouds, and with cloud scrolls, outlined in gold upon a mottled red ground. The panels hang from dragons' heads at the upper corners, and are encircled by gilded foliations; the intervening ground is sprinkled with sacred jewels and conventional flowers. Date, about 1700.   CVI.

1. SAKÉ-POT (*Choshi*), of Satsuma faïence, with a minutely crackled glaze, decorated in enamel colors—blue, red, and green—with gilding. Of square outline, with a spout curving upward from below and a scrolled handle, it has a cover fashioned in the form of a chrysanthemum, and a second ring of petals encircling the rim of the mouth, below a dotted blue band which intervenes. The upper surface of the saké-pot, and the four side panels, are filled with sprays of the fir, plum, and bamboo—the three floral emblems of long life; the panels are framed in blue and studded with gilded flowers.

2. FLOWER-VASE (*Hana-ike*), of Satsuma faïence, enameled with a similar finely crackled glaze, and decorated in delicate colors with gilding. The body is covered with gracefully waving sprays of the *Paulownia imperialis*, displaying large conventional flowers; the neck is encircled by formal foliations of pointed shape in two rings, spreading upward and downward. The mottled brown staining of the surface indicates that the vase has been used as a saké-bottle. The two pieces are referred to the same period—the end of the eighteenth century.   CVII.

1. TEACUP (*Cha-wan*), of Satsuma faïence, decorated in colors, covered outside with a trelliswork pattern of *svastika* design painted in bright green, outlined with gold, so as to stand out in slight relief upon the white background, which is finely crackled with brown lines. The fretted ground is broken on either side by a badge or crest, the one in front being composed of a double garland of wistaria-flowers, with three leaflets at the top, the other of a formal spray of Paulownia, with a central flower of five florets and lateral flowers of three, springing from three gilded leaves, representing the official and private crests of the owner. Bands of diaper penciled in red and gold encircle the rims. Date, 1800–1850.

2. FLOWER-VASE (*Hana-ike*), of Satsuma faïence, of graceful ovoid form, with two handles composed, as it were, of plain and brocaded fillets tied in knots. The surface, of the usual finely crackled texture, is decorated with delicate scrolls of a vine with many colored leaves and curling tendrils. Waving spirals encircle the foot, which is partly gilded, and the rim of the lip is defined by a heavy line of gold. Date, 1750–1800.   CVIII.

SAKÉ-BOTTLE (*Tokuri*), of Hirado porcelain, modeled in the shape of a gourd, with a slightly compressed waist, and drawn in above to a small mouth, which is closed by a round stopper. The aperture is tightened by a cap of yellow silk, the fringe of which is seen in the illustration. There is a floral decoration outside, executed in white slip, worked in slight relief, and finished with the graving tool; it consists of sprays of chrysanthemum-flowers, intermingled with a few blades and a single penciled head of grass. The investing glaze is of soft, white tone with a tinge of green. There is no mark attached. The date is 1750–1800.   CIX.

1. SAKÉ-BOTTLE (*Tokuri*), of Hirado porcelain, modeled in the form of a vase, with a bulging, globular body tapering into a slender, upright neck. It is decorated in soft-toned cobalt-blue, with a miniature garden-scene, a sketch of a rockery and a paling, with a palm, peonies, and other flowers, behind the fence. At the back there is a group of five small boys dancing round a couple of fighting-cocks. Date, 1750–1800. The *Sometsuké*, or blue and white, decorated at this period with Chinese boys playing, was made especially for the use of a prince of the Matsu-ura family residing at Hirado, and its sale was prohibited.

2. INCENSE-BURNER (*Kōro*), of Hirado porcelain, molded in the form of a puppy squatting on the ground, its head, which is detachable, being the cover, the line of junction being the lower edge of the ribbon which is represented as tied round the neck. The flanks are decorated with chrysanthemum-sprays, which have the flowers worked in white relief, the leaves penciled in blue; on the back is a panel similarly ornamented with a carp leaping from waves, and a foliated patch with a blue ground is painted between the ears. No mark. Period, 1750–1800.   CX.

WATER-JAR (*Midsu-sashi*), of Hirado porcelain, of bowl-like form with upright sides; of circular section below, it becomes gradually quadrangular, with rounded corners toward the upper rim. It is decorated with bamboos painted in underglaze cobalt-blue, shaded in soft tones of grayish tint; a small clump of bamboo rises in front, with three-jointed stems, from which branches of foliage spread over the bowl, while the other side is painted with a hanging spray of foliage extending along the upper rim. Date, 1750–1800. CXI.

HIRADO BLUE AND WHITE CENSER (*Kōro*), of depressed globular form, with a pierced outer casing and a rounded openwork cover, poised upon a pillar with a square base, which is mounted on a square pedestal with four scroll feet—all molded in one piece. There are two projecting loop-handles of scrolled form proceeding from the mouth of monstrous unicorn heads, and the pillar has a pair of two-horned, three-clawed dragons coiled round it, modeled in salient openwork relief, with the scaly spinous bodies enameled white. Through the outer casing of the censer, which is pierced in a trellis pattern, the decoration is seen penciled inside in delicate blue, consisting of a flock of sea-birds on one side and a pair of butterflies on the other. The rims of the bowl and cover are encircled by borders of conventional ornament, painted in the same grayish blue: the intervals of the dragon forms are filled in with cloud scrolls, and the base of the pillar enveloped in rolling sea-waves; the pedestal is surrounded by a chain of rectangular fret, and the feet with spiral bands. There is a mark painted in minute blue characters under one of the feet, of which the first character of the potter's name is blurred and illegible. It reads: *Hirado san Mikawachi . . . Jake sei*—i. e., " Made by . . . Jake at Mikawachi in Hirado." CXII.

HIRADO BLUE AND WHITE VASE (*Hana-ike*), 12¾ inches high, of round beaker-shaped form, with a widely flaring mouth, and two solid handles molded in the guise of frogs crawling, as it were, up the neck. It is decorated, inside and out, in underglaze cobalt-blue of grayish tone with a water scene. Two trunks of drooping willow-trees rise from the interior of the vase, decorating its surface with a mass of foliage, and sending, besides, several branches over the rim to cover the upper portion of the exterior with gracefully curving sprays. The lower portion is painted with scrolled waves to indicate the water from which the frogs are supposed to spring. The scene depicted on the vase, it is suggested, reminds a Japanese of the famous calligraphist and poet, Ono no Dofu, who lived during the tenth century A. D., and who is always represented watching frogs leaping out of a stream into willow-trees—illustrative of successful perseverance. There is no mark. It is to be referred, probably, to the beginning of the nineteenth century. CXIII.

1. JAPANESE HOT-WATER BOTTLE (*Shaku-date*), used with a ladle (*shaku*) inside at tea-ceremonies; brown stoneware, invested with an opaque olive-brown glaze, flecked with minute yellowish spots of lustrous aspect, terminating in an irregularly undulating line before it reaches the base, so as to show the natural color of the fired clay; near the top it is overlaid with splashes of deep yellow color with

crackled surface, becoming reddish as they mingle with the surrounding ground. Idzumo ware, made at Fujina, in the province of Idzumo, in the beginning of the nineteenth century.

2. JAPANESE TEA-JAR (*Cha-iré*), made of folds of translucent paper, gilded in the interior, and coated externally with lacquer to imitate glazed pottery, from which it can hardly be distinguished. The cover is made of ivory, the bag of brocaded silk.

3. JAPANESE TEA-JAR (*Cha-iré*), of cylindrical form, tapering upward to the shoulder; made of dark-brown stoneware, covered with a brilliant yellowish-brown glaze of mottled aspect and partially crackled surface, invested round the top with a layer of dark olive color, which runs down behind in a vertical streak, mingling with the other glaze. Seto-ware, made in the province of Owari about 1700. CXIV.

JAPANESE TEA-JARS (*Cha-iré*).
1. Of oval form, with a sharply ridged shoulder contracting to a small mouth. A paste of light grayish material, invested with a yellowish-brown glaze of brilliant tint, overlaid with a splash of verdigris color which runs down on one side in two finely crackled green streaks, ending in olive drops. Shigaraki pottery, made in the province of Omi about 1850.

2. Of wide, depressed form, with a prominently ridged center, simulating a covered bowl. Composed of a red clay and covered with a brown glaze, over which is spread a thick enamel of mottled gray tone passing into brilliant olive tints, running down irregularly in unctuous drops. Takatori stoneware, made in the province of Chikuzen about 1750.

3. Of oval shape, with a horizontally ridged surface, and two slightly projecting strap handles. A paste of light-brown material, covered with a yellowish-brown glaze, overlaid on either side of the shoulder by an irregular splash of paler yellow with a brilliant crackled surface. Idzumo stoneware, from Fujina, in Idzumo province, about 1750. CXV.

VASE (*P'ing*), 12 inches high, of ancient Korean faïence, dating from the thirteenth century A. D., covered with a gray-brown glaze, crackled where it is thick as it collects round the neck and above the circular rim of the foot. It is decorated with floral designs and diapered grounds, inlaid in an ivory-white slip of brilliant crackled texture. The body, defined by encircling rings, is inlaid with two boldly designed sprays of formal flowers, with flying insects like wasps filling in the intervals of the floral decoration, and a bird of rough archaic outline perched upon one of the flowers. The remainder of the surface is filled in with simple diapers, two broad bands extending round the neck and shoulder of the base, two narrower bands round the base. The bottom, curiously wrinkled underneath, is only partially—for about half of its surface—coated with a gray-brown glaze, so as to expose the material, which is a drab-colored faïence. CXVI.

II. TEXT CUTS.

BALUSTER-SHAPED VASE (*Mei P'ing*), of good form, vertically grooved so as to be of five-lobed section. The decoration, which is lightly etched at the point in the paste, consists of birds and graceful sprays of bamboos, with lambrequins round the neck studded with single blossoms, and rings of palmations encircling the rims above and below. The finely crackled turquoise glaze, which invests the whole, varies in soft translucid tints, according to its depths, so as to enhance the effect of the engraving underneath. French mounting of the most graceful and artistic style. Height, 6½ inches.

PAIR OF VASES (*Yi Tui P'ing*), of hexagonal outline, with spreading feet, and slender necks furnished at the side with two open loop handles emerging from projected heads of dragons. The spring of the foot is encircled by a fillet,

binding rings of leaves, which spread upward and downward, worked in slight relief in the paste. The finely crackled monochrome glaze of rich and translucent turquoise tint, together with the form and technique, indicate the reign of *Wan-li* (1573–1619), of the *Ming* dynasty. The mounting is French ormolu work of the eighteenth century. Height, 12 inches. No. 1.

OCTAGONAL EGGSHELL LANTERN (*To-t'ai Têng*), of the *K'ang-hsi* period (1662–1722), decorated in brilliant enamel colors with the eight Taoist immortals (*Pa Hsien*) crossing the sea in procession. The other side of this lantern is illustrated in Plate XI, where it is described in full detail. Height, 13 inches. A full account of each of the *Pa Hsien* is given on pages 292 and 293. No. 2.

YUAN DYNASTY BOWL (*Yuan Tz'ŭ Wan*), a small bowl of hard dense ware of grayish fabric, invested with a thick lustrous glaze of ivory-white tone, minutely crackled with a network of dark lines. It is only partially enameled underneath, the lower third and the foot being left bare. Diameter, 4¼ inches.

JAR, of archaic iron-gray stoneware, with a crackled glaze of stone-gray celadon color; *Kwang-yao* of the *Yuan* dynasty.

BOWL, of *Yuan* dynasty ware, of reddish-gray body, with crackled purplish glaze, mottled with brown. No. 3.

SQUARE BOTTLE (*Fang P'ing*), one of a pair, of the *K'ang-hsi* period, enameled with a remarkably iridescent ground of coral-red of intense tone, with reserved medallions painted in enamel colors with gilding upon a white ground. The panels on the front and back, shaped like finger-citrons, are filled with pomegranates and asters, with a cock crowing; the panels on the sides, shaped as begonia-flowers and plum-blossoms, contain goldfish and moss, crabs and shrimps. The bottoms are unglazed. Louis XVI mounts. Height, 14 inches. No. 4.

LARGE VASE (*P'ing*), of *Lang Yao* porcelain of *K'ang-hsi* date, with a brilliant *sang-de-bœuf* glaze of crackled texture, displaying the characteristic mottling and streaked play of color. The base is coated underneath with a grayish "rice-colored" (*mi-sê*) crackled glaze, mottled with brown. A rare example of the class, with an old European mounting. Height, 20 inches. No. 5.

OVOID VASE (*Yuan P'ing*), one of a pair, coated with brownish-red monochrome glaze of *K'ang-hsi* date, which have been cut across horizontally and mounted in silver in Europe as bowls with covers. The enamel, of deep rich tone mottled with darker spots, is finely pitted on the surface. The bases are enameled pure white. Height, 8 inches. No. 6.

LARGE VASE (*Ta P'ing*), of the *Ming* period, coated with a celadon glaze (*Lung-ch'üan yu*) of darkest green tint, not crackled, but dotted all over with minute bubblelike points. The decoration, which is boldly worked in the paste in slight relief under the glaze, consists of a pair of phœnixes flying through a floral ground of sprays of the tree-peony (*Pæonia moutan*). The foot is encircled outside by a band scored with crossed lines. It is unglazed at the base, showing a paste of grayish-yellow color. Height, 2 feet 5 inches. No. 7.

VASE (*P'ing*), coated with a minutely crackled turquoise glaze of pure soft tone, over a delicately etched decoration of dragons and bats enveloped in scrolls of clouds. A gadroon band extends round the vase, succeeded by a chain of rectangular fret at the foot, also incised at the point in the paste under the glaze. There is an etched seal underneath, inscribed *Ta Ch'ing Chia ch'ing nien chih*, "Made in the reign of Chia-ch'ing of the Great Ch'ing [dynasty]." The openwork mounting is of modern French work, executed in gold. Height, 8 inches. No. 8.

FRUIT-DISH (*Kuo P'an*), one of a pair of rare type, of *K'ang-hsi* date, which are molded in the shape of leaves with convoluted folded margins, and decorated *sur biscuit*, in colored enamels. The dish is enameled with a *truité* ground of apple-green; the handle, a knotted branch of prunus, colored purple, passes over the rim of the dish, to decorate the interior, in relief, with sprays of flowers and buds which are colored red, dark blue, and gold.

The companion dish is overlaid inside with branches of fruit, instead of flowers, which are painted in similar colors. The stands are designed in gilded bronze as graceful mermaids of classical form, seated with their fish-legs intertwined, and supporting the dishes with extended arms. Diameter, 10 inches. No. 9.

GOURD-SHAPED VASE (*Hu-lu P'ing*), one of a pair of old stone-gray crackled gourds that have been mounted in Europe, with scrolled handles of graceful design springing from classic masks. Height, 10¾ inches. No. 10.

VASE (*P'ing*), one of a pair, of *K'ang-hsi* porcelain painted *sur biscuit* in delicate enamel colors, the base being unglazed, only marked with the cross-lined pattern of the stuff on which the paste was pressed. They are molded with ribbed surfaces as if composed of a series of jointed bamboo-stems, the joints of which are used as panels for the decoration of floral sprays. The flowers, including the lotus, chrysanthemum, aster, peony, peach, plum, magnolia, pink, iris, and narcissus, with palm-leaves and twigs of bamboo, are relieved by enameled grounds of white, yellow, purple, and two shades of bright green. At the base of the neck a ring of lotus-petals modeled in slight relief is tinted red and bound round with a green strip of reed. Height, 8½ inches. No. 11.

SNUFF-BOTTLE (*Pi Yen Hu*), decorated in enamel colors and gilding with groups of the varied paraphernalia of the liberal arts known as *Po Ku*, or the "Hundred Antiques," displayed in salient relief upon a pale-green background of lozenge-pattern fret. Marked in red underneath with a seal similar to that described in No. 25. No. 12.

SMALL JAR WITH COVER (*Hsiao Kuan*), enameled with a pale pea-green glaze (*tou-ch'ing yu*), the typical celadon of the *Ch'ien-lung* period. It is decorated in relief in the paste with archaic designs taken from ancient bronzes, bands of fret of different pattern, rings of scrolled palmations, and other foliated designs of conventional ornament, which show out in pale relief in the parts less thickly coated with glaze. There is an impressed seal underneath —*Ta Ch'ing Ch'ien lung nien chih*, "Made in the reign of Ch'ien-lung of the Great Ch'ing [dynasty]." The jar is elaborately mounted in metal, parcel gilt, and inlaid with colored enamels. An openwork floral scroll extends around the foot, inclosing bats and peaches, linked chains are attached to the upright loop-handles, a lizardlike dragon is coiling up the shoulder, and a lion with one of its fore feet upon a ball surmounts the cover. Height, with mount, 6 inches. No. 13.

TALL VASE (*Hua P'ing*), one of a pair, artistically decorated in brilliant blue and white of the *K'ang-hsi* period, with idealized floral scrolls consisting of encircling bands and upright sprays of graceful arabesquelike design. The broad band round the body of the vase is interrupted by four circular medallions inclosing phœnixes in the midst of clouds, the intervening sprays displaying blossoms like asters and lilies with anomalous buds and leaves of diverse form, all springing from the same stalk, the general effect of which is highly decorative. Mounted in bronze of old European work. A similar unmounted vase in the Walters Collection shows the mark underneath—a double ring. Height, 16 inches. No. 14.

BOTTLE-SHAPED VASE (*P'ing*), one of a pair, of *Nien Yao* of the *Yung-chêng* period, enameled with a monochrome glaze of ruby-red tint derived from copper. The glaze, of a beautiful uniform tone, exhibits the characteristic stippled texture which is due to its *soufflé* method of application. They are mounted with an artistic setting of the Louis XV period as ewers, with the lip formed of the outspread wings of a swan alighting upon a clump of bulrushes. Height, 16½ inches. No. 15.

PORCELAIN PILLOW (*Tz'ŭ Chên*), decorated in bright enamel colors of the *K'ang-hsi* period, with a foliated diamond-shaped panel of floral brocade composed of scrolls of peony relieved by a yellow ground, and with bands of formal diaper and fret round the two ends. The colors, all overglaze, include a bright green, nankin-yellow of primrose tint, manganese-purple, coral-red, and black, with a sparing addition of gold. Length, 19 inches. No. 16.

SAUCER-SHAPED DISH (*Kuo P'an*), of the *K'ang-hsi* period, painted in blue under the white glaze with conventional scrolls of lotus, spreading over the interior and covering the under border with a symmetrical arrangement of large blossoms, which are fully expanded, so as to display in each flower the cup-shaped fruit studded with the seeds in the midst of a whorl of petals. Round the base of the dish, underneath, a groove is left unglazed, so that it has a second sharply prominent inner rim, a characteristic of some of the finest large dishes of the time. In the middle the mark is penciled in blue, encircled by a double ring, *Ta Ch'ing K'ang-hsi nien chih,* "Made in the reign of K'ang-hsi of the Great Ch'ing [dynasty]." Diameter, 15 inches. No. 17.

WINE-CUP (*Chiu Chung*), of eggshell thinness and bell-like form with upright rim, translucidly white, with the exception of a formal scroll of underglaze blue penciled round the foot outside, which shows clearly through inside when the delicate fragile cup is held up to the light. The mark, written in minute characters, almost requiring a lens to read them, within a double ring, is *Ta Ch'ing K'ang-hsi nien chih,* "Made in the reign of K'ang-hsi of the Great Ch'ing [dynasty]." Diameter, 2⅛ inches.

WINE-CUP (*Chiu Pei*), one of a pair, of delicate eggshell fabric, with a white glaze having a slight tinge of blue. The decoration is lightly molded, or impressed in the paste, in the interior of the cups, so as to show through in shaded tones when held up to the light, like a water-mark in paper. It consists of a pair of five-clawed dragons in the midst of flames and scrolled clouds, pursuing effulgent jewels. The mark, boldly written in underglaze blue, in an oblong double-lined panel, is *Ta Ming Wan li nien chih,* "Made in the reign of Wan-li (1573–1619) of the Great Ming [dynasty]." Diameter, 2¼ inches. No. 18.

TALL CYLINDRICAL EWER (*T'ung Hu*), of the *K'ang-hsi* period, modeled in the shape of a three-jointed section of bamboo, with the rim projected upward in front in the form of a tiara; there is a short curved spout on one side, and on the other there are two studs fashioned as grotesque lions' heads and perforated for the copper handle. It is enameled, inside and outside, as well as over the base, with a finely crackled monochrome purple glaze of rich aubergine tint. The elaborate mounts are in French metal-work of the Louis XVI period. Height, 19 inches. No. 19.

TALL VASE (*Hua P'ing*), of perfect form and beautifully soft turquoise tint, dating from the finest period of the reign of *K'ang-hsi.* A crested dragon (*ch'ih-lung*) of archaic form, with waving scrolls of mane and long mustaches, projects, in full undercut relief, upon the shoulders of the vase, with its branching tail coiled closely round the neck. The ground color is a pure turquoise of finely crackled texture, collecting as it " runs " in greenish drops, and mottled with brownish tints over the dragons. It is magnificently mounted in the most artistic French work of the seventeenth century. Height, with mount, 22 inches. No. 20.

SMALL BALUSTER VASE (*Hsiao Mei P'ing*), enameled with dark-brown, almost black, monochrome glaze, thickly flecked with iridescent spots of metallic aspect. A typical specimen of the " iron-rust " (*t'ieh-hsiu*) glaze of the Chinese. It has been mounted in Europe with flowing handles, a spreading open foot, and a cover in ormolu. Height with mount, 8½ inches. No. 21.

LARGE VASE (*P'ing*), one of a pair, of ovoid form, bulging in the middle, alternately ridged and grooved in vertical lines so as to be of foliated section. They are coated with a monochrome glaze derived from cobalt of pale-blue color, the Chinese " sky-blue " (*t'ien-ch'ing*), which is of grayish tone, and becomes nearly white over the prominent ridges. Dating from the *K'ang-hsi* period, they are mounted in ormolu of Louis XVI work, with handles of fish having garlands of oak with acorns hanging from their mouths, tied together at the ends with bows. Height, 21 inches. No. 22.

SNUFF-BOTTLE (*Pi Yen Hu*), of Yi-hsing " boccaro " ware, being made of fine red faïence, enameled outside in soft colors with a miniature mountain landscape of temples, pavilions, and bridges. No. 23.

BOWL (*Wan*), one of a pair, of the *K'ang-hsi* period, enameled *sur biscuit* with a finely crackled monochrome purple glaze of aubergine tint. The base is partially

coated with a wrinkled grayish enamel. European mounts of bronze. Diameter, 7 inches. No. 24.

SNUFF-BOTTLE (*Pi Yen Hu*), with an outer pierced casing carved with nine lions sporting with brocaded balls, between borders of conventional scrolls, and with a fret band etched round the rim, enameled white. The mark under the foot is a red seal inscribed *Chia ch'ing nien chih,* " Made in the reign of Chia-ch'ing (1796–1820)." The stopper, mounted with a button of glass and amethyst, has the usual miniature spoon of ivory attached to it inside for ladling out the snuff. No. 25.

VASE (*P'ing*), coated with a deep rich glaze of greenish celadon color, crackled throughout. A band is reserved in the glaze round the shoulder of the vase and filled in with a ring of rectangular fret succeeded by formal scrolls, all worked in relief in slip and colored iron-gray. The handles are oval garlands of rosettes in the same relief-work. It is elaborately mounted in ormolu of old European workmanship. Height, with mount, 14 inches. No. 26.

TRANSMUTATION VASE (*Yao-pien P'ing*), one of a pair, of European form and design, festooned, as it were, with curtains gathered up by ribbons in front and hanging in knotted folds at the sides, and coated with a transmutation glaze of early *Ch'ien-lung* date, exhibiting all the characteristic brilliant tints as it runs down in heavy drops, streaked and mottled with crimson, purple, and brown, in variegated clouds. European mounts. Height, 14 inches. No. 27.

VASE (*P'ing*), of *Nien Yao* of the *Yung-chêng* period, of the same ruby-red monochrome glaze as the pair described under 15. The neck of the vase has been cut down, and it has been mounted in Europe in gilded bronze as a cistern, placed in an elaborate stand supported by three dolphins, and perforated for a tap, which is fashioned in the shape of a griffin. Height, with mount, 12 inches. No. 28.

SQUARE BOTTLE (*Fang P'ing*), one of a pair, with powder-blue grounds of the *K'ang-hsi* period, enameled over in gold with flowers and birds. Bottoms unglazed, European mounts of the eighteenth century. Height, 8½ inches. No. 29.

VASE (*P'ing*), of decoration similar to the pair described under No. 11, and mounted in the same style, to form a center-piece of a set, intended to figure as a *garniture de cheminée.* The artistic setting, which is beautifully executed in gilded openwork designs of Oriental scrolls, is signed " Fᶜ Boucheron, Paris." Height, 10 inches. No. 30.

LITTLE COVERED BOWL (*Hsiao Kai Wan*), one of a pair, of finely crackled turquoise enamel of *Ch'ien-lung* date, mounted in European metal-work, and placed upon square pedestals of German porcelain which are marked F., probably for Fürstenburg. Height, with mounts, 7 inches. No. 31.

SNUFF-BOTTLE (*Pi Yen Hu*), of rounded vaselike form, molded in a basket-work pattern, with lions'-head handles, and enameled with a minutely crackled turquoise glaze of the usual mottled tone. No. 32.

SHELL (*Lo-ssŭ*), one of a pair, fashioned of pure white *pâte* in the shape of whelks, and enameled *sur biscuit* with a finely crackled turquoise glaze of uniformly blue tint. The round covers are molded in the form of lotus-leaves, with conical shells on the top as handles. One of the shells is marked in the interior, which is unglazed, with the Chinese numeral 3 penciled in black; the other is incised with a line surmounted by a dot. The mounts are French work of the eighteenth century. Height, 7½ inches. No. 33.

MUG (*Chiu Pei*), of the *K'ang-hsi* period, painted in brilliant blue, with a formal mountain landscape containing temples and open pavilions on wooded hills and houses on the banks of a wide river. The base is encircled by a ring of conventional foliations, and the upper rim by a band of chrysanthemum-sprays. The bottom is unglazed. Mounted in Europe, with a silver lid engraved with a crest. Height, 18 inches. No. 34.

CYLINDRICAL VASE (*T'ung P'ing*), of *K'ang-hsi* porcelain, brilliantly decorated in enamel colors in the same style as the vase described under No. 268. It has been cut down and mounted in Europe as a mug, with a coronet and coat of arms etched upon the lid. Height, 9½ inches. No. 35.

VASE (*P'ing*), of white enameled porcelain of ancient bronze form and design, with two loop handles springing from grotesque heads, and archaic designs worked in slight relief in the paste under the white glaze. The seal, impressed in the paste underneath, is *Ta Ch'ing Ch'ien-lung nien chih*—i. e., "Made in the reign of Ch'ien-lung (1736–95) of the Great Ch'ing [dynasty]." The mounting is European. Height, 9½ inches. No. 36.

BOWL (*Wan*), enameled with a pale *soufflé* glaze of sky-blue (*t'ien-ch'ing*) derived from cobalt, mounted in Europe upon a pedestal representing a clump of bulrushes, together with a pair of fish of finely crackled turquoise, the "peacock-green" (*kung-chüo lü*) glaze of the Chinese ceramist. Height, 7½ inches.

CUP WITH COVER (*Kai Wan*), of the *Fên-Ting* class, painted in blue after the early style of the *Ming* dynasty. The handle of the cover is fashioned in the shape of a phœnix and colored blue. Both the cup and the cover are decorated outside with a pair of five-clawed dragons pursuing jewels in the midst of clouds and flames, painted in soft-toned shades of blue under the soft-looking glaze, which is of ivory-white tone and finely crackled throughout—in the interior of the piece as well as outside. Height with cover, 4¼ inches; diameter, 3 inches.

FLOWER-VASE (*Hua P'ing*), molded in the form of a growing Shantung cabbage (*Brassica chinensis*, L.; in Chinese, *Po-ts'ai*), mistaken for an opening Nelumbo, with a sprout springing from the base, making a smaller receptacle for a separate flower. The leaves stand up in duplex tier, shaped in naturalistic detail with finely dentated margins, and colored outside in two shades of green etched over with the natural venation in black, the stalks being left white. The interior is enameled with the soft, pale-green monochrome glaze characteristic of some of the finest vases of the *Ch'ien-lung* period, to which, no doubt, this quaint specimen belongs. Height, 4¾ inches. No. 37.

WINE-CUP (*Chiu Pei*), of swelling, bowl-like form and most delicate texture, decorated over the white glaze in gold with sprays of chrysanthemums. The hall-mark of *Ching Ssŭ T'ang Chih* is penciled underneath in red. Diameter, 2¾ inches.

WINE-POT (*Chiu Hu*), a miniature square vessel of the *Ming* period, fashioned in the shape of an old bronze casting. Of solid make, with an arched handle on the top, and a short hexagonal spout projecting from one side, it is enameled turquoise-blue overlaid with splashes of aubergine-purple, both these glazes being of minutely crackled texture.

WINE-CUP (*Chiu Pei*), decorated in soft enamel colors with the eight propitious symbols (*pa-chi-hsiang*) of Buddhist origin, arranged in four pairs encircled by waving fillets, and with borders of conventional scrolls round the rims. The mark, penciled in red underneath the foot, is *Tao kuang kêng hsü nien chih*, "Made in the year kêng-hsü (1850) of the reign of Tao-kuang." Diameter, 2¾ inches. No. 38.

GOURD-SHAPED BOTTLE (*Hu-lu P'ing*), one of a pair, of the *K'ang-hsi* period, decorated on a white ground with conventionalized scrolls studded with formal cruciform flowers, painted in mottled blue of very brilliant tone. European mounts, the cover representing a bee in the middle of a garland of flowers. Height, 10 inches. No. 39.

FISH-BOWL (*Yü Kang*), one of a pair, of depressed globular form, the traditional shape of the alms-bowl of Buddha, enameled with a finely crackled turquoise glaze of mottled hue, of the same date as the vase illustrated in Fig. 20. The two bowls are elaborately mounted in artistic French work of style similar to that of the vase. Diameter, 9 inches. No. 40.

PILGRIM BOTTLE (*Pei Hu P'ing*), with a central boss, a channeled foot, and four looped handles at the sides. The surface is worked in slight relief with white flowers and butterflies, etched with the graving-tool, and brought out by a monochrome ground of pale cobalt-blue. Artistically mounted in Europe for suspension. Height, with mount, 12 inches. No. 41.

VASE (*P'ing*), one of a pair, painted in brilliant blue of the *K'ang-hsi* period. The body is decorated with figures of Chinese ladies standing, or seated on barrel-shaped seats, arranged in couples, beside pots of peonies, and holding flowers in their hands. Palms fill in the intervals, and a formal band of blue defines the base of the neck, which is covered with sprays of blossoming prunus. The mark, penciled in blue underneath, is a leaf encircled by a fillet, inclosed within a double ring. Height, with mounts of European work, 7½ inches. No. 42.

FIVE-NOZZLED ROSADON (*Wu Tsui P'ing*), enameled with a pea-green celadon glaze (*tou-ch'ing yu*) of the *Yung-chêng* or early *Ch'ien-lung* period. Artistically mounted in Europe with grape-knobbed covers, connected by chains, and with garlands of vine stretched round the necks. Height, with mount, 12 inches. No. 43.

LARGE CELADON DISH (*Lung-ch'üan P'an*), of circular form, with vertically ribbed sides and foliated rim, decorated with floral designs etched in the paste under the rich glaze, which is of greenish tone. The large medallion occupying the bottom inside is filled with branches of a fruit tree, apparently the *Nephelium litchi*. The slope is chased with upright sprays of peony-flowers, sixteen in number, of identical design, in panels corresponding to the foliations of the border. The panels on the convexity underneath are worked with leafy sprays in slight relief. The rim is lightly etched. Under the foot there is a wide ring of paste uncovered with glaze, with regular edges, as if ruled by a compass, the bare field of which, 1½ inches broad, is of brick-dust color. Diameter, 22 inches. No. 44.

COVERED BOWL (*Kai Wan*), pierced with trellis panels and decorated in enamel colors of the best *K'ang-hsi* period. The sides, pierced with six panels of hexagonal trellis-work inclosing sprays of flowers, are painted with bands of diaper and with borders of dotted green studded with prunus-blossoms alternately white and overglaze blue of purplish tone. The cover, which is surmounted by a blue lion, is encircled by a belt of trellis, succeeded by a band of floral pattern similar to that on the bowl. It has been artistically mounted in bronze in Europe as a flower-basket raised upon a four-footed stand. Height, with mount, 7½ inches. No. 45.

OBLONG VASE (*Fang P'ing*), of lozenge-shaped section, enameled with a pale monochrome glaze of *K'ang-hsi* date of pure celadon tint (*Tung ch'ing*). It is molded with symbols under the glaze, displaying the *yin-yang* emblem between the eight trigrams (*pa kua*) in sunk panels on each of the four sides. Height, 11 inches. No. 46.

VASE (*P'ing*), enameled with a coral-red monochrome glaze of beautiful color, the charming effect of which is enhanced by the European ormolu mounts of light sprays and festoons of grapevine which wind round the vase. The graceful form, with spreading foot, indicates the *Yung-chêng* period, and the white enamel with which the foot is coated underneath is of pale greenish tone. Height, with mount, 9¾ inches. No. 47.

SNUFF-BOTTLE (*Pi Yen Hu*), with carved decoration filled in with enamel colors of the *Ch'ien-lung* period. The two panels contain the star-gods of happiness, rank, and long life, with their attributes, mounted on cloud pedestals, displayed upon a background of scrolled sea-waves. The framework is carved in pierced work, with the symbols of the eight Taoist immortals (*Pa Hsien*) inclosed in scrolls. The upper rim is gilded. No. 48.

VASE (*P'ing*), of ancient brownish-red stoneware of the *Han* dynasty (B. C. 206–A. D. 220), coated with a thin but lustrous glaze of camellia-leaf green. The bottom, only partially enameled over about one third of its surface, shows the color of the material. Height, 9¼ inches. Diameter, 10 inches. No. 49.

PILGRIM BOTTLE (*Pao Yueh P'ing*), with two open flowing handles fashioned in the form of archaic two-horned dragons (*ch'ih-lung*), decorated in enamel colors and gilding of the *Ch'ien-lung* period, in connection with details previously outlined in underglaze blue. The dragon-handles are in shaded red touched with gold. Round the neck and in the hollow of the foot are bats displayed in the midst of clouds. The body is emblazoned on each side with a central *shou* (longevity) monogram, surrounded by the eight Taoist emblems (*pa an-hsien*) tied in pairs with waving fillets, intermingled with floral sprays and cloud scrolls, inclosed in a wide panel by a circular line of blue and gold. The convexities of the vase between the panels are occupied by the eight Buddhist symbols (*pa chi-hsiang*) with scrolls and flowers. The seal penciled in blue underneath has the ordinary seal-character inscription of the reign of *Ch'ien-lung* (1736–95). Height, 19½ inches. No. 50.

LARGE JAR WITH COVER (*Mei Hua Kuan*), of the *K'ang-hsi* period, decorated in brilliant hue with blossoming branches of prunus (*mei hua*) alternately rising and descending to cover the surface of the jar as well as the top of the cover. The flowers are reserved in white upon a mottled blue background, which is penciled with a reticulation of darker blue lines. A band of triangular fret defines the upper and lower borders of the jar, and another encircles the projecting rim of the cover, which is surmounted by a globular knob colored plain blue. A band of conventional foliations, extending midway up the neck of the jar, completes the decoration. The mark under the foot is a double ring. Height, with cover, 17 inches. No. 51.

LARGE DEEP PLATE (*Kuo P'an*), of Chinese porcelain of early *K'ang-hsi* date, with designs painted in underglaze cobalt-blue, filled in with enamel colors—blue, green, yellow, and red, with gilding. The rim is gilded. The brocaded grounds of diaper round the border are in underglaze blue, as well as the outlines of the diversely shaped panels, which are painted inside with pictures in colors. The field is filled with birds flying through sprays of chrysanthemum and peony, with a coronet near the top, under which is a shield emblazoned with the heraldic lion of Holland. Diameter, 18½ inches. No. 52.

SMALL OVAL JAR (*Ch'a Kuan*), one of a pair, decorated with a pale-blue monochrome ground etched in darker blue with floral designs. The sides are vertically ribbed, interrupted by three circular medallions. Of the *K'ang-hsi* period, the mark underneath is a palm-leaf inclosed in a double ring. The mounts are European, and the covers, of Oriental powder-blue, are not original. Height, without cover, 5½ inches. A third little jar in the collection, with a similar decoration and mark, only with symbols penciled around the neck instead of sprays of flowers, is mounted with a Persian cover of chased copper. No. 53.

BLUE AND WHITE GARNITURE of the famed Lange-Eleizen pattern; period, *K'ang-hsi*. The mark on the foot —*Chia-ching nien chih*—is apocryphal. Height, 17½ inches. No. 54.

VASE (*P'ing*), with flanged lip, of white enameled porcelain, of the *Ch'ien-lung* period, coated with a rich glaze of somewhat greenish tint over a decoration molded in slight relief in the paste. This consists of four encircling bands of conventional floral sprays, defined by prominent rings; the neck is surrounded by two rings of formal scroll design, and the foot by a continuous chain of rectangular fret, succeeded by a spiral gadroonlike border. Height, 15 inches. No. 55.

BRUSH-POT (*Pi T'ung*), of wide cylindrical form, swelling at the mouth, with the decoration partly worked in relief in "slip," painted in underglaze blue and in overglaze en-amel colors, including coral-red, yellow, greens of varied shade, and black. The pictures of a scholar dreaming are intended to be an illustration of the half stanza of verse— *Mêng pi shêng hua*, "Dreaming the pencil blossoms into flowers." The seal, inscribed underneath in underglaze blue, is *Ta Ch'ing Yung-chêng nien chih*, "Made in the reign of Yung-chêng (1723–35) of the Great Ch'ing [dynasty]." Diameter, 8 inches. No. 56.

LIBATION-CUP (*Chüeh*), of white Fuchien porcelain (*Chien Tz'ŭ*). Of hornlike form, it is fashioned in the outline of a knotted branch of prunus, giving off a blossoming twig, which is worked in relief outside near the rim. The rest of the surface is decorated in the same salient relief with other archaic designs—a flying stork on one side, a four-clawed dragon, half hidden in the clouds, on the other, and a fish emerging from waves underneath; a deer is outlined near the foot in front, and floral lozenges project on either side. The glaze, of satiny texture, blends intimately with the ivory-white paste. Height, 2¾ inches. No. 57.

SEAL (*Yin*), one of a pair, of oblong form and square section, with lions mounted upon the top as handles, seated upon brocaded squares of rich floral pattern, painted *sur biscuit*, in brilliant enamel colors of the *famille verte*, dating from the *K'ang-hsi* period. Height, 3 inches. No. 58.

INSCRIPTIONS, on the two seals with lions as handles, of which one is represented in Fig. 58. That on the left is engraved, the characters appearing in white reserve. The other is carved in relief. No. 59.

WINE-CUP (*Chiu Pei*), one of a pair, of ivory-white Fuchien porcelain (*Chien Tz'ŭ*), molded of floral form, with everted rim, and supported by three small feet. The stanza of verse etched in the paste upon the side is *Tsui hou liu chün, cho ming yueh*, "When drunk with wine, save a little, as a libation to the bright moon." Diameter, 3½ inches. No. 60.

HANGING WALL-VASE (*Kua P'ing*), with flattened back perforated for suspension, a stand molded in porcelain as part of the piece, and two open-scrolled handles. It is decorated in delicate enamel colors and gilding with foliated panels, surrounded by floral designs, and with conventional palmated borders. The larger panel is painted with the picture of a hunting scene; the smaller panel above contains an ode in praise of hunting, signed by the Emperor *Ch'ien-lung*. The back of the vase and the interior of the mouth are coated with the pale-green enamel which distinguishes the imperial porcelain of the time, and the base is coated with the same, reserving a white panel for the mark of *Ta Ch'ing Ch'ien-lung nien chih*, "Made in the reign of Ch'ien-lung of the Great Ch'ing [dynasty]," which is penciled in underglaze blue in one line of antique script. Height, 8½ inches. No. 61.

"HOOF-SHAPED" VASE (*Ma-t'i P'ing*), having a dome-shaped body rounding in to a cylindrical neck, decorated in delicate enamel colors of the *Ch'ien-lung* period, with a picturesque landscape representing the woody islet Yen yü shan, in the Western Lake at Hangchou, with temples and pavilions on the hillside, pine-trees and willows, waterfalls and bridges, and a boat crossing the lake. A descriptive ode in four stanzas of rhyming verse is penciled in black on the other side of the vase, which is also illustrated. Height, 7 inches. No. 62.

BOWL (*Wan*), with flanged brim, of the *Tao-kuang* period, decorated on one side with sprays of flowers, hung with an endless knot—a Buddhist symbol of longevity— painted in colors, and relieved by an enameled monochrome background of coral-red. On the other side a verse is inscribed in white characters reserved in the red ground. The seal, enameled in red on a pale-green ground under the foot, is *Ta Ch'ing Tao-kuang nien chih*—i. e., "Made in the reign of Tao-kuang (1821–50) of the Great Ch'ing [dynasty]." Diameter, 7 inches. No. 63.

SNUFF-BOTTLE (*Pi Yen Hu*), of flattened form, decorated on one side in enamel colors with a little garden scene, a rockery and peonies and a boy with a basket feeding a hen and chicken. On the other side an ode upon the ceramic art, written by the Emperor *Ch'ien-lung*, is penciled in black, with the imperial seal attached in red. The mark inscribed underneath in red enamel is *Ch'ien lung nien chih*, "Made in the reign of Ch'ien-lung (1736–95)." No. 64.

SNUFF-BOTTLE, same as that represented in Fig. 64, but greatly enlarged in order to show the inscription, a poem by the Emperor *Ch'ien-lung* in praise of the ceramic art. A translation is given on page 31. No. 65.

CENSER (*Hsiang Lu*), of archaic aspect, dating from the *K'ang-hsi* period, with a decoration roughly painted in cobalt-blue under a crackled glaze of grayish tone, traversed by deep brown fissures. The decoration consists of a pair of four-clawed dragons grasping the effulgent jewel of magic power, with cloud scrolls and forked flames filling in the intervals. Diameter, 5 inches. No. 66.

BOWL (*Wan*), designed in the form of a lotus-blossom, with an outer ring of eight petals molded round the foot, and the rim of eightfold foliated outline. It is enameled with a monochrome ground of coral-red, with a decoration painted upon it of two five-clawed dragons pursuing effulgent jewels; and with a tiny floral spray on each of the foliated panels round the foot, depicting in order the prunus and bamboo, narcissus, begonia, chrysanthemum, jasmine, orchid, convolvulus, aster and lilac, and plum blossoms. The foot is enameled, like the interior, pale green, with a white panel reserved in the middle, which is penciled in red, with the seal *Hsieh Chu Tsao*, in antique script. Diameter, 7 inches. No. 67.

TEAPOT (*Ch'a Hu*), of the finest *Ku Yueh Hsüan* type, decorated with two broad panel pictures of landscapes penciled in bright overglaze cobalt-blue enamel. The rest of the surface is covered with bands of floral design, containing tiny sprays of many different kinds of flowers, delicately painted in enamel colors. The cover is ornamented with a similar floral ground, painted in the same characteristically translucent enamels, and the knob is made to simulate a chrysanthemum. There is a seal penciled underneath in overglaze blue enamel inscribed *Yung chêng nien chih*, "Made in the reign of Yung-chêng (1723–35)." No. 68.

QUADRANGULAR VASE (*Fang P'ing*), of fine dark-colored paste, invested with two coats of glaze, in the style of the ancient imperial productions of the *Sung* dynasty. The base, which is thinly glazed, is incised in the middle with the two characters *Hsüan ho*, which are filled in with the same grayish-white enamel that forms the overglaze of the vase. Height, 3¼ inches. No. 69.

EGGSHELL BOWL (*To-t'ai Wan*), of light fragile structure, with a small base, spreading sides, and a wide rim notched at regular intervals with six indentations. Invested with a pellucid glaze of slightly grayish ivory-white tone. The decoration, lightly incised in the paste in the interior of the bowl round the sides, so as to show in transparency when it is held up to the light, consists of a pair of five-clawed imperial dragons pursuing a flaming jewel enveloped in clouds. The inscription, which is also faintly engraved in the bottom of the bowl, inside, in a bold archaic style, is *Yung lo nien chih*—i. e., "Made in the reign of Yung-lo (1403–24)." Height, 2¾ inches; diameter, 8½ inches. No. 70.

WINE-CUP (*Chiu Pei*), of eggshell thinness, decorated, partly in underglaze blue, partly in enamel colors of the *K'ang-hsi* period, with a pair of mandarin ducks in a lake with lotus and other water-plants growing in it and a kingfisher flying above. The stanza of verse at the back and the peculiar mark are explained in Chapter IV, page 42. A precisely similar cup, painted entirely in blue, with the same stanza inscribed at the back, has the ordinary mark written underneath of *Ta Ch'ing K'ang hsi nien chih*, "Made in the reign of K'ang-hsi of the Great Ch'ing [dynasty]." Diameter, 2½ inches. No. 71.

EGGSHELL BOWL (*To-t'ai Wan*), decorated in the artistic style of the "rose-backed" plates with the soft brilliant

enamels and gold of the *famille rose*. The richly brocaded floral grounds inclosing foliated medallions of fruit, and the varied diapers surrounding the panel picture of a Chinese family scene, with a lady seated and two children playing, which fill the interior of the bowl, are well shown in the illustration. The exterior is decorated with similar minutely painted diapers and floral designs, with four circular medallions of antique dragons on a dark-blue ground, and with four large foliated panels containing charming sprays of peony and chrysanthemum. It derives additional interest from being dated, which very rarely occurs on pieces of the class. The mark underneath is the ordinary six-character inscription of the reign of *Yung-chêng*, which is penciled under the foot in underglaze blue written in stiff archaic style, encircled by a double ring. Diameter, 7¼ inches. No. 72.

MEDALLION BOWL (*Yueh-kuang Wan*), decorated in enamel colors with a brocaded floral ground interrupted by four circular medallions. The ground, outside, etched with a scroll pattern, is crimson (*rouge d'or*), and is covered with sprays of conventional flowers painted in delicate colors; the medallions display fruit and flowers on a white ground, pomegranates, peaches, and longan fruit, peonies, China rose, narcissus, and daisies. The interior is painted in underglaze blue with a basket of flowers surrounded with four sprays of fruit, flowers, and branched Polyporus fungus. The seal, penciled under the foot in the same blue, is *Ta Ch'ing Tao kuang nien chih*, "Made in the reign of Tao-kuang of the Great Ch'ing [dynasty]." Diameter, 6 inches. No. 73.

RICE-BOWL (*Fan Wan*), decorated outside with butterflies, painted in delicate enamel colors, and relieved by an enameled monochrome ground of coral-red. The rim is gilded. The mark, penciled in red under the foot, is *Shên Tê T'ang Chih*, which is said to be an imperial hall-mark of the reign of *Tao-kuang*. Diameter, 5½ inches. No. 74.

TEAPOT (*Ch'a Hu*), of the *K'ang-hsi* period, decorated in blue and white, with the borders and rims enameled pale yellow, and the overarching handle penciled in black upon a yellow ground in imitation of basketwork. The panels on the side are filled, two with pictures of domestic scenes, and one with bamboo growing from rocks. The upright rim has small panels with sprays of the emblematic flowers of the four seasons. The knob on the cover, carved in openwork with the character *lu*, "rank," is encircled by a four-clawed dragon painted blue. The bottom is *en biscuit* with the exception of a sunk panel in the middle, which is inscribed *sous couverte*, *Yi Yü T'ang chih*, "Made at the Hall of Ductile Jade." Height, 9 inches. No. 75.

VASE (*P'ing*), of the *Ch'ien-lung* period, with a decoration, etched at the point in the paste, of a pair of five-clawed imperial dragons in the midst of cloud scrolls and lightning-flames, pursuing the magic jewel, which is represented as a round disk emitting a spiral effulgent ray from its center. It is invested with a turquoise glaze of charmingly soft mottled tones and minutely crackled texture. There is a hall-mark engraved in the paste underneath, *Ssŭ Kan Ts'ao T'ang*. The mounting is European work of the eighteenth century. Height, with mount, 12 inches. No. 76.

WINE-CUP (*Chiu Pei*), one of a pair, of four-lobed form with indented rim, painted in enamel colors, with a procession of the eight Taoist immortals (*Pa Hsien*) crossing the sea. The interior is sprinkled with a few white jasmine-flowers (*mo-li hua*), touched with the same delicate tints. There is a mark under the foot, *Hsieh Chu Tsao*, penciled in red, in antique script within a square panel. Diameter, 2½ inches. No. 77.

WINE-CUP (*Chiu Pei*), of perfect form and technique, painted outside in pure colors upon a translucently white ground with a floral decoration. This consists of a clump of bamboos with dianthus pinks growing from the ground beneath, and a bat with a propitious emblem hanging from a ribbon in its mouth flying above. There are butterflies at the back, and a half stanza of verse penciled in black,

"Vows for good fortune and a thousand fruitful years!" A blossom and a bud of the fragrant jasmine are painted inside the cup at the bottom. The hall-mark, *Chih Hsiu Ts'ao T'ang*, is penciled in red under the foot. Diameter, 2½ inches. No. 78.

WINE-CUP (*Chiu Pei*), decorated upon a white ground in delicate enamel colors with a floral group composed of the three emblems of longevity, the evergreen fir (*sung*), the graceful leafy bamboo (*chu*), and the blossoming winter prunus (*mei*). The hall-mark of *Pao Shan Chai* is penciled in red under the foot. Diameter, 2¼ inches. No. 79.

WINE-CUP (*Chiu Pei*), one of a pair, each painted in shaded red with fifty bats, covering the ground inside and outside, as emblems of hundredfold happiness. The circular form of the longevity character (*Shou*) is outlined in red on the bottom of the cup, filled in with gold. The hall-mark under the foot is *Fu Ch'ing Ta'ng chih*, "Made at [or for] the Hall of Happiness and Good Fortune." Diameter, 2½ inches. No. 80.

TALL EWER (*Chiu Hu*), of blue and white porcelain of the *Wan-li* period. It has a flowing bandlike handle, and a long curving spout attached to the neck by a spiral buttress; the slender neck swells into a bulb near the mouth, which has a six-sided cover crowned with a knob. It is decorated with phœnixes and storks flying in the midst of clouds, and with scrolled bands and foliated borders round the rims. The mark, penciled in blue under the foot within a double ring, is *Ch'ang ming fu kuei*—i. e., "Long life, happiness, and honor!" The handwriting, as well as the style of decoration of the wine-pot, indicate the *Ming* dynasty. It is studded all over with uncut turquoises and garnets arranged alternately in gilded settings of Oriental work. The rims show traces of gilded rings, and are mounted in chased metal. Height, 13½ inches. No. 81.

WINE-POT (*Chiu Hu*), molded in the form of the character *fu*, "happiness," and decorated *sur biscuit* in the typical "three colors" (*san ts'ai*) of the *K'ang-hsi* period—viz., yellow, green, and purple. The rims and borders are colored light green; the spout has a pale-yellow ground with diverse forms of *shou* (longevity) penciled upon it, alternately pale purple and green; the rest of the surface is covered with bands of lotus-scrolls, with white and purple blossoms and green foliations, relieved by a pale-yellow ground outlined in purple, interrupted by panels of foliated outline in the middle, which are framed in green relief. These panels are painted with symbolical pictures in the same soft colors; on one side a pine, *ling-chih* fungus, and grass growing from rocks, an axis-deer, and a stork; on the other side a peach-tree, rocks with bamboo, a couple of birds flying together, and a tiger. The base, unglazed, is cross-hatched with the lines of the stuff of which the paste was molded. Height, 9 inches. No. 82.

VASE (*P'ing*), decorated in blue and white of the *K'ang-hsi* period. The body displays two groups of symbols around oval panels in the middle, which are inscribed in antique script, *Ch'ien*, "Heaven," and *Shou*, "Longevity"; in front is a palm-leaf fan, ending in a fly-whisk, and a branch of peach-blossoms; behind, a rolled-up scroll and a spray of chrysanthemum. Light chains of fret encircle the shoulder and the rim of the mouth. There is no mark underneath. Height, 8 inches. No. 83.

VASE (*P'ing*), modeled in the form of a tall bowl with a vaulted cover, the line of junction being indicated by a prominent ridge. It is enameled with a crackled glaze of light gray-brown color, interrupted by transverse bands worked in the paste and colored black, a gadroon band round the foot, and two basketwork bands overlaid with circular longevity (*shou*) characters filled in with crackled glaze. The two loop-handles, roughly shaped as elephant heads, are colored black, also the rim of the mouth, and the under surface of the foot. Height, 6 inches. No. 84.

GOURD-SHAPED VASE (*Hu-lu P'ing*), richly decorated in enamel colors of the *K'ang-hsi* period, with no gilding. The two segments are hung with lambrequins of floral brocade, in which chrysanthemum-flowers are conspicuous, tied with hanging bows of red ribbon; the intervals being filled in with medallions of storks. The neck is studded with four large circular *shou* characters in yellow, accompanied by four smaller *svastika* symbols in red. Encircling bands of floral brocade and formal ornamental scrolls of diverse pattern complete the decoration of the vase, which is a striking example of brilliant coloring, as well as of artistic decoration. Height, 18 inches. No. 85.

FIGURE OF K'UEI HSING (*K'uei Hsing Hsiang*), the Stellar God of Literature, painted in enamel colors. Poised with one foot upon the head of a fish-dragon, which is swimming in waves, one hand is uplifted to wield the pencil-brush, while the other grasps a cake of ink. The cloak waving loosely above his head and hanging down in long ends, and the general pose of the figures, are intended to give the impression of movement. Height, 14½ inches. No. 86.

EGGSHELL VASE (*To-t'ai P'ing*), of delicate texture and undulatory surface, decorated over the translucently white glaze with a spray of chrysanthemum and a single head of spiked millet, beautifully painted in a neutral sepia tint. The one touch of color is the vermilion outline of the seal, which is attached to the stanza of verse, quoted from an ode written upon the chrysanthemum by an old poet of the *T'ang* dynasty, which is inscribed on the back of the vase. Height, 8¼ inches. No. 87.

VASE (*P'ing*), of the *K'ang-hsi* period, with a swelling domelike body and a tall cylindrical neck, resembling somewhat in shape a Buddhist *dâgaba*. The body is a pale-blue monochrome derived from cobalt, the shoulder is surrounded by a ring of coffee-brown, and the neck is painted in dark blue, with a two-horned dragon of archaic design pursuing a jewel disk. Old European mounts. No mark. A pair of similar vases, from the Marquis Collection in Paris, not mounted, have the dragons on the neck painted in maroon and blue, and the light-blue body of the vase penciled in darker blue with lotus medallions and *shou* characters. They are marked underneath *Shou Fu*, "Longevity and Happiness." Height, 10½ inches. No. 88.

WIDE-NECKED VASE (*Hua Tsun*), with slightly spreading foot, decorated in enamel colors of the *K'ang-hsi* period without underglaze blue or gold. It is modeled in relief with foliated panels and spirally waving scrolls painted with brocaded bands and chains of fret, and the field, thus divided into panels, is delicately painted with landscapes, sprays of flowers, birds and butterflies, vases and censers, symbols and emblems, and the varied apparatus of literary culture in China. Among the symbols the eight Buddhist emblems of good fortune (*pa chi-hsiang*) occupy a conspicuous position, and the apparatus of the four liberal arts of the scholar, viz., writing, painting, music, and chess. The base is plainly enameled, with no mark inscribed. Height, 19 inches. No. 89.

RITUAL WINE-POT (*Chiu Hu*), of ancient bronze form, with a rounded body mounted on four cylindrical feet, a wide loop-handle, and a straight spout; the cover wanting. Painted in blue, with conventional scrolls of sacred-fungus design, and with sprays of Indian lotus supporting the eight Buddhist symbols of happy augury (*pa chi-hsiang*) encircled by waving fillets. A chain of interrupted rectangular fret round the shoulders and a ring of spiral fret at the base of the spout complete the decoration. The mark underneath, outlined in blue, is the seal *Ta Ch'ing Ch'ien lung nien chih*, "Made in the reign of Ch'ien-lung of the Great Ch'ing [dynasty]." Height, 7 inches. No. 90.

SNUFF-BOTTLE (*Pi-yen-hu*), with Buddhist symbols (*pa chi-hsiang*) molded in relief. No. 91.

THE MARK on the foot of the tall vase shown in Fig. 93. It consists of the sacred *ling-chih* fungus enveloped in tufts of grass. No. 92.

GOURD-SHAPED VASE (*Hu lu P'ing*), one of a pair, of the *K'ang-hsi* period, painted in pure full tones of shaded blue. It is decorated in two sections with a floral ground of interlacing peony scrolls inclosing panels of diverse form. The three quatrefoil medallions on the upper section contain sprays of blossoming prunus, and birds. The three panels on the lower section contain quadrupeds displayed in white upon a mottled-blue background, an elephant in a panel of pomegranate shape, a lion with one forefoot on a ball in a ficus-leaf, and a *ch'i-lin* in a palm-leaf. Bands of chrysanthemum scrolls round the rim, above and below, and two double chains of triangular fret, separated by encircling rings, in white relief, complete the artistic decoration. The mark (Fig. 92) is a sacred fungus with tufts of grass inclosed in a wide double ring. Height, 16¾ inches.   No. 93.

LARGE PLATE (*Kuo P'an*), decorated in brilliant enamel colors of the *K'ang-hsi* period. The rim is gilded over coffee-brown, and the slope of the plate is encircled by a red scroll and a chain of fret in overglaze blue between plain rings of yellow, pale purple, and apple-green. The broad band of peony scrolls round the border has red and purple blossoms tipped with gold, springing from a wavy, slender, black stem, relieved by a ground of pale green dotted with black, and five archaic dragons are wending their way round through the floral scrolls. The field is occupied by a tall, graceful vase, of *Ming* dynasty style, filled with a bouquet of peonies, surrounded by a varied selection from the paraphernalia of the liberal arts, which have been described in Chapter IV under the name of *Po Ku*, the "Hundred Antiques." Diameter, 18 inches.   No. 94.

VASE (*P'ing*), richly and profusely decorated in brilliant enamel colors of the *K'ang-hsi* period. The body is decorated in panels, displayed upon a ground of lotus scrolls, with the slender forms of two dragons winding through, relieved by a background of coral-red. Two of the panels contain mountain scenes: one shows four old men playing *gô*, with the board placed upon a rock; the other, a man on horseback, with an attendant carrying a lyre, on his way to visit a friend who is awaiting him at the door of his mountain retreat; a third panel has a tiger standing in the foreground; another a clump of chrysanthemums growing from rocks. The remaining two contain pictures of the *Po Ku*, or "Hundred Antiques." The neck is covered with a *svastika* pattern brocade, interrupted by two panels of water scenes—an old man fishing with a rod in one, a man poling a boat in the other. The shoulder is encircled by a broad band of floral brocade, with medallions containing the apparatus of the four liberal arts—the case of books of the scholar, the bundle of scroll pictures of the artist, the folding board and boxes for white and black men of the *gô*-player, and the lyre in its brocaded case of the musician. A chain of rectangular fret, penciled in overglaze blue round the rim of the mouth, and another, black upon a green ground, round the foot, complete the decoration. No mark attached. Height, 16½ inches.   No. 95.

VASE (*Hua P'ing*), of the *K'ang-hsi* period, decorated in red and pale green, with touches of gold. The neck and foot are encircled by successive ornamental bands of fret brocade, diaper, and gadroon of varied design; the shoulder has a broad band of brocade interrupted by medallions containing chrysanthemum-blossoms. The body of the vase is decorated with four panels separated by a ground of chrysanthemum scrolls richly worked in red and gold. The panels, which are illustrated in succession in Figs. 97, 98, and 99, are filled with the apparatus of the liberal arts and the materials of the scholar, which have been described in Chapter IV. Height, 15 inches.   Nos. 96–99.

ORNAMENTAL VASE (*Hua P'ing*), of imperial porcelain of the reign of *Ch'ien-lung*, richly decorated in enamel colors, with gilding, with no underglaze blue. It has two handles on the neck, of open scroll design, fashioned as dragons, on which hang suspended gilded movable rings; and rims of gold define the lip and the foot, as well as the top of the neck and of the body. The fret borders, above and below, are penciled in light blue upon a pale vermilion ground. The vase is decorated in panels filled with flowers and butterflies and various emblematic designs, the spaces between the panels being decorated with conventional floral

sprays, relieved by a plain yellow enameled ground. The flowers represented in the four large panels on the body of the vase are emblematic of the four seasons. In the first panel (spring) which is illustrated in the picture we see the *Magnolia yulan* and *Pæonia moutan*, growing from rocks, and a pair of butterflies flying in the air. The next panel (summer) contains hydrangea shrubs, with pinks (dianthus) and flags (iris). The next (autumn) an oak with acorns and russet-tinted leaves, overshadowing chrysanthemums of varied tint. The last (winter) displays a leafless prunus-tree in full blossom (*mei hua*), and the monthly rose (*yueh chi*), which flowers in China the whole year round.

The seal, penciled underneath in blue on a white panel reserved in the pale-green ground, is *Ta Ch'ing Ch'ien lung nien chih*, "Made in the reign of Ch'ien-lung of the Great Ch'ing [dynasty]." Height, 11½ inches.   No. 100.

LARGE CIRCULAR DISH (*Ta Kuo P'an*), of the finest imperial porcelain of the reign of *Yung-chêng*, artistically decorated in enamel colors, on a white ground, a companion piece to the dish which has been illustrated in colors in Plate XLVIII, and inscribed with the same mark underneath. The floral decoration consists of sprays of peony (*Pæonia moutan*), magnolia (*Magnolia yulan*), and "hait'ang" (*Pyrus spectabilis*), which throw off branches to decorate the under border as they spring from the foot and then spread over the rims to decorate the interior of the disk. The pyrus-blossoms are pink, the large peonies nearly white just tipped with pink, and the magnolia-flowers snow-white, being filled in with an opaque enamel of a different tone in the white of the translucent ground. Diameter, 19¾ inches.   No. 101.

SNUFF-BOTTLE (*Pi-yen-hu*), inscribed with the character *shou*, "longevity."   No. 102.

CIRCULAR DISH (*P'an Tzŭ*), of saucer-shaped form and eggshell texture, decorated with scrolls of Arabic writing (for a translation of which see page 72) penciled in black and filled in with gold. The outer rim is encircled by a light band of floral scrolls composed of alternate sprays of peony and chrysanthemum, relieved by a gilded ground. Diameter, 8 inches.   No. 103.

WINE-FLASK (*Chiu P'ing*), of Tz'ŭ-chou ware, fashioned in the shape of a small pilgrim bottle, with two loop-handles for suspension, and a mouth drawn in to a fine point. It is painted on one side with a spray of flowers in darker and lighter shades of brown. Height, 6½ inches.

GOURD-SHAPED BOTTLE (*Hu-lu P'ing*), of Tz'ŭ-chou ware, decorated in two shades of brown, with the character *fu*, "happiness," on the upper segment, and a spray of prunus-blossom, as the floral emblem of longevity, on the lower segment. Height, 7½ inches.

TWIN GENII OF PEACE AND HARMONY (*Ho Ho Erh Hsien*), the merry genii of the Taoist cult, molded together in white Tz'ŭ-chou ware, and painted in brown of two shades. They are intended to hold an incense-stick before a Taoist shrine, the joss-stick being inserted in the tube which is seen projecting from the shoulder of one of the figures. Height, 6 inches.   No. 104.

LARGE RICE-BOWL (*Fan Wan*), of the *K'ang-hsi* period, with a fretwork design involving the *svastika* symbol carved in relief outside and enameled white, the recesses being inlaid with a grass-green monochrome. The fretwork is interrupted by four circular medallions, which are decorated, in delicate enamel colors and gilding, with small pictures of flowers and insects. A band of spiral fret is penciled in red round the rim of the foot, and the upper border is gilded. The mark is a lotus-flower modeled underneath in slight white relief. Diameter, 7¼ inches.   No. 105.

SMALL WATER-BOWL (*Shui Kang*), modeled after the form, and decorated in the style, of the large garden fish-bowls of the *Ming* dynasty. The sides are ornamented with four foliated medallions, filled alternately with flowers and rocks, and with fruit and birds, painted in brilliant colors, the intervals being brocaded in blue, with a diapered ground inclosing small single blossoms painted in enamel colors, and the rims encircled by gadroon and foliated borders in colored enamels. The seal, penciled in blue under the glaze, within a double circle, is *Ta Ming Wan li nien chih*, "Made in the reign of Wan-li of the Great Ming [dynasty]." The silver cover, of pierced floral design, is Japanese. Height, with mounts, 5 ¼ inches.　　No. 106.

FISH-BOWL (*Yü Kang*), of rounded shape, with the lower part vertically fluted outside and enameled with a monochrome glaze of pale-green celadon tint, while the shoulder is decorated with a pair of three-clawed dragons of archaic type enveloped in clouds, under a pure translucidly white glaze. The scrolled clouds are worked round in relief in the paste, so that the forms of the dragons are partially hidden; the parts that appear being painted in greenish celadon touched with maroon, and having brownish-red flames issuing from their bodies. The technique is probably that of the *Yung-chêng* period; the bottom is unglazed, and there is no mark. Diameter, 10 inches.　　No. 107.

VASE (*P'ing*), of imperial porcelain of the *Ch'ien-lung* period, richly decorated in enamel colors of the *famille rouge*, with gilding. Of regular ovoid form, it has two solid handles fashioned in the shape of elephants' heads projecting from the gracefully receding neck. The neck and foot are covered with floral scrolls painted in delicate colors relieved by a ground of crimson (*rouge d'or*) etched all over with spiral foliations. The swelling body, defined by two bands of conventional scrolls worked in relief, is enameled with a pale monochrome glaze thickly strewn with tiny rings of darker tint, looking like minute bubbles, of *soufflé* color, and overlaid with a vertical rain of crimson flecks, sprinkled on evidently from the point of a brush. This is one of the so-called *Chün Yu*, or "Chün glazes" of the period, artificial facsimiles of the celebrated Chün-chou glazes of the *Sung* dynasty, although these were really mottled productions of the *grand feu*, and not fired in the muffle stove like this vase. The foot is enameled pale green underneath, with a panel reserved in the middle for the seal, which is penciled in underglaze blue, *Ta Ch'ing Ch'ien lung nien chih*, "Made in the reign of Ch'ien-lung of the Great Ch'ing [dynasty]." Height, 15 inches. No. 108.

VASE WITH FLARING MOUTH (*Ling-chih P'ing*), modeled in the form of the sacred fungus *Polyporus lucidus*, swelling into a large head at the top, and having the stem covered with a number of branchlets, bearing smaller fungus blades, all roughly worked in relief in the paste. The whole is enameled with a crackled glaze of grayish tint, overlaid with irregular splashes of two kinds, a dull purplish blue, and a variegated *flambé* glaze of mottled olive-brown and crimson tints. The ground color is seen in the intervals of the splashes, and it also covers the foot, which is not marked. Height, 13 inches.　　No. 109.

DOUBLE GOURD-SHAPED VASE (*Hu-lu P'ing*), enameled with a finely crackled turquoise glaze of grayish tone over a floral decoration worked in the paste underneath, in the style of the *Ming* dynasty or early *K'ang-hsi* period. The lower section is worked with a broad band of freely designed scrolls of the polyporus fungus mingled with blades of grass traversed by a dragon of archaic type. The upper section is decorated with a band of peony scrolls, from the upper border of which springs a line of spiral clouds encircling the base of the neck. The base is coated with a *truité* enamel of ivory-white tint. The mounts are of old bronze work etched with similar floral designs. Height, 8 inches.　　No. 110.

CYLINDRICAL VASE (*Hua T'ung*), with the rim of the mouth marked with four slight indentations, and the sides molded with two prominent handles fashioned as lions' heads with oval rings suspended from their mouths. It is enameled inside and out, as well as under the foot, with a celadon glaze of bluish tint, which is known as *Ju Yu*, being the traditional shade of the ancient Ju-chou wares of the *Sung* dynasty. The glaze is traversed irregularly by crackled lines, which are colorless in some parts, as under the foot, and become reddish brown in others. The rim of the foot is plastered brown, simulating the natural color of the *pâte* of the old *Sung* dynasty ware, which is a ferruginous faïence. Height, 15 inches.　　No. 111.

VASE (*P'ing*), of the *Ch'ien-lung* period, decorated in blue and white with archaic dragons of conventional design, carrying sprays of flowers in their mouths, which spread over the surface to cover it with formal scrolls, enveloping the large longevity (*shou*) characters, which are penciled on the body of the vase. A chain of continuous rectangular fret runs round the shoulder, and borders of scrolls and foliations surround the rims. The broad everted lip is painted with a circlet of four pairs of small dragons. Height, 13 inches.　　No. 112.

VASE (*P'ing*), with a two-horned, four-clawed dragon modeled upon it in full relief, bestriding the shoulder and enveloping the neck within the scaly, snakelike coils. The dragon is coated with a purplish-brown mottled glaze, the eyes and other small details being touched with dark brown. The rest of the vase is enameled with a grayish, white ground, mottled with cloudlike splashes of olive-brown passing into bluish variegated tint as they fade into the surrounding ground. The foot is coated underneath with a similar glaze mottled with brown. Height, 19 inches.　　No. 113.

CYLINDRICAL VASE (*T'ung P'ing*), of *K'ang-hsi* blue and white, artistically decorated with sprays of lotus and peony and with foliated borders, of similar design to the pair of jars described under Fig. 178, and mounted in the same style to form a *garniture de cheminée* with them. The mark under the foot is a double ring. The elaborate European mounts make it appear as a slender-necked vase with ring handles. Height, without mounts, 12 inches.　　No. 114.

GOURD-SHAPED VASE (*Kua P'ing*), of regular oval shape, modeled in the form of an ordinary melon (*kua*), with eight vertical grooves, and coated with a turquoise enamel of finely crackled texture and mottled greenish tone, the typical "peacock-green" (*Kung-chüo lü*) of the Chinese. Elaborately mounted with a pedestal and cover of European work of the last century. The piece is to be attributed from its technique to the early part of the seventeenth century. Height, 15 inches.　　No. 115.

VASE (*P'ing*), of tall archaic form, with the bulging part of the body encircled by two prominent ribs, a horizontally ridged neck, and a swelling mouth, the rim of which is held in the jaws of two horned crested dragons, with their necks curving upward and downward to form the flowing handles, which are ornamented with a row of studs in their outer surface. Below the point of attachment of each handle an oval foliated boss projects from the surface, engraved with cloud scrolls, and a ring of similar knobs is embossed round the shoulder of the vase. The enamel is a crackled glaze of *clair-de-lune* (*Yueh-pai*) tint, deepening to azure blue in the thicker parts. The crackled lines are reddish brown. The foot is coated underneath with the same crackled glaze, and inscribed with a seal, penciled in underglaze blue, *Ta Ch'ing Yung chêng nien chih*, "Made in the reign of Yung-chêng of the Great Ch'ing [dynasty]." Height, 21 inches.　　No. 116.

BOTTLE-SHAPED VASE (*P'ing*), with the neck curving over to end in a duck's head; an ancient bronze design. There is a circularly rimmed aperture in the convexity of the neck at the top. It is invested with a celadon glaze of typical sea-green tint. Height, 7 ¼ inches.　　No. 117.

VASE (*P'ing*), of form somewhat similar to that of the vase shown in Fig. 163, with a mouth swelling into a broad recurved lip of indented outline worked with conventional scrolls, enameled with a brilliant transmutation (*yao-pien*) glaze of the *Ch'ien-lung* period. A ground of grayish crackled texture is invested with a rich *flambé* coating, passing into deep crimson mottled tints flecked with spots of light purplish blue. The foot is enameled underneath with a pale purplish glaze, not crackled, and there is no mark inscribed. Height, 10¾ inches.　　No. 118.

"Double Fish" Dish (*Shuang Yü P'an*), a typical specimen of ancient Lung-ch'üan Yao of the *Sung* dynasty (960–1279), having a pair of fish worked in the paste, so as to project inside in strong relief as if swimming around. The little dish has a plain horizontal rim, and the convexity of the border, underneath, is vertically ribbed. It is invested with a crackled celadon glaze of greenish-brown tones approaching olive-green, shot and flecked with a brighter grass-green, which the Chinese liken to the tint of onion sprouts. The rim of the foot, which is unglazed, shows the reddish-buff color of the fabric. Diameter, 5½ inches.　　　　No. 119.

Saucer-shaped Dish (*P'an*), of old Lung-ch'üan celadon of the *Ming* dynasty (1368–1643). It has a foliated rim, and the sides are fluted in the interior so as to be ribbed underneath. A spray of peony is etched inside under the glaze. The glaze is a typical celadon of sea-green tint, varying in depth of tone according to its thickness. The under-surface of the dish has been photographed to show the irregular ring in the bottom, which distinguishes the class, when the paste, left bare, is of the usual reddish-buff color. Diameter, 11½ inches.　　　　No. 120.

Crackled Cup (*Ko Yao Pei*), modeled after an ancient design, simulating a lotus-leaf with convoluted everted rim, to which a lizardlike dragon is clinging, forming a handle for the cup. It is coated inside and out with a gray, stone-colored enamel, crackled by a network of deeper dark lines connected by superficial colorless lines. The foot-rim is stained brown, the traditional shade of the old *Ko Yao* of the *Sung* dynasty. Height, 4 inches.　　　　No. 121.

Small Censer (*Hsiang Lu*), of primitive *Ko Yao* of the *Sung* dynasty. Of globular form, with three small mammillated feet, it is coated with a speckled glaze of grayish tint, crackled throughout with a close network of brown lines. The feet show at their points a fabric of dark iron-gray color, and are encircled at their bases with brown lines of stain. It has been mounted in China upon an elaborately carved stand, and has a rosewood cover with a fungus-shaped knob of white jade. Height, 2 inches.　　No. 122.

Water Receptacle (*Shui Ch'êng*), of ancient *Sung* dynasty crackle, coated inside and outside, as well as under the foot, with a thick unctuous translucent glaze of dark brownish-gray tone, traversed by a reticulation of dark lines. The mouth is tinged a coppery red; the foot-rim shows a darkish iron-gray fabric. Height, 1½ inch; diameter, 3 inches.　　　　No. 123.

Miniature Vase (*Hsiao P'ing*), of primitive *Ko Yao* of the *Sung* dynasty. It is molded with two mask handles in relief, and invested with a rich glaze of light gray tint, crackled by a reticulation of dark lines, and is coated underneath with the same crackled glaze. The foot-rim shows a pale iron-gray paste. Height, 3 inches. No. 124.

Water-Pot (*Shui Ch'êng*), of ancient Chün Yao of the *Sung* dynasty (960–1279). Of solid dense structure, it has an archaic dragon roughly modeled in bold relief on one side so as to lift its head above the rim. The rich crackled glaze is of the pale-blue shade known as *clair de lune* (*yüeh pai*). It is stained at one point with a characteristic patch of deep crimson, shaded with a purple border, which is seen on the left side of the illustration. The mark, deeply cut in the paste under the foot, is the numeral *san* (3). The foot-rim shows a fabric of reddish-gray stoneware. Height, 2½ inches.　　　　No. 125.

Shallow Bowl (*Hua Pên*), modeled after the form of one of the ancient Chün-chou bowls of the *Sung* dynasty, which were used for the cultivation of narcissus bulbs, and enameled to reproduce the "pear-blossom red" (*hai-t'ang hung*) of the period. It is circular in form, with a rounded lip of sixfold foliated outline and vertically ridged sides, and is mounted upon three scrolled feet. The glaze is a mottled red of the *grand feu*, derived from copper, exhibiting a pink ground flecked with darker purplish spots, and it becomes changed to apple-green on the ridges and more

prominent parts. The bottom, coated with a grayish enamel, has six spur-marks round the rim, and the numeral *san* (3) on one side, cut in the paste, and it is stamped in the middle with the seal *Ta Ch'ing Yung chêng nien chih*, "Made in the reign of Yung-chêng of the Great Ch'ing [dynasty]." Diameter, 11 inches.　　　　No. 126.

Club-shaped Vase (*Pang-chih P'ing*), one of a pair of tall vases of early *K'ang-hsi* date, enameled with a crackled turquoise glaze of pure tone and uniformly bluish tint, over an artistic decoration previously molded and etched in the paste. This consists of scrolled sprays of peonies extending over the lower two thirds of the body, succeeded by a band containing ogre-like *t'ao-t'ieh* heads, displayed upon a spiral background; the shoulder is encircled by a chain of rectangular fret, and the neck by rings of formal scrolls. The foot is coated underneath with the same *truité* turquoise enamel. The highly decorative mounts are of European workmanship of Louis XV date. Height, 27 inches.　　　　No. 127.

Wine-Ewer (*Chiu Hu*), with a flowing cylindrical handle, an upright curving spout, and a bell-shaped cover surmounted by a knob. An early *K'ang-hsi* piece, it is decorated in panels of foliated outline, filled with formal trees, painted in deep blue, with cross-hatched strokes in a style not common in Chinese art. The intervals are filled in with floral scrolls and scattered blossoms, and the rims are defined by chains of fret of varied pattern. The metal mounting is of Oriental workmanship. Height, 13½ inches.
　　　　No. 128.

Broad-mouthed Vase (*Hua Tsun*), modeled in the form of an ancient sacrificial wine-vessel, with a horizontally grooved body and four vertically projecting broken ribs; the two handles being fashioned in full openwork relief as alligatorlike dragons. It is invested with a crackled glaze of transmutation type variegated with vertical splashes of grayish purple and olive-green, in the same way as the square vase of similar type illustrated in Plate XXIII. In the bottom, which is only partially glazed, a coarse reddish paste is exposed. Height, 12½ inches.　　　　No. 129.

Vase (*P'ing*), modeled in one of the graceful forms characteristic of the *Yung-ch'êng* period, and charmingly decorated on a pellucid white ground in the delicate enamel colors of the time. A magnolia-tree spreads round the vase to cover it with sprays of snow-white blossoms and buds; a gayly plumaged bird is clinging to one of the branches, and bright butterflies are flying round. The intervals are filled in with tree-peonies, branches of *Hibiscus rosa sinensis* and of pink-blossomed *Pyrus japonica*. The swelling rim of the foot is scattered with peach-blossoms and small sprays of chrysanthemum. There is no mark under the foot. Height, 16½ inches.　　　　No. 130.

Vase (*P'ing*), with three lions projected in full openwork relief upon the shoulder, represented in pursuit of brocaded balls tied with fillets, which are executed in similar salient relief. The lions are of the usual grotesque form, with gilded bodies, touched with yellow, green, and purple enamels, outlined in dark brown. The ground of the vase is covered with close spiral curves penciled in dull brownish red, and it has no claims to either beauty or antiquity. Height, 16½ inches.　　　　No. 131.

Wide-mouthed Vase (*Hua Tsun*), enameled inside and outside with a crackled glaze of grayish-white tint mottled with pale-reddish spots, traversed by a well-marked, deep network of dark lines. The bases of the neck and of the body are defined by rings uncovered by enamel and colored iron-gray, succeeded on the neck by another prominent ring round the top of the shoulder. The shoulder is studded with four handles executed in relief in "slip" as butterflies with suspended rings. The neck is surrounded by a band of the same iron-gray color, composed of a chain of interrupted rectangular fret between two formal scrolls, and the upright rim of the mouth is encircled by a single ring of conventional scrolls of the same pattern. The foot, colored iron-gray, is dotted at regular intervals with small buttons of gray enamel, as if to cover spur-marks. Height, 11 inches. No. 132.

LARGE HEAVY VASE, of the *Sung* dynasty ; exceedingly dense body and deep indented glaze of livid red, purple, and gray. Height, with mount, 14¼ inches. No. 133.

SMALL ARCHAIC VASE, with coarsely crackled ivory-white glaze, crudely decorated in blue. No. 134.

SNUFF-BOTTLES, (1) decorated in blue and white ; (2) of white paste, modeled in high relief, and surmounted by the so-called dog Fo ; (3) of *Fên-ting* white paste, with a perforated and reticulated design. No. 135.

GOURD-SHAPED VASE (*Hu-lu P'ing*), modeled in the shape of a large double gourd, with a branch of the same plant worked in salient undercut relief, spreading down from the top to cover the upper half of the vase with a reticulation of trailing vines bearing small gourds, leaves, and tendrils. The intervals of the leafy network are occupied by five flying bats—emblems of the five happinesses, the gourd itself being the emblem of long life, as the Taoist receptacle of the *elixir vitæ*. The vase is covered with a *soufflé* monochrome glaze of pale azure-blue tint (*t'ien-ch'ing*), while the bats and small gourds are touched with a mottled red derived from copper, which runs down to stain the surface of the vase in several spots. Height, 17 inches. No. 136.

THREEFOLD-GOURD VASE (*San Hu-lu P'ing*), of composite form and three-lobed section, simulating three gourds tied together at the waists, so that the three bodies have coalesced into one, while the necks remain distinct. The band with which they are girdled is worked in relief, and the ends tied together in a bow so as to hang down on one side. It is enameled with a transmutation (*Yao-pien*) glaze of grayish crackled texture, darkening to mottled crimson, and becoming purplish toward the edges, leaving the rim colorless, as well as the prominent parts of the ends of the ribbons. The foot is coated with the same grayish-white crackle. Height, 13½ inches. No. 137.

CUP (*Pei*), of *Ch'ien-lung* date, pierced with a broad band of openwork carving composed of interlacing circles extending round the sides, interrupted by five solid medallions, on which are posed in salient undercut relief the figures of the star-god of longevity (*Shou Hsing*) and of the eight immortals (*Pa Hsien*), grouped in pairs, holding their various attributes, with backgrounds of clouds. The figures are molded in brown *pâte*, and touched with colored enamels of dull tone, including white. A scroll of chrysanthemums is lightly worked round the foot in an opaque white of different tone from the lustrous white glaze underneath, and with which the rest of the cup is enameled. The foot is in white *biscuit* unglazed. The lining of the cup is of beaten silver, gilded. Diameter, 3½ inches. No. 138.

TEAPOT (*Ch'a Hu*), one of a pair, artistically modeled in the form of a fully expanded lotus-blossom, the sides being molded with rings of petals, and the rim studded with the seeds that naturally project from the cuplike fruit in the middle. The handle is the bowed body of a dragon (*ch'ih-lung*) which is clinging to the bowl by its jaws and four feet as well as by its bifid tail. The spout is the hollowed body of an alligator rising with gaping mouth to form the lips. The bottom, which is unglazed, is carved to represent a lotus-leaf, and a second veined peltate leaf with its stalk attached forms the lid. It is enameled with a *truité* turquoise glaze of softly mottled tones, deepening into purple where it thickens, round the rim of the cover, for example. Height, 4 inches. No. 139.

VASE (*P'ing*), of three-lobed outline, with indented mouth, and a vertically grooved body of solid form, molded with the figures of three lions projecting in salient relief from the sides. It is enameled with a transmutation (*yao-pien*) glaze of the *Ch'ien-lung* period, of a grayish pale-colored crackled ground, splashed with olive-brown and crimson patches of variegated mottled tints. The mouth, inside, and the foot are coated with a light purple, the

latter only partially, so as to expose a yellowish *pâte* in the intervals. Height, 9¾ inches. No. 140.

YUAN DYNASTY BOWL (*Yuan Tz'ŭ Wan*), composed of a coarse reddish-gray stoneware coated with a crackled glaze of pale purple tint, mottled with darker spots, and becoming brown at the edges. On the under side of the bowl the glaze has run down in a thick unctuous mass, so as to cover only part of the surface, stopping in an irregularly curved line, and leaving about a third of the side, as well as the foot, uncovered. Diameter, 6½ inches. No. 141.

JAR (*Kuan*), of ovoid form and archaic aspect, composed of a rough dark iron-gray stoneware, coated with a thick deeply crackled glaze of light stone-gray celadon tint. The upper rim is stained brown. It resembles the ancient jars so highly prized by the natives of Borneo and other islands of the Eastern Archipelago, and is probably a production of the Kuangtung potteries (*Kuang Yao*), of the *Sung* or *Yuan* dynasty. Height, 5 inches. No. 142.

MINIATURE TRIPOD CENSER (*Hsiao Ting Lu*), with two loop handles, invested inside and out with a gray crackled glaze of the same character as that described under No. 121. Height, 2 inches. No. 143.

BROAD-NECKED VASE (*Hua Tsun*), with mask handles fashioned in relief as lions' heads holding rings, enameled with a superficially and minutely crackled glaze of mottled tones, passing from pale translucid celadon to crimson and ruby tints. The glaze has "run," so that the lower part of the vase is densely coated and dark-colored while the upper rim and the prominent handles remain almost colorless. In the interior it has collected in *flambé* drops of brightly mottled purple. The foot has been ground on the wheel to remove the superfluous enamel. The base is coated yellowish gray with a crackled network of brown lines. Height, 13 inches. No. 144.

VASE (*Hua P'ing*), of a ritual form modeled after that of the Buddhist *dâgaba* illustrated in Fig. 349, decorated in brilliant enamel colors of early *K'ang-hsi* date, greens predominating, with a pure vermilion red, an orange yellow, a brownish purple, and touches of black, without gold or underglaze blue. The neck is enveloped in the coils of a four-clawed dragon pursuing an effulgent jewel among green clouds and red lightning-flames ; its base is encircled by a diapered band inclosing medallions of lotus-flowers, and the upper rim by rings of *svastika* pattern diaper and of chrysanthemum brocade. The body of the vase has ornamental fret borders, a graceful chain of conventional lotus sprays below, and four *shou*, "longevity," characters emblazoned on the shoulder above, between the four circular panels with foliated rims, which form the main decoration. One of these panels contains fish tossed in the waves, with a large one rising from the water, exhaling red flames, as if about to be metamorphosed into a dragon. The opposite panel has an eagle of majestic aspect perched upon a rock on the seashore. The other two panels display Taoist scenes. In one, two old men, seated on a rocky shore, are looking at a temple rising in the waves and a stork flying across carrying a tally of fate in its beak. In the other, one of the genii is bestriding the branch of a tree, which is taking the form of a dragon's head in front, his pilgrim's gourd and rolled scroll slung on a branch behind, as he crosses the sea in this strange craft. Height, 18¼ inches. No. 145.

BEAKER-SHAPED VASE (*Hua Ku*), of graceful form and finished technique, modeled in the lines of an ancient bronze sacrificial vessel, and coated all over, inside the mouth as well as outside and under the foot, with a bright yellow glaze of uniform orange tone, the typical "imperial yellow" monochrome of the *Ch'ien-lung* period. Height, 8½ inches. No. 146.

VASE (*P'ing*), of finished technique, dating from the *Yung-chêng* period, enameled with a plain white glaze of pure translucent tone. A dragon of archaic type is projected in bold, undercut relief upon the shoulder of the vase, and colored with a bright-blue overglaze enamel of mottled tint derived from cobalt. Height, 8½ inches.   No. 147.

WINE-POT (*Chiu Hu*), of rustic form, decorated *sur biscuit* in the three colors of the *demi-grand feu*—viz., turquoise-blue, aubergine-purple, and touches of pale green—all of finely crackled texture. It is roughly fashioned to simulate jointed bamboo, with branches of pine attached as handle and spout, from which sprays of foliage spread out to decorate the surface in relief. A sprig of bamboo surmounts the false cover, which is immovable, the wine being poured in through a hole in the bottom of the wine-pot, which is coated all round with the turquoise glaze. Height, 5 inches.   No. 148.

GLOBULAR BOWL (*Shui Ch'êng*), one of a pair, of lavender crackle, traversed by a network of brown lines. It is mounted upon a tall tripod stand of European work. Diameter, 4 inches.   No. 149.

VASE (*P'ing*), of the *K'ang-hsi* period, of graceful form and fine technique, artistically decorated with conventional floral designs, painted in red and gold with touches of pale green. The body is studded with five large blossoms of the idealized flowers known as *pao hsiang hua*, "flowers of paradise," connected by delicate wavy foliations. A gadroon border with beaded foliations surrounds the base, the shoulder is encircled by a band of brocaded pattern, and the rim of the mouth by a similar band, running round under the lip, which shows signs of gilding. A series of scrolled palmations springs up from the base of the neck, and it is ornamented above with strings of beads hung with tassels suspended from a ring of scroll fret. Height, 17 inches.   No. 150.

WATER-POT (*Shui Ch'êng*), for the writer's table, molded in the shape of a white univalve shell, and lightly tinted with pink and yellow enamels at the edges; the three feet are tiny shells, and a lizardlike dragon (*ch'ih-lung*) is coiled upon the top of the shell, executed in full undercut relief. Height, 2 inches.   No. 151.

VASE (*P'ing*), one of a pair of tall bottle-shaped vases, with a monochrome ground of pale-green celadon tint, decorated in "slip" with flowers and birds in relief. The floral decoration is composed of blossoming prunus-trees, bamboos, chrysanthemums, and lotus-plants, naturalistically modeled, so that most of the flowers stand out in white relief, but some of the leaves and other details, and the birds which are perched upon the branches, are penciled in underglaze cobalt-blue. The pedestal, flowing open handles, and other mounts are in European bronze work of ornate style. Height, with mounts, 2 feet 6 inches.   No. 152.

TEA-JAR (*Ch'a Kuan*), a typical specimen both in style and coloring of blue and white porcelain of the *Ming* dynasty. It is painted in brilliant blue, with the eight Taoist immortals (*Pa Hsien*) crossing the sea in procession, holding up in their hands their peculiar attributes. The scrolled waves lift up crested tops in the intervals, and the clouds dip down in formal scrolls from above to form a kind of canopy for each figure. The borders are decorated with encircling bands of conventional scrolls. The mark, penciled under the foot in blue, inclosed within a double ring, is *Ta Ming Wan-li nien chih*, "Made in the reign of Wan-li (1573–1619) of the Great Ming [dynasty]." Height, 6 inches.   No. 153.

VASE (*P'ing*), bottle-shaped, with a projecting rim at the top, and a globular body, from the upper part of which proceeds a short, solid mouthpiece. It is decorated with floral sprays of peony, lotus, jasmine, and aster, enameled in bright colors, surrounded by scrolls of green leaves, and relieved by an intensely black ground. A band of white, lightly penciled in red with a triangular fret, separates the neck from the body. The upper rim is mounted with metal, and the mouthpiece is fitted with a nozzle of Oriental workmanship. It was evidently decorated in China for the Mohammedan market, and has been subsequently mounted, perhaps in Persia, as part of a *narghili*. Height, 10½ inches.   No. 154.

DOUBLE-FISH VASE (*Shuang Yü P'ing*), one of a pair, with details molded in slight relief under a celadon monochrome glaze of typical sea-green tint. Mounted in ormolu of European work. Height, 6 inches.   No. 155.

TALL CLUB-SHAPED VASE (*Ta Pang-chih P'ing*), elaborately decorated in enamel colors with a few touches of gilding in the style of the *K'ang-hsi* "famille verte." The body is decorated with a battle scene. The heroine of the fight is on horseback in front, clad in mailed costume, brandishing a sword in one hand, a spear in the other, and having a small babe wrapped in her girdle, out of whose head proceeds a thin red line which unfolds above into clouds displaying the gilded form of a dragon. An umbrella-shaped tent with imperial insignia in front is pitched on the hillside, in the direction in which the commander-in-chief is riding, surrounded by his staff carrying flags and banners. The neck of the vase is decorated with a picture of the "five ancients" (*wu lao*), the divinities of the five planets, examining a scroll with the *yin-yang* dual symbol inscribed upon it, the surroundings being of Taoist character, with pines and storks, spotted deer, and rocks covered with sacred fungus. The shoulder slope is filled with a broad band of lotus scrolls traversed by dragons, interrupted by medallions containing lions sporting with brocaded balls. A brocaded band of plum-blossom succeeds, and encircling rings of triangular fret and of gadroon pattern complete the decoration. Height, 30½ inches.   No. 156.

VASE (*P'ing*), bottle-shaped, with a swelling globular body and two projecting rings on the neck, dating from the *K'ang-hsi* period. It is enameled with a dark-brown coffee-colored monochrome ground, interrupted by four circular medallions painted in dark underglaze blue with flowers, and by a ring round the shoulder with alternate lozenges and circles displayed upon the white ground. The mark under the foot is a palm-leaf penciled in blue. It is mounted with a chased bronze cover of Persian work. Height, with cover, 8½ inches.   No. 157.

THREEFOLD GOURD VASE (*San Hu-lu P'ing*), with a vertically grooved body simulating three coalescent gourds with the necks distinct, so as to form three orifices for the vase. It is one of a pair enameled with a finely crackled turquoise glaze of unusually deep tones, becoming almost black in the depths of the grooves and near the foot, which is unglazed at the base. They have been mounted in Europe with three-footed stands, tasseled cords tied round the waists, and covers inlaid with three disks of crackled turquoise porcelain, hung round with festoons and tassels and surmounted by circular garlands of flowers. Height, without mounts, 8 inches.   No. 158.

CELADON VASE (*Lung-ch'üan P'ing*), of the *Ming* period, of whitish paste coated with a rich unctuous-looking glaze of pale greenish tone. The decoration, which is worked in relief in the paste under the glaze, is in three horizontal bands defined by prominent rings. The lower band is vertically ribbed. The middle band has waving scrolls of chrysanthemums under a ring of diamond pattern fret. The upper band contains interlacing sprays of the mountain peony. A spot of iridescent purple black is to be noticed on the shoulder, shaded with red clouds, starting from a slight pit in the glaze, and indicating the presence of iron in the materials. The base is enameled underneath with the same celadon glaze. Height, 17 inches.   No. 159.

TRIPOD CENSER (*Ting Lu*), with short cylindrical feet, and two spreading loop-handles of rope pattern, coated with a *Lang Yao* glaze of the *K'ang-hsi* period. The glaze, of the usual crackled texture, displays the characteristic *sang-de-bœuf* coloring in streaky mottled tones, passing in some parts of the surface into pale apple-green, while the rims and more prominent parts are nearly white. The stand and cover are of rosewood, carved in China in a string-net pattern, and mounted with a steatite knob. Height, 4¼ inches; breadth, 5 inches.   No. 160.

VASE (*P'ing*), bottle-shaped, one of a pair, with wide-spreading necks, enameled with a monochrome coral-red glaze, penciled over with two floral scrolls in gold of arabesque-like design on the bodies and with light floral borders round the edges. They have been mounted in Persia with copper rims and covers, minutely chased all over with figures, hunting-scenes, ornamental bands, and panels containing birds and flowers. Height, 7½ inches. No. 161.

QUADRANGULAR VASE (*Fang P'ing*), of oblong section, with rounded indented corners, molded with two handles fashioned as lions' heads suspending rings. There is a floral decoration on the front and back, incised in the paste, and inlaid with green and white enamels, the surrounding ground being a purplish brown of brilliant iridescent tints. The decoration consists of flowers growing from rocks, a blossoming prunus with a twig of bamboo, on one side, chrysanthemums and grass, with a pair of butterflies flying, on the other. The mark, incised in the paste under the glaze in archaic script, is *Chêng-tê nien chih*—i. e., "Made in the period Chêng-tê (1506–21)." It seems really, however, to be a reproduction of the time of *Ch'ien-lung*. Height, 7½ inches. No. 162.

VASE (*P'ing*), of depressed ovoid form, with a short narrow neck widening into a flaring mouth with coarsely serrated rim. A five-clawed imperial dragon envelops the vase within its coils as it pursues the magic jewel, which is represented on one side as a disk emitting branching rays of effulgence, the intervals being filled in with the scrolled clouds in which the dragon is disporting. The details are modeled in relief in the paste, and finished with the graving-tool. The investing glaze is a minutely crackled turquoise-blue of the *Ch'ien-lung* period, clouded with characteristic mottling of greenish tone, and becoming darker where it thickens. Round the foot, where it has "run" into a thick mass, it becomes deep crimson, affording a striking example of the manifold transformations of the protean copper silicates under varied degrees of oxidation. Height, 10½ inches. No. 163.

CYLINDRICAL VASE (*Hua T'ung*), of the *Wan-li* period, decorated upon a white ground with enamel colors—red, green, yellow of brownish tone, and manganese-purple—without underglaze blue. The rim of the mouth is colored light brown; the shoulder and base of the vase are encircled by bands of spiral fret penciled in red. The body is decorated with trees growing from behind an open rockery, lit up by the yellow-brown disk of the sun, and filled in with a background of red trellis-work. A peach-tree is conspicuous with scarlet blossoms, and a clump of bamboo, with graceful green foliage; orchids and other flowers are blossoming at the foot, and a pair of birds is flying across above. The neck is covered with a diaper of foliated pattern, brocaded with branches of fruit and sprays of flowers. The base is unglazed, with the exception of a spot of white in the center. Height, 15 inches. No. 164.

FIGURE OF A CAT (*Mao Hsiang*), naturally modeled in a grayish paste of light porous fabric, and enameled with a crackled gray glaze splashed with transmutation colors of bronzelike tones passing into olive-brown, to imitate tortoise-shell. Height, 7½ inches. No. 165.

SMALL WINE-POT (*Chiu Hu*), of rustic form, molded in the shape of a lotus capsule with striated sides and the seeds projecting all round at the top, and mounted upon three spiral feet; the flowing handle is a roughly tuberculated stalk, and the curved spout another, while a small folded leaf projects on either side as a decoration. The enamel colors, applied *sur biscuit*, are green and yellow. Height, 3 inches. No. 166.

CYLINDRICAL VASE (*Hua T'ung*), decorated in colors of the *Wan-li* period, with floral arabesques, painted partly in underglaze blue, partly in emerald-green and vermilion enamels. The groundwork is a bold design of leaf scrolls studded with large blossoms like those of the wild rose, executed in blue, which is brocaded with small green leaves and filled in with a diaper pattern penciled in red. The light bands of scroll which encircle the rims are out-

lined in red upon a white ground. The bottom is unglazed, only marked by concentric lines of the wheel. The vase is mounted with a collar and lid of copper, which is elaborately chased with bands containing figures of men, four-footed animals, and birds, and with floral and foliated designs of Persian work. Height, 13½ inches. No. 167.

CYLINDRICAL EWER (*T'ung Hu*), modeled in the form of a jointed tube of bamboo with a tiaralike projection at the top. The handle is a one-horned dragon with bowed back and bifid curling tail, and it is colored red with gilded details; the spout springs from a lion's head, and the cover is surmounted by the figure of a unicorn. The surface is covered with sprays of flowers and butterflies of naturalistic design painted in enamels of the *Ch'ien-lung* period. The flowers include separate sprays of the tree-peony, rose, hydrangea, lotus, peach-blossom, magnolia, chrysanthemum, lily, hibiscus, convolvulus, aster, orchid, and nandina berries. Height, 14½ inches. No. 168.

CLUB-SHAPED VASE (*Pang-chih P'ing*), of the *K'ang-hsi* period, decorated in blue and white with panels of varied form, inclosed in a *soufflé* ground of brilliant powder-blue. There are six panels on the body, of which the two below—square, with indented corners—are painted with landscapes; the two fan-shaped panels above contain peonies and chrysanthemums growing from rocks. and the other two—of rounded foliated outline—are filled with vases of flowers and peacock's feathers; censers, and the paraphernalia of the scholar. There are two panels in the neck, shaped like leaves of the *Ficus religiosa*, one of which has a kingfisher inside perched upon a peony-branch; the other, incense-burning apparatus and a folding fan. The mark under the foot is a double ring penciled in blue. Height, 18 inches. No. 169.

VASE (*Hua P'ing*), of the *Ch'ien-lung* period, fashioned on an archaic bronze model, with decorations executed in relief and engraved in the paste, invested with a finely crackled turquoise glaze, which varies in tone according to the depth, so as to enhance the effect of the decoration underneath. This decoration consists of a broad band of peony scrolls round the body and a ring of upright palmations on the neck, completed by encircling bands of ornamental scroll and fret designs of varied pattern. The foot, only partially glazed, shows a grayish-buff *pâte* in the intervals. Height, 13½ inches. No. 170.

VASE (*P'ing*), of the *K'ang-hsi* period, very brilliantly decorated in enamel colors, with rich borders of scroll and fret, floral brocade and conventional foliations. The two large panels on the body contain a grotesque lion sporting with a brocaded ball tied with waving fillets, and a unicorn (*ch'i-lin*) of orthodox traditional form with flames proceeding from its body; the panels are separated by vertical bands containing lozenge-shaped symbols of success (*fangshêng*). The vase, slightly cut down, has been fitted with European bronze mounts. Height, 8½ inches. No. 171.

VASE (*P'ing*), of the *Fên Ting*, or "soft paste" class, painted in soft-toned blue in characteristic style with fine and clearly defined strokes, under a soft-looking ivory-white glaze of crackled texture and undulatory surface. It is decorated with nine grotesque lions: five grouped on the body of the vase, and four on the neck, supported on banks of scrolled clouds and enveloped in flames, disporting with brocaded balls tied with waving fillets. The receding slope of the shoulder is encircled by a band of cloud scrolls, traversed by five flying bats, symbols of the five happinesses, and the foot has plum-blossoms, the floral emblem of long life, scattered over a reticulated ground of mottled blue. The foot is crackled underneath; no mark. Height, 8¾ inches. No. 172.

GROTESQUE UNICORN MONSTER (*Tu Chüeh Shou*), molded in porcelain of the *Ming* period, with a lionlike body, having a horn, shaped like the horn of a rhinoceros, curving up from the middle of the forehead. The body, etched with a graving-tool, is coated with a snow-white crackled glaze; the ears, beard, and flowing tail are overlaid with bright blue; the mane and spiral coils of hair are touched with dark green. The interior, which is hollow, is partially lined with crackled glaze, showing a grayish paste in the intervals. Length, 6 inches.   No. 173.

SMALL VASE (*Hua P'ing*), of turquoise crackle of the *Ming* dynasty. It is molded of archaic design, with a ribbed body vertically grooved and a mouth with an eight-fold foliated rim. Round the body and neck of the vase are coiled the forms of two three-clawed lizardlike dragons, modeled in complete undercut relief, in pursuit of the jewel-ball, which is attached in front midway between the heads of the monsters. The *truité* glaze changes from its pure turquoise tint to olive-gray in the thinner parts, and deepens into purple where it collects in thick drops. The foot is unglazed, showing a yellowish-gray *pâte*. Height, 5 ½ inches.   No. 174.

BEAKER-SHAPED VASE (*Hua Ku*), of crackled celadon, dating from early in the *Ming* dynasty, if not older. The flaring mouth has a rim alternately projected and indented as if formed of eight foliations, and the vase is marked with slight vertical ribs starting from the points of the foliations. The prominent band around the middle of the vase is etched with triangular lines and clouds showing indistinctly under the thick glaze. The glaze, which spreads over half of the interior of the vase, and also covers the base, is a celadon of green tint and lustrous aspect, crackled with a network of dark-brown lines, although inside and under the foot the reticulated lines are colorless. The foot-rim shows a *pâte* of reddish-yellow color. Height, 11 inches.   No. 175.

PILGRIM BOTTLE (*Pei-hu P'ing*), of the rounded form and oval section known also as *Pao-yueh P'ing*, from its resemblance to that of the full moon. Decorated in blue and maroon under the white glaze, with five-clawed imperial dragons rising from the sea into the clouds in pursuit of the wish-granting jewel, which is depicted in the middle of the vase as an effulgent disk. There is a seal under the foot, penciled in the same underglaze cobalt-blue, with the inscription *Ta Ch'ing Ch'ien-lung nien chih*, "Made in the reign of Ch'ien-lung (1736–95) of the Great Ch'ing [dynasty]." Height, 12 ¾ inches.   No. 176.

VASE (*P'ing*), of the coarser Ting-chou ware of the *Ming* period known as *T'u Ting*. The decorative designs are either molded in relief or etched at the point in the grayish-white paste, which is coated with an ivory-white crackled glaze, become greenish in tone where it thickens. The neck swells above into a bulbous enlargement, which is grooved like a bulb of garlic. A dragon of archaic design is coiled round in salient relief, pursuing a jewel among clouds. The bulging body is engraved with floral scrolls, a band of gadroon pattern runs round below and a band of spiral fret above, succeeded by a chain of rectangular fret etched round the shoulder. The foot is coated with the same soft-looking crackled glaze. The foot-rim shows a hard fabric, which can not be scratched by a steel point. Height, 13 ½ inches.   No. 177.

JAR (*Kuan*), one of a pair, with bell-shaped covers, richly decorated in blue and white of the *K'ang-hsi* period, and mounted in European work of the eighteenth century in the same style as the vase in Fig. 114. It is decorated with clumps of lotus intermingled with reeds, alternating with hanging branches of peonies and sprays of asters. Foliations of brocaded design spread upward and downward from the borders, which are encircled also with floral bands. The cover is painted with sprays of peony at the top, succeeded by a conventional floral border. The mark under the foot is a diamond-shaped symbol (*fang-shêng*), tied with a fillet, inclosed in a double ring. Height, 17 inches.   No. 178.

FIVE SNUFF-BOTTLES, of the reigns of *Yung-chêng* and *Ch'ien-lung*.   No. 179.

SMALL VASE (*Hsiao P'ing*), of white *Fên Ting* porcelain, fashioned after an antique model, with a flaring bell-shaped

mouth. The rims are lightly etched with scroll borders, and the vase is encircled with three foliated bands worked in slight relief in the paste. The glaze, of characteristically soft ivory-white tone, is not crackled, but has the undulatory pitted texture known as *chü-p'i wên*, or "orange-peel marking." Height, 5 ½ inches.   No. 180.

VASE (*P'ing*), of bulbous form, with vertical grooves, so as to be of six-lobed section, invested with a mottled *flambé* glaze of dark brownish-crimson tint, flecked with lighter spots at the edges. The interior is coated with a grayish, superficially crackled glaze, which also appears on the lip and more prominent points of the surface. The foot is enameled with a greenish, uncrackled glaze, and has no mark inscribed. Height, 13 inches.   No. 181.

BEAKER-SHAPED VASE (*Hua Ku*), of the *K'ang-hsi* period, painted in colors—greens of diverse tone, brownish-yellow, vermilion, and shaded purples, relieved by a black enameled ground. It is decorated in two divisions. The lower half is covered with blossoming prunus-trees with white flowers and buds, and a bird perched on one of the branches, filled in with colored sprays of asters and grass and bunches of peaches and persimmons. The upper half has peach-trees with red and purplish flowers and peony shrubs with large shaded vermilion blossoms, mingled with the prunus, a Reeves' pheasant in the foreground on a rock, and other birds flying among the trees. The foot is enameled white, with no mark attached. Height, 18 inches.   No. 182.

LARGE VASE (*Ta P'ing*), of the *Ch'ien-lung* period, enameled with a monochrome glaze of greenish celadon tint, deepening in tone as it thickens in the recesses of the decoration, which is worked in relief in the paste underneath. This consists of a pair of five-clawed imperial dragons, one just emerging from the scrolled waves, which surround the base of the vase, the other enveloping the body and neck within its scaly coils. Flames issue from the bodies of the monsters, the intervals are filled in with scrolled masses of clouds, and the jewel which they are pursuing is represented on one side as a disk emitting threefold branching rays of effulgence. The base, unglazed, shows a comparatively coarse, yellowish paste. Height, 21 ¼ inches.   No. 183.

JAR (*Kuan*), painted in blue and white, of the *K'ang-hsi* period, with a band of Amazons riding down a mountain valley toward a military encampment, the tents of which are seen over the hills in the distance. They have long pheasant-feathers stuck in their fur caps, and are carrying flags and banners, with spears slung on their backs; one has a drawn sword in each hand. The mark under the foot is a palm-leaf encircled by a wide double ring. Height, 9 inches.   No. 184.

GOURD-SHAPED VASE (*Hu-lu P'ing*), one of a pair, intricately fashioned with carved openwork casings and movable appendages, and richly decorated in delicate enamel colors and gilding of the *Ch'ien-lung* period. Through the open trellis bands, inclosing foliated panels with *svastika* symbols, glimpses are caught of a solid cylindrical core painted with bats flying among clouds. The waists are belted with movable rings, with two projecting scrolled handles, by which the rings can be made to revolve. The foot is enameled red underneath, with the seal, penciled in gold, inscribed *Ta Ch'ing Ch'ien-lung nien chih*, "Made in the reign of Ch'ien-lung of the Great Ch'ing [dynasty]." Height, 16 ½ inches.   No. 185.

SMALL TEAPOT (*Ch'a Hu*), carved in openwork designs, and richly decorated in enamel colors and gilding of *Yung-chêng* or early *Ch'ien-lung* date. The globular body, which represents a brocaded ball, is studded with four floral bosses with gilded, pierced centers, and has the intervals filled in with brocaded designs relieved by an enameled black ground. Two grotesque lions, colored pink (*rose d'or*), are crouching upon the ball, of which one forms the handle, while the other has a tube projecting from its back as the spout. The cover is crowned by a floral knob set in the middle of a gilded openwork boss, encircled by the same delicate floral scrolls as decorate the rim of the tea-pot. Height, 4½ inches. No. 186.

VASE (*P'ing*), of *K'ang hsi* blue and white. The long, graceful neck is decorated with floral scrolls, conventional bands of ornament, and palmated foliations. The body displays a pair of hexagonal vases with arrows inside, as well as in the tubular handles, which are mounted on tripod tables, alternating with two pairs of lamps, each pair being suspended side by side with cords hung with tassels. The mark under the foot is a flower sprig. Height, 10½ inches. No. 187.

WATER RECEPTACLE (*T'ai-po Tsun*), so called because it is modeled in the shape of the wine-jar (*tsun*) of the famous poet Li T'ai-po, enameled outside with a mottled " peach-bloom " glaze of reddish tone, variegated on one side with a cloud of apple-green. There is an etched decoration in the paste under the glaze in the form of three medallions of archaic dragon scrolls. The mark, written underneath in blue in large characters, is *Ta Ch'ing K'ang-hsi nien chih*, " Made in the reign of K'ang-hsi of the Great Ch'ing [dynasty]." Diameter, 5½ inches. Bronze mount and stand. No. 188.

VASE (*Hua Tsun*), of the *Ch'ien-lung* period, modeled in the form of a bronze sacrificial wine-vessel, with the handles fashioned as elephants' heads, and the sides worked in relief and etched under the finely crackled turquoise glaze, which is of the usual mottled tone. The body is encircled by a broad band filled with lizardlike dragons holding scrolls of sacred fungus (*ling-chih*) in their mouths, the neck with a ring of conventional palmations, and the foot by a continuous chain in double outline of rectangular fret. The foot, partially glazed, shows a white *pâte* of fine texture. Height, 9 inches. No. 189.

GOURD-SHAPED VASE (*Hu-lu P'ing*), of pale-colored *Lang Yao* of the *K'ang-hsi* period. The glaze, which is slightly crackled in parts, is of liver tint, thickly flecked with light spots, and it is of minutely pitted texture. The vase is enameled so as to leave a well-defined white rim round the mouth and at the base; the foot is coated with a pure white glaze underneath, with no mark inscribed. Height, 16 inches. No. 190.

VASE (*P'ing*), of grayish crackle, executed in the style of the ancient *Ko Yao*. The glaze, which runs in thick unctuous masses, is a gray celadon, traversed by a network of reddish-brown lines connected by more superficial color-less lines. It is stained brown, as if accidentally, under the handles and ornamental rings. The two handles are fash-ioned in the form of lions' heads, surrounded by fringes of curled mane, and are perforated for rings. They are col-ored iron-gray, like the three encircling bands of fret which are worked round the vase. The interior of the vase is created with the same gray crackle; the foot, un-glazed, is stained a reddish brown. Height, 15 inches. No. 191.

VASE (*P'ing*), of later *Ch'ien-lung* date, enameled with a finely crackled yellow monochrome ground of clouded tone. The decoration, which is molded in relief in the paste and finished by engraving, consists of a group of three lions sporting with a brocaded ball tied with waving fillets, and a single bat flying across the neck of the vase above; the enamel colors used comprise a bright green and purple, with a sparing addition of white. The base is coated with the same *truité* yellow enamel, with no mark inscribed. The fabric is peculiarly thin and light. Height, 12 inches. No. 192.

STATUETTE (*Hsiang*), of a mandarin of high rank, richly enameled in brilliant colors of the *K'ang-hsi* period, with smiling features of Chinese type, and flowing mustaches, painted black in openwork relief. The official robes with wide hanging sleeve are brocaded with four-clawed drag-ons on a pale-purple ground, and display the square insig-nia of the highest rank embroidered with storks behind as well as in front. The girdle is set in ancient style, with oblong and circular plaques, which are executed in relief

and colored " old gold," of tint different from the ordinary yellow derived from antimony, which is used on the bro-cade designs. The hat and the baton of rank, once held in the hands, are both lost. Height, 17½ inches. No. 193.

DELICATE AND GRACEFUL VASE (*P'ing*), of the best *K'ang-hsi* period; *pâte sur pâte* modeling of *ch'i-lin* amid surges in fine white beneath a beautiful translucent glaze, set off with *ch'i-lin* in a strong peach-bloom tint. Height, with mounts, 9 inches. No. 194.

BALUSTER VASE (*Mei P'ing*), finely decorated in bright enamel colors of the best *K'ang-hsi* period, with two promi-nent handles pierced for rings fashioned in the form of grotesque lions' heads, and reserved in pure white " bis-cuit." It is decorated in horizontal bands separated by chains of rectangular and spiral fret penciled on purple grounds. The broad band round the middle has a pair of archaic dragons (*ch'ih-lung*) in the midst of graceful scrolls of lotus, relieved by an enameled black ground. A band of peony scrolls spreads round the foot displayed upon the same black ground, and sprays of peony wind round the shoulder of the vase with a bright-green background etched with a spiral pattern. A ring of palmations encir-cles the neck, filled in with black. The foot is enameled white underneath, with no mark inscribed. Height, 11¼ inches. No. 195.

LANG YAO VASE (*Lang Yao P'ing*). A small bottle-shaped vase with bulging body, displaying the same rich *sang-de-bœuf* coloring as the large vase which is illustrated in Plate LIX. The foot is coated underneath with a crackled apple-green glaze mottled with tints of olive. Height, 9 inches. No. 196.

VASE (*Hua P'ing*), decorated in brilliant enamel colors of the *K'ang-hsi* period. Formal rings of conventional palm-leaves spread upward and downward to ornament the neck and foot with scrolled foliations, of which four on the neck display the dual *yin-yang* symbol with black and gilded red segments. The body of the vase is covered above with lambrequins of floral brocade, exhibiting, in regular rotation, sprays of the emblematic flowers of the four seasons—the peony of spring, the lotus of summer, the chrysanthemum of autumn, and the prunus of winter—grouped with other flowers. The rest of the surface un-derneath is decorated with butterflies and with scattered sprays of peony and plum-blossom. The foot, enameled white, has no mark. Height, 16¾ inches. No. 197.

BOX FOR SEAL VERMILION (*Yin Sê Ho*), of circular shape, composed of two equal parts, of which one is the cover. It is coated with a typical " peach-bloom " glaze, having a light pinkish-red ground mottled with clouds of darker red, and passing into apple-green toward the mid-dle. The mark, written in blue in orthodox style, is *Ta Ch'ing K'ang-hsi nien chih*, " Made in the reign of K'ang-hsi of the Great Ch'ing [dynasty]." Diameter, 2¾ inches. No. 198.

GROUP OF SNUFF-BOTTLES, of the *K'ang-hsi* period. No. 199.

VASE, of the *K'ang-hsi* period; imperial yellow glaze. Height, 11½ inches. No. 200.

SMALL PILGRIM BOTTLE (*Pei Hu P'ing*), of the *K'ang-hsi* period, invested with a copper-red glaze of the " peach-bloom " type and coloring. It has two open flowing handles of wavy outline, and a dragon of archaic form (*ch'ih-lung*) is worked in bold relief in a medallionlike coil upon the shoulder both in front and behind. The rims are lightly mounted in metal. There is no mark under the foot. Height, 8 inches. No. 201.

VASE (*Hua P'ing*), of the " peach-bloom " class with foliated base, the neck of which has been cut, but mounted with gold and silver in Japan in the lines of the original form. This is a companion piece to the vase which was illustrated in Plate LII, and the description will be found accompanying that plate. No. 202.

DOUBLE-FISH VASE (*Shuang Yü P'ing*), modeled in the form of a pair of fish rising from waves, with their bodies blending into one, and their gaping mouths coalescing to make a single oval rim. They are enameled in soft coral-reds of graduated tone, over details etched in the paste; the waves at the foot are colored blue and green, and the eyes of the fish are touched with points of black enamel. Height, 7 1/2 inches.   No. 203.

VASE (*Hua P'ing*), of flattened ovoid form, with an oval mouth of four-lobed outline, the indentations of which are continued down the vase as far as the rim of the foot. It is coated with a lustrous glaze of crackled texture, which is of a pale-green celadon tone, thickly flecked with clouds of dull cherry-red; become more intense in the grooved parts, where the glaze is deepest. The inside of the mouth and the base of the vase are lined with a gray-green enamel of similar shade, flecked with red, but not crackled. It is a specimen of crackled apple-green (*p'ing-kuo ch'ing*) of the *K'ang-hsi* period. Height, 7 3/4 inches.   No. 204.

LANG YAO VASE (*P'ing*), of form similar to the one illustrated in Plate LIX, showing the way in which the color is apt to "run," so as to be partially obliterated in the furnace. The upper half of the vase is a pale gray-green crackle with brown reticulations, only slightly tinged with pink, while the lower half displays all the rich *sang-de-bœuf* tones of color, shot with a dark speckled mottling. The two parts are separated by an irregularly undulating line, evidently of fortuitous origin. The base is coated with a typical apple-green crackled glaze slightly clouded over with olive tints. Height, 18 inches.   No. 205.

VASE (*P'ing*), of the *K'ang-hsi* period, of graceful form, coated with the mottled cobalt glaze known as "powder-blue" or "mazarin-blue," and decorated over the blue glaze of the *grand feu* with sprays of large-blossomed chrysanthemum and bamboo painted in gold and fixed in the muffle. An inscription in ten characters, penciled in gold on the back of the vase, now half obliterated, is a stanza taken from an ode on the chrysanthemum. Height, 10 inches.   No. 206.

VASE (*P'ing*), of the *K'ang-hsi* period, of rare type and magnificent coloring, having the decoration executed in cobalt-blue and copper-red of the *grand feu*, enhanced by a *sang-de-bœuf* background of the type of the *Lang Yao* monochrome vases of the time. The crackled ground exhibits the usual brilliantly mottled tones, passing from paler ruby shades into the deepest crimson. There is a floral decoration worked in relief in the paste, the shoulder is defined by a prominent ring, and the neck, which has, by the way, been cut at the top, is horizontally ribbed. On the front of the vase a lotus plant is modeled, growing naturally in water represented by crested waves; the large folded leaves, lifted upon rough tuberculated stalks, are painted in blue; the flowers and buds are shaded in wavy lines of red within blue outlines; a couple of swallows painted in blue complete the scene, one flying, the other perched upon a leaf-stalk. The foot is enameled white, with a tinge of green. No mark. Height, 14 1/2 inches.   No. 207.

CLUB-SHAPED VASE (*Pang-chih P'ing*), painted in brilliant colors with gilding of the *K'ang-hsi* period. The panels of diverse form which decorate the vase are of powder-blue *soufflé* ground, outlined and painted in gold. The panels on the neck display a mountain landscape and sprays of plum-blossom. The larger panels on the body contain a picture of a temple in the sea representing the Taoist paradise, with a stork flying near, bringing a "rod of Fate" in its beak; a mountain scene with fishing-boats; a pair of fighting-cocks; and a pine scene with a couple of deer; the smaller panels show a flock of geese, an aquatic monster, and four sprays of flowers. The intervening ground is painted with chrysanthemum scrolls traversed by dragons (*ch'ih-lung*); the neck, with butterflies and flowers on a pale-green background dotted with black, with phœnixes in clouds coiled in medallions, and storks penetrating the floral ground. The shoulder has a ring of floral brocade,

interrupted by four foliated medallions, with pictures of fish and fishermen, flowers, and apparatus for chess and incense. Height, 18 inches.   No. 208.

SMALL VASE (*Hua P'ing*), with a one-horned three-clawed dragon modeled upon it in full undercut relief, coiling round the shoulder at the base of the long cylindrical neck. The ground of the vase is a "peach-bloom" glaze of nearly uniform deep tint, except the slightly prominent rim, which is defined by a clear line of white. The dragon is enameled a bright apple-green of uniform shade, contrasting vividly as a complementary color with the red background. The mark, penciled beneath the foot in underglaze blue, is *Ta Ch'ing K'ang-hsi nien chih*, "Made in the reign of K'ang-hsi of the Great Ch'ing [dynasty]." Height, 9 inches.   No. 209.

WINE-CUP (*Chiu Pei*), a little bowl-shaped cup of egg-shell texture, with a gently expanded rim, which is defined by a line of white. The rest of the surface, both inside and outside, is invested with a mottled glaze of the characteristic "peach-bloom" type, flecked with spots of darker, duller red, and variegated with clouds of apple-green tint, the latter being more marked near the base. The mark, penciled under the foot in cobalt-blue, encircled by a single ring, is *Ta Ming Hsüan-tê nien chih*—i. e., "Made in the reign of Hsüan-tê (1426–35) of the Great Ming [dynasty]," but the technique and peculiar style of coloring indicate rather the *Kang-hsi* period (1662–1722). Height, 1 3/4 inch; diameter, 2 3/8 inches.   No. 210.

BALUSTER-SHAPED VASE (*Mei P'ing*), of the *K'ang-hsi* period, enameled with a brilliant crackled glaze of emerald-green passing into olive at the edges, invested with a thick overglaze of peach-bloom red, irregularly mottling the green substratum with clouds of crushed-strawberry color. A lightly etched decoration in the paste underneath the glaze of a border of sea-waves round the foot of the vase, and two dragons mounting among clouds up the sides, is barely visible through the dense and variegated overlying mantle. The middle of the foot, bounded by a broad rim of "biscuit," is marked with concentric lines of grayish-white crackle. Height, 6 3/4 inches.   No. 211.

TRIPLE GOURD-SHAPED VASE (*Hu-lu P'ing*), of the *K'ang-hsi* period, a companion piece to the tall vase which is illustrated in Plate LXI. The middle section is enameled in colors upon a white ground with butterflies in the midst of sprays of flowers and leaves, defined above and below by rings of spiral and rectangular fret penciled in coral-red. The upper and lower sections are enameled with a black iridescent ground of "raven's-wing" hue, over designs executed in relief in the paste underneath; these designs represent on the upper part three lionlike monsters surrounded by flames of fire, on the lower part three lions of the ordinary grotesque type sporting with embroidered balls encircled by waving fillets. Traces of gilding can be detected on this vase. Height, 28 inches.   No. 212.

SET OF FIVE PIECES (*Wu Shê*), arranged as a *Garniture de Cheminée*, composed of three ovoid jars with covers, and two cylindrical beakers. The pieces are enameled with a monochrome ground of coffee-brown shade, leaving white reserves of varied form, scroll pictures, leaf-shaped panels, flowers, lambrequins and bands of floral brocade, and the like, which are decorated in bright enamel colors with gilding. The larger panels are filled with hill landscapes with temples and pagodas; the flowers that fill the brocaded bands and stud the intervals include peonies, asters, and blossoms of the peach and plum. Height, 10 1/2 and 11 inches.   No. 213.

VASE (*Hua P'ing*), of the *K'ang-hsi* period, with the body enameled with a *tzŭ-chin* glaze of light yellowish-brown tint, and the neck decorated in blue and white with a band of diaper inclosing three medallions of flowers, succeeded by a ring of *svastika* pattern fret, and upright sprays of pinks. The mark, underneath the foot, is a double ring penciled in blue. Height, 8 inches.   No. 214.

VASE (*Hua P'ing*), of the *K'ang-hsi* period, of complex form and mixed decoration. The globular body has the lower half enameled with a *tzŭ-chin* (or *bruni*) glaze of *café-au-lait* color, which is succeeded by a ring of grayish-white crackle, and this by a band of floral sprays painted in blue. The upper part, which is shaped like a "beaker," poised upon the globe, is decorated in blue and white with pinks (dianthus) growing from rocks and with sprays of daisies. No mark. Height, 7 inches. No. 215.

BOTTLE-SHAPED VASE (*Hua P'ing*), of the *K'ang-hsi* period, enameled with a brown *tzŭ-chin* glaze of chocolate-color, and decorated over the glaze, in white slip, with two formal baskets of flowers on the body, and a conventional scroll round the upper rim, hung with beaded pendants. The foot is enameled white underneath. Height, 10¼ inches. No. 216.

WINE-POT (*Chiu Hu*), molded in the shape of a peach, with a hole in the bottom for the introduction of the wine. The handle and curved spout are fashioned as small branches, which send off leafy twigs to decorate the surface on which they are worked in relief in the paste. The paste, which is gray in color, is invested with aubergine-purple and turquoise glazes of the *demi-grand feu*, mingling as they meet in brilliant intermediate tints. Height, 5½ inches. No. 217.

MINIATURE FLOWER-VASE (*Hua Ch'a*), of purest white porcelain of the *K'ang-hsi* period, charming in design and perfect in technique. It is molded in the shape of a flowering twig of the *Magnolia yulan*, lifting up a blossom, as white as the finest jade from which the flower takes its name, to form the vase, and buttressed by two buds, which rise from the same twig as it winds round in openwork relief to form the support. The sepals of the flowers are delicately etched under the white glaze, which is rich and translucid. Height, 5 inches. No. 218.

WATER RECEPTACLE (*Shui Ch'êng*), of eggshell, *Fên-Ting*, porcelain, with uncrackled white glaze of soft tone. It has two handles molded in open relief upon the sides of the bowl in the shape of a pair of archaic dragons (*ch'ih-lung*). Height, 2½ inches. No. 219.

VASE (*P'ing*), of *Ting-Yao* porcelain, bottle-shaped, with depressed bulging body and long cylindrical neck. It is coated with a deep ivory-white glaze crackled throughout with brown lines, overspread with light clouds of buff tint partially investing the brown reticulation. The rim of the mouth is defined by a line of white. Height, 8 inches. No. 220.

VASE (*P'ing*), of *Ting-Yao* porcelain of tall, graceful form, tapering gradually downward from the rounded shoulder. The rich glaze is minutely crackled throughout with brown lines of varying depth and color, invested with mottled buff tints clouding the surface. Height, 8¾ inches. No. 221.

VASE (*P'ing*), of delicate *Fên-Ting* fabric of the *K'ang-hsi* period, invested with a soft-looking undulatory glaze of ivory-white tone, traversed by a few sparse lines of crackling. The molded decoration consists of a four-clawed dragon in relief, pursuing a disk with dotted, "jeweled" surface and spiral center, enveloped in flaming rays. Height, 8½ inches. No. 222.

MINIATURE VASE FOR DIVINING-RODS (*Shih-ts'ao P'ing*), of oblong quadrangular form and square section, with ribbed corners, and ridged sides studded with four central bosses which are carved in openwork as branches of peaches. The paste, of *Fên-Ting* texture, is invested with a soft-looking crackled glaze of ivory-white tone. Height, 4 inches. No. 223.

BALUSTER VASE (*Mei P'ing*), of the *Fên-Ting* or "soft paste" class, dating from the reign of *K'ang-hsi*. Of remarkably light weight, owing to the porous texture of the material, which is, in reality, very hard, it is invested with an undulatory glaze, pitted like the peel of an orange, with uncrackled surface, under which the decoration is pen-

ciled in pure soft-toned blue. The strokes of the brush are neatly defined in the way that is characteristic of this material, which differs from ordinary porcelain as vellum does from paper. The chaste decoration consists of three formal upright sprays of lotus, each composed of a single peltate leaf, an expanded blossom and a bud, with simple rings of rectangular fret round the shoulder and foot. Height, 13 inches. No. 224.

SMALL VASE (*P'ing*), of graceful form and finished technique, decorated on each side with a five-clawed imperial dragon enveloped in flames, painted in maroon, the underglaze red of the *grand feu*, which is derived from copper. The mark, penciled underneath, in underglaze cobalt-blue of brilliant tint, is *Ta Ch'ing K'ang-hsi nien chih*, "Made in the reign of K'ang-hsi of the Great Ch'ing [dynasty]." Height, 8½ inches. No. 225.

VASE (*P'ing*), of tall ovoid form, with the decoration molded in relief and painted in colors of the *grand feu*, blue, maroon, and celadon. Four-clawed, two-horned dragons are depicted on the obverse and reverse sides of the vase, rising from the waves of the sea, with brown bodies and blue manes, the jewels which they are pursuing in the air are shaded in brown, emitting spirally effulgent rays; and flames proceeding from the limbs of the monsters fill in the interstices. The rocks that rise out of the blue crested waves are painted in celadon. The mark, penciled underneath in blue, within a double ring, is *Ta Ch'ing K'ang-hsi nien chih*, "Made in the reign of K'ang-hsi of the Great Ch'ing [dynasty]." Height, 17¼ inches. No. 226.

VASE (*P'ing*), decorated in underglaze blue, maroon, and celadon, all colors of the *grand feu*, with a combat between the tiger, king of land animals, and the dragon, prince of the powers of the air. The tiger is standing in the foreground of a rocky landscape, with large pines rising in the background having their knotted trunks painted in brown and the foliage in blue; the rocks are tinted celadon, and the clumps of Polyporus fungus growing on the rocks are outlined in maroon, pierced through by blue blades of grass. The four-clawed dragon, of fierce aspect, is half hidden in scrolled clouds, which roll round the vase, worked on in white "slip" in slight relief. The mark, penciled in blue within a double ring, is *Ta Ch'ing K'ang-hsi nien chih*, "Made in the reign of K'ang-hsi of the Great Ch'ing [dynasty]." Height, 16¾ inches. No. 227.

CLUB-SHAPED VASE (*P'ang-chih P'ing*), of the *K'ang-hsi* period, artistically decorated in brilliant enamels, with a touch or two of gold, without any underglaze blue. It is painted in panels of diverse form, the intervals being filled in with butterflies and floral sprays of lotus, peony, chrysanthemum, begonia, pink, and aster. The panels contain symbols of rank and honor with the apparatus of the liberal arts and other antiques (*po ku*); grotesque monsters on rocks, with eagles flying in the air; storks on a pine, with peaches floating in the water beneath; phœnixes under a dryandra-tree, peacocks with peonies, and warblers in a blossoming prunus-tree. The shoulder of the vase is encircled by a band of diaper with butterflies in medallions, and the neck has quatrefoil panels containing flowers and butterflies, separated by a spiral diaper traversed by lizard-like dragons (*ch'ih-lung*) of archaic design. Height, 17½ inches. No. 228.

VASE (*P'ing*), painted in underglaze red of maroon tint derived from copper, covered with a white glaze of harmonious translucent tone. The decoration consists of five horizontal bands of scrolled sea-waves, containing dragons and other grotesque monsters, and four bands of diaper of lozenge fret pattern. A fifth band of fret winds round the prominent lip of the vase, succeeded by two rings of formal foliations. A double white ring round the body breaks the monotony of the decoration and defines the shape. The mark, written under the foot in underglaze cobalt-blue, is *Ta Ch'ing K'ang-hsi nien chih*, "Made in the reign of K'ang-hsi (1662–1722) of the Great Ch'ing [dynasty]." Height, 10¾ inches. No. 229.

EGGSHELL PLATE (*To-t'ai P'an*), enameled on the back round the border with a crimson (*rouge d'or*) ground, and decorated in front in brilliant enamel colors of the *famille rose*, with gilding. The field is filled with a picture of the Dragon Festival annually celebrated on the fifth day of the fifth moon, with a dragon-boat being towed in procession, painted over the white glaze in sepia. This is framed by encircling bands of floral brocade, and the border of the plate is filled in with diapers of varied pattern inclosing panels of scroll ornament and formal flowers, all richly painted in delicate enamels, among which pink (*rose d'or*) predominates. Diameter, 8 inches.   No. 230.

COVERED BOWL (*Kai Wan*), of the *K'ang-hsi* period, with lions' heads as handles, an archaic dragon surmounting the cover, and Taoist figures molded in relief in the midst of scrolled clouds round the sides. It is an example of the class of *San Ts'ai* or "three colors," being enameled *sur biscuit* in yellow, green, and purple of grayish tone. The foot is unglazed. Diameter, 4 inches.   No. 231.

CYLINDRICAL VASE (*T'ung P'ing*), of the *K'ang-hsi* period, decorated in blue and white in the same style as the vase of similar shape illustrated in Figs. 268 and 35, which are enameled in colors. The decoration consists of horizontal bands, with alternate grounds of white and mottled blue. The central band contains archaic dragons (*ch'ih-lung*), with branches of sacred fungus; the other bands floral scrolls with felicitous symbols and brocaded panels, and the neck is encircled by stiff upright palm-leaves of formal design. Height, 11 inches.   No. 232.

CENSER (*Hsiang Lu*), of circular shape, bulging below, coated with a finely crackled glaze of ivory-white tone invested with cloudy tints of buff. Carved rosewood stand and cover of Chinese work. Height, 4 inches; diameter, 8 inches.   No. 233.

VASE-SHAPED EWER (*Hu P'ing*), with a flowing handle fashioned in the outline of a dragon, a tall overlapping cover, and no spout nor projecting lip. It is decorated in blue of the *K'ang-hsi* period with foliated panels of floral brocade, connected by straps and links, and separated by diapered grounds, and the rims are encircled by light bands of triangular fret. The base is unglazed. Height, 11 inches.   No. 234.

PLATE (*P'an-tzŭ*), of *Ch'ien-lung* porcelain, coated with a celadon glaze of pale greenish tone, enameled over the glaze in opaque white derived from arsenic. In the field is a little garden scene with peonies, cockscombs, asters, and millet, and a cock crowing on a rockery, a favorite decoration of the time. The border is filled with a scroll of conventional flowers executed in the same white enamel. The rim is encircled by a formal border penciled in overglaze blue, and is colored iron-brown at the edge, with traces of gilding; on the inner slope of the border is a band of chrysanthemum scrolls painted in the same cobalt-blue. Diameter, 8¾ inches.   No. 235.

SMALL CENSER (*Hsiang Lu*), mounted upon four mammillated feet, having an overlapping cover pierced in openwork with a trellis framework inclosing two *svastika* symbols. Coated with a thick stone-gray glaze of *Ko Yao* type crackled with brown lines. An ancient piece, with the interior of the cover deeply stained with incense-smoke. Height, 3 inches.   No. 236.

CYLINDRICAL VASES (*P'ing*), a set of three, of the *K'ang-hsi* period, with diapered borders and rim bands of fret penciled in underglaze blue, inclosing panels of varied form, painted with flowers in brilliant enamel colors with gilding. The central vase has two large oblong panels on the body: the first containing a lotus growing with reeds having one large leaf of pale green splatched with black of purple iridescent tint and a smaller leaf tipped with overglaze blue; the other containing a spray of peony; the neck is decorated with a spray of poppies and a begonia with a grasshopper feeding on its leaves. The two side vases have small medallions inclosed in the diapered bor-

ders, displaying dragons and peonies at the top; fish, shells, censers, lions, and lilies down the sides; palm-leaves and musical stones bound with fillets at the bottom; the large panels are painted on one side with blossoming branches of prunus mingled with twigs of bamboo, on the other side with hanging branches of *Hibiscus rosa sinensis;* the necks are decorated with two small sprays of peony. The mounts are in European work of the eighteenth century. No marks underneath. Height, without mounts, 11 inches.   No. 237.

VASE (*P'ing*), one of a pair of small bottle-shaped vases, enameled with a finely crackled turquoise glaze of the *K'ang-hsi* period. They are elaborately mounted in gilded European bronze-work, with foliated covers surmounted by strawberries as knobs, garlands of flowers hanging in festoons round the rims and foliated pedestals. Height, with mounts, 8½ inches.   No. 238.

TALL BEAKER of *K'ang-hsi* porcelain, decorated in the characteristic enamels of the period, showing a court interior, with a dancing-girl, accompanied by an orchestra, performing before the imperial circle. Height, 30 inches.

No. 239.

JAR (*Kuan*), of tall ovoid form, with a rounded cover, artistically decorated in polychrome enamels (*wu ts'ai*) of the finest *K'ang-hsi* period. Lines of underglaze cobalt-blue define the rims, but the decoration is entirely executed in brilliant enamels, among which overglaze cobalt-blue is conspicuous. The jar displays two duplicate pictures of family life, groups of ladies with slender, graceful figures, and children in courtyards filled with flowers and with various emblems of rank and culture. The cover is painted with vases, incense apparatus, propitious symbols, and paraphernalia of the liberal arts. Bands of floral sprays, with rings of formal diaper and foliated pattern, complete the decoration. The mark underneath is a double ring, penciled in underglaze blue. Height, 15 inches.   No. 240.

VASE (*P'ing*) with a pedestal (*tso*), of decorated porcelain of the *famille verte*, dating from the reign of *K'ang-hsi*. Of similar style to those illustrated in Figs. 11 and 30, it is fluted and painted with the same floral designs in green, yellow, and manganese purple, with touches of black. Height, with stand, 8½ inches.   No. 241.

CLUB-SHAPED VASE (*Pang-chih P'ing*), of the *K'ang-hsi* period, covered with a *soufflé* coral-red ground, interrupted by reserved medallions of varied form outlined in gold, and decorated in delicate enamel color. On the body are four panels, two of quatrefoil shape, two in the form of leaves of the sacred fig (*Ficus religiosa*), which are filled with flowers and butterflies; and on the neck three circular panels with butterflies. Round the shoulder is a band of diaper, enameled in green, inclosing medallions containing insects. Height, 11 inches.   No. 242.

CUP WITH COVER (*Kai Wan*), of crackled *Fên-Ting* ware, painted under the glaze in soft shades of cobalt-blue. The texture of the material is light and delicate; the glaze, of soft aspect and ivory-white tone, is traversed with a reticulation of brown lines. The decoration, consisting of pomegranates, spreads over the rims of both cup and cover into the interior. The under surface of the foot and the top of the cover rise in the middle into small pointed cones, in the traditional fashion of the teacups of the reign of *Hsüan-tê* (1426–35), after which this one is modeled.   No. 243.

CLUB-SHAPED VASE (*Pang-chih P'ing*), of the *K'ang-hsi* period, displaying the sacred figures of the Taoist Triad, painted in colors, with a rich gold-brocaded background of Mazarin blue. The gilded designs are scrolls of chrysanthemum, rings of spiral, and rectangular fret, of gadroon pattern, and of diaper with floral medallions, and the neck is studded with four large circular *shou* (longevity) characters. Reserves having been left in the powder-blue ground for the figures, they were first sketched in underglaze blue, and subsequently filled in with enamel colors of the muffle stove, bright green, coral-red, dark purple, and black. Height, 17 inches.   No. 244.

VASE (*P'ing*), with a yellow-brown ground of the *tzŭ-chin* class, inclosing a number of panels raised in slight relief and painted in blue with various symbols. A large *shou* (longevity) character is emblazoned on the front and back, interrupted by an oblong panel containing a fish, erect in the midst of waves, exhaling a slim dragon. The smaller panels on the neck contain peaches with the character *shou* inscribed upon them ; and in the intervals on the body are small oblong panels displaying another form of the same ubiquitous character below, and round panels with Buddhist emblems, the wheel of the law bound with a fillet and a pair of fish above. Height, 9 inches. No. 245.

SMALL VASE (*Hsiao P'ing*), of white porcelain of the *Fên-Ting* type, of light loose material, invested with soft-looking, sparsely crackled glaze of somewhat grayish tone. Of hexagonal outline and section, with a spreading foot, the bulging shoulder is overlaid with two branching twigs of prunus-blossom (*mei hua*), modeled in full relief with openwork. Height, 6¾ inches. No. 246.

" HAWTHORN " BOTTLE (*Mei-hua P'ing*), a large, conspicuous vase of the *K'ang-hsi* period, with a rounded body gradually tapering in to a tall, slender neck, decorated with blossoming sprays of prunus (*mei hua*), displayed in white reserve upon a brilliant background of pulsating mottled blue, penciled with a reticulation of darker lines. The leafless branches spring from the base and wind round in every direction so as to cover the whole surface of the vase with a close floral investment of white flowers and buds, with the exception of a narrow band under the prominent white lip, which is lightly penciled in blue with a triangular fret. The foot is coated white underneath, with no mark. Height, 17 inches. No. 247.

RICE-BOWL (*Fan Wan*) and TEACUP (*Ch'a Wan*), of *K'ang-hsi* blue and white porcelain with pierced openwork designs. The bowl has an outer casing of hexagonal trellis connecting four circular openwork medallions of floral designs. Through the trellis-work are seen four couples of Chinamen with fans, and ladies holding flowers, painted in blue. The interior is decorated with two boys playing in a garden, within a medallion, and a border of *svastika* pattern diaper interrupted by four panels containing peaches. The mark, in a double ring, is *Ta Ming Ch'êng-hua nien chih*, " Made in the reign of Ch'êng-hua of the Great Ming [dynasty]." Diameter, 6¼ inches. The cup is pierced with a band composed of interlacing circles interrupted by six solid medallions painted in blue with landscapes. To be used, it must have a thin lining of silver or other metal. The bottom is left *en biscuit*. Diameter, 4½ inches. No. 248.

TWO SAUCER-SHAPED DISHES (*P'an-tzŭ*) : (*a*) of semi-eggshell texture, enameled inside in brilliant colors with a floral decoration composed of a flowering-bulb of narcissus, a spray of roses, and two branching stems of *Polyporus lucidus*, the variegated fungus of Taoist sacred lore. The mark written underneath, within a double ring, in cobalt-blue, in the style affected by the private potters of the period, is *Ta Ch'ing Yung-chêng nien chih*, " Made in the reign of Yung-chêng of the Great Ch'ing [dynasty]." Diameter, 8¼ inches. (*b*) Of decorated *Ch'ien-lung* porcelain, designed after a well-known imperial pattern of the preceding reign of *Yung-chêng*. Branches of peaches spring from the circular rim which surrounds the foot and pass over the edge of the dish to ornament the interior with large fruit and pink flowers growing on the same twigs. This is the symbolical fruit of life, and is accompanied by the emblems of all kinds of happiness in the shape of five bats, which are painted in shades of red, three in the field of the saucer, two upon its outer border. There is a seal underneath, inscribed in underglaze blue, *Ta Ch'ing Ch'ien-lung nien chih*—i. e., " Made in the reign of Ch'ien-lung of the Great Ch'ing [dynasty]." Diameter, 8¼ inches. No. 249.

SMALL BALUSTER VASE (*Hsiao Mei P'ing*), of the *Yung-chêng* period, invested with a monochrome ground of ruby red tint (*chi hung*), derived from copper. This *soufflé* glaze,

strewn with little points, covers the whole surface with the exception of an irregular panel on one side, where it gradually fades into a nearly white ground. The panel is painted with a picture of the Taoist immortal Tung Fang So, speeding over the clouds, carrying the branch of peaches, which he has stolen from the tree of life in the paradise of the divinity Hsi Wang Mu, thrown across his shoulders. It is etched in sepia with touches of gold and a few points of light overglaze blue and crimson *rouge d'or*. The foot of the vase is enameled with an ornamental scroll, partly obliterated, penciled in black and gold. Height, 8 inches. No. 250.

VASE (*P'ing*), of oval, melon-shaped form and six-lobed outline, coated with a white glaze minutely crackled with a fine reticulation of dark lines, giving a general gray effect. The technique points to the *Yung-chêng* period (1723-35), but there is no mark inscribed. Height, 8¾ inches. No. 251.

VASE (*Hua P'ing*), of white porcelain of the *Yung-chêng* period, with a dragon coiled in undercut relief round the neck enameled crimson (*rouge d'or*). A few single peach-blossoms are painted in delicate colors on the rippled white surface of the vase, of which two, upon the shoulder, are seen in the illustration, two others are near the foot on the opposite side. The mark, which was inscribed underneath, has been ground away on the lathe. Height, 8¼ inches. No. 252.

BALUSTER VASE (*Mei P'ing*),* artistically decorated upon a translucent white ground of perfect tone, in brilliant enamel colors, with fruit and flowers. Branches, springing from the base on one side, spread upward in all directions over the vase, covering it with large pomegranates and peaches and bunches of yellow dragon's-eye fruit (*Nephelium longan*), mingled with sprays of scarlet pomegranate-flowers and pink peach-blossom. The mark, written underneath in underglaze blue within a double ring, is *Ta Ch'ing Yung-chêng nien chih*, " Made in the reign of Yung-chêng (1723-35) of the Great Ch'ing [dynasty]." Height, 13¼ inches. No. 253.

SMALL TEA-JAR (*Ch'a Kuan*), with lotus plants worked in relief round the base and round the top of the cover, painted in enamel colors with gilding. It is decorated with a picture of a two-storied temple, with gilded roof hung with gold bells, standing in the midst of sea-waves ; swallows are flying in the air. The ornamental border above is composed of panels of gilded diaper alternating with wave scrolls penciled in black. Height, 5 inches.

No. 254.

SMALL TEA-JAR (*Ch'a Kuan*), with an openwork scroll round the foot, decorated in enamel colors with gilding. Sprays of the tree-peony are painted on a white ground within two lotus-leaf-shaped panels of convoluted outline, surrounded by a field of floral brocade, composed of blue-leaved bamboo and overglaze white plum-blossom on a spiral black ground. This specimen and that shown in Fig. 254 are examples of the " India china " class, being parts of tea sets painted for exportation to Europe in the first half of the eighteenth century. Height, 5 inches. No. 255.

VASE (*P'ing*), of white *Fên-Ting* porcelain, molded with a whorl of conventional palm-leaves round the shoulder, connected by eight ridges with foliations encircling the bulbous mouth. It is covered with a soft-looking, sparsely crackled glaze of slightly grayish tone. Height, 6½ inches. No. 256.

VASE (*P'ing*), of tall slender form, decorated, in enamel colors of the *Yung-chêng* period, with a picture of the Taoist goddess Hsi Wang Mu crossing the sea upon a

---

* The name *Mei P'ing* means " Plum Vase," this peculiar form being considered to be most appropriate for the display of branches of blossoming prunus (*mei hua*) at the New-Year's festival. The imperial porcelain of the period, of which this piece is a striking example, represents, according to Chinese connoisseurs, in the perfection of its technique and in the artistic style of its decoration, the highest achievement of their ceramic art.

gigantic lotus-petal, holding a branch of the sacred fungus of long life, accompanied by an attendant carrying a peach, with a basket full of flowers and Buddha's-hand citrons, on the frail craft beside her. In the background is a temple standing in the sea, with a peach-tree laden with fruit close by ; a stork is perched upon the roof, and its mate is flying across, carrying scrolls in its beak. The clouds, of roseate hue, are illumined by the vermilion disk of the sun. Height, 18½ inches. No. 257.

SMALL VASE (*Hsiao P'ing*), covered over two thirds of its surface with a pale celadon glaze of clouded hue, and on the other third with an irregular cloud of brilliantly mottled red. Of the deepest *sang-de-bœuf* shade in the middle, the cloud becomes of pinkish tint toward the edges, and then gradually fades away into the celadon ground. It is evidently due to copper silicate soaking through the investing glaze under the solving influence of the furnace. The glaze is flecked throughout with a multitude of tiny bubbles, giving a charming effect, and suggesting the *soufflé* application of the two colors. Height, 4 inches. No. 258.

VASE (*P'ing*), of the *K'ang-hsi* period, with a coral-red *soufflé* ground of charming color. A four-clawed dragon in pursuit of a jewel encircled by flaming rays of effulgence is modeled in slight relief on the surface of the vase etched with the graving-tool, glazed and reserved in brilliant white. The rest of the ground is imbued with coral-red, shot with minute mottled flecks, and shading off gradually into paler tints as it approaches the white relief modeling. A broad rim round the foot underneath is left in white "biscuit," the middle is sunken and enameled white of greenish tone. Height, 8½ inches. No. 259.

VASE (*P'ing*), of the *K'ang-hsi* period, a magnificent specimen of the brilliant *soufflé* glaze known as "powder-blue," the clear blue ground being flecked all over with darker spots. The rims are clearly defined by two lines of white. The foot is invested underneath with a rough brownish-black coating, so as to leave an ovoid patch of the brilliantly white glaze in the middle, and another patch at the edge. Height, 17¾ inches. No. 260.

VASE (*Hua P'ing*), of graceful form, decorated, in green and purple with touches of white, with peonies, chrysanthemums, and daisies, growing from rocks, and with butterflies flying in the intervals of the floral decoration. This is relieved by a minutely crackled ground of pure yellow color. The details of the designs are delicately etched in the paste with a graving-tool. The foot is coated underneath with the same *truité* yellow glaze with no mark attached. Height, 10 inches. No. 261.

TEAPOT (*Ch'a Hu*), of "armorial china" decorated with gilded arabesque borders outlined in red, and with gilded floral sprays on the spout and handle, while three sprays of flowers are painted on the cover in enamel colors. There is an identical armorial design on the front and back painted in enamels with gold of early *Ch'ien-lung* date. It consists of a fanciful coat-of-arms mingled with branches of flowers and having a bouquet in a vase standing upon a pedestal on one side. In the middle are two shields, *accollés*, with a gilded dual coronet above, beneath which is a red bearded face emerging between wings, and as supporters are two yellow eagles touched with red. Height, with cover, 5½ inches. No. 262.

DOUBLE VASE (*Shuang P'ing*), formed, as it were, of two vases coalescing, the line of junction being indicated by a vertical groove. The shape resembles that of the *Ch'ien-lung* vase of the *famille rose* illustrated in Plate LXXVI, and, like that, it is intended to have a cover. It is a typical example of the *Ku Yueh Hsüan* class, decorated in bright, delicate enamel colors, *rouge d'or* predominating, with Chinese copies of European pictures of miniature-like finish, and tiny landscapes of European scenery, inserted in framed panels, surrounded by floral scrolls and ornamental borders of purely Chinese style, executed in the same translucent colors. It once had a seal of four characters penciled underneath in black enamel, but the bottom of

the vase has been broken, and only parts of the last two characters, *nien chih*, remain. The first two were, probably, *Ch'ien-lung*, indicating the date, 1736–95. Height, 5½ inches. No. 263.

VASE (*Hua P'ing*), of European style, molded with a pedestal overlaid with branches of fruit in solid relief, and with a delicate interlacement of wild-roses and other flowers filling in the hollows of the flowing bandlike handles. The faces of the vase are decorated in gold with scrolls of sea-waves below, and phœnixes with expanded wings and spreading tails above, and on the outer surface of the handles are centiped-like dragons with winged insect heads of very un-Chinese aspect. The gilded decoration is completed by a few light floral scrolls, and the edges of the handles, as well as the square rim of the mouth, are heavily gilded. Height, 11¾ inches. No. 264.

SMALL VASE (*Hsiao P'ing*), of white uncrackled *Fên-Ting* porcelain, with a globular body, spreading foot, and swelling lip, and wide loop handles springing from the mouths of dragons. The body is delicately etched at the point in the paste, under the soft-looking ivory-white glaze, with the figures of two imperial five-clawed dragons disporting in clouds. Height, 6½ inches. No. 265.

WATER RECEPTACLE (*Shui Ch'êng*), in the shape of a small globular bowl-like vase of perfect technique, with a small circularly rimmed mouth, which is mounted with a silver ring. It is soberly decorated with two small sprays of peony rising from the base, penciled in underglaze red of maroon tint, the leaves of which, outlined and veined in the same red, are touched with bright-green enamel. The mark written underneath in blue, in the style of the "peach-bloom" vases, is *Ta Ch'ing K'ang-hsi nien chih*, "Made in the reign of K'ang-hsi of the Great C'hing [dynasty]." Height, 3½ inches. No. 266.

VASE (*P'ing*), of charming design and finished technique, enameled with a pellucid white glaze over a relief decoration delicately molded and etched in the paste underneath. Of quatrefoil section, the body of the vase is covered, in four large panels, with symmetrically arranged scrolls of idealistic flowers and bats; ornamental scrolls of conventional design encircle the upper and lower borders of the body and the rim of the mouth, continuous chains of rectangular fret run down the shoulder and foot, and a band of palmations extends midway up the neck. There is a seal etched in the paste under the foot inscribed *Ta Ch'ing Ch'ien-lung nien chih*, "Made in the reign of Ch'ien-lung of the Great Ch'ing [dynasty]." Height, 10 inches. No. 267.

CYLINDRICAL VASE (*T'ung P'ing*), of the *K'ang-hsi* period, richly decorated in brilliant enamel colors, one of a pair mounted in European work to form a set with the three vases of the same shape and size illustrated in Fig. 237. The body is decorated in four bands ; the first and third contain formal flower scrolls displayed upon a bright pale-green ground; the second has a pair of dragons in the midst of flames pursuing jewels with a coral-red background; the fourth is plain red, relieved by a linked chain of green winding round below. A band of hexagonal diaper at the foot, of flowers on a yellow ground round the shoulder, and a ring of palmations in green filled in with red on the neck, complete the decoration. The mark underneath is a double ring in underglaze blue. Height, 11 inches. No. 268.

SNUFF-BOTTLE, decorated in blue and white, with peach-bloom dragon ; mark, *Ch'ien-lung*. No. 269.

VASE (*P'ing*), of hexagonal section with two tubular handles, enameled with transmutation (*yao-pien*) colors of early *Ch'ien-lung* date. The groundwork, a crackled glaze, is invested with irregular splashes of green passing into olive-brown and mingled with purplish grays. Height, 7¼ inches. No. 270.

VASE (*P'ing*), of graceful form and very fine technique, dating from the *Ch'ien-lung* period, vertically grooved, with a bulbous body, and a long neck swelling into a bulb above under the circular lip. A dragon of archaic type is executed upon the shoulder of the vase in full undercut relief, with its long bifid tail coiling upward to encircle the neck. The dragon is enameled green, while the surface of the vase is coated with a monochrome-yellow enamel of soft tone, which also lines the foot. Height, 9 inches. No. 271.

BEAN-SHAPED SNUFF-BOTTLE, with archaic *k'i-lin* in blue and green on yellow ground ; *K'ang-hsi* period. No. 272.

VASE (*Hua P'ing*), of the *Ku Yueh Hsüan* class, molded of the characteristically short, very white, vitreous-looking paste, and crisply decorated in bright enamel colors of peculiar delicacy and finish. A pair of quails stand out prominently in the foreground, backed by an autumnal scene of trees with crimson-tinted leaves, marguerite daisies, and a rockery with roses. A pink scroll border worked in relief, succeeded by a blue fret, encircles the shoulder, and a gilded line defines the swelling lip. The couplet of verse which has suggested the motive for the little picture is inscribed on the reverse side of the vase. Height, 7 inches. No. 273.

WINE-CUP (*Chiu Pei*), molded in the form of an ancient bronze libation-cup, and colored with enamels to imitate the surface of patinated bronze. The *genre* is known as *ku t'ung ts'ai*—i. e., " archaic bronze coloring." The ground shade is olive-brown flecked with tea-green, which is penciled with gilded scrolls and encircling bands of fret, while the hollow parts of the designs, which are artificially roughened or pitted, are partially filled in with a grayish-blue enamel of mottled tint passing into green. The seal underneath, outlined in gold, is *Ch'ien-lung nien chih*, " Made in the reign of Ch'ien-lung." Length, 5 inches. No. 274.

SMALL VASE (*Hsiao P'ing*), of eggshell thinness and purest white color. It is encircled near the neck and foot by faint rings in the paste. There is no mark attached, but it must be a production of Ching-tê-chên, dating from the *Yung-chêng*, or, perhaps, the early *Ch'ien-lung*, period. Height, 6 inches. No. 275.

SMALL VASE (*Hsiao P'ing*), a typical example of " soft porcelain," so called, dating from the reign of *K'ang-hsi*. Light in weight, the body being of loose texture, it is invested with a white glaze of somewhat grayish tone and slightly undulatory surface, crackled (*k'ai-p'ien*) throughout. It is decorated under the glaze with a monstrous lionlike quadruped standing at the foot of a spreading pine, with a bat flying overhead, painted in blues of subdued tones ; the flames which proceed from the shoulders and hips of the monster being tinged red, and its eyes lightly touched with rings of the same underglaze color, derived from copper. Height, 7 inches. No. 276.

WATER RECEPTACLE (*Shui Ch'êng*), of ovoid form rounding into a small circular mouth, above which is coiled in salient relief a dragon (*chih-lung*) of archaic type. The bowl is etched at the point with scrolls of lotus and peony under the white translucent glaze ; the dragon is enameled reddish brown touched with gold, The seal, etched beneath the glaze in the paste underneath, is *Ta Ch'ing Ch'ien-lung nien chih*—i. e., " Made in the reign of Ch'ien-lung of the Great Ch'ing [dynasty]." Height, 4 1/2 inches. No. 277.

SMALL BEAKER (*Hsiao Tsun*), modeled after an ancient bronze form and design, with an archaic band of scroll round the middle, and vertical dentated ridges down the corners and sides. The handle is formed of a large lizardlike dragon (*ch'ih-lung*) in undercut relief, with four smaller ones wriggling over its body, and four others are crawling over the neck of the vase, which is enameled white, while the dragons are all painted in soft colors of the *Ch'ien-lung* period. Height, 4 1/2 inches. No. 278.

DOUBLE GOURD-SHAPED VASE (*Hu-lu P'ing*), decorated in polychrome enamel colors, shades of pink predominating, of the *Ch'ien-lung* period. The decoration is that commonly known by the name of *Po Hua*, or " The Hundred Flowers," the ground being completely covered with a dense mass of floral sprays, presenting a huge bouquet, as it were, culled from the Chinese flora, naturally and artistically rendered. The neck, slightly cut, is mounted with a metal collar, round the foot is a band of formal foliations, painted in shaded blue and green, relieved by a pink ground, between heavily gilded rims. The base, enameled like the inside of the mouth, pale green, has a red seal in a white reserve panel, inscribed in bold, well-written style, *Ta Ch'ing Ch'ien-lung nien chih*, " Made in the reign of Ch'ien-lung of the Great Ch'ing [dynasty]." Height, 21 inches. No. 279.

FLOWER - POT (*Hua P'ên*), of *Ch'ien-lung* porcelain, molded of rounded octagonal form, with a projecting lip, a perforated bottom, and four scrolled feet, and decorated outside with flowers and butterflies arranged in eight panels. The front panel in the illustration contains a picture of the three symbolical plants of long life—the pine, bamboo, and prunus ; the panel on the left of this, flowering bulbs of narcissus and roses ; the panel on the right, orchids with sprays of a red-foliaged plant and butterflies ; the other five panels exhibit, in succession, the pomegranate and chrysanthemum, the *Begonia discolor*, the *Hibiscus rosa sinensis*, the *Dielytra spectabilis*, and the azure-tipped marguerite daisy, the yellow jasmine, and scarlet fungus (*Polyporus lucidus*). Height, 9 1/2 inches. No. 280.

SNUFF-BOTTLE, with brilliant decoration on a deep-red ground ; mark, *Ch'ien-lung*. No. 281.

EGGSHELL VASE (*To-t'ai P'ing*), of the *Ch'ien-lung* period, decorated in soft, enamel colors with gilding. It is overlaid with a close-set floral decoration consisting of chrysanthemums and *hai-t'ang* flowers and daisies, attached in salient relief, and painted in red, green, and gold. Two oval panels are reserved in intervals of the floral relief-work, and painted in delicate colors with scenes of domestic life, a party of ladies drinking wine out of tiny gilded cups, and a group in a garden looking at fighting-cocks. Light floral scrolls penciled in gold round the upper and lower rims complete the decoration. Height, 8 3/4 inches. No. 282.

VASE (*Hua P'ing*), of three-lobed outline, covered with an olive-green monochrome glaze thickly flecked with tiny spots of lighter green, the typical *soufflé* glaze known as " tea-dust " (*ch'a-yeh mo*). Upon this as a background stands out a white branch of pomegranate, modeled in full undercut relief, with the fruit bursting open to show the seeds inside, and flowers and leaves naturalistically rendered. When this, as it winds round, leaves a small interval in the shoulder of the vase, a branched stem of the *Polyporus lucidus* is worked in, also enameled white. The foot is stamped underneath with the seal *Ta Ch'ing Ch'ien-lung nien chih*, " Made in the reign of Ch'ien-lung of the Great Ch'ing [dynasty]." Height, 8 inches. No. 283.

ARTICULATED VASE (*Chieh P'ing*—*chieh* meaning joined or spliced), cut horizontally into two parts in a waved four-lobed line of foliated outline. Of old bronze form and design, the details are worked in relief in the paste, representing vaguely four monstrous ogre (*t'ao-t'ieh*) faces, so much conventionalized as to form a broad band of ornamented scroll-work. The celadon glaze which covers the vase varies from pea-green to lighter shades, according to its depth, so as to enhance the effect of the molded designs. The seal underneath, penciled in blue under the same celadon glaze, is *Ta Ch'ing Ch'ien-lung nien chih*—i. e., " Made in the reign of Ch'ien-lung of the Great Ch'ing [dynasty]." Height, 6 inches. No. 284.

LACE-WORK VASE (*T'ou-hua P'ing*), of palest celadon porcelain of the reign of *Ch'ien-lung*. The sides are pierced with a floral design representing conventional peonies in the midst of leafy scrolls, which is filled in with glaze so as to form a delicate " rice-grain " transparency, giving the effect of lace-work. The vase, of almost eggshell thinness, is covered with a glaze of pale sea-green tone, while the borders, molded with bands of conventional ornament in slight relief, are picked out in white. Height, 7 inches. No. 285.

SNUFF-BOTTLE; twin gourds with decoration in brilliant enamels on yellow ground; mark, *Ch'ien-lung.*   No. 286.

EGGSHELL VASE (*To-t'ai P'ing*), richly decorated, in soft enamel colors and gilding of the *Ch'ien-lung* period, with illustrations of the different processes of sericulture. The pictures show in succession the hatching of the eggs, the feeding of the silkworms in the different stages of their growth, as they are kept in open baskets on curtained bamboo shelves, the winding of the silk from the chrysalids, and the weaving of the spun thread in hand-looms of complicated structure. Women and children carry on all the branches of work, boys are bringing in baskets of mulberry-leaves slung on their shoulders from the trees outside, and one is seated at the loom helping the women. The decoration of the vase is completed by light sprays of red and pink roses underneath the gilded rim. Height, 10½ inches.   No. 287.

SIX SNUFF-BOTTLES (*Pi Yen Hu*), of various designs, chiefly of the *Yung-chêng* and *Ch'ien-lung* periods: 1. Decorated in enamel colors of the *Yung-chêng* period (288). 2. A royal blue double gourd (289). 3. Blue and white flower design on a brown crackled ground (290). 4. Perforated design in reticulated work upon a ground of broken sticks; dark-green glaze (291). 5. Intricate designs in high relief of lions chasing wheels and fire emblems; *Ch'ien-lung* period (292). 6. A double bottle with a coral-red decoration, of the *Ch'ien-lung* period.   Nos. 288–293.

RICE-BOWL (*Fan Wan*), decorated in colors with the symbolical plants of long life, the pine and sacred fungus, the bamboo and prunus. The painted decoration is identical inside and outside, and it has the foliage and flowers pierced through in parts and filled in with glaze in "rice-grain" fashion, so as to appear as a partial transparency. The seal, penciled underneath the underglaze blue, is *Ta Ch'ing Chia-ch'ing nien chih*, "Made in the reign of Chia-ch'ing (1796–1820) of the Great Ch'ing [dynasty]."   No. 294.

MELON-SHAPED SNUFF-BOTTLE, with decoration of vines in blue and white; mark, *Yung-chêng.*   No. 295.

SNUFF-BOTTLE; celadon on modeled decoration; *Ch'ien-lung* period.   No. 296.

VASE (*P'ing*), representing a modern attempt at reproduction of the celebrated *Lang Yao sang-de-bœuf* of the reign of *K'ang-hsi.* The crackled glaze exhibits brilliant tones of coloring, but it is somewhat thin in aspect, especially toward the top of the vase; at the bottom it has "run" and congealed, and a bare mark can be detected on one side where a thick drop has had to be removed on the lathe.   No. 297.

FLOWER-VASE (*Hua P'ing*), of ovoid form, semi-eggshell texture, and partially crackled undulatory glaze, decorated in delicate enamel colors with gilding of the *Ch'ien-lung* period. The two panels have the foliated rims modeled in relief in the paste, and the sprays of blossoming prunus, painted in red and gold, as well as the white swallows, are also worked in relief, so as to project from the intervening ground, which is filled in with dotted circles sketched in blue. The panels are painted with pictures of domestic life in the style of the so-called "Indian china" of the eighteenth century, which was mostly painted in the workshops of Canton for the European market. Height, 11½ inches.   No. 298.

VASE (*P'ing*), a typical specimen of the soft-looking porcelain of the reign of *K'ang-hsi*, painted in blue under a crackled glaze of ivory-white tone, commonly known as *ch'ing-hua Fên Ting*—i. e., "Fên-Ting porcelain painted in blue." The rim of the foot shows a paste of loose texture, but very hard, the bottom being covered with the same crackled glaze as the vase, which is very light in weight when compared with ordinary porcelain. The decoration, penciled in soft shades of blue, is a rocky landscape with a pair of grotesque lions sporting under the shade of a gnarled pine, through the branches of which the full moon is visible. Shrubs of prunus and bamboo are growing from

the rocks, completing the vegetable trio of longevity; and a couple of bats are flying together in the background as symbols of happiness. Height, 15½ inches.   No. 299.

TWO SNUFF-BOTTLES of the *Ch'ien-lung* period: 1. Blue and white. 2. Modeled in high relief and decorated in brilliant colors.   Nos. 300, 301.

CENSER (*Hsiang Lu*) of ivory-white Fuchien porcelain. It is modeled as a round basket with pierced openwork sides worked into sprays of peony, and has a band of bamboo as handles attached by floral studs. Under the bottom, which is unglazed, is a stamped seal in the form of a Chinese "cash" inclosing the sacred *svastika* symbol. Height, with pedestal, 5½ inches.   No. 302.

LION (*Shih-tzŭ*), of white Fuchien porcelain (*Chien tz'ŭ*), seated upon an oblong pedestal, with the right forefoot placed upon a ball with a cord attached to it, the other end of which the lion holds in his mouth. From the back of the stand a tube rises on the right to hold the stick of incense. There should always be a pair of these lions before the shrine, and the companion would have a cub in place of the brocaded ball. Height, 5 inches.   No. 303.

LUSTRATION EWER (*Ch'ing Shui Hu*), of complicated form, intended for Buddhist ritual use. It is richly decorated in colors of the *K'ang-hsi* period, with diapers inclosing floral medallions and bands of conventional ornament, relieved by a *tzŭ-chin* ground of "old gold" tint. The monstrous head of a dragon projects from one side of the globular receptacle, modeled with formidable rows of teeth and black mustaches curling upward, from which emerges the long curved spout, reminding one of the celestial dragons that officiated at the miraculous baptism of the infant Buddha. Height, 8 inches.   No. 304.

SNUFF-BOTTLE; gray crackle of the *K'ang-hsi* period; mark, *Ch'êng-hua nien chih.*   No. 305.

HANGING BASKET (*Hua Lan*), with two hooks springing from the rim for the attachment of chains by which it is suspended to a crossbar, richly decorated in enamel colors of the *K'ang-hsi* period. The sides are pierced in openwork and painted in yellow, green, and black to simulate wicker. Through the interstices of the open casing the decoration of the cylinder, which fits inside, appears; it is crisply painted in red with a scrolled ground of lotus-flowers and a border of spiral fret. Height, 9 inches. No. 306.

BASKET (*Hua Lan*), of *K'ang-hsi* porcelain decorated in enamel colors. The bowl, of depressed globular form, has an arched handle, strengthened by side pieces, springing from the shoulder, and a round cover surmounted by a lion as handle. The sides of the bowl are pierced in six panels of hexagonal trellis interrupted by chrysanthemum-flowers which are painted alternately red and pale purple, and the cover is pierced with a similar trellis-work. The handle is painted in black lines on a yellow ground to imitate basket-work. Foot glazed white underneath. Height, 5 inches.   No. 307.

PIERCED GLOBE FOR SCENTED FLOWERS (*Hsiang Ch'iu*), of light biscuit porcelain of the *K'ang-hsi* period, carved with trellis medallions inclosing floral designs of the peony and lotus inlaid with colors, including a brilliant green in combination with the usual enamels of the old *famille rose.* It has a tiny round cover on the top for the introduction of flowers, which are placed as a sacred offering before the domestic shrine. Diameter, 4 inches.   No. 308.

ROSE-WATER SPRINKLER (*Hsiang Shui P'ing*), one of a pair, of the reign of *K'ang-hsi*, with powder-blue grounds, interrupted by three reserved medallions, quatrefoil, pomegranate and fan-shaped, which are filled with wild-flowers growing from rocks, penciled in shaded underglaze blue with white grounds. Tipped with metal mounts. Height, 7½ inches.   No. 309.

MINIATURE VASE (*Hsiao P'ing*), of Fuchien porcelain, with a bulbous mouth, and a dragon in salient relief winding round the neck of the vase and projecting its head on one side. Ivory-white glaze. Height, 4½ inches.   No. 310.

SNUFF-BOTTLE, with green and white dragon; mark, *Tao-kuang.*   No. 311.

VASE (*P'ing*), of the *Ch'en-lung* period, decorated in blue and white in the ordinary way with a mountain landscape of temples and pavilions on the shore of a lake. This is covered with splashes of *flambé* glaze, laid on over the original white ground, so as nearly to conceal the painted design under variegated clouds of purple, crimson, and olive-brown tints, the glaze becoming crackled in the thinner parts. The interior of the vase is coated with the same crackled and variegated enamel. Height, 15 1/4 inches.   No. 312.

ARROW RECEPTACLE (*Chien T'ung*), of square section, mounted in a socket pedestal of the same material. A production of the finest *K'ang-hsi* period, it exhibits a combination of many of the methods of decoration that distinguished the porcelain of the time, such as openwork molding, pierced-work carving, and relief modeling, all artistically painted in richly varied designs, laid on over the white glaze in the brilliant enamel colors of the fully-equipped ceramic palette of the period. Height, 29 inches.   No. 313.

SMALL VASE, with globular body and expanding mouth, intended for use as a hand spittoon (*t'an ho p'ing*). It is decorated over the white glaze, in two shades of coral-red, with a pair of five-clawed imperial dragons in the midst of flames and clouds pursuing jewels, with light bands of gadroon and spiral fret, and with a scroll of conventional flowers round the mouth. There is no mark underneath, but the technique and style are those of the *Ch'ien-lung* period. Height, 3 1/2 inches.   No. 314.

CYLINDRICAL BEAKER (*Hua T'ung*), with flaring mouth, of *laque burgautée* inlaid on porcelain, of the *K'ang-hsi* period. The decoration is a mountain landscape with temples, pagodas, and open pavilions, overlooking a lake upon which boats are sailing, a tall willow with drooping branches forming the background. The rims are encircled by light borders of diaper pattern inlaid in the same thin plaques of mother-of-pearl. Height, 11 inches.   No. 315.

VASE (*P'ing*), of the *K'ang-hsi* period, with a few encircling parallel rings lightly tooled in the paste, coated *sur biscuit* with enamels of different colors, yellow, green, and olive-brown, above a white glaze of soft ivory tint. The paste is grayish. The effect, which somewhat resembles that of tortoise-shell, is known to the Chinese by the name of *hu p'i wên*, "tiger-spotted." Height, 8 1/2 inches. No. 316.

SNUFF-BOTTLE, with foliations in soft parts, white on dark-blue ground; *Ch'ien-lung* period.   No. 317.

BEAKER-SHAPED VASE of Hirado porcelain, with the decoration partly painted in shaded blue, partly pierced and filled in with glaze so as to appear as a transparency. Height, 11 1/2 inches.   No. 318.

PIERCED CUP (*T'ou-hua Wan*), with the sides carved in openwork, with a broad band of *svastika* pattern connecting five solid medallions, upon which are attached, in full relief, figures of the longevity star god, Shou Hsing, and of the eight Taoist immortals, arranged in pairs. The figures are *en biscuit*, the clouds in the background are worked in slip, as well as the floral scrolls, which are carried round the rims of the cup over the white glaze which invests the rest of the surface. The foot is unglazed. Period, *Ch'ien-lung.* Diameter, 3 3/4 inches.   No. 319.

TAZZA-SHAPED CUP (*Pa Pei*), of the *Ch'ien-lung* period, decorated in enamel colors on a white ground, with formal archaic designs, including six conventionally ornamented pendants hung with symbols round the bowl, and a ring of brocaded palmations encircling the stem. Height, 4 3/4 inches.   No. 320.

MUG (*Pei*) of *Ch'ien-lung* "rice-grain" work, having the sides pierced with a broad central band of star pattern filled in with glaze, so as to be seen in transparency. The conventional bands of ornament that surround the rims and the flowers that stud the points of junction of the handle are penciled in underglaze cobalt-blue of grayish tone and picked out with gold. Height, 4 3/4 inches.   No. 321.

PIERCED CUP (*T'ou-hua Wan*) of delicate texture, dating from the *Ch'ien-lung* period, carved in openwork (*à jour*) with a trellis pattern of intersecting circles, broken by five circular medallions of floral design, and with a narrow conventional border round the rim. The white glaze is of rich unctuous texture, and of the slightly greenish tone characteristic of Ching-tê-chên. The foot is left *en biscuit.* Diameter, 3 3/4 inches.   No. 322.

GOURD-SHAPED VASE (*Hu-lu P'ing*), enameled with an iridescent deep-brown glaze (*tzŭ-chin yu*) overlaid with a decoration, roughly executed in white slip, of sprays of conventional flowers springing from rocks. The neck is mounted with a copper rim, and the mouth is plugged with a corklike stopper of Persian metal-work chased with figures and birds. Height, 10 inches.   No. 323.

SMALL BALUSTER VASE (*Hsiao Mei P'ing*) enameled of a pale sky-blue (*t'ien-ch'ing*) tint derived from cobalt, sparsely crackled with rare brown lines, having a spray of blossoming prunus worked upon it in slight relief and finished with the graving-tool. The foot, of the same blue tint underneath, is colored iron-gray round the rim. The neck, slightly chipped, is mounted with a copper rim. Height, 8 inches.   No. 324.

DECORATED VASE (*Hua P'ing*), painted in delicate enamel colors with gilding of the *Yung-chêng*, or later *K'ang-hsi*, period. The large characters outlined in brocaded strokes on the two sides of the vase are *shou*, "longevity," and *fu*, "happiness." The character *shou* is interrupted by a peach-shaped medallion, containing a picture of the three stellar divinities, Fu, Lu, and Shou of the Taoist Triad, with attendant sprites. The character *fu*, on the opposite side, is interrupted by a circular medallion displaying a picture of the Taoist goddess, Hsi Wang Mu, crossing the sea on a raft. The intervals are filled in with colored cloud scrolls, above which a couple of storks are flying, bringing peaches. Height, 17 inches.   No. 325.

LIBATION-CUP (*Chüeh*), of old brown "boccaro," of Yi-hsing-hsien. The paste is seen underneath in the unglazed part, indicating the material to be a dark grayish-brown faïence. The cup has an open handle invested in two branches of scrolled fungus and rests on three scroll feet. The molded decoration outside consists of floral scrolls and a quatrefoil border. It is enameled inside and out with a brownish-yellow crackled glaze, overlaid with irregular splashes of mottled purplish-gray color, partially concealing the yellow ground. Length, 4 1/2 inches.   No. 326.

BUTTERFLY-SHAPED SNUFF-BOTTLE; imperial yellow glaze.   No. 327.

LARGE VASE (*Ta P'ing*), decorated in brilliant enamel colors of early *K'ang-hsi* date, with the picture of a battle scene taken from the *Hsü Shui Hu*, a celebrated romance recounting the deeds of notorious brigands. The heroine, the "White Lady," who is riding a lion, and the principal generals mounted on horseback, carry small flags with their names inscribed. Greens of different shade predominate among the colors; the dark cucumber-green, the pale apple-green, and the purple exhibit the finely crackled texture, characteristic of some of the splendid monochrome glazes of the period. Height, 30 inches.   No. 328.

LIBATION-CUP (*Chüeh*), of the *K'ang-hsi* period, painted in colors, with hieratic designs taken from ancient bronzes. The two lizardlike dragons modeled in full openwork relief under the broad lip of the cup are colored green, and there is another pair, colored blue, clinging to the sides of the bandlike handle. Short dentated ridges project vertically from the bowl, which is painted with the features of the *t'ao-t'ieh* ogre emerging from spiral clouds. The rim, both inside and outside, is surrounded by a band of dragons and sacred fungus, displayed upon a pale-green background dotted with black. Length, 4 3/4 inches.   No. 329.

SNUFF-BOTTLE; imperial yellow crackle.　　No. 330.

SNUFF-BOTTLE; blue and white with red dragon.

　　No. 331.

VASE (*Hua P'ing*), of the finest porcelain of the *Yung-chêng* period, artistically painted in delicate colors upon a translucently white ground with flowers and birds. A *yulan* magnolia, springing from the foot of the vase, spreads gracefully round to decorate it with snow-white flowers and buds, and beneath the tree are peonies, with pink and white blossoms, and roses, yellow and red. A flowering branch of *Pyrus spectabilis* (*hai-t'ang*) with shaded pink flowers winds across the interval, having a small gayly plumaged bird perched upon it, which is seen in the foreground, and the mate is flying in the background. The neck is strengthened by a European mounting designed as a trailing vine. Height, 8½ inches.　　No. 332.

CYLINDRICAL RECEPTACLE FOR SCENTED FLOWERS (*Hsiang Hua T'ung*), adopted for offering blossoms of the *mo-li hua* (*Jasminum sambac*) or other fragrant flowers before the domestic shrine. Closed at the top, the bottom is perforated and shaped for a screw cover for the introduction of the flowers, and the sides are pierced in the intervals of the painted decoration, so that the fragrance may penetrate and be diffused. The group of figures on the sides represents the Taoist Triad, the three stellar divinities of happiness, rank, and longevity, and on the top is painted, in the same bright enamel colors of the *Ch'ien-lung* period, the Taoist immortal Tung Fang Sô, speeding over the clouds, with a branch of peaches, the fruit of life, on his shoulder. Height, 6½ inches.　　No. 333.

FOUR SNUFF-BOTTLES: 1. Blue and white; mark, *Ch'ien-lung* (334). 2. With foliations in relief; mark, *Tao-kuang nien chih* (335). 3. With dark, lustrous-brown glaze over dark-blue decoration; *Ch'ien-lung* period (336). 4. In the form of a bud, and covered with a yellow glaze (337).

　　Nos. 334–337.

BEAKER-SHAPED VASE (*Hua Ku*), of the *K'ang-hsi* period, artistically decorated, in bright enamel colors, with a pair of magpies in plumage of glossiest black, recalling the tint of the brilliant monochrome glaze of the period commonly known as "raven's-wing." The birds are perched upon rocks, with a prunus-tree in the background, which extends its blossoming branches in all directions to cover the rest of the surface of the vase with a charming floral decoration. The mark underneath is an antique form of the character *fu*, "happiness," in a small oblong panel, inclosed within a double circle. Height, 13½ inches.　　No. 338.

EGGSHELL DISH (*To-t'ai P'an*), painted in the delicate enamel colors, with gilding, of the *famille rose*. The diapered band encircling the rim is pink (*rose d'or*), the floral brocade which succeeds it is displayed upon a lilac diaper, and the convoluted edge of the central panel has the outline, which is that of a peony-petal folded over at intervals, penciled in gold. The graceful figures in the panel, upheld by light sprays of equisetum moss, represent the fairy goddess, Hsi Wang Mu, with a *ju-i* scepter, and an attendant carrying a peach, painted in sepia tints lightly touched with gold. Diameter, 7¾ inches.　　No. 339.

SNUFF-BOTTLE, in the shape of a gourd overgrown by a gourd-vine.　　No. 340.

LARGE VASE (*Ta P'ing*). The opposite side of the piece illustrated in Fig. 328, showing the rest of the picture of the battle scene. The banner in the middle of the shoulder of the vase is that of the imperial army, being emblazoned *Ta Sung*, "The Great Sung," the name of the dynasty that reigned 960–1279. The group on the neck of the vase represents the commander-in-chief with a flag inscribed with his rank, *shuai*, surrounded by his staff; they are gazing upward on the god of war appearing on wheels of fire as an omen of victory. Height, 30 inches.　　No. 341.

PORCELAIN PILLOW (*Tzŭ-Chên*). One of the square ends of the pillow shown in Fig. 16, decorated with a scene from a comedy painted in overglaze enamel colors. The other

end is painted with a companion picture, taken apparently from the same play. Diameter, 6 inches.　　No. 342.

FIGURE OF KUAN TI (*Kuan Ti Hsiang*), the Chinese god of war. Seated in a dragon-armed chair of carved wood, in a conventional attitude, with one foot raised upon a pile of rock, the other resting on a lion. The figure is decorated in antique style, *sur biscuit*, with minute and careful finish, in the rich enamel characteristic of the finest *K'ang-hsi* period, combined with lavish gilding to throw out the delicate pierced work of the coat-of-mail. Height, 11 inches.　　No. 343.

SNUFF-BOTTLE, with soft enamel decoration, of *Ch'ien-lung* period; mark, *Ch'êng-hua*.　　No. 344.

BLUE AND WHITE SNUFF-BOTTLE.　　No. 345.

THE TWIN GENII OF PEACE AND HARMONY (*Ho Ho Erh Hsien*), decorated in bright enamel colors with gilding of the *Ch'ien-lung* period. One carries in his hand a blossom and leaf of the sacred nelumbium, or lotus, the other holds a round box, full of precious gifts of happy omen. The pedestal simulates a bank of clouds, being worked with tiers of scrolls under the glaze of celadon tint with which it is enameled. Height, 12 inches.　　No. 346.

SNUFF-BOTTLE, with Shou-Lao and a deer in brilliant enamels, on a *sang-de-bœuf* ground; *Ch'ien-lung* period.

　　No. 347.

FIGURE OF SHOU LAO (*Shou Lao Hsiang*), the Stellar God of Longevity. A small statuette of conventional design painted in enamel colors of the *Tao-kuang* period. A peach, the symbolical "fruit of life," is held in one hand, and the robe is brocaded with longevity (*shou*) characters. Height, 8 inches.　　No. 348.

RELIC SHRINE, or DÂGABA (*T'a*), richly decorated in enamel colors with gilding of the *Ch'ien-lung* period. The hollow dome in the center, with an open door, symbolizes the vault of heaven, and it is covered with arabesque-like scrolls of conventional "paradise flowers" (*pao hsiang hua*). The spirelike summit is ringed to represent the twelve upper celestial tiers of the Buddhist universe; it is surmounted by a sacred umbrella, supporting in its top a precious jar (*pao-p'ing*) bound with fillets. Underneath it is enameled pale green, like some of the finest imperial vases of the time. Height, 16 inches.　　No. 349.

BLUE AND WHITE SNUFF-BOTTLE.　　No. 350.

SNUFF-BOTTLE, covered with a dark, apple-green crackle; *K'ang-hsi* period.　　No. 351.

OBLONG PLAQUE (*Ch'a P'ing*), mounted in a frame of carved wood with a stand as a screen picture. It is painted in colors, with a representation of the eight Taoist immortals, or genii (*pa hsien*), crossing the sea in procession, on their way to the Elysian Fields, the *Shou Shan*, or "Longevity Hills," of Taoist story, which are represented here as clad with fruit trees and gigantic evergreen pines. The enamels are those of the ordinary private pottery of the *Ch'ien-lung* period. Size, 18 × 11½ inches.　　No. 352.

BLUE AND WHITE SNUFF-BOTTLE; mark, *Ch'ien-lung*.

　　No. 353.

FLOWER RECEPTACLES (*Hua Cha*), of white *Fên-Ting* porcelain of the *K'ang-hsi* period, delicately molded in the shape of a bunch of nelumbium bound round with a reed. The folded peltate leaf, with its naturally convoluted margin, forms the vase. The leaf-stalk curls round and is tied, as it extends upward, into a bundle with a fully expanded flower, showing the cupped lotus fruit in the middle, a bud, and a smaller leaf; all modeled in natural detail with the aid of the graving-tool. The soft-looking glaze, of ivory-white tone, has an undulating pitted surface. Height, 6 inches.　　No. 354.

VASE (*Hua P'ing*), of brown Kuangtung stoneware (*Kuang Yao*), modeled in the form of an archaic ritual wine-vessel of bronze, with a string band in relief encircling the neck and oxen's heads as handles. It is covered with a pale, greenish-blue glaze of crackled texture, which "runs" in thick drops. Height, 5 inches.　　No. 355.

SAUCER-SHAPED PLATE (*P'an-tzŭ*), of eggshell porcelain of *Ch'ien-lung* date, painted in enamel colors of the *famille rose*, within panels and floral designs reserved in a richly enameled ground of mottled crimson tint. The large central panel is painted with a picture of fighting-cocks and peonies displayed upon a partially unrolled scroll. Sprays of plum-blossom fill in the spaces above and below ; and the border of the plate is decorated with small panel sketches of mountain and water scenery, alternating with sprigs of orchid. Diameter, 9 inches. No. 356.

"HAWTHORN" JAR (*Mei-Hua Kuan*), of the *K'ang-hsi* period, with clumps of prunus-blossom, alternating with single flowers, studding the ground of mottled blue, which is traversed by a reticulation of darker blue lines. The flowers, originally reserved in white, have been filled in, subsequently, with bright-green and brick-dust-red enamels, so as to form a kind of formal floral diaper of these two colors. Mark, double ring in underglaze blue. Height, 8 inches. No. 357.

WINE-POT (*Chiu Hu*), of the *K'ang-hsi* period, with looped handle and cover, intended to be connected by a chain, enameled deep reddish brown of the "dead-leaf" type (*tzŭ chin*), and decorated over the brown monochrome glaze in enamel colors with gilding. It is painted, on the two sides, with the picture of a Taoist female divinity carrying a basket of the sacred longevity fungus (*ling-chih*) suspended by a stick, and the cover is overlaid with small sprays of flowers. Height, 6 inches. No. 358.

BOWL (*Wan*), of the *K'ang-hsi* period, having the interior painted in blue and white with chrysanthemum scrolls and with a floral border round the rim. The outside, originally a plain monochrome brown, has been pierced on the lathe with a broad band of flowers and birds in European style, executed, apparently, in Europe. Diameter, 6 inches. No. 359.

TEAPOT (*Ch'a Hu*), of the "armorial china" type, richly decorated in enamels of the *famille rose* class, with gilding. This decoration consists of brocaded floral grounds and diapered bands inclosing foliated panels filled with sprays of chrysanthemum, peony, and other flowers. An oval panel reserved in the middle of the brocaded ground looks as if it were intended for a coat-of-arms, but is filled instead with a formal flower, which is painted in black touched with gold. The tray, shown in Fig. 378, of the usual hexagonal form, with foliated and indented rim, is decorated with similar designs. No. 360.

SAUCER-SHAPED DISH (*P'an tzŭ*), of eggshell texture, painted in bright enamel colors of the *famille rose* class with gilding. The decoration, of "armorial china" type, consists of floral bands and gilded diapers of Chinese style, inclosing emblems, partly European, partly Chinese, designed for the bridal service of the Dutch couple whose names and monograms are inscribed in gilded letters. Their miniature portraits have also been copied by the Chinese artist, whose work dates from about the middle of the eighteenth century. Diameter, 8 inches. No. 361.

TEAPOT WITH CUP AND SAUCER (*Ch'a Hu, Wan, Tieh*), part of a service painted in enamel colors with Chinese designs for the European market, early in the seventeenth century. The foliated panels contain grotesque *k'i lin*, on a floral brocaded ground, and the intervals are filled in with branches of prunus-blossom and birds. The teapot has a band of floral diaper round the shoulder, and the cover is mounted with a floral knob. No. 362.

BOWL (*Wan*), decorated in overglaze blue, red, and green enamels with a conventional floral ground studded at regular intervals with single blossoms. The formal borders of Indian style that encircle the rims are relieved by a ground of crackled yellow, the upper edge is gilded, and there is a rim of green round the foot. Bowls of this peculiar style have been attributed by some to Persia, by others to Hindustan, or to Siam ; they would seem, however, to have been made in China for this last country after the native taste. Diameter, 7 inches. No. 363.

PLATE (*P'an tzŭ*), one of a pair, artistically decorated in soft colors of the *famille rose*, with the backs enameled in deep pink (*rose d'or*) round the border. The interior is painted with a landscape representing the Hsi Hu Lake at Hangchou. Temples are seen on the rocky islands, approached by bridges of varied form, small boats are sailing in the lake and another is being towed along the bank. A range of mountains, dimly outlined in pink, stretches across in the far distance. The border is filled in with a diapered pattern on a pale-pink ground, interrupted by three foliated panels, which contain sprays of flowers and fruit, peonies and asters, peaches, pomegranates, and melons. Diameter, 8 inches. No. 364.

RECEPTACLE FOR WATER (*Shui Ch'êng*), of the faïence called "boccaro," made at Yi-hsing-hsien. The paste of comparatively pale color, approaching buff, is coated with reddish-brown and purple-gray glazes, to imitate the tints of an autumnal leaf, in the shape of which the little dish is molded. The stand of carved ivory is mounted upon a second stand of rosewood. Length, 5 inches. No. 365.

GOURD-SHAPED VASE (*Hu-lu P'ing*), of the *K'ang-hsi* period, enameled with a monochrome celadon glaze of pure tone and pale-greenish shade. The decoration, which is beautifully executed in slight relief in the paste, touched with the graving-tool, consists of a close interlacement of waving scrolls of the tree-peony (*Pæonia moutan*). The rim of the mouth is defined by a line of white glaze, and the interior is lined with white enamel, as well as the foot underneath, where there is no mark inscribed. Height, 17½ inches. No. 366.

TALL BEAKER (*Hua Ku*), decorated in cobalt-blue of brilliant tints developed under the pure translucent glaze characteristic of the *K'ang-hsi* period. The surface of the vase is divided by a light horizontal band of triangular fret into two sections, which are decorated with sprays of magnolia springing from rocks, so that the flowers stand out in snowy-white relief from a shaded background of pulsating blue. The mark, written underneath in three columns of two characters, within a large double ring, is *Ta Ch'ing K'ang-hsi nien chih*, "Made in the reign of K'ang-hsi (1662–1722) of the Great Ch'ing [dynasty]." Height, 20 inches. No. 367.

CREAM-JUG (*Nai Kuan*), of the *famille rose* class, with a cover surmounted by a knob, modeled in European form, as part of a tea-set, and decorated with enamel colors in the style of the *rouge d'or* dishes. Foliated panels, containing sprays of peony, hibiscus (China rose), jasmine, and other flowers, are inclosed in a gilded ground of diaper pattern. No. 368.

VASE (*Hua P'ing*), of Kuangtung stoneware, with ring handles suspended on lions' heads. The opaque body of dark-brown paste is covered with a thick, translucent glaze of bright-green tint mottled with brown and becoming grayish blue at the edges. Height, 10½ inches. No. 369.

VASE (*P'ing*), of Kuangtung stoneware, made of light but hard material, of brown color, with a pair of lizardlike dragons projecting in openwork relief from the base of the neck. It is enameled with a translucent crackled glaze of rich emerald-green color, passing into purplish gray toward the rim of the vase and over the more prominent parts of the molding. Height, 13½ inches. No. 370.

CENSER (*Hsiang Lu*), of Fuchien porcelain, with a floral design composed of bamboos and peonies growing from rocks molded in relief under the typical ivory-white translucent glaze with which it is invested. A circular seal, stamped under the foot, displays the inscription in archaic script, *Hsüan-tê nien chih*, "Made in the reign of Hsüan-tê (1426–35)." Diameter, 8 inches. No. 371.

VASE (*Hua P'ing*), of Fuchien porcelain (*Chien tz'ŭ*). The neck is ornamented with a band of fret succeeded by a ring of triangular foliations, and the body with four identical sprays of prunus modeled in relief, all worked in the paste under the pure white glaze, which is of ivory-white tone. Height, 7½ inches. No. 372.

HOOF-SHAPED VASE (*Ma T'i P'ing*), of Fuchien porcelain, covered with a molded decoration in relief, displaying the eight Buddhist symbols of good augury, enveloped in waving fillets and leafy scrolls. The white glaze of creamy tone has a slight bluish tinge. Height, 6½ inches. No. 373.

WATER RECEPTACLE (*Shui Ch'êng*), of ancient Kuang-tung faïence (*Kuang Yao*), modeled in the form of a bronze sacrificial wine-vessel. The paste, of buff color, is invested with a celadon glaze of pale sea-green shade. Height, 2½ inches; length, 6 inches. No. 374.

OKIMONO, of Hirado ware; three Chinese boys rolling a snowball. No. 375.

DOUBLE FISH-VASE (*Shuang Yü P'ing*), modeled in the form of a pair of fish springing upright from the waves, the bodies of which have coalesced to make a single mouth for the joint vase. The dorsal fins project on either side as handles; the other fins, the scaly bodies, the eyes and other details, as well as a fringe of waves round the foot, are worked in the paste, as part of the decoration of the vase, and come out in varied shade through the celadon glaze of pale blue-green tint with which they are invested. The vases are mounted as jugs with stands in an appropriate setting of bulrushes. Height, 10 inches. No. 376.

VASE (*P'ing*), one of a pair, decorated with a pale-blue *soufflé* ground, derived from cobalt, penciled in a darker shade of the same underglaze color, with a brocaded design of prunus-blossoms and triangles. Pedestals and stoppers in the form of crowns of European work. Height, 4 inches. No. 377.

SMALL TEA-TRAY (*ch'a pan*), from the same set as the teapot shown in Fig. 360, painted in colors, with a similar crestlike badge in the middle. No. 378.

GOURD-SHAPED VASE (*Hu-lu P'ing*), of the *K'ang-hsi* period, with the lower two thirds of the globular body covered with a glaze of *café-au-lait* color, succeeded by a girdle of grayish-white crackle, and a narrow band of blue and white diaper, the upper part being decorated in blue with flowers and lambrequins of floral brocade. European silver mounts. No mark. Height, 7 inches. No. 379.

MISHIMA BOWL, of dark stoneware, enameled with a white glaze with the incised designs filled in with encaustic black clay. See page 338.

CONICAL ARCHAIC BOWL of Korean faïence, of yellowish color stippled with darker spots. See p. 339. No. 380.

SHAPED DISH, of "Old Japan" Imari ware, richly decorated in brilliant colors with gilding. See p. 335. No. 381.

OLD KOREAN BOWL, with a lightly incised decoration under a buff-tinted celadon glaze, sparsely and superficially crackled. See page 338. No. 382.

TEMPLE VASE, of Takatori pottery, enameled with a crackled green glaze of mottled tint, decorated in slip in low relief with Buddhist figures. No. 383.

ORNAMENT (*Okimono*), of Hirado porcelain molded in the shape of a white colza turnip with blue-tinted leaves, with a rat crouched upon the bulb. No. 384.

VASE, of Kyōto faïence, with a grayish sparsely crackled glaze decorated in enamel colors and gilding with flowers and insects in the "Nishiki," or brocaded, style. No. 385.

INCENSE-BURNER (*Kōro*), of Hirado blue and white porcelain, with a picture on the inner cylinder, seen through the openwork trellis, of five children playing in a garden, under a pine-tree, which spreads over the pierced cover. See page 367. No. 386.

CENSER (*Kōro*), of white Hirado porcelain, molded in the form of a grotesque unicorn lion, with a movable head as a lid, with the details modeled in relief in the paste and lightly chased under the glaze. No. 387.

OKIMONO, of white Hirado porcelain, with the figure of a Shōjō, with smiling face and long hair sweeping the ground, standing beside a tripod wine-jar with a bamboo ladle in his hand. No. 388.

INCENSE-BURNER (*Kōro*), of Imari ware, fashioned in the shape of a cock perched upon a stump of wood and painted in enamel colors, black, brown, and red, with touches of gold and silver. *Circa*, 1700. No. 389.

SAKÉ-BOTTLE of Okawaji ware, with a crackled celadon glaze. Fully described on page 366. No. 390.

SMALL CENSER (*Kōro*), of Hirado porcelain, with a pierced outer trellised casing overspread with three sprays of chrysanthemum-flowers modeled in slight relief. Silver openwork cover. No. 391.

SATSUMA FIGURE of Chinese boy (*Kara-ko*), holding a palm-leaf fan, richly decorated in enamel colors and gilding. No. 392.

SAKÉ-BOTTLE of Satsuma ware, decorated in soft enamel colors and gold with sprays of *Paulownia imperialis*. Silver Kiku stopper.—SATSUMA VASE, decorated in enamel colors with a selection from the precious objects called *Takara-mono* described on page 373. No. 393.

CHINESE LION (*Kara Shishi*), of Hirado porcelain of the eighteenth century, with its left fore-foot upon an openwork ball of quatrefoil brocade pattern. The details are lightly etched under the white glaze, which is of pale greenish tone. No. 394.

SATSUMA FIGURE of Hotei, the Monk of the Hempen Bag, painted in enamel colors and gold. See p. 373. No. 395.

SMALL CYLINDER, with perforated side, of Hizen blue and white porcelain; mark of Shonsui. No. 396.

VASE, of Kyōto porcelain, decorated in rich enamel colors with gilding, with elaborate floral scrolls and panel pictures of Buddhist figures described on p. 362. No. 397.

LARGE DISH, of "Old Imari" ware, painted in underglaze blue in combination with enamels and gilding in the typical *chrysanthemo-péonienne* style. See p. 365. No. 398.

LARGE COVERED JAR, of "Old Imari" ware, decorated in colors and gold with pictures of outdoor scenes and brocaded bands with pierced trellis-work panels. No. 399.

WATER-POT, of Hizen porcelain molded in the shape of a fish-dragon, and painted in underglaze blue with touches of black enamel and gold. See page 366. No. 400.

SAKÉ-POT, of Hizen porcelain, decorated with dragons in the midst of flower-strewn waves, painted in dark green and other enamel colors. See page 366. No. 401.

CAKE-DISH, of Hirado porcelain, painted in blue with a group of seven Chinese boys playing under a pine-tree. See page 367. No. 402.

HIRADO CENSER, of pale celadon tint, with openwork cover and trellis casing displaying the badge of the Tokugawa house. See page 368. No. 403.

FIGURE OF BUDDHA, standing upon a lotus pedestal modeled in Hirado porcelain, and painted in blue with touches of brown and black. See page 368. No. 404.

VASE, of Hirado porcelain, decorated in three sections, the middle lightly chased with scrolls enameled white, the other two decorated in colors relieved by a russet-red ground. See page 368. No. 405.

SMALL JAR of Satsuma faïence, with conventional floral scrolls in enamel colors and gold. Old silver cover, a lotus-leaf. No. 406.

SATSUMA FIGURE of Chinese boy, holding up a jewel, richly decorated in enamel colors and gilding. No. 407.

SATSUMA CENSER, fashioned as a bowl on a tripod stand pierced with three medallions and delicately painted in enamel colors and gold. See page 373. No. 408.

TRIPOD CENSER with mask handles, of Kutani porcelain, decorated in enamel colors. Cover of lacquered metal. More details are given on page 376. No. 409.

SATSUMA CENSER, modeled in the shape of a court hat, with pierced work and painted decoration of floral scrolls. See page 373. No. 410.

BOWL, of Kutani porcelain, artistically decorated in brilliant enamel colors with sprays of iris painted upon a soft milk-white ground. See page 376. No. 411.

INDEX.